D1591381

Municipal Management Series

Emergency Management: Principles and Practice for Local Government

The International City Management Association is the professional and educational organization for chief appointed management executives in local government. The purposes of ICMA are to enhance the quality of local government and to nurture and assist professional local government administrators in the United States and other countries. In furtherance of its mission, ICMA develops and disseminates new approaches to management through training programs, information services, and publications.

Managers, carrying a wide range of titles, serve cities, towns, counties, and councils of governments in all parts of the United States and Canada. These managers serve at the direction of elected councils and governing boards. ICMA serves these managers and local governments through many programs that aim at improving the manager's professional competence and strengthening the quality of all local governments.

The International City Management Association was founded in 1914, adopted its City Management Code of Ethics in 1924, and established its Institute for Training in Municipal Administration in 1934. The Institute, in turn, provided the basis for the Municipal Management Series, generally termed the "ICMA Green Books." ICMA's interests and activities include public management education; standards of ethics for members; *The Municipal Year Book* and other data services; local government research; and newsletters, *Public Management* magazine, and other publications. ICMA's efforts for the improvement of local government management—as represented by this book—are offered for all local governments and educational institutions.

Contributors

William A. Anderson

Barbara A. Block

Guy E. Daines

Thomas E. Drabek

Tom Durham

David F. Gillespie

David R. Godschalk

Gerard J. Hoetmer

Gary A. Kreps

Shirley Mattingly

Ronald W. Perry

John H. Pickett

John C. Pine

Claire B. Rubin

T. Joseph Scanlon

Lacy E. Suiter

Advisory Committee

William A. Anderson

Duane A. Baltz

Thomas E. Drabek

John A. Granito

Gerard J. Hoetmer

Joseph LaFleur

John H. Pickett

Allen K. Settle

John Sorensen

Graham W. Watt

Municipal Management Series

Emergency Management: Principles and Practice for Local Government

Editors

Thomas E. Drabek
University of Denver

Gerard J. Hoetmer
ICMA

Published by the

International
City
Management
Association

Municipal Management Series

Emergency Management: Principles and Practice for Local Government

Effective Communication

The Effective Local Government Manager

Effective Supervisory Practices

Housing and Local Government

Local Government Police Management

Management of Local Planning

Management of Local Public Works

Management Policies in Local Government Finance

Managing Fire Services

Managing Human Services

Managing Local Government: Cases in Decision Making

Managing Municipal Leisure Services

The Practice of Local Government Planning

The Practice of State and Regional Planning

Small Cities and Counties: A Guide to Managing Services

The views expressed in this book are those
of the contributors and are not necessarily
those of ICMA or the Federal Emergency
Management Agency.

Library of Congress Cataloging-in-Publication Data

Emergency management: principles and practice for
  local government / editors, Thomas E. Drabek,
  Gerard J. Hoetmer.
      p.   cm. — (Municipal management series)
    Includes bibliographical references (p.   )
    and index.
    ISBN 0-87326-082-1
    1. Emergency management—United States.
2. Civil defense—United States. 3. Local government—
United States. 4. Federal government—United States.
I. Drabek, Thomas E.,   II. Hoetmer, Gerard J.
III. International City Management Association.
IV. Series.
HV551.3.E44 1991
363.3'48'0973—dc20   91-7132
                                                  CIP

Copyright © 1991 by the International City
Management Association, 777 N. Capitol Street, Suite
500, N.E., Washington, D.C. 20002. All rights reserved,
including rights of reproduction and use in any form
or by any means, including the making of copies by
any photographic process, or by any electronic or
mechanical device, printed, written, or oral or
recording for sound or visual reproduction, or for
use in any knowledge or retrieval system or device,
unless permission in writing is obtained from the
copyright proprietor.

Printed in the United States of America.

97969594939291
54321

Contents

Tables

Figures

Foreword

This volume, the first comprehensive text in its field, originated in efforts by the Federal Emergency Management Agency (FEMA) to educate not only front-line emergency management professionals but also elected and appointed local government officials in the principles and practice of emergency management.

In 1983, FEMA and the National Association of Schools of Public Affairs and Administration (NASPAA) sponsored a conference on emergency management in public administration education. Conference participants noted the need for "an integrated research base and body of knowledge (in emergency management) relevant to public administration" and recommended two approaches to achieve that end: (1) assembling existing research materials, course outlines, case studies, and other materials to form the requisite body of knowledge and (2) developing new curriculum materials to bring emergency management into the mainstream of public administration education.

Among the steps taken by FEMA as a result of the conference was the formation of a National Review Panel to develop and implement a plan for introducing emergency management into public administration education. The review panel's recommendations included the creation of a textbook that would form the core of an emergency management curriculum as well as provide practical guidance for local government administrators. *Emergency Management: Principles and Practice for Local Government*, is a direct outgrowth of the review panel's recommendation. The book was developed through a cooperative agreement with FEMA, which provided partial funding for the project.

Emergency management as it is practiced today is comparatively new; and, as a number of the chapters in this volume note, the field is still evolving fairly rapidly. A variety of forces have affected and will continue to affect its evolution, including changing federal priorities; research findings in diverse fields; and shifts in patterns of population distribution and urbanization. These and other influences on emergency management are explored throughout the volume.

The emergency management function in local government takes widely diverse forms, but a number of basic activities must be undertaken by every emergency management department—whatever its size, whatever its budget, and whatever its position in the local government structure. *Emergency Management: Principles and Practice for Local Government* addresses the needs of the emergency manager in any local government, and it does so in the context of two complementary concepts: comprehensive emergency management (CEM) and the integrated emergency management system (IEMS).

CEM is based on the four phases of emergency management: mitigation, preparedness, response, and recovery. IEMS, which provides both a strategic and operational framework for the implementation of CEM, calls for the assessment of potential hazards and available resources and the development of a plan to bring resources into line with risk.

It is our hope that this book will serve two purposes: first, that it will be a catalyst, assisting emergency management to take its rightful place in the mainstream of public administration education; second, that it will become a standard reference for local government professionals, students of public administration, and practicing emergency managers, offering them the practical, state-of-the-art information and guidance that they need.

Emergency Management: Principles and Practice for Local Government, is part of ICMA's Municipal Management Series. The volumes in the series form the basis for the courses developed by ICMA's Training Institute, which has offered in-service training specifically designed for local government administrators since 1934.

The development of this volume was a cooperative effort that required the expertise and commitment of a number of organizations and individuals. First and foremost among these is the Federal Emergency Management Agency, which provided substantial support for the project.

ICMA would like to thank the editors of the volume, Thomas E. Drabek, professor of sociology, University of Denver; and Gerard J. Hoetmer, assistant executive director for program development, public policy, and consortia, ICMA. We are also grateful to the chapter authors not only for the excellence of the material they contributed but also for their cooperation and commitment during revision.

ICMA extends thanks to the members of the advisory committee, who, in consultation with the editors, developed the scope, coverage, and architecture of the volume: William A. Anderson, Head, Hazard Mitigation Section, National Science Foundation; Duane Baltz, project officer, Office of Training, FEMA; John A. Granito, vice president emeritus, State University of New York at Binghamton; Joseph LaFleur, director, Pennsylvania Emergency Management Agency; John H. Pickett, coordinator, Office of Emergency Preparedness, Dallas, Texas (retired); Allen K. Settle, professor of public administration and political science, California Polytechnic State University; John Sorensen, group leader, Hazard Management Group, Energy Division, Oak Ridge National Laboratory; and Graham W. Watt, public management consultant, Graham W. Watt & Associates.

A number of ICMA staff members and other individuals contributed to this project: Sandra Chizinsky Leas, who oversaw the project; Jane Anderson Nunez, who copyedited chapters 2, 5, and 6; Jane E. Lewin, who copyedited all other chapters and the introduction; Andrea Posner, who obtained permission for use of copyrighted material and shepherded the manuscript through the production process; Breck Marshall, who researched sources; Dawn M. Leland, who managed illustrations and production; and Mary W. Blair and Tonya L. Horsley, who provided administrative assistance. The project was conducted under the general direction of Barbara H. Moore, Director of Publications.

William H. Hansell, Jr.
Executive Director,
ICMA
Washington, D.C.

Introduction

This book is about local emergency management. Emergency management is the discipline and profession of applying science, technology, planning, and management to deal with extreme events that can injure or kill large numbers of people, do extensive damage to property, and disrupt community life. When such events do occur and cause extensive harm, they are called disasters.

In popular usage today the term *disaster* is widely and casually used to describe everything from a flooded basement to a defeat in football to the sinking of the *Titanic*. In ancient times the word was spoken with more care and expressed a deep sense of dread. The original Latin meaning signified the unfavorable aspect of a star; *disaster* thus connoted a harmful influence that came from the heavens and was beyond human control.

Some of this fear of the unknown, of the uncontrollable and unexpected, still lies behind our sometimes cavalier use of the word and occasionally rises to the surface. It is most likely to surface among survivors of disaster, although it may manifest itself as near-exhilaration. Having escaped death, survivors feel the glow of good fortune; at the same time, they are sharply aware of their own mortality and are impelled to reach out to those who can confirm their experience, sharing both their sense of well-being and their sense of loss.

Survivors of earthquakes, hurricanes, floods, and the like may feel a heightened respect for the forces of nature; some may also turn to religion to give context to their ordeal. Others may begin to feel an especially close kinship with their families or with other people who have gone through the same experience. Something of that aspect of what survivors undergo has been described by William James, who was teaching at Stanford at the time of the 1906 San Francisco earthquake. According to James, the phenomenon of "earthquake love," or the euphoric condition found among the survivors, was "a kind of uplift . . . that takes away the sense of loneliness that gives the sharpest edge to the more usual kind of misfortune that may befall a man."[1] In the words of a survivor of the 1979 tornadoes in Wichita Falls, Texas, surviving disaster "is a once-in-a-lifetime experience and makes you place more importance on human relationships and less on material possessions."[2]

Distinguishing between emergencies and disasters

Defining the term *disaster* in its most general sense is easier than deciding whether it applies to a particular event in a particular community. The field of emergency management generally makes a distinction between emergencies and disasters. Emergencies are "routine" adverse events that do not have communitywide impact or do not require extraordinary use of resources or procedures to bring conditions back to normal. A house fire, a burglary, a heart attack, or a broken water main is within the scope of the standard operating procedures of most local fire, police, emergency medical service, and public works departments. It is only when these departments are unexpectedly torn from their standard operating procedures or are required to obtain resources outside of their normal authority that they must move beyond the emergency level of operations.

Catastrophic disasters   The term *catastrophic* must be associated with any definition of disaster. A catastrophic disaster is one that affects an entire nation and requires extraordinary resources and skills for recovery—some of which must come from other nations. The 1990 Iran earthquake, which killed more than 50,000 people, was a catastrophic disaster. Hurricane Hugo in 1989 was not, although it required that 265,000 people be evacuated and left 93,000 people in need of shelter and 398 in need of medical attention. Had Hurricane Hugo directly struck a major metropolitan area, however, it might well have been a catastrophic disaster.

A catastrophic disaster is one that results in many times more damage than that wreaked by Hugo. To prepare for such an eventuality, in July 1982 President Reagan approved National Security Decision Directive 47 (NSDD-47), which declared it was the government's policy "to develop systems and plans to ensure that sufficient medical personnel, supplies, equipment, and facilities will be available and deployed to meet essential civilian and military health care needs in an emergency." Under this policy, a Nationwide Medical Response System was established to supplement state and local medical resources during catastrophic disasters and to provide back-up medical support to the military and Veterans Administration medical care systems during a conventional conflict overseas.

The medical system's two major components are (1) medical response at the scene, including disaster medical assistance teams that will assist localities with triage, medical care, and medical equipment and supplies; and (2) patient evacuation to acute care beds.

In a sense, therefore, what constitutes a disaster depends largely on the community itself: the jurisdiction's size, its resource base, and its experience with a particular hazard. It is thus a fundamental precept of emergency management that each community establish distinct levels, or stages, that define the progression from an emergency to a disaster. These stages or levels of emergency provide guidance for first responders; even more important, they provide benchmarks so local decision makers will know when to institute warnings, when to seek supplemental or special resources, and when to undertake extraordinary procedures or evacuations. Because officials in Basel, Switzerland, failed to identify accurately an emergency with the potential to escalate into a disaster—and to make the necessary transition to the disaster response mode—a 1986 storage-house fire turned into one of the worst chemical disasters in Western Europe since the 1976 dioxin disaster in Seveso, Italy. Such events underscore the importance of having a clear definition of a disaster—and of the progression from emergency to disaster—within the context of a particular community. The principle applies to all kinds of situations, not only those that involve hazardous materials.

Numerous other examples occurred in the years before the late 1970s. Until that time, many local public safety officials were ill prepared to respond adequately to incidents involving hazardous materials. Such incidents can produce (among other things) boiling liquid expanding vapor explosions (BLEVEs)—which occurred with frightening and tragic consequences in a number of communities, principally because the emergency management capabilities were not adequate to deal with hazardous materials incidents. Thus, emergencies with limited initial impact turned quickly and unexpectedly into disasters.

Today, improved skills and resources in dealing with hazardous materials help ensure that most hazardous materials incidents do not create disasters. Nevertheless, because of the unpredictable and volatile nature of the products involved

(*continued on page xx*)

Emergency levels defined

Level 1 emergency

Defined   Any unexpected occurrence that can be met with a single department's normally available resources. "Normally available resources" may include the response of other city departments in a routine capacity.

Responsibility   The department that would normally handle the situation is responsible for the decision making to properly resolve the incident.

Notifications   None.

Action   The responsible department may set up an on-site command post if it so desires. No citywide action is required.

Press relations will be handled by the responsible department. Needed logistical support, additional personnel, or other resources will be the additional responsibility of the responsible department.

Level 2 emergency

Defined   Any unexpected occurrence that requires response by two (2) or more city departments above a routine capacity, or where outside agencies have responded to render such assistance. Such emergencies require a cooperative effort and a commitment of personnel, equipment, or resources that would be expected to upset the normal working routine of either or all of the responding departments.

Responsibility   The primary decision-making responsibility rests with the department that would normally handle the situation, but a cooperative effort with departments that are responding in support is *required*. The cooperative efforts should be designed to properly resolve the incident.

Notifications   The mayor should be alerted to the situation by the originating department.

Action   The senior representative of the responsible department should set up an on-site command post and notify all responding departments of the location.

The responsible department may also set up an administrative command post (usually at its main facility or dispatch area) and should notify all responding departments and the mayor of the location.

Press relations will be handled by the responsible department. Needed logistical support, additional personnel, or other resources will be the added responsibility of the responsible department. Emergency purchases should be referred to the mayor, who may expedite those requests with the assistance of the purchasing division.

Level 3 emergency

Defined   Any extraordinary occurrence of such magnitude that all city departments and resources must be utilized or where a combination of city departments and outside agencies have been mobilized to handle the situation.

Responsibility   The primary responsibility for decision making rests with the Emergency Management Board. The on-site commanders may make those decisions necessary to protect life and property and to stabilize the situation. Decisions designed to properly resolve the entire emergency shall be the responsibility of the Emergency Management Board.

This level of emergency usually results in a "Declaration of Emergency" by the mayor, who invokes the emergency powers of the office.

Notifications   The following personnel will be notified (or, in their absence, an alternate from their department): mayor, chief of staff, chief of police, fire chief, public works director, and others as directed by the mayor.

(*continued on next page*)

(continued from previous page)

The initiating department shall have the responsibility for making the above notifications. The initiating department can get assistance in any instance by notifying the police dispatch supervisor of the need for such assistance.

Action The senior representative of the initiating department shall establish an on-site command post and notify all responding departments of the location.

The chief of police shall activate the City Emergency Command Center. All members of the Emergency Management Board shall report to the Command Center and, whenever possible, shall bring with them a hand-held radio on their own operating channel.

Press relations will be assumed by the Command Center. The further acquisition of personnel, equipment, or other resources will become the duty of the Emergency Management Board.

All support staff should report to the fire department's command room. The fire department will assume the communications functions necessary during a level 3 emergency.

All other department heads and those with designated responsibilities elsewhere in this plan should report to their regular areas. (Other instructions may be given at time of mobilization.)

Source: Emergency Management Plan, Salt Lake City Corporation, Office of the Mayor.

---

and the specialized resources and skills required to deal with them, such incidents continue to require qualitatively different forms of readiness and response than the forms needed in a strictly "routine" emergency.

The role of the emergency program manager

The local emergency manager's task is to use a variety of resources, techniques, and skills to reduce the probability and impact of extreme events—and, should a disaster occur, to bring about a quick restoration of routine. Although emergency managers are key players in a disaster situation, they need not be "in charge"; rather, their responsibility is to ensure that someone *is* "in charge"—and that that person has access to the resources, skills, and knowledge necessary to manage the situation effectively. The single most crucial aspect of effective emergency management is making sure *before* a disaster occurs that *in* a disaster responsibility, authority, and channels of communication are clearly delineated.

The two concepts that currently help define the roles and responsibilities of emergency management are comprehensive emergency management (CEM) and the integrated emergency management system (IEMS). These two concepts also underlie this volume. The practical implications of CEM and IEMS are discussed in detail throughout the book, but here the two terms are broadly defined. Briefly, CEM calls for an integrated approach to the management of emergency programs and activities: each element of CEM relates to every other element. IEMS helps a community define these relationships in both strategic and operational terms. In other words, CEM provides emergency management with a conceptual framework, and IEMS shows how the framework can be translated into action.

More specifically, CEM is a way of fitting together the many elements of emergency management into an inclusive framework that encompasses all hazards and all levels of government (as well as the private sector).[3] It includes four phases: mitigation, preparedness, response, and recovery. One depiction of CEM shows it as a circle, which indicates the continuity of the four phases of emergency management: current thinking in the field is that communities should prepare for recovery before disaster strikes so that difficult decisions about reconstruction and mitigation are less subject to the extreme pressures that characterize the immediate aftermath of disaster.

IEMS is a way of spelling out the details of CEM. On the strategic side, IEMS requires that a community undertake a hazard and risk analysis, assess its current capabilities in the areas of mitigation, preparedness, response, and recovery, and devise action steps to close the gap between existing and required levels of capability. Operationally, IEMS provides the framework to support the development of emergency management capabilities based on functions (warning, shelter, public safety, evacuation, and so forth) that are required for all hazards.

Types and probability of disasters

Researchers have traditionally identified three types of disasters: natural, technological, and civil. Violent natural events (for example, earthquakes, floods, tornadoes) that have an extreme impact on human beings are natural disasters. Events that have an extreme impact on human beings but are caused by human omission or error are technological disasters. Deliberate human acts—such as wars—that cause extensive harm are categorized as civil disasters.

Recently a fourth type of disaster has come under discussion: ecological disasters. These are events that are caused principally by human beings and that initially affect, in a major way, the earth, its atmosphere, and its flora and fauna, rather than human beings. Unlike other types of disaster, ecological disasters are usually insidious rather than dramatic, but ultimately they are just as deadly. The destruction of the planet's rain forests and the extinction of entire species can be categorized as ecological disasters. Certain forms of technological disaster—such as leakage from a toxic waste site (as discussed below)—can cause or contribute to ecological damage.

The fourfold classification of disasters is valuable to research as well as to the development of strategic approaches to emergency management. For example, different types of disasters have different effects on human behavior and require different types of organizational response. Information about these differences can be helpful to emergency managers, particularly during the preparedness and response phases of emergency management. Of course, the fourfold classification can be further subdivided on the basis of a number of other variables, such as speed of onset, predictability, and other characteristics that may affect an event's degree of destructiveness.

Figure 1 Different disasters produce different results. The chart shows frequently observed short-term effects of major natural disasters.

Effect	Type of disaster			
	Earthquake	High winds	Tidal wave, flash flood	Flood
Deaths	Many	Few	Many	Few
Severe injuries requiring intensive medical care	Many	Fair number	Few	Few
Increased risk of infectious disease	Potential problem in all major disasters (probably rises with overcrowding and deteriorating sanitation)			
Scarcity of food	Rare (May occur because of factors other than shortage of food)	Rare	Common	Common
Major population movements	Rare (May occur when urban areas are heavily damaged)	Rare	Common	Common

The growing probability

No place on earth is disaster free. Moreover, the potential for highly destructive events is increasing as the world's population increases, as certain potentially dangerous technologies become more widespread, and—especially—as populations become more concentrated in urban areas. Of the more than 5.2 billion people who inhabit the earth today, 41 percent live in urban areas. It is projected that by the year 2020, the world population will be close to 10 billion, 60 percent of which will be crowded into urban areas, most of them located in coastal regions at risk from hurricanes, coastal flooding, and tsunamis.

The ecological effects of this vast mass of humanity are a particular cause of concern. As the world's population increases, so does the potential for global warming created by the buildup of gases such as carbon dioxide and methane in the atmosphere—and global warming could lead to an increase in the number of natural disasters. Although scientists continue to discuss the impact of global warming in terms of probabilities, the consensus from the National Academy of Sciences is that the earth mean temperature will increase by from 1.5 to 4.5 degrees Celsius in the next century,[4] and, according to Stephen H. Schneider, a noted climatologist, "Change of this magnitude could dramatically alter accustomed climatic patterns, affecting agriculture, water supplies, disease patterns, ecosystems, endangered species, severe storms, sea level and coastal flooding."[5]

In addition, some experts believe that these climatic changes could come without warning—like an avalanche or lightning—when carbon dioxide suddenly surges and breaks a "threshold." Thus, the complex interactions subsumed under the deceptively simple label "global warming" will no doubt generate some ominous ecological changes during the next decade.

Natural disasters

The North American continent faces the likelihood of numerous natural disasters every year. But whereas geography and climate determine where natural disasters occur, their impact is influenced largely by the built environment, above all in the case of earthquakes. Moreover, many natural disasters are consequences of other natural disasters; for example, landslides result from heavy rains, floods, or earthquakes.

Earthquakes The majority of casualties caused by earthquakes occur when built structures collapse. In the 1985 Mexico earthquake, for example, more than four hundred large, unreinforced buildings collapsed or were severely damaged, trapping an estimated ten thousand victims. Modern reinforced buildings can resist collapse, but unreinforced buildings and adobe and dry stone houses are highly unstable, even when they are only a single story high. In the more recent earthquakes in Armenia (1988), Iran (1990), and the Philippines (1990), as in the Mexico earthquake, the collapse of unreinforced buildings and of dry stone houses caused heavy loss of life.

For more than a half century, California authorities have been attempting to prepare the state's population for the so-called Big One by enacting codes and zoning ordinances to mitigate the impact of a major quake. Not until recently, however, have authorities in other high-risk earthquake zones, such as the area around the New Madrid fault in Missouri, begun similar mitigation efforts. (The New Madrid area was the site of the great earthquakes of 1811– 12, five of which were 8.0 or more in magnitude.)

Despite California's preparedness and mitigation actions, estimates are that a major quake on the Hayward fault would cause more than three thousand casualties and over forty billion dollars' worth of property damage. (In 1990,

Table 1. Selected major U.S. earthquakes.

Date	Location	Magnitude (Richter scale)	Deaths	Damage (millions of 1979 dollars)
1811–12	New Madrid, Missouri	7.1–8.6	Unknown	Unknown
August 31, 1886	Charleston, South Carolina	Unknown	60	Unknown
April 18, 1906	San Francisco, California	8.2	700	2,000
March 11, 1933	Long Beach, California	6.3	115	266
April 1, 1946	Unimak, Alaska	Unknown	173	90
April 13, 1949	Olympia, Washington	Unknown	8	80
July 25, 1952	Kern County, California	7.2	12	150
August 18, 1959	Hebgen Lake, Montana	7.1	28	26
March 27, 1964	Prince William Sound, Alaska	8.4	131	1,020
February 9, 1971	San Fernando, California	6.4	58	900
October 17, 1989	San Francisco, California	7.8	62	3,750

Table 2. Location and damage estimates for potential future earthquakes.

Location	Intensity (Richter scale)	Kind of damage	Deaths[a]	Serious injuries[a]	Property damage (billions of 1987 dollars)	Study (date)
San Francisco	8.3	Vibration	3,500–12,840	13,300–49,700	40.2	USGS (1981)
San Francisco	8.3	Fire	n.a.	n.a.	4.8–19.1	AIRAC (1987)
San Francisco	8.3	Vibration	n.a.	n.a.	8.5	Calif. (1987)
Los Angeles	7.5	Vibration	5,100–24,000	20,100–95,500	66.4	USGS (1981)
Los Angeles	7.5	Fire	n.a.	n.a.	6.3–21.6	AIRAC (1987)
Los Angeles	7.5	Vibration	n.a.	n.a.	10.0	Calif. (1987)
Memphis area	8.6	Vibration	440–3,840	1,760–15,300	36.6	FEMA (1985)
Seattle area	7.5	Vibration	1,130–3,820	620–11,400	n.a.	USGS (1975)
Salt Lake City	7.5	Vibration	390–3,635	1,560–14,500	n.a.	USGS (1976)

[a]Estimates exclude potential dam failures.

the National Earthquake Prediction Evaluation Council, a group of seismologists that advises the U.S. Geological Survey, set at 67 percent the odds that an earthquake of 7 or more on the Richter scale would occur along the Hayward or the San Andreas fault within thirty years.)

In addition to the casualties and damage that earthquakes cause directly, largely by affecting the built environments, they also cause secondary disasters that significantly increase losses. Examples of secondary disasters caused by earthquakes are ground failures and liquefaction (when a stable granular material like sand enters a fluid state). Some of the worst damage created by the 1989 Loma Prieta earthquake occurred in San Francisco's Marina district, where landfill that had been created shortly after the 1906 San Francisco earthquake liquefied.

Two other types of secondary event caused by earthquakes are landslides and tsunamis (the latter are commonly but erroneously called tidal waves). In May 1970, an earthquake dislodged a massive landslide of ice, snow, and earth from the slopes of the Andes, burying a Peruvian city of fifteen thousand. The Loma Prieta earthquake also triggered thousands of landslides throughout the San Francisco–Santa Cruz–Monterey Bay region and along the Big Sur coastline as much as eighty-one miles from the epicenter. These

(*continued on page xxviii*)

The New Madrid Fault   The New Madrid Fault System extends 120 miles southward from the area of Charleston, Missouri, and Cairo, Illinois, through New Madrid and Caruthersville, in Missouri, following Interstate 55 to Blytheville and on down to Marked Tree, in Arkansas. It crosses five state lines and cuts across the Mississippi River in three places. The fault is active, averaging more than three hundred measured events per year (1.0 or more on the Richter scale)—almost one per day. Tremors large enough to be felt (2.5–3.0 on the Richter scale) are noted six or seven times annually. Every fourteen to fifteen months the fault releases a shock of 4.0 or more, capable of producing local minor damage. Magnitudes of 5.0 or greater occur about once per decade; these events can do significant damage in a small region and can be felt in several states. The highest earthquake risk in the United States outside the West Coast is along the New Madrid Fault. Damaging tremors are not as frequent along that fault as in California, but when they do occur, they are twenty times more damaging because of the underlying geology.

A damaging earthquake in this area, 6.0 or greater in magnitude, occurs about every eighty years (the last was one in 1895). There is a 50 percent chance of such a quake by the year 2000. This would cause serious damage to masonry buildings throughout southeast Missouri and less serious damage from Memphis to St. Louis. A major earthquake in this area, 7.5 or greater, happens every two to three hundred years (the last one was in 1812). There is a 10 percent chance of such a disaster by the year 2000 and a 25 percent chance by 2040. A New Madrid Fault rupture of this size would be felt throughout half the United States and would do damage in twenty or more states. Missouri could anticipate at least a billion dollars' loss from such an event.

The great New Madrid earthquake of 1811–1812 was actually a series of over 2,000 shocks in three months, five of which were 8.0 or more in magnitude. Eighteen of these rang church bells on the eastern seaboard. It was the largest burst of seismic energy east of the Rockies in the history of the United States and was several times larger than the San Francisco quake of 1906.

When will another great earthquake happen the size of those in 1811–1812? Several lines of research suggest that catastrophic upheavals like those of 1811–1812 vist the New Madrid region every five to six hundred years. Hence, emergency planners, engineers, and seismologists do not expect a repeat of the intensity of the 1811–1812 series for at least one hundred years. However, even though the chance is remote, experts assign a 1 percent probability for a 8.0 or greater event by the year 2000 and a 3 percent probability of an earthquake that size by the year 2040. Earthquake probabilities for known active faults always increase with time because stresses within the earth slowly and inexorably mount, year by year, until the rocks can take no more and a sudden rupture becomes inevitable. Our greatest concerns are the 6.0–7.6 sized events, which do have significant probabilities in the near future. A 6.0 shock has a 90 percent chance by the year 2040. One or more damaging earthquakes of this magnitude or bigger are virtually certain within the lifetimes of our children.

What can we do to protect ourselves? Education, planning, proper building construction, and preparedness are proven means to minimize the impact of such hazards. Earthquake mitigation programs reduce casualties and property losses to but a fraction of what they would have been.

Source: Center for Earthquake Studies, Southeast Missouri State University.

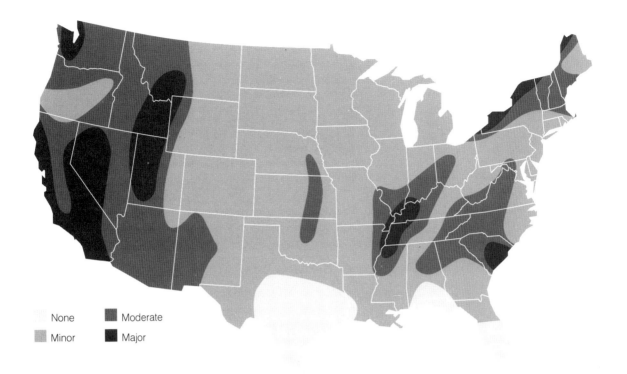

Figure 2 Earthquake risks.

The severity of an earthquake The severity of an earthquake can be expressed in terms of both *intensity* and *magnitude*. However, the two terms are quite different, and they are often confused by the public.

Intensity is based on the observed effects of shaking ground on people, buildings, and natural features. It varies from place to place within the disturbed region depending on the location of the observer with respect to the earthquake epicenter.

Magnitude is related to the amount of seismic energy released at the hypocenter of the earthquake. It is based on the amplitude of the earthquake waves recorded on instruments which have a common calibration. The magnitude of an earthquake is thus represented by a single, instrumentally determined value.

Earthquakes are the result of forces deep within the earth's interior that continuously affect the surface of the earth. The energy from these forces is stored in a variety of ways within rocks. When this energy is released suddenly, for example by shearing movements along faults in the crust of the earth, an earthquake results. The area of the fault where the sudden rupture takes place is called the *focus* or *hypocenter* of the earthquake. The point on the earth's surface directly above the focus is called the *epicenter* of the earthquake.

The Richter magnitude scale Seismic waves are the vibrations from earthquakes that travel through the earth; they are recorded on instruments called seismographs. Seismographs record a zigzag trace that shows the varying amplitude of ground

(continued on next page)

(continued from previous page)

oscillations beneath the instrument. Sensitive seismographs, which greatly magnify these ground motions, can detect strong earthquakes from sources anywhere in the world. The time, location, and magnitude of an earthquake can be determined from the data recorded by seismograph stations.

The Richter magnitude scale was developed in 1935 by Charles F. Richter of the California Institute of Technology as a mathematical device to compare the size of earthquakes. The magnitude of an earthquake is determined from the logarithm of the amplitude of waves recorded by seismographs. Adjustments are included in the magnitude formula to compensate for the variation in the distance between the various seismographs and the epicenters of the earthquakes. On the Richter scale, magnitude is expressed in whole numbers and decimal fractions. For example, a magnitude of 5.3 might be computed for a moderate earthquake, and a strong earthquake might be rated as magnitude 6.3. Because of the logarithmic basis of the scale, each whole-number increase in magnitude represents a tenfold increase in measured amplitude; as an estimate of energy, each whole-number step in the magnitude scale corresponds to the release of about 31 times more energy than the amount associated with the preceding whole-number value.

Earthquakes with magnitude of about 2.0 or less are usually called microearthquakes; they are not commonly felt by people and are generally recorded only on local seismographs. Although the Richter scale has no upper limit, the largest known shocks have had magnitudes in the 8.8 to 8.9 range.

The Modified Mercalli Intensity Scale

The effect of an earthquake on the earth's surface is called the intensity. The intensity scale consists of a series of certain key responses such as people awakening, movement of furniture, damage to chimneys, and, finally, total destruction. Although numerous intensity scales have been developed over the last several hundred years to evaluate the effects of earthquakes, the one currently used in the United States is the Modified Mercalli (MM) Intensity Scale. It was developed in 1931 by the American seismologists Harry Wood and Frank Neumann. This scale, composed of twelve increasing levels of intensity that range from imperceptible shaking to catastrophic destruction, is designated by roman numerals. It does not have a mathematical basis; instead it is an arbitrary ranking based on observed effects. To the nonscientist, the Modified Mercalli intensity value assigned to a specific site after an earthquake is a more meaningful measure of severity than the magnitude because intensity refers to the effects actually experienced at that place.

The *lower* numbers of the intensity scale generally deal with the manner in which the earthquake is felt by people. The *higher* numbers of the scale are based on observed structural damage. Structural engineers usually contribute information for assigning intensity values of VIII or above.

The following is an abbreviated description of the twelve levels of Modified Mercalli intensity.

I. Not felt except by a very few under especially favorable conditions.
II. Felt only by a few persons at rest, especially on upper floors of buildings. Delicately suspended objects may swing.
III. Felt quite noticeably by persons indoors, especially on upper floors of buildings. Many people do not recognize it as an earthquake. Standing motor cars may rock slightly. Vibration similar to that created by the passing of a truck. Duration estimated.
IV. During the day, felt indoors by many, outdoors by few. At night,

some awakened. Dishes, windows, doors disturbed; walls make cracking sound. Sensation like heavy truck striking building. Standing motor cars rock noticeably.

V. Felt by nearly everyone; many awakened. Some dishes, windows broken. Unstable objects overturned. Pendulum clocks may stop.

VI. Felt by all, many frightened. Some heavy furniture moved; a few instances of fallen plaster. Damage slight.

VII. Damage negligible in buildings of good design and construction; slight to moderate in well-built ordinary structures; considerable damage in poorly built or badly designed structures; some chimneys broken.

VIII. Damage slight in specially designed structures; damage considerable in ordinary substantial buildings with partial collapse. Damage great in poorly built structures. Fall of chimneys, factory stacks, columns, monuments, walls. Heavy furniture overturned.

IX. Damage considerable in specially designed structures; well-designed frame structures thrown out of plumb. Damage great in substantial buildings, with partial collapse. Buildings shifted off foundations.

X. Some well-built wooden structures destroyed; most masonry and frame structures destroyed with foundations. Rails bent.

XI. Few, if any (masonry) structures remain standing. Bridges destroyed. Rails bent greatly.

XII. Damage total. Lines of sight and level are distorted. Objects thrown into the air.

Source: U.S. Geological Survey.

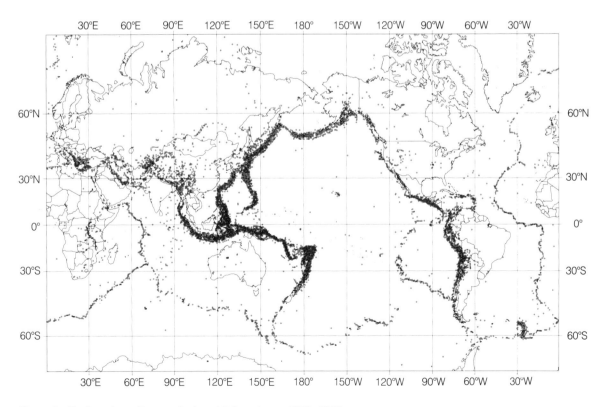

Figure 3 Earthquakes with magnitudes of 5.0 or above, 1963–1988.

landslides caused tens of millions of dollars' worth of damage and blocked many transportation routes, hampering rescue and relief efforts.

Tsunamis—massive, towering waves caused by earthquakes or tremors—can travel thousands of miles across the ocean before striking shore. Populated coastal areas throughout the Pacific are vulnerable to tsunamis. The city of Hilo, Hawaii, for example, is now located twelve miles farther inland than it was in the mid-1940s, when a tsunami destroyed portions of the city located nearer the shore. In response to the threat of tsunamis, countries with shores on the Pacific have developed a spotter system and cooperate in warning one another of tsunamis.

Volcanic eruptions are another potentially deadly result of seismic activity. Like earthquakes, volcanic eruptions are most common at the edges of major tectonic plates, where the earth's crust is unstable. The Pacific Ocean rim is sometimes known as the "ring of fire" because of the frequency and intensity of its seismic activity.

The most famous volcanic eruption in history was the eruption of Vesuvius, which destroyed the city of Pompeii in A.D. 79. More recent examples of volcanic eruptions are Mount St. Helens in Washington State (1980) and Mount Kilanea in Hawaii (1989).

Flooding   Flooding is the natural disaster from which human beings are most at risk. Although few injuries result from floods, more deaths and property damage (particularly from landslides) can be attributed to flooding than to any other type of natural disaster. According to the National Flood Insurance Program, roughly eight million structures are located in hazardous floodplains in the United States. The figures that follow show the cost of flood damage in the United States over a five-year period:

1985	$367,863,787
1986	126,219,031
1987	104,769,883
1988	47,665,559
1989	419,684,755[6]

The most dangerous floods are flash floods. They can occur anywhere, even in arid lands; usually develop suddenly and without warning; and are much more likely to cause fatalities than slow flooding is. In an arid area, for example, a deluge of rain in nearby hills may fill dry riverbeds, turning them quickly into torrents. Flash floods can have a variety of other causes as well—such as the collapse of a dam or a tidal surge from a hurricane's sudden change of course. One of the most devastating flash floods in U.S. history struck Johnstown, Pennsylvania, in 1889, killing 2,200 people. More recently, to name just two occurrences, the 1976 Big Thompson Canyon flash flood near Estes Park, Colorado, killed 139; and in 1990, Shadyside, Ohio, suffered 51 fatalities.

Some scientists predict that global warming will raise the level of ocean waters by three feet by the year 2010. If this prediction holds true, major flooding along low-lying U.S. coastal states will increase, and elsewhere in the world the results of the higher water levels may be catastrophic.

Hurricanes   Hurricanes, or typhoons (as they are known in the western Pacific), are masses of warm, moist air rotating around a low-pressure area. These air masses develop seasonally over the Atlantic and Caribbean, the eastern Pacific off Mexico, and the western Pacific. When they reach speeds of seventy-four miles per hour, they are called hurricanes.

Although fewer deaths and injuries result from hurricanes than from earthquakes or floods, hurricanes still are potentially deadly. They can easily change course, subjecting coastal areas to a tidal or storm surge whose effects are very much like those of a flash flood. And a hurricane like Hugo, which in 1989 inflicted more than seven billion dollars' worth of damage on South Carolina, would have been catastrophic if it had directly hit a major metropolitan area like Miami. Moreover, although improvements in advance warning systems during the past fifty years have significantly reduced deaths and injuries from hurricanes, expanded development in vulnerable coastal areas has caused property damage to increase significantly. One study showed that "as of 1985 almost 75% of U.S. coastal residents from Texas to Maine have never experienced a direct hit by a major hurricane. Many of those 43 million residents had moved to coastal sections during the [previous] twenty-five years."[7] Unless cities and counties along the coast from Texas to Maine are prepared to warn and evacuate their citizens quickly, major hurricanes in coming years have the potential to be catastrophic disasters.

Some climatologists are concerned that global warming will increase the size and frequency of hurricanes; other hurricane experts are particularly concerned about the level of summer rainfall occurring in West Africa—a breeding ground of Atlantic hurricanes.

William Gray, professor of atmospheric science at Colorado State University, notes that the changing levels of summer rainfall in West Africa correspond to patterns in the occurrence of higher-category hurricanes (categories 3, 4, and 5). Particularly heavy rains create conditions favorable to the formation of more and stronger Atlantic hurricanes. The years between 1970 and 1987 were a time of drought in West Africa and were marked by relatively few big Atlantic storms. But the heavy rains occur in twenty- to twenty-five-year cycles, which means that an increase in the level of rainfall is about due—along with a corresponding increase in the number and size of hurricanes. Gray predicts an increase in the number of killer hurricanes in the 1990s. He also warns that "the return of more intense hurricanes will have much greater impact because of the greatly increased population and property values along the hurricane-prone coastlines over the last 20 years."[8]

Tornadoes Tornadoes, which are among the most violent natural events to strike North America, generally develop when severe thunderstorms are present. Thunderstorms typically occur when a fast-moving cold front collides with warm, moist air. Tornado funnels are created when the stable boundary of air within the thunderstorm is disrupted, allowing warm, moist air to suddenly spiral up toward the cool, dry air of higher altitudes. Tornadoes can travel at speeds of up to seventy miles per hour, with funnel wind speeds reaching six hundred miles per hour.

The states most at risk from tornadoes are Oklahoma, Florida, and Indiana,

Table 3. Saffir/Simpson hurricane scale ranges.

Scale number (category)	Central pressure		OR	Winds (mph)	OR	Surge (feet)	Damage
	Millibars	Inches					
1	≥980	≥28.94		74–95		4–5	Minimal
2	965–979	28.50–28.91		96–110		6–8	Moderate
3	945–964	27.91–28.47		111–130		9–12	Extensive
4	920–944	27.17–27.88		131–155		13–18	Extreme
5	<920	<27.17		>155		>18	Catastrophic

which in a typical year have 6 to 8 tornadoes per 10,000 square miles. Massachusetts, Kansas, Illinois, and Iowa average annually 5 to 6 tornadoes per 10,000 square miles. And Mississippi, Missouri, Nebraska, and Texas typically experience 4 to 5 tornadoes per 10,000 square miles per year.

One of the worst tornado disasters in the United States occurred in Wichita Falls, Texas, in 1979, when tornadoes cut an 8-mile swath across the city, obliterating everything in their path and destroying more than 4,000 homes. Although 1,700 people were injured and 171 were hospitalized, only 46 people died, principally because of the city's effective warning system. Of those who died, 25 were killed in their cars, and 16 of those had deliberately sought safety in their vehicles—an action that tornado education programs urge citizens to avoid.

According to the National Weather Service's National Severe Storm and Warning Center, which tracks tornadoes, issues warnings on them, and keeps records on tornadoes and other severe weather conditions, the number of tornadoes recorded in the United States increased from 4,795 in the 1950s to more than 8,000 in the 1970s and 1980s. The increase in the number of tornadoes recorded during the past two decades is principally due to more-reliable and better-developed tornado reporting systems and extensive development in previously uninhabited prairie land.

Technological disasters

Unlike most natural disasters, technological disasters (which may or may not involve hazardous materials) usually are preceded by little or no warning. In some cases, technological disasters are insidious, and victims may not know they have been affected until many years later. A 1990 report from the U.S. Department of Energy, for example, noted that airborne leaks of high doses of radioactive iodine from the Hanford Nuclear Reservation near Richland, Washington, had occurred from 1944 to 1947, affecting 13,500 people living near the plant. These toxic radioactive leaks are now being blamed for high incidences of cancer, thyroid dysfunction, and heart problems among residents of the surrounding area. Similar evidence of health problems caused by hidden toxic waste sites like that at Love Canal, near Niagara Falls, New York, has generated significant federal legislation to safeguard citizens from such dangers, including the Comprehensive Environmental Response, Compensation and Liability Act of 1980.

Although there are many kinds of technological disasters, the most common involve fires or explosions. Other kinds of technological disasters include transportation accidents, such as airplane crashes; structural failures, such as the collapse of the skywalk at the Kansas City Hyatt Hotel; and rail and highway hazardous materials incidents. Less likely, but more feared by the public, are nuclear power plant failures such as the one that occurred in 1986 at Chernobyl in the Soviet Union.

The number of technological incidents is increasing, primarily because hundreds of new substances are created each year, giving rise to that many more opportunities for human error. For example, about 2 billion tons of the more than 2,400 materials identified as hazardous by the U.S. Department of Transportation are transported annually; and the Environmental Protection Agency estimates that 266 metric tons of hazardous waste are generated each year.[9]

Although technological disasters are wholly unpredictable, maps showing where facilities are located or where hazardous activities are being conducted can reveal areas at risk from such disasters. Major transportation corridors, for example, are likely places for hazardous materials incidents.

In 1968, to help bring federal agency expertise to bear on incidents involving spills of oil and hazardous substances, Congress established the National Contingency Plan (NCP). The two primary legal authorities for the NCP are the Clean Water Act, which established a fund for federal responses to oil spills;

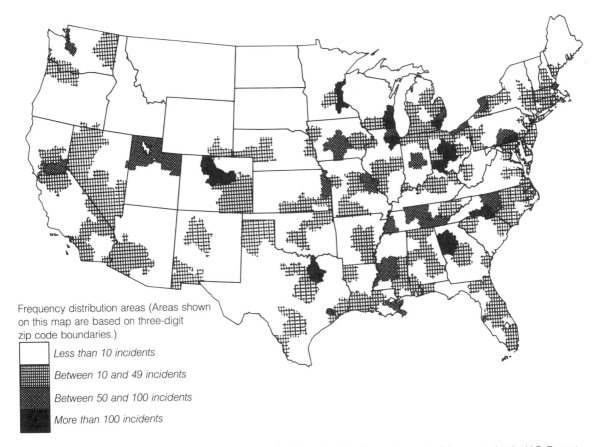

Figure 4 Rail and highway incidents involving hazardous materials reported to the U.S. Department of Transportation, 1989.

and the Comprehensive Environmental Response, Compensation and Liability Act (CERCLA), which established the Superfund for federal responses to release of hazardous substances. The National Response Team (NRT) is responsible for coordinating federal planning, preparedness, and response actions related to oil discharges and hazardous substance releases.

Partly in response to the December 1984 disaster in Bhopal, India, when a cloud of deadly methyl isocyanate gas escaped from a Union Carbide chemical plant, killing more than twenty-five thousand people and leaving tens of thousands injured, Congress enacted legislation mandating disaster planning wherever hazardous materials are in use. The Superfund Amendments and Reauthorization Act (SARA) is designed to assist localities and citizens in preparing for and responding to hazardous materials incidents. Title III of SARA (also known as the Emergency Planning and Community Right-to-Know Act) requires that detailed information about the nature of hazardous substances in or near communities be made available to the public.

Both of these congressional actions (NCP and SARA Title III) have considerably improved the ability of local communities to prepare for and respond to the increasing number of technological incidents and disasters.

Civil disasters

Wars, civil disturbances, massacres, and other deliberately destructive human actions have characterized human life since the dawn of time. The likely results of civil disasters—besides large-scale loss of life—are squalid camps of refugees, widespread illness and injury, the destruction of property, and long-term social and economic disruption. Particularly since the founding of the United Nations, international preparedness and cooperation have been put forth as a principal means of preventing such disasters or coping with them should they occur.

Terrorism is a civil incident with the potential to lead to civil disaster. The miniaturization of highly destructive weapons and political unrest have made terrorism of particular concern in Europe and the Middle East. The United States has also been affected by terrorist activity; the 1988 bombing of Pan Am flight 103 over Scotland is an example.

Like terrorism, random incidents of violence and civil disturbances such as riots can become catalysts for widespread destruction and unheaval. Racial and social inequality and deep-seated political differences have the potential to create civil unrest—such as that experienced by Miami during the 1980s. Given the right conditions, civil unrest can escalate to civil disaster. In short, civil disaster is not necessarily the result of conflict with another nation; the seeds of civil disaster may lie entirely within one nation's borders.

Response to a major incident   At 5:10 P.M. on January 2, 1988—a bitter cold holiday weekend—a four-million-gallon oil tank collapsed, and a wave of oil washed over the containment dike at an Ashland Oil terminal near Pittsburgh. About one million gallons of oil escaped into the Monongahela River through storm sewers—a major oil spill. Ashland employees promptly notified the National Response Center and the Coast Guard; they in turn notified EPA, which dispatched the designated on-scene coordinator.

Local authorities were the first responders on the scene. They and Ashland's cleanup contractor worked to prevent the oil from reaching the river. However, initial response actions were hampered by several factors. Because the initial evaluation took place in the dark, the early reports greatly underestimated the spill's magnitude. All electrical and telephone lines were disconnected at the terminal after a report of a gasoline leak, and about 250 people were evacuated because of the fear of explosion or fire. The resulting confusion made site access difficult and impeded the first responders' efforts.

The Coast Guard, the first federal agency on the scene, controlled river traffic and mobilized a national strike force team. The EPA on-scene coordinator arrived at first light the next morning, along with the EPA technical

assistance team. Ashland agreed to assume full responsibility for the costs of the cleanup and accepted EPA's direction of the response action. The incident-specific regional response team (RRT) was activated on January 4. The RRT included seven federal agencies, two state agencies each from Pennsylvania, West Virginia, and Ohio, and one Kentucky agency. The RRT members acted as conduits for information to and from their agencies.

Three types of monitoring took place: monitoring of the rivers to define spill mass and track spill movement, monitoring of intakes to protect water supplies, and monitoring of the effects on fish and wildlife. Several federal and state RRT member agencies tracked the spill and took samples until mid-February, when the spill had dispersed to the point where sample results were inconclusive. The sampling extended down the Ohio River to Illinois. Provision of information by the emergency response agencies enabled downstream water suppliers to implement treatment procedures and increase storage volume before the spill affected their intakes.

Source: The National Response Team, *A Report on the National Oil and Hazardous Substances Response System*, Annual Report (Washington, D.C.: National Response Team, March 1989).

Organization of this book

This book consists of twelve chapters divided into four parts: "History and Foundations of Emergency Management" (chapters 1–5), "Comprehensive Emergency Management" (chapters 6–9), "Daily Operations and Legal Issues" (chapters 10 and 11), and "The Future of Emergency Management" (chapter 12).

In chapter 1, "The Evolution of Emergency Management," Thomas Drabek sets the stage for the rest of the volume by reviewing the development of emergency management as a field of research and practice. Gary Kreps's chapter 2, "Organizing for Emergency Management," begins the discussion of "foundations" by examining the organizing principles and practices that make for effective emergency management at the local level. Kreps focuses on planning and the ability to improvise, the two pillars of effective preparedness. In chapter 3, "Coordinating Community Resources," David Gillespie describes how to achieve the level of coordination that is essential to good emergency management, focusing particularly on the roles of community organizations, the private sector, and critical community systems. Joseph Scanlon's chapter 4, "Reaching Out: Getting the Community Involved in Preparedness," covers public perception of emergency management, citizens' responses to warnings and evacuations, and the crucial role of the mass media in disaster education, warning, and response. Tom Durham and Lacy Suiter, in chapter 5, "Perspectives and Roles of the State and Federal Governments," explore in detail the relationship between local emergency management and other levels of government.

Part 2 of the volume describes the activities and responsibilities involved in emergency management during each of the four phases of CEM—mitigation, preparedness, response, and recovery. David Godschalk's chapter 6, "Disaster Mitigation and Hazard Management," reviews the most politically sensitive and difficult phase of comprehensive emergency management and suggests ways of overcoming resistance to mitigation. In chapter 7, "Planning, Training, and Exercising," Guy Daines discusses the three principal activities associated with the preparedness phase of emergency management. The response phase of CEM is discussed by Ronald Perry in chapter 8, "Managing Disaster Response Operations," which covers leadership during crises, victims' responses to disaster, and the role of the emergency operations center. Chapter 9, "Recovery from Disaster," by Claire B. Rubin, concludes this section of the book by analyzing the characteristics of a successful community recovery; coming full circle, Rubin stresses the importance of incorporating mitigation efforts into the recovery process.

Part 3 consists of two chapters. In chapter 10, "Day-to-Day Management," Barbara Block and John Pickett detail the daily operations of managing an office of emergency management. John Pine's chapter 11, "Liability Issues," reviews the forms of organizational and individual liability that can result from emergency management activities and suggests ways in which local governments and emergency management personnel can protect themselves from suit.

Part 4 consists of a single chapter—chapter 12—on the future of the profession. William Anderson and Shirley Mattingly consider the effects of demographic change; a number of emerging issues that will shape the political and social context within which emergency managers must operate and make decisions in the years to come; and the relationship between practitioners and the academic community.

Symbolically, this last chapter is the first chapter of a closer working relationship between disaster researchers and emergency management practitioners. Unfortunately, many localities that experience disaster make the same mistakes—mistakes that could perhaps be prevented if the individuals in charge of emergency management were more familiar with research findings. But because the emergency management community has only begun the long process of professionalization, the transfer of knowledge from researchers to practitioners has been slow and erratic. That situation is beginning to change, and this book is one part of that change; the professional certification program being established by the National Coordinating Council on Emergency Management is another.

The political and administrative context in which local emergency program managers must operate is also changing. Many local government chief executives are beginning to see the benefits of effective emergency management in daily operations. The principles of emergency management, in fact, are fundamental to the efficient operation of other local government departments, particularly police and fire. In the case of police, the communication, coordination, and cooperation that are essential to emergency management are equally essential to the effective delivery of day-to-day police services—because effective policing can no longer depend solely on the police department. A multidepartmental, community approach is required. To deal with the underlying causes of crime, police departments need to work with recreation departments, social service agencies, and other government agencies. Similarly, a fire department that only responds to fires is doing but a small percentage of its job; it also needs to be involved in mitigation (through code enforcement and inspections), in preparedness (through fire safety education), and in recovery (by providing information and assistance after a fire).

The city manager of Pampa, Texas, integrated emergency management principles into daily operations and management throughout the local government. Not only did the delivery of regular services improve as a result, but also, after a massive explosion at an industrial plant that employed a large number of Pampa citizens, the city was able to respond to the disaster and recover from it quickly. The community recovered successfully because it had regularly applied the lessons of good emergency management. It is our hope that this book will enable readers to do the same.

1 Quoted in Fenton Johnson, "Aftershock in San Francisco," *New York Times Magazine*, June 17, 1990, 2.

2 Robert C. Bolin, *Long-Term Family Recovery from Disaster* (Boulder, Colorado: Institute of Behavioral Science, The University of Colorado, 1982), 131.

3 As of late 1990, ecological hazards (defined later in this introduction) are not among the hazards encompassed by CEM.

4 Stephen H. Schneider, "Cooling It," *World Monitor* (July 1990): 30.

5 Ibid.

6 Figures provided by Jeff Donahue of the National Flood Insurance Program, telephone interview, July 26, 1990.

7 Paul J. Herbert and Robert A. Case, "The Deadliest, Costliest, and Most Intense United States Hurricanes of This Century (and Other Frequently Requested Hurricane Facts)" (Miami, FL: National Hurricane Center, National Oceanic and Atmospheric Administration/National Weather Services, 1990).

8 William Gray, "Outlook for Atlantic Hurricane Activity During 1990" (Paper presented at the National Hurricane Conference, Houston, TX, April 1990).

9 Figures given in Raymond D. Scanlon, "Introduction," in *Hazardous Materials, Hazardous Waste: Local Management Options*, ed. Raymond D. Scanlon (Washington, DC: International City Management Association, 1987), 4.

Part one: History and foundations of emergency management

The evolution of emergency management

People have always devised strategies for coping with disaster: forms of mitigation, preparedness, response, and recovery have existed as long as human society has. In recent years, such activities have become the domain of an emerging profession. The purpose of this chapter is to place the development of the emergency management profession into historical context.

The chapter begins by considering the two principal policy streams that have shaped emergency management in the United States: responses to natural disasters and civil defense programs.

Although little can be done to control extreme natural events, improved warning, response, and mitigation practices have done much to limit the damage they cause. The notion that the federal government ought to play a consistent and important role in disaster response has gained increasing strength in the course of this century. How that role should be implemented has been less clear, and the numerous shifts in federal policy and practice have greatly influenced emergency management at the state and local levels. Moreover, social developments—extensive settlement of earthquake- or flood-prone lands, the increasing production, use, and transportation of hazardous materials—have added to the breadth and complexity of the hazards faced by communities nationwide.

As for efforts to respond to the threat of war, the earliest human settlements give evidence of them. And the destructive capacity of weaponry has steadily grown, so that nations are now threatened by devastation of unimaginable proportions. In the United States, as with natural and technological disasters, the key to civil defense has been the history of federal policy. The chapter examines the evolution of that policy, including the eventual alliance—albeit a somewhat uneasy one—between civil defense efforts and the management of other disasters. The chapter examines the creation of the Federal Emergency Management Agency (FEMA), the emergence of comprehensive emergency management, and the development of the integrated emergency management system.

In recent years, emergency management policy and practice have begun to feel the influence of social science research findings. Even today, however, far more is known than is ordinarily applied; one of the goals of this book is to broaden the application of current findings. With this in mind, the chapter examines the growing body of research being undertaken in the behavioral sciences.

The chapter concludes with a look at the policy issues facing emergency management today and in the years to come, considering in some detail the trends that are expected to influence emergency management as a practice and as a profession.

Patterns of response to disaster

Ancient peoples responded to natural disasters by inventing frameworks to explain the origin of the disasters and prevent future occurrences. According to the folklore of the Hawaiian islands, for example, when the goddess who controlled

Figure 1–1
One of
the most
devastating
floods in U.S.
history struck
Johnstown,
Pennsylvania,
in 1889.

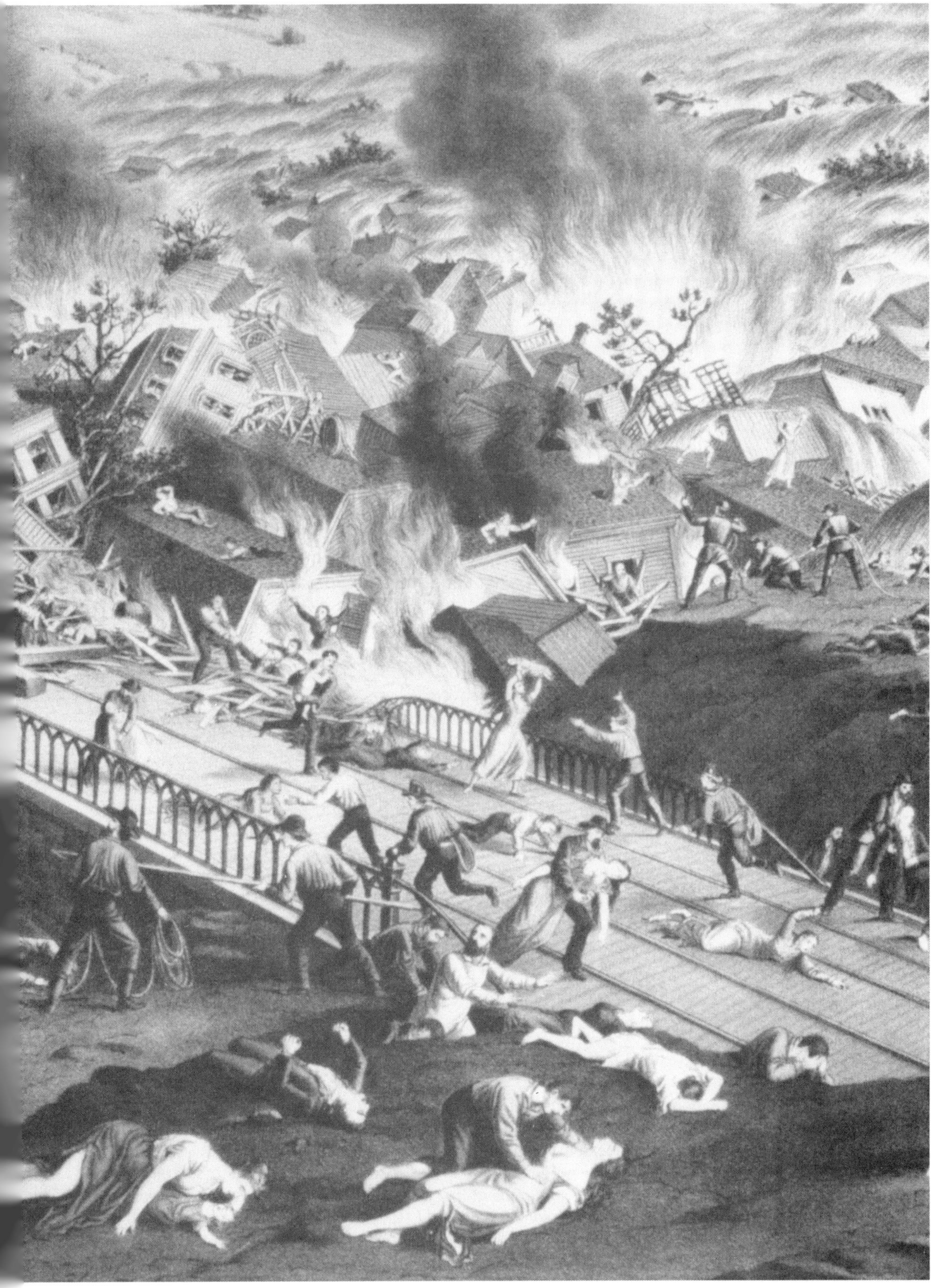

the volcanoes became angry, she caused molten lava to pour forth from an otherwise quiet mountaintop. Surveys of other cultures reveal parallels.

Although such supernatural explanations of disasters still exist throughout the world, scientific views of such events have gained ground—and are the basis for the modern profession of emergency management.[1] One of the crucial differences between the scientific and the nonscientific view of disaster concerns the nature of the human actions designed to prevent or to respond to such events. Rather than attempt to appease a supernatural being who controls wind, rain, or tides, scientific efforts focus on specific protective actions—from building codes, to insurance, to evacuation.

One of the earliest instances of such efforts occurred in response to the Great Fire of London, which struck in 1666. During a five-day period, 13,200 houses, nearly 90 churches, the guild hall, the royal exchange, the customs house, other government buildings, and numerous hospitals and libraries burned to the ground. Nearly two-thirds of the city was destroyed.

The losses of 1666 stimulated the gradual adoption of building codes and insurance, two of the most important forms of nonstructural disaster mitigation ever devised. For centuries, fire victims had relied chiefly on donations from friends and relatives. After the Great Fire, these were augmented by settlements from private insurance organizations. Such settlements gradually became commonplace, especially after lending institutions began requiring insurance to protect their investments. In 1752, nearly a century after the Great Fire of London, Benjamin Franklin founded the first successful fire insurance company in America.[2]

Emergency management in America: Responses to disaster

In 1803, American responses to disaster took a significant turn, beginning a pattern of federal involvement that continues to this day.[3] When an extensive fire swept through Portsmouth, New Hampshire, community and state resources were taxed severely by the recovery effort. This situation was dramatized to Congress, which responded with the first legislative action making federal resources available to assist a state and a local government. This congressional act of 1803 is commonly regarded as the first piece of national disaster legislation.[4]

Congress responded similarly many times during the decades that followed. Hurricanes struck the coastal areas of Texas, Florida, Louisiana, and elsewhere, prompting the release of federal funds for disaster assistance. Victims of the San Francisco earthquake of 1906 received congressional aid. Although the earthquake was not matched in scope by floods or tornadoes, these, too, evoked congressional action. Between 1803 and 1950, more than one hundred disasters of various types across the nation were combatted with federal resources made available under ad hoc legislative decrees.

Expansions under Roosevelt

During the Depression, President Franklin Roosevelt recast the partnership among local, state, and federal agencies, advocating a far more active role for the federal government and establishing a number of new programs and agencies to implement his New Deal.

In 1933, for example, the Reconstruction Finance Corporation was granted authority to provide loans for the repair and reconstruction of certain public facilities that had been damaged by earthquakes; other disasters were eventually included in this program. In 1934, the Bureau of Public Roads was given continuous authority to provide grants for the repair of federal-aid highways and bridges that had been damaged by natural events. During the next sixteen years, thirty-nine million dollars were spent to repair flood-damaged roads and bridges on the federal-aid road system.[5]

The Flood Control Act of 1936 provided for a wide variety of projects, many of which were completed under authority granted to the Army Corps of Engineers. Reflecting the proactive approach advocated by engineers, hundreds of dams, dikes, and levees were erected to reduce vulnerability to floods.

These are but a few illustrations of the growing federal role in emergency management. Although many of the ventures supported by President Roosevelt led to new or expanded federal activities, it is important to note that during the nation's struggle to escape from the Depression, many state and local governments also initiated emergency management programs.

The Federal Disaster Act of 1950

In August 1950, Congressman Harold Hagen of Minnesota presented to the House Committee on Public Works a list of 128 separate laws that Congress had passed since 1803. Each of these had been enacted after specific disasters, which, in Hagen's view, established a clear precedent for supplemental federal assistance to state and local governments. Although two earlier acts had permitted federal resources to be applied to disaster relief, the Federal Disaster Act of 1950 created, for the first time, *permanent* and *general* legislation pertaining to disaster relief.[6]

Interestingly, the legislation was prompted by everyday problems—flood-damaged roads and bridges that prevented people from getting to work and transporting produce to nearby cities. Although rarely life threatening, the floods had created hardships that were beyond the capacities of local governments to remedy. According to a recent legislative history of disaster relief, Hagen described the primary purpose of the bill as that of "getting assistance to rebuild the streets and farm-to-market highways and roads":

The existing law limited its program to the primary and secondary federal-aid road systems. Without a change in the law, there was no way in which federal dollars could be regularly used for the repair of county and township roads. . . . During the course of the hearings, local officials recited one example after another to prove to the Congress that they were in dire need of relief. County finances in many counties were reaching the breaking point from the costs for repairing roads, bridges, and culverts from previous disasters, with no resources available to combat the present flooding.[7]

Figure 1–2 A levee used as a refuge during Mississippi River flooding in 1912.

The 1950 act established the legal basis for a continuing federal role in disaster relief, formalizing and stabilizing an impressive array of already-existing federal programs. Congress described its intent as follows:

To provide an orderly and continuing means of assistance by the Federal Government to state and local governments in carrying out their responsibilities to alleviate suffering and damage resulting from major disasters, to repair essential public facilities in major disasters, and to foster the development of such state and local organizations and plans to cope with major disasters as may be necessary.[8]

Figure 1–3   In drought-plagued Liberal, Kansas, dust particles darken the sky (ca. 1930).

Figure 1–4   Remains of the Cocoanut Grove nightclub after a 1942 fire.

Program fragmentation

Although a number of disasters struck the United States following passage of the 1950 Federal Disaster Act, the Alaskan earthquake of March 27, 1964, presented unprecedented challenges and evoked expanded federal participation in recovery efforts. Unfortunately, this participation continued to reflect the general legislative pattern of the pre-1950 era: programs were created or expanded either in response to specific disasters or because federal agency executives perceived new needs. Congress passed legislation, for example, following Hurricanes Betsy and Camille (1965 and 1969), Tropical Storm Agnes (1972), and the San Fernando earthquake (1971). Additional acts liberalized the circumstances under which federal surplus equipment could be used and provided special assistance to groups such as farmers and stockmen.

These and other actions compounded the growing fragmentation among programs. Following Hurricane Camille, Senator Birch Bayh of Indiana held hearings in Mississippi and Virginia to garner support for an Omnibus Disaster Assistance Act, passed as the Disaster Relief Act of 1970. Although the act was intended to lessen fragmentation of relief programs, criticism from many local and state government officials continued. Further hearings culminated in passage of the Disaster Relief Act of 1974, Title II of which authorized federal assistance for both federal and state disaster preparedness and warning programs. Title III of the act authorized disaster assistance and the creation of the Federal Disaster Assistance Administration—the precursor to the Federal Emergency Management Agency (FEMA).[9]

Civil defense in the pre-atomic era

Although civil defense became particularly important after the creation of the atomic bomb, with its potential to inflict civilian casualties of unheard-of dimensions, an important legacy had been established before that era.

Figure 1–5   Hurricane Camille (1969) left this pile of debris on the doorstep of the city hall in Long Beach, Mississippi.

Well before the discovery of the New World, settlement patterns in Europe reflected efforts at civil defense. Castles were built on high ground so that approaching troops could be observed and the rulers within defended. After the invention of artillery, walls were constructed around settlements to guard against that new threat. More modern—and more abstract—concepts of civil defense derive from the writings of political philosophers, particularly Thomas Hobbes. Hobbes articulated the view that government has a duty to protect its citizens.[10]

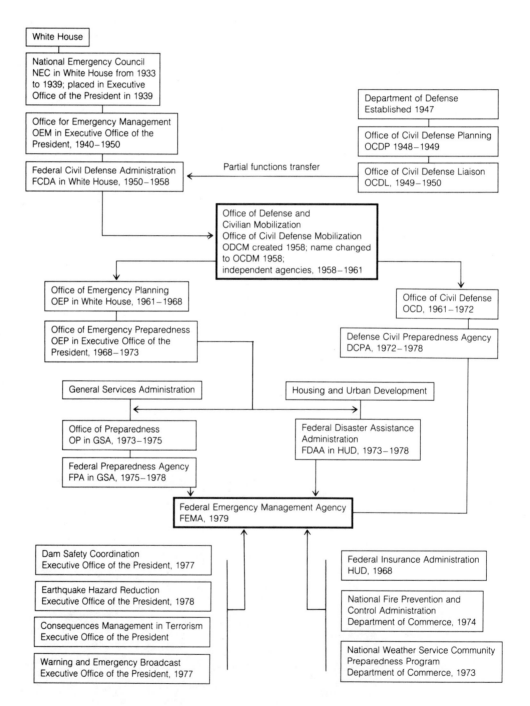

Figure 1-6 Development of federal organizations with emergency management responsibilities.

A less philosophical though no less important perspective emerged from the experiences of a young Swiss by the name of Jean Henri Dunant, whose presence at the Battle of Solferino led eventually to the creation of the International Red Cross. (The accompanying sidebar details Dunant's role in developing an organization that is central to the delivery of disaster relief worldwide.) In the United States, it was Clara Barton, the well-known Civil War nurse, who took on the task of establishing the American Red Cross, still operating under the federal charter awarded by President William McKinley in 1900.

The early years of the twentieth century brought weapons of great destructive power, and the horrors of chemical warfare and civilian bombing in Europe spurred U.S. efforts to organize for civil defense. In 1916, Congress enacted the United States Army Appropriation Act, the first legislation pertaining to civil defense. This act established the Council of National Defense (CND), which consisted of the secretaries of war, navy, agriculture, commerce, labor, and the interior. The CND established the War Industries Board and encouraged states to create state defense councils. The state councils were encouraged, in turn, to create local defense councils. In 1917, the CND established the State Councils Section to provide liaison between the state councils and the federal council. Although these agencies received little nurturing in the years following World War I, they established a pattern of partnership and communication within the intergovernmental structure.

From Castiglione to Geneva   As president of a grain company in Algeria (then a French possession), Jean Henri Dunant was in Italy seeking the approval of Napoleon III to build some windmills to grind grain. The Franco-Austrian war was being fought in East Lombardy, and Napoleon was directing his troops from Castiglione. On the morning of 24 June 1859, Dunant heard the noise of a fierce battle, later known as the Battle of Solferino. When all was quiet, Dunant rode to the battlefield and was shocked by the sight of hundreds of wounded soldiers scattered across the fields. He organized some of the townspeople to assist with medical treatment—without regard to which nation the wounded represented.

Memories of this experience haunted Dunant in the months that followed. Three years later he published *Un Souvenir de Solferino (A Memory of Solferino)*. Although he acknowledged that wars probably could not be prevented, Dunant believed that the wounded must be cared for and proposed the establishment of a neutral agency to meet this need. His ideas hit a responsive chord, especially in his homeland. In 1863, less than a year after the book's publication, a small group—the Committee of Five—met in Geneva to lay the groundwork for implementing Dunant's proposal.

Later that same year, the committee sponsored a conference attended by representatives of sixteen countries, all of whom agreed to establish an independent organization when they returned home. The International Red Cross and Red Crescent Movement was launched.

In 1901, Dunant, along with Frédéric Passy, who founded the French Union for Peace and the French Association for Arbitration between Nations, was awarded the first Nobel Peace Prize.

Source: Richard Deming, *Heroes of the International Red Cross* (New York: Meredith Press, 1969). See also Pam Brown, *Henry Dunant* (Watford, England: Exley Publications, Ltd., 1988).

The councils were not without their critics. In assessing such programs, Thomas Kerr has noted, for example, that their missions went far beyond defending the population against attack:

Since the United States was never in danger of attack, the civil defense programs assumed an essentially nonprotective quality. Instead of being mainly concerned with programs designed to cope with the effects of actual attack, the civil defense effort was largely given over to the mobilization of popular support for the war effort. . . . Attention was turned to such activities as maintaining anti-saboteur vigilance, encouraging men to join the armed forces, facilitating the implementation of the draft, participating in Liberty Bond drives, and helping to maintain the morale of the soldiers.[11]

When World War I ended, other priorities surfaced. During the roaring twenties and the depression of the thirties, civil defense policy aroused minimal interest. As hostilities intensified in Europe during the end of the 1930s, however, more attention was directed at defense issues.

In 1939, President Roosevelt issued a statement on espionage, requesting all

---

Clara Barton and the American Red Cross After her heroic work organizing medical assistance for thousands wounded in the Civil War, Clara Barton retreated to Europe to rest. In Geneva, she learned of the emerging Red Cross societies and of the principles they had formulated regarding the treatment of wounded soldiers. These principles, formally expressed in the "Geneva Convention for the Amelioration of the Condition of the Wounded of Armies in the Field," were ratified by a dozen European nations in 1864. However, President Ulysses Grant and his successors rejected the convention because they did not wish to become involved in European treaties.

A pamphlet Barton published in 1878 called for a "peacetime mission," a principle that greatly increased public acceptance of her views. Barton emphasized that Red Cross societies should respond to natural disasters as well as to those of human origin. In what came to be recognized as the "American amendment," Barton defined the need for emergency management and proposed that it be met by the Red Cross:

Although we in the United States may fondly hope to be seldom visited by the calamities of war, yet the misfortunes of other nations with which we are on terms of amity appeal to our sympathies; our southern coasts are periodically visited by the scourge of yellow fever; the valleys of the Mississippi are subject to destructive inundations; the plains of the West are devastated by insects and drought, and our cities and country are swept by consuming fires. In all such cases, to gather and dispense the profuse liberality of our people, without waste of time or material, requires the wisdom that comes of experience and permanent organization.

Barton pressured influential people for nearly a dozen years. In the early 1880s, she and others founded the American Association of the Red Cross. In 1882, under President Chester Arthur, the United States formally ratified the Geneva Convention. President Arthur's signature cleared the way for Barton's newly formed organization to join other national societies that made up the International Red Cross movement. Barton's efforts are generally recognized as the most significant influence on U.S. ratification of the treaty.

Source: Excerpt from *THE AMERICAN RED CROSS: A History* by Foster Rhea Dulles. Copyright 1950 by the American Red Cross. Reprinted by permission of HarperCollins Publishers Inc. The excerpt from Clara Barton's *The Red Cross of the Geneva Convention: What It Is* (1878) is quoted in Dulles, p. 14.

citizens, including state and local officials, to turn over relevant information to the FBI; local police officials began to do so almost immediately.[12] In addition, the FBI began surveying plants under contract to manufacture defense materials and prepared a plant protection manual for use by local police chiefs.

Shortly after making his statement, President Roosevelt established an Office for Emergency Management (OEM). The liaison officer for emergency management was an administrative assistant to the president who was subsequently named secretary of the CND and of the council's advisory commission.[13]

As the world crisis intensified, the coordination responsibilities of the OEM were expanded, as it coordinated a range of defense-related issues among complex governmental structures. In the area of defense housing, for example, the OEM worked with numerous federal, state, and local agencies—which, in turn, worked with private builders.

In 1941, President Roosevelt abolished the CND and established the Office of Civil Defense (OCD) within the Office of Emergency Planning. Like its predecessor, the OCD was linked with what was by then a nationwide network of 44 state and 1,000 local defense councils.[14]

The first head of the OCD was New York City Mayor Fiorello LaGuardia, who resigned within a year amid controversy. His replacement was James M. Landis, dean of the Harvard University Law School. Landis's primary achievement was to strengthen the fledgling protective services programs, especially the Civil Defense Corps, which coordinated approximately ten million volunteers to provide shelter instruction, camouflage of vital facilities, evacuation readiness, and other services. When the war came to an end, bringing hopes of a lasting peace, President Truman abolished the OCD.

The nuclear threat and civil defense

Although the advent of nuclear weapons made it much more difficult to protect civilian populations, the nuclear threat was not high on the public agenda during

The Red Cross today Henri Dunant's vision is now implemented by a complex organization that integrates the efforts of millions of people. The International Red Cross and Red Crescent Movement has three units (described below) and is coordinated through policies adopted at the International Conference by its standing commission and council of delegates.

The International Committee of the Red Cross (ICRC) is an independent Swiss institution that continues as the founding body of the Red Cross and the guardian and promoter of the Geneva Convention. It acts as a neutral intermediary during armed conflicts, providing protection and assistance to military and civilian victims.

The League of Red Cross and Red Crescent Societies (LORCS) was created in 1919 as the international federation of national Red Cross and Red Crescent societies. It facilitates the activities of its members' societies and promotes the establishment and growth of new societies. LORCS plays an operational role in international emergency relief actions.

The 146 national Red Cross and Red Crescent societies serve as auxiliaries to public authorities in their own nations. Although their activities vary from country to country, they all give priority to health and relief services. Their independence allows them to take action regardless of differences of race, religion, or political opinion.

Source: Adapted from a July 1988 press release issued by the League of Red Cross and Red Crescent Societies, Petit-Saconnex, Geneva, Switzerland.

the years of relative peace that immediately followed World War II. Civil defense programs and funding levels reflected this political reality.

The discussion that follows highlights some of the initiatives and reorganizations of the postwar years.

Civil defense studies and proposals

Between 1945 and 1949, various agencies undertook studies of civil defense. The authors of the U.S. Strategic Bombing Survey recommended evacuation planning and creation of shelters for those who would have to remain.[15] In its *Defense against Enemy Actions Directed against Civilians, Study 3B-1*, the Office of the Provost Marshal General advocated a national shelter policy; stockpiles of civil defense supplies; an effective attack warning system; plans for dispersing industry and evacuating individuals from likely target areas; and training programs in civil defense activities.[16] In 1946 the War Department appointed a Civil Defense Board (CDB) to conduct a third study; the CDB report echoed many of the recommendations of Study 3B-1, adding that major civil defense efforts are civilian in nature and should be undertaken by civilian organizations.[17] Nevertheless, the CDB proposed that any future civil defense agency be established within the "Department of Armed Forces" (the unification of the armed forces was in process at the time).

In March 1948, President Harry Truman appointed Russell J. Hopley, president of Northwestern Bell Telephone, to direct the newly formed Office of Civil Defense Planning (OCDP). The primary mission of the OCDP was to prepare a program report that would include a plan for a permanent civil defense agency. Six months later, the OCDP issued a report, *Civil Defense for National Security*, proposing a federal office of civil defense. Overall responsibility for national civil defense, however, was outlined as a joint responsibility of federal, state, and local governments. Debates about the structural placement of such a program continued until March 1949, when President Truman temporarily resolved them by assigning civil defense responsibility to the National Security Resources Board (NSRB).

Shifts in civil defense policy

Shortly after the civil defense function was assigned to the NSRB, three events altered subsequent policy.[18] First, in August 1949 the Soviets detonated an atomic bomb. The diffusion of nuclear capability represented a new threat, particularly as the Cold War heated up. Second, in June 1950, North Korea sent troops into South Korea; five months later, soldiers from the People's Republic of China joined North Korean troops against the small contingent of troops that had been dispatched by the United Nations. A prolonged conflict seemed inevitable. Third, the NSRB issued a report proposing that "the operational responsibilities of civil defense would rest with the state and local governments and the federal government would assist in ways *it* believed to be appropriate."[19] Although the "Blue Book," as the NSRB report came to be called, echoed many of the ideas of the earlier OCDP report, it recommended that legislation be submitted to Congress establishing a federal civil defense administration reporting directly to the president. In December 1949, President Truman established the Federal Civil Defense Administration (FCDA).

These three events and other converging forces provided the setting for the rapid passage of the Federal Civil Defense Act of 1950. The act provided the FCDA with the authority to initiate planning and "to provide the states and their political subdivisions with guidance, coordination and assistance, training, and matching grants on a fifty-fifty basis for the procurement of supplies and equipment."[20] In addition, the FCDA was to undertake an evacuation and sheltering program.

Many in Congress remained resistant, however, especially when it came to funding. For example, critics from big cities expressed fears of potential boondoggles. "Some legislators from rural areas resented the use of federal tax funds for projects that would only benefit urban areas."[21] The agency requested $403 million to initiate its activities, projecting an eventual total expenditure of $3 billion. The response from Congress was a clear harbinger of future civil defense policy: $31.75 million was approved.

Dwight Eisenhower was elected president, the Korean conflict ended, and the world was introduced to a new vocabulary of weaponry: H-bombs and intercontinental ballistic missiles. Although Val Peterson, the new administrator of the FCDA, make little headway with Congress, he succeeded in introducing two important ideas: (1) civil defense should be regarded as "national survival insurance" in case deterrence failed, and (2) civil defense activities such as disaster planning, rescue, and relief work have peacetime value.

Placement of the FCDA in the federal structure continued to be debated, culminating in a decision to consolidate FCDA's programs with those in the Office of Defense Mobilization (ODM)—an agency President Truman had created during the Korean conflict to manage the economic and production control measures authorized under the Defense Production Act of 1950. Later, the ODM had been assigned to coordinate all federal emergency preparedness measures *except* civil defense. The new Office of Civil Defense Mobilization (OCDM) created from the combined FCDA and ODM was located within the executive office of the president. Because this arrangement also had shortcomings, however, review and debate continued.

In 1961, responsibilities were again divided between two agencies. Most civil defense functions were assigned to the Office of Civil Defense (OCD), an agency of the Department of Defense. The OCDM continued to function within the executive office but was renamed the Office of Emergency Preparedness (OEP). OEP staff determined the civil defense roles of federal agencies, coordinated overall federal civil defense, and oversaw planning for governmental continuity and for national resource mobilization.

From fallout shelters to crisis relocation planning

In 1961, shortly after taking office, President John Kennedy voiced concern about the state of U.S. civil defense programs. Although scholars have speculated widely about the reasons for Kennedy's interest in civil defense, there is no question that his commitment prompted a re-examination of policy.[22] Three reports completed during the Eisenhower administration—the Gaither Report, the Rockefeller Report, and the RAND Corporation Report—had concluded that an expanded sheltering program could reduce the effects of a nuclear attack, assist in subsequent recovery, and, perhaps most important, strengthen the effects of deterrence.[23] Records from the period document disagreement among Kennedy's staff, but the president and Secretary of Defense Robert McNamara pressed the issue during what they referred to as "extraordinary times." In a speech televised nationally on 25 July 1961, the president made a strong appeal:

In the event of an attack, the lives of those families which are not hit in a nuclear blast and fire can still be saved if they can be warned to take shelter and if that shelter is available. We owe that kind of insurance to our families and to our country.

In contrast to our friends in Europe, the need for this kind of protection is new to our shores. But the time to start is now. In the coming months, I hope to let every citizen know what steps he can take without delay to protect his family in case of attack. I know you would not want to do less.[24]

The case for civil defense   Through his case studies of changing civil defense policies in the United States, Switzerland, Great Britain, and the Soviet Union, Lawrence J. Vale has identified a number of rationales used by political leaders and bureaucrats to justify their efforts:

To protect civilians from the effects of natural or technological disasters, conventional warfare, nuclear accidents, and fallout from a nuclear conflict in a neighboring country

To deter conventional or nuclear warfare

To gain public support for current defense policy

To enable government to take more risks in nuclear brinksmanship

To protect civilians, the economy, and the government from the effects of nuclear weapons.

Vale proposes that these justifications reflect four broad rationales. First is the notion of *humanitarian insurance*; that is, it is reasonable for citizens to expect their government to initiate programs to protect them from various threats, including war. Second is the rationale of *deterrence*: potential adversaries will be less likely to attack a nation that can protect its population. A third rationale reflects notions of *crisis management*: an effective civil defense program can influence international crises and short-circuit efforts at nuclear blackmail. The fourth rationale is the *survival of the state*. Plans to ensure state survival include relocating and sheltering the general population, securing shelter for government leaders, and taking economic measures such as protecting and dispersing industrial plants.

Source: Lawrence J. Vale, *The Limits of Civil Defense in the USA, Switzerland, Britain and the Soviet Union: The Evolution of Policies since 1945* (New York: St. Martin's Press; and London and Basingstoke: Macmillan; 1987).

The day after this speech, Secretary of Defense McNamara outlined proposals before the Senate Appropriation Committee and requested $207.6 million to initiate an expanded fallout shelter program. Although the proposals were presented as consistent with efforts that had been made during the Eisenhower years, they did represent significant increases in funding levels and in federal participation. Congress approved the request, and the nation experienced what social historians would later call the "fallout shelter craze."

After the assassination of President Kennedy in 1963 and the election in 1964 of Lyndon Johnson, any priority allotted to civil defense initiatives gave way before other pressures: inner-city riots, the escalating conflict in Vietnam, and Johnson's vision of a Great Society.

In 1972, the OCD was renamed the Defense Civil Preparedness Agency (DCPA); in 1973, the OEP was abolished. These changes were designed to improve coordination between the federal level and state and local governments. The Federal Preparedness Agency (FPA) and the Federal Disaster Assistance Administration (FDAA) were created to carry out related federal programs.

By the mid-1970s, increasing weapons stockpiles spurred the development of crisis relocation planning (CRP), an alternative to the home-based fallout shelters of the 1960s.[25] The goal of CRP was to disperse populations in high-risk areas during periods of heightened international tension. This strategy seemed appropriate to current weapons technologies and was a logical extension of the successful hurricane evacuation programs many coastal states had adopted. In its effort to plan for peacetime as well as for wartime emergencies, CRP was a precursor of emergency management as it is practiced today.

Figure 1–7 Tornado near Denver, Colorado, airport, 1975.

The legitimization of comprehensive emergency management

During the years of federal efforts to implement CRP, emergency management professionals throughout the nation and at all levels of the intergovernmental system wanted more control over their programs. They felt the strains and inconsistencies of the formal and informal organizational agreements that limited their actions and reduced their effectiveness. The findings of a National Governors' Association (NGA) project substantiated their views and gave them a unified voice in which to demand change.

The NGA project was undertaken in 1977, with DCPA funding. Under the direction of Hilary Whittaker, a small research team analyzed the intergovernmental system of disaster preparedness. The stimulus for the project was an NGA policy statement describing the governors' increasing concern about "the lack of a comprehensive national emergency policy, as well as the dispersion of federal responsibilities among numerous federal agencies, which has hampered states' ability to manage disaster situations."[26] (The next sidebar highlights some of the study's major findings.)

In 1979, President Jimmy Carter created the Federal Emergency Management Agency (FEMA) by means of two executive orders that pulled together programs and personnel scattered throughout the federal bureaucracy. According to the final report released by the NGA, he did so despite "strong resistance by some of the federal agencies concerned" and in response to "strong pressure . . . by state and local elected officials, as well as civil defense and emergency service organizations."[27]

Highlights of the National Governors' Association report To investigate the intergovernmental system for emergency management, a National Governors' Association project team undertook extensive interviews with state, county, and municipal officials and private-sector representatives; reviewed federal and state legislation and primary source documents; and conducted field studies of thirty natural and technological disasters in eight geographic regions of the United States.

The following are some highlights of the report's findings:

1. "Many state emergency operations are fragmented." Researchers found not only that "uncoordinated federal programs encourage state fragmentation" but also that state emergency management offices lacked understanding of the crucial relationship between, on the one hand, long-term recovery and mitigation of future disasters and, on the other hand, preparedness and response for more immediate disasters.
2. "Few states are aware of the relationships of emergency management to state policy and community development planning. In addition, federal-state-local emergency management roles and strong state emergency management policy have not been delineated and articulated."
3. Although "most states have natural disaster preparedness and response mechanisms well in hand, . . . no particular office . . . is responsible for mitigation and recovery activities; thus, these vital functions are inadequately planned and coordinated, and are often undertaken only on an ad hoc basis in various state agencies."
4. "Important efforts are made by several states to develop integrated policy and centralized management beyond natural disasters and preparedness/response operations. However, no state . . . has centrally integrated policy and coordination for all phases, for all types of emergency, and at all levels of participation."

Source: National Governors' Association, *1978 Emergency Preparedness Project: Final Report* (Washington, DC: National Governors' Association, 1978), xiv.

This reorganization, reports and actions backed by groups such as the NGA, and various social science research findings combined to give increasing legitimacy to comprehensive emergency management (CEM), a concept that was fully articulated for the first time in the NGA report and that would eventually become the cornerstone of the emergency management profession. CEM had its origins in the "dual use" concept of emergency planning that had begun to gain popularity during the 1970s. CEM represented a new view of emergency planning that had analytical, administrative, and political implications.

As a broad concept, CEM quickly attracted a broad base of support. As FEMA staff attempted to implement it, however, the complexity of the approach became apparent, especially in relation to several unusual events. Like earlier events, Love Canal and Three Mile Island helped shape evolving views of emergency management and the organizational arrangements best suited to its implementation.

Residents of Love Canal, a neighborhood in Niagara Falls, New York, lobbied for state and federal funds to relieve them of mortgages on homes that they believed to have been contaminated by toxic substances long forgotten in a nearby dump. Leaders of the newly organized neighborhood associations coordinated demonstrations such as the one held at the 1980 Democratic National Convention in New York City. There, many carried inflated children's boats on which they had painted the words "Boat People." The neighborhood leaders reasoned that because FEMA staff had been dispatched to assist with the emergency created by the arrival of Cuban exiles in Florida, the victims of the toxic dump were also entitled to FEMA's help. Ultimately, FEMA personnel and other federal staff succeeded in creating complex federal-state arrangements through which many of the homes were purchased.

The incident at Three Mile Island (TMI) also put pressure on the newly organized agency. FEMA found itself fielding questions about management failures at TMI. These failures underscored the need for CEM to be implemented as quickly as possible at all levels within the intergovernmental system. They also illustrated the pronounced degree of strain within and between levels of government and facets of the private sector. Eventually, FEMA was given major new responsibilities, including planning for population protection.

Population protection planning dates back to the earliest civil defense programs. As mentioned earlier, however, it was during the 1970s that the concept of CRP (crisis relocation planning) was tested and expanded. A 1978 directive issued by President Carter increased the priority assigned to civil defense, thereby reinforcing the policy of mutually assured destruction (MAD) that had emerged during the Kennedy years. However, state and local directors who attempted to implement the directive by initiating CRP encountered resistance and, in some cases, hostility. Many activists argued that since nuclear war was not survivable, CRP efforts were misguided. Some even argued that CRP programs could lull politicians and senior military officials into viewing nuclear war as an acceptable option.[28]

These tensions heightened with the election of President Ronald Reagan and the appointment of Louis Giuffrida as director of FEMA. Giuffrida did support a comprehensive approach to emergency management, but his priorities had little in common with those of John Macy, FEMA's first director. When President Reagan called for an "enhanced civil defense program," Giuffrida announced the adoption of four objectives by which this would be accomplished:

1. Provide for the survival of a substantial portion of the U.S. population in the event of a nuclear attack preceded by a strategic warning, and for continuity of government should deterrence and escalation control fail.
2. Provide an improved ability to deal with natural disasters and other large-scale domestic emergencies.
3. Enhance deterrence and stability in conjunction with our strategic offensive and other strategic defense forces. Civil defense, as an element of the strategic balance, should assist in maintaining perceptions that this balance is favorable to the United States.
4. Reduce the possibility that the United States could be coerced in a time of crisis.[29]

Clearly, this relative mix of priorities emphasized attack preparedness. Whereas many local emergency managers felt overwhelmed by the technical aspect of CRP, public interest in the concept intensified. Depending on the community ethos, local directors either enforced the federal stance or distanced themselves and their agencies from it. Federal officials might have pressed for local and state compliance, but by 1984 it had become clear that compliance would not happen. In the mid-1980s, after conducting case studies of four emergency management initiatives, Peter May and Walter Williams summarized the failure of efforts to implement CRP:

FEMA officials kept a low profile in the face of opposition, letting state and local civil defense professionals take the heat. Moreover, FEMA officials were willing to fund CRP "under the table" if only state and local governments would accept the money. The federal government was reluctant to take no for an answer. The "feds" said, in effect, take the CRP funds, do what you choose as long as it is emergency planning, and call the activity what you want, or need, to make it acceptable at the local level.[30]

As local resistance to CRP intensified, an alternative policy was announced. The phrase *population protection* replaced CRP; evacuation planning was nested within CEM, and an all-hazard approach was emphasized. Local and state emergency managers were urged to ask such questions as the following:

What hazards confront your community?

What resources are available?

What needed resources are not available?

Over what period of time could your local government reasonably acquire these resources?

What mitigation actions could be taken to reduce future vulnerability?

The issues raised by these and related questions were arranged into an overall planning framework that defined the integrated emergency management system (IEMS). IEMS will be discussed more fully in later chapters. In essence, it requires that emergency managers complete both hazard and response capability assessments. Once capability shortfalls have been identified, a multiyear development plan is prepared that targets federal, state, and local sources of required resources. The multiyear plan also describes recovery and mitigation efforts aimed at decreasing future vulnerabilities.

The framework defining IEMS reflects the broad planning orientation implicit in the earliest statements on CEM and provides a useful implementation process for bringing an all-hazard approach to emergency management. Civil defense activities can be effectively incorporated within this framework and emphasized in accordance with the level of local community support.

Contributions of behavioral sciences

The two principal policy streams that have shaped emergency management in the United States—natural disaster responses and civil defense programs—have come together over time, though the alliance remains an uneasy one. A third significant influence on the profession is behavioral science research, which has implications for all aspects of emergency management now and in the future.

On 6 December 1917, the French munitions ship *Mont Blanc*, loaded with TNT, collided with a Belgian relief ship near the dock of Halifax, Nova Scotia. A young Canadian doctoral student named Samuel Henry Prince documented the response.[31] His work is regarded as the first empirical study of response to disaster to reflect social science principles and orientation.[32]

Although a number of researchers investigated responses to the Depression and World War II, only a few social science studies of disasters were undertaken between Prince's and the 1950s, when a number of research programs were initiated. Of these, an effort based at the University of Chicago attained the greatest visibility. Under a contract with the Army Chemical Center of the Department of the Army, staff members Charles E. Fritz and Eli Marks of the National Opinion Research Center directed field teams that interviewed victims and emergency officials in the aftermath of more than seventy disasters, including tornadoes, explosions, earthquakes, airplane crashes, and industrial fires.

The conclusions reached were published in a number of publications; a monograph series issued by the National Academy of Sciences–National Research Council was especially influential. As topics such as responses to warnings, panic behavior, evacuation, and convergence were systematically analyzed according to social science methods, it became clear that much of what the public—

Behavioral assessments of local coordinators One of the earliest social science research programs in the area of civil defense was carried out at Iowa State University during the 1960s and early 1970s. Gerald Klonglan, Charles Mulford, and their assistants conducted numerous surveys focused primarily on characteristics of effective local coordinators. Although one of the principal results of the investigations was simply to reveal the complexity of the issue, several factors did emerge as consistently related to effective performance, for example, job satisfaction and frequency of meetings with other local coordinators. Surprisingly, the relationship between civil defense programs and community elites turned out to be more critical than director characteristics. This, in turn, was related to levels and types of training and to horizontal relationships, such as time spent with one's counterparts elsewhere in the state or region.

The surveys also revealed something startling, especially given the policy

emphasis the researchers had assumed was prevalent: "Preparedness for nuclear attack is not salient for most coordinators. One clear implication for DCPA is that appeals made to local coordinators on the basis of . . . the all-hazards approach are likely to be more readily acted upon than others." Thus, behavioral analyses revealed that regardless of the policy emphasis at the federal level—and the resulting directives—many local government officials took a broader view of preparedness. Civil defense activities, particularly those focused on nuclear attack preparedness, were viewed by many as only one dimension of community preparedness, and certainly not the most critical one.

Source: Charles L. Mulford, Gerald E. Klonglan, and Dan L. Tweed, *Profiles on Effectiveness: A Systems Analysis* (Ames: Department of Sociology and Anthropology, Iowa State University, 1973).

including emergency officials—believed about behavior in disasters reflected myth rather than fact.

Today, emergency management studies are conducted by researchers with various specialties, including the physical and natural sciences as well as sociology, psychology, anthropology, geography, economics, political science, and public administration. The study topics reflect the particular disciplines of the researchers. A psychologist might ask how well victims are sleeping after a tornado; a geographer might map the rebuilt environment and ask whether the new spatial patterns will place the community at greater risk; a political scientist might explore the process by which a community makes mitigation decisions.

Emergency management requires research of many types. Some research should reflect the strengths of the theories and methods of single disciplines; other investigations will require more interdisciplinary approaches. Although research based on single disciplines will continue to enrich the understanding of emergency managers, they must become increasingly skilled at making cross-disciplinary syntheses and applications.

In the course of some thirty years of research, what has been learned? Although a detailed view is outside the scope of this text, the next four sections briefly highlight study findings from each of the four phases of comprehensive emergency management. Later chapters draw heavily on such research, and it is imperative that emergency managers stay current with expanding knowledge in the field.[33]

Major research centers and their orientations   Disaster Research Center (DRC), University of Delaware, Newark, Delaware. Major emphasis: sociology, especially organizational and mass media responses. Founded in 1963 at The Ohio State University, the DRC continues the quick response research tradition established earlier by NORC (National Opinion Research Center) field teams. Through grants from, and contracts with, the National Science Foundation, various civil defense agencies, and other federal and state agencies, the DRC staff has completed hundreds of field studies, established a major archive of disaster data, created a computer-based library, and produced numerous valuable publications.

Natural Hazards Research and Applications Information Center (NHRAIC), University of Colorado, Boulder, Colorado. Major emphasis: geography; also serves as an interdisciplinary clearinghouse. The NHRAIC has provided an important forum for interdisciplinary studies. Since the early 1970s, an annual summer workshop has brought together both practitioners and social science researchers. In its function as a clearinghouse, the center sponsors a widely used monograph series and publishes a bimonthly newsletter with a worldwide circulation of eight thousand. The center's hazards library, currently

being automated for computer-based searches, houses approximately ten thousand items.

University Center for Social and Urban Research, University of Pittsburgh, Pittsburgh, Pennsylvania. Major emphasis: sociology. The center has been funded to survey attitudes toward civil defense as well as other management issues. The resulting quantitative data complement an extensive qualitative database that was used to create a prototype computer-based information retrieval system for research findings pertaining to crisis behavior.

Center for Technology, Environment, and Development (CENTED), Clark University, Worcester, Massachusetts. Major emphasis: geography, with a special focus on technological hazards. Founded in 1978, CENTED has more than thirty faculty members from a variety of disciplines, including geography, biology, chemistry, and economics. Six interdisciplinary research groups conduct projects on topics such as hazard assessment, development and the environment, regional development, energy, water resources, and the climate and society. CENTED also houses a specialized library with over four thousand items dealing with more than ninety technological hazards.

Preparedness   *Most citizens accept emergency management as an appropriate and acceptable function of government.* It is true that many programs compete for a community's attention and funds, and emergency management may not seem to rate high on the public agenda. Research indicates, however, that the public assumes that preparedness efforts are being undertaken. When disaster strikes an unprepared community, the rage residents often express may reflect a feeling of betrayal. Wise emergency managers ensure that all local officials keep public expectations in sight. Failing to do so can put the entire emergency management program—and those it was designed to protect—at risk.

Response   *Disaster victims react actively, not passively.* Picture a father carrying an injured child from a crowded stadium that had been the scene of an explosion moments earlier. What would you expect him to do as he nears the entrance to the parking lot and spots a taxi cab? Will he direct the driver to the hospital designated by emergency planners—or to the nearest hospital or medical center?

Victims of a disaster respond quickly, with actions that are well intentioned but that can wreak havoc with poorly conceived plans—those created without a realistic understanding of what people are likely to do when disaster strikes. Good emergency planning relies on valid information about what people are likely to do.

Recovery *In cases of civil disorder, looting is widespread, collective, public, and undertaken by local people with community support. In natural disasters, looting is limited, individual, and private and is undertaken by outsiders who take advantage of the situation but are strongly condemned for their actions.* The public, and many emergency managers, associate looting with disaster. When people are asked to evacuate, fear of looters is one of the most common reasons for refusing. Emergency managers familiar with research in the area know that looting in the aftermath of a natural or technological disaster is rare, and they can therefore allocate their resources effectively, posting only enough personnel to be able to assure residents and businesses that their property is safe.

Mitigation *Typically, the public underestimates risk; people generally believe that they are safe from hazards.* The public's persistent unwillingness to acknowledge risk makes tenacity a fundamental requirement for emergency managers. Recognizing the denial that typifies the public view of hazards is the first step in designing a program for change.

Issues facing emergency management today

Emergency management is still an emerging profession. The gradual professionalization of any occupational group is characterized by changing views of mission, role, and methods. In the coming years, the field of emergency management will be shaped, as well, by international tensions, new technologies, and other social forces.

In September 1983, the newly established Senior Executive Policy Center (SEPC), a short-lived component of the National Emergency Training Center, launched its first policy conference. Meeting to identify and define significant policy issues were forty top-level policymakers from the private sector; federal, state, and local government; national public-interest organizations; and the voluntary sector. (The policy issues ultimately adopted by the SEPC are described in the next sidebar.) In the keynote address, eight professional issues—described in the sections that follow—were identified as central to the future of the profession itself.[34]

Integrated disaster-loss database Neither nationwide nor worldwide do emergency managers have a comprehensive picture of "the problem": although a number of special-interest groups document what they perceive as pressing social needs, accurate and verifiable data on the annual frequency and cost of disasters are unavailable. Without a comprehensive database of disaster losses, emergency managers are less effective in budget negotiations and in the determination of priorities than they would be if such a fundamental tool were available.

Training and certification Much more is known about emergency management than is being applied in the field, and the role of universities and specialized training institutes remains undefined. Despite several federal initiatives in this area and a number of efforts by professional associations, there is no

---

A view from the trenches: Nine key policy issues   In 1983, policymakers meeting at FEMA's Senior Executive Policy Center spent three days identifying and defining policy issues that would have significant influence on the field of emergency management. The nine issues they selected are listed below.

Liability   The "cloud of uncertainty" surrounding personal liability for actions taken by paid and volunteer emergency staff must be eliminated.

Intergovernmental issues   The roles, responsibilities, and authority of federal, state, and local emergency management personnel before, during, and after emergencies must be clarified.

News media issues   The news media must be encouraged, educated, and assisted so that they can most effectively and accurately inform the public about emergency preparedness and response.

Management issues   The effectiveness of those working in emergency management must be improved, through the identification and transfer of organizational and management techniques used successfully in other types of organizations and through the development of approaches that may be unique to the emergency environment.

Hazardous materials   Hazardous materials are a significant problem in

that they require broad attention from emergency management professionals at all levels of government.

Nuclear facilities   Issues associated with nuclear facilities create a unique and discrete aspect of emergency management. Operators, regulators, and state and local officials need opportunities to exchange information and opinions in order to improve their working relationships, the quality of preparedness planning, and local understanding of the operation of fixed nuclear facilities.

Public support   Only an aware and informed public will prepare itself for disaster and support government preparedness efforts. Alternative strategies must be developed to educate the public and to gain the necessary public support.

Research and information   The exchange of information between researchers and practitioners must be improved.

Use of volunteers   Volunteers are an invaluable resource in all phases of emergency management. Most communities are unfamiliar with effective methods of recruiting, training, mobilizing, and rewarding volunteers, and such information must be evaluated and disseminated.

Source: Senior Executive Policy Center, *Issues in Emergency Management* (Emmitsburg, MD: National Emergency Training Center, FEMA, 1983), 4–5.

---

clear consensus on issues such as how training should be funded, who should conduct it, and who should determine standards.

Integrated community warning systems   Although warning systems have been improved for specific threats such as tornadoes and hurricanes, a host of policy issues related to integrated warning systems remain undecided. All levels of the intergovernmental system must cooperate to determine how such systems should be funded, implemented, administered, maintained, and evaluated.

Liability   A wide variety of legal issues confront the emergency management community. Both decision makers and operations personnel need to increase their understanding of potential liability associated with emergency actions. Strategies need to be devised for legal reform in a large number of areas, ranging from decisions to issue warnings to "good Samaritan" legislation.

As a specific example, behavioral research indicates that the public is concerned about potential liability following rescue efforts; some individuals who acted heroically worried afterward about potential legal actions. Although most states have enacted good Samaritan laws, the laws vary widely in the degree of protection they afford. It will be a terrible tragedy if the current litigious environment erodes the willingness—and ability—of volunteers to take action in a crisis.

Mental health of first responders Although the evidence is somewhat inconclusive, studies conducted in a variety of disciplines suggest that responders to disasters that entail high death tolls can experience great trauma. Digging through debris and finding bits of human remains appears to exacerbate the stress first responders confront regularly.

A number of issues need to be explored: What therapeutic interventions are appropriate? Who should decide when and where they will be used? Should participation be voluntary? Is intervention best administered through existing, work-related disability programs or through alternative mechanisms?

Post-disaster mitigation What types of mitigation should be mandated following certain disasters? In many communities, conflicts within the intergovernmental system and among private interests have brought this issue to the forefront of the political agenda. Among the issues are the following: What are the costs, both real and perceived, of various mitigation proposals? How do stakeholders representing different sectors of the community perceive these costs? How do mitigation proposals reflect different visions of the community and its future with respect to development and growth? The inherently normative nature of emergency management becomes most clear when such far-reaching policy issues are being considered.

Civil defense Although treaties have brought about the destruction of an entire class of weapons, massive nuclear arsenals—and the threat of nuclear destruction—remain. In addition, chemical weapons, more cheaply produced than nuclear weapons and made from readily available substances, are becoming widely distributed throughout the world, including nations characterized by political instability. Despite these continued threats, many citizens perceive civil defense programs as dangerous in themselves, arguing that rather than contribute to deterrence, such programs may lull the populace into an unrealistic view of the post-attack environment.[35] As noted earlier in the chapter, federal efforts to initiate crisis relocation planning failed to be implemented, at least in part because of local resistance to the policy. If emergency managers wish to maintain credibility and legitimacy, they cannot allow their programs to be perceived as instruments of war.

Emergency managers must come to understand that they have a political as well as a technical role—in other words, that their actions have political implications. The choices they make may outrage some whose perspectives and concerns differ, and they will have to live with the consequences of their decisions. Emergency management, like other professions, has an ethical dimension. Given the seriousness and complexity of the decisions emergency managers will confront, this aspect of emergency management education, both pre-service and in-service, cannot be overemphasized.

From flood to all-hazard insurance The National Flood Insurance Program has been implemented with much success since its inauguration in 1968. Although the Office of Emergency Preparedness recommended adoption of all-hazard insurance in 1972, such a plan is still far from being realized.[36] Years ago, angry hurricane victims were informed that their homes had been damaged by water, not wind, and that their homeowners insurance did not apply to water damage.

Even today, unless they have flood insurance, homeowners do not have coverage for water-caused damage; nor do mudslide victims. But whatever the cause, damage to one's home is damage, and alternative approaches to disaster insurance should be created so that homeowners are covered for all hazards. One way to begin is to mandate that those who build in disaster-prone areas share the costs of that choice by participating in insurance programs.

Conclusion

Although no one can predict the future, certain identifiable trends have shaped the past and will influence the future. A survey of sixty-two emergency managers throughout the United States revealed four major sources of influence on the field of emergency management: disaster events, interest groups, policy adjustments, and long-term developmental trends.[37]

Disaster events As has been illustrated throughout this chapter, emergency management approaches and priorities are often shaped by individual events. War and international tensions, for example, affect civil defense programs, and events like the 1979 incident at Three Mile Island shaped the long-term development of emergency management in America.

Interest groups Disasters have been—and will be—used by interest groups to promote their own policy proposals. For example, further regulation of the transportation and storage of toxic substances seems likely but is expected to be vehemently opposed by the firms that will be affected. The development of emergency management will inevitably be influenced by conflicts among opposing interests and the policy choices that evolve from those conflicts.

Policy adjustments Policy originating at any level of government is dynamic; adjustments are continual. Although other examples could be cited, recent legislation pertaining to hazardous waste illustrates the impact of policy adjustment on the development of emergency management. With the passage of the Resource Conservation and Recovery Act of 1976, the Environmental Protection Agency (EPA) was assigned responsibility to enforce minimum standards for the processing, storage, transfer, and disposal of hazardous waste. Ten years later, the Superfund Amendments and Reauthorization Act (SARA) stipulated that all firms that produce or store such substances must maintain information files in the form of material safety data sheets. Furthermore, SARA Title III required that this information be made available to those responsible for emergency planning—and that they, in turn, document the establishment of local planning committees.[38]

Long-term developmental trends Five trends are expected to have particular significance in the field of emergency management. First and most important is the trend toward increasing professionalism and more formal credentials. The National Association of Schools of Public Affairs and Administration, the International City Management Association, and the National Coordinating Council of Emergency Management and other organizations have suggested two major approaches to improving emergency management education and professionalism: (1) the development of independent undergraduate and graduate-level degree-granting programs in emergency management and (2) the inclusion of emergency management courses in public administration programs.[39] Such university-based programs will complement the continuing training programs offered at FEMA's Emergency Management Institute and through state emergency management offices. As is the case with other occupational groups, professional associations will play a key role in defining the content of training programs and monitoring the results.

The second significant trend concerns the domain of local emergency management, which will become clearer and more widely accepted. Coordination among local and extralocal agencies will emerge as the unique and primary responsibility of the local emergency management department—whatever the type or phase of disaster. Although circumstances could emerge that would reverse this trend, local emergency managers will likely continue to emphasize preparedness for natural and technological hazards and to assign lower priority to civil defense. The use of the all-hazard approach will continue to expand.

The third influence on the evolution of the field in the coming years is the structural location of the emergency management function within local government. Mid-sized jurisdictions may find it desirable to establish an independent and largely autonomous agency, whereas others will opt for one of the many alternative designs. To some extent, the locations selected will reflect emergency managers' perceptions of where their base of support is likely to be strongest. The decentralized quality of the American political system is likely to encourage continued variability in the structural location of the emergency management function.[40]

Fourth, during the next two decades, increasing numbers of emergency management departments will adopt a growing array of new technologies. Widespread adoption of minicomputers will be one of the most significant influences on the field.[41]

The fifth trend will be nurtured by the first four: emergency management and emergency management professionals will be viewed increasingly positively by the public. As emergency managers receive advanced training, use sophisticated technologies, and demonstrate greater understanding and acceptance of the coordination function, and as local and state professional associations expand their activities, emergency managers will achieve greater visibility, and their image will improve.

As this chapter has illustrated, emergency management has changed significantly over the years. And it will continue to change. As new risks threaten human populations, new tools, planning processes, policies—and conflicts—can be anticipated. The search for increased safety is unending.

1 In the most extensive survey ever undertaken of residents of earthquake-prone areas, Ralph Turner and his associates documented the continuing pervasiveness of nonscientific beliefs. More than one-fifth (21 percent) of the southern Californians surveyed indicated that psychics or mystics could predict earthquakes; 3 percent indicated that religious leaders could do so. In addition, "three out of five people are fatalistic about the general impact of an earthquake, but fewer are fatalistic when it comes to the possibility of taking steps to protect themselves. . . . The belief is overwhelming that something can be done for the groups in special danger (i.e., 85% agreed)." See Ralph H. Turner, Joanne M. Nigg, Denise Heller Paz, and Barbara Shaw Young, *Earthquake Threat: The Human Response in Southern California* (Los Angeles: Institute for Social Science Research, University of California, Los Angeles, 1979), 144.

2 B. J. Thompson, "The Evolution of the Fire Service," in *Managing Fire Services*, ed. Ronny J. Coleman and John A. Granito (Washington, DC: International City Management Association, 1988), 11.

3 The history of American responses to disaster—particularly the section entitled "Expansions under Roosevelt"—is based in part on Thomas E. Drabek, *The Professional Emergency Manager: Structures and Strategies for Success*, monograph no. 44 (Boulder: University of Colorado, Institute of Behavioral Science, 1987), 35–36.

4 Bruce B. Clary, "The Evolution and Structure of Natural Hazard Policies," *Public Administration Review* 45 (January 1985): 20–28. Jamie W. Moore and Dorothy P. Moore trace federal involvement in floods to 1850, when Congress authorized surveys of the Mississippi Delta after a series of destructive floods (*The Army Corps of Engineers*

and the Evolution of Federal Flood Plain Management Policy, Boulder: University of Colorado, Institute of Behavioral Science, 1989, p. 1).

5   For a detailed account of these and related disaster programs, see William J. Petak and Arthur A. Atkisson, *Natural Hazard Risk Assessment and Public Policy: Anticipating the Unexpected* (New York: Springer-Verlag, 1982), and Clark F. Norton, *Emergency Preparedness and Disaster Assistance: Federal Organization and Programs* (Washington, DC: Congressional Research Service, Library of Congress, 1978).

6   A 1947 act had permitted federal surplus property to be given to state and local governments for disaster relief, and a 1948 act had provided for an "Emergency Fund for the President" to be used for disaster relief. See Frank P. Bourgin, *A Legislative History of Federal Disaster Relief, 1950–1974* (Washington, DC: FEMA, n.d.), chap. 1, 4–6.

7   Ibid., 5.

8   Ibid., 7.

9   Ibid., chap. 7, 31–94.

10 See Lawrence J. Vale, *The Limits of Civil Defense in the USA, Switzerland, Britain, and the Soviet Union: The Evolution of Policies Since 1945* (New York: St. Martin's Press, 1987).

11 Thomas J. Kerr, *Civil Defense in the U.S.: Band-aid for a Holocaust?* (Boulder, CO: Westview Press, 1983), 10.

12 Arnold Miles and Roy H. Owsley, *Cities and the National Defense Program* (Chicago: American Municipal Association, 1941), 11.

13 Ibid., 12.

14 Ibid., 11.

15 U.S. Strategic Bombing Survey, *The Effects of Atomic Bombs on Hiroshima and Nagasaki* (Washington, DC: Government Printing Office, 1946), 3.

16 Kerr, *Civil Defense in the U.S.*, 20.

17 Ibid., 21.

18 This discussion of civil defense policy is based in part on Drabek, *The Professional Emergency Manager*, 32–33.

19 Kerr, *Civil Defense in the U.S.*, 27. The official citation for the report is Executive Office of the President, National Security Resources Board, *United States Civil Defense*, NSRB doc. no. 128 (Washington, DC: Government Printing Office, 1950).

20 B. Wayne Blanchard, *American Civil Defense 1945–1984: The Evolution of Programs and Policies* (Emmitsburg, MD: National Emergency Training Center, FEMA, 1984), 3–4.

21 Kerr, *Civil Defense in the U.S.*, 45.

22 It is instructive to contrast Blanchard, *American Civil Defense 1945–1984*, 11–17, with Kerr, *Civil Defense in the U.S.*, 116–132, and with Vale, *The Limits of Civil Defense*, 63–69.

23 U.S. Congress, Joint Committee on Defense Production, *Deterrence and Survival in the Nuclear Age: The "Gaither Report" of 1957*, 94th Cong., 2d. sess., 1976; Rockefeller Brothers Fund, *International Security—The Military Aspect: Report of Panel II of the Special Studies Project* (Garden City, NY: Doubleday and Co., 1958); RAND Corporation, *Report on a Study of Non-Military Defense: Report R-322-RC, July 1, 1958* (Santa Monica, CA: RAND Corporation, 1958).

24 Quoted in Vale, *The Limits of Civil Defense*, 64.

25 The discussions of CRP and the legitimization of comprehensive emergency management are based

in part on Drabek, *The Professional Emergency Manager*, 34–43.

26 National Governors' Association, *1978 Emergency Preparedness Project: Final Report* (Washington, DC: National Governors' Association, 1978), ii.

27 Ibid., xii.

28 For further arguments about the efficacy of civil defense programs, see Henry Eyring, *Civil Defense: A Symposium Presented at the Berkeley Meeting of the American Association for the Advancement of Science, December, 1965* (Washington, DC: American Association for the Advancement of Science, 1966); Ronald W. Perry, *The Social Psychology of Civil Defense* (Lexington, MA: D. C. Heath and Company, 1982); and Joseph Scanlon, "The Roller Coaster Story of Civil Defense Planning in Canada," *Emergency Planning Digest* 9 (April–June 1982): 2–14.

29 Louis O. Giuffrida, *Emergency Management: The National Perspective* (Emmitsburg, MD: National Emergency Training Center, FEMA, 1983).

30 Peter J. May and Walter Williams, *Disaster Policy Implementation: Managing Programs under Shared Governance* (New York: Plenum Press, 1986), 123.

31 See Samuel Henry Prince, "Catastrophe and Social Change: Based upon a Sociological Study of the Halifax Disaster" (Ph.D. diss., Columbia University, 1920). For an assessment of Prince's impact, see Joseph Scanlon, "Disaster's Little-Known Pioneer: Canada's Samuel Henry Prince," *International Journal of Mass Emergencies and Disasters* 6 (November 1988): 213–32.

32 For a detailed survey of the history of social science research and a discussion of sociological findings, see Thomas E. Drabek, *Human System Responses to Disaster: An Inventory of Sociological Findings* (New York: Springer-Verlag, 1986). Additional histories are included in Gary A. Kreps, "The Worth of the NAS-NRC (1952–1963) and DRC (1963–present): Studies of Individual and Social Responses to Disasters," in *Social Science and Natural Hazards*, ed. James D. Wright and Peter H. Rossi (Cambridge, MA: Abt Books, 1981); and in E. L. Quarantelli, "Disaster Studies: An Analysis of the Social Historical Factors Affecting the Development of Research in the Area," *International Journal of Mass Emergencies and Disasters* 5 (November 1987): 285–310.

33 The findings and conclusions are summarized and adapted from Drabek, *Human System Responses*, 23, 133, 232, 284, 321.

34 The description of policy issues draws heavily on Thomas E. Drabek, *Some Emerging Issues in Emergency Management* (Emmitsburg, MD: National Emergency Training Center, FEMA, 1984).

35 Lydia Dotto, *Planet Earth in Jeopardy: Environmental Consequences of Nuclear War* (Chichester, England: John Wiley and Sons, 1986).

36 Office of Emergency Preparedness, Executive Office of the President, *Disaster Preparedness, 1–3* (Washington, DC: U.S. Government Printing Office, 1972).

37 This discussion draws heavily on Thomas E. Drabek, *The Local Emergency Manager: The Emerging Profession*, Part 1 (Emmitsburg, MD: National Emergency Training Center, FEMA, 1988); and Drabek, *The Professional Emergency Manager*.

38 For a case study of the constraints on local officials trying to implement SARA Title III requirements, see Charles E. Faupel and Conner Bailey, "Contingencies Affecting Emergency Preparedness for Hazardous Wastes," *International Journal of Mass Emergencies and Disasters* 6 (August 1988): 131–154.

39 Michael T. Charles and John Choon K. Kim, eds., *Crisis Management: A Casebook* (Springfield, IL: Charles C Thomas Publishers, 1988), xiii.

40 Gerard J. Hoetmer, "Emergency Management: Individual and County Data," *Baseline Data Report* 15 (Washington, DC: International City Management Association, August 1983).

41 Thomas E. Drabek, "Microcomputer Implementation Patterns among State and Local Emergency Management Agencies," in *Simulators V: Proceedings of the SCS Simulators Conference, 1988*, ed. A. Ben Clymer and Vince Amico (San Diego, CA: Simulation Councils, Inc., 1988), 330–34.

Organizing for emergency management

Simply put, a disaster is a sudden and dramatic emergency. When disaster strikes, the demands facing threatened communities are obvious and compelling. People must be protected to the extent possible. Victims must be cared for. Basic services must be restored. Physical structures must be repaired or replaced. An affected community must respond immediately and vigorously. Fortunately, such immediate response is precisely what occurs most of the time. Local individuals, groups, and organizations respond quickly, not always predictably or efficiently perhaps, but in such a way that important demands are met in a timely manner.

But responding to an event is very different from responding to the *possibility* of an event. To most people, natural and technological hazards are not major concerns—until a disaster occurs. This indifference is easy to understand. In any given year the chance that a disaster will severely affect individual citizens is very low. People tend not to worry about what is unlikely to affect them directly. This apparent lack of concern does not mean that people do not fear disaster or that they deny its possibility, but rather that they tend to think more about immediate, daily problems than about emergencies and catastrophes. Moreover, public knowledge about most hazards is limited. Thus, public education is required to sensitize citizens to the dangers of potential hazards.

Interestingly, it is local communities that must deal directly with the immediate problems of disaster, and yet it is at the local level that a readiness posture is most difficult to sustain. The reason is that from a national perspective, disasters occur more often and create higher total damages and costs.[1] So it is not surprising that the push for emergency planning comes from the top down: from national to regional to local levels. Therefore, grassroots support for disaster preparedness is often difficult to sustain.

All of this points to an important fact of life for every local emergency manager: there are no quick fixes. Most of the time, the threat of a disaster at some future time cannot compete with everyday issues in terms of ability to motivate local officials, the private sector, and the public.[2] The challenge for the emergency manager is somehow to overcome indifference about, and sometimes outright opposition to, disaster planning and preparedness. This chapter presents practical suggestions for meeting that challenge. Many of the recommendations will be detailed further in later chapters. The goals here are to describe what goes on during a disaster situation, delineate the problems that face affected communities, and suggest some ways of organizing to solve these problems.[3]

The first section of the chapter highlights two foundations of emergency management—improvisation and preparedness. Each will be illustrated by an actual emergency situation.[4] These examples will show that improvising during an emergency is a basic strength of local communities and that the ability to improvise can be increased by modestly preparing beforehand.

The second section of the chapter offers a set of principles of emergency preparedness. These principles can be applied to any level of government, but the emphasis here is on the local level. The principles are based on a realistic view of the disaster environment and of the potential for emergency preparedness.

The third section of the chapter gets to the heart of the matter: identifying specific emergency management needs and related functions. The approach (adapted from previous studies by ICMA) involves asking local officials to visualize their own situation in terms of a checklist of emergency management requirements, using a question-and-answer approach.[5] The same approach is then used to develop a related list of disaster preparedness functions. In effect, organizing for emergency management requires developing ways to perform these functions.

The fourth section of the chapter discusses different ways of organizing emergency management within local governments. Although there is no one best way to organize emergency management, the choice as to its precise location within a local government is a critical one. The section provides guidelines for making that choice.

The fifth section examines the role of the professional emergency manager by asking what it means to perform that role effectively. The sixth section focuses on program implementation and review. Some additional suggestions are offered for ensuring that the disaster preparedness functions identified earlier are implemented to the fullest extent possible and that they are routinely evaluated, even though a major disaster may never actually occur during the tenure of current local officials.

Foundations of emergency management: Improvisation and preparedness

Emergency preparedness—even if it is only modest—can make an important difference if a disaster takes place. Such preparedness should be based on an understanding of what typically happens during disasters.

Those with responsibility for emergency management never have to start from scratch. Although disasters are nonroutine events, communities and regions are remarkably adaptive in meeting disaster-related demands, regardless of their level of preparedness. In thinking about organizing for emergency management, it is important to understand how and why communities adapt so well. One important reason is that most (including federally declared) disasters are far from massive in comparison with the remaining human and material resources. This means that affected communities can usually mobilize quickly through their own efforts and through assistance provided from the outside. This is not to deny that there are critical problems and needs, of course. But the resilience of individuals and communities in coping with physical harm and social disruption must never be underestimated. Many if not most of the problems posed by disaster are at least partially organizational and informational in character. Offering solutions to them is a major objective of emergency management.

When there has been very little planning for an emergency, the ability to improvise assumes singular importance. Even a modest level of preparedness, however, clearly makes a difference and enhances any necessary improvisation. The first sidebar illustrates people's innate ability to improvise in the face of disaster. The second illustrates the beneficial effects of preparedness. In reviewing these two cases, consider the following questions, which highlight the central argument of this section and lay the groundwork for a discussion of emergency preparedness principles.[6]

Both operations show a functioning organization. In the first it is created during the emergency, whereas in the second it exists before the event. Both organizations therefore are able to respond to the basic demands of the particular disaster situation—damage assessment in the first example and pre-impact warning and evacuation in the second. Both organizations have legitimated domains

The ability to improvise: A case in point   A tornado strikes a metropolitan community on a Friday morning, carving a path of destruction three and a half miles long. Hundreds of homes and other buildings are either destroyed outright or sustain major structural damage. Recognizing the potential danger these unsafe structures pose to their inhabitants and knowing that many buildings will have to be condemned, the mayor and other city officials turn the problem over to the city building and zoning department. On Friday evening, the mayor tells the city building commissioner, "Do what you have to do, whatever you have to do. If somebody gets in your way, run over them, and if they get up, [tell them] 'I'm gonna run you over.' "

The building commissioner, in turn, knowing that he and his staff of four cannot begin to inspect effectively all of the damaged buildings, decides to enlist the assistance of a regional building association. As the only individual legally empowered to condemn buildings and realizing that the city will soon be flooded with private contractors and insurance claims adjustors, the building commissioner prepares to take charge of what will quickly become an extensive operation. A previous agreement by members of the regional building association (which resulted from an earlier tornado) expedites the arrival of volunteer building commissioners and inspectors from surrounding communities, who begin appearing early Saturday morning.

As the person in charge, the local building commissioner makes several immediate decisions. First, to protect volunteers from any legal repercussions, they are "hired" on the spot for one dollar each, with each individual receiving a temporary appointment card. These "employees" are then divided into teams, each led by an inspector appointed by the commissioner. Teams are assigned to different sections of the affected area and are told to fan out to cover all of the area. Buildings are then categorized as belonging to one of three classes: (1) light damage (habitable buildings), (2) moderate to heavy damage (buildings with apparent structural damage but still habitable in a crunch), or (3) heavy to severe damage (structurally unsound and uninhabitable). Three separate inspections are completed over the next few days until all unsalvageable buildings are condemned and eventually destroyed. The city's fire department is assigned the task of handling the destruction of these buildings.

of responsibility. The necessary human and material resources are mobilized. There are clear understandings about who is going to do what before action is taken. On its own terms, each operation appears quite successful. The ability to improvise, however, is the key reason for success in the first operation, whereas predisaster preparedness is the key reason for success in the second.

Although the operations are similar in important ways, there are subtle differences that could become very important in more severe circumstances. Both operations can be considered successful, but there are grounds for evaluating the second one as superior. The second demonstrates less confusion about who is going to be responsible; there is no need to make decisions about who is in charge. Hence, the mobilization of key resources is also faster and easier. In addition, the second operation has more potential for successful continuing improvisation if conditions change, because of its greater initial clarity about roles and responsibilities.

These differences point to the genuine value of disaster preparedness. There is no substitute for experience, of course, but in its absence, emergency pre-

The role of preparedness: A case in point A river runs through a large metropolitan area. A state police unit wires the city fire department that the river is at flood level, that floodwaters are causing considerable damage upstream, and that flood conditions are expected to reach the city within several hours. A fire department communications operator contacts the fire chief, who puts the department on standby alert. The fire department is schooled in evacuation procedures through predisaster preparedness activities. After being notified by the operator, the fire chief goes to the site of the initial city police command post (the first one in the field) and informs police personnel of his intention to evacuate low-lying manufacturing and residential areas. It is agreed that the fire department will handle the evacuation of selected low-lying areas.

Upon receiving additional information from the local police and water departments, the chief decides to divide the fire department's equipment and personnel into two sections, one on each side of the river, to ensure an adequate distribution of resources for both evacuation and fire protection.

Working through the normal chain of command, he orders fire personnel to mobilize and relocate people and possessions currently within one thousand feet of the bank on each side of the river. Fire department personnel and equipment are then deployed according to the chief's dictates. Although the media have already warned the threatened population, fire department personnel move door to door to evacuate all residents in the selected lowland areas.

There is sufficient time before flooding both to evacuate those threatened and to recheck the areas covered. Several threatened individuals choose to remain, arguing that they must protect their property. Some of those who remain are eventually stranded and must be evacuated by fire department boats. As conditions become more severe, larger boats are requested by the fire department, and several are volunteered. The evacuation is terminated shortly after impact, when all those stranded have been successfully evacuated. In the face of considerable property damage, no deaths or serious injuries result from the flood.

paredness becomes an important resource. The differences probably were not of great consequence in the conditions described. In the case of more widespread destruction from an earthquake or multiple tornadoes, however, the damage assessment operation described would become much more difficult. In the case of a more damaging flood with a wider scope of impact, there would be greater potential to expand the described flood evacuation operation because of its firm foundation in preparedness.

These examples illustrate that effective emergency management requires both improvisation and preparedness. Without improvisation, emergency management loses flexibility in the face of changing conditions. Without preparedness, emergency management loses clarity and efficiency in meeting essential disaster-related demands. Equally important, improvisation and preparedness go hand in hand. One need not worry that preparedness will decrease the ability to improvise. On the contrary, even a modest effort to prepare enhances the ability to improvise.[7]

Principles of emergency preparedness

The goal of emergency management is the rapid restoration of normal routines. Efforts must be made to anticipate possible impacts of a range of different hazards and to develop countermeasures to neutralize or soften these impacts. Written disaster plans dealing with specific problems and needs are merely parts of a broader process that involves knowledge, planning, training, and public education as each is related to the range of hazards faced by a community. This section examines the general principles of this preparedness process. Many other principles could also be offered, but the eight that follow are among the most important.[8]

Preparedness and improvisation are foundations of emergency management To prepare is to organize for emergency response before an event. What does that mean? It means that various domains of responsibility (such as warning, damage assessment, and other emergency management functions) are identified and assigned to entities capable of performing them. It means that how these responsibilities are going to be performed has been worked out in at least a preliminary way. It means that the human and material resources needed to get the job done are available and can be mobilized quickly. Simply put, preparedness is clarity about what may be needed, what should be done, and how it will be done.

To improvise is *to organize for emergency response during an event.* Improvisation implies that various domains of responsibility and the way in which they are to be performed may have to be worked out on the spot. Human and material resources may have to be moved around because there are too many in some locations and not enough in others. Even in the best of cases, at least some degree of confusion about appropriate courses of action is inevitable, because conditions and needs can change quickly during the emergency period. Emergency managers must recognize the need for flexibility and know that, if need be, there is more than one way to get the job done.

Improvisation and preparedness are not opposites; ideally, they go hand in hand.

Preparedness is a continuous process The development of a written plan at a specific time is only a small part of the total preparedness process. It is a serious mistake to assume that preparedness is complete merely because a written document has been produced. Plans need to be kept up-to-date and must be changed to meet new conditions and requirements. An out-of-date plan may be worse than no plan at all if time is wasted in trying to put it to work.

Preparedness reduces unknowns during an emergency The goals of preparedness are to anticipate problems and project possible solutions. It is often impossible to keep a given disaster from happening, but once it does happen, it is possible to soften its impacts on the physical and social environment. By isolating the range of problems that might occur and by defining possible solutions to them, preparedness reduces the level of uncertainty. No matter how well prepared a community is, of course, the unexpected will still occur—but preparedness increases the ability to deal with uncertainty.

Preparedness is an educational activity If a plan is going to work, those involved in emergency response must be familiar with it and must teach other individuals, groups, and organizations what their roles will be. In other words, the emergency manager is also a trainer who ensures that the written plan can be put to work for and by the people who may have to implement it.

Preparedness is based on knowledge Anticipating problems and devising solutions requires accurate knowledge. Emergency managers must know the difference between myths and reality in preparing for a disaster. Popular

Myths and realities of disaster response

Myths

Because people faced with a great danger will panic, warnings should be withheld until the last minute.

Even those who do not act irrationally are often immobilized by disaster and will need help with such basic tasks as getting fed, housed, and clothed.

Partly because of widespread individual pathological reactions and partly because of the overwhelming damage to the resources of disaster-affected communities, local social units are severely limited in their ability to handle emergency demands effectively. Outside help is essential.

The social disorganization that results from disaster impact allows antisocial behavior to surface. Because social control is weak or absent, those in the disaster area become easy victims of looting and other forms of criminal activity.

Community morale is very low in disaster-stricken areas. Steps must be taken to overcome demoralization of the affected population.

A community stricken by a disaster may descend into total personal and social chaos. Immediate, firm, and unequivocal control is required, often from the outside.

Realities

Information about danger should be disseminated—not withheld because of fear that people will panic. They will not.

Residents of disaster-affected areas respond actively and do not wait for community officials to tell them what to do.

The ratio of disaster damages to community and regional resources is usually low to modest. Local social units generally have enough material resources and personnel to deal with the situation. Outside aid should be consistent with local requirements and not sent indiscriminately.

Although symbolic security measures should be taken, massive deployment of forces for security is usually unnecessary. Looting and other antisocial behaviors are not major problems in most disaster situations.

Community morale is generally high immediately after a disaster. Quick restoration of essential community services tends to sustain it.

Communities mobilize rapidly to meet emergency demands even under severe circumstances. Timely coordination is more important than control. Although it is often difficult to achieve, coordination is essential and should be maintained under local authority.

Source: Adapted from Russell R. Dynes, E. L. Quarantelli, and Gary A. Kreps, *A Perspective on Disaster Planning*, Report Series 11 (Newark: Disaster Research Center, University of Delaware, 1972), 15–39.

---

conceptions of community response to disasters usually focus on personal and social breakdown. Most of these conceptions either are patently false or are true only under carefully defined circumstances.[9] The accompanying sidebar summarizes both the myth and reality of disaster response.

Preparedness evokes appropriate action Planning is sometimes seen as a way to increase the speed of response in an emergency. Speed is undeniably important in some respects, but appropriateness of response is a far more important overall goal.

Education and knowledge about what really happens during an emergency tend to evoke appropriate responses. For example, it can be assumed that local groups and organizations will mobilize quickly (with or without planning) to respond to the most immediate needs of victims. To the untrained eye, the disaster environment may appear a bewildering array of interlocking social units as new groups emerge and existing organizations take on responsibilities that are sometimes quite different from their normal ones. The emergency manager is cautioned not to conclude that what is happening is disorganized or that it must somehow be rigidly controlled. To the contrary, what takes place is adaptive and necessary. In the early emergency period, a planning objective more appropriate than efforts at rigid control is ensuring that valid information about shorter- and longer-term needs is generated as soon as possible—a process that takes time, because the earliest estimates are usually less reliable than more delayed ones. From a preparedness standpoint, damage assessment is every bit as important as damage containment.

Resistance to emergency preparedness is a given   The value of preparedness is neither self-evident nor readily endorsed by local officials. One reason, alluded to earlier, is that the probability of disaster is not that high at the local level. Another is the mistaken assumption that civilian disasters can be handled by a command and control model or through direct military intervention if need be.[10] Another reason is overconfidence: Some public officials think they already know what to expect and what to do during a disaster and that they will be able to improvise as they go along. Still another reason is that disaster planning diverts resources from ostensibly more pressing concerns. Planning efforts require leadership from public officials to overcome these obstacles.

Modest planning is a reasonable goal   Particularly at the local level, a modest degree of preparedness is all that can reasonably be expected unless emergencies occur repeatedly. That is why a focus on principles is so important. Although it is tempting to make written plans highly detailed, the temptation should be resisted. First, it is impossible to plan for every contingency. Second, situations change constantly, and specific details quickly become out-of-date. Third, the presence of too many details gives the impression that everything is of equal importance, which is not the case. Fourth, a complex and detailed plan is intimidating to potential users and tends to be ignored. Although it cannot neglect details, especially at the organizational level, disaster planning should be as streamlined as possible.

A checklist approach to emergency management

The examples of emergency response given earlier (damage assessment and protective action) highlight only two of many disaster demands that can be prepared for in one way or another. The problem is to identify preparedness needs so that those responsible for emergency operations can develop ways of meeting them. This section is based on ICMA's checklist approach to identifying preparedness needs.[11] Rather than cover everything on ICMA's checklist, the section describes a general process that local officials and emergency managers can apply.

The discussion begins with disaster warning as a case in point, because it constitutes an obvious and critical problem in the early emergency period. More brief discussions then show how other preparedness needs can be pinpointed in the same way. The section concludes by translating the identified preparedness needs into a set of broader emergency management functions.

The checklist approach allows local officials and emergency managers to compare their community capabilities and resources against a checklist of disaster-related needs. The trick is to make the checklist neither too simple nor too complicated. If it is too simple, important matters will be bypassed. If it is too complicated, it cannot be used efficiently to develop a working set of emergency preparedness functions. The idea is to strike a balance between simplicity and complexity, in this and all other phases of program implementation.

Preparedness needs: Disaster warning as a case in point

Over the years, disaster researchers have developed a fairly good understanding of how people respond to disaster warnings.[12] When danger is recognized as imminent and personally threatening, people seek safety, and their behavior is generally adaptive. Thus, rather than act irrationally and thereby increase the danger, people take action to protect themselves, their families, and others. People will seek confirmation of official warning messages and will supplement official information with communications from relatives, neighbors, and friends. Thus, when evacuation is officially or informally deemed appropriate, the decision to leave is a group rather than an individual decision. The resulting movement out of harm's way is most often orderly and goal directed. Documented instances of panic are quite rare. Even under the impact of severe disasters, most people continue to be concerned about the safety of their families, friends, and neighbors.

Because people can be assumed to act rationally when threatened, a key responsibility of public officials is to get warning messages to them in a timely way. An all-hazard alerting system is an important part of emergency management planning. It should include notification of key public officials, mechanisms for warning the community at large, and provisions for special populations such as handicapped people or people not speaking native languages.[13] The applicable questions for public officials are as follows:

Are weather and other indicators of potential emergencies monitored continuously?

Would key emergency personnel be notified rapidly of a disaster or a potential disaster situation? What if a key individual were out of town?

Who is responsible for alerting the general public about an actual or potential emergency situation?

Has the role of the media in alerting the public been coordinated with media representatives?

Has the general public been educated about the meaning of the alerting signals and about corresponding actions to take?

Are there special provisions for alerting particular population groups such as handicapped or institutionalized people or those speaking non-native languages?

If the answer to these questions is *yes*, then this preparedness need has been handled. What remains is to ensure that this continues to be the case in the future. If the answer is *no* or *do not know*, then there is a preparedness problem that needs to be addressed. Without a public education component, for example, there is less assurance that citizens will recognize alerting signals, know what to do when an alert occurs, and know how to cope with the effects of impact. Without a procedure for notifying key officials during off-duty hours or when communications are down, the mobilization of emergency response becomes more difficult.

Identifying other preparedness needs

Many other emergency management needs can be identified by the same question-and-answer method. The questions that follow are not exhaustive but do highlight some key emergency preparedness needs (the needs are indicated in italics before each set of questions).

Roles of elected and appointed officials: Have official and unofficial responsibilities during a disaster been designated for the community's key elected and appointed officials? Is anyone formally, perhaps legally, in charge of emergency management?

The point of this first set of questions is that key elected and appointed officials are responsible for providing for the protection of the lives and property of their constituents. Most citizens give little attention to emergency management in everyday affairs, but they will expect government leaders to manage a disaster effectively. Citizens expect to be warned, to be informed, to have basic public services restored soon, and to have their individual needs met. Fulfilling these responsibilities requires preparedness.

Planning as a continuous process: Who is responsible for emergency management planning? Do emergency planners work regularly with other departments and community groups in performing planning functions?

The point of the second set of questions is that preparedness should have some legitimacy and be continuous. Legitimacy means that preparedness has the attention, cooperation, and respect of government officials and the public. Continuity means that preparedness activities are integrated into the routine operations of government: relationships should be established that require frequent contact between emergency management personnel and other government personnel.

All-hazard approach to planning: Does the emergency management plan consider the full range of natural and technological hazards confronting the community?

The point here is that a local emergency management capability should be geared to all the types of hazards likely to occur (for example, natural disasters, industrial accidents, transportation accidents). And wherever or whenever a disaster of any kind has occurred, there should be a means of detecting it quickly.

Connections between management of "routine" emergencies and disasters: To what extent are disaster management problems and responses similar to and different from those related to everyday emergencies?

The preceding question requires more extended comment. The general point is that there are similarities and differences between the handling of routine emergencies and disasters.[14] With respect to similarities, the organizational structure implemented during a disaster should extend as much as possible from that used for everyday crises. Certain functions will have to be added (such as warning, damage assessment, coordination of agencies and volunteers, intergovernmental relations), but it is important to ensure as much continuity as possible. If, for example, emergency communications are used routinely, they need not be taken down from the shelf and dusted off to meet disaster needs. If public safety, police, fire, public works, and (perhaps) emergency management units form a cluster of organizations that routinely work together, as they often do in the United States, then emergency management can draw on the formal and informal arrangements that have built up over time. Similarly, hospitals, emergency medical groups, and social service agencies often form a second identifiable cluster of organizations that can be expected to cooperate both in routine emergencies and in major disasters. And certainly public utilities, public and private transportation organizations, and private industries engage in emergency planning and deal with minor emergencies fairly routinely, as well. Although such everyday emergency operations and planning are not necessarily integrated into a larger system, they do provide a base upon which to build an integrated communitywide effort when the need arises. Disaster management never has to start from scratch.

On the other hand, disasters do differ both quantitatively and qualitatively from everyday emergencies. Disasters, for example, force organizations into more and different kinds of interactions with other groups and organizations (such as business with government, local government with national bureaucracies). Moreover, during a disaster, organizations lose some of their autonomy (through such things as pooling of personnel and resources, integration of groups, loss of site control by business and industry). Performance standards may also change. The standard U.S. approach to structural fires, for example, is rapid mobilization and response; however, dealing with fires involving unidentified substances may necessitate delayed responses or even different kinds of responses. Similarly, emergency medical service professionals have adopted procedures emphasizing swift delivery of patients to hospitals; for large numbers of casualties, however, such routine procedures may have to be amended by triaging to avoid overwhelming the available hospitals and medical personnel. Thus, those involved in disaster planning must be sensitive both to similarities and to differences between everyday emergencies and major disasters. Emergency managers must build on the similarities, and they must also plan for the differences.[15]

Intergovernmental relations: Are there formal and informal cooperative arrangements (such as mutual aid) with regional and national governments for disaster assistance?

Eligibility for outside assistance: What are the requirements and procedures for receiving regional and national government assistance? Who has the authority to apply for this assistance? What information is required?

Records management: Have procedures been developed and implemented to gather and record disaster-related information?

The point of the last three sets of questions is that communities do not respond to a disaster in a vacuum. Links to other communities and regions and to the national level are important components of emergency management, and preparedness can help to ensure that effective cooperation occurs during an emergency.[16] Mutual aid agreements among neighboring communities and cooperative arrangements with regional organizations and with the federal government can be developed well before they are actually needed. Eligibility requirements and application procedures for outside assistance should be part of the knowledge base of the responsible local officials. Moreover, data on local government expenditures must be maintained in accordance with regional and federal requirements for reimbursement, in case a disaster is officially declared. Without prior thought and planning, information retrieval can be a problem during the emergency period.

Translating preparedness needs into emergency management functions

The preceding exercise was designed to show that there are many readily identifiable preparedness needs. Such needs should be made the basis of emergency management functions. There is no exhaustive list of emergency management functions, just as there is no exhaustive list of hazards that could become disasters. Accordingly, it is wise to plan for disasters generally (comprehensive emergency management) rather than for specific hazards. It is also wise to think in terms of general functions rather than to develop a highly detailed operational plan.

Why use an all-hazard rather than an agent-specific approach? Disasters do differ in important ways, such as their predictability; length of forewarning; speed of onset; magnitude, scope, and duration of impact; and possibility of secondary impacts.[17] Special provisions (such as radiation monitoring) may indeed be required for unique characteristics of specific hazards. But for many disaster management needs and problems, the particular type of disaster (natural, technological, or other) does not matter. The warning function can serve as a case in point. Regardless of whether the threat is a hurricane, a chemical spill, a flood, a tidal wave, or a nuclear emergency, what matters is whether people will understand, believe, and respond to warning messages. There must be an alerting system that works, and warning messages must be accurate, precise, consistent, and timely. Similarly, because any number of disasters can generate demands for search and rescue, damage assessment and control, emergency medical services, or restoration of essential public services, the important preparedness issues arise not from differences between hazards but from organizational problems that any number of hazards commonly create.

There are also practical reasons for a general preparedness approach. It is efficient in its use of time, effort, money, and other resources. An all-hazards approach helps avoid duplication of effort, gaps in disaster responses, and possible conflicts arising from divergent approaches to planning. It is a politically desirable strategy because it eliminates the need to sell different plans to different constituencies. General preparedness increases the efficiency and effectiveness of disaster response through an integrated community planning effort.[18]

Why base disaster planning on general rather than specific functions? As noted earlier, there is a tendency to write disaster plans that are too detailed. When a large document has been developed (and put on the shelf), it creates a false impression that preparedness has been achieved. But preparedness is more a process than a product, encompassing all of the following:

Convening meetings to share information

Conducting drills or exercises to go over specifics

Updating plans and strategies as conditions change

Formulating understandings and mutual aid agreements

Maintaining standby human and material resources

Engaging in public education

Engaging in disaster training

Maintaining a current, practical understanding of present and future hazards

Coordinating and integrating organizational disaster plans.

Separated from the rest of the tasks that make up the preparedness process, a written plan decreases rapidly in value from the time it is written and put on the shelf.[19]

An exhaustive list of general functions would be quite long, but the following ten functions are useful as minimum requirements for responding to an emergency or disaster. (Several will be discussed in greater detail in subsequent chapters.) Additional functions will evolve from a community's specific checklist of preparedness needs.

Mobilizing emergency personnel and resources

Warning the public

Figure 2–1 Personal copy of the "Chief Executive Officer's Checklist." Designed to be folded and kept in a wallet, the checklist is part of *The CEO's Disaster Survival Kit* put out by FEMA and the U.S. Fire Administration.

CEO's disaster survival kit

Background information

Notified by _____
Time _____
Type of emergency _____
Location
CEO reporting point, open routes and means; communications channels
Incident size-up
Type
Magnitude
Best/worst case
Damage
Injuries/deaths
Area (size)
Property damage
Other impacts
Resources
Incident command status
Int./ext. resources committed
Int./ext. resources required
EOC status and location
Other authorities notified?

CEO's disaster survival kit

1   Immediate action

Begin personal log

Establish contact with Office of Emergency Management

Direct staff to assess and report on problems, resources, shortfalls, policy needs and options

Chair assessment meeting

Issue emergency declarations as needed

Set reporting procedures

Remind staff to keep complete logs of actions and financial records

Begin liaison with other officials

CEO's disaster survival kit

2   Personal

Tell family destination and how to contact

Take medications, toiletries, and clothes

Take list of peers to contact for advice

Remember that your role is policymaking, not operational

Take personal tape recorder

Other things to remember:

_____

_____

CEO's disaster survival kit

3   Legal

Contact legal advisors

Review legal responsibilities and authorities:

• Emergency declarations

• Chain of succession

• Intergovernmental aid

• Social controls (curfews)

• Price controls

• Other restrictions

Monitor equity of service based on needs and risks

Maintain balance between public welfare and citizen's rights

Have status of contracts reviewed

CEO's disaster survival kit

4   Political

Recognize accountability

Check provisions for public officials

Space at EOC

Periodic updates

Staff updates on politically sensitive issues, such as life and property losses, service interruptions

Establish and evaluate policy decisions throughout the incident

Confer with other selected officials when problems arise

Use elected officials to request assistance from public and private organizations

---

CEO's disaster survival kit

5   Public information

Check plans to inform public and manage media

Designate single PIO

Evaluate media capabilities

Establish media center

Channel all releases first through CEO in EOC

Establish news media update and access policies

Taking protective action

Caring for victims

Assessing the damage

Restoring essential public services

Informing the public

Record keeping

Planning the recovery

Coordinating emergency management activities.

Mobilizing emergency personnel and resources   Emergency personnel and resources should be mobilized when local emergency managers detect or are notified of an environmental threat. That moment is the effective beginning of an emergency response. The origin of the alert depends on the nature of the threat. In the United States, for example, notice of tornadoes and riverine floods usually comes from the National Weather Service. Notification of a hazardous materials transportation accident may come from either the shipper of the material or its carrier. In the event of a nuclear power plant accident, notification may come from the plant operator, the Nuclear Regulatory Commission, or a state department of emergency services. Citizens themselves may be an important source of information on environmental threats.

Because authorities may be notified by one or more sources, an emergency response plan should contain provisions for two kinds of activity. First, a procedure should exist that allows local authorities to receive around-the-clock notification of threats. Usually this is accomplished by designating a duty officer to monitor incoming communications and relay them to key emergency personnel (such as elected officials, police chiefs, fire chiefs, public works directors, medical services administrators, heads of voluntary agencies). Second, once notified, these key emergency personnel must have procedures to mobilize personnel and material resources of their own units in a timely manner.[20]

Warning the public and taking protective action   Warning and taking protective action are grouped together because they both involve making provisions to protect the public from harm. Warning has already been discussed in some detail. The key is to provide timely messages that are authoritative, accurate, and precise.[21] Citizens need to be able to determine whether they are at risk and, if so, what they can do to protect themselves and their families.

Protective action varies with the type and magnitude of the threat. Although there are cases in which only one kind of protective action is most appropriate (such as evacuation in the face of a riverine flood), it is often reasonable to suggest various protective options for the same threat. In the event of a light ashfall from a volcanic eruption, for example, the public might be advised to stay indoors and wear protective masks. But if the ashfall is expected to be heavy or if mudflows threaten, then evacuation might be the better choice. Protective actions must be most exhaustively considered in cases of technological hazards (such as chemical or nuclear hazards) that might result in the need to control access to affected areas, monitor toxic releases, measure exposure levels, and make provisions for decontamination and specialized medical treatment.[22]

Caring for victims   Caring for victims encompasses a variety of functions—from search and rescue, to care of the injured and dead, to providing temporary services for displaced populations, to ensuring victims access to public and private disaster assistance programs. Following a disaster, a number of community, regional, and national organizations will mobilize to meet specific aspects of victims' needs, and these organizations will tend to converge.[23] For instance, much of the initial search and rescue is handled by victims themselves, but public safety agencies, search and rescue groups, and perhaps the military are all also likely to be involved quickly. Hospitals and emergency medical services will attend to the injured and dead. Voluntary agencies will provide food, shelter, and clothing. Government organizations, private insurance companies, lending institutions, and law firms—perhaps with lists of eligibility requirements and the necessary forms in hand—will also converge on the disaster site.

The principal problems associated with care of victims generally do not stem from scarcity of human and material resources but from organizational difficulties, such as overlapping responsibilities, uneven distribution of resources, inadequate communications, and conflicts between local and outside organizations. Local emergency managers should consider these problems as inevitable. Some will be handled on the spot; others can be overcome through planned efforts to integrate clusters of organizations dealing with related victim needs and to coordinate overall victim care efforts as much as possible.

Assessing the damage   Damage assessment should be a continuous process that begins during impact and continues well into the post-impact period. Considered in this way, damage assessment becomes a source of continuous information about the community's condition.[24] Emergency managers need such information to decide how resources should be used, shifted, or discontinued (for example, a diking operation requires continuing assessment until waters recede; physical structures subjected to an earthquake may have to be rechecked several times following aftershocks). If it is not planned for, systematic damage assessment is one of the activities that can fall through the cracks in the face of immediate pressure to get things done. Too often the result is that estimates of damages and needs are grossly inaccurate.

Damage assessment for technological hazards may involve special difficulties. By way of illustration, in the case of a nuclear hazard, specialized instruments are needed to measure accurately the magnitude and location of a release of radioactive material or to confirm that no release has occurred. Mobilization of this specialized equipment may take time, meaning that those threatened or responding to the emergency may be forced to operate under considerable uncertainty during the waiting period. Therefore, if a local community faces a possible nuclear threat, it would be prudent to determine in the planning stages the closest locations of radiological equipment and of personnel trained to use it.[25]

Restoring essential public services   If essential public services (utilities, communications, transportation, public safety services, and legal and other government programs) are disrupted, they should be restored as soon as possible. The restoration will help to minimize social disruption and to restore normal community routines. In larger and more developed communities, water, power, telephone, public safety, public works, and mass transit organizations are likely to have disaster plans of their own. Public utilities in the United States, for example, are prepared both for emergencies—everyday, localized breakdowns that can be handled by local resources and personnel—and for disasters and catastrophes—statistically rare events that require external aid because local resources will not be sufficient.[26] Those involved in communitywide disaster planning should be aware of and coordinate that decentralized planning effort to the extent possible. In smaller, less developed, and more isolated communities, those engaged in disaster preparedness will probably have to resolve disaster-related problems themselves, working directly with those providing public services.

Informing the public In a disaster, tremendous confusion can develop if each group and organization supplies different information to the public. Because such confusion can damage the public's confidence that those in charge can manage the situation effectively, emergency response plans should contain definitive procedures for communicating to the public. If possible these plans should designate a point for the direct release of disaster-related information to the public and to the news media. Ideally, those responsible for the routine government public information function (if there is one) should also be responsible for disaster-related public information.[27]

Record keeping As noted earlier, information retrieval can be a problem during the emergency period unless given prior thought and planning. Record keeping relates to all other functions because each has a record-keeping component. Although the principal focus here is the record keeping required for local governments to obtain regional and federal government reimbursement if a disaster is officially declared, record keeping also has a broader and arguably even more important function. Reasonably complete compilations of damages, deaths, physical and mental traumas, and allocations of public and private resources provide an invaluable public service by making it possible to learn from the disaster experience.

Planning the recovery Recovery planning is not always thought of as an emergency-period function, but it really is, and as such it should be given consideration in the disaster preparedness effort. As implied in the preceding discussion of record keeping, there is an immediate and practical reason for making recovery planning a normal part of emergency management: a community seeking state or federal aid has to be familiar with the requirements and procedures for receiving this aid. Effective recovery planning involves monitoring ongoing community development plans, learning about eligibility requirements for external postdisaster aid, and maintaining regular contact with government agencies that administer disaster assistance programs.

A major focus of recovery planning is the reconstruction of physical structures and infrastructures. Historically, the most common pattern—for both the public and the private sectors—is to rebuild on the same locations. Although there has been relatively little research in this area, the historical pattern may not be the wisest. For one thing, the community may simply recreate the earlier vulnerability to disaster. Nothing would have changed when maybe it could have. For another, the postdisaster period may be one of increased support for mitigation efforts. This suggests that local officials should consider beforehand how they would replace destroyed structures and infrastructures. Changes might be possible that would reduce vulnerability.[28]

Coordinating emergency management activities Coordination is the last—but certainly not the least important—disaster management function. There is a strong tendency to view emergency planning as analogous to military planning; that is, to assume that a command and control model works best. (*Command and control* refers to a rigidly structured operation in which authority flows from the top down.) The command and control model has important limitations, however, even in the military.[29] More important, research indicates that such a model does not accurately capture what really goes on during a disaster. In fact, a command and control model would probably not be viable even if attempted.

The notion that the command and control model is appropriate for emergency management is based on several premises: massiveness of disaster impacts, weakness of victims, fragility of affected social systems, breakdown of social control, and the need for a single encompassing structure to replace non-functioning organizations. According to this model, disaster planning should focus on creating a strong authority, perhaps imposed from the outside, to overcome the disintegrating effects of disaster events.

None of these premises is valid. Earlier discussion pointed out the resiliency of a disaster-stricken community. It is simply inaccurate to assume that communities affected by major disasters descend into personal and social chaos and that immediate, firm, and unequivocal leadership is required, usually from the outside. Communities mobilize rapidly to meet disaster demands even under severe circumstances. Timely coordination is more important than hierarchical authority. This is certainly the case among local community groups and organizations involved in disaster response, and it is even more true of intergovernmental relations. Although often difficult to achieve, coordination is essential and should be maintained under local control to the extent possible.

This does not mean that the need for authority does not exist. Clearly there must be people and organizations that are in charge and that have legitimated authority in certain domains. Authority, however, has many possible roots. It may be legitimated by involvement in everyday emergencies, by technical competence, by preparedness, by being at the center of disaster-related communications, or by other factors that are hard to anticipate. During the emergency period, authority tends to be more decentralized than centralized. As already noted, there is a good deal of continuity with predisaster routines.

Thus, effective emergency management should not be based on a command and control model but on what might be called an emergent resource coordination model.[30] Prototype organizations of this model are emergency operations centers, which certainly can be planned but will emerge in some form anyway simply because the situation demands it.[31] Such an emergent organization can serve as an effective communications center, information clearinghouse, place to resolve confusion and disagreements, and source of authority in its own right—when that authority is needed.

The coordination model is effective if it accomplishes the following:

Efficient mobilization of personnel and resources

Timely communication of information within and between local clusters of organizations

Timely communication with the public

Resolution of conflicts over goals, tactics, and resources

Effective interaction with regional and national government units when needed

Effective exercise of authority when needed.

Coordination is hard to define and difficult to sustain. During a disaster, strained relationships within and among relief organizations are practically inevitable, because of the very nonroutine nature of the tasks involved. But a spontaneous spirit of cooperation usually prevails, at least for a time, and helps keep the process moving along. But preparing for or, better, already having in place a planned emergency operations center is clearly a prerequisite for effective longer-term coordination.

Even so, according to disaster studies of the last thirty years, preparedness and actual disaster response have their limits. Much of what goes on will inevitably have to be improvised. Gaps and inefficiencies will exist, yet things will still get done. Trying to impose efficiency and effectiveness through a command and control model will not work as a general management strategy. Although an emergent resource coordination model is no panacea, either, it is at least more in keeping with predisaster routines and with the fluid conditions of the emergency period.

Once again, improvisation and preparedness are the twin foundations of emergency management, and a disaster-impacted community's ability to improvise is a given, unless the ratio of damages to resources (impact ratio) is extraordinarily high. Preparedness is in the hands of local officials and emergency managers. The barriers to emergency management are significant and cannot be overcome unless these officials and emergency managers resolve to play leadership roles.

Types of emergency management organization

How is the emergency management function performed by local governments? The keynote is diversity. The best data available are those developed by ICMA, which in 1982 surveyed more than six thousand of the nearly forty thousand local governments in the United States.[32] Data from more than fifteen hundred of the jurisdictions surveyed provide some clues about the different ways local communities address emergency management.

Although some emergency planning is conducted in most municipalities and counties, the ICMA survey shows that who is actually doing the planning varies considerably. In cities, the city manager (23 percent), part-time emergency preparedness coordinator (19 percent), full-time emergency preparedness coordinator (14 percent), or fire chief (16.2 percent) was most likely to have emergency management responsibility. In counties, full-time emergency preparedness coordinators (44 percent) or part-time emergency preparedness coordinators (33 percent) were found to have the responsibility. Only 33 percent of the cities responding had either a full-time or a part-time emergency preparedness coordinator.[33]

At the smallest scale are single individuals who play some kind of emergency management role voluntarily, as part of another job, part time, or full time. Because there are many more small than large jurisdictions in the United States, this arrangement is undoubtedly the most common. In these cases, the emergency management role is identified and, in some sense, legitimated by local government, but tangible resources available for preparedness are modest at best. This resource scarcity does not necessarily mean that important emergency management activities are precluded. To the contrary, many dedicated people accomplish a great deal with minimal resources.[34] But it does mean that the emergency management vision can easily exceed its grasp, not only in smaller local governments but in larger ones as well.

The larger the city or county, the more likely it is to have a dedicated emergency management unit. Although staff size is generally small (three or fewer full-time employees), the organizational character of emergency management activities becomes more apparent.[35] Among those local governments that have an emergency management department, there is variation in the degree of organizational autonomy. The department may be either an independent agency or embedded within some other unit. An independent agency, as illustrated in Figure 2–2, is a relatively autonomous unit with a direct line of authority to the top level of local government. Figure 2–3 shows an emergency management department housed within another government unit, such as law enforcement, public works, or fire protection.

Both figures considerably simplify organizational structures in order to highlight the locational distinction, and far more diversity exists in the location of actual emergency management units than is implied by the figures. Among independent emergency management units, actual authority and coordination

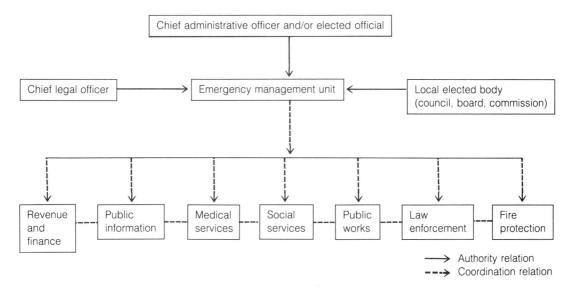

Figure 2–2   Organization chart showing an independent emergency management unit.

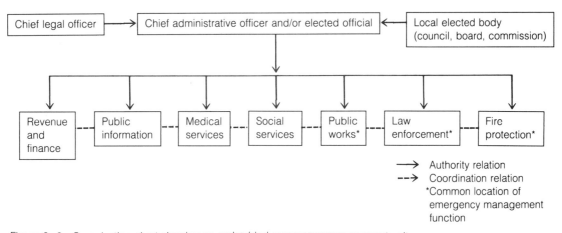

Figure 2–3   Organization chart showing an embedded emergency management unit.

relations vary widely from place to place. Among embedded units, location within the government structure varies. Regardless of whether an agency is independent or embedded, its preparedness activities may be either narrowly defined (for example, focused on traditional civil defense activities) or broadly defined (an all-hazard approach).[36] Yet another source of diversity is the basic difference between municipalities and counties. A county emergency manager, who must work with a number of different municipalities, confronts a set of problems very different from those faced by the emergency manager of just one city, large or small.

As the ICMA survey notes, to know that most municipalities and counties have disaster plans is not necessarily to know very much about what is actually going on in any given locality.

A comprehensive understanding of local government emergency management strategies and arrangements does not exist. The conclusion Thomas Drabek reached after studying more than sixty city and county emergency management offices seems quite reasonable: given the wide variation in political and organizational realities among local governments, there cannot be any standard design for emergency management. Local directors must therefore seek to locate their agency where it will be maximally supported and protected.[37]

A traditional and central function of any emergency management unit is coordinating the various mitigation, preparedness, response, and recovery activities of local government. With a small staff and modest resources, any emergency management unit, whatever its position or approach, will find that its ability to perform that function depends on the credibility given to it by the local government's top elected and appointed officials. Without that credibility, the agency is likely to be ignored before an emergency and bypassed during it. Credibility is not freely granted; it must be earned. As will be discussed in a later section, successful emergency managers are able to take a great deal of initiative in earning it.[38]

The major potential advantage of having an independent emergency management unit is its central location between the formal powers of government and the agencies providing routine and emergency-related services. Although disaster preparedness by different groups in the public and private sectors is valuable in itself, it is even more valuable when these plans are integrated into a communitywide disaster preparedness program. In such a program, human and material resources are identified, perhaps placed on a standby basis, and updated as needed. Community coordination and control problems are anticipated and addressed. A tentative communitywide division of labor ensures that the necessary emergency management functions are performed. The emergency management unit illustrated in Figure 2–2 would be in an excellent position to facilitate these outcomes—but without formal legitimacy and earned credibility, such location would count for little.

A major potential advantage of an embedded agency is its more direct involvement in the day-to-day activities of government. Similarities exist between responses to everyday emergencies and to major crises, and the organizational structure implemented during a disaster should be based to the degree possible on that used for routine emergencies. When clusters of agencies work together regularly, the formal and informal arrangements that develop over time can be drawn on during a disaster. If the emergency management unit is a part of one of these clusters, it is more likely to have developed social networks and understandings that are tied to actual situations and not merely to hypothetical circumstances. Therefore, although the ideal of a communitywide emergency management system may seem more clearly delineated in Figure 2–2, attaining the ideal may be just as likely with the arrangement shown in Figure 2–3. As with the independent emergency management unit, a prerequisite for the success of the embedded unit is that it have earned credibility for itself through competent performance. The professional emergency manager must develop strategies to enhance the performance and credibility of his or her role and department. That is the topic of the next section. In closing this section, let's return to an earlier key point. The principal problem for local emergency planning and preparedness is that disasters (fortunately) do not occur often enough to represent a sustained threat. Because of this, emergency planning and preparedness are not given high priority in ongoing organizational and community affairs (except for the usual flurry of activity right after an event). That is a fact of life for professional emergency managers. The best they can generally hope for is modest planning and preparedness. They should not allow their vision to exceed their grasp, just as they recognize that even modest planning and preparedness can make a difference. The government bodies that are responsible for protecting the public need to be aware of those hazards that are more likely to result in emergencies and disasters in their communities. Fortunately, general planning needs, principles, and functions can be applied to virtually all hazards. Although it must take account of the threat posed by specific hazards, the preparedness process can and should be generic.

The professional emergency manager: Credibility through performance

The role of the emergency management professional is neither easily performed nor well understood. Nor is it a readily accepted role in many local jurisdictions. At this point in the development of emergency management, a professional role is unfolding amid uncertain expectations rather than in relation to well-defined standards of performance. The more successful emergency managers, in particular, are necessarily engaged in role making. Drabek's benchmark study of professional emergency managers from sixty-two cities and counties identifies strategies and characteristics of successful performance in that role.

The first phase of Drabek's research involved intensive study of twelve directors singled out as effective (a judgment later validated within the design of the study). The second phase of the study compared these twelve directors and their agencies with a random sample of fifty other directors and agencies selected to ensure variability across geographic region, community size, and city-county designation. The discussion that follows summarizes some key findings from this study.[39]

What does it take to be a good director of a local emergency management agency? Why are successful directors perceived as such by executives who lead other units of the local emergency management system? Following lengthy interviews with each of the twelve successful directors to determine how they performed their jobs, Drabek then interviewed executives from seven types of local organizations from each director's local jurisdiction to get the executives' perceptions of the respective director's performance. The executives were from law enforcement and fire protection agencies, public works departments, elected bodies, Red Cross associations, local businesses, and medical organizations. When asked to report on and to evaluate the activities of their local emergency management directors, the responses of seventy-nine executives emphasized three broad categories: professionalism, individual qualities, and emergency management activities.

Professionalism

Successful directors were perceived as having established a legitimate niche as emergency management coordinators. They were seen as integrators, mediators, facilitators, or compromisers rather than as autocrats. They were also perceived as having specialized knowledge. All occupational groups in the process of becoming professionalized must identify special areas of knowledge unique to their field. Successful directors were seen as highly knowledgeable about existing and pending legislation, operating rules and regulations, and key federal and state agencies. Through a wide variety of actions, successful directors had developed and sustained an image of commitment to their profession. Many local executives were impressed with the tenacity of their emergency management directors in the face of small budgets and limited authority. Finally, some of the successful directors were perceived as being recognized by specialized professional groups outside the community (for example, the National Coordinating Council of Emergency Managers and the American Civil Defense Association). Although it was usually communicated very subtly by the directors themselves, this professional recognition enhanced directors' credibility among other agency heads at the local level.

Individual qualities

Several different qualities related to the personality of the individual were found to be associated with success as an emergency manager. Those noted most frequently were communication skills, organizational ability, human relations skills, and control under stress. In addition, all the successful directors were seen as having some unique skill. It did not seem to matter exactly what the skill was—for example, prior military experience, ability to work with volunteers, or technical background or training. The key is that the skill was seen as important to the director's job performance. The general conclusion is that successful directors drew on resources they had by virtue of their employment histories. Finally, the success of some of the directors was perceived to be related to their effective performance during an actual emergency. In other words, real-life disasters had provided several directors with the opportunity to prove their worth—both personal and organizational.

Emergency management activities

Under the heading of emergency management activities, three characteristics were associated with success. First, many local executives praised the approach to disaster preparedness used by the director. One quality viewed as most relevant to the director's success was a shift from a traditional (and narrow) civil defense approach to a comprehensive emergency management approach. Most executives did recognize the legitimacy of civil defense, but they were more concerned about nonmilitary disasters, which are generally perceived to be more likely to affect a community directly. Many executives also expressed appreciation for the increased visibility of emergency management within the community. This suggests that successful directors recognized the costs of physical isolation and made sure that they maintained contact with important constituencies. Specific accomplishments were noted as a distinctive quality of successful directors. Although the accomplishments varied widely, they were all perceived to be program related (for example, making an equipment purchase, establishing a training program, undertaking a disaster exercise and critique, making a polished presentation).

The overall picture provided by the Drabek study is one of credibility earned through performance. Drabek's study shows that successful directors were dedicated professionals who worked hard to improve emergency management capability in their localities. Regardless of their location in the government structure, they had established a niche for their program and used local networks to maintain that niche. These networks included top elected officials, local government agencies, local businesses, the mass media, voluntary associations, and disaster-relevant governmental agencies at state and federal levels. In interviews with Drabek, successful directors communicated a sense of realism about the obstacles they faced, and they could articulate reasonable strategies for overcoming them. They were role makers rather than simply role players, but their vision did not exceed their grasp.

Program implementation and review

An active community emergency response will take place with or without disaster preparedness, but even a modest preparedness effort will markedly improve response. The implementation and review of local emergency management programs can and should proceed even in the absence of an actual disaster. Whether a disaster occurs or not, preparedness programs must be examined and evaluated routinely. If preparedness slackens and the unlikely disaster catches the community unprepared, the fiscal, legal, and political costs to those charged with protecting the public can be considerable.[40] This section offers a framework for going about the task of program implementation, including regular evaluation or review.

The success of emergency management is based on the extent to which preparedness functions (such as the ten highlighted earlier) have been implemented. Although many other functions could have been included, creation of an exhaus-

Figure 2–4 Emergency preparedness functions: implementation framework.

Preparedness functions	Implementation components				
	Performing organization	Performance description	Interorganizational arrangements	Planning and training schedule	Program review schedule
Mobilizing emergency personnel and resources					
Warning the public					
Taking protective action					
Caring for victims					
Assessing the damage					
Restoring essential public services					
Informing the public					
Record keeping					
Planning the recovery					
Coordinating emergency management activities					
(Other functions)					

tive list is counterproductive, because some improvisation is inevitable during an emergency and, in fact, is essential during a major disaster. Thus, the aim should be for modest but sustained preparedness tied to minimum response requirements.

The implementation framework is summarized in Figure 2–4. The ten functions (other special ones can be added if necessary) are listed vertically, and five implementation components, including review or evaluation, are listed along the top.

The next five sections of this chapter highlight the kinds of issues that need to be considered for each of the implementation components. Annexes could readily be developed for hazards that have unique response requirements.

Performing organizations A cluster of organizations is likely to be involved in any given functional area. The first function, for example—which is mobilization of emergency personnel and resources—relates to initial notification of emergency conditions. Such notification can come from multiple sources, and the ensuing mobilization will probably be accomplished by yet another cluster of different organizations. Members of each cluster need to be identified, to the extent possible. A key point is to identify a focal (central) organization or person within each cluster. In the case of mobilization of resources, it may be a duty officer from a designated organization who monitors incoming communications and relays them to other members of the cluster. In the case of the coordination function, it may—and probably should—be the local emergency management office.

Performance description It is not enough simply to designate who is going to be involved in various disaster-related domains. It is also critically important to anticipate how the tasks associated with these domains will be performed. What are the personnel and resource requirements? How will the members of a given cluster of organizations work together to get the job done? What problems can be anticipated and ironed out as part of an ongoing preparedness effort? The answers to these questions should not be in a detailed operational plan but in a succinct performance scenario that can be amended as needed through cooperative discussions among those involved. Once again, the rule is to keep it simple and avoid the temptation to become too detailed.

Interorganizational arrangements   Because there are likely to be clusters of organizations involved in the same domains, it might be useful for them to develop formal or informal understandings with each other as part of a preparedness program. During an actual emergency, these understandings would develop out of necessity—sometimes smoothly and sometimes not. It is far better to get things clarified, to the extent possible, under calmer conditions. That may prove easier to accomplish than one might think, because members of many organizational clusters interact routinely. Relying on understandings that already exist can increase the continuity between everyday and emergency situations.

Planning and training schedule   Any preparedness program must be sustained if it is to be successful. If all the effort that so often goes into developing highly detailed plans—plans that typically are put on the shelf and forgotten— were used instead to keep far simpler plans up-to-date, then the local emergency management program would be much better off. It is hard to overemphasize the importance of taking a modest preparedness program and making it a continuous process. This is accomplished not through constant training exercises, which are impractical, but through periodic ones to maintain a reasonable state of readiness. Rather than constantly rewrite plans, emergency managers should convene periodic meetings among key participants to keep everyone current about existing arrangements and to learn from them about important changes in their own personnel and operations. Planning and training need not be highly formalized—just regular.

Program review schedule   Assuming that preparedness has become an ongoing process, what is required next is a periodic fresh look at what is being done. Such a review is probably best accomplished by someone from the outside. Important problems and issues are perhaps being overlooked, new technologies may be available, or new hazards may have to be considered. Because emergency management is still an emerging profession, selection of outside evaluators can be difficult. It is best to rely for advice on professional associations; FEMA offices at federal, regional, and state levels; and FEMA's national training center at Emmitsburg, Maryland.

Whatever counsel they obtain from outside, in the final analysis local communities must implement their own preparedness programs. Resources are scarce, and the bulk of them should therefore be expended locally, where they can do the most good. This discussion has in a sense come full circle to the twin foundations of emergency management—preparedness and improvisation. Even modest preparedness increases the ability to improvise during an actual emergency. And in the face of minimal resources, it takes considerable improvisational skills to become prepared in the first place. Emergency managers, then, must also be innovators if they are to make progress.

Conclusion

This chapter is based on a simple question: What does it mean to organize for emergency management? It means recognizing that improvisation and preparedness are the foundations of emergency management. It means understanding that there are guiding principles of emergency management that can be applied widely. Emergency management needs must be identified and translated into emergency management functions. Emergency management must find a niche in the local community and establish credibility through performance. A local emergency management role must be performed with professional and organizational skills and no small amount of tenacity and grace. And finally, a clearly articulated and understood emergency management program must be implemented and evaluated as a routine activity of local government.

1   For good summaries of recent disaster-related damages and losses in the United States, see James D. Wright, Peter H. Rossi, Sonia R. Wright, and Eleanor Weber-Burdin, *After the Clean-Up: Long Range Effects of Natural Disasters* (Beverly Hills, CA: Sage Publications, 1979). See also Peter H. Rossi, James D. Wright, Eleanor Weber-Burdin, and Joseph Pereira, *Victims of the Environment: Loss from Natural Hazards in the United States 1970–80* (New York: Plenum Press, 1983).

2   For a good summary of the state and local politics of hazards and disasters, see Peter H. Rossi, James D. Wright, and Eleanor Weber-Burdin, *Natural Hazards and Public Choice: The State and Local Politics of Hazard Mitigation* (New York: Academic Press, 1982).

3   This chapter is based, in part, on work supported by the National Science Foundation under Grants No. CEE–9121135, CEE–8400486, and CES–8703518. Any opinions, findings, conclusions, or recommendations expressed are those of the author and do not necessarily reflect the views of the National Science Foundation. The author wishes to thank Thomas Drabek, Gerard Hoetmer, and Susan Bosworth for critiques of earlier versions of this chapter.

4   The examples are based on material in the archives of the Disaster Research Center at the University of Delaware. The author's archival research is summarized in a number of articles and the following book: Gary A. Kreps, ed., *Social Structure and Disaster* (Newark: University of Delaware Press, 1989).

5   For a manager's checklist, see the appendix of Lisa Stevenson and Marie Hayman, *Local Government Disaster Protection* (Washington, DC: International City Management Association, 1981).

6   The first example is adapted from Joel Enoch, *Origins, Networks, and Restructuring: An Analysis of Three Methodologies*, Master's thesis (Williamsburg, VA: The College of William and Mary, 1988), 54–55. The second example is adapted from Susan Lovegren Bosworth and Gary A. Kreps, "Structure as Process: Organization and Role," *American Sociological Review* 51 (October 1986): 703.

7   This point is a principal conclusion of Bosworth and Kreps, "Structure as Process," 712.

8   These principles are discussed in detail in Russell R. Dynes, E. L. Quarantelli, and Gary A. Kreps, *A Perspective on Disaster Planning*, Report Series 11 (Newark: Disaster Research Center, University of Delaware, 1972), 1–5, 15–39.

9   For further discussions of this point, see Ronald W. Perry and Michael K. Lindell, "The Psychological Consequences of Natural Disaster: A Review of Research on American Communi-

ties," *Mass Emergencies* 3 (1978): 105–115. See also Robert Bolin, "Disaster Characteristics and Psychosocial Impacts," and Bonnie L. Greene, "Conceptual and Methodological Issues in Assessing the Psychological Impact of Disaster," both in Barbara J. Sowder and Mary Lystad, eds., *Disasters and Mental Health* (Washington, DC: American Psychiatric Press, 1986).

10 This assumption is critiqued nicely in E. L. Quarantelli, *Criteria Which Could Be Used in Assessing Disaster Preparedness Planning and Management* (Newark: Disaster Research Center, University of Delaware, 1987), 6–7.

11 Readers are strongly encouraged to consult the ICMA Local Government Emergency Management Handbook Series No. 2, titled "How Prepared Is Your Community for Its Next Emergency: A Manager's Checklist" (see also Endnote 5). This material provides many insights about effective emergency and hazards management.

12 For summaries of research findings, see E. L. Quarantelli and Russell R. Dynes, "Response to Social Crisis and Disaster," *Annual Review of Sociology* 3 (1977): 23–49; Gary A. Kreps, "Sociological Inquiry and Disaster Research," *Annual Review of Sociology* 10 (1984): 309–30; Ronald W. Perry, *Comprehensive Emergency Management: Evacuating Threatened Populations* (Greenwich, CT: JAI Press, Inc., 1985); Thomas E. Drabek, *Human System Response to Disaster: An Inventory of Findings* (New York: Springer-Verlag, 1986); and John H. Sorensen, Barbara M. Vogt, and Dennis Mileti, *Evacuation: An Assessment of Planning and Research* (Oak Ridge, TN: Oak Ridge National Laboratory, 1987).

13 See Gerard J. Hoetmer, "How Prepared Is Your Community for Its Next Disaster," *Emergency Management Review* 1 (1984): 6–9. See also Ronald W. Perry, "Evaluating Emergency Response Plans," *Emergency Management Review* 1 (1984): 20–24.

14 For discussions of this issue, see Russell R. Dynes and B. E. Aguirre, "Organizational Adaptation to Crisis: Mechanisms of Coordination and Structural Change," *Disasters* 3 (1979): 71–74; Thomas E. Drabek, "Managing the Emergency Response," *Public Administration Review* 45 (1985): 85–93; and E. L. Quarantelli, *Organizational Behavior in Disasters and Implications for Disaster Planning* (Emmitsburg, MD: FEMA National Emergency Training Center, 1984).

15 Quarantelli, *Assessing Disaster Preparedness Planning and Management*, 1–4.

16 For discussions of intergovernmental relations and disaster management, see Peter J. May and Walter Williams, *Disaster Policy Implementation: Managing Programs under Shared Governance* (New York: Plenum Press, 1986). See also Ron-

ald W. Perry and Joanne M. Nigg, "Emergency Preparedness and Response Planning: An Intergovernmental Perspective," in Mary Lystad, ed., *Mental Health Response to Mass Emergencies: Theory and Practice* (New York: Bruner-Mazel Publishers, 1988), 346–70.

17 See Russell R. Dynes, *Organized Behavior in Disaster* (Lexington, MA: D. C. Heath, 1970), 62–66.

18 Quarantelli, *Assessing Disaster Preparedness Planning and Management*, 6–8.

19 Ibid., 8–9.

20 Perry, "Evaluating Emergency Response Plans," 21.

21 Drabek, *Human System Response*, 70–97 and 100–12.

22 For an excellent comparison of nuclear and nonnuclear hazards, see Ronald W. Perry, "Population Evacuation in Volcanic Eruptions, Floods, and Nuclear Power Plant Accidents," *Journal of Community Psychiatry* 11 (1983): 36–47.

23 The benchmark study of convergence is Charles E. Fritz and J. H. Matthewson, *Convergence Behavior in Disasters* (Washington, DC: National Academy of Sciences–National Research Council, 1957).

24 Dynes, Quarantelli, and Kreps, *A Perspective on Disaster Planning*, 11.

25 Perry, "Evaluating Emergency Response Plans," 21–22.

26 Quarantelli, *Assessing Disaster Preparedness Planning and Management*, 2.

27 For a thorough summary of research on the role of the mass media in disasters, see Gary A. Kreps, "Research Needs and Policy Issues on the Mass Media," in *Disasters and the Mass Media: Proceedings of the Committee on Disasters and the Mass Media Workshop, February 1979* (Washington, DC: National Academy of Sciences–National Research Council), 35–74.

28 For a summary of research findings on disaster recovery, see Drabek, *Human System Response*, 250–316.

29 For an excellent discussion of organizational

problems during military operations, see Randall Collins, "Sociological Theory, Disaster Research and War," in Gary A. Kreps, ed., *Social Structure and Disaster* (Newark: The University of Delaware Press, 1989), 365–85.

30 This is a central argument of Dynes, Quarantelli, and Kreps, *A Perspective on Disaster Planning*, 12–13; and of Quarantelli, *Assessing Disaster Preparedness Planning and Management*, 6–8.

31 Drabek, "Managing the Emergency Response," 90.

32 See Gerard J. Hoetmer, "Emergency Management," *Baseline Data Report* 15 (April 1983): 1–13 (Washington, DC: International City Management Association). See also Gerard J. Hoetmer, "Emergency Management: Individual and County Data," *Baseline Data Report* 15 (August 1983): 1–13 (Washington, DC: International City Management Association).

33 Hoetmer, "Individual and County Data," 1–2. Percentages have been rounded.

34 See Thomas E. Drabek, *The Professional Emergency Manager* (Boulder, CO: Institute for Behavioral Science, 1987), 90–105.

35 Drabek, *Professional Emergency Manager*, 50–77.

36 This distinction is developed more fully in Dennis Wenger, E. L. Quarantelli, and Russell R. Dynes, *Disaster Analysis: Emergency Management Offices and Arrangements* (Newark: Disaster Research Center, University of Delaware, 1987). See also Drabek, *Professional Emergency Manager*, 50–77.

37 Drabek, *Professional Emergency Manager*, 107.

38 Drabek, *Professional Emergency Manager*, 77–105. See also Wenger, Quarantelli, and Dynes, *Disaster Analysis*, 43–71.

39 Drabek, *Professional Emergency Manager*, especially the fourth, fifth, and eighth chapters.

40 For a case in point, see Robert Wolensky, *Power, Policy, and Disaster: The Political Organizational Impact of a Major Flood* (Stevens Point: Center for the Small City, University of Wisconsin–Stevens Point, 1984).

3 Coordinating community resources

In emergency management, coordination refers to agreed-upon relationships between independent organizations—relationships that provide for the sharing of critical resources. Coordination is vitally important during all four phases of emergency management: mitigation, preparedness, response, and recovery. Mitigation is stronger when the entire community has been involved in hazard vulnerability assessments. Preparedness is improved by mutual aid agreements and other forms of interjurisdictional planning. Response efforts are more effective when key governmental units and private organizations cooperate. And recovery is faster when tasks and responsibilities are allocated across the widest possible resource base.

Coordination, therefore, channels resources into a common direction for the overall benefit of a community and is an essential element in viable emergency management systems. The more complex the community—that is, the more the community contains special districts, overlapping jurisdictions, or numerous organizations with highly specialized responsibilities—the more important it is to establish coordination. However, coordination is important to emergency managers in every community regardless of degree of complexity. Moreover, several current trends are increasing the importance of coordinating community resources.

One such trend is the growing awareness and adoption of the integrated emergency management system (IEMS). IEMS is a management strategy developed by FEMA to implement comprehensive emergency management (CEM).[1] IEMS has three principal parts:

1. An assessment of hazard vulnerabilities
2. An inventory of community capabilities to deal with hazards
3. Steps to reduce the gap between vulnerability and capability (by working across various districts and jurisdictions and working with many different kinds of professionals).

The concept underlying IEMS is the importance of focusing on functions common in all disasters (such as damage assessment, communication, evacuation, control, and support services) and of promoting partnerships among various kinds of professionals and across jurisdictional boundaries in mitigating, preparing for, responding to, and recovering from disasters. Coordination is a key factor in establishing and maintaining such partnerships.

A second trend increasing the significance of coordination is that settlement patterns are producing greater concentrations of people. Many people live in floodplains, on slopes subject to mudslides and landslides, in unreinforced dwellings near earthquake faults, next to spillways of water dams, and in other places that are vulnerable to natural disasters. These settlement patterns mean that disasters affect larger populations; disaster situations may therefore be more complex, involving the close proximity of diverse interests and the interplay of different hazards.

A third trend that underscores the importance of coordinating community resources is the increasing risk of technological disaster. Large quantities of hazardous materials such as gasoline, nuclear waste, and liquid natural gas are moved by truck and rail through heavily populated areas. In addition, hazardous facilities such as oil refineries and nuclear power plants are often located near population centers. The hazardous materials may present dangers in themselves, or they may complicate the dangers arising from natural disasters. The identification and handling of hazardous materials is a specialized area of emergency management, and coordination between general emergency management and hazardous materials specialists is critically needed.

The fourth trend emphasizing the need to coordinate community resources is the growing professionalization of emergency management, a professionalization prompted by the increasing complexity of hazards and the consequent need for more knowledge about all phases and aspects of disasters. Government education and training programs for emergency managers have expanded; ICMA materials on emergency management have been written specifically for local government managers; and the National Emergency Training Center at Emmitsburg, Maryland, has been training emergency management personnel since 1980. In addition, state emergency management agencies offer courses and training seminars (as well as prepare and disseminate hazard risk information and serve as resources for local emergency management officials). In 1965, 86 percent of emergency managers had had 24 or fewer days of training, and only 3 percent had had 100 or more days of training. By 1985, these figures were reversed, with only 36 percent having had 24 or fewer days of training and 29 percent having had 100 or more days.[2] With more training and greater knowledge, emergency managers have a broader span of control. This, too, increases the need for coordination.

Organizational complexity also contributes to the growing need for coordination. Numerous private-sector initiatives complement the government programs. Insurance companies offer risk protection for most hazards. And although the National Flood Insurance Program is subsidized by the federal government, it is implemented through private insurance companies. Many small firms offer risk assessments, preparedness training, and technical assistance. As the number and variety of organizations involved in disaster mitigation, preparedness, response, or recovery increase, coordination becomes increasingly important.

In addition, certain not-for-profit organizations are central actors in the disaster networks of almost every community; the American Red Cross is probably the most widely known. The Red Cross—which has a congressional mandate to offer disaster services and to facilitate the health and safety of citizens—is involved in public education, hazard and capability assessments, and community coordination. A number of religious organizations, too, are involved in disaster relief efforts. The National Voluntary Organizations Active in Disaster lists twenty-six organizations as disaster service or relief organizations, mostly churches but also the Boy Scouts of America and some ham radio groups. Emergency managers must ensure that the separate efforts are all unified.

All these developments underscore the increasing importance of coordination to emergency managers. Thus, emergency managers must understand the meaning of coordination, the factors that impede and facilitate it, and its potential benefits; the types of community resources that are coordinated in different phases of emergency management; the critical community subsystems that must be coordinated if there is to be an effective response to disaster; and several kinds of coordination techniques that help promote a level of coordination appropriate to the community's need.

Coordination: Definition, underlying factors, and benefits

Coordination has been defined in different ways. Richard Hall and others define it as "the extent to which organizations attempt to ensure that their activities

Figure 3–1   The 1989 explosion at the Phillips Petroleum plant in Pasadena, Texas, points out the need for coordinated, public and private comprehensive planning.

take into account those of other organizations."[3] In considering decision making among community organizations, Roland Warren and others emphasize a "deliberate degree of adjustment to each other."[4] In the view of Michael Aiken and others, coordination ensures that the "comprehensiveness of, compatibility among, and cooperation among elements are maximized."[5] In general, then, coordination is the cooperation of independent units for the purpose of eliminating fragmentation, gaps in service delivery, and unnecessary (as opposed to strategic) duplication of services.

The word *integration* is often used interchangeably with *coordination*, even though the two words have different meanings. *To integrate* means to draw separate parts together into a unified whole. In contrast, *to coordinate* means to bring into common action or to harmonize. In coordinated systems, independent actors work with a common purpose. The opposite of coordination is anarchy, where each unit pursues its objectives irrespective of others. Because the large number of actors involved in emergency management creates a potential for conflict, it is essential to promote coordination.

Coordination may be voluntary or mandated. Voluntary coordination usually emerges in response to mutual needs. Two communities adjacent to each other may coordinate if each believes it will benefit from pooling a resource—for example, police personnel during response to a disaster. This kind of voluntary coordination contributes importantly to emergency management and community welfare. Mandated coordination is required by a higher authority. For example, every jurisdiction in a state may be required to designate an emergency manager who must submit certain information to the state. Mandated coordination can result in systems coordinated across diverse jurisdictional boundaries.

Coordination should occur in both planning and service delivery.[6] Coordinated planning means that organizations make decisions together, whereas coordinated service delivery refers to cooperation in providing services—when, for example, the staff of one organization directly contacts the staff of another organization in the expectation that its request for services will be agreed to.

Coordinated service delivery includes direct service linkages and administrative linkages. Direct service linkages deal with the specific needs of victims and include search and rescue, damage assessment, emergency communication, evacuation, and referral. For emergency managers, these linkages come into play mostly in the disaster response period. Administrative linkages, in contrast, are designed to meet the needs of a whole class of clients or victims rather than the needs of specific victims. They connect or consolidate the management of services and affect the service delivery system.

Administrative linkages include fiscal linkages (joint budgeting, joint funding, fund transfers, and purchase of service); personnel practices (consolidated personnel administration, staff transfers, and staff sharing); planning and programming (joint planning, joint programming, joint evaluation, and information exchanges); and administrative support services (joint record keeping, grant management, and central support services).

Generally, administrative linkages are more difficult to establish than direct service linkages because they require a larger investment of resources, especially staff time, and are often viewed as a threat to the decision-making powers of individual organizations. Moreover, the benefits from administrative linkages are usually not realized in the short term. In the long run, however, despite potential shortcomings, administrative linkages have the greatest effect on service delivery.

Factors impeding coordination

There are seven principal obstacles to coordination within community emergency management systems:

1. The tendency of organizations to seek autonomy
2. Staff commitment to professional ideologies and work autonomy
3. Differences in organizational technologies and resource needs
4. Fear that the identity of the group or organization will be lost
5. Concern about the redirection of scarce resources
6. The proliferation of organizations and interest groups across multiple political jurisdictions
7. Differences in costs of and benefits from participating in coordination.

Figure 3–2 Red Cross
workers assisting victims
of Hurricane Hugo,
1989.

Although these factors are potential obstacles in day-to-day operations in a community, additional constraints emerge during the immediate response period.[7] Key personnel may be unable to assume their responsibilities, equipment may be damaged or inaccessible, lines of authority may be confused or challenged, and the urgency of the need may complicate communication.

Certain forms of coordination threaten organizational autonomy. For example, it is more difficult to gain acceptance for joint budgeting and staff transfers than for forms of coordination involving purchase of service, information, and staff training. Once jointly funded programs are accepted, they are difficult to maintain because they achieve an identity separate from the supporting parent organizations. This puts a strain on the willingness of the organizations to continue their support.

Differences in professional beliefs and practices can complicate efforts to coordinate. For example, newscasters believe that the public's "right to know" gives them the right to enter, observe, and report what they see in disaster areas, whereas the police or others in command maintain that *their* responsibility to protect the public gives them the right to control who enters, observes, and reports the disaster-response activities.

Differences in technology and resources can also make relationships between organizations more difficult to form or maintain. For example, the adoption of a new communication system may enhance the speed or efficiency of the adopting unit while also cutting the unit off from other agencies unable to afford a new system.

Fear about the loss of organizational identity is associated both with joint budgeting programs and with staff transfers. Jointly budgeted programs are usually identified by the name of the program and not by the names of the supporting organizations. When such programs achieve success, they tend to move toward acquiring an independent identity, which then entails the obstacles described above with respect to autonomy. Staff transfers invite comparisons between organizations, with the possibility that key personnel will move to the other organization.

Proposals to redirect scarce resources impede coordination by threatening both organizational autonomy and organizational identity. In 1985, municipal emergency managers in St. Louis raised these issues explicitly when their county government advanced a proposal to assume metropolitanwide responsibility for disaster response.

The increasing complexity of contemporary disasters has expanded the range of expertise and the kinds of organizations needed to deal effectively with disasters, and the growing number of organizations and interest groups that must work across political jurisdictions impedes coordination. Increased numbers alone make coordination more difficult, but the problems are magnified when different interests and political jurisdictions are involved.

Finally, differences in costs and benefits can also impede coordination. For example, with joint budgeting, usually one organization spends more money than the other. This can engender conflicts about authority and confusion about how to credit the successes of jointly funded programs.

Awareness of these obstacles to coordination is the first step toward overcoming them. The principal technique emergency managers use to overcome them is clearly written proposals that benefit the community as a whole. Proposals should take into account the potential threats to each organization's autonomy (perhaps by developing guidelines of fair exchange), the mixing and matching of various professional groups, the range of technologies and resources that need to be strategically linked, and the political compromises necessary to achieve coordination. In addition to countering the obstacles, emergency managers can try to take advantage of the factors facilitating coordination.

Factors facilitating coordination

At least five factors facilitate coordination:

1. Shared goals or expectations about what the organizations will and will not do
2. Shared leaders or overlapping board memberships
3. Diversity of roles and interests
4. Similarity in technologies and resource needs
5. High rates of environmental change.

Organizations with common clients, services, and activities interact more often than those operating in different spheres. Some researchers—for example, William M. Evan—have suggested that resource exchanges are lowest between organizations with very similar or very different goals.[8] Others—for example, J. Kenneth Benson—say coordination is highest only when organizations have overlapping goals and ideologies.[9] It has been suggested, as well, that coordination is improved when organizations have compatible reward structures, time orientations, and expectations.[10]

Cooperative relationships develop when leaders are predisposed to cooperate. It is important for leaders to perceive that they have similar interests and that some type of interaction is necessary to achieve organizational goals. Leaders must also accept the legitimacy of the other organizations and the need each has for the other. Moreover, coordination is more successful when the effort is guided by skilled leaders.

Within a single organization, diversity of roles and skills stimulates communication and innovation; and in a highly innovative organization, new efforts are likely to overlap with the work of other organizations, thereby increasing the need for the organization to coordinate its activities with those of other organizations. C. L. Mulford and M. A. Mulford have shown that the larger the organization, its staff, and its budget, and the greater its number and variety of services, the more the organization needs to interact with other organizations.[11]

Interaction between organizations increases when the tasks performed are concentrated rather than spread out; stable; and similar. Moreover, the greater a community's capacity to support relationships (a capacity determined by overall resource base, number and size of organizations, level of economic well-being, and so forth), the more likely that coordination will occur. Organizations seek relationships with other organizations as a means of coping with rapid change and uncertainty in the environment. For example, by controlling resources needed by others, an organization acquires prestige within the system and improves its bargaining position in relation to competitors.

Emergency managers can take advantage of factors that facilitate coordination by developing proposals to extend already established patterns of cooperation. They can do this by drawing up a list of organizations and the critical services or resources they offer, their goals, their technologies, and their board memberships; reviewing the list to identify shared goals, similar technologies, similar resources, and overlapping board memberships; and noting potentially viable exchanges between one organization and another. Building on already established exchanges, managers can then write proposals for coordinated systems to benefit the community as a whole.

Benefits of coordination

The benefits of coordination may include

1. Financial stability
2. Increased staff creativity

3. Public support or perception of legitimacy
4. Broader geographical representation
5. Prestige
6. Reduced fragmentation of services
7. Continuity of services
8. Reduced duplication of services.

Perceived benefits underlie every instance of coordination. The assessment of these benefits may be formal or informal, quantitative or qualitative, and may or may not distinguish between the criteria of efficiency and effectiveness. But in one way or another, a judgment must be reached as to whether the benefits outweigh the costs. It is important to understand, however, that the benefits of coordination are not distributed evenly across the various levels of the emergency management system. For example, line staff have different perspectives on organizational effectiveness than do administrators at the community, state, or federal levels. In other words, different levels in the system use different criteria to evaluate the outcomes of coordination, as the discussion of interest groups, below, illustrates.

David Rogers and Charles Mulford identify four principal interest groups in coordinated systems: support groups, coordinating groups, administrative groups, and demand groups.[12] Support groups are interested in policy and strict fiscal accountability—in showing *that* something was done rather than *how* it was done. These groups, which generally include state and federal legislators and agency administrators, are responsible for securing and dispensing funds or accounting for funds.

Coordinating groups, which include professional staff and administrators employed by the entities or agencies in a coordinated system, are responsible for ensuring the efficiency and effectiveness of the overall delivery system. Coordinating groups focus much of their effort on mediating conflicts between member organizations and on minimizing the independent actions of the organizations in the system.

Administrative groups, consisting of administrators and managers of individual organizations, are more concerned with the impact of coordination on their own organization than with the overall system. Because organizational administrators are responsible for managing their organization and are usually evaluated in terms of their organization's success in achieving its goals, administrative groups focus on demonstrating productivity to maintain public support. The primary evaluation criterion of these groups is the degree of investment required by the coordination effort, with investment a function of organizational autonomy, organizational resources, or both.

Demand groups include the general public and clients of the organization. They are interested primarily in the effectiveness of the services delivered and the ease of gaining access to needed services; they are not very concerned with efficiency. Demand groups evaluate on the basis of ultimate outcomes and their own level of participation in decisions that affect the availability of and access to services.

The different priorities of these interest groups lead them to evaluate coordination differently. Rogers and Mulford suggest that support groups and coordinating groups prefer strategies that are formalized and ordered by authority because such strategies give more power and control to the coordinating system. In contrast, administrative groups prefer strategies that require less investment of resources and that allow the individual organizations to maintain greater control over their own activities. There is little evidence to suggest that demand groups prefer one strategy to another. Because demand groups are interested in service delivery and participation in decision making, they will accept whichever strategy best serves those ends.

Regardless of the criterion used to evaluate the outcomes of coordination, research indicates that coordination allows more services to be provided at the same level of funding.[13] There are many reasons for this. The exchange of ideas among agencies increases creativity and prevents the development of an inflexible and monolithic public service structure. And whereas an individual organization is more likely to lack resources, centralized coordinated systems obtain resources by presenting their needs as those of a single unit. Of course, if the resources are not available, a unified approach will still fail. Nevertheless, there is strength in numbers and in unity. The process clarifies community goals. Moreover, with central planning, broader community goals are substituted for the narrow goals of any single organization. Finally, use of demand groups is associated with high levels of public support for coordinated systems.

Types of community resources

For effective disaster mitigation, preparedness, response, and recovery, five resources need to be coordinated: information, people, money, physical space, and equipment. The nature of the resource exchanged depends partly on the phase of the disaster. Although the exchanges associated with each of the four major phases differ from one another, in the following discussion the main distinction is between predisaster (mitigation and preparedness) and postdisaster (response and recovery) types of resources.

Information

Although the general and pervasive nature of information makes it difficult to describe in an exact way, one may differentiate the kinds of information that must be exchanged. In predisaster stages, for example, coordination requires the sharing of information about hazard assessments, planning, training programs and exercises, and the sharing of knowledge or opinions related to all four phases of emergency management. In other words, in predisaster phases, the sharing of information builds a capacity to respond effectively. During these phases, information is used to establish, refine, and maintain mitigation and preparedness.

In contrast, information exchanged in the postdisaster stages includes medical assessments, damage assessments, and crisis counseling. In other words, during postdisaster stages, information guides action. An effective response to disaster requires the accurate and timely transfer of information—and one of the most serious problems in disasters is disruption of the flow of information. (For example, telephone lines are often knocked out or overloaded. In the case of the Miamisburg derailment, the danger of a chemical fire after the derailment was so imminent that a formal emergency operations center [EOC] with regular telephones was not established until the fourth day—see sidebar on pages 64–65.) To some extent, emergency communication follows planned guidelines but, as was indicated in Chapter 2, a disaster often calls for improvisation as well.

The kind of information needed during the response period is further distinguished from the kind required in predisaster phases (and from the kind required in recovery) by the urgency of the need for specific information and by the shortage of time available for getting and relaying it.

People

Lending or exchanging personnel is an essential aspect of coordination. As part of preparedness, an organization's experienced staff or persons with special expertise are assigned specific tasks and responsibilities in other organizations. Emergency managers and other key resource people serve on the boards of various organizations to promote concerted mitigation and preparedness efforts. Hazard assessment experts and planners share appraisals and discuss mobilization strategies to uncover snags and conflicts.

Following a disaster, especially during the immediate response period, coordination of volunteers and emergency workers becomes critical. For one thing, people tend to converge on the disaster area, spurred on by curiosity and the desire to help. Despite the altruism, convergence can create more problems than it solves. Convergence poses special problems that need to be anticipated and planned for, not simply reacted to.

During the predisaster phases and the recovery phase, people tend to assume specialized roles that relate to their education, past experience, and training— but during the response phase, victims who are able and people who are nearby

The Miamisburg derailment   The importance of coordination was highlighted in the wake of the train derailment and phosphorus fire in Miamisburg, a southwest Ohio community of 18,000. Three federal agencies, eight departments of state government, and numerous local organizations were involved in the five-day response effort. Coordination between state and city units was excellent, but both a federal agency and the representative of a private firm challenged the city's authority to manage the response effort, and conflicting information was released to the public.

At 4:29 P.M. on July 8, 1986, fifteen cars of a forty-four-car freight train derailed, causing a phosphorus-filled tanker to erupt in flames. The local fire chief was one of the first on the scene. On the basis of information in a hazardous materials handbook, the chief immediately ordered the evacuation of about a third of the community. This order was backed by the city manager, who had clear authority at the local level. The evacuation was supervised by a police lieutenant and carried out by police and fire department personnel and fifteen volunteer fire fighters. A formal declaration of emergency was made by the city as a step toward being eligible for state and federal assistance.

The first challenge to the city's authority came about 1½ hours after the accident. The train master, representing the company that owned

the tracks, sought to control response operations and clear the derailed cars from the tracks before government accident officials arrived. When the city manager pointed out that the train master was taking responsibility for public safety, the train master agreed to leave control in the hands of the city's designated emergency manager.

On that first day, Ohio's governor provided a hotline for citizens to call with concerns and questions and assigned a liaison between the state departments and the city.

By the second day, the chemicals appeared to be stabilizing, but technical reports from the regional HAZMAT team indicated continued uncertainty about the potential for explosion. In addition, the public and the media criticized the city for not lifting the evacuation order. Citizens made "thousands of calls" asking whether it was safe to return home, and despite advice to stay away, some did return.

Near dusk on the second day, the abutment under the tanker gave way and the car crashed down, sending up a huge flare and a plume of smoke. The emergency broadcast system was activated, police were deployed in designated sectors, and the Regional Transit Authority and ambulance services were called upon to help evacuate nursing homes and people with special needs; the Convention Center was used for sheltering. After about two hours, the entire city was evacuated.

simply take action, using whatever knowledge and experience they have to cope with immediate, practical problems. As trained personnel begin to mobilize, it is critical to coordinate their work with the informal response efforts already under way.

Money

The exchange of any resource involves a cost, and money reflects the value assigned to the particular exchange. In predisaster situations, direct monetary exchanges include grants and fees for service. Within government, grants are usually made from higher to lower levels. Services provided for a fee include functions such as hazard assessment, education, and training. During the imme-

---

On the third day, a dispute surfaced about the safest way to handle the situation. The U.S. Environmental Protection Agency (EPA) "objected highly to the way the city was managing the disaster" and to the fact that it had been excluded from decision making. An EPA official informed the city manager of federal regulations allowing the EPA to take control of the response effort. The city manager, however, said that unless directed otherwise by a federal court order, the city would continue to manage the response effort. Nevertheless, a meeting was set up to learn more about the plan favored by the EPA. All officials on the scene except those from the EPA and the explosive experts agreed that the city's plan to vent the rail car was the safest. The plan was implemented and it worked. The city's authority was not questioned again.

On the fourth day, a formal emergency operations center (EOC) was belatedly established in the city council chamber. Until then, communication had been via walkie-talkie and cellular phone, and decisions had been made at the site or in the city's conference room.

The absence of an EOC may have contributed to the release of conflicting information. The U.S. Department of Transportation's Federal Railroad Administration and the National Transportation Safety Board conducted press conferences without briefing the city. When the city spokespersons later

went before the press, they were asked to respond to information released previously by one of the federal agencies, and, of course, they could not. With a properly organized EOC and a well-trained staff, such an incident might not have occurred. In contrast, the coordination of press efforts between state and city units prevented any conflict or confusion.

The fire was extinguished early on the fifth day. The evacuation order was lifted. Two fire fighters were assigned to monitor the site around the clock. Railroad officials began negotiating with the owners of the tanker to remove the car and the phosphorus. The Ohio Health Department and the U.S. Centers for Disease Control announced plans for a long-term follow-up of health problems. The pressure and urgency of the response period was over. No one had died as a direct result of the derailment, although one person died when his camper caught fire. Many residents were treated for mild respiratory problems and irritated eyes.

Principal source: Linda R. Woodhouse, "How City of Miamisburg Averted Disaster: Five-day Tanker-Car Fire Spotlights Hazardous Materials Issues," *Nation's Cities Weekly* 9 (July 21, 1986):1–6. Reprinted with permission from *Nation's Cities Weekly*, the official publication of the National League of Cities.

diate response period, altruism and concerns about survival displace direct exchanges of money. Companies and stores open their doors and dispense food, tools, and whatever materials they have on hand to help the response effort.

Insurance settlements and disaster loans are important direct exchanges of money following disaster. These disbursements are usually made at least several weeks after the event.

The predisaster stages are governed mainly by concerns for efficiency or working within cost guidelines. Although there are tremendous financial costs from disasters, the emphasis during the immediate disaster response period is on getting the job done. Issues of financial accounting and responsibility resurface during the recovery period, but damage assessment and other response activities do figure in the financial accounting.

Buildings and land

The arrangement of buildings and land used to carry out emergency management functions during predisaster stages affects the pattern of relationships between the organizations in a community. For example, evidence indicates that organizations located in close proximity are more likely to share resources, which suggests, in turn, that patterns of building occupancy affect the exchange of resources in mitigation and preparedness.[14] If an emergency manager finds that organizations involved in emergency service delivery are spread about, he or she should draw upon the forms of coordination discussed below (see the section on forms of coordination) to facilitate contacts.

During predisaster phases, land sites and buildings are identified for possible use in emergency operations, sheltering, and other functions. Agreements on the use of specific buildings and land sites strengthen community preparedness: the larger the number of potentially useful sites, the more prepared the community. Efforts to assess both geographical areas of vulnerability and the resistance of buildings to hazards contribute to mitigation. After a disaster, a limited number of sites are selected for emergency operations centers, medical services, and sheltering.

In addition to their involvement in local sheltering efforts, emergency managers should familiarize themselves with federal and state programs that provide housing for disaster victims whose homes have been destroyed. For example, FEMA provides mobile homes until victims' homes are repaired or alternative housing is found, but emergency managers must be familiar with the regulations that govern the location of mobile homes on private property and the length of time they can be occupied.

Equipment

Throughout the predisaster period, equipment such as educational tools, special materials for disaster exercises, and the gear necessary to conduct hazard assessments is shared. Like buildings and land, field equipment is identified and inventoried during predisaster phases to build resource capacity.

Postdisaster exchange of equipment is critical in saving lives and delivering services. Special communications equipment is often brought into disaster areas from neighboring communities, as is heavy equipment (to remove debris), four-wheel-drive vehicles, or boats.

Critical community systems

Six community subsystems stand out as particularly important in emergency management: medical care, social services, public works, private business, regulated utilities, and the media. Each of these subsystems controls resources critical to effective disaster response. The task of coordinating these subsystems within and between communities is difficult, time consuming, imperfect, and never finished. Yet working to establish and continually improve coordination can save lives and reduce losses from disaster.

Some understanding of critical community subsystems is essential to establish and maintain coordination. The focus in this section will be on the immediate response period, since this is the target period for all emergency management coordination efforts. The general goal of coordination is to ensure that the resources of these subsystems mesh in a way that reduces the potential for conflict, fragmentation, gaps in service, and unnecessary duplication (see sidebar on pages 68–69). The following capsule descriptions of each critical subsystem include discussion of problems that can occur in disaster response and strategies for using coordination to reduce these problems.

Emergency medical care

The emergency medical system includes a wide variety of services and resources, from the first aid offered by medical technicians in the field to basic life support provided in hospitals. Every state has laws and regulations governing emergency medical services. Social, economic, and cultural traditions create further variations in medical services from one locality to another. Field support may operate under the auspices of fire departments, police departments, private companies, or volunteer organizations. Whatever the auspices, however, a physician located at a designated base hospital is responsible for emergency medical decisions.

Disasters place extensive and often unexpected demands upon the medical system. There may be large numbers of patients, a shortage of trained staff, and damage to medical facilities and equipment. Moreover, mass convergence of volunteers is likely, and dealing with altruistic but untrained help can be a problem in itself. Finally, victims with only minor injuries will be the first to arrive at hospitals—and these self-referrals, combined with the altruistic actions of volunteers, complicate hospital admissions by letting in people who might be adequately served elsewhere.

Most of the regular communication in a hospital is by telephone, but telephones are often inoperative or overloaded during the immediate response period of a disaster. At the same time, the public demand for information is high. Thus, many of the problems of medical care result from unexpected and excessive demands.

Some of the problems of medical care following a disaster can be reduced through coordination. The flow of patients can be controlled through predisaster plans for triage and routing. To create such plans, the emergency manager begins by taking inventory of medical facilities and personnel, including technicians, nurses, and doctors living in the area. Information about work shifts and the number of personnel on duty at any given time is also required for effective coordination. Medical supplies must be inventoried, too, as must drug manufacturers, distributors, and retail stores carrying medical supplies. Plans also require the development of effective ways of getting information on the number and extent of injuries and of managing the flow of victims to hospitals.

Social services and mental health

Food and clothing, mass shelter, crisis intervention, and grief counseling are crucial services provided by social service and mental health professionals during disaster response. Organizations such as the American Red Cross and the Salvation Army, as well as many local groups, provide such services. In addition, all states have public mental hospitals, and there are more than four hundred community mental health centers nationwide, as well as private clinics and hot

(*continued on page 70*)

Terrible Tuesday: The Wichita Falls tornadoes Wichita Falls is located in the Red River Valley region of Texas, between Dallas and Oklahoma City, Oklahoma. It is a city with almost 100,000 people spread over about fifty square miles. The situation there after three tornadoes hit in 1979 illustrates some of the complexities of coordinating response efforts across critical community systems.

Shortly after 6 P.M. on April 10, 1979, three tornadoes converged and struck Wichita Falls. Winds in excess of 200 miles per hour cut a mile-wide, eight-mile-long path of destruction. Property damage was extensive: about 6,000 homes were demolished or severely damaged, more than 80 businesses were destroyed, and nearly 300 businesses suffered major damage. One shopping center was devastated and another seriously damaged. Two schools were wrecked, one was badly damaged, and eight others were moderately damaged. Two fire stations were destroyed. Several churches and a nursing home were destroyed. A civic stadium and art museum suffered major damage. More than 5,000 families were left homeless. There were 46 deaths, 171 hospitalizations, and more than 1,600 injuries.

Educational public service announcements during February and March had reminded residents of the dangers of tornadoes. Radio and TV coverage and sirens on the day of the disaster warned most residents, but the warnings were given far enough in advance that some people mistakenly tried to leave the area by car rather than stay home. (Sixty percent of the dead and 51 percent of the seriously injured were in cars.) Once the tornadoes struck, both television stations and five of the six radio stations were knocked out, and the one remaining radio station had limited ability to transmit.

A tornado earlier in the day in Vernon, about fifty miles away, precipitated

preparedness action in Wichita Falls. In the middle of the afternoon, or more than two hours before the tornadoes would hit, the emergency manager set up the emergency operations center (EOC) at police headquarters. The city's disaster plan, tested six days earlier in a simulated exercise with mass casualties, was activated at around 4 P.M. Warning sirens were sounded. The tornadoes touched down shortly after 6 P.M., severing all seven electrical trunk lines to the city. For the first twenty-four hours, the power loss and the limited output from the backup generator made the city heavily dependent on battery-operated radio communications. Emergency communications were adequate within the city, but communication with the outside was severely limited.

Fire fighters were sent to damaged areas to help turn off gas lines and to help mobilize search and rescue operations (there were very few fires). Police provided security and assisted in search and rescue. Off-duty police officers conducted door-to-door searches, while on-duty officers responded to requests for assistance.

Within an hour, two field command posts were set up to handle communications between the disaster zone and the EOC, to control field activities, and to deal with the dead. The creation of two additional command centers was not planned but was considered necessary because of the wide scope of destruction. (There was some trouble keeping key people in the EOC because everyone wanted to be in the field helping and making sure that everything possible was being done.) Apart from the fact that city, county, and state officials had slightly different perceptions as to which unit was the lead agency, the separate command posts worked well.

Overall, in fact, the entire public agency system worked well. Within two hours, the state highway patrol had sealed off the city to prevent outsiders from converging. (Volunteers were not allowed to enter on their own; they lined up around the EOC to get authorization and direction to help.) Security systems were established in residential neighborhoods. A request by the city for air force help was relayed by radio to Shepard Air Force Base and then to a B-52 crew in flight, which landed shortly thereafter and started to help. The air force sent an officer to the EOC to coordinate military assistance: the air force helped with search and rescue and with the transporting of injured people.

Few of the injured were transported by ambulance or authorized vehicles (such as those provided by the air force); most were taken to medical facilities by volunteers. Volunteers also made sandwiches and served coffee, cleared debris, bandaged the injured, helped with traffic control, hauled water, and gave blood. Directing the volunteers, however, especially those from out of town, took a lot of the emergency manager's time and energy.

The Red Cross assisted with emergency communications at the command posts because it had battery-operated radio equipment. The Red Cross also undertook damage assessment and sheltering operations, opening several shelters around the city. But no more than 330 people were in them at one time. One reason for the small number may have been exaggerated fears of looters. Many people guarded their homes with rifles, and even emergency workers had to proceed carefully.

Like the public agencies, the hospitals were on alert before the twisters hit. At the time the tornadoes struck Wichita Falls, a medical team was being assembled to assist Vernon. Staff physicians and nurses reported to the hospitals as directed in their emergency plans, although several went to the wrong hospital. Triage of injured at the scene was impossible.

Victims were plastered with mud, glass, and fiberglass insulation. Nearly every doctor in town went to the hospitals, and some doctors from neighboring communities showed up, too. Because the city water was contaminated, hospitals were in critical need of water, which local dairy farmers brought in.

The regulated utilities worked intensively to restore power and prevent further destruction. Electric company personnel began almost immediately to repair severed power lines and worked through the night. Part-time electricians and maintenance staff pitched in, providing much-needed assistance. The destruction went far beyond any emergency contingencies planned for by the company. It was twenty-four hours before electrical service was restored. Gas company crews closed gas lines, and their quick action prevented fires. Telephone service was virtually destroyed, and the telephone company had to install temporary lines for partial service. It was almost a week before regular phone service was restored.

Private businesses responded with heavy equipment and other necessary supplies. Bulldozers and trucks, essential to move debris, were provided by building contractors. McDonald's restaurants provided canteens.

This case illustrates positive aspects of coordination across the critical resource systems controlled by emergency managers. Emergency managers can use the example of Wichita Falls to begin or improve coordination in their own jurisdictions.

Principal source: Federal Emergency Management Agency, *Case Study No. 22, Tornado: Wichita Falls, Texas, April 10, 1979* (Emmitsburg, MD: National Emergency Training Center, Learning Resource Center).

(*continued from page 67*)

lines. Special efforts are required, however, to coordinate the necessary services to elderly residents, handicapped residents, children, and non-English-speaking residents.

Coordination of shelter is often incomplete and fragmented among various organizations. This creates problems of service duplication in some areas and service omission in others. Although the American Red Cross has a long history of involvement in shelter operations and a congressional mandate to assume responsibility for shelter, this is not always understood by community leaders, especially in rural areas. Communitywide agreements about who will provide shelter can reduce serious duplication and omission, but such agreements are rare.

Another problem may be the mental health effects of disaster. Emergency responders often deny or play down mental health symptoms during the response period. Only recently have research interests developed in this area.[15] What is known, however, is that negative mental health effects can be reduced through planning, beginning with plans based on a realistic view of the potential for people to help themselves. Any plan should educate the public about what happens in the event of specific disasters and what to do in each case. Planning should take into account community and social networks already in place, the inevitable emergent networks of altruistic groups, and the designated authorities and professionals. Aggressive outreach is necessary.

Public agencies

Local police, fire, water, and sewer departments—and sometimes the military— are central in the initial response to disasters. Police departments help by enforcing laws to protect life and property; undertaking search and rescue, evacuation, and mass public control; helping to maintain communication; and managing hazardous material incidents. Fire departments provide fire control, search and rescue, emergency medical care, and management of hazardous materials. Water and sewer departments help restore or maintain water supply levels, prevent contamination, and manage dams and flood control facilities. The extensive resources and preparedness of the military allow it to assist community response efforts in many ways, including warning, search and rescue, mass feeding and shelter operations, medical treatment, restoration of minimum community services, and maintenance of law and order.[16]

Disasters create demands that exceed the standard emergency training given to police, fire fighters, and local government personnel. Traditional training and orientation are geared to the specific emergencies expected in the jurisdiction: for example, fires, traffic accidents, floods (if in a floodplain), airplane crashes (if in an air traffic zone). This focus tends to generate incorrect expectations about citizen behavior; that is, citizens' involvement in response efforts tends to be overlooked.

The narrow focus of local preparedness may make the military an especially valuable resource when the demands from a disaster exceed the community's capacity to respond. And although the power and structure of the military differ significantly from those of the civilian emergency system, there need not be concern about military control. Military assistance is almost never provided unless requested, and it is always under civilian authority. Both the armed forces and National Guard assist only during times of most critical need and disengage rapidly once the critical period has passed.

The confusion and uncertainty associated with disaster require flexible coordination. The first step is to obtain community consensus on the need to prepare for disaster. Emergency managers must educate citizens and the governing body and strive to replace inertia with a proactive stance. Emergency management is based on a planned, yet flexible, system of disaster response that can assume different patterns depending on the needs and constraints of a particular disaster.[17]

The private sector

The private sector includes the construction industry, the chemical industry, volunteers, and volunteer organizations. The heavy-duty equipment used in the construction industry can be essential to clearing roads or removing debris. Since operating such equipment requires specialized training, it is important for the emergency manager to coordinate with construction industry representatives during the predisaster phase. New chemicals and their associated dangers are being discovered weekly, and the specialized training required to deal with incidents involving hazardous materials has been introduced to the emergency management field only recently. Hazardous material response teams depend heavily on the expertise of the chemical industry, which has established a national information center and hotline as well as a network of hazmat response teams.

As noted earlier, volunteers and volunteer organizations are widely involved in emergency management, particularly in the response phase. Many emergency managers are themselves volunteers, particularly in smaller communities. Volunteers help with damage assessment, communications, transportation, debris removal, search and rescue, and public information. Because disasters are infrequent in any given locality, preparedness is rarely a line item on the local budget. Limited financial resources make volunteers and volunteer groups crucial to emergency management efforts.

Research on volunteers has emphasized the mass convergence response and the difficulty of integrating formal organizational activity with convergence. David Gillespie and Ronald Perry note that volunteer groups are often viewed as part of the problem rather than as a resource.[18] But volunteers can help established organizations increase their effectiveness: for example, since responsibilities for disaster communication are fragmented among a variety of organizations, volunteers with CB and ham radio capability are important in drawing together widely dispersed channels of communication.[19]

Local control, widespread involvement, and flexibility appear to be keys to quick and effective mobilization of volunteer resources following disaster. The American Red Cross has developed excellent plans for volunteer response, but the emergency management field has little basic knowledge about coordinating relationships, especially across organizations. Although disasters inspire tremendous immediate altruism, the motivation for mitigation and preparedness dissipates rapidly. Emergency managers, therefore, must be continually engaged in recruiting volunteers, training them, updating the plan, and generating commitment to mitigation and preparedness efforts.

The regulated sector

The regulated sector includes private organizations that are heavily regulated by government—organizations such as power companies, public transportation companies, and telephone companies.

Because power company personnel, like police officers and fire fighters, are trained to handle specific emergencies such as repairing a broken line or generator, repair crews can be overwhelmed by the extensive breakdowns resulting from a disaster. The widespread power failures that may accompany disasters require skills, tools, and experience beyond those normally brought to bear by power company personnel.

Because power sources are critical to saving lives and protecting property, coordination between power companies and government agencies takes prece-

(*continued on page 74*)

Figure 3–3   Volunteer organizations active in disasters.

Organization	Professional staff	Trained staff	Trained volunteers	Untrained staff	Untrained volunteers	Facilities for stationary feeding	Equipment for mobile feeding	Mass shelter facilities	Trucks	Vans	Buses	Station wagons	Rescue equipment	Communication equipment	Clothing	Bedding	Used furniture	Materials for rebuilding homes	Collection and distribution of donated goods other than clothing	Collection, sorting and sizing of used clothing	Cleaning debris from private property	Cleaning homes	Free labor to repair or rebuild homes	Welfare inquiry service	Registration and information service	Counseling service	Crisis intervention and long-term recovery capability	Training	Financial assistance	Comments (see key below)
American National Red Cross	×	×	×	×	×	×	×	×	×	×	×	×	×	×	×	×	−	×	−	−	−	−	−	×	×	×	−	×	×	A
Ananda Marga (Amurt)	×	×	×	−	−	−	−	−	−	−	−	−	−	×	×	×	×	−	×	×	−	−	−	×	×	×	−	×	×	
B'nai B'rith	×	−	−	−	×	−	−	−	−	−	−	−	−	−	−	−	−	−	×	×	×	−	−	−	−	−	−	−	−	
Church of the Brethren	×	×	×	×	×	×	−	×	−	−	−	−	−	−	−	−	−	−	−	×	×	×	−	×	−	−	−	−	−	B
Christian Reformed World Relief	×	×	×	×	×	×	×	×	×	×	×	×	×	−	×	×	×	×	×	×	×	×	×	×	×	×	×	×	×	B
Church World Service	×	×	×	−	−	−	−	−	−	−	−	−	−	−	×	×	−	−	−	−	−	−	−	−	−	−	−	−	×	H
Goodwill Industries	×	×	×	×	×	−	−	−	×	×	−	−	×	×	×	−	−	−	−	−	−	−	−	−	−	−	−	×	×	
Lutheran Church of America	×	−	−	−	×	×	×	×	−	−	−	−	−	−	×	×	−	−	−	−	−	−	−	×	×	×	×	×	×	H
Mennonite Disaster Service	×	×	×	−	×	−	−	−	−	−	−	−	−	−	−	−	−	−	−	−	×	×	×	−	−	−	−	−	−	B
National Catholic Disaster Relief Committee	×	×	×	×	×	×	−	×	−	−	−	−	−	−	×	×	×	−	−	−	−	−	−	−	−	×	×	−	×	H
National Catholic Conference and Catholic Charities	×	×	×	×	×	−	×	−	−	−	−	−	−	−	×	×	×	−	−	−	−	−	−	−	−	×	×	−	×	H
The Salvation Army	×	×	×	×	×	×	×	×	×	×	×	×	×	−	×	×	×	×	×	×	−	−	−	×	×	×	×	×	×	C
Seventh-Day Adventists	×	×	×	×	×	×	×	×	×	×	×	×	×	×	×	×	×	×	×	×	×	×	×	×	×	×	−	×	×	D
Southern Baptist Convention	×	×	×	×	×	×	×	×	×	×	×	×	−	−	×	×	×	−	×	×	×	×	×	×	×	×	×	×	×	E
Society of St. Vincent de Paul	×	×	×	×	×	×	×	×	×	×	×	×	×	×	−	−	×	×	×	×	×	×	×	×	×	×	×	×	×	F
United Methodist Church Committee	×	×	×	×	×	×	×	×	−	×	×	×	−	−	×	×	×	×	×	×	×	×	×	−	×	×	−	×	×	H
Volunteers of America	×	×	×	×	×	×	×	×	×	×	×	×	×	×	×	×	×	×	×	×	×	×	×	×	×	×	×	×	×	G

Key

A Congressional mandate. If there is no other resource, Red Cross will meet needs.
B Expertise in establishing inter-faith organizations.
C Bulk food distribution; warehouse ready supplies.
D Private mobile homes available for major disasters.
E $100,000 revolving fund and more if needed.
F Maybe only in one or a few larger councils.
G Ambulances and air transportation and rescue.
H Revolving loan funds available.

How one city is faring after the quake of '83   Coalinga, California, is an example of why disaster-stricken cities shouldn't count on state and federal aid alone to dig out from under the economic rubble.

State and federal programs reimbursed this central California town for 99% of the $3.8 million it spent to recover from a 46-second earthquake in 1983. But six years later, the city is still struggling to get back on its economic feet and it's using a box full of other fiscal tools to do it.

"State and federal agencies said the damage to Coalinga amounted to $31 million," recalled Public Works Director Alan Jacobsen.

"But two years later, we put the figure at about $50 million in damage to buildings and infrastructure, and that doesn't include economic losses. So, we turned to as many other sources as we could think of. The first step was to get the entire city, 2.5 square miles, declared a redevelopment area," he said.

When that occurred, the assessed valuation of existing property was frozen.

The difference between the old assessed value and the value of any new development translates into tax dollars that go into the coffers of the city's redevelopment agency. The difference between the two rates is called the tax increment. This year revenue from the districting passed the $500,000 mark.

The agency issued $5 million in bonds two years ago to finance redevelopment projects in its downtown area.

"But we have another four or five blocks that need to be restored," said Mr. Jacobsen. "Altogether we demolished about 55 commercial buildings."

The agency expects to issue another $8 million in debt to pay for more redevelopment.

Tax increment financing can be used for commercial projects as well as for housing in the redevelopment area.

The California Community Redevelopment Agencies Association sponsored a one-day seminar for Bay Area cities and counties that may want to set up similar redevelopment areas as part of their quake recovery strategy.

"We also expect to see some legislation to speed up the process of creating a redevelopment area," said Milt Farrell, executive director of the association. "Usually it takes a year, but obviously cities hit by the quake can't wait that long."

To further modernize its downtown during redevelopment, Coalinga set up a district to run utility lines underground and replace street lights.

Part of the project was funded by $500,000 borrowed from Fresno County's unused "Rule 20A" as it is called. The California Public Utilities Commission requires Pacific Gas & Electric to set aside a portion of its profits to finance placement of utilities underground.

Coalinga borrowed against the dollars PG&E allocated to Fresno County to reach this goal. The city also borrowed another $1.5 million from its own water and gas companies.

"But we're still not finished," said Mr. Jacobsen. "Each downtown block not restored represents another $1 million in lost revenues. The redevelopment area was set up for 30 years."

Source: Marjorie Murray, "How One City Is Faring after the Quake of '83," *City and State*, 6 November 1989.

(*continued from page 71*)
dence over all other activities. Minimal cost is involved in developing inventories of equipment, identifying experienced personnel, establishing mutual aid agreements, and maintaining interorganizational and interjurisdictional disaster planning. Additional low-cost efforts that emergency managers should promote include stockpiling critical spare parts, setting up alternative emergency arrangements, introducing corrosion control procedures, and promoting strategic redundancy. The expense involved in taking these precautions compares favorably with the high cost of replacing equipment.

The media

Although radio and TV stations, like power, transportation, and telephone companies, are regulated by government, they are grouped here with the unregulated medium—newspapers—because of the common functions these organizations provide in disaster and because research has tended to approach all media as a single category. The media provide the public with hazard warnings, safety instructions, official announcements, evacuation procedures, directions on getting to medical and mass care facilities, status reports on the condition of lifelines, and damage assessment information. Radio and television stations are required to maintain and test emergency communications equipment. The Emergency Broadcast System (EBS) is governed by the Federal Communications Commission, and local emergency managers are responsible for getting emergency information to EBS and for ensuring that the information is translated for non-English speakers and made available to those with visual and hearing disabilities.

Because the media have occasionally sensationalized reports of disaster, many emergency managers and the public question the validity of media reports. The media have tended to portray worst-case illustrations, have highlighted particularly dramatic episodes, and have given currency to myths about behavior during disasters. For example, following the 1985 earthquake in Mexico City, the headline in the *St. Louis Post-Dispatch* stated, "Mexico Tries to Quell Panic"—whereas in fact, as TV footage revealed, extensive volunteer efforts were under way in a determined and orderly manner. Furthermore, media organizations devote disproportionate attention to the immediate postdisaster period. Mitigation, preparedness, and recovery are covered less frequently and given less prominence than the first seventy-two hours after disaster strikes.[20]

Accurate and timely information is critical to saving lives and protecting property in a disaster. Coordination between the media and the emergency operations center (EOC) and other official communication systems contributes importantly to rumor control and assessments of report validity and strengthens coordination generally among local, county, state, and federal information officials. Coordination with the media can also improve the quality of status reports about response efforts (such reports should be used at command centers).

Forms of coordination

When independent organizations, as controllers of critical resources, are coordinated to work toward continuous improvement in a community's ability to prevent or respond to disaster, the resource base of the community is expanded. The emergency manager has a number of ways to pursue coordination of community resources. The simplest are to share data banks and enter into mutual aid agreements to provide contingency exchanges or service contracts. Other ways are to share or rotate board members, and develop cooperative councils. The most complex form of coordination can also be undertaken: joint planning and programs.

CITYLINK *In the wake of the Loma Prieta earthquake as the League of California Cities scrambled to gather information and rush aid to affected cities, the following message came over the CITYLINK Bulletin Board network from Mike Bridges, Deputy City Manager, Oakland:*

To: LEAGUE OF CITIES
From: etloaki

Hello from Oakland.

So we have had major damage as you have seen on TV. The Cypress Ave Freeway section is a major disaster. In addition we have lost our City Hall and three subsidiary buildings for city staff in the downtown. We have received excellent support from various cities. Thanks to all for your offers.

We have an incredible task of rebuilding our services and offices to house our staff. We have become the officeless.

To Whittier:
Do you have any recommendations on how to deal with FEMA? We are putting our best people on working on the claims forms. I remember a conference I attended in Whittier (Municipal Management Assistant of So Cal) and heard about your quake and recovery efforts.

In general it has been an interesting study on the ability of employees and management staff to deal with the disaster and the recovery of city services.
Bye for now. . . . .
Mike Bridges
rats. . . . . .

Within a few hours, the City of Whittier responded:
To: etloaki
cc: citytalk <bboards>
From: etiwhit
Subject: RESPONSE TO EARTHQUAKE RE FEMA

TO OAKLAND:
In response to your question about dealing with FEMA: The answer to the question is document, document, document! FEMA is relatively good about reimbursing for city expenses in dealing with a disaster and reimbursing for the loss of public buildings, facilities and infrastructure. You do, however, have to be aggressive in seeking reimbursement; assign one management staff member to oversee the effort. Even though you have quality people assigned, you need to have a continuity of liaison between FEMA and the City of Oakland. Don't forget that what FEMA will not reimburse, the state should, and the latter has a number of eligible expenses which the feds will not recognize. Example: Whittier hired a consultant to do its FEMA reimbursement submittals at a cost of $75,000. The cost of the consulting service was not an eligible federal expense but will be reimbursed by the State of California. Net cost—0.

Also, don't forget to get consultant reviews of your public facilities. An engineer's evaluation of the City of Whittier's water system turned up at about half a million dollars in earthquake damages, which would have otherwise gone unnoticed until such facilities were regularly reviewed. The earthquake damages discovered in that review are FEMA eligible.

Also, note that FEMA may be easier to deal with than private insurance companies. Insurance companies will fight hard over the question of whether a facility can be rehabilitated rather than demolished and try to compromise claims to the lowest common denominator: two years of negotiations in Whittier over one public building.

Also, on the FEMA reimbursement program, watch the deadlines carefully. You have to have all damage submitted within six months and all work completed within 18. Both deadlines are difficult, because you may not know yet all that you are dealing with—see water facilities comment above. Therefore, be aware of, and, if necessary, get deadline extensions. Let us know if we can help further. Whittier.

Source: "Why Is CITYLINK Important?" Reprinted with permission from the December 1989 issue of *Western City* magazine, the monthly publication of the League of California Cities.

Local Exchange   During two 1989 disasters, Hurricane Hugo and the West Coast earthquake, the Local Exchange communications and information service was available for transmitting instant consultations and emergency advice. The network is operated by National League of Cities, ICMA, and Public Technology, Inc. During the hurricane, NLC registered the Municipal Association of South Carolina so that the state municipal league could expedite communications between state leagues and concerned city officials from across the country.

Using Local Exchange during the earthquake—when voice contact was difficult—PTI President Costis Toregas

contacted Oakland local government officials to offer the name of a key contact in Kansas City who had experience with fallen concrete and understood the special needs in counseling rescue workers under stress.

Asynchronous transmission, such as that of Local Exchange, is particularly useful in emergency conditions since it allows the sender to put a message into the system and the receiver to pick it up at a convenient time and location.

Source: Adapted from *Public Management* 71 (December 1989): 19. *Public Management* is published by ICMA.

Common data banks   Sharing data banks is a natural extension of hazard vulnerability and capability assessments. Hazard vulnerability inventories collect the following information:

The incidence of particular hazards in the community

The severity of these hazards as reflected in injuries, loss of life, and property damage

The probabilities of recurrence for each hazard

Geographical, economic, cultural, or other conditions that increase the estimated severity assigned to particular hazards.

Capability assessments take stock of the types of resources and coordination available to mobilize response efforts. Increasing the awareness of hazard vulnerability by sharing data helps to promote coordination agreements. Maintaining, updating, and sharing resource inventories increases a community's capacity for effective response.

Mutual aid agreements   Mutual aid agreements are mandated in legislation or negotiated as legal contracts. Mutual aid agreements are of two kinds. First, organizations may draw up agreements for reciprocal assistance. If a disaster affects community A but not community B, then B will assist A, and vice versa. Second, organizations may establish contingent acquisition agreements between emergency service providers, vendors, and contractors. These are nonreciprocal service contracts under which the service is provided and the payment is received only under disaster conditions. Many communities negotiate agreements of this second kind with, for example, the American Red Cross to handle damage assessment and to establish mass sheltering facilities.

Board memberships   Organizational boards generally have either fund-raising or administrative functions. Especially when the board handles administrative issues, sharing or exchanging board members provides a useful way to promote coordination. Boards represent the most important focal point for promoting coordination when they control the organizations' principal resources, when the organizations' technology is not highly specialized, when the board members hold high status in the community, and when the organization is facing a crisis of survival that requires it to reach out beyond its usual practices and routines.

Cooperative councils Cooperative councils are valuable forums for information exchange. Councils generally focus broadly on community-level goals and criteria for measuring progress, and can be developed to represent communities or areas of almost any size. The wider the range of community participation, the greater the legitimacy associated with council membership. Two noteworthy examples of cooperative councils involved in emergency management are the Church World Service and the St. Louis Disaster Resource Council. The Church World Service is a national council that works through ministerial associations to provide training, seed money, and assistance to local church groups in developing emergency management capability. The St. Louis Disaster Resource Council is an effort headed by the city emergency management office and the county civil preparedness office to promote disaster mitigation and preparedness across organizational and political boundaries in the metropolitan area. The council's membership includes government agencies and private for-profit and not-for-profit organizations.

Joint planning and programs Joint planning and programs are an advanced form of coordination that is difficult to promote. One result of joint planning is to clarify the specific costs and benefits that will accrue to each group if a given proposal is implemented. Because organizations rarely benefit equally from coordination, the potential for problems increases as the number of organizations involved in joint planning or programs increases. Emergency managers must work to keep in perspective the ultimate purpose of joint planning and programs: effective mitigation, preparedness, response, and recovery.

Summary

Coordination enables emergency managers to channel critical resources into mitigation, preparedness, response, and recovery. In this chapter, the importance of coordination for emergency management was illustrated with specific reference to medical care, social services, public works, private business, regulated utilities, and the media. The chapter also explained how emergency managers can attack and sometimes overcome the factors that impede coordination, and how they can take advantage of the factors that facilitate coordination. Finally, five techniques that emergency managers can use to build coordinated systems were presented.

Success in building coordinated systems is worth an emergency manager's effort. Coordination can increase the financial stability, staff creativity, public support, geographical representation, and prestige of the organizations involved, while decreasing fragmentation and duplication of services.

1 Louis O. Giuffrida, *Integrated Emergency Management System: Capability Assessment and Standards for State and Local Government*, FEMA Publication CPG 1-102 (Washington, DC: 1983).

2 Thomas E. Drabek, *The Local Emergency Manager: The Emerging Professional (Part I)*, National Emergency Training Center, FEMA Monograph Series (Emmitsburg, MD: 1988).

3 R. H. Hall, J. P. Clark, P. C. Giordano, P. V. Johnson, and V. Roekel, "Patterns of Interor-

ganizational Relationships," *Administrative Science Quarterly* 22 (September 1977): 457–74.

4 R. Warren, S. M. Bergunder, and A. F. Rose, *The Structure of Urban Reform: Community Decision Organizations in Stability and Change* (Lexington, MA: D.C. Heath, 1974).

5 M. Aiken, R. Dewar, J. Hage, and G. Zeitz, *Coordinating Human Services* (San Francisco: Jossey-Bass, 1975).

6 S. M. Davidson, "Planning and Coordination of

Social Services in Multiorganizational Contexts," *Social Service Review* 50 (March 1976): 115–37.

7   Thomas E. Drabek, *Human System Responses to Disaster: An Inventory of Sociological Findings* (New York: Springer-Verlag, 1986).

8   William M. Evan, "The Organizational Set: Toward a Theory of Interorganizational Relations," in *Complex Organizations and Their Environment*, ed. Merlin B. Brinkerhoff and Philip R. Kunz (Dubuque, IA: William C. Brown Co., 1972), 326–340.

9   J. Kenneth Benson, "The Interorganizational Network as a Political Economy," *Administrative Science Quarterly* 20 (June 1975): 229–249.

10 J. E. Tropman and M. J. Dluhy, "Some Problems in Federal-City Collaboration in the 1960s: An Analysis," *Journal of Social Welfare* 2 (Winter 1976): 47–58.

11 C. L. Mulford and M. A. Mulford, "Interdependence and Intra-organizational Structure for Voluntary Associations," *Journal of Voluntary Action Research* 9 (1980): 20–34.

12 D. L. Rogers and C. L. Mulford, "Consequences," in *Interorganizational Coordination: Theory, Research, and Implementation*, ed. D. L. Rogers, D. A. Whetten, and Associates (Ames: Iowa State University Press, 1982): 73–94.

13 Neal Gilbert and Harry Specht, *Coordinating Social Services: An Analysis of Community, Organizational, and Staff Characteristics* (New York: Praeger, 1977).

14 T. Hutton and D. Ley, "Location, Linkages, and Labor: The Downtown Complex of Corporate Activities in a Medium Size City, Vancouver, British Columbia," *Economic Geography* 63, no. 2 (1987): 126–41.

15 Mary Evans Melick, "The Health of Post-disaster Populations: A Review of Literature and Case Study," in *Perspectives on Disaster Recovery*, ed. Jerri Laube and Shirley A. Murphy (Norwalk, CT: Appleton-Century-Crofts, 1985).

16 William A. Anderson, "Military Organizations in Natural Disaster," *American Behavioral Scientist* 13, no. 3 (January/February 1970): 415–22.

17 A good example of such a system is the Incident Command System that has been adopted in California. See Boise Interagency Fire Center, *National Interagency Incident Management System* (Boise, ID: Boise Interagency Fire Center, 1983).

18 David F. Gillespie and Ronald W. Perry, "An Integrated Systems and Emergent Approach to Mass Emergencies," *Mass Emergencies* 1 (1976): 303–12.

19 Thomas E. Drabek, Donald Q. Brodie, Jessica Edgerton, and Paul Munson, *The Flood Breakers: Citizens Band Radio Use During the 1978 Flood in the Grand Forks Region* (Boulder: Institute of Behavioral Science, University of Colorado, 1979).

20 Joseph Scanlon has developed an empirically based sequential model of how the media respond to disaster. See Joseph T. Scanlon, "Coping with the Media: Police-Media Problems and Tactics in Hostage Takings and Terrorist Incidents," *Canadian Police College Journal* 5, no. 3 (1981): 129–48.

Reaching out: Getting the community involved in preparedness

At 6:02 P.M., April 10, 1979, tornadoes leveled one-fifth of Wichita Falls, Texas, destroying 4,250 housing units, injuring 1,720 persons, killing 46. Some of the deaths were avoidable. Cars are not a safe place to be in a tornado, but more than half of those killed died in cars, attempting to escape. Others died in slightly damaged homes (they had not gone to basements or other locations where there is some protection). But many escaped injury because, when they heard the warning, they knew what to do.[1]

On May 2, 1983, barely more than four years later, Coalinga, California, was hit by an earthquake registering 6.7 on the Richter scale—a quake that made one-fifth of the city's 2,500 homes uninhabitable, started fires in the city's center, and leveled most of the old, downtown buildings. But it began with a rolling motion that "gave residents time to duck beneath doorways or under tables or hurry into open spaces on lawns or in the city's wide streets."[2] Only fifty-three people were injured, most with cuts, a few with broken bones. No one died. The first warning was the beginning of the quake itself, but people knew what to do.

Effective emergency preparedness requires planning, and it requires public support and involvement. This chapter explains the various steps in obtaining that support and involvement, from analyzing hazards to setting up a disaster education program to sorting out preparedness options and preparing for recovery. The chapter also explains how to use networking and disaster education to involve individuals and organizations in the preparedness process. The chapter replaces myths about disaster with solid information and touches on the role of the media in emergency management. The chapter concludes by emphasizing the need to test and update emergency plans.[3]

Taking the preliminary steps

The reason communities are often inadequately prepared for disasters is that they have no sense of need. Because disasters are uncommon, emergency preparedness is rarely a priority among local officials, politicians, or the public.[4] Even communities with disaster experience often lack effective planning. Community leaders reason that if a disaster hits once, it won't hit again; if they muddled through once, they can do so again; or the next disaster will be like the last one. This last view can be especially risky. History may, in fact, repeat itself: where floods and hurricanes have struck before, they will strike again. But all floods are not the slow-onset floods of springtime; some are flash floods. All hurricanes are not simply wind and rain storms; some generate huge, destructive tidal waves (tsunamis), and others bring tornadoes.

The only way to overcome a reluctance to plan is for someone in the community to take the initiative. That someone must be a person with authority—perhaps the mayor, perhaps an appointed administrator. Such a person can show leadership in four ways. First, by ensuring that there is action within the municipal structure: emergency plans must be established to guarantee that the government can carry on in a disaster. Second, by obtaining the support of the community's political leadership: though disasters are rare, they can be politically devastating (if the community is prepared, the public will be grateful; if it is not, the public will demand to know why). Third, by supervising the development of a network of involved citizens and agencies. Fourth, by setting an example: attending key meetings, participating in exercises, insisting that directives are followed, and rewarding effective emergency preparedness action (this fourth way is discussed in Chapter 10, "Day-to-Day Management").

Hazard analysis

The first step in effective planning is performing a hazard analysis—going through the process of identifying the hazards that face the community and the level of risk they represent. A hazard creates a potential for damage. Risk is a function of the way the hazard is handled. For example, a chemical plant may deal with hazardous chemicals but be low risk because of good safety procedures. Though a few inches of snow will be easily cleared away in the Canadian capital, the same snowfall will cause chaos in the U.S. capital. Risk evaluation, furthermore, can be complex. Specialists knew Mount St. Helens could erupt, create a lava flow, and send a rush of water downriver. But they did not anticipate that, in communities hundreds of miles from the mountain, ground transportation would be halted when engines became ash-clogged. And one final note of caution. All hazards carry some level of risk. For example, nuclear power plants, which are reputed to be safe, have posed a threat three times in recent years: at Three Mile Island in the United States (1979), at Windscale in England (1983), and at Chernobyl in the Soviet Union (1986).

Hazard analysis begins with a listing of hazards and continues with a determination of risk. Taking these two steps in public will involve individuals and groups in the planning process. As a start, ask the local historical association or, perhaps, a group of history teachers to trace the community's hazard history. Or ask geographers or environmental groups to identify threats from the environment. Or go to industry. Ever since Bhopal, the chemical industry has been especially supportive of emergency preparedness and has instituted a program called CAER, Community Awareness and Emergency Response (in Europe, the equivalent program is called APELL, Awareness and Preparedness for Emergencies at the Local Level).[5] Under these programs, industries that use chemicals now realize—for example—that they need to share information with local hospitals so that victims of toxic incidents can be promptly and accurately treated.

Community groups should be encouraged to look for material to illustrate the community's disaster history and possible future: maps showing floodplains and high-water levels; charts that plot prevailing winds; pictures of past disasters. These can be displayed in public buildings, including city hall; exhibited at the annual fair; or used in flashback stories by local media.[6]

Community groups should probably work separately to develop a list of hazards and then collaborate to assess risk. If there are disputes about hazards or risks, better that they take place in such a forum rather than at council, for risk is seen as a technical matter and not a policy question; ironing it out in a technical committee rather than in a policymaking body therefore makes sense. The groups should *not* determine what ought to be done about the risk; that is for local government.

A hazard analysis may sound somewhat involved, even costly. It's not. Citizens rarely view emergency planning as a priority, but once they are asked to help, they are not likely to refuse. The costs will probably be confined to providing a room for meetings, arranging the occasional lunch or reception, and supplying secretarial help for typing or duplicating reports.

Assessment of community attitudes and needs

In addition to listing hazards and evaluating risk, it is important to know the community as it is and as it will be. For example, are ethnic patterns changing? From what sources do different language and ethnic groups receive their information? What are community attitudes toward hazards, risk, disaster? Some of this information may already be available to the local government. Officials in various departments—say, social or health services—will be familiar with language groups. Elected officials may know how to reach various elements in the community.

But it's important to know more than that such groups exist or how to reach them. It's important to understand how the community perceives hazards and what the residents consider an appropriate response should a threat develop. The creation of an emergency plan also requires information about population density, the availability of transportation, and so forth. All such information is best obtained by a survey.

Large communities, which may already be using professional survey firms, can piggyback a disaster study onto another project. Smaller communities may be able to find a university professor to do the research, perhaps for a small fee. Or the project may interest a graduate student or undergraduate who can use some financial assistance.

Whatever the results, the survey will be another step toward preparedness. If it identifies concerns, it will strengthen the case for action. If it reveals ignorance, it will strengthen the case for education.

Planning within the government

While hazards and risks are being evaluated and data being gathered, local government must begin its own planning. A city manager suggests that "for selected employees, disaster preparedness and planning . . . be made a part of their normal job descriptions, requiring an annual assessment and evaluation prior to granting pay raises and promotions. Department managers should also require the same of their subordinates."[7] Who should be assigned such responsibilities? That decision is up to the manager. But responsibility must not be left only to low-level staff or to one person with insufficient authority. Staff in every department of the local government must be assigned specific tasks and given the authority and support to carry them out.

Experience demonstrates that such an approach works. After managing a hijacking at Toronto International Airport, the police chief of Toronto Township decided that his force needed an emergency plan and assigned staff to develop one. Then he made the plan a police priority. He used the same approach when he became chief of the Peel (Ontario) Regional Police Force: no Peel officer could be promoted unless he or she knew the emergency plan. In November 1978, Peel police were widely praised when they managed, without incident, to evacuate 217,000 people following a train derailment and toxic spill near Mississauga (see sidebar on p. 82).[8]

Networking to evaluate resources

Although taking action within the local government is important, emergency planning also requires broad community involvement. One way to get it is by networking—breaking down the planning process into tasks that are then assigned to different groups, for example, a health committee, a social service committee, a transportation committee, and a media relations committee (see sidebar on p. 83).

The Mississauga derailment   When the chief of police of Toronto Township, a rural municipality near Toronto, was called to Malton (now Toronto) International Airport, he found himself on the international stage. There had been a hijacking and, as local chief, he was in charge. Fortunately, a dangerous situation ended without bloodshed. But the chief was not pleased. Neither he nor his department had been prepared for such a crisis, and he decided that that would never happen again. He assigned staff to develop an emergency plan and made it a police priority.

When he later took over the new police force in Peel Region, a suburban city just west of Toronto, he brought with him the lessons he had learned from Malton: anything can happen anywhere; don't let yourself be caught by surprise. He insisted that his new department, too, plan for all types of emergencies. These plans included

1. Arrangements for site control of any incident, whether a crime, a disaster, or a major accident
2. On-site command exercised from a mobile, well-equipped command vehicle
3. A control area outside the major impact zone, where emergency agencies could work freely
4. Good media relations, with the media allowed to pass through police lines to a controlled area, where they can be supervised
5. Superb communications, including arrangements for twelve unlisted,

unsequenced (each line unrelated to any other line) phone lines, secure (unknown even to the chief) until an incident should occur
6. Frequent exercises
7. Required monthly review of the plan by all officers.

At 11:53 P.M. on a November holiday weekend in 1978, the planning paid off. A freight train derailed near a level crossing in Mississauga (part of Peel Region). The train carried toxic chemicals—caustic soda, toluene, styrene, chlorine, and propane. Some cars began to leak; others exploded. Within twenty-four hours, police had to evacuate more than 217,000 people.

That evacuation went so smoothly that Peel Region received praise from all over the continent, and attention from all over the world. Good planning— planning arising from the chief's experience with the hijacking—had paid off.

Of course, Peel police weren't alone. They had help from neighboring Metro Toronto, from the Red Cross, the Ontario Provincial Police, the Royal Canadian Mounted Police, and Metro Toronto Ambulance (an agency with its own sophisticated plans). All of this assistance was critical, but Peel Region benefited most from the fact that it had a plan. The plan was applicable to a range of emergencies; it was known; and all the systems needed to make the plan work, including good communication systems, were in place.

Each committee may begin work on its own, but the committees will eventually need to work together. A health committee considering the handling of mass casualties will soon realize that the ambulance system could not handle a major incident. Should the community call on outside ambulance services? Should it use other types of vehicles—buses, taxis, private cars? How should these be commandeered? Such matters must obviously be discussed with the transportation committee. A social service committee, discussing how to establish and run shelters, will also need transportation, not only to move victims but also to obtain supplies.

The overall goal of the committees is to evaluate community resources before the need to use them arises. Only when a tornado hit the mining area of Sudbury in northern Ontario (1985) was it discovered that many residents had either basic or advanced first-aid training.[9] It's also important not to overlook any resource. People die in a disaster—there are bodies, grieving relatives, distraught families—and funeral directors and their staffs are well prepared to deal with bodies, the bereaved, and those suffering emotional stress.

Finally, it may be wise to reach beyond community boundaries. In May of 1980, when ash from the eruption of Mount St. Helens hit Cheney, Washington, the city manager looked north:

I realized that help was not going to come from within the state. Every available water truck is going to be sucked up by [larger jurisdictions] able to pay . . . outrageous prices. . . . I said, it's so simple . . . British Columbia. Just go up there north of the border. We got a map of British Columbia and started calling up the RCMP [Royal Canadian Mounted Police] stations up there [to get phone numbers of local mayors, managers, and city engineers]. We made four phone calls. [The town of] Trail said, "We can only give the truck up *for a week*." [The town of] Nelson said, "How can we get it down to you?" [The town of] Fernie said, "You bet."[10]

(Canada and the United States have understandings that allow emergency equipment to move freely and rapidly across the border.)

The payoff of networking in Edmonton In 1987 in Edmonton, Alberta, several years of networking and creating specialized planning groups paid off.

The first specialized planning group—the Edmonton area pipeline and utility operators' committee—was formed in 1979 after a pipeline rupture forced the evacuation of 19,000 people. The committee worked out or initiated:

Standard procedures for safe construction in and around pipeline rights-of-way

An annual seminar promoting safety

A "one-call" system to provide callers with information about existing installations.

The second specialized group—the general emergency planning committee of Edmonton—consisted of only three persons in 1980: the city's emergency planning officer, the police department's emergency planning officer, and the fire chief. But as problems and needs were identified, the committee gradually expanded, in a classic example of networking. First to be added was a physician representing the ambulance service. Then came representatives from inside the city (from the federal penitentiary and the University of Alberta) and from outside it (from the petrochemical

industry, mainly in nearby Strathcona County; from the international airport outside the city limits; and from the province's emergency agency, Alberta Public Safety Services).

Finally, in 1984, the need to plan for the crowds expected when the Pope visited Edmonton led to the creation of the third specialized planning group: a health care advisory committee. It included emergency physicians, blood transfusion units of Edmonton and Strathcona County, ambulance personnel, and representatives of a paramedical training center.

These three committees became part of the overall Edmonton city emergency planning system and were the source of a number of initiatives:

A mutual aid arrangement with Strathcona County

A regional hazard analysis, including "worst case" scenarios, developed by the chemical industry under the Community Awareness and Emergency Response program

Carefully designated dangerous-goods routes

A regular inventory of medical disaster facilities

A disaster center with "hot lines" to key agencies

(continued on next page)

Building networks takes time but is not as complicated or difficult as might appear. The first groups to involve are the obvious agencies—police, fire, ambulance services, hospitals. Others soon follow—social services, public works, public transit. If each committee is free to add members—not only government agencies, but also private organizations—the list will grow steadily. Once one organization is involved, other similar organizations will want to take part, too. Get one school bus company involved, and the others will follow. (Always stress that such involvement is voluntary.)

Disaster education

As the committees are developing their plans, it's important to begin another step, too—increasing the public's awareness of what can happen and (as information becomes available) of what can be done. This step may take considerable effort. A 1983 study by ICMA found few communities with a public education program, and those that had one usually limited it to a few articles in a municipal publication or the local newspaper.[11]

(continued)

A systematic program of table-top exercises and other simulations. (When possible, the exercises have involved more than one agency. The transit system, for example, will take part in a hospital exercise; hospitals will participate in a simulation of a toxic spill.)

On Friday, July 31, 1987, the networking paid off.

Late that afternoon, Edmonton and Strathcona County were hit by a devastating tornado. Homes, factories, and businesses were extensively damaged. Transportation and communication were disrupted. Between 300 and 400 people were injured; 27 were killed.

Even before the tornado had finished its attack, the city's key personnel—the police chief, fire chief, transit head, ambulance head, and a representative of the chemical industry—had been called to city hall to meet with the mayor and the emergency planning officer. The telephone system was partly down, partly in disarray; thus, many of those in attendance could be notified only because the "hot lines" worked. The group formulated a response to the disaster.

Because key officials were together,

the transit system representative was able—within seconds—to inform the committee that buses were available if a hospital severely flooded by concurrent heavy rains had to be evacuated. The chemical specialist was able to reassure those present that the spill of radioactive sand—one of fourteen toxic incidents caused by the tornado—was not dangerous. Police and other advisors guaranteed the ambulance service that some new, unlicensed vehicles were properly insured and could be put into service immediately. By 10 A.M., Monday, August 3, the municipality, the province, the federal government, a number of volunteer agencies, and the private sector had created and opened a one-stop center where victims could obtain almost everything they needed, from counseling and the handling of insurance claims to a temporary place to live.

As early as Saturday, August 1, the morning after the tornado struck, Edmonton's planners had conducted a quick review of their response to the disaster and had begun to take steps to improve their plans.

Source: Based on material provided by R. Bruce Wilson, Emergency Planning Consultant, 10608-147 St., Edmonton, Alberta, Canada T5N3C7.

Figure 4–1 The mayor's message from the *Citizen's Emergency Action Guide*, Live Oak, Texas.

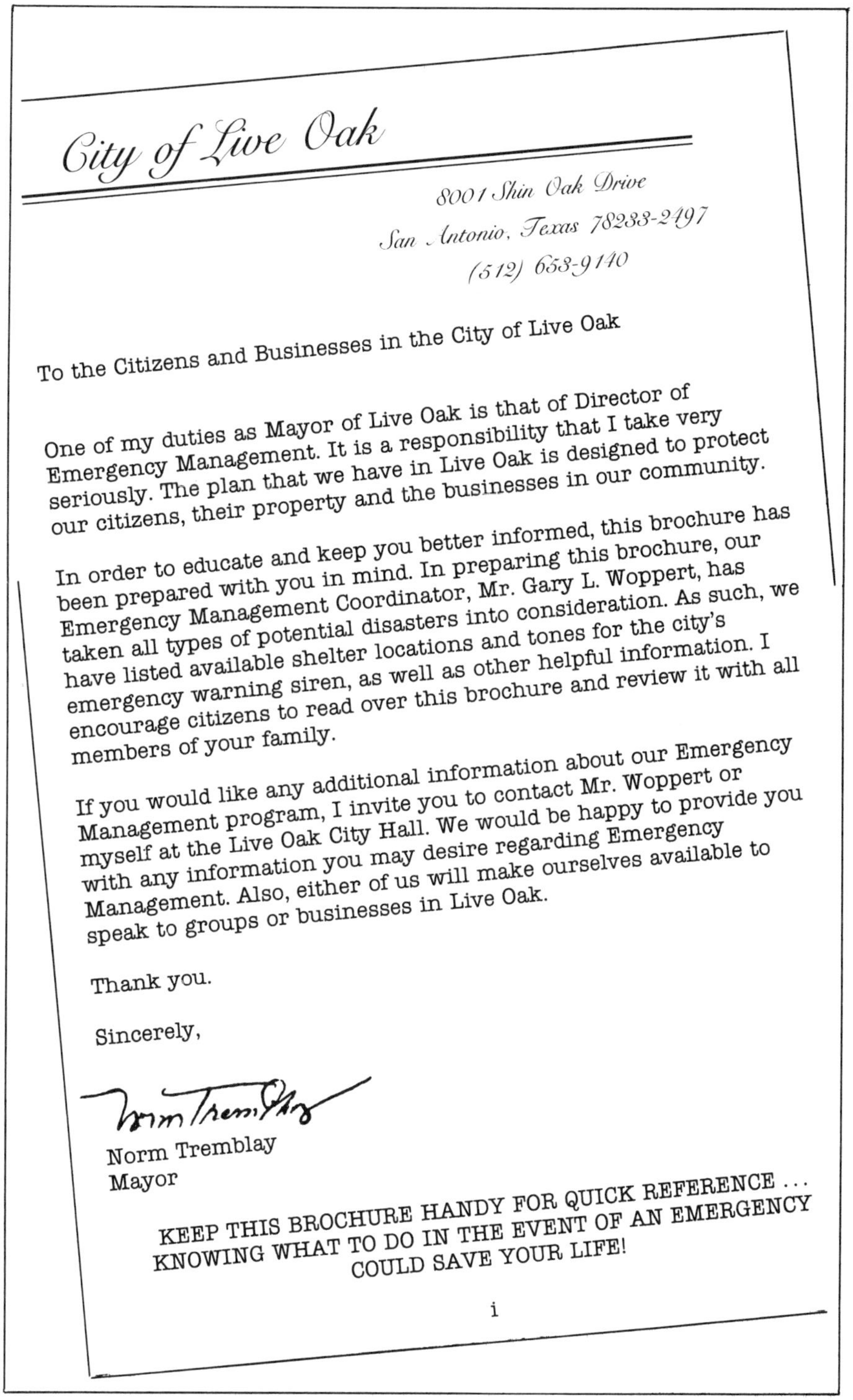

City of Live Oak

8001 Shin Oak Drive
San Antonio, Texas 78233-2497
(512) 653-9140

To the Citizens and Businesses in the City of Live Oak

One of my duties as Mayor of Live Oak is that of Director of Emergency Management. It is a responsibility that I take very seriously. The plan that we have in Live Oak is designed to protect our citizens, their property and the businesses in our community.

In order to educate and keep you better informed, this brochure has been prepared with you in mind. In preparing this brochure, our Emergency Management Coordinator, Mr. Gary L. Woppert, has taken all types of potential disasters into consideration. As such, we have listed available shelter locations and tones for the city's emergency warning siren, as well as other helpful information. I encourage citizens to read over this brochure and review it with all members of your family.

If you would like any additional information about our Emergency Management program, I invite you to contact Mr. Woppert or myself at the Live Oak City Hall. We would be happy to provide you with any information you may desire regarding Emergency Management. Also, either of us will make ourselves available to speak to groups or businesses in Live Oak.

Thank you.

Sincerely,

Norm Tremblay
Mayor

KEEP THIS BROCHURE HANDY FOR QUICK REFERENCE . . .
KNOWING WHAT TO DO IN THE EVENT OF AN EMERGENCY
COULD SAVE YOUR LIFE!

i

Yet E. L. Quarantelli has observed that other approaches to preparedness are more costly:

Vast amounts of money are always required, for example, to prevent disasters by structural means such as constructing huge dams or seawalls, refitting or disaster proofing buildings, changing climatic conditions. . . . These are highly desirable activities in many cases. But they are very expensive. Educational activities cost less, at least as far as money is concerned (though not necessarily in terms of time and effort).[12]

Figure 4–2 Employees at First Interstate Bank in California are given a "survival tips" card that folds to wallet size.

Before an earthquake
Store extra water, food and medicines
Securely anchor tall furniture and hot water tanks
Take first aid and CPR training
Designate an out-of-state relative or friend to be a funnel of information to other family members:

Name: _____

Phone #: _____

GR-0400 15M 5/87

DON'T WAIT
FOR THE QUAKE

First Interstate Bank

SURVIVAL TIPS

When an earthquake strikes the solid earth may pitch and roll like the deck of a ship for a minute or two. Although the motion is frightening, your chances of survival are better if you remain calm and:

During the shaking

If indoors, stay indoors. Hide under sturdy furniture. Stay near the center of the building. Stay away from glass.

Don't use candles, matches, or other open flames.

Don't run through or near buildings where there is danger of falling debris.

If outside, stay in the open away from buildings and utility wires.

If in a moving car, stop but stay inside.

After the shaking

Check for injuries—give first aid.

Check water, gas, and electric lines. If damaged, shut off at mains. If gas leakage is detected, open windows, leave house and report to authorities.

Turn on radio or television for emergency bulletins.

Stay out of damaged buildings; aftershocks can shake them down.

Call your out of state telephone contact . . . and:

Tell them how and where you are.

Ask if other family members have left messages.

Tell them when you will try to call again at a specific time.

Possible approaches As the sidebar on page 87 indicates, disaster education can be done in many ways.[13] Good public information planning not only makes use of ongoing activities but also seizes opportunities, using events elsewhere to publicize local efforts. Ontario Hydro, which runs several nuclear power plants, used Chernobyl to publicize its emergency plans.

Education about emergency planning can be fitted into existing organizations. Some time before the ash from Mount St. Helens landed on Yakima, Washington, some lower-income neighborhoods had been organized to receive federal block grants: "Those lower income areas had their areas cleaned up quicker and were more organized than anyone else in the community. . . . Everyone knows everybody else on their block—[they] have their own little

Approaches to disaster education

Create displays in public buildings or gathering places to portray past disasters and responses.

Set up markers to remind residents of past incidents.

Publicly honor those whose buildings meet standards for earthquake resistance or other mitigation requirements.

Arrange tours to show local officials key locations, such as high-water marks.

Ask the local telephone company to include emergency information in its annual directory, e.g., maps showing floodplains or the location of emergency shelters.

At times of seasonal risk, ask utility companies to include "stuffers" with their bills, identifying hazards and instructing citizens what to do should disaster strike.

Ask major employers to include similar information with payroll checks.

Post seasonal information in a variety of places—on milk cartons, bread wrappers, shopping bags, hunting and fishing licenses.

Clearly mark hospital and snow emergency routes.

Label public buildings as disaster shelters.

Post placards on municipal vehicles publicizing disaster-related activities.

Train municipal staff who routinely handle calls (such as complaints or requests for information) to give out emergency information.

Create a "hazard hotline," and track the calls to obtain information about changing interest in emergency management.

Create a speakers' bureau to guarantee that any service organization, parent-teacher group, or church group can learn about emergency planning.

---

crime watch thing going and those other kinds of things . . .—and they *know* each other."[14] Jack Kartez, William Kelley, and Michael Lindell recommend taking advantage of such existing structures: "Make use of the block watch, crime watch, and neighborhood planning groups that have developed in recent years. Maintaining agreed-upon procedures with the citizen coordinators of these groups can provide one means to pass vital information to citizens or to locate senior citizens and homebound citizens needing special attention."[15]

APELL, the European program for dealing with toxic chemicals, suggests that churches may be an effective way to reach the community.

Finally, disaster education must include children. For one thing, children will eventually *be* the community. For another, children are a route to adults, especially to those who do not speak the predominant language. Approaching parents through children has been especially successful in fire education, where schoolchildren bring home questions about fire safety. Firefighters and police can include emergency information in talks to schools. In the United States, the television program "Sesame Street" created the exciting "Stop, Drop, and Roll" song to tell children about fire. The producers of "Sesame Street" also developed the bilingual kit *Get Ready for Hurricanes*, which includes the song "Hurricane Blues."

In determining approaches to disaster education, it's important to remember that anyone can play a role in a disaster. For example, initial rescue work is usually done by survivors: "Eighty to ninety per cent of the victims in the

Figure 4-3 A page from *Get Ready for Hurricanes*, a bilingual kit developed by the Children's Television Workshop, producers of "Sesame Street." The kit was funded by FEMA, the National Weather Service, and the American Red Cross.

Mexico City earthquake were rescued in the first few hours by their friends, neighbors, and people who happened to be there. They just went in and pulled people out."[16]

It's important to remember, too, that different kinds of incidents lead to different kinds of problems, even for the same kinds of groups. In Newfoundland, when power went out, dairy farmers discovered they no longer had the labor or skills required to milk by hand. In Prince Edward County, when snow blocked the roads, dairy farmers could do their milking but couldn't deliver their milk.

Myths to be dispelled The most crucial aspect of disaster education may be overcoming misunderstandings about disaster, many of which have been given currency by the media. Here are some common myths about disaster:

1. In a disaster, the victims will be shocked, confused.
2. People will panic.
3. There will be looting.
4. Given large numbers of injured and dead, some police, firefighters, and ambulance attendants will leave their posts to check on their families.
5. Overall, however, organizations will perform better than victims.

The facts—based on seventy years of research—are different:

1. Disaster victims cope very well. They help their families, their neighbors, their co-workers.

2. Panic is so rare that it is not a problem.
3. Looting is rare. Crime rates fall after disasters.
4. People with emergency responsibilities do not leave their posts in a disaster. In more than five hundred field studies, the Disaster Research Center at the University of Delaware did not discover a single example of role abandonment.
5. Organizations are at a disadvantage in disasters. Victims can look around them, see what has to be done, then do it. Communication and transportation damage may make it impossible for organizations to do the same. They are ready and willing to help but may not have adequate access to information or equipment.

The myths become dangerous when organizations act on them. Fearing panic, radio stations hold back warnings. To prevent looting, police devote their resources to security. On the assumption that victims can't cope, impact areas are evacuated. Imagining the victims to be helpless, outsiders rush to help, causing congestion.

All these actions cause problems. In 1985, when the stadium in Bradford, England, caught fire, police told spectators all was well and not to panic; some spectators died because they remained where they were when they should have fled. When Cyclone Tracy destroyed Darwin, Australia, in 1974, the authorities persuaded many residents to leave. Studies show that those who stayed amid the destruction and retained their family units coped the best. In the worst man-made explosion until Hiroshima, a French munitions ship exploded in Halifax harbor on December 6, 1917, killing or injuring 22 percent of the population. Relief supplies poured in from Canada and the United States—but

> so great was the outpouring of assistance, personal and material, . . . that the administrative situation in Halifax became extremely strained. The congestion swamped the workers and added temporarily to the difficulties of the situation. Accordingly, the Relief Committee on December 12 requested that no more volunteer helpers come to Halifax without first communicating with them and that parties desiring to donate supplies first notify the Committee of the character and quantity of the goods offered. In this way the congestion was relieved.[17]

Replacing myths with fact isn't easy, but the effort must be made. And the key target is the media. Even as they are reading this, some readers will be thinking, "Haven't I seen, heard, or read news reports of looting and of dazed, shocked survivors?" You almost certainly have; the problem is that the media continually report as if the myths were true. They report attempts to prevent looting as if there were looting. They state, "There was no panic," as if panic were to be expected. Because of such reporting, officials and the public believe the myths. Changing this requires two strategies: educating officials, and working with the media to try to prevent such misleading reporting.

Developing the plan

The preliminary steps, then, are identifying hazards, assessing the community's attitudes and needs, beginning the planning process within the government, evaluating resources, and initiating a public education program. The rest of the chapter focuses on community involvement in the actual development of the emergency plan. Opportunity for public debate and discussion is essential, for example, in evaluating preparedness and mitigation options. Similarly, a warning system conceived without an understanding of how residents are likely to respond to a warning will be of little use in the case of an actual disaster.

The sections that follow offer guidelines on assisting victims, improving post-disaster communication, working with the media, planning for recovery, and testing and updating the plan. The emphasis throughout is on *strengthening the plan by involving the community and making the best use of its material and personal resources.*

Preparedness options

As risks are identified, various options for dealing with them will emerge. It may be possible to prevent disasters or their effects. It may be possible to warn people. It may be possible to assist victims with an effective response. Before undertaking a full-blown public education effort, a local government must decide which option or combination of them it will use.

For a flood hazard, for example, the options may include building dikes to prevent flooding; building floodways to carry water past the community; passing zoning regulations to prevent development (or further development) on floodplains; developing long-term plans to relocate developments currently in floodplain areas; putting up signs to show where floods would occur; designing systems to warn when a threat has been identified; and developing a plan for an actual flood. Each of these approaches will require its own form of public education: one educational program, for example, to sell the idea of dikes or floodways, another to persuade residents not to build on floodplains, and yet another to make people aware of how warnings will be given and what to do if they are.

Of course, one action does not preclude another. In London, England, flood barriers on the lower Thames should stop high tides that would cause a surge of water up the Thames—but they will not prevent a flood threat from inland, so London is also developing floodways to carry water around residential areas. That approach has been used successfully in Winnipeg, Manitoba.

No matter which approach or combination of approaches is favored, proposals must be made public before decisions are made. The public can be told advantages, disadvantages, and costs; they should not be presented with conclusions. When a local authority in England showed a videotape favoring one particular solution, the public responded by arguing that the "consultative process" was a facade. To guarantee public involvement in the discussion of options, meetings should be well publicized, and an effort should be made to reach out to all segments of the community that might be affected.

Even if some threats are more likely than others, plans must account for a wide range of possibilities. It makes no sense to build dikes to prevent flooding if those dikes will liquefy (turn to mud) in an earthquake. It makes no sense to install sirens for tornado warnings unless the sirens can also be used for other threats. (A siren that means "turn on your radio" is useful for any threat; one that is understood to mean "go to your basement" is not much use in a flood.)

This does not mean planning for the absurd. Although a Russian satellite has already landed in northern Canada and an American one in Australia, small communities need not plan for satellite crashes. But genuine threats must not be ignored. Hurricanes, for example, are usually seen as a threat to communities along the Gulf of Mexico or the Atlantic Coast. Yet they can go north and inland—as Metro Toronto discovered in 1954, when rain brought by Hurricane Hazel created devastating flash floods.

Mitigation

Although nothing can stop a hurricane, a tornado, or an earthquake, it is possible to reduce, or mitigate, their effects. A community can, for example, build dikes to restrain flood waters or make its buildings earthquake resistant. Although this approach sounds sensible, it may be difficult to sell. Most people are convinced that disasters won't occur, so they see no reason to spend money to mitigate their effects. Politically, mitigation may be very unpopular.

Riverfront properties are commercially very attractive, and a plan to block new construction along a flood-prone river will provoke an outcry from developers. Requirements that owners fortify their buildings against earthquakes will provoke similar reactions. Such requirements cost money. And even if mitigation actions are charged to general tax revenues, there may be opposition. Taxpayers do not want to spend their money helping residents who have made what they regard as poor choices: building in a floodplain or purchasing a structure not resistant to earthquakes.

Once again, the best approach may be networking and public debate. Builders, developers, insurance agents can be asked to discuss how a community should identify hazards. Must a property be identified as flood prone in any sales document? If not, what liability occurs, and to whom? Can such properties be insured? If not, why not? Even if no one wants to deal with current realities, everyone may agree that buildings must be brought up to certain standards when they are sold or renovated.

Local officials may believe that the public cannot understand technicalities. The evidence is otherwise; Peter Sandman noted that "when the general public has felt it was exercising real influence on a decision, it has shown a surprising ability to master the technical details."[18]

Ironically, successful mitigation efforts may create new problems: the public may assume that no further action is needed. Residents may believe that this new security blanket—a dike, a floodway, an earthquake-resistant building—will eliminate risk. It is up to the local government to continue education efforts to correct this misconception.

Warning systems

Some disasters—building collapses, industrial explosions—come with little warning. Others—floods, hurricanes, tornadoes—are preceded by advance notice. And although a toxic incident may occur without warning, the proper response—perhaps evacuation, perhaps staying indoors—is communicated the same way a warning is: as the final step in a formal warning system.

Key elements   Warning systems have several key elements. First, the problem must be detected. Then, the threat must be evaluated. Next, a decision must be made about what to do. Finally, that decision must be acted on: only then is a public warning issued. Even then, the warning is effective only if those hearing it understand it and are willing to respond with action.

The process of deciding whether to issue a warning can be complicated. Given an earthquake prediction with a low probability—"there's a 10 percent chance of a 3.5 earthquake within ten days"—it may be difficult to decide whether a warning is required. Given an emission of radioactive gases, there may be debate about whether residents should be told to stay under cover or asked to leave. Even if officials believe a serious threat exists, they may be reluctant to issue a warning lest they be seen as panicky—or lest the warning provoke panic. Ironically, though, one of the most serious problems in disasters is not panic, but *unwillingness to believe and react even to obvious signs of danger.* That's why occupants of an office building in North Bay, Ontario, remained in the building for three hours although it reeked of natural gas. An ancient Chinese proverb says, "There are thirty-six ways to behave. The best is to run." Disaster experts wish more people followed that advice.

To overcome the reluctance to act, disaster warnings must

Be specific about the danger

Be specific about what to do

Be specific about who is being warned

Be issued by all possible sources

Be based on previous education.

An effective warning that meets these criteria would sound something like this:

There is a tornado coming. It is just minutes away. Head for your basement. Take a portable radio with you and keep it on. Stay there until you hear the all clear. This warning applies to everyone in Town city.

The announcement would be backed up by sirens.

J. S. Tyhurst, one of the first scholars in the field, found that people were not upset by warnings if those warnings were clear and specific about the danger and the proper response. When the truth is clearly stated, people know what to do.

Sometimes it's obvious who the warnings are intended for. At other times, it's not. A tornado watch for "Jones County" may have little meaning to someone on a cross-country trip. A message creeping across the TV screen on a motel TV set could be coming from anywhere.

Because those who hear warnings usually try to confirm them by checking elsewhere, it's crucial that warnings come from all possible channels. If, for example, sirens sound but there are no messages on the radio and just the usual programs on TV, and if family members and neighbors aren't reacting, people will conclude that the warning is false.

Peel police got people to leave Mississauga because they clearly identified the threats: there were dangerous gases and the chance of an explosion; told people what to do: leave; left no doubt about who they were talking to: they went to every door; and had the message put on all possible channels: it was announced over the radio, shown on maps on TV, and repeated by people using bullhorns.

The most critical aspect of a warning, however, may be that it will have been preceded by education. Those who are well informed about hazards and the risks they present will recognize warning signs and react appropriately. Research suggests that they will react especially well if they know where they are to go and how to get there.[19]

Role of media   If radio, television, and print are available, they are essential to any warning system. When tornadoes threatened Woodstock and Barrie, Ontario, no warning was given over local radio or TV because a power failure had knocked all local media off the air, and none had back-up power. After impact, officials were unable to tell residents what was being done. In Woodstock, where water and sewer lines were broken, power lines were down, and the debris included dead animals, the Medical Officer of Health had no way to warn residents of dangers to public health.

The first step in educating the media about disaster is to get them to make their own emergency plans (the media approached must include specialized media, community papers, black media, ethnic media, and religious broadcasters). Do local radio and television stations have emergency power? Have they worked out a staffing plan for emergencies? Do they have back-up facilities (such as an alternative printing plant for a newspaper)? Do they have the necessary equipment to report on an emergency: boats for a flood, snowmobiles for a snow emergency? In small communities, radio stations may broadcast less than twenty-four hours a day. How can staff be reached during off hours to activate a station? (The U.S. Federal Communications Commission allows stations to change both their range and broadcasting hours for emergency service.)

Next, the media must be integrated into any warning system. They must know how information will reach them and how to confirm warnings from elsewhere. They must be persuaded to inform their audiences ahead of time about how the warning system will work and of their role in it. Ideally, radio and television stations will have prerecorded messages available using voices that are well-known and highly regarded in the community. In many parts of the United States, warnings must go out in Spanish. In Canada, French is an absolute necessity.

Finally, the media must understand that warning messages will be undermined if they are interspersed between other less-serious programming or are allowed to creep across the TV screen so that they won't interrupt a comedy.

Assistance to victims

Disaster preparedness must also focus on potential victims—those who may lose their homes, their loved ones, their livelihood. Whether disaster victims suffer differently from victims of other, less widespread events such as automobile accidents is a matter of debate. Disaster victims are different in the sense that there are many of them and a lot of help may be needed, but also in the sense that they can share their problems with and help one another.

A good community plan will anticipate that victims suddenly find themselves in need of assistance. In one approach, which has become known as "one-stop shopping," all victim services are in one place. In Edmonton, Alberta, after the 1987 tornado, local, provincial, and federal levels of government joined forces with voluntary agencies and the private sector, took over a school, and established a victim service center within sixty hours of the disaster. In one visit, a victim could collect car insurance, register for unemployment insurance, receive emotional counseling, find a new apartment, and arrange for utilities—including telephone service—for his or her temporary home. The authorities were so well prepared they let a local TV station follow the first family through the center. That family left the center ninety minutes after arriving, the father happily displaying the key to the family's new apartment. A telephone crew was already en route to install the family's new telephone.

The one-stop shopping center in Edmonton was put together after the disaster, but it resulted from good predisaster networking. Direction was provided by three key emergency agencies: Emergency Preparedness Canada (federal), Public Safety Services (provincial), and the office of the emergency measures coordinator (municipal). These three agencies had worked together before the disaster; getting along after it meant more of the same.

In planning for victims' needs, it is important to remember that disaster victims may well be outsiders, which may lead to many problems. For example, in 1988, when flash flooding knocked out all the highways around Terrace in northern British Columbia, many travelers were forced to seek help. After being rescued by helicopter, they were without supplies, money, or transportation. Similar problems arise in snow emergencies. And when an F-28 Air Ontario Fokker jet crashed near Dryden, Ontario, on March 10, 1989, most of the forty-seven survivors came from Thunder Bay, a nearby city.[20]

Problems are especially likely to arise when a threatened population is evacuated to a community with a different cultural and ethnic mix. When major fires hit northern Ontario in 1990, many people, including Native Americans, were flown out to relief centers in the neighboring province of Manitoba. When Cyclone Tracy hit Australia's northernmost city, Darwin, evacuees were flown to cities 1,800 to 2,500 miles away. In such situations, billets may be difficult to find, and misunderstandings may result from different cultural expectations.

Postdisaster communication

Another problem created by disasters is an enormous demand for information. Those outside the area will want to know what has happened to relatives and friends. Victims will want to know what services are available. Families will be trying to reunite. After the Dryden air crash, Red Cross volunteers spent hours on the telephone relaying messages between victims and anxious relatives.

Making connections among survivors and between survivors and relatives can be difficult because disasters knock out transportation and communications. Increased demand for information overloads telephones. Movement of the injured to hospitals, the homeless to relatives and friends, and evacuees to shelters makes it difficult for people to locate one another.

One way to ease the situation is to have predesignated registration centers. Residents can be taught that, given a disaster, they should register at a specified school or church or public building. They can leave word where they came from, where they are going, and, most important, the name of someone who will know where they are. (Many victims move several times in the wake of disaster. Without such a contact, they will soon be lost sight of.) Good planning will have seen to it that volunteer agencies are prepared for this process of registration.

The information collected at a registration center is useful not only to victims but also to those conducting search and rescue activities. Fire fighters, police, and other search and rescue personnel may spend hours searching for those who left unharmed. When the ferry *Herald of Free Enterprise* sank at Zeebrugge, Belgium, in 1987, the Kent County Constabulary in England set up a public inquiry office where anxious persons could ask about relatives. The office received thousands of phone calls. When the ferry was finally raised, these data proved invaluable in identifying victims and locating relatives.

Postdisaster information for victims may take other forms. A "hot line," for example, can allow victims to call in for information about what is happening and what is being done for them. Relatives can call for information about family members. For this approach to work, staff must be available to handle an inevitably overwhelming number of calls; and it's crucial that staff be able to use all local languages. Telephone lines must be in place before the disaster, or advance arrangements must be made with the phone company.

In smaller communities, a public meeting may be the best way to get information out. A meeting allows all questions to be handled at one time and guarantees that everyone hears the same answers. It can also be politically effective. After victims of floods in northern British Columbia expressed their concerns to a cabinet minister who had flown in, he persuaded the cabinet to make changes in aid procedures.

All these approaches to postdisaster communication work only if those in charge have something to say. Public communication is of value only if information is being collected and decisions are being made. Without adequate planning, community leaders will discover they cannot respond to the questions they will inevitably be asked.

Post-impact role of the media

When the 1977 power blackout struck New York City, the *New York Times* staff worked by candlelight, and the paper was printed in New Jersey. After the 1987 Edmonton tornado, the daily *Edmonton Journal* chartered a jet to fly staff and production material to nearby Calgary to get out a limited edition of the paper.

In addition to being part of the education process and part of the warning system, the media are also an important part of the post-impact information system. First, though, they must be able to operate. Second, they must know where to obtain post-impact information and how to check out specific information. Benjamin Singer has shown that local media, especially radio, can provide a key link between the public and officials.[21] Thus, when calls come in from the media, officials must be ready: the public will be listening. (Local media audiences rise sharply during an emergency.)

Under ordinary conditions, media relations are generally confined to local media; after an emergency, local media will feed stories to wire services, radio services, and the various TV networks. This may happen incredibly quickly. When a USAF jet crashed into a hotel in Indianapolis in 1987, one of the first to report the news was Tom Brokaw of NBC News in New York. An NBC affiliate fed him coverage from the scene via satellite.

National media coverage may stimulate hundreds, even thousands, of calls from friends and relatives to those in the affected community. It is possible for long-distance operators to block operator-assisted calls by telling all but essential customers that circuits are busy. It is not possible to screen calls that are direct dialed within a single community. It is possible to adjust service, making it easier for some clients to make calls, through a process called line load control—but this works only if there has been planning and the customers requiring such service have been designated in advance. Finally, it is possible to create an emergency telephone service by using portable offices, which include switching systems, or by rerouting calls and thus bypassing damaged parts of the system.

It may be useful to ask the media to report not only what *is* affected but what is *not*. For example, by making clear that flooding has not affected certain portions of a city, the media may reduce the anxiety of those who are listening and watching.

Sometimes news media are already present when disasters occur. When the fire broke out in the soccer stadium in Bradford, the game was being telecast live. That was true when a riot started at the beginning of a soccer match at the Heisel Stadium in Belgium. And it was true of a 1989 incident at a soccer game in Sheffield, England. But media coverage can lead to response problems if the officials watching television or listening to the radio assume that the coverage is accurate. When the fire occurred at the stadium in Bradford, TV covered it live, but the telecast showed people trying to escape from the stands by climbing the fence and getting onto the field—it did not show the people who were going out under the stands, where they became trapped and died.

Initial media coverage may be based on reports fed from local media outlets. That situation won't last long. The major media will send news crews to the site, sometimes in incredible numbers. At Gander, Newfoundland, in the wake of the 1985 Arrow air crash that killed 256, 325 media personnel were on site within twelve hours. NBC even brought in a satellite ground station from England. (See sidebar on page 96.) After the 1983 Coalinga earthquake, helicopters from southern California radio and TV stations created an aerial traffic jam. At such times, media coverage outdoes communications from local officials: officials at Three Mile Island discovered that the best way to keep informed was to watch TV.

And, just as the journalism textbooks suggest, media personnel will ask very specific questions: How many injured? How many dead? How much damage? How effective was the warning? What was the cause (if it's not obvious)? What exactly are the effects? Some of these questions may be at odds with the priorities of emergency response. Local authorities don't want a count or a damage estimate; they want to know if everyone is looked after. As for inquiries into fault, they can be left until later.

Yet the media representatives cannot be pushed aside. Their reports will shape state, provincial, and federal officials' image of what has happened. Local communities will find assistance easier to get if higher levels of government receive an accurate picture from TV. It's therefore essential that someone be assigned to collect information so that it can be passed on to outside as well as local media.

Large communities may have experienced public information staff. In smaller communities, the media blitz can be overwhelming. A municipal official who has never talked to anyone but reporters from the local weekly newspaper may

The media at Gander   Gander, in central Newfoundland, is far from major media centers. Yet on December 12, 1985, Gander itself became a major media center. A chartered Arrow jet carrying U.S. soldiers from the 101st Airborne home from the Middle East crashed near Gander Airport. More than 325 media representatives descended on the town.

Local officials, airport staff, the Royal Canadian Mounted Police, and the Canadian Aviation Safety Board (CASB) were nearly overwhelmed. But because they followed some simple rules, there were few problems with the media.

First, local officials were honest about what they did and didn't know. For example, they were uncertain about the precise number of passengers aboard the plane. The spokespersons admitted to that uncertainty.

Second, they refused to speculate. Because the plane had landed in a freezing drizzle and the pilot had not de-iced, there was speculation that icing had caused the crash. The CASB confirmed that the pilot had not de-iced but stressed that it was far too early to speculate on causes of the crash.

Third, officials made clear what the media representatives could and could not do. The representatives were told they would have no immediate access to the site, and that decision was enforced by careful site control.

Fourth, officials explained things that might have been confusing. For example, in the United States, conversations on flight recorders are made public, but Canadian law prohibits this. The difference between the two laws was explained immediately and carefully.

Fifth, officials promised to find out things they did not know—and did so.

Sixth, they made certain that media personnel were well informed about when news conferences would be held. When activity at the site was shut down overnight, the media representatives were told this and told there would be no further briefings until the next day.

Seventh, with access to the crash site limited, media personnel were allowed to choose their own representatives for pool assignments on flights over the crash site (they invariably chose the best persons).

---

be dazed by the TV lights and microphones. One way to handle this problem is to ask local media personnel to serve as community information officers. After the Air Ontario jet crashed near Dryden, the community invited the general manager of the local radio station to the emergency operations center to deal with media phone calls. Another solution is to call outside for help. Since the media personnel themselves come from outside, they can hardly object to media relations personnel coming from outside, too. After a tornado struck St. Bonaventure, Quebec, in 1985, the Quebec emergency agency, Protection Civile, sent just one person, a public information officer. The mayor dealt with local media; the information officer dealt with the outsiders.

No matter who handles media relations, honesty is essential—don't hide things. If you don't know, say so. Collecting information takes time. How could anyone expect you to be fully informed just after a disaster has hit your community? One thing you can say right away is what you are doing. If you have adequate planning, this should be simple. But in addition to adequate planning, efficient information collection is also important. If the community itself is the best and most reliable source of information, it will be the dominant source for the media representatives. If community officials are seen as not well informed, the media representatives will go elsewhere.

Incidentally, during the postdisaster phase, it's well to remember that different media—local, regional and state, national, even international—have different needs and that local media personnel will be around when the disaster ends. Local officials overwhelmed by media superstars—people whose faces, names, or voices they recognize—may neglect local media representatives, to their later regret. At Three Mile Island, local media personnel resented the fact that the press corps accompanying President Jimmy Carter was given access denied to local reporters. At Fort Campbell, Kentucky, where the soldiers killed in the Gander air crash had been based, local media representatives were pleased to get exactly the same treatment that was accorded the media representatives accompanying President Ronald Reagan.

The good news about postdisaster media convergence is that it ends quickly. In Gander, most media representatives arrived late on Thursday, the day of the crash, and most were gone by Sunday afternoon, less than seventy-two hours later.[22]

Recovery

In the wake of disaster, public officials may be subjected to a number of conflicting pressures. Local business and other community leaders will want to restore "business as usual" as quickly as possible. At the same time, public support for mitigation action—which must be carefully planned and takes significant time to implement—may be at an all-time high. Disasters present an opportunity for dramatic change, for better or for worse, and it's important that public officials not be swept along by the seemingly overwhelming pressure to return to normal life as quickly as possible. Kathleen Loewy and David Sink have described an incident in Florida in which the pressure to return to normalcy was irresistible. The mayor had resigned just after a disaster, and

the council hurriedly selected an acting mayor who was immediately confronted by three land developers. They wanted to get the community back on its feet again. They wanted permission to begin cleaning debris and staking out lots for waterfront condos and beach houses. . . . Several members of council were not sure about the haste of the whole affair. . . . Their concerns were shouted down in the din of ensuing council meetings. . . . When council finally did pass zoning regulations, one year after the hurricane, . . . the action came as a symbolic and meaningless gesture. . . . Over 4,000 new condos were in place, 2,500 were under construction and 4,500 more were on the drawing board.[23]

Quarantelli has described a case in Kansas where the same tornado hit two communities, but with two different results:

In one of those cities, the tornado led to a massive re-working of the central business district and a variety of other things, while in the other city it did not, though urban renewal was an issue. We questioned the differences. . . . The difference is that some group decided to take advantage of this opportunity. . . . Opportunities may come into being, conditions may be ripe, but unless there is someone taking the ball and running with it, nothing is likely to happen.[24]

If change is to happen, it must come quickly. As each day passes, support for dramatic action will weaken. That means that development plans must be ready before disaster strikes. A disaster is not just a calamity but an opportunity, and a manager who is prepared can use it to alter the public agenda.

Testing and updating the plan

Other chapters in this book tell how to write an emergency plan. This chapter makes it clear that emergency planning involves far more than the creation of a document. As Quarantelli has noted:

The plan itself may be the least important part of the whole disaster planning process. Planning involves meetings and interorganizational contacts and communication. It involves training exercises and disaster rehearsals. It involves assessing risks and creating linkages among relevant groups. It involves creating certain kinds of social climates and attitudes favorable to coping with disasters. Most important of all, disaster preparedness involves thinking about disaster situations. [Few] if any of these activities require writing a document.[25]

It is easy—as well as misleading—for communities to convince themselves that, because they have a paper plan, all is well. Paper plans, especially detailed ones, will not be opened during a disaster. Moreover, "disaster plans, by tradition, are lengthy and dry procedural documents. . . . Plans contain essential information but they often go unread by key departments. Holding multi-agency emergency exercises at least annually is essential to breathing life into plans."[26]

Plans will work only if people become accustomed to them through exercises designed to train them and increase their disaster awareness. Simulations are essential; but they must be realistic. If exercises are always dramatic events, an air crash, a massive explosion in a school, this won't convince exercise participants or the public that threats are real. Disaster exercises are not games but opportunities to publicize genuine risks. An ideal simulation should focus on what might really happen. For example, if the most likely threat is seasonal, the exercise should be just before the threat season.

Disaster exercises can be full-scale simulations involving many agencies. But exercises on a much smaller scale can still be effective. The following four approaches are useful, yet can be accomplished with limited resources:

1. Simply require individuals or agencies to think through their role in an incident. A test of homes for senior citizens, for example, could be based on the premise that each of those homes has been isolated. Each home could then work out whether staffing and supplies are adequate, and for how long.
2. Undertake a table-top exercise, in which a scenario is devised and those concerned respond to it. A chemical company, for example, can report dangerous gases heading in a particular direction. The emergency response agencies can outline what resources they would have and how they would use them.
3. Undertake a small-scale simulation. Hospital officials can inform staff that a fire has started in one room and can then observe as the first response procedures are carried out. (This works quite well as long as patients on that ward are quietly told what is to happen.)
4. Use drills. Drills usually test safety procedures. The most common are fire drills in public buildings. Fire drills work well provided that the buildings are actually evacuated and that any residents needing special help are identified.

Any of these approaches can be used to test on-site command posts and off-site EOCs (emergency operations centers). Another alternative is to send staff to training programs that use simulations—programs such as the ESM (Emergency Site Management Course) at the Canadian Emergency Preparedness College. (In a four-and-one-half-day course, the college staff put students through three major simulations.) All these approaches will increase disaster awareness, and most cause far less disruption than a major simulation does.

Some communities have found it useful to ask the media to cover exercises as if they were real events. This helps officials learn what the media do and how to cope with them.

Whatever approach is taken, it is essential that the process be critiqued by knowledgeable, impartial, outside observers, who might be academics or emergency personnel from other communities or from other levels of government.

Putting a plan together, making it known, testing it, and even using it in a real disaster are just part of the process. A plan must also be continually updated, and those it affects must be re-educated, re-informed. Without updating and re-education, any plan will become obsolete. New problems develop; residents retire, die, move away. Even an excellent plan won't work forever.

Changes must be publicized, perhaps during annual events or by special announcements. If you wanted to inform residents of changes in the emergency plans for tornadoes, for example, here are guidelines for a program:

1. Schedule a well-publicized evacuation exercise.
2. Afterward, in cooperation with local merchants, close off one block of the central business district to traffic and hold a "tornado day" sale.
3. Announce the sale in advertisements that also include emergency information.
4. On the day of the sale, hand out leaflets and buttons to those entering the downtown area.
5. Have stores sponsor "quizzes" on emergency plans.

The media may agree to carry seasonal educational messages. Each year, before winter or the hurricane or tornado season, newspaper, radio, or television special announcements can remind residents of the danger and instruct them on what to do in case of an emergency. The instructions will vary with local conditions but, for almost any emergency, residents should be told to prepare a kit that includes a battery-operated radio, a flashlight, bottled water, and some canned food.

Above all, municipal officials must make sure their own house is in order. The municipality's internal plan must be tested and updated regularly. Changes should be reported to the council in an annual report on community preparedness. There should be a budget item for emergency preparedness. No matter how small the amount, it will guarantee that preparedness comes up for annual review. Each year, every municipal department should be asked if it has items for this budget.

There is no question that disasters make it easier to keep planning up-to-date. The city of Corner Brook, Newfoundland, which had just created an emergency plan, found it easy to revise that plan when a 1981 toxic incident led to evacuation of a city suburb. The 1978 Mississauga derailment made it easier for the chief of Peel police to focus public attention on emergency preparedness.

In the absence of disasters, someone must see that planning is kept current. That someone may be the emergency manager, the local government manager, or the mayor. When the Emergency Communications Research Unit at Carleton University in Ottawa reviewed a series of incidents to see whether there had been planning, it found that, in almost every case in which the essentials were present, the mayor had provided predisaster leadership—not necessarily doing the planning, but insisting that it be done. The study also found that the mayor had been encouraged to act by someone else.[27]

Clearly, if emergency planning is to get done well, it must be seen as a priority. That means it must have both top-level political and administrative support. The emergency manager will find it helpful to persuade the mayor to attend an emergency management course (special courses are given for politicians) or to show up at simulations, play a role in table-top exercises, meet with the groups doing risk assessment—in short, generally indicate interest and support.

Conclusion

It is easy to talk about leadership. It is much harder to make leadership effective. This chapter has shown, step by step, how to involve the community in emergency planning at every stage, from hazard evaluation to recovery. It has explained

networking—the process of gradually expanding the community's involvement—and has covered in detail the myths about disasters. It has dealt, as well,
with such important topics as media relations and the planning of exercises.
Drawing on the suggestions in this chapter, a manager should be able to develop
a plan and make it known to—and accepted by—the entire community.

1 Gerald G. Fox, "Disaster Planning: A Tale of Two Cities," *Public Management* (January/February 1981): 7–11.
2 Allen K. Settle, "Legal Issues in Emergency Management: The Coalinga Earthquake" (paper presented at the American Society for Public Administration, Anaheim, CA, April 1986).
3 Many examples in this chapter are drawn from field studies conducted by the Emergency Communications Research Unit (ECRU) at Carleton University in Ottawa with funds obtained mainly from Emergency Preparedness Canada (the Canadian equivalent of FEMA) and also from other agencies, including the Canadian Police College, the National Research Council of Canada, the Canadian Association of Fire Chiefs, and the Defence Research Board.
4 Gerard J. Hoetmer, "Emergency Management," *Baseline Data Reports* 15, no. 4 (Washington, DC: International City Management Association, April 1983).
5 United Nations Environment Program, Industry and Environment Office, *APELL Awareness and Preparedness for Emergencies at Local Level* (Paris: UNEP, 1988).
6 An example of a more formal hazard history (of London, Ontario) is Kenneth Hewitt and Ian Burton, *The Hazardousness of a Place* (Toronto: University of Toronto Press, 1971).
7 Roger L. Kemp, "Public Officials' Role in Emergency Management" (n.p., n.d.).
8 Joseph Scanlon with Massey Padgham, *The Peel Regional Police Force and the Mississauga Evacuation: How a Major Police Force Handled a Chemical Emergency* (Ottawa: The Canadian Police College, 1979).
9 Bruce Wilson, "City of Edmonton: An Emergency Plan That Works," *Emergency Preparedness Digest* (July-September 1988):17–23.
10 Jack D. Kartez, "Emergency Planning Implications of Local Governments' Responses to Mount St. Helens" (Boulder, CO: Natural Hazard Research, 1982, Working Paper no. 46).
11 Hoetmer, "Emergency Management."
12 E. L. Quarantelli, "Disaster Education: Its Substantive Content and the Target Audiences" (Paper presented at conference on Emergency '88, London, England, November 29, 1988).
13 Ronald W. Perry and Joanne M. Nigg, "Emergency Management Strategies for Communication of Hazard Information," *Public Administration Review* (January 1985): 72–77.
14 Kartez, "Emergency Planning Implications."
15 Jack D. Kartez, William J. Kelley, and Michael K. Lindell, "Conditions for Implementation," in *Strategies and Policy Perspectives*, ed. Louise Comfort (Durham, NC: Duke University Press, 1988), 126–146.
16 E. L. Quarantelli, "The Controversy on the Mental Health Consequences of Disasters," in Robert J. Ursano, ed., *Groups and Organizations in War, Disaster and Trauma* (Bethesda, MD: Uniformed Services University of the Health Sciences, 1987).
17 Dwight Johnstone (Unpublished manuscript on the Halifax explosion, circa 1919).
18 Peter M. Sandman, "Explaining Risk to Non-Experts" (Paper presented at conference on Global Disasters and International Information Flow, Washington, DC, October 8–10, 1986).
19 Ronald W. Perry, Michael K. Lindell, and Marjorie Greene, *Evacuation Planning in Emergency Management* (Lexington, MA: D. C. Heath and Company, 1981).
20 Joseph Scanlon, Gillian Osborne, and Ann Simard, "The Dryden Air Crash, March 10, 1989" (unpublished manuscript).
21 Benjamin Singer and Lyndsay Green, *The Social Functions of Radio during a Community Emergency* (Toronto: The Copp Clark Publishing Company, 1972).
22 For a detailed account of media relations, see Joseph Scanlon, Suzanne Alldred, Al Farrell, and Angela Prawzick, "Coping with the Media in Disasters: Some Predictable Problems," *Public Administration Review* (January 1985): 123–133.
23 Kathleen K. Loewy and David Sink, "Political Realities of Local Emergency Managers" (paper presented at the American Society for Public Administration, Anaheim, CA, April 1986).
24 Quarantelli, "Controversy on the Mental Health Consequences of Disasters."
25 Quarantelli, "Controversy on the Mental Health Consequences of Disasters."
26 Jack D. Kartez, William J. Kelley, and Michael K. Lindell, *Adaptive Planning for Community Emergency Management: A Management Brief* (Pullman: Washington State University, 1987).
27 Joseph Scanlon, "Political Leadership and Canadian Emergency Planning: The Role of the Mayor," in *Cities and Disaster: North American Studies in Emergency Management*, Richard T. Sylves and William L. Waugh, Jr., eds. (Springfield, IL: Charles C Thomas, 1989).

Perspectives and Roles of the State and Federal Governments

The practice of emergency management in the United States has undergone a significant transition since passage of the Federal Civil Defense Act of 1950. Emergency management's scope has expanded from an earlier emphasis on civil defense to today's all-hazard approach, which addresses natural, technological, and civil hazards. Disasters themselves often serve as the impetus for change: the Bhopal, India, disaster, for example, prompted Congress to enact legislation to prevent a similar type of accident from occurring in the United States. Title III of SARA sets forth detailed emergency planning and chemical reporting requirements for state and local governments, in cooperation with industry. SARA Title III has accelerated the trend toward increased preparedness for technological disasters. As government responsibilities have expanded during the past forty years and new programs have been established, new intergovernmental relationships have arisen and ongoing relationships have been redefined.

This chapter examines the roles and responsibilities of the state and the federal governments in emergency preparedness, response, recovery, and mitigation, with an emphasis on the impact of state and federal programs on local government. Emergency management is maturing rapidly as a discipline and is assuming its own identity within an intergovernmental system; in this context, the chapter highlights some important programs, initiatives, and trends in emergency management that are related to state and federal government activities.

State role and responsibilities

Local government has traditionally focused on preparedness and response, and the federal government on preparedness and recovery; state government serves as the pivot in the intergovernmental system. As one former governor explained, "The state has to become the key instrument for collecting information and assessing the problem, and deciding the course of action. . . . The state is the quarterback."[1] In its pivotal role, the state is in a position to determine the emergency management needs and capabilities of its political subdivisions and to channel state and federal resources to local government, including training and technical assistance, as well as operational support in an emergency.

Role of the governor

Without exception, the authority and responsibility for emergency management at the state level rest with the governor (or his or her designated representative). State laws may vary in their delineation of emergency-related authority and responsibilities, but the powers or options to do the following are typically vested in the governor:

Suspend state statutes

Procure materials and facilities without regard to limitations of existing law

Direct evacuations

Control entrance to and exit from disaster area

Authorize release of emergency funds

Activate emergency contingency funds and reallocate state agency budgets for emergency work

Issue state or area emergency declarations and invoke appropriate state response actions

Apply for and monitor federal disaster and emergency assistance.[2]

The unpredictability of natural, technological, and civil hazards, coupled with the potential for intense media scrutiny during an emergency, has spurred the nation's governors to give increasing attention to the state emergency management function. The Three Mile Island incident is a classic example of how a governor can suddenly be thrust into the media spotlight under stressful conditions. And the response and recovery efforts surrounding the Valdez, Alaska, oil spill demonstrate that disasters are becomingly extraordinarily complex and costly. Legal issues, such as protection from liability in a disaster, are yet another dimension of emergency management with which governors (as well as administrators at the local level) must be conversant.

Recognizing the importance of emergency management, the National Governors' Association (NGA) has assumed a leadership role in raising the visibility of the state emergency management function. The increased incidence of technological disasters across the nation, for example, has prompted a number of states to reexamine their emergency authorities and their emergency management legislation. Congress recognized the pivotal role of the governor in emergency management when it designated the governor as the lead player in SARA Title III, with responsibility for establishing the state emergency response council and appointing local emergency response committees across the state.

State organizational framework

The governor has statutory authority and responsibility for emergency management at the state level, but the day-to-day emergency management function is normally vested in a lead state agency. The responsibilities of the lead agency include the following:

Developing and implementing an emergency management program

Coordinating the activities of other agencies in the development of the state emergency operations plan

Supporting and facilitating local government preparedness efforts (to ensure that disasters are handled at the lowest government level)

Coordinating, on behalf of the governor, state government resources and activities during a disaster

Assuming any or all of the emergency powers of the governor

Coordinating state recovery efforts, including obtaining federal disaster assistance.

Location of the state emergency management office

The specific functions, responsibilities, and lines of authority of the state emergency management office may vary somewhat, but they generally fall under one of five organizational models: (1) office of the governor (eleven states), (2) division or bureau under civilian department (fourteen states), (3) division or bureau under the adjutant general (twenty-two states), (4) bureau under the state police (two states), or (5) agency under a state council that oversees departmental activities (one state).

The importance of the location of the state emergency management office was the subject of a 1978 study undertaken by the National Governors' Association.[3] In examining the effectiveness of the five state models in relation to the four phases of emergency management, the study suggested that mitigation and recovery functions are better managed by program- and policy-oriented offices of state government, whereas preparedness and response are better managed by more tactically oriented departments such as the state police or adjutant general. The study concluded, however, that the overall effectiveness of the emergency management function in state government is not determined by the location of the office but by the relationship between the emergency management office and the governor's office. In analyzing the organizational models, the authors note that "some offices are strong and some are weak for a variety of historical, turf, political, and conceptual reasons. Clearly, there is not a state 'model' to follow; rather, it is the governor's understanding, concern, and sup-

Title III of the Superfund Amendments and Reauthorization

Act One of the most significant and far-reaching pieces of legislation, in its impact on emergency management organization at the state and local levels, is Title III of the Superfund Amendments and Reauthorization Act (SARA) of 1986. Passed by Congress in response to increased concern about the nation's vulnerability to major chemical accidents such as the one that occurred in Bhopal, India, SARA Title III places the responsibility for chemical emergency preparedness squarely on the shoulders of the governor. Under Title III, the governor of each state must appoint a state emergency response commission, designate emergency planning districts, appoint local emergency planning committees (LEPCs), supervise and coordinate the activities of the LEPCs, review emergency plans, receive chemical release notifications, and establish procedures for receiving and processing requests from the public for information related to hazardous chemicals in each community and to the local emergency plans required under Title III.

Title III is significant in at least two fundamental respects. First, there is its organizational impact. Although many states and communities had so-called integrated emergency planning committees in place before 17 October 1986, Section 301 of the act prescribes, for the first time, an organizational structure at the local level, including the membership and responsibilities of the local committees. The groups that must be represented on the LEPCs include a number of interests and disciplines not traditionally represented on local committees: the media, community organizations, environmental groups, and representatives of business and industry. In essence, the organizational and planning requirements outlined under Title III have provided local emergency management with a new constituency and, in the process, a new visibility in many communities.

Second, Title III has in many instances forged a new working relationship between government and industry. The provisions of Title III cannot be implemented without the full cooperation of industry, particularly the chemical industry. In complying with the planning and reporting requirements of Title III, many local committees are discovering new resources and areas of expertise through their work with local industry. This partnership of local government and industry may prove to be the greatest long-term benefit of Title III.

port, coupled with the state director's coordination and strategy-building skills, that determine the strength of the organizational framework."[4]

Role of the state emergency management office

As noted in the introduction to this chapter, the role and responsibilities of the state emergency management office have changed significantly, both in focus and scope, since passage of the Federal Civil Defense Act of 1950. During the 1950s and 1960s, the state "civil defense" office was primarily responsible for coordination with its designated federal counterpart to disseminate information on civil defense, to maintain civil defense communications, and to provide for civil defense training programs. The increased incidence of technological disasters in the 1970s and 1980s precipitated the transition to an all-hazard approach to emergency management and the emergence of state offices with a much broader scope of responsibility. The state emergency management office, as one report notes, has evolved from being a relatively small and obscure line agency with limited planning, training, and response capabilities to its present status as an integral part of state government.[5]

State emergency management agencies may vary in organizational structure, but most are organized to provide the following basic functions: (1) emergency management planning, (2) emergency management training and exercising, (3) emergency operations, and (4) disaster assistance.

State emergency operations plan   Each state has a state emergency operations plan that identifies the state emergency authorities, incorporates the statewide hazard analysis, and specifies the roles and responsibilities of state departments and agencies in preparedness, response, recovery, and mitigation activities.

The state emergency operations plan is the official document that guides state action in the event of a disaster. Given the broad range of natural and technological hazards for which states and their localities must be prepared, coupled with the proliferation of federal and state regulations pertaining to disasters, emergency authorities and responsibilities must be clearly delineated in state statutes and in the state emergency operations plan in order to avoid interagency and intergovernmental conflict when disaster does occur. Chemical accidents, for example, typically require interagency coordination involving state emergency management staff, the state environmental agency, state public safety personnel, and local authorities. Ambiguity or uncertainty with respect to lines of authority and responsibility may lead to conflict in emergency operations and in cleanup.

Emergency management training   In many instances, local officials become aware of the existence and role of the state emergency management office through the latter's training and exercise function. Each state has a FEMA-funded training officer who coordinates the delivery of federally funded emergency management training programs throughout the state. The training courses are designed to enable states and communities to prevent disasters whenever possible, to achieve preparedness, to respond to disasters of all types, and to be in a better position to recover from natural, technological, or civil disasters, including nuclear attack. FEMA develops and delivers training and education programs to the states through its National Emergency Training Center (NETC) in Emmitsburg, Maryland, the site of the Emergency Management Institute and the National Fire Academy.

Universities are beginning to assume a more prominent role in the delivery of emergency management training and education. As emergency management continues to gain wider acceptance as an important function of government, more and more colleges and universities are offering emergency management courses, particularly in their schools of public administration and urban and regional planning. (North Texas State is the first university to offer a separate undergraduate degree in emergency management.) In essence, state offices recognize the important role and potential contribution of the university system in the area of emergency management training, and increasing collaboration between the two groups is expected.

The state office is also responsible for coordinating all emergency training associated with exercises for the nation's nuclear plants, or "fixed nuclear facilities." The Nuclear Regulatory Commission requires each nuclear facility owner to be able to demonstrate an evacuation capability for a fixed radius surrounding the facility. This requirement translates into a significant level of annual training for emergency workers, hospital officials, elected officials, and other state and local personnel responsible for evacuation planning and exercising. The Tennessee Emergency Management Agency, for example, conducts annual training for an estimated thirty-five hundred state and local officials in preparation for an exercise for a single nuclear plant.

Training has become an important tool for the state emergency management office in promoting hazard awareness across the state and in enhancing political support for emergency management. Training has also become instrumental in promoting a closer working relationship with industry—especially with respect to contingency planning for hazardous materials. SARA Title III, in particular, has served as a catalyst in improving coordination and cooperation between government and industry in the field of hazardous materials. The extensive planning and training requirements under Title III and the accelerated timetable for implementing the provisions of the act have essentially mandated that key officials in the public and private sectors join forces to develop local plans and conduct training. In many instances, industry has taken the lead role.

Increasingly, state offices are developing customized emergency management training curricula to reflect priorities and requirements within their own states. The California Specialized Training Institute, for example, offers courses on urban search and rescue and other aspects of response planning for earthquakes. Tennessee's vulnerability to hazardous materials accidents has served as the stimulus for the creation, beginning in 1980, of a comprehensive hazardous materials training curriculum that is delivered to thousands of emergency response personnel across the state. Finally, many states are taking innovative approaches to the delivery of emergency training to an increasingly broad audience: Tennessee and California are among a growing number of states using teleconferencing to deliver training statewide.

Emergency operations Local government has the primary responsibility for emergency response, but there are times when a disaster overwhelms local government's capacity for effective response. The state office's emergency operations function includes those activities that are essential to a coordinated response in support of a local jurisdiction, such as alerting and warning, emergency communications, and the broadcast of emergency information to the public.

The state emergency operations center (EOC) is the state command post for coordination during disasters. When a disaster occurs, the state EOC becomes activated, and the governor mobilizes and deploys state personnel, equipment, and other resources to the disaster scene in support of local government.

The most important state resource in a disaster consists of the scores of state agency personnel who are trained to assess damage to public and privately owned facilities; to assist local government in warning and notification and, if necessary, the evacuation of the threatened populace; to open and operate shelters; and to assist in cleaning up the affected area. The state emergency operations plan outlines the roles, responsibilities, and resources of key state agencies that can support local government in the event of a disaster.

Disaster assistance   The state emergency management office's disaster assistance function refers to those activities designed to get a community back on its feet following a disaster. In its role as intermediary, the state office provides direct support to local government, when requested, and coordinates the delivery of federal disaster assistance to local jurisdictions (Chapter 9, on recovery, discusses state and federal disaster assistance in more depth). More specifically, the state emergency management office serves the following functions in a disaster:

Damage assessment, which is based on procedures developed by the state office to determine the scope and magnitude of damage to a local jurisdiction following a disaster. Damage assessment is a critical step in disaster response and recovery, and reporting procedures and format must be clearly understood by local authorities.

Coordination and deployment of state disaster assistance resources. In many instances, state programs and resources are sufficient to assist local jurisdictions following a disaster.

Request for a presidential declaration of a major disaster or emergency under P.L. 93–288, Disaster Relief Act of 1974, as amended. When a disaster occurs that "is of such severity and magnitude that effective response is beyond the capability of the state and affected local govern-

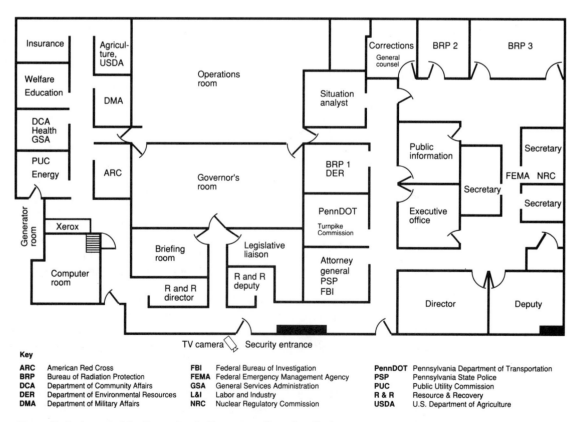

Key

ARC	American Red Cross	**FBI**	Federal Bureau of Investigation	**PennDOT**	Pennsylvania Department of Transportation
BRP	Bureau of Radiation Protection	**FEMA**	Federal Emergency Management Agency	**PSP**	Pennsylvania State Police
DCA	Department of Community Affairs	**GSA**	General Services Administration	**PUC**	Public Utility Commission
DER	Department of Environmental Resources	**L&I**	Labor and Industry	**R & R**	Resource & Recovery
DMA	Department of Military Affairs	**NRC**	Nuclear Regulatory Commission	**USDA**	U.S. Department of Agriculture

Figure 5–1   Layout of the Pennsylvania Emergency Operation Center.

ment(s)" and federal assistance is required to save lives and protect property, the state office prepares the presidential declaration request for the governor's signature.

Coordination with FEMA and other agencies to provide disaster assistance to eligible recipients under the public assistance or individual assistance programs, or both. The "state coordinating officer," usually a representative of the state emergency management office, works closely with his or her federal counterpart to coordinate the delivery of disaster assistance benefits in the jurisdictions included in the presidential disaster declaration.

Relationship with local government

The state emergency management office has the responsibility for administering federal funds (primarily from FEMA) to assist local government in developing and maintaining an all-hazard emergency management system. In this capacity, the state office has a unique relationship with local government, a relationship governed by two related objectives: (1) to ensure that federal dollars are used in a manner consistent with federal policy (including the requirement for attack preparedness), and (2) to provide direct support to local governments as they develop emergency management capability. Support in the latter context includes provision of technical assistance in the preparation of local emergency operations

---

When is it appropriate to request a presidential declaration? One of the most controversial and misunderstood aspects of disaster assistance is the fundamental issue of what constitutes a major disaster. Federal authorities have attempted to apply quantifiable indicators and formulas to the assessment process, but judging a request for a disaster declaration essentially depends ultimately on whether the disaster was of such magnitude and severity that a combination of state and local resources is simply not adequate to respond effectively to the situation.

To minimize conflict and controversy, particularly in a marginal disaster, state and local officials can take three interrelated actions. First, to avoid inflated or unrealistic expectations, they can ensure that key decision makers and the media understand the actual impact of disaster on local and state resources; for instance, damage figures may be in the millions of dollars, but if resources are available, including private insurance, for effective recovery, it is not necessary to

obtain a presidential disaster declaration. Second, it is important that local officials work with the state emergency management office to review damage assessment procedures and forms; an accurate picture of damages to public and private facilities is essential to determining the overall impact of the disaster. Predisaster training programs, offered by the state office, address the key features of damage assessment. Third, state and local officials should keep accurate records of local resources applied during the response and recovery phases and determine the level of resources (including tax revenues) available for the remainder of the recovery process. In a declared disaster, certain categories of local expenditures (such as personnel costs associated with disaster response) can be reimbursed on a matching basis, which reinforces the importance of accurate record keeping. These three steps, taken collectively, should facilitate the intergovernmental decision-making process with respect to a presidential declaration of a major disaster or emergency.

plans; training support; and direct funding assistance through FEMA's Emergency Management Assistance (EMA) program.

The EMA program, administered by the state emergency management office, provides federal matching funds to all states—and through them to approximately twenty-seven hundred local jurisdictions—to "increase the operational capability for emergency management at state and local levels of government, including development and maintenance of trained, experienced staff of full-time emergency management personnel."[6] In practice, approximately half the jurisdictions that receive EMA funds have populations of twenty-five thousand or less, and the average allocation for jurisdictions in this population category is $5,500 per fiscal year.[7] Although funding levels have actually decreased in recent years in terms of real dollars, the EMA program remains an important tool for the state emergency management director and the principal source of external funds for local jurisdictions. The EMA program will be discussed in greater detail in a later section.

In most states, the emergency management function at the local level is carried out in large part by volunteer civil defense or emergency management personnel and by ambulance and emergency medical personnel, fire fighters, and other related professional groups that are involved in a multidisciplinary approach to

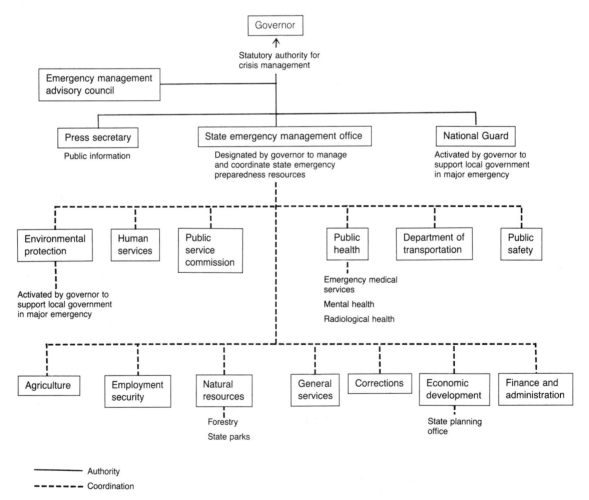

Figure 5–2 State agencies with emergency management responsibilities. This model depicts state emergency management under the governor.

emergency management. These groups form the nucleus of the emergency management (or emergency services) councils, which have become important mechanisms for coordinating the policies, programs, and activities of these organizations and for improving the relationship between the state emergency management office and local government.

Other state agencies

Emergency management, by definition, requires extensive coordination. A major function of the state emergency management office is to coordinate state resources and activities so that when a disaster does occur, a range of resources can be deployed in a timely manner to support local government response and recovery operations. Figure 5–2 depicts some of the key state agencies that have emergency preparedness, response, recovery, or mitigation responsibilities. The basic tenet of emergency management in an intergovernmental system is that the problem should be addressed, whenever possible, at the local level. If the disaster is of such magnitude that local resources are overwhelmed, however, state resources are available to assist local government, and if these resources are insufficient, then federal resources can be made available. The accompanying sidebar outlines

---

State agency emergency management functions in support of local government

Emergency management function	Principal state agencies
Direction and control in emergency	State emergency management (through governor)
Warning and notification	State emergency management
Communications	State emergency management Public safety
Public information	Governor's office State emergency management
Shelter and mass care	American Red Cross Human services
Evacuation	State emergency management National Guard
Law enforcement	Public safety National Guard
Damage assessment	
Public buildings	General services
Electric power	Public service commission
Unemployment	Employment security
Housing	Human services
Farms	Agriculture
Water supply	Environmental protection
Roads and bridges	Transportation
State agency coordination for damage assessment	State emergency management
Hazardous materials	
Identification and assessment	Environmental protection
Emergency response	State emergency management
Cleanup	Environmental protection
Radiological monitoring	Environmental protection

---

the primary emergency management functions provided by state government, as well as the state agencies that typically have responsibility for those functions.

State environmental protection   Most state agencies do not become involved in emergency management until a disaster occurs, at which time each agency is called upon to carry out its predetermined responsibilities. One exception to this general rule is the state environmental protection agency. Title III of SARA accelerated a trend that began in the 1970s—namely, the increased attention given to technological hazards, and specifically to accidental releases of hazardous chemicals.

The state environmental protection agency and state emergency management office are becoming more closely aligned in response to the increasing number of reported incidents involving hazardous substances. Statutory responsibilities for hazardous materials preparedness vary from state to state (for example, half of the Title III state emergency response councils are chaired by the state EPA; the other half are chaired by the directors of the state emergency management office). One of the most positive aspects of Title III is that it has prompted greater coordination among state and local agencies in hazard identification, hazard analysis, disaster response, and cleanup responsibilities.

Emergency medical services   When a disaster occurs, medical and health care personnel are suddenly called upon to provide emergency services to a poten-

Role of the National Guard   The National Guard, which includes the Army and Air National Guard, is a unique resource available to the governor when public safety is in jeopardy or during other extraordinary circumstances. Although its federal reserve role has been strengthened (units support active U.S. military forces around the world), the National Guard of each state remains, constitutionally, a state-administered force. The Guard's mission is (1) to provide units trained and equipped to protect life and property and (2) to preserve peace, order, and public safety, under the orders of state and federal authorities.

The National Guard's resources and expertise are extensive and include the following: trained medical personnel, evacuation units, search and rescue capability, aviation support, ground transportation, forest fire support, and emergency shelter capability (through the network of National Guard armories). These resources are most often activated to assist civil authorities in responding to and recovering from disasters involving natural or technological hazards, including flooding, drought, forest fires, and ice storms and other severe weather. More recently, state authorities have used National Guard resources to support drug enforcement operations.

Generally, governors are reluctant to activate the National Guard. In addition to the cost entailed, there are psychological factors involved. As a military force, the National Guard represents the governor's ultimate recourse in a disaster including a civil disturbance, and governors do not wish to be perceived as having to routinely rely on the military sector to handle situations that can in fact be handled by state and local officials. Nevertheless, there are occasions when National Guard resources are needed. Guard personnel respond to an average of 400 to 500 call-ups per year across the nation, mostly for natural disasters and other emergencies.

tially large number of people under very stressful conditions. Intergovernmental coordination is therefore extraordinarily critical in the field of emergency medical services (EMS). To encourage such coordination, Congress in 1973 passed P.L. 93–154, the Emergency Medical Services Systems Act (EMSSA), which provides funding to more than one hundred community or regional EMS authorities to develop comprehensive EMS delivery systems. The law further specifies fifteen separate functions that must be included in such systems. The state EMS agency, which in most states is a division of the state health department, is responsible for statewide coordination and implementation of EMS activities. The EMSSA requires "disaster linkage"—that is, the coordination of local, regional, and state disaster plans—but one authority notes that EMS planning is still fragmented, owing in part to the great number of agencies and levels of government involved in EMS.[8] To develop more successful EMS preparedness programs, "persons with responsibility for emergency management at different levels of government need to exchange information with local, regional, and state EMS officials and providers, as well as with public and private health care organizations . . . . EMS disaster preparedness planning should be an element in comprehensive local, regional, state, and federal preparedness programs, not a separate effort."[9]

Summary

In summary, as the scope of emergency management has expanded, the state office has achieved legitimacy in state government. Emergency management has become a clearly defined function. In view of the spectrum of natural and technological hazards to which a state is typically vulnerable, the state director has become an increasingly important member of the governor's cabinet. Title III of SARA has further accelerated the trend toward the formation of integrated emergency management councils at the state and local levels. Although the state office has taken on new responsibilities and achieved greater visibility, the basic role of the office has remained unchanged: to support local government in all aspects of disaster mitigation, preparedness, response, and recovery.

Role and responsibilities of the federal government

As pointed out in Chapter 1, numerous changes have occurred over the years in federal organization and functions related to emergency management. Since the New Deal and World War II, the federal emergency management function has been assigned to a number of agencies, each with its own acronym; new programs and organizations have been created and then summarily dissolved; and periodic attempts have been made to improve management and coordination by consolidation of civil defense programs under one agency. This administrative pattern prompted one congressional committee member to observe that federal emergency preparedness in the United States has "a history that resembles an alphabet soup."[10]

Federal government organization of the emergency management function may have undergone a number of changes, but the basic role of the federal government in emergency management has remained essentially the same: to protect life and property in a disaster and to assist state and local governments in the recovery process. Various aspects of the efforts to implement that role—federal policy, programs, and funding levels—have clearly changed over the years, often as the direct result of a disaster. The Cuban missile crisis, Hurricane Agnes, and the Three Mile Island incident are examples of emergencies that have had a profound effect on federal emergency management policy.

Role of the president

There are three principal categories of emergencies under which the president has traditionally exercised emergency powers: economic emergencies, national security emergencies, and natural and technological disasters.[11] In the economic sphere, for example, the Great Depression led to the enactment of the Federal Emergency Relief Act of 1933, which opened with a declaration that the depression had created a serious emergency because of widespread unemployment and the inadequacy of state and local relief funds. Since 1933, Congress has authorized the president to declare economic emergencies in a number of situations in response to perceived threats to national welfare, security, or defense.

National security has always been a central responsibility of the chief executive, and with the passage of the Federal Civil Defense Act of 1950, civil defense became a recognized arm of the U.S. national security system. Chapter 1 chronicled the series of executive orders enacted since 1950 to implement the act. Civil defense is a component of the national security strategy, which is coordinated by the National Security Council (NSC). The policies and strategies of the NSC are translated into national security decision directives (NSDDs), which in the aggregate guide the preparation of foreign and defense policy. In February 1987, President Ronald Reagan issued NSDD 259, which redefined U.S. civil defense policy and, among other provisions, assigned priority to the development of survivable state and local crisis management capabilities, including a network of emergency operating centers able to withstand the effects of nuclear attack, other technological disasters, and natural disasters.

The third category of emergency powers enjoyed by the president, as authorized by Congress, is response to and recovery from major disasters. P.L. 93–288, the Disaster Relief Act of 1974, as amended, authorizes the president to declare an "emergency" or "major disaster" for an area affected by a disaster, and where state and local resources are inadequate to respond effectively and to undertake recovery. Once a presidential declaration has been made, FEMA may direct any federal agency to assist state and local governments directly. In recent years, the definition of "emergency" has been expanded to include technological emergencies and civil disturbances; and, in effect, P.L. 93–288 has become a vehicle for the president to authorize the use of federal resources in a relatively wide variety of situations that overwhelm state and local response and recovery capabilities. For example, in 1980 funds were authorized under P.L. 93–288 to help the state of Florida resettle Cuban refugees.

Creation of the Federal Emergency Management Agency

One of the most persistent problems in the relatively brief history of emergency management has been in fragmentation of government functions, particularly at the federal level.[12] Before 1979, federal responsibility for civil defense and for mitigation, preparedness, response, and recovery for natural and technological hazards was spread among six separate federal agencies. There was a growing consensus among the Carter administration, the National Governors' Association, Congress, and the emergency management community that the federal emergency management function needed to be reorganized, and more specifically that a lead agency was needed to coordinate federal programs related to emergency management. Reorganization Plan No. 3 of 1978, which proposed the creation of FEMA (the Federal Emergency Management Agency), rested on four fundamental principles:

1. Federal authorities to anticipate, prepare for, and respond to major civil emergencies should be supervised by one official responsible to the president and given attention by other officials at the highest levels.

2. An effective civil defense system requires the most efficient use of all available resources. . . . The communications, warning, evacuation, and public education processes involved in preparedness for a possible nuclear attack should be developed, tested, and used for major natural and accidental disasters as well.
3. Whenever possible, emergency responsibilities should be extensions of the regular missions of the federal agencies.
4. Federal hazard mitigation activities should be closely linked with emergency preparedness and response functions.[13]

The creation of FEMA represented a milestone in the evolution of emergency management in the United States. As one observer noted, "In light of the many changes in policy and organization since the 1950s, the creation of FEMA can be viewed as a grand experiment involving a recasting of the federal role in emergency management and a new approach to fulfilling that role."[14]

FEMA'S role and responsibilities

FEMA was created to be the catalyst in an intergovernmental system of emergency management. As envisioned by the coalition of groups at the state and local levels that supported the reorganization, FEMA would become the lead agency—the central point of contact for emergency managers, volunteer agencies, business and industry, the fire service community, the law enforcement community, and other groups with responsibility for public safety and protection of property in the event of a disaster. From a federal perspective, the reorganization would centralize planning and coordination for natural, technological, and civil hazards within one independent, lead federal agency. As the sidebar on page 114 indicates, FEMA's statutory responsibilities, and the programs established to carry out those responsibilities, are diverse. Emergency management organization and resources also show considerable diversity at state and local levels, which presents FEMA with a challenge in developing programs that can be applied to a broad range of communities addressing a broad range of hazards.[15]

To carry out its statutory responsibilities, FEMA is organized at the national level into the following five divisions or directorates: (1) Federal Insurance Administration (FIA), (2) External Affairs Directorate, (3) National Preparedness Directorate, (4) U.S. Fire Administration, and (5) State and Local Programs and Support Directorate. Ten FEMA regional offices work with state emergency management offices and local agencies to coordinate FEMA programs, administer FEMA funding, and make certain that state and local programs reflect national program objectives.

The directorate with the most day-to-day contact with state and local emergency management, private sector leaders, elected and appointed officials, and other state and local groups is the State and Local Programs and Support Directorate (SLPS). The following section highlights some of FEMA's efforts under that directorate.

Activities of FEMA's State and Local Programs and Support Directorate

Since its creation in 1979, FEMA has faced the formidable task of developing a cohesive, integrated national program for emergency management that addresses the unique requirements of the fifty states and their localities. Historically, at least two factors have hindered the development of a strong, integrated program: first, national legislation and policy are typically hazard specific (earthquakes, dam safety, flooding, fixed nuclear facility accidents), an orientation that has shaped the state and local programs designed to implement the national policy; the result, in many instances, has been a hazard-specific, compartmentalized

**FEMA's statutory responsibilities
and the national programs designed
to implement the policy**

Statutory and executive authority	Programs administered
Federal Civil Defense Act of 1950, as amended	Program for population protection, preparedness, and response in emergency conditions ranging from a peacetime disaster to an enemy attack.
Federal Fire Protection and Control Act of 1974	Programs to reduce national fire loss, including training and education.
National Flood Insurance Act of 1968 and the Flood Disaster Protection Act of 1973	Program to provide flood insurance and to encourage better floodplain management.
Disaster Relief Act of 1974, as amended	Programs to provide assistance to individuals and to state and local governments in presidentially declared disaster areas.
National Security Act of 1974, as amended; Strategic and Critical Materials Stockpiling Act, as amended; and Defense Production Act of 1950, as amended	Programs to provide for continuity of government, emergency resource assessment and management, post-attack economic recovery and stabilization, and policy guidance for stockpiling strategic materials.
Earthquake Hazards Reduction Act of 1977	Programs to identify and reduce earthquake vulnerabilities and consequences.
Nuclear Regulatory Commission FY 1980 Appropriation Authorization Act and related presidential directives	Off-site emergency preparedness for fixed nuclear facilities.
Executive Order 12148	Oversight of the national dam safety program.
Comprehensive Environmental Response and Liability Act and Executive Order 12316	Specific emergency response activities, including those of the National Response Team.

approach to emergency management. Second, state and local emergency management agencies have traditionally been very dependent on FEMA for funding support. The relatively static level of federal funding, coupled with fiscal constraints at the state and local levels, has weakened the capacities of state and local governments to develop comprehensive emergency management programs.[16]

Having recognized that it was fostering a single-hazard orientation, FEMA developed a more integrated, functional, multihazard approach to emergency management, an approach known as the integrated emergency management system, or IEMS. Through IEMS, FEMA has identified fifteen functions common to most disasters, such as operations planning, direction and control, emergency communications, alerting and warning, sheltering, and evacuation. In implementing the IEMS approach to emergency management, FEMA signaled a shift away from single-hazard planning and emphasized the development of preparedness and response capability for all hazards, including hostile attack.

Although FEMA has the lead role in coordinating national functions related to natural, technological, and civil hazards, the implementation of these programs rests with state and local government. Three well-defined federal programs, in particular, have shaped state and local emergency management: Emergency Management Assistance (EMA), the National Earthquake Hazards Reduction Program (NEHRP), and Radiological Emergency Preparedness (REP).

Emergency Management Assistance Emergency Management Assistance, a program within the Office of Civil Defense (SLPS), provides grants to state and local governments to cover as much as 50 percent of salaries, travel expenses, and other administrative costs essential to day-to-day operation. The goal of the program is to "develop and maintain a cadre of emergency managers and supporting staff to coordinate state and local response activities during emergencies."[17] In fiscal year 1987, EMA funds supported 5,523 local emergency management personnel and 1,251 state emergency management personnel. In return, the participants in the EMA program are expected to develop and maintain an emergency operations plan that incorporates all hazards faced by that jurisdiction, including hostile attack; to participate in an exercise of the plan; and to submit reports to the state emergency management office.

EMA is the primary funding mechanism and program for implementing the provisions of the Federal Civil Defense Act of 1950, as amended, at the state and local levels. The 1981 amendment to the act permits the "dual use" of civil defense program funds (including EMA) for peacetime disasters, including natural and technological disasters, "to the extent that the use of such funds for such purposes is consistent with, contributes to, and does not detract from attack-related civil defense preparedness." To assist state and local governments in meeting national program objectives, FEMA has issued a series of "civil preparedness guides" (CPGs) on a number of subjects, including the *Guide for Development of State and Local Emergency Operations Plans*.[18] In practice, FEMA's is a somewhat sensitive situation. As the lead federal agency with the responsibility for national civil preparedness, FEMA must ensure that state and local programs, at least those that receive EMA funding, address civil defense preparedness. At the same time, the agency acknowledges the political implications of overemphasizing attack preparedness in an era of limited federal funding to support preparedness for more likely disasters.[19]

National Earthquake Hazards Reduction Program Until the late 1970s and early 1980s, few state and local officials outside of California recognized the potential impact of earthquakes on their communities. Yet the U.S. Geological Survey has determined that at least forty-three states are vulnerable to a damaging earthquake. Earthquakes are unique in their unpredictability and in their potential for inflicting significant damage over a multistate area.

In 1977, Congress passed the Earthquake Hazards Reduction Act, which created the National Earthquake Hazards Reduction Program (NEHRP). The goals of the NEHRP are to reduce future losses of life and property from earthquakes and to prevent the severe socioeconomic disruption that a catastrophic earthquake could cause. The act further directed FEMA to take the lead agency role in coordinating federal research, hazard mitigation, and disaster preparedness activities. Figure 5–3 outlines the major elements of the NEHRP and the federal agencies that have primary responsibility for implementing the program: FEMA (lead agency), the U.S. Geological Survey (USGS), the National Institute of Science and Technology (NIST), and the National Science Foundation (NSF).

Civil defense initiatives under National Security Decision Directive 259 "It is the policy of the United States to have a civil defense capability as an element of our overall national security posture." President Reagan's signing of National Security Decision Directive 259 on 4 February 1987 provided the impetus for a series of FEMA initiatives to enhance the civil defense program. Directive 259 cites a number of national program objectives, including improving state and local crisis management and population protection capabilities. The conceptual basis for the NSDD is an emphasis on the development of a "civil defense infrastructure capable of rapid expansion in a national security emergency" or a series of "surge" actions (such as rapid dissemination of emergency public information) that can be implemented over a short period of time.

To improve state and local crisis management, FEMA has reallocated resources to three functional areas: national attack warning systems (NAWAS), protected radio emergency broadcast systems (EBS), and emergency operations centers (EOCs). To improve population protection capabilities, FEMA is developing standby materials that can be disseminated by the mass media during a crisis as part of a series of actions that can be taken during a "surge" period (a period of heightened tension).

FEMA's rationale in upgrading the NAWAS and EBS systems and other hardware is twofold. First, because of minimal funding and upkeep in previous years, these systems and facilities had deteriorated to a point that their reliability and ability to survive a disaster would be jeopardized without additional funding. Second, these systems have dual use benefits in peacetime emergencies, particularly during severe weather. Many critics would argue, however, that until Congress becomes serious about nuclear attack preparedness and authorizes funding levels commensurate with the scope of the potential threat, current programs will have negligible impact. As the chairman of the House Armed Services subcommittee that oversees FEMA's civil defense programs remarked in a 1987 hearing, "I think civil defense, with respect to nuclear attack, is an illusion" (Ronald Dellums [D-CA], hearing before Subcommittee on Military Preparedness Installations and Facilities, Committee on Armed Services, House of Representatives, March 5, 1987). Nevertheless, FEMA's mandate continues to be the development of a national civil preparedness capability through increased emphasis on enhancing state and local crisis management capabilities, particularly EOCs.

Radiological Emergency Preparedness   The third major preparedness program administered by FEMA's State and Local Programs and Support Directorate is Radiological Emergency Preparedness (REP), which addresses intergovernmental coordination in emergency response planning for radiological accidents at fixed nuclear facilities and for radiological accidents involving the transportation of nuclear materials.

The Three Mile Island incident in 1979 heightened concern about the potential for a serious mishap at a nuclear facility and demonstrated the need for close coordination among federal agencies, utility owners and operators, and state and local agencies with public safety responsibilities. The federal role in radiological emergency response and preparedness is defined in the Interagency Agreement, updated in 1980, which established the Federal Radiological Preparedness Coordinating Committee, chaired by FEMA, to ensure that key federal agencies coordinate their activities and responsibilities, particularly as related to state and local governments. Figure 5–4 outlines the structure of the federal agency coordination and cooperation with state and local gov-

Figure 5–3 The nine elements of the National Earthquake Hazards Reduction Program and the agencies primarily responsible for their implementation.

Leadership	Lead agency activities	FEMA
Earthquake potential and hazard assessment	Earthquake potential assessment: Source zone characterization and long-term forecasts	USGS
	Earthquake hazard assessments	USGS
Earthquake prediction research	Prediction methodology	USGS
	Earthquake prediction experiments	USGS
	Theoretical, laboratory, and fault zone studies	USGS
	Induced seismicity	USGS
Earthquake engineering research	Strong ground-motion data collection, processing, and analysis	USGS
	Siting and geotechnical engineering research	NSF
	Structural analysis and design research	NSF
	Computer methods and expert systems research	NSF
	Architectural and nonstructural components research	NSF
	Research facilities	NSF
	Research for standards	NIST
Earthquake planning and mitigation	Development of design practices and manuals	FEMA
	Federal response planning	FEMA
	State and local earthquake hazard reduction	FEMA
	Multihazard planning	FEMA
	Insurance	FEMA
	Earthquake systems integration	NSF
Fundamental earthquake studies	Implications of plate tectonics	NSF
	Earthquake processes	NSF
Information systems and dissemination	Engineering information services	NSF
	Seismologic data and information services	USGS
	Education and information transfer	FEMA
Postearthquake studies		FEMA/NSF/ USGS/NIST
International cooperation	International research	NSF/USGS/
	International Decade for Natural Disaster Reduction	FEMA/NIST

Key
NIST National Institute of Science and Technology
NSF National Science Foundation
USGS U.S. Geological Survey

Role of state and local government in the National Earthquake Hazards Reduction Program The effectiveness of the National Earthquake Hazards Reduction Program hinges on the level and quality of state and local programs for reducing the impact of earthquakes. To facilitate earthquake preparedness efforts, FEMA provides funding to states that are seismically vulnerable, and the states in turn work with local jurisdictions to reduce earthquake hazards. The Bay Area Regional Earthquake Preparedness Project, for example, has been active in developing preparedness guidelines for five local jurisdictions, including guidelines for hospitals and medical facilities, schools, and other critical facilities. Utah has collaborated with the private sector in Salt Lake City to develop a videotape on earthquake awareness and preparedness that received an award from the Academy of Television Arts and Sciences. The Central U.S. Earthquake Consortium, a seven-state earthquake preparedness organization based in Memphis, uses a computer-based data management resource inventory system to coordinate the deployment of resources in the event of an earthquake on the New Madrid Fault. The Southern California Earthquake Preparedness Project has developed a local incentive grant program to provide direct grants to local jurisdictions for innovative projects that are transferable. In many respects, the earthquake preparedness program is an excellent example of how an intergovernmental system for emergency preparedness can function.

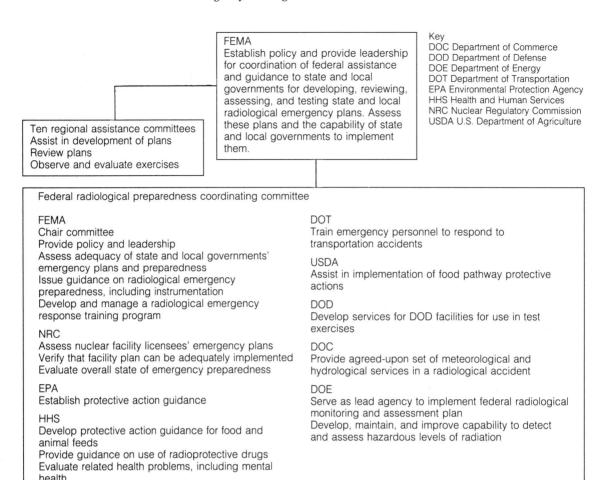

Figure 5–4 Significant responsibilities of federal agencies and committees in providing emergency planning guidance for radiological emergencies. (As of July 1990, there were eight additional federal agencies participating in the coordinating committee: Department of Housing and Urban Development, Department of the Interior, Department of State, Department of Veterans Affairs, Federal Bureau of Investigation, General Services Administration, National Aeronautics and Space Administration, and National Communications System.)

ernment and depicts the primary responsibilities of federal agencies in radiological emergency response and preparedness.

In most states, the state emergency management office is the central coordinating agency in the development of radiological emergency preparedness plans, and the state office conducts extensive training with local officials in exercising these plans. For a nuclear facility to receive an operating license or to be relicensed, the facility must demonstrate to the Nuclear Regulatory Commission, through a successful exercise of a radiological preparedness plan, that the local population can be warned in a timely manner and, if necessary, safely evacuated and sheltered in the event of an accident. Although the likelihood of an accident at one of the nation's fixed nuclear facilities is remote, the technical training that local officials receive can become an asset in responding to other emergencies. In many instances, for example, the nuclear facility operator will fund improvements to the local emergency operations center, particularly the communications system, to ensure that the warning and notification system will function properly.

FEMA's Office of Training

Another section of FEMA important from a state and local perspective is the Office of Training, whose activities extend over all five directorates. Formally established in 1987, it oversees the training functions of the Emergency Management Institute and the National Fire Academy, which together constitute FEMA's National Emergency Training Center (NETC). Training is carried out through a resident program at the NETC central campus at Emmitsburg, Maryland, and through an outreach program administered by state emergency management offices.

Emergency Management Institute   The Emergency Management Institute (EMI), a part of NETC, is the national center for the development and delivery of civil defense and emergency management training programs. Approximately 4,000 emergency management professionals take a range of courses at EMI each year, while about 70,000 participate in nonresident training sponsored by and coordinated through the state emergency management office.

The curricula at EMI are designed both to meet the practical training needs of state and local emergency managers and to support the development of a national civil defense program. EMI's program also supports FEMA's goal of developing a trained cadre of emergency management professionals across the nation. The course series that have been offered in the past, on a resident or nonresident basis, include professional development, executive development/management, natural hazards, radiological preparedness, hazardous materials, and national emergency preparedness. The institute is not an accredited academic institution and therefore cannot grant college credit or degrees, but certain courses have been recommended for credit equivalency under the Non-Collegiate Sponsored Instruction Program of the American Council on Education.

National Fire Academy   The National Fire Academy, also located at NETC, is the national focal point for advancing the professional development of fire service personnel. The academy also trains professionals in allied fields such as code enforcement, architecture, city management and administration, planning, and emergency medical services. On-campus and off-campus courses address a broad range of subjects reflecting national priorities, including fire service technology, fire incident management, fire prevention and risk management, public fire education, fire service management, and hazardous materials. In addition, the academy's curriculum plan allows individuals to take a designated series of courses to become better qualified as fire service technical specialists, command and staff officers, or executive fire officers.

The academy's off-campus programs are delivered by state and local fire training agency staff, adjunct academy faculty, and Fire Academy trained trainers. More than 200,000 participate in these off-campus programs. Courses are offered in every state and are usually taught on weekends to allow for maximum participation of volunteer fire personnel.

FEMA's National Preparedness Directorate

The largest portion of FEMA's budget supports the National Preparedness Directorate (NPD), which addresses the national and federal preparedness provisions and authorities designated in the Federal Civil Defense Act of 1950, the National Security Act, and the Defense Production Act. The NPD develops and coor-

Innovation and research at the Emergency Management Institute   The integrated emergency management course (IEMC), one of the most popular courses offered by the Emergency Management Institute (EMI), stresses a community approach to emergency management; it is unique in that the entire executive staff of a community is put through the course, including elected and appointed officials, legal counsel, emergency managers, and other key management personnel. The course, which has been taught in the field as well as at EMI, provides an excellent opportunity for management staff to develop and exercise emergency management programs and to interact under simulated and often stressful conditions. A number of cities from across the nation have sent their staffs to the IEMC course, including Atlanta, Baltimore, Boulder, Los Angeles, and Philadelphia. The IEMC has also been taught in the field in cities including Des Moines, Kansas City (Missouri), Portland (Oregon), and San Francisco. Information on the IEMC and other courses can be obtained through the training officer of the state emergency management office.

In addition to the IEMC, the EMI has pursued other innovative approaches to delivering emergency training. The Emergency Education Network (EENET) is FEMA's system for providing video training and educational programming via satellite to fire service and emergency management personnel and other professionals nationwide. Administered by FEMA's Office of Training, EENET uses satellite videoconferencing (one-way video and two-way audio) to broadcast live training activities to thousands of sites across the United States. EENET's broadcasts have been used in conjunction with such programs as Title III of SARA to deliver a substantial amount of technical material to a broad audience. Through toll-free telephone systems, participants can interact with experts in the EENET studio in Emmitsburg, Maryland.

As the national focal point for emergency training, the EMI also serves an important research function. Emergency management is a dynamic field: programs and priorities change, new players (the insurance industry, for example) continue to enter the picture, and techniques for application of research continue to evolve. The EMI has an important role in keeping a finger on the pulse of emergency management, including emerging trends, issues, and technologies.

---

dinates national policies and programs for all federal departments and agencies concerning national security emergency management. It does this principally by (1) assessing emergency management resource requirements and assuring the effective management of the nation's resources during a national emergency; (2) conducting research and developing programs to protect the population and key defense-related industries from the effects of domestic or national security emergencies; and (3) developing mobilization plans for FEMA and coordinating these plans with the Department of Defense, the National Security Council, and other federal agencies.

What is the role of local government in an emergency that threatens national security? How does local government fit into the national preparedness efforts of FEMA and other federal agencies? One of the tenets of national preparedness planning is that the nation's ability to respond to and recover from a national emergency is, in large part, a function of how effectively problems can be managed at the local level. The Office of Civil Defense (SLPS) coordinates with NPD to achieve this. The objectives of the civil defense program, as reflected in the NSDD 259, include developing population protection capabilities, developing state and local government crisis management capabilities, and promoting voluntary participation by citizens and institutions in community civil defense. A priority of FEMA is to improve national warning and communications systems so that state and local officials can continue to function in a major emergency.[20] Finally, local government has an important role in the Continuity of Government (COG) program, which delineates the measures that governments at all levels must take to maintain their ability to carry out executive, legislative, and judicial functions in the event of a major emergency. The goals of the COG program are to preserve lawful leadership and authority, prevent the unlawful assumption of authority, preserve vital government documents, and ensure that systems necessary for continued government direction and control are in place before a crisis.[21]

Other federal agencies

Although FEMA has the principal responsibility for coordinating federal programs and resources that affect state and local emergency management, several other federal agencies also have roles and responsibilities in mitigation, preparedness, response, and recovery. The Corps of Engineers, for example, provides a number of services related to flood hazard mitigation and flood emergency operations. Its Flood Plain Management Services provide technical information and advisory services to state and local governments to identify areas subject to flooding and flood losses and to assess the risk of flooding for proposed building sites. Under its Flood Emergency Operations program, the corps can make available specialized emergency assistance, including flood fighting and rescue operation, in times of actual flooding or when flooding is imminent; assistance under this program is provided as a supplement to state and local resources.[22]

The U.S. Geological Survey (USGS) plays a very important role in the National Earthquake Hazards Reduction Program, particularly in the areas of earthquake prediction research, engineering seismology, regional hazards assessment, and data and information services. For state and local governments to develop earthquake mitigation and preparedness programs, they need accurate and credible information on the nature and scope of the earthquake problem. In addressing these information requirements, the USGS emphasizes applied research and has conducted workshops across the country bringing together scientists, engineers, emergency management personnel, business and industry representatives, and members of other key groups with a role in earthquake preparedness. The regional workshops and other USGS projects have made important contributions toward an understanding of the earthquake hazard in the United States.

Other federal agencies also have significant programs related to natural hazards. The U.S. Soil Conservation Service (Department of Agriculture), for example, provides technical assistance in the conservation, development, and use of soil and water resources, including watershed protection and flood protection projects, flood plain studies, resource conservation and development, emergency watershed protection, and soil and snow surveys. The National Weather Service, in addition to its weather-related forecasts and warnings, provides forecasts of water levels of the nation's rivers so that when floods threaten a community, forecasts and warnings can be passed on to the public through mass media and weather radio. The U.S. Coast Guard, meanwhile, is responsible for coordinating federal and state response to discharges of oil and other hazardous pollutants into the nation's river system. In essence, there are a number of federal agencies that have statutory responsibility for mitigation, preparedness, response, and recovery activities related to natural hazards. Local officials should at least be aware of the range of services provided by federal agencies.[23]

Traditionally, emergency management at the federal level has focused on natural hazards, as evidenced by the fact that the Disaster Relief Act of 1974 defines "major disaster" in the context of natural hazards. Technological disasters have usually been relegated to a separate category of "other catastrophes," although the Robert T. Stafford Disaster Relief and Disaster Assistance Act, P.L. 100–707, as amended, does cover technological disasters. Only recently has the federal government assumed an active role in mitigation, preparedness, response, and cleanup for technological disasters. In addition to FEMA, two other federal agencies have significant roles and responsibilities for technological hazards, and specifically for hazardous materials: the Environmental Protection Agency (EPA) and the Department of Transportation (DOT).

The EPA has major responsibility for hazardous materials incident preparedness, response, and cleanup. Under the aegis of the Comprehensive Environmental Response, Compensation, and Liability Act (CERCLA), the EPA prepared the National Contingency Plan (NCP), which outlines federal responsibilities for hazardous materials monitoring, response, and cleanup. The principal mechanisms for implementing the plan are (1) the National Response Team, consisting of fourteen federal agencies—responsible for national coordination of hazardous materials preparedness and also capable of emergency response—and (2) the regional response teams, one per federal region—capable of responding to hazardous materials releases when more than one state is involved or when other extraordinary circumstances necessitate federal support. Another of EPA's major roles in hazardous materials preparedness is to provide technical expertise to federal, state, and local agencies in hazard identification and analysis. For instance, under SARA Title III, the agency is responsible for identifying "extremely hazardous substances"; the chemicals identified become the basis for preparing local emergency response plans. The EPA also coordinates with FEMA in developing and delivering hazardous materials training, with emphasis on vulnerability assessment and risk analysis.

DOT is also an important source of training and technical information related to the transportation of hazardous (including radioactive) materials. The DOT *Emergency Response Guidebook* is particularly useful to state and local emergency first responders and other officials.[24] The DOT also has regulatory authority pertaining to hazardous materials; for example, one DOT regulation requires carriers of hazardous materials to have in their possession shipping papers that identify the nature and properties of the materials—information that can be critical in a disaster response.

As the discussion of FEMA and other federal emergency management programs has made clear, although the federal government has historically been involved in mitigation, preparedness, response, and recovery programs for natural hazards, there is now a clear trend toward a greater federal presence in the management of technological hazards. An examination of the federal role in natural versus technological disasters reveals an interesting contrast.[25] Federal programs for natural disasters focus on mitigation and recovery activities for "acts of God" that are relatively well understood by the public. The federal role in technological hazards, on the other hand, tends to involve more specialized technical expertise and to be more regulatory in nature. Management of technological hazards also has a potential for creating much more public controversy, such as in the case of long-term relocation of a community away from a toxic site, a situation that presents federal agencies with an entirely different set of management problems from those that arise in the aftermath of a natural disaster. The complexity of technological hazards, combined with the public's relative unfamiliarity with them, often complicates emergency response and recovery. As one observer notes, "The major burden of hazard management in developed societies has shifted from risks associated with natural processes to those arising from technological development and application."[26]

Hazardous materials transportation accidents prompt new government-industry initiatives Significant attention has been focused on the SARA Title III program, but states and communities are actually far more vulnerable to accidents involving the transportation of hazardous materials than to the accidental release of hazardous materials by a chemical plant or other fixed site. In Tennessee, for example, more than a thousand accidents per year involve the transportation of hazardous materials, primarily on the road system.

Through the Department of Transportation (DOT), the federal government is developing an aggressive national program to address the transportation of hazardous materials. A number of complex efforts need to be undertaken: determining the regional flow patterns of hazardous materials; promoting uniformity in federal, state, and local regulations governing the transportation of hazardous materials; and developing or enhancing statewide response teams that are adequately trained and equipped to respond to hazardous materials accidents. As was the case with SARA Title III, a national program that addresses transportation-related accidents will require extensive coordination and cooperation among all levels of government and the chemical industry. Each player has a role and responsibility in preparedness for chemical emergencies.

As one step in assessing state and local planning and training requirements, DOT is working with states to develop a database identifying regional flow patterns for hazardous materials. FEMA, in turn, is placing more emphasis on hazardous materials preparedness. (EMI has a separate curriculum devoted to hazardous materials.)

The chemical industry, through the Chemical Manufacturers Association (CMA), has developed a network of programs to assist state and local government and the public in gaining access to information on chemicals and chemical products. CHEMTREC (Chemical Transportation Emergency Center), for example, is a twenty-four-hour center established by the CMA to provide immediate advice to callers on how to cope with chemicals involved in a disaster and to notify shippers and manufacturers of the chemicals so they can take appropriate action. Following the Bhopal, India, accident, the CMA established the Community Awareness and Emergency Response Program (CAER), a voluntary industry-government cooperative preparedness program that was the forerunner of SARA Title III.

States are in a pivotal role in establishing a comprehensive hazardous materials transportation program. In fact, a growing number of states are enacting or considering legislation to integrate transportation of hazardous materials with the state's SARA Title III program. Because transportation of hazardous materials is exempt from SARA Title III (except for an actual release), more and more states are using the local emergency planning committees as the nucleus for expanded training to address transportation-related accidents, notably training for first responders. Several states, for example, are placing priority on developing a regional emergency response capability for hazardous materials accidents (transportation and fixed site). The foundation for a regional response capability is the availability of local officials with hands-on training in the technical aspects of hazardous materials response. Local emergency response personnel are typically the first to arrive on the scene of a hazardous materials accident. In the final analysis, perhaps the most important training for local officials is in how to assess the situation accurately, because, as statistics point out, most casualties related to hazardous materials accidents can be prevented.

International emergency management

On a global basis, disasters are becoming more frequent, more serious, and more deadly. In developing countries, in particular, growing populations and economic pressures are pushing increasing numbers of people into more hazardous locations, usually in major population centers. The more developed countries, including the United States, are not immune from the escalating costs associated with disaster recovery.

Accompanying the steady worldwide increase in damages and casualties from disasters has been the evolution of an international relief system that functions with varying degrees of success following a major disaster. In general terms, the system consists of donor agencies and groups that collect and channel resources and intervenor organizations that actually carry out the disaster relief activities in the field.[27] Examples of intervenors include international relief agencies (such as the U.N. Disaster Relief Organization, the Red Cross, and CARE), as well as church-affiliated and nongovernmental organizations.

Figure 5–5 depicts the complex network of organizations involved in international disaster relief—international organizations, foreign governments, volunteer groups, church-affiliated groups, and others. Adding to the complexity is the fact that these organizations may be motivated by different factors, including

Figure 5–5   Relationships and funding channels in the international relief system.

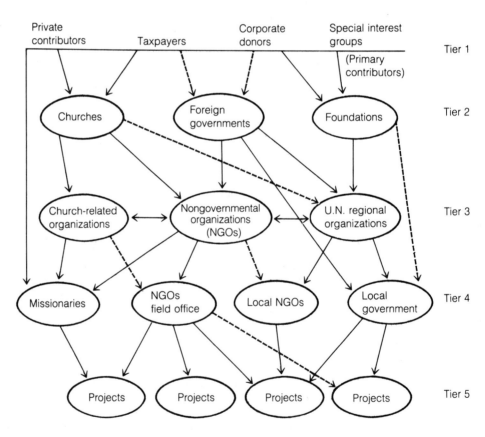

Nine lessons learned from previous international disaster relief operations

1. Because disaster assistance has been viewed predominantly from the standpoint of the intervenors, many common approaches to relief facilitate delivery of assistance. To provide effective aid, agencies must view disaster assistance from the standpoint of the victims and their requirements. For example, disaster-stricken Third World communities often become dependent on donations of goods and services for their daily existence. When these extensive donations are abruptly ended, special problems arise.
2. Many postdisaster needs can be determined on the basis of natural hazard, season, and location.
3. "In almost every disaster, outside agencies underestimate the basic resources still available in communities."
4. Material assistance following disasters is generally far in excess of actual needs; is generally in proportions larger than needed or usable; often requires services and facilities that could be used for more essential tasks; often causes conflicts among relief agencies; generally adds to the problem of congestion; and in some cases may disrupt the local economy.
5. Relief materials from within the disaster-affected country itself are more likely to be compatible with normal use patterns than are those

delivered from a different culture; the most useful materials provided by intervenors are those obtained in or near the disaster area.
6. Re-establishment of the local economy and of job security is usually more important for disaster victims than material assistance is.
7. Assistance provided by international relief agencies rarely plays a major role in the immediate response phase.
8. Because it is unrealistic to assume that foreign assistance sent to a disaster area will be applied in the immediate response phase, emphasis should be shifted from speed of emergency response to developing an appropriate response to intermediate or advanced recovery needs.
9. Contributions from outside donors are most effective in predisaster and reconstruction phases.

Source: Frederick Cuny, *Disasters and Development* (New York: Oxford University Press, 1983): 104–5. Source for statement 3, E. L. Quarantelli and Russell R. Dynes, "When Disaster Strikes (It Isn't Much Like What You've Heard and Read About)," *Psychology Today* 5 (February 1972): 66–70. Source for statement 9, Frederick C. Cuny and Eduardo A. Perez, *Improvement of Low-Cost Housing in Fiji to Withstand Hurricanes and High Winds* (Washington, DC: Office of Foreign Disaster Assistance, Agency for International Development, 1982).

humanitarian reasons, political or geopolitical factors, economic goals, or perhaps even military objectives.[28] The fundamental objective of the five-tiered system is to collect resources and channel them as efficiently as possible to the disaster-stricken area. The first three tiers represent the international level, the fourth tier the regional or country level, and the final tier the project level, where resources are actually distributed to disaster victims.

Despite an increase in the knowledge and expertise now available to minimize the impact of natural hazards, earthquakes, floods, severe weather, and other natural hazards continue to inflict major damage and interrupt the lives of people all over the world. The new information apparently is not being effectively disseminated. The underlying idea for designating the 1990s as the International Decade for Natural Disaster Reduction was first enunciated by Frank Press, president of the National Academy of Sciences, in his keynote address to the

1984 Eighth World Conference on Earthquake Engineering. The goals and ideals embodied in observation of the decade have since been put into a conceptual framework by the National Academy of Sciences, the National Academy of Engineering, and the Institute of Medicine, as follows: (1) the creation and dissemination of scientific and engineering knowledge pertinent to the reduction of losses from natural hazards, (2) the development of new institutional mechanisms and societal strategies for applying that knowledge to the reduction of losses from natural hazards, and (3) the application of that knowledge and those mechanisms and strategies to achieve reductions in losses.[29] Although observing the decade will constitute a major organizational undertaking, a strong consensus has emerged from a broad coalition of groups that such a collaborative global effort is needed to make an impact on international hazard reduction.

Conclusion

In analyzing the roles, responsibilities, and perspectives of the state and federal governments in emergency management, the following interrelated conclusions can be drawn:

Emergency management has become a legitimate function of state and federal governments.

State and federal governments have more responsibility for a broader range of hazards than ever before, in part because American society is increasingly dependent on chemical products and technology.

Funding levels to support state and federal emergency management are not increasing significantly, which means that intergovernmental coordination and sharing of resources are more important than ever.

Increasingly, disaster mitigation and preparedness must be undertaken from a global perspective; climatic changes and natural disasters are becoming global problems that require global strategies and solutions.

This chapter has demonstrated that emergency management is an intergovernmental process and that each level of government has a unique role and responsibility in that process. The system is interdependent: when one government level is flawed or becomes weak, the entire emergency management system suffers.

1 National Governors' Association, *Management Notes: Emergency Management* (Washington, DC: National Governors' Association, Office of State Services, 1986), 4.
2 Ibid., 5.
3 National Governors' Association, *1978 Emergency Preparedness Project: Final Report* (Washington, DC: National Governors' Association, Office of State Services, 1979).
4 NGA, *Management Notes*, 9.
5 U.S. General Accounting Office, *States Can Be Better Prepared to Respond to Disasters*, Report CED 80–60 (Washington, DC: U.S. General Accounting Office, 31 March 1980).
6 FEMA, *Civil Preparedness Guide* 1–3 (Washington, DC: FEMA, June 1987).
7 The allocation formula for EMA funds has been a topic of discussion at several meetings between FEMA and state and local emergency management officials. From FEMA's perspective, the issue is how to maximize the impact of limited federal

dollars to develop an emergency management capability or infrastructure. From a state and local perspective, the fundamental issue is how to convince Congress that more funds need to be appropriated for EMA.
8 Kathleen J. Tierney, "Emergency Medical Preparedness and Response in Disasters: The Need for Interorganizational Coordination," *Public Administration Review* 45 (January 1985): 80.
9 Ibid., 83.
10 Clark F. Norton, *Emergency Preparedness and Disaster Assistance: Federal Organization and Programs*, Report No. 78–102606 (Washington, DC: Congressional Research Service, April 1978), 2.
11 J. Malcolm Smith and Cornelius P. Cotter, *Powers of the President during Crises* (New York: Da Capo Press, 1979), 15.
12 The problems and challenges of administering emergency management programs in an intergovernmental setting are the focus of an excellent

compendium of articles by researchers and practitioners in the January 1985 issue of *Public
Administration Review*.

13 Message from the president of the United States
transmitting a "Reorganization Plan to Improve
Federal Emergency Management and Assistance" (19 June 1978), quoted in Reorganization
Plan No. 3 of 1978, House Document 95–356,
95th Cong., 2d sess., 1978, pp. 2–3.

14 Peter J. May, "FEMA's Role in Emergency Management: Examining Recent Experience," *Public
Administration Review* 45 (January 1985): 40.

15 Gerard J. Hoetmer, "Emergency Management,"
Baseline Data Reports 15, no. 4 (Washington, DC:
International City Management Association, April
1983), 13.

16 Alvin H. Mushkatel and Louis F. Weschler,
"Emergency Management and the Intergovernmental System," *Public Administration Review*
45 (January 1985): 51.

17 44 Code of Federal Regulations, Section 302.

18 FEMA, *Guide for Development of State and Local
Emergency Operations Plans* (Washington, DC:
FEMA, 1988).

19 Elder Witt, "The Civil (Defense) War between
the States and the Federal Government," in *Governing the States and Localities* (Washington, DC:
Congressional Quarterly, June 1988), 21.

20 FEMA's strategy to enhance local government
capability to respond to disasters, including nuclear
attack, is highlighted in the testimony of Julius
Becton, director of FEMA, before the Subcommittee on Military Installations and Facilities,

Committee on Armed Services, House of Representatives, 9 March 1988.

21 FEMA, *Guide for the Development of a State and
Local Continuity of Government Capability* CPG
1–10 (Washington, DC: FEMA, July 1987).

22 Information on these and other Corps of Engineers programs can be obtained from the district
engineer of the nearest U.S. Army Corps of Engineers district.

23 FEMA's publication *Disaster Assistance Programs* DAP-21 (Washington, DC: FEMA, August
1988) is an excellent compendium of federal programs that are designed to supplement state and
local relief and recovery and mitigation efforts.

24 U.S. Department of Transportation, *Emergency
Response Guidebook* (Washington, DC: Department of Transportation, 1984).

25 Roger E. Kasperson and K. David Pijawka,
"Societal Response to Hazards and Major Hazard Events: Comparing Natural and Technological
Hazards," *Public Administration Review* 45 (January 1985): 17.

26 Kasperson and Pijawka, "Societal Response," 7–
17.

27 Frederick C. Cuny, *Disasters and Development*
(New York: Oxford University Press, 1983), 107.

28 Cuny, *Disasters and Development*, 110–15.

29 James K. Mitchell and Abram B. Bernstein, eds.,
"Toward a Less Hazardous World: A Proposal
to Establish an International Decade of Hazard
Reduction," interim report (Washington, DC:
National Academy of Sciences, January 1987).

Part two:
Comprehensive emergency management

6 Disaster mitigation and hazard management

The estimated cumulative toll from two 1989 disasters, Hurricane Hugo and the Loma Prieta earthquake, amounted to more than ten billion dollars.[1] Costly reactions to those and other floods and earthquakes, and to technological disasters such as Three Mile Island and Chernobyl, have been thoroughly documented. But there are few published accounts of averting disasters or minimizing their effects through foresighted and ultimately less expensive mitigation programs.

This lack of information on mitigation could well be remedied during the 1990s, which have been designated by the U.N. General Assembly as the International Decade for Natural Disaster Reduction.[2] Rather than simply respond to disasters when they occur, the focus of the U.N. effort is to reduce deaths, injuries, property damage, and community losses by anticipating disasters' destructive effects and taking advance hazard management actions. Such advance actions, collectively termed *mitigation*, are designed to lessen the impact of disaster on the social and built environments.

What does mitigation involve? FEMA defines it as "acting before a disaster strikes to prevent permanently the occurrence of the disaster or to reduce the effects of the disaster when it occurs. It is also used effectively after a disaster to reduce the risk of a repeat disaster."[3] According to FEMA, the benefits of effective mitigation include the following:

Saving lives and reducing injuries

Preventing or reducing property damage

Reducing economic losses

Minimizing social dislocation and stress

Minimizing agricultural losses

Maintaining critical facilities in functioning order

Protecting infrastructure from damage

Protecting mental health

Lessening legal liability of government and public officials

Providing positive political consequences for government action

Because it reduces risk, mitigation is as important as preparedness in providing effective local emergency management. But mitigation is not as well understood as other aspects of emergency management; moreover, mitigation is particularly complex because its activities are often the primary responsibility of a number of different local government departments, such as planning, housing and community development, building inspection, public works, and natural resources and environmental protection. This does not mean that the local emergency manager lacks a mitigation role. On the contrary, the emergency manager plays a crucial role in coordinating, motivating, and monitoring mitigation.

Mitigation deals primarily with four basic elements: hazard, risk, vulnerability, and disaster. *Hazards* are natural, technological, or civil threats to people, property, and the environment. *Risk* is the probability that a hazard will occur during a particular time period. *Vulnerability* is susceptibility to injury or damage from hazards. And a *disaster* is a hazard occurrence resulting in significant injury or damage. Thus, a flood is a natural hazard; flood risk is defined in terms of the hundred-year flood—that flood with 1 percent probability of occurrence in any given year; the people or buildings located within the hundred-year flood zone are vulnerable; and a flood disaster is a flood that injures a number of people, causes significant property damage, or both.

The emergency manager's job with respect to mitigation is to analyze the hazards faced by the community, identify their associated risks, and reduce vulnerability to the hazards, thus mitigating their potential disaster impact. To do this well, the emergency manager needs to have both a political and a technical understanding of hazard mitigation. On the political side, the manager is the major local advocate of good mitigation practice who can convince local leaders to adopt and fund mitigation plans and policies. On the technical side, the manager is the local expert who can handle and explain the specialized terms, methodologies, and programs involved in hazard mitigation.

How does the emergency manager build mitigation into local policy? This chapter offers proven strategies for making mitigation an important public agenda item and describes effective arguments for countering opposition; it shows how mitigation's recent acceptance as an important aspect of federal emergency management policy can translate into local policymaking leverage. On the technical side, the chapter describes effective tools and techniques for identifying, analyzing, and managing different types of hazards. The underlying theme throughout is that of improving the local emergency manager's practice of disaster mitigation.

Evolution of federal mitigation policy

Initially, federal emergency management policy focused narrowly on civil defense preparedness and case-by-case disaster relief. Although during the 1930s and 1940s the U.S. Corps of Engineers and the Tennessee Valley Authority carried out numerous structural mitigation projects, the presence of mitigation in domestic public policy is relatively recent. Mitigation first appeared in federal emergency management policy as part of floodplain management during the 1960s. Since then the concept has been gradually extended to cover a variety of natural and technological hazards. In the process, mitigation has advanced from being an optional element to being required in many federal programs. It has been assigned importance equal to that of other phases of emergency management and has become an important part of the comprehensive emergency management system. Today federal management policy has a broad all-hazard approach with a strong, proactive mitigation component.

This evolution is illustrated by the development of federal flood policy from the mid-1960s, shown in the accompanying sidebar. One of the first uses of mitigation was the requirement in Presidential Executive Order 11296 of 1966 to reduce development of floodplains, as a way of mitigating future flood losses. The mitigation concept was then integrated into the 1986 National Flood Insurance Act, which required local governments to regulate development within their floodplains in order to be eligible for national flood insurance.

During the 1970s, mitigation was also incorporated into the Coastal Zone Management Act (1972), which encouraged states to identify hazard areas as part of their coastal management programs. In 1973 the Flood Disaster Protection Act put teeth into flood hazard mitigation by cutting off federally insured loans to floodplain property in communities that did not meet the requirements for participation in the National Flood Insurance Program (NFIP). By 1974 the adoption of state and local postdisaster mitigation plans had become a requirement under the Disaster Relief Act for receiving future federal disaster aid, and

Evolution of federal flood mitigation policy

1966   Presidential Executive Order 11296 requires federal agencies to reduce floodplain development.

1968   National Flood Insurance Act requires floodplain management in exchange for national flood insurance coverage eligibility.

1972   Coastal Zone Management Act encourages coastal planning, including hazards identification.

1973   Flood Disaster Protection Act prohibits federally insured loans to floodplain property in communities not under the National Flood Insurance Program.

1974   Disaster Relief Act requires state and local mitigation plans in order to receive federal aid (Section 406, later numbered 409) and authorizes Hurricane Preparedness Planning Program.

1977   Presidential Executive Orders 11988 and 11990 mandate federal agencies to refrain from financing or permitting development in floodplains and wetlands unless no practicable alternatives exist.

1977   National Earthquake Hazards Reduction Act authorizes development and implementation of measures to mitigate earthquake hazards.

1979   Presidential Executive Order 12127 creates FEMA to coordinate federal disaster management.

1980   FEMA establishes Interagency Hazard Mitigation Teams through interagency agreement.

1980   FEMA requires state and local governments to assume 25 percent of public assistance program costs.

1982   Coastal Barrier Resources Act withdraws federal flood insurance and financial assistance from undeveloped coastal barriers.

1983   FEMA initiates Integrated Emergency Management System.

1987   National Flood Insurance Act is amended to provide prepayment of insurance to relocate or demolish structures in imminent danger of collapse from coastal erosion and wave action.

1988   Disaster Relief Act is amended to allow FEMA to participate with states in hazard mitigation projects on a 50–50 matching grant basis.

1990   FEMA initiates Community Rating System (CRS) to reduce flood insurance premiums in communities with effective hazard mitigation strategies.

Source: Adapted from D. R. Godschalk, D. J. Brower, and T. Beatley, *Catastrophic Coastal Storms: Hazard Mitigation and Development Management* (Durham, NC: Duke University Press, 1989), 52.

an extensive program of hurricane preparedness had been authorized. Presidential executive orders in 1977 strengthened the policy of avoiding development in floodplains. And the 1977 National Earthquake Hazards Reduction Act provided resources for developing and implementing measures to mitigate earthquake hazards, focusing national attention on this hazard.

The 1979 creation of FEMA marked the first time that planning for all peacetime and wartime disasters had been established in a single agency. During the 1980s, FEMA initiated a series of actions to promote mitigation, including establishing Interagency Hazard Mitigation Teams (which go to the sites of major disasters to lay out a mitigation plan), increasing the level of state and local contributions to postdisaster public assistance in order to create a sense of shared responsibility for reducing potential disaster costs, and adopting the integrated emergency management system (IEMS), which not only included the full spectrum of disasters but also gave mitigation equal billing with the other phases of emergency management. In addition, in 1982 Congress enacted the Coastal Barrier Resources Act, withdrawing federal flood insurance and financial assistance for infrastructure from undeveloped coastal barriers in order to reduce public financial obligations to support private development projects in these flood- and hurricane-prone areas. In 1987, Section 1306 of the National Flood Insurance Act was amended to allow prepayment of flood insurance claims to owners of structures threatened by coastal erosion or wave action who relocate or demolish the structures *before* they collapse. (For relocating to a nonthreatened area, owners may obtain 40 percent of the value of structures in imminent danger of collapse. For demolition, owners may obtain 110 percent of market value or full insured coverage, whichever is less.) In 1988 the Disaster Relief Act was amended to allow FEMA to pay up to 50 percent of the cost of state hazard mitigation projects. And in 1990 FEMA initiated the Community Rating System (CRS) to reward local hazard mitigation efforts by reducing flood insurance premiums in communities that adopt relocation, hazard area acquisition, and other mitigation policies.

Clearly, federal flood hazard policy is demonstrating an increasing emphasis on mitigation. As federal policy has evolved, mitigation has been used to:

Modify or contain the flood hazard through structures such as dikes

Protect people, property, and facilities in flood-prone areas, through requirements related to insurance, building elevation, and floodproofing

Limit development and use of flood hazard areas, through setback regulations, density reduction, relocation of threatened structures, and keying insurance availability or premiums to levels of hazard and mitigation.

Thus, mitigation works to change the nature of the threat, decrease vulnerability to damage, and reduce exposure to the hazard.

In addition to flood mitigation, the federal government has initiated efforts to mitigate earthquake and landslide hazards, hazardous materials exposure, and a number of other natural and technological hazards.[4] These mitigation efforts are incorporated into a four-phase model of comprehensive emergency management, discussed in the next section.

Comprehensive emergency management

The four phases of comprehensive emergency management are preparedness, response, recovery, and mitigation. The sequence is set in motion by a disaster (see Figure 6–1). Although in practice the phases overlap, each has its own aims and also serves as a building block for the next phase.

Preparedness is undertaken before a disaster occurs, to build emergency management capacity. It focuses on the development of emergency operations plans and systems. Response takes place immediately before, during, and directly after a disaster. The purpose of response is to minimize personal injury and property damage through emergency functions such as warning, evacuation, search and rescue, and provision of shelter and medical services. Recovery begins immediately following a disaster with efforts to restore minimum services to the stricken area and continues with longer-term efforts to return the community to normal. Immediate recovery activities include assessing damage, clearing debris, and restoring food supplies, shelter, and utilities. Longer-term recovery activities include rebuilding and redeveloping the community and implementing mitigation programs.

Mitigation can take place both during recovery from a past disaster and during preparedness for a potential disaster. In each case, the aim is to reduce risk through anticipatory actions. Mitigation activities include preparing land use and

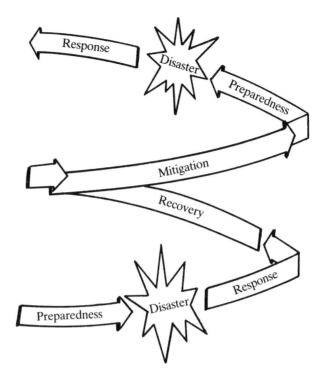

Figure 6-1   Emergency management phases.

development management plans for hazard areas, reducing hazards by relocating buildings away from hazard areas, strengthening building codes, and educating decision makers and the community about risks.

Preparedness, response, and short-term recovery call for tactical skills in inter-agency coordination and decision making to cope with emergency operations under disaster conditions. Recovery in the longer term and mitigation call for strategic skills in planning, policy design, and implementation to reduce risk and limit the impact of potential disasters (see sidebar on page 136).

Comprehensive emergency management coordinates the full set of actors and activities that come into play when disaster strikes. FEMA's goal is to provide federal, state, and local government agencies with the capability to cope with all potential hazards during all four phases of emergency management. Rather than create separate systems for each type of hazard, FEMA advocates an all-hazard approach, which is based on the fact that many emergency management functions are appropriate to a range of hazards.[5]

FEMA created the integrated emergency management system (IEMS) to build state and local capacity for a coordinated response to multiple hazards. Once a local emergency manager has identified all the natural and technological hazards faced by the community, analyzed the risks posed by these hazards, and prepared an emergency management strategy to deal with them, a year-by-year program can be undertaken to implement the IEMS strategy. Mitigation, as a part of IEMS, follows analogous steps of hazard identification, hazard analysis, and strategy preparation.

The local hazard mitigation process includes the following three steps:

1. Identifying all local hazards: their characteristics; locations; probabilities of occurrence; and potential impact on people, property and the environment; also identifying appropriate actions to reduce structural and nonstructural damage.

The four phases of comprehensive emergency management

Phases	General measures
Mitigation: Actions taken to eliminate or reduce the degree of long-term risk to human life and property from natural and technological hazards. (Mitigation assumes that society is exposed to risks whether or not an emergency occurs.)	Building codes Disaster insurance Hazard information systems Land use management Hazard analysis Land acquisition Monitoring/inspection Public education Research Relocation Risk mapping Safety codes Statutes/ordinances Tax incentives/disincentives
Preparedness: Actions taken in advance of an emergency to develop operational capabilities and facilitate an effective response in the event an emergency occurs.	Continuity of government Emergency broadcast system Emergency communications Emergency operations centers Emergency operations plans Emergency public information materials Exercise of plans/systems Mutual aid agreements Resource management Training response personnel Warning systems
Response: Actions taken immediately before, during, or directly after an emergency occurs, to save lives, minimize damage to property, and enhance the effectiveness of recovery.	Emergency plan activation Emergency broadcast system activation Emergency instructions to the public Emergency medical assistance Staffing the emergency operations center Public official alerting Reception and care Shelter/evacuation Search and rescue Resource mobilization Warning systems activation
Recovery: Activity to return vital life support systems to minimum operating standards and long-term activity designed to return life to normal or improved levels.	Crisis counseling Damage assessment Debris clearance Decontamination Disaster assistance centers Disaster insurance payments Disaster loans and grants Disaster unemployment assistance Public information Reassessment of emergency plans Reconstruction Temporary housing

Source: Adapted from R. J. Coleman and J. A. Granito, eds., *Managing Fire Services* (Washington, DC: International City Management Association, 1988), 325.

2. Analyzing the probable risks of disaster occurrence and the vulnerability of people, property, and the environment to injury or damage. The analysis is based on inventories of structures and populations at risk, estimates of economic loss, studies of risk perception, and projections of mitigation costs and benefits.

The integrated emergency management system The goal of the integrated emergency management system (IEMS) is to develop and maintain a credible emergency management capability nationwide by integrating activities along functional lines at all levels of government and, to the fullest extent possible, across all hazards.

State and local governments can achieve this goal by (1) determining the hazards and magnitude of risk in a logical, consistent manner; (2) assessing the existing and required capability with respect to those hazards; and (3) establishing realistic local and state-tailored plans that lay out necessary actions for closing the gap between existing and required levels of capability. These efforts are related and must be undertaken sequentially. The identification of hazards forms the basis for assessing capability and determining the capability shortfall. The shortfall, in turn, leads to preparation of a multiyear development plan. These initial steps are the starting point for integrating emergency management activities on a multihazard, functional basis.

Although IEMS underscores capability development, the process recognizes that current operations must be conducted according to existing plans and with existing resources, and that these operations can contribute to the developmental effort. The process, therefore, includes two paths: one focusing on current capabilities and activities (steps 1–7), and the other emphasizing capability improvement (steps 8–13).

STEP 1: Hazard analysis Knowing what could happen, the likelihood of it happening, and having some idea of the magnitude of the problems that could arise, are essential ingredients for emergency planning. The first step, then, is for the jurisdiction to identify the potential hazards and to determine the probable impact each of those hazards could have on people and property. This task need not be complicated or highly sophisticated to provide useful results. What is important is that all hazards that pose a potential threat to the jurisdiction are identified and addressed in the jurisdiction's emergency response planning and mitigation efforts.

STEP 2: Capability assessment The next step for the jurisdiction is to assess its current capability for dealing with the hazards that have been identified in step 1. Current capability is determined against standards and criteria FEMA has established as necessary to perform basic emergency management functions; e.g., alerting and warning, evacuation, and emergency communications. The resulting information provides a summary of the capabilities that exist and upon which current plans should be prepared (step 3), and leads to the identification of the jurisdiction's weaknesses (step 8).

STEP 3: Emergency operations plans A plan should be developed with functional annexes common to the hazards identified in step 1. Those activities unique to specific hazards should be described separately, perhaps in appendixes to the appropriate functional annexes. This approach is a departure from previous guidance, which stressed development of hazard-specific plans. Existing plans should be reviewed and modified as necessary to ensure their applicability to all hazards that pose a potential threat to the jurisdiction. The exact

3. Preparing, recommending, and maintaining a community mitigation strategy, including all of the technical and political, policy and program, plan and budget, and regulation and education aspects.

The following sections will address each of these three steps: hazard identification, hazard analysis, and mitigation strategy preparation.

---

format of the plan is less important than the assurance that the planning process considers each function from a multihazard perspective.

STEP 4: Capability maintenance   Once developed, the ability to take appropriate and effective action against any hazard must be continually maintained or it will diminish significantly over time. Plans must be updated; equipment must be serviced and tested; personnel must be trained; procedures and systems must be exercised. This is particularly important for jurisdictions that do not experience frequent, large-scale emergencies.

STEP 5: Mitigation efforts   Mitigating the potential effects of hazards should be given high priority. Resources utilized to limit the effects of a hazard or reduce or eliminate the hazard can minimize loss and suffering in the future. For example, proper land-use management and stringent building and safety codes can lessen the effects of future disasters. Significant mitigation efforts can also reduce the level of capability needed to conduct recovery operations, thereby reducing the capability shortfall that may exist. The results of these efforts will be reflected in future hazard analyses (step 1) and capability assessments (step 2).

STEP 6: Emergency operations   The need to conduct emergency operations may arise at any time and must be carried out under current plans and with current resources despite the existence of plans for making improvements in the future. The operations, however, can provide an opportunity to test existing capabilities under real conditions.

STEP 7: Evaluation   The outcome of

the emergency operations (step 6) should be analyzed and assessed in terms of actual vs. required capabilities and considered in subsequent updates of steps 2 and 8. Identifying the need for future mitigation efforts should be an important part of each evaluation. Tests and exercises should be undertaken for the purpose of evaluation, especially where disasters occur infrequently.

STEP 8: Capability shortfall   The difference between current capability (step 2) and the optimum capability reflected in the standards and criteria established by FEMA represents the capability shortfall. The areas not currently meeting the assessment criteria should receive primary consideration when preparing the jurisdiction's multiyear development plan (step 9).

STEP 9: Multiyear development plan   Based on the capability shortfall identified in step 8, the jurisdiction should prepare a multiyear development plan tailored to meet its unique situation and requirements. The plan should outline what needs to be done to reach the desired level of capability. Ideally, this plan should cover a five-year period so that long-term development projects can be properly scheduled and adequately funded. The plan should include all emergency management projects and activities to be undertaken by the jurisdiction regardless of the funding source.

When used in conjunction with the hazards analysis and capability assessment results, these plans should be helpful in convincing local chief executives of the need for improvements and in presenting a logical, realistic schedule of the

Hazard identification

Hazard identification means determining the full range of potential hazards faced by a community and grouping them according to characteristics, impacts, and potential mitigation actions. A community might face floods, tornadoes, and chemical spills, for example, each of which would have different effects and

---

projects and activities that should be given priority over the next five years. At the state level, this information should be used to develop a statewide multiyear plan for supporting local development efforts and in determining priority state requirements for federal financial and technical support through Comprehensive Cooperative Agreements.

STEP 10: Annual development increment   With the multiyear development plan serving as a framework for improving capability over time, the next step is to determine in detail what is going to be done next year. Situations change each year, and perhaps more or less was accomplished the year before than had been planned. These factors should be reflected in modifications to the multiyear development plan and in determining next year's annual increment. Through this process, emergency managers can provide their local officials and state counterparts with detailed descriptions of what they plan to accomplish in the coming year and their requirements for financial and technical assistance in support of these efforts. During the initial implementation of IEMS, no major change is contemplated to reporting procedures now in effect. FEMA is exploring opportunities, however, for simplifying reporting and tracking through automation.

STEP 11: State/local resources   State and local governments are expected to contribute financially and in-kind to capability development and maintenance efforts, as they have done in the past. Some activities identified in the annual increment may be accomplished solely with local resources, while others may require state and/or federal support. Whatever

the source of funding and other support, each project and activity should represent a necessary building block in the jurisdiction's overall capability development program.

STEP 12: Federal sources   The federal government will continue to provide policy and procedural guidance, financial aid, technical support, and staff resources to assist state and local governments in developing and maintaining capability. FEMA's Comprehensive Cooperative Agreements with states will remain the vehicle for funding FEMA-approved projects and activities on an annual basis.

STEP 13: Annual work increment   As capability development projects and activities are completed, the jurisdiction's capability shortfall will be reduced. These improvements will be reflected in the capability assessment and capability shortfall (steps 2 and 8) as the results of the process are reviewed each year. Emergency operations plans should then be revised to incorporate these improvements. Multiyear development plans also should be modified in view of these changes and the experience gained during exercises and the conduct of actual emergency operations. Each state should provide a method for recording and consolidating local annual work increments.

Source: Excerpted from FEMA, *The Integrated Emergency Management System: Process Overview*, CPG 1-100 (Washington, D.C.: U.S. Government Printing Office, 1983).

require different mitigation actions. Or a community may find that its primary hazards are coastal flooding, erosion, and hurricanes, all of which would threaten the same sections of the community and be mitigated by similar methods. In some cases a community may face collateral hazards triggered by a primary hazard; for example, in the 1964 Alaskan earthquake, landslides caused the major property losses and tsunamis caused 119 of the 131 fatalities.

Types of hazards

The type of hazard affects the choice of mitigation strategy. Mitigation of chemical emergencies, for instance, is accomplished by reducing the likelihood of harmful releases through techniques such as processing plant containment, disposal control, and transportation tracking and routing; relocating the community, as at Love Canal, is a last resort. Different strategies are used to mitigate earthquake hazards, focusing on improving the resistance of buildings and structures to earthquake shocks, ground faults, soil failure, and the effects of collateral hazards.

Disasters can be classified by origin into three major groups: *natural*, *technological*, and *civil*. Certain functional characteristics are also important for the emergency manager preparing a mitigation strategy. These characteristics include predictability, speed of onset, extent of impact, intensity, warning time, recurrence, controllability, and destructive potential.[6]

Grouping together hazards with similar functional characteristics allows the emergency manager to develop mitigation strategies that apply to more than one hazard. For instance, for hazards with a high degree of locational predictability, such as floods and hurricanes, the same area-specific building code provisions, density limitations, and special district mitigation funding programs could be applied. Or for hazards with a slow speed of onset and adequate warning time, such as floods and certain technological and civil hazards, similar methods could be used to maintain adequate shelter and evacuation route capacity. As Chapter 2, "Organizing for Emergency Management," makes clear, it is more efficient to maintain "generic," all-hazard mitigation strategies than to have separate, overlapping strategies for each hazard.

Natural hazards   The major natural hazards include hurricanes, tornadoes, riverine floods, earthquakes, expansive soils (with high shrink-swell potential), landslides, severe winds, and tsunamis. According to an analysis by William Petak and Arthur Atkisson, the losses from all these hazards in the United States are expected to increase sharply by the year 2000 unless major mitigation initiatives are undertaken (see Table 6–1). Threatened individuals and businesses acting on their own will not necessarily take the needed steps to reduce these hazards, so the initiative must come from government and must be spearheaded by local emergency managers.

Natural hazards have varying characteristics but generally follow a well-understood causal sequence. Hurricanes, for example, result when ocean water condenses, releasing latent heat. They generally occur in certain geographic areas at the same season each year and have a warning time of a few days, high intensity but low probability of occurrence, and a very high destructive potential and no possibility of control. Earthquakes result from the movement of subsurface tectonic plates in localized fault zones. They do not have a seasonal pattern or a warning period but do occur in definite geographic areas. Earthquakes have very high intensity and destructive potential. Landslides, which result from a weakening of soil structure or support, occur in known hazard areas and can have either a sudden or a gradual onset and a moderate or high intensity and destructive potential. Landslides can often be mitigated by protective actions or structures.

Table 6–1 Annual U.S. natural hazard losses for 1970 (actual) and 2000 (projected); all in 1970 dollars.

Hazard	Per capita ($) 1970/2000	Annual (mil.$) 1970/2000	Deaths 1970/2000	Housing units 1970/2000
Hurricane[a]	8.36/22.92	1,697.2/5,869.2	99/256	56,406/95,994
Tornado	8.12/20.38	1,656.0/5,219.1	392/920	36,212/52,119
Riverine flood	13.57/12.40	2,758.3/3,175.3	190/159	—
Earthquake	3.83/6.07	781.1/1,553.7	273/400	20,485/22,868
Expansive soil	3.93/3.89	798.1/997.1	—	—
Landslide	1.82/3.40	370.3/871.2	—	—
Severe wind	.06/.19	18.0/53.4	5/11	547/748
Tsunami	.07/.16	15.0/40.4	20/44	234/335

[a]Hurricane losses are combined hurricane winds and storm surge, calculated separately.

Identification of certain natural hazards is facilitated by standard maps. The NFIP, for instance, provides maps of all areas in the United States that are subject to flooding, based on a standard definition of a floodplain under various degrees of risk. Other hazards are not so well defined and mapped. Earthquake loss studies, for example, have not yet been standardized or applied to all areas at risk. Where outside hazard identification has not been undertaken, the local emergency manager will have to make do with historical records of hazard occurrences or arrange for special local hazard studies.

Technological hazards Chemical emergencies and nuclear accidents constitute the major technological hazards. These hazards have grown with the spread of advanced technology and are believed to constitute the major emergency management problem in developed countries because they present the greatest risk and are the most difficult to manage. Most mitigation of technological hazards must be done at the national level, but localities can reroute hazardous cargo and enact zoning, monitoring, and disclosure requirements. Relocation of a contaminated community, as at Love Canal, New York, or Times Beach, Missouri, is a last resort.

Technological hazards resulting from an accident are characterized by rapid onset, low predictability and warning time, and high intensity and destructive potential. Technological hazards resulting from long-term exposure are characterized by gradual onset, low predictability and warning, and varying intensity and destructive potential. Unlike natural hazards, technological hazards usually stem from the failure of a system designed by humans and hence are subject to human control, for example, through rigorous safety standards and well-developed emergency procedures.

Lack of experience with technological hazards makes identification and prevention all the more difficult. Fear, uncertainty, and overestimation of risk can surround technological hazards with intense political conflict. Under such circumstances, mitigation proposals can themselves be hazardous, as when opposition groups attack proposals for, and proposers of, centralized hazardous waste management facilities.[7] In some cases, such as nuclear power plants, extensive hazard analyses are required by federal law; in other cases, such as solid waste sites, the local emergency manager will have to arrange for local analyses. Although there is no guaranteed method of dealing with conflict over technological hazards, open and participatory decision processes are less likely to arouse public distrust.

Civil hazards Famine and hostile attack constitute the major civil hazards. Even though these have not been faced by U.S. populations in recent decades, they have been the cause of a number of disasters in other countries. More-over, given the uncertain impact of the greenhouse effect on climate and the instability of relationships among world powers, it is possible that future generations of Americans may also have to face one or more civil hazards, including terrorism.

Civil hazards are characterized by low predictability and warning and cat-astrophic intensity and destructiveness. At the local level, they are uncontrollable. The only mitigating actions that can be taken are those of preparedness—instituting plans and programs to cope with potential disrup-tion or destruction of physical and social systems.

Hazard impact groups

Hazards can be grouped according to whether they primarily affect people, property, or both. Some disasters, such as droughts, do not affect property; others, such as slow-rising floods, may affect property almost entirely. Most hazards, however, threaten both people and property: evacuation cannot always remove at-risk populations before disaster strikes, and even with strong building codes and land use plans, some property will be damaged by most major dis-asters. Where both people and property are at risk, mitigation strategies usually set protection of people as the first priority and protection of property as the second. Special priority is given also to protection of lifeline systems that are vital to community health and safety, such as transportation, communications, water supply, sewage treatment, and electrical power systems; to essential public facilities that are vital to postdisaster response, such as hospitals, fire stations, and police stations; and to facilities with a potential for significant loss, such as dams, chemical plants, and densely occupied large buildings.

Delineating areas of potential property damage allows emergency managers to identify threatened lifeline systems, to tabulate potential property losses, and to demonstrate the economic and public safety value of mitigation programs. Prudent emergency managers will also identify in advance those populations at risk from technological hazards, such as those within the evacuation zone of a nuclear or chemical plant. They will use census and other population data to identify categories of at-risk populations that will require special assistance in any type of disaster, such as school children, infirm and elderly residents, hospital patients, nursing home residents, and prison inmates.

Thanks to advances in warning systems, deaths and injuries in the United States from recurring natural hazards such as hurricanes and floods have dropped significantly since 1900, when six thousand died in a hurricane in Galveston, Texas. But advances in warning capability have leveled off, while people continue to settle in areas at risk from natural hazards. Thus, as Table 6–1 indicates, by the year 2000, the U.S. death toll from hurricanes is expected to rise again because of the increase of population in vulnerable coastal areas.

Types of mitigation actions

Mitigation actions can be grouped into two basic types: structural and nonstruc-tural. Structural actions include efforts to contain a hazard, as with dams or dikes, and to strengthen exposed buildings and structures to withstand disaster stresses, as with building codes and disaster-proofing.

Nonstructural actions use the government's regulatory, taxing, spending, and management powers to limit the extent to which people and property are in harm's way. These include land use plans, zoning and subdivision regulations, building codes, capital improvement programs, land acquisition, preferential taxation, and insurance.

To inform citizens and decision makers about a comprehensive mitigation program, findings from the hazard identification can be described in map and report form and summarized in a matrix. The matrix could list all potential local hazards on one axis, grouped by predictability or hazard area of type of impact, and could list types of mitigation actions on the other axis.

Hazard analysis

Once potential hazards, their impacts, and possible mitigation actions have been identified, a hazard analysis can be conducted to provide information on the location and extent of risk and vulnerability, the roles played by different groups, the potential extent of losses, and the benefits that can be realized from mitigation. For each identified hazard, the hazard analysis should clearly state both actual and perceived levels of risk and vulnerability. The analysis, which will include engineering as well as economic components, should be prepared in both written and mapped form to specify the characteristics as well as the locations of the hazards. In the report, techniques for determining risk and vulnerability should be clearly documented, and findings and conclusions should be presented in a form that is useful and understandable to the public and decision makers.

Risk and vulnerability mapping

Risk is the probability of a hazard occurrence, and vulnerability is the susceptibility of people and property to injury or damage. Risk and vulnerability mapping is simply a procedure for locating areas with different degrees of hazard probability and susceptibility. For instance, hurricanes are categorized on a scale of 1 (least destructive) to 5 (most destructive), and a hurricane flood map can highlight the areas of the community subject to storm surge flooding during hurricanes of various intensities, thereby indicating the areas that should be evacuated under certain storm conditions (see Figure 6–2). Maps of the value

(*continued on page 146*)

Figure 6–2 This map of Lee County, Florida, shows the risk of hurricane flooding according to storm category.

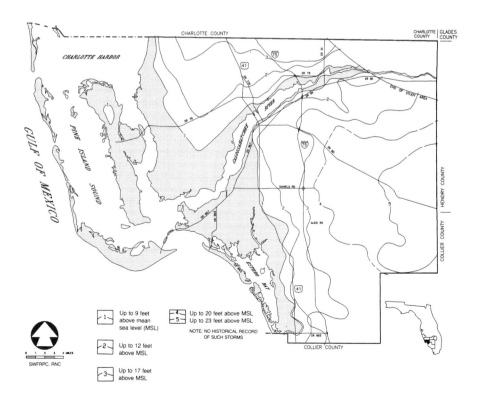

Hazard analysis   Managing hazardous threats and actual disasters poses an increasingly sophisticated challenge to government. The first step in effective emergency management is understanding the nature and implications of the hazards to which we are, or may become, vulnerable. The preparation of a vulnerability analysis provides such understanding and sets of agendas for efforts to prevent disasters, minimize risks, and manage the consequences of actual disasters.

Emergency managers at all levels of government and in the private sector need to work toward establishing common terms and definitions for use in preparing vulnerability analyses. This would provide a point of commonality for nationwide studies and comparisons as well as enhanced communications and emergency management planning.

The following glossary defines several key terms.

Elements at risk   Population, buildings, businesses, civil works, economic activities, public services, utilities, infrastructure, and so forth

Emergency/disaster   Event that demands substantial crisis response requiring the use of governmental powers and resources beyond the scope of one line agency or service

Hazard/hazard agent   Source of danger that may or may not lead to an emergency or disaster and is named after the emergency/disaster that could be so precipitated

Incidence   Number of disasters or emergencies precipitated by a given hazard or group of hazards during a given historical period

Local conditions   Local environmental conditions such as topography, geology, geography, and so forth, that increase or decrease hazard effects

Physical properties of hazards   Hazard magnitude (e.g., severity of a hazard measured in terms of wind speed for windstorms or earthshock for earthquakes), rate of onset, frequency, and so forth

Probability   Number of chances per year or other time span that a disaster of a certain magnitude will occur

Risk   Susceptibility to death, injury, damage, destruction, disruption, stoppage, and so forth

Risk reduction measures   Actions taken to minimize or eliminate vulnerability to disasters (e.g., land-use patterns, development planning, mitigation measures)

Vulnerability   Degree to which population, property, environment, and social and economic activity are at risk.

Accurate predictions about time, place and magnitude of all potential emergencies are nearly impossible to make. Hence, broad-based preparedness, response, and recovery plans will always be needed. The basic questions a hazard analysis must answer are not those relating to predictions, but rather:

If hazard agent X develops into a crisis of Y magnitude, what would be the most likely impact upon the Z vulnerability of people and property at risk in a given area?

Can we prevent X from occurring, decrease Y and/or minimize Z? If so, to what extent and in what combination can measures be taken to do so in a cost-effective manner?

Can hazard X be prevented or substantially controlled from developing into a crisis, or must we concentrate on mitigating/preventing subsequent damage to people and property?

How do the interrelationships of the X, Y, and Z factors of one potential emergency compare with those of others we face?

A hazard analysis should be designed to answer these questions using hard, objective data to the extent possible. A properly prepared and periodically updated hazard analysis is the emergency manager's primary tool for managing hazards and should:

Enable emergency managers to set priorities and goals commensurate with the degree of local public need for protection

Provide descriptive information on every major hazard affecting a given area and a methodology for comparison of vastly different types of hazards

Justify management decisions for altering program and staffing assignments that may vary from previous norms

Substantiate decisions about resource allocations and justify budget requests

Encourage identification of technological and research needs in emergency management

Provide tools to raise the level of understanding of public officials to influence the adoption of prevention/ mitigation measures and the expenditure of scarce resources to do so

Enable the establishment of a viable national database of hazard, vulnerability, and other relevant and comparable information for national comprehensive emergency management (CEM) planning.

The effectiveness of a hazard analysis depends upon its being performed in the context of CEM, and therefore should address:

All hazards   Natural, manmade and attack—both those known to occur and cause damage, and those having a reasonable likelihood of occurrence and damage-producing effects

Four management phases   Mitigation, preparedness, response, and recovery—actions taken in any or all of the phases can positively or negatively affect vulnerability of the population and property at risk

All government levels and the private sector   Each has a separate but interdependent role in disaster management and information and experience to apply to hazard analysis.

In addition, a hazard analysis should be designed to answer the questions and fulfill the purposes aforementioned. For all hazards analyzed, the following information should be provided:

Nature and scope of hazards and where they are likely to occur

References to secondary emergencies or disasters that can be or have been triggered by a primary event

Detailed description of historical events as examples of what occurs when a particular hazard develops into an emergency/disaster

Historical incidence data nationally and/or statewide including information on hazard severity scales applied to measure the magnitude of the event

Location of fixed sites that may pose dangers (e.g., nuclear power plants)

Mapping of hazardous zones based on past occurrences or potential events (e.g., hurricane paths, floodplains, railroads, highways)

Historical damage data expressed in dollars and aggregated for a period of years or months for a selected number of hazards

Suggested mitigation measures

Listings of emergency and disaster declarations issued.

Source: Adapted from Hilary Whittaker and Jaynelle Marie Ketchum, *Comprehensive Emergency Management Bulletin #2* (Washington, DC: National Governors' Association, May 1982) (out of print).

(*continued from page 143*)
of buildings and structures in each area would allow the emergency manager to calculate vulnerability in dollar terms for each type of storm flood. Similar mapping could be done for each likely hazard.

Flood risk has been mapped nationally under the NFIP. Techniques also exist for mapping vulnerability to earthquakes and landslides, but as mentioned earlier, they have not been applied on a national basis.[8] The growing availability of computerized mapping programs, along with the continuing development of hazard analysis methods, should hasten the extension of risk and vulnerability mapping throughout the country. In the meantime, the local emergency manager must use various local, state, and federal resources to compile risk and vulnerability maps.

Estimating economic losses

Estimating potential economic losses from a disaster in terms of dollars and cents is a powerful tool for alerting policymakers to the advantages of mitigation. Estimating economic losses actually incurred is a vital part of the postdisaster recovery process. Predisaster estimates are based on the dollar value of public and private property vulnerable to various hazards. Postdisaster estimates are based on inspection of actual damage and are used in a number of recovery activities, including planning for reconstruction, issuing repair permits, acquiring damaged properties, and applying for federal disaster assistance. The basic element of both predisaster and postdisaster economic loss estimation is the inventory of buildings and structures at risk.

For estimates of potential economic losses, for example, the value of residential and commercial property that would be damaged by hurricanes of 25-, 50-, and 100-year frequencies could be calculated on the basis of flood hazard maps, tax assessment records, and building permit data. A similar calculation could be

---

Elements to include in an inventory of buildings and structures at risk

Geographic location, with a property identification number keyed to a standard map of record, such as a tax map, which is referenced to state plane coordinates or latitude/longitude so that the property can be located following a disaster that destroys streets or other landmarks normally used to locate an address or building

Construction type, such as wood frame, reinforced masonry, steel frame, and so forth; number of stories; and age of structure, which is used to indicate the ability of the structure to withstand hazard forces, as well as its value

Hazard resistance, an overall measure of ability to withstand various hazards, such as an earthquake (seismic resistance) or a flood (floodproofing)

Economic value, usually recorded in terms of replacement cost, but sometimes recorded as cash value or assessed tax value if these values are the only ones readily available

Number of occupants, that is, family or household size, number of employees, students, patients, and so forth, preferably noted in terms of occupancy at different times of the day

Use of the premises, classified according to land use categories such as single-family residential, mobile home, apartment, hotel, office, school, hospital, retail commercial, industrial, theater, and so forth.

made for vulnerable public facilities, such as schools, public office buildings, roads and bridges, and water and sewer systems. This loss estimation technique is most developed for hurricanes, floods, and earthquakes, but it can also be adapted for other hazards.[9]

SLOSH (Sea, Lake, and Overland Surges from Hurricanes)   The "Sea, Lake and Overland Surges from Hurricanes" (SLOSH) numerical storm surge prediction model, developed by the National Oceanic and Atmospheric Administration, is an example of computer technology initially intended as a meteorological forecasting instrument that has been found to have even greater value as a long-range hurricane emergency planning tool. Its speed and flexibility have enabled quick and comprehensive surge predictions. Its speed is of most value when it is used as an operational forecasting tool, its flexibility when it is used for long-range emergency planning. . . .

The SLOSH model has allowed the evacuation planner and, in turn, the emergency manager, to formulate quantitative hurricane evacuation plans. The enhanced hazard and vulnerability analyses afforded by SLOSH not only provide a thorough base of technical data, but also define the evacuation problem numerically and graphically, thus permitting the development of a clear operations plan. The calculation of the geographic extent of hurricane vulnerability defined by SLOSH also enables the emergency manager to portray vulnerable land areas to the public by producing clear, color-coded public information maps. Finally, the extensive set of data, operational strategies, and public information efforts resulting from such quantitative studies can be used to develop coherent plans that can be tested and evaluated in various types of emergency exercises.

The comprehensive hurricane population preparedness program, established by the prototype Tampa Bay Plan and adopted by FEMA, consists of four major interrelated elements:

The Technical Data Report documents the findings of all methodological, data gathering, and technical analysis tasks of the study. The report defines and quantifies the evacuation problem and the response necessary for warning, evacuation, and shelter.

The Evacuation Implementation Element is a concise summary guide that includes key maps, charts, tables, and other information from the Technical Data Report and serves as the reference document for official decision making in the emergency operations center during a hurricane's approach. A separate Evacuation Implementation Element for each local jurisdiction, tailored to that jurisdiction's standard operating procedures, is most effective.

The Public Information Program consists of simple, easy-to-understand printed tabloids, pamphlets, or brochures describing to each resident his/her evacuation zone, assigned route, shelter, and the overall concept of the plan. The tabloid should include clear, color-coded maps and instructions tailored for each major jurisdiction and printed for every household in the region. The printed tabloid should be supplemented by emergency broadcast system radio and television programs during an event that convey the same graphic information.

The Emergency Operations Simulation Exercise is a total-system, regional hurricane evacuation exercise simulating the actual approach and/or landfall of a major hurricane, the evacuation decision-making process, communications, and the actual emergency operations called for in the completed plan.

A comprehensive program [cont.]

Assessing risk perception

How risks are perceived shapes the way people respond to them. If local officials do not perceive hazard risks as important, they will not give mitigation programs high priority. Decision makers can be surveyed to assess their perceptions of

---

incorporating these four elements typically takes from one to two years to complete. All elements should be updated at least every two to three years.

The basic evacuation planning methodology that is employed in such comprehensive studies integrates several quantitative analyses stemming from SLOSH-based hazard and vulnerability analysis. Briefly, they are:

Hazard analysis. A comprehensive analysis of the potential hurricane hazards that could confront the region

Vulnerability analysis. A detailed identification of the areas and population of the region vulnerable to specific hurricane hazards

Population data analysis. A systematic enumeration of the dwelling units, population, and available vehicles within the identified vulnerable areas

Behavioral analysis. A statistically significant survey and historical identification of the probable tendencies of potential future evacuees of the region

Shelter resource analysis. A region-wide inventory of the characteristics and capacity of existing public shelters

Shelter surge analysis. A quantitative analysis of the storm surge vulnerability of existing as well as potential future public shelter structures

Institutional facility surge analysis. A quantitative analysis of the storm surge vulnerability of all hospitals, nursing homes, prisons, and other residential facilities requiring special evacuation procedures.

Surge roadway inundation analysis.

Estimations of the time of inundation of critical points on evacuation routes relative to hurricane landfall

Gale force winds arrival analysis. Estimations of the time of the arrival of gale force winds relative to hurricane landfall

Shelter duration analysis. An analysis of the expected shelter stay duration throughout the life of the storm

Freshwater roadway inundation analysis. A regionwide identification of roadways historically inundated from rainfall flooding

Evacuation zone formulation. A regionwide delineation of areas defined by SLOSH as vulnerable evacuation zones based on common hazard vulnerability and common evacuation routes

Evacuation routes assignment. The assignment of volumes of vehicles from specific zones to specific routes in order to develop optimum intra- and inter-county evacuation strategies

Shelter assignment. The assignment of persons within specific evacuation zones to specific shelters on the basis of evacuation routing strategies

Clearance time quantification. The calculation of times for the movement of masses of vehicles associated with the evacuation of persons from SLOSH-defined vulnerable areas to specific evacuation destinations

Evacuation time estimation. An estimation of the total time needed to issue and implement evacuation orders based on the addition of clearance time to pre-landfall hazards (e.g., surge roadway inundation or gale force wind) arrival time.

risk from natural and technological hazards and the importance they accord such hazards on the public agenda. National surveys show that mitigating such risks is rarely at the top of local public policy priorities.[10] Given the periodic turnover in elected and appointed officials, such surveys should be carried out regularly. If decision makers are to support adequate mitigation programs and budgets, it

---

The use of SLOSH technology in the above analyses begins with the selection of parameters to characterize each of 200 to 300 hypothetical hurricanes to be simulated in individual model runs. Each simulation represents the effect of a potential hurricane on the region. The full spectrum of probable storms—including "worst probable" combinations of intensity, track, size, and forward speed—are simulated to produce a comprehensive hazard analysis.

Before the actual simulations are run by the computer, those individual geographic grid cells representing critical evacuation points are selected (there are usually about 50), and the program is directed to create time history data for each of them in each hypothetical hurricane.

Although SLOSH technology allows for the examination of a hurricane with a specific track, intensity, and other parameters, current hurricane forecasting cannot determine a specific track and landfall point sufficiently early to aid an evacuation decision. To help produce an evacuation decision which does not underestimate the evacuation area, a focused range of a single parameter (e.g., track) is combined using a special, more generalized SLOSH run termed a "maximum envelope of water" (MEOW). The geographic distribution of surge predicted by a MEOW run represents the highest surge that could be expected in each grid cell due to any of the 10 to 15 individual hurricanes simulated in the MEOW. The degree to which maximum surge height generalizations are made depends on characteristics of the basin and its historical hurricane climatology.

Before conducting a vulnerability analysis, a couple of less significant water height features must be superimposed onto the SLOSH-generated surge height by the emergency planner. These are (1) the astronomical tide range above mean sea level (MSL) (in order to consider the hurricane approach coinciding with daily high tide) and (2) a 20% stillwater addition (in order to compensate for model inaccuracy based on a current survey of model performance).

The vulnerability analysis itself entails systematically subtracting the land elevation of each grid cell from the SLOSH-generated surge height, since the SLOSH elevations are referenced to MSL.

The inundation patterns that emerge from individual SLOSH simulations and MEOWs provide the basis for various evacuation scenarios requiring significantly different emergency operational response. Each level of evacuation encompasses cumulatively more area—and thus more evacuation zones—that must be completely cleared if threatened by that type and/ or intensity of hurricane. The actual number of evacuation levels varies from region to region, the ideal being the creation of enough levels to avoid over- or under-evacuation, yet sufficiently few to allow the development of a relatively simplified response plan and public information program. For example, the Tampa Bay Plan has five different evacuation levels, whereas the current Southeast Louisiana Study has resulted in twelve distinct evacuation levels.

Source: Excerpted from David A. Griffith, "Hurricane Emergency Management Applications of the SLOSH Numerical Storm Surge Prediction Model," in Sallie A. Marston, ed., *Terminal Disasters: Computer Application in Emergency Management* (Boulder: Institute of Behavioral Science, University of Colorado, 1986), 83–90.

is vital for the local emergency manager to ensure that they have an accurate grasp of risks.

Assessing the public's risk perceptions is important in determining how people will behave during an actual disaster as well as how they understand and will act upon the need for mitigation. Behavioral surveys are a standard tool for estimating the percentage of the exposed population that will evacuate, when they will evacuate, and where they will seek shelter. Results of these surveys are used to quantify the need for shelters and evacuation routes.[11] Results also show the public's level of understanding of hazard conditions. In addition to ensuring that up-to-date behavioral surveys are provided, the emergency manager also needs to participate actively in continuing public education efforts to ensure that people exposed to hazards know the risks they face and the steps they can take as individuals to reduce these risks.

Estimating mitigation benefits and costs

Once the economic loss estimates have been completed, the emergency manager can estimate the potential benefits of mitigation. In its most basic form, this estimate requires three steps: (1) projecting reduced disaster-related losses anticipated in the absence of a mitigation program; (2) projecting disaster-related losses under the mitigation program, less the costs of the program itself; and (3) comparing the projected level of loss *without* the mitigation program to the projected level *with* the program. A more disaggregated approach tabulates benefits for different types of specific public objectives, such as economic efficiency, environmental quality, and individual safety (see sidebar).[12] Note that not all costs and benefits can be stated in dollars. The reduced losses (that is, the benefits) usually far outweigh the costs of the mitigation program.

Example of a benefit/cost calculation for floodplain management (data from ten cities)

	Benefits	Costs
Economic efficiency	Reduction in average annual flood damages: $10.994 million	Annual cost of floodplain management program: $0.345 million
Environmental quality	Environmental resource conservation: 3,513 acres of open space preserved in floodplains	Environmental resource damage: 2,545 residential and 379 nonresidential building sites filled to meet floodplain elevation requirements
Public safety	Reduced exposure to risk: 21,920 persons and 9,444 dwellings diverted from floodplains	Increased construction costs due to floodproofing for buildings in floodplains: $1.590 million
	NFIP coverage of property in floodplains: $556 million	Annual flood insurance premiums paid by individuals and firms: $2.694 million

Source: Adapted from R. J. Burby et al., *Cities Under Water: A Comparative Evaluation of Ten Cities' Efforts to Manage Floodplain Land Use* (Boulder: Institute of Behavioral Science, University of Colorado, 1988), 188–191.

A given mitigation program, for example, may increase the cost of public and private construction in hazard-prone areas by 10 percent and may require a 5 percent increase in the annual emergency management budget. On the other hand, the same mitigation program may reduce expected disaster property damage and personal injury by 50 percent. In most cases, it can be shown that an ounce of predisaster mitigation is worth a pound of postdisaster response. Quantifying the costs and benefits of mitigation can be a powerful way to counter the objections of mitigation opponents.

Preparing mitigation strategies

Once the hazard identification and analysis have been done, the emergency manager can begin to create community awareness of and support for mitigation. Preparing mitigation strategies, the third step in the mitigation process, involves working with local planners, decision makers, and community leaders to build mitigation into both public policy actions and private development practice. This work involves operating in the "shared governance" arena, where responsibilities and decision making are spread among a number of public and private actors, including federal, state, and local government agencies as well as private builders, developers, financial institutions, and other interests.[13]

At this stage the emergency manager makes a tentative selection of the mitigation techniques that seem feasible for the jurisdiction, works with local planners to explore how these techniques can be integrated into comprehensive plans and development regulations, looks for linkages with other public and private efforts such as recreation and open space preservation, and starts to educate community leaders and the public about the importance and value of mitigation.

Natural-hazard mitigation strategies preserve and restore the innate mitigative features of the natural environment, strengthen exposed buildings and facilities to withstand hazard impacts, facilitate the evacuation and sheltering of exposed populations, relocate threatened development out of hazard areas, and limit future development in hazard areas. Technological-hazard mitigation strategies redirect the movement of hazardous materials, neutralize hazardous material disposal areas, relocate away from population concentrations those facilities using or producing hazardous materials, strengthen containment systems for hazardous substances, and reduce hazard generation in manufacturing and industrial processes.

The Lee County, Florida, mitigation strategy illustrates how hurricane and flood hazard mitigation can be successfully built into a local comprehensive plan. Thanks to close coordination between the emergency management division and the planning division, this Gulf Coast county gained approval of an innovative hurricane and flood hazard reduction strategy that includes charging the costs of mitigation to the county residents, linking future development to the capacity of evacuation systems, and requiring postdisaster redevelopment to include actions to reduce vulnerability. Because some 20 percent of the county land area and some 40 percent of its assessed tax value lie within the hundred-year flood zone, debate over mitigation proposals was fierce. After numerous public hearings and information meetings, however, the elected officials were convinced of the need for mitigation, and the proposed strategy was formally adopted in the goals, objectives, and policies of the 1989 Lee County Comprehensive Plan (see sidebar on page 152).

The Santa Rosa, California, postearthquake experience illustrates how a committed community has been able to adopt and maintain an effective continuing seismic safety program over some two decades.[14] Following two 1969 earthquakes that caused more than six million dollars' worth of damage to public and private facilities, mostly in the central business district, the city adopted a strategy combining downtown redevelopment and citywide abatement of structural hazards. In the downtown area, earthquake-damaged

Hazard mitigation goals, objectives, and policies in the 1989 Lee County, Florida, Comprehensive Plan

Goal: Planning, coordination, and implementation   To protect the public from the effects of natural and technological hazards. . . .

Objective   The county shall maintain a system . . . for protecting the population at risk to injury or death from the natural and technological hazards defined in the 1984 Lee County Hazard Vulnerability Analysis or subsequent updates.

Policy   The Lee County Comprehensive Emergency Management Plan shall be used as the operational guide in preparing for, responding to, and recovering from natural and technological hazards requiring emergency actions. . . .

Policy   The county . . . shall implement a program of education and information describing the risks of hazards such as hurricanes, tropical storms, severe thunderstorms, tornadoes, lightning, freezes, and attack from hostile governments; and actions necessary to mitigate the dangers which these present. . . .

Goal: Protection of life and property   To protect human life and developed property from natural disasters.

Objective: Development in hazard areas   Development (other than minor structures) within the V Zones shall not be allowed seaward of the Coastal Construction Control Line; . . . New development on barrier islands shall be limited to densities that meet required evacuation standards; new development requiring seawalls for protection from coastal erosion shall not be permitted; and allowable densities for undeveloped areas within A Zone areas will be considered for reduction. . . .

Policy   Rezonings to allow higher densities shall not be permitted on barrier and coastal islands if the capacity of critical evacuation routes would thereby be exceeded. . . .

Policy   Through the plan amendment process, land use designations of undeveloped areas within the A Zone shall be considered for reduced density categories . . . in order to limit the future population exposed to coastal flooding and hurricane damage.

Goal: Limitation of public expenditures in hazard areas   To restrict public expenditures in areas particularly subject to repeated destruction by hurricanes, except to maintain required service levels, to protect existing residents, and to provide for recreation and open space uses.

Goal: Hazard mitigation   To provide . . . means to minimize future property losses from tropical storms and hurricanes.

Objective: Development regulations   By 1990, all development regulations shall be reviewed and revised to require that the vulnerability of future development in the A Zone . . . be reduced.

Policy   Regulations and incentives will be examined for additional setbacks in critical erosion areas, conservation and enhancement of dunes and vegetation, floodproofing of utilities, and appropriate requirements for structural wind resistance and floodplain management. . . .

Objective: Public funds   By 1990, the county shall establish a funding source to provide funds for hazard mitigation and disaster recovery needs.

Policy   The county shall consider impact fees or a Hazard Mitigation MSTU (Multiple Service Taxing Unit) to cover the public costs of hazard mitigation, floodproofing, evacuation, search and rescue, acquisition of hazard-prone property, reconstruction of public facilities, construction or improvements to shelters, and similar needs.

Source: Lee County, Florida, 1989 Comprehensive Plan.

buildings were removed and replaced with a quake-resistant regional shopping center that not only added to hazard mitigation but also contributed to economic development. (Such "piggybacking" of mitigation with other community goals often is an effective technique.) A citywide hazard abatement ordinance was adopted requiring a structural review by the city of certain types of hazard-prone buildings; the owners were then required to bring the buildings up to current seismic safety code standards within a year of the review. Between 1971 and 1978, some 250 buildings were reviewed through the program, and many of them were found to need, and subsequently received, rehabilitation to meet standards. This was a major accomplishment, given that the older buildings were usually built of unreinforced masonry and were highly vulnerable to earthquake damage. Moving slowly but surely, the city staff convinced elected officials of the importance of mitigation and kept the program flexible and responsive enough to avoid controversy. Steady growth and a rise in property values encouraged owners, especially new owners, to comply with rehabilitation recommendations. In addition to the ordinance, the city adopted a seismic safety element in its general plan, reaffirming its commitment to abate structural hazards and to regulate land use in areas of significant natural hazard.

Mitigation tools and techniques

The array of mitigation tools and techniques includes plans, development regulations, taxation and spending programs, insurance, and hazard information systems. Choosing among these approaches is both a technical and a political process. On the technical side, each tool available to the community can be cross-checked against a list of all local hazards to define the set of tools most likely to be effective in dealing with the full slate of community hazards (see Figure 6–3). For example, for nearly all types of hazards, identification of urban service areas in land use plans can be used together with hazard zone identification to separate service areas, with their encouragement of urban development, from hazard areas, with their concomitant risks. However, specialized tools like soil reports are useful primarily for earthquake and landslide mitigation. On the political side, the emergency manager must assess the likelihood of local acceptance of new or unfamiliar approaches to mitigation. For example, it might be easier to persuade local elected officials to adopt hazard overlay districts and density bonuses for hazard mitigation in the zoning ordinance than to adopt a more complicated transfer-of-development-rights program.

Plans

Emergency management plans lay the groundwork for emergency operations. For mitigation, it is important to work also with the community's comprehensive or land use plans, which specify the locations of future growth and development, as well as the adopted goals, objectives, and policies of the community. Comprehensive or land use plans should point out hazard areas, such as floodplains or fault zones, and provide policies and standards to control development there to reduce vulnerability. Such plans may include sections on evacuation, recovery, and reconstruction. Some states, such as Florida, require local comprehensive plans to include these sections; most states do not. Hazard mitigation elements of both local comprehensive plans and local emergency management plans should be all-encompassing. The sidebar on page 155 lists the mitigation issues a community must consider in formulating a flood management plan under the NFIP, for example.

Plans are necessary but not sufficient mitigation tools. They can generate consensus about the need to take mitigation action and commit to mitigation programs. But to reduce hazards effectively, plans must be regularly updated,

Figure 6–3   Tools and hazards matrix.

Tools	Hazards					
	Flood	Earthquake	Landslide	Hurricane	Nuclear accident	Toxic spill
Land use plan						
Urban services area	+	+	+	+	+	0
Hazard zone identification	+	+	+	+	+	+
Evacuation plan	+	+	+	+	+	+
Reconstruction guides	+	+	+	+	+	0
Hazardous materials transportation	0	0	0	0	0	+
Zoning						
Hazard overlay districts	+	+	+	+	+	0
Mitigation performance standards	+	+	+	+	0	0
Hazard mitigation bonus	+	+	+	+	0	0
Nonconforming requirements	+	+	+	+	0	0
Subdivision regulations						
Hazard disclosure	+	+	+	+	+	0
Hazard area dedication	+	+	+	+	0	0
Soil reports	0	+	+	0	0	0
Building code						
Elevation requirements	+	−	−	+	0	0
Wind resistance requirements	+	+	+	+	0	0
Public health regulations						
Hazard overlay districts	+	+	+	+	+	0
Construction standards	+	+	+	+	+	+
Public facility programs						
Siting requirements	+	+	+	+	+	0
Capital improvement programs	+	+	+	+	+	0
Land acquisition						
Hazard/open space	+	+	+	+	+	+
TDR (transfer of development rights)	+	+	+	+	+	0
Taxation						
Preferential hazard assessment	+	+	+	+	+	0

Key
+   Complementary
0   Neutral
−   Conflicting

monitored, and evaluated. More important, they must be implemented, whether through regulations, budgets, or ongoing decision making.

Regulations

The most widely used tools for implementing plans and managing development are regulations, such as zoning ordinances, subdivision regulations, building codes, and public health regulations. Zoning ordinances regulate the use of land and structures and set standards for setbacks and yards, building height and bulk, lot size, density, and treatment of nonconforming uses and structures. Zoning can be used to limit development or reconstruction in hazard-prone areas, to establish performance standards that reduce vulnerability, and to create incentives for development that incorporates hazard mitigation.

Subdivision regulations govern not only the conversion of raw land into building sites but also the provision of improvements such as streets and utilities. These regulations can be used to require the floodproofing of infrastructure, the dedication of hazard areas for open space, the clustering of buildings on least hazardous site areas, and the disclosure of risks to prospective lot buyers. An example of the use of subdivision regulations to mitigate hazards is the requirement by some Utah counties that for sites in potential debris flow areas, developers obtain soil and engineering reports and topographic maps identifying hazardous conditions. At-risk properties are placed on a debris flow hazard list and can be developed only if engineering solutions can be found to stabilize slopes or buildings can be sited in ways that eliminate risk.

Building codes set safety standards for construction materials, design, and procedures. Codes can be used to protect new construction in hazard areas by specifying design standards for resistance to the stresses of natural and technological hazards, such as floods, high winds, earth movement, or explosion. Building codes can also set standards for retrofitting existing buildings to make them less vulnerable, such as older buildings in earthquake-prone areas.

Public health regulations govern the design and operation of public utilities such as water and sewer systems and facilities for disposal of solid and hazardous wastes. These regulations can set health and safety requirements for industrial processes and can also be used to protect against contamination from hazardous substances by governing system location and design, especially in areas prone to natural hazards.

Concerns in the development of a flood management program under the NFIP

Human safety

Diversion of development to areas safe from flooding

Disclosure to prospective buyers and renters that structures are located in flood-prone areas

Adverse effects of floodplain development on existing development

Encouragement of floodproofing

Flood warning and preparedness plans

Alternate access and escape routes

Minimum floodproofing and access standards for hospitals, nursing homes, police stations, and other public facilities in flood-prone areas

Improvement of local drainage

Coordination of plans with those of neighboring communities

Requirement that new construction in subsidence areas be elevated above base flood level plus expected ten-year subsidence

Requirement that developers delineate floodways

Maintenance of flood-carrying capacity by restricting alteration of watercourses

Setbacks for new construction in high-hazard coastal areas

Additional elevation above base flood level for new construction in special flood hazard areas (land within the 100-year floodplain) and high-hazard coastal areas (land subject to high-velocity storm surge)

Consistency among state, regional, and local plans

Prohibition of the use of fill to elevate structures within flood-prone areas

Prohibition of hazardous materials facilities in floodways and high-hazard coastal areas

Source: Adapted from Richard Hamann and Jeff Wade, *Mitigation of Hurricane Losses: Federal, State and Local Programs*, SGR-100 (Gainesville: Florida Seagrant College Program, University of Florida, 1990), 26–27.

Regulations that impose extra requirements on development in hazard areas are sometimes criticized for the additional costs associated with higher standards. Nevertheless, as long as these regulations are uniformly applied to all similar hazard areas, they are defensible because they protect public health and safety. Moreover, their long-term economic costs should be less than the economic benefits of reduced vulnerability.

Spending and taxing programs

Relocation of threatened structures, public acquisition of hazard-prone lands, and floodproofing of public facilities are examples of government mitigation spending programs. Relocation of threatened structures is now an allowable expense under the NFIP and can also be assisted by local programs of technical assistance. Land acquisition can take the form of outright purchase or the less expensive purchase of easements or development rights.[15] Often land acquisition in hazard areas can be "piggybacked" on acquisition programs for recreational and environmental open space. Floodproofing can protect roads and utility systems from stresses caused by future disasters.

Financing the public costs of mitigation requires dependable revenue sources. Taxing powers can be used to provide private owners with incentives to undertake mitigation actions. For instance, "preferential" or "use value" taxation taxes land in hazard areas on the basis of its actual income production rather than its market value, providing the owner agrees to maintain low-density use of the land. Taxing powers also can be used to provide revenue for mitigation programs through special impact fees or hazard district taxes.[16] In Illinois, for example, the marine motor fuel tax helps to fund redevelopment of damaged waterfront areas for boat landing facilities.

Insurance

Hazard insurance spreads the costs of disasters among a broad group of policyholders. Even though insurance programs are operated at the national or state level, the local emergency manager should be aware of their provisions. Pointing out to local decision makers that mitigation actions can lower insurance premiums is often effective in convincing them to adopt a local mitigation program.

The National Flood Insurance Program is the only federal hazard mitigation insurance program now in effect. Under NFIP, private property owners in flood hazard areas are eligible to purchase federal flood insurance if their locality has qualified through instituting elevation, floodproofing, and zoning regulations to reduce the vulnerability of exposed property. As mentioned earlier, recent amendments allow insurance payments for demolishing or relocating threatened structures as well as those damaged by floods. The NFIP requirements are powerful incentives for both individual and community flood hazard mitigation.

Many states also have established wind damage insurance pools that allow residents to purchase wind damage insurance to complement the federal flood insurance. Neither flood nor wind damage insurance risks have been attractive to the private insurance sector.

Hazard information systems

Hazard information systems are another crucial implement of effective mitigation. Such systems record, update, analyze, and display data about the location, intensity, scope, and impacts of hazards.

The emergence of computer software for hazard analysis and mitigation has added a new tool to the emergency manager's kit. Computerized hazard mitigation information systems are available to map hazard areas, maintain hazard identification and analysis databases, and test mitigation scenarios.

At the operational level, computer programs have been developed to evaluate evacuation scenarios against hazard spread and impact patterns and to support emergency management decisions.[17] In addition, geographic information systems (GIS) allow long-range mitigation strategies to be formulated and tested. GIS capabilities offer opportunities to model alternative land use and transportation patterns under various hazard mitigation approaches and to compare the costs and benefits of various mitigation packages.[18]

Mitigation and public policy

The goal of mitigation is to save lives and dollars while preventing the community fabric from being torn apart by disasters. Although mitigation is not free, its short-term economic and political costs are most often greatly outweighed by its long-term community benefits. But if the emergency manager does not actively demonstrate to community leaders the values of mitigation, then the community is less likely to undertake the proactive efforts necessary for effective implementation of a program.

Mitigation actions can be controversial. Developers may argue that mitigation needlessly increases the costs of housing and other development projects. Environmentalists usually support mitigation that protects the natural environment but may argue that proposed strategies do not go far enough. Conservative political groups may object to mitigation on principle, arguing that it increases government influence in the private sphere. Residents of hazard-prone areas may object to postdisaster restrictions on rebuilding their houses.

The emergency manager must be able to counter these objections, ideally by educating concerned groups about the benefits of mitigation. For instance, widespread public opposition to a proposed program to acquire flood-prone properties in Baltimore County, Maryland, was overcome when community leaders were placed on a task force charged with solving the problem of repeated flooding. Once they understood the favorable benefit-cost ratio of the acquisition strategy, the leaders became strong supporters. By 1980, the county had purchased 189 flood-prone homes at a cost of approximately eleven million dollars.

Another effective argument is that hazard mitigation is good business. By totaling the potential dollars-and-cents savings from mitigation efforts, emergency managers can convince even skeptical decision makers that it is in everyone's interest to reduce risks.

Yet another argument for hazard mitigation is that not to reduce risk is irresponsible. When public officials are made aware that they could even be viewed as liable for malfeasance because they knew of potential disasters yet did not act to reduce risk, they are likely to become more receptive to mitigation policy proposals.[19] Most of the strategies for reducing local government liability involve mitigation actions (see sidebar on page 158).

Finally, it can be argued that mitigation often furthers other community goals. Additional recreation and open space, preservation of critical environmental areas, safer housing, and more efficient transportation systems are some of the objectives that mitigation can help to achieve.

Mitigation needs a champion to stand up and argue for it. In Portola Valley, California, a geologist was hired to document the hazards of the earthquake fault that lay under the town and to convince public officials to adopt regulations for seismic safety. In Tulsa, Oklahoma, following repeated floods, the mayor championed the enactment of expanded flood hazard mitigation and succeeded in creating a new department of stormwater management and gaining a seventy-five-million-dollar commitment to solve flooding and drainage problems.

Strategies for reducing potential hazard-related liability

1. Avoid municipal actions which may cause or worsen hazards, such as operation of a landfill in an area of high groundwater or construction of a dike in a floodway. The avoidance of such activities can be facilitated by an inventory of hazards and the mapping of natural hazard areas. Such information then can be reflected in the public facilities plan, the land use plan, and community regulations. If community activities are to occur in hazard areas, the community should comply with all applicable federal, state, and local regulations including its own, and it should design and maintain structures consistent with sound geologic, architectural, and engineering practices.

2. Prevent private actions which will increase hazards or hazard losses. Landowners have no "right" to create or exacerbate hazards. The control of private actions can be accomplished through upgraded zoning subdivision control, building codes or other special codes, and careful evaluation of permit applications. Developers can be made to submit much of the information needed for analysis. Certifications of "safety" and compliance by registered architects, engineers, and geologists can also be required. To the extent possible, responsibility for mitigating hazards on private lands should be placed squarely in the laps of those wishing to use such lands.

3. Require disclaimers of public liability when private uses are permitted in a hazard area (e.g., a bluff erosion area). Such disclaimers can help reduce potential liability suits by successors in title to the permittee, although disclaimers are no panacea, particularly where negligence is involved.

4. Submit all policy-related decisions to the local governing body for debate and approval so they become "discretionary," "planning," or "legislative" rather than "ministerial" acts.

5. Develop a hazard preparedness plan to deal with problems when (or if) they occur (such as a hurricane evacuation plan). This may help support the reasonableness of community action.

6. Carefully comply with state and federal statutory requirements and the community's own regulations in planning, regulation, acquisition, and other activities to avoid due process problems and possible subrogation suits (e.g., under the National Flood Insurance Program).

7. Ensure that all hazard mitigation measures, including permit approvals and denials, are based upon adequate data; also, provide equitable and evenhanded administration and enforcement of hazard regulations to avoid due process and possible "taking" challenges.

8. Encourage private landowners in hazard areas to carry insurance (e.g., flood insurance, earthquake insurance). A landowner compensated by insurance after a loss is less likely to sue the municipality.

9. Upgrade hazard mitigation plans and measures as data, mitigation technologies, and mitigation strategies improve.

Source: Jon A. Kusler, "Liability as a Dilemma for Local Managers," *Public Administration Review* 45 (January 1985): 121. Reprinted with permission from *Public Administration Review* © 1985 by the American Society for Public Administration (ASPA), 1120 G Street, N.W., Suite 500, Washington, DC 20005. All rights reserved.

The wise emergency manager will look for allies in promoting the mitigation cause. In addition to federal and state emergency management officials, potential supporters include local and regional planning staffs, environmental interest groups, chambers of commerce, elected officials, and businesses and people at risk. Mobilizing broad support greatly increases the chances of securing a strong and effective mitigation policy.

1 For damage estimates from these 1989 disasters, see Interagency Hazard Mitigation Team Report, *Hurricane Hugo* (Washington, DC: FEMA, 1989); and Dames and Moore, *The October 17, 1989 Loma Prieta Earthquake* (Los Angeles: Dames and Moore, 1989).

2 See Advisory Committee on the International Decade for Natural Hazard Reduction, *Confronting Natural Disasters: An International Decade for Natural Hazard Reduction* (Washington, DC: National Academy Press, 1987).

3 FEMA, *Mitigation Program Development Guidance* (Washington, DC: FEMA 1987). See also FEMA, *Making Mitigation Work: A Handbook for State Officials* (Washington, DC: FEMA, 1986).

4 For earthquakes, see the report to Congress by FEMA, *National Earthquake Hazards Reduction Program: Fiscal Year 1987 Activities* (Washington, DC: U.S. Government Printing Office, 1988); FEMA, *Estimating Losses from Future Earthquakes* (Washington, DC: FEMA, 1989); Earthquake Engineering Research Institute, *Reducing Earthquake Hazards* (El Cerrito, CA: 1986); Dames and Moore, *The Loma Prieta Earthquake*. For landslides, see National Research Council, *Reducing Losses from Landsliding in the United States* (Washington, DC: National Academy Press, 1985), as well as FEMA, *Landslide Loss Reduction: A Guide for State and Local Government Planning* (Washington, DC: FEMA, 1989). For hazardous materials exposure, see National Response Team, *Hazardous National Emergency Planning Guide* (Washington, DC: Environmental Protection Agency, 1987).

5 David R. Godschalk and David J. Brower, "Mitigation Strategies and Integrated Emergency Management," *Public Administration Review* 45 (January 1985): 64–71.

6 D. S. Mileti, *Natural Hazard Warning Systems in the United States: A Research Assessment* (Boulder: Institute of Behavioral Science, University of Colorado, 1975).

7 See Rae Zimmerman, "Public Acceptability of Alternative Waste Management Services," in *Psychosocial Effects of Hazardous Toxic Waste Disposal on Communities*, ed. Dennis Peck (Springfield, IL: Charles C Thomas, 1989), 197–237.

8 See S. French and M. Isaacson, "Applying Earthquake Risk Analysis Techniques to Land Use Planning," *Journal of the American Planning Association* 50, no. 4 (Autumn 1984): 509–22; M. Jaffe, J. A. Butler, and C. Thurow, *Reducing Earthquake Risks: A Planner's Guide* (Chicago: American Planning Association, 1981); and D. Erley and W. J. Kockelman, *Reducing Landslide Hazards: A Guide for Planners* (Chicago: American Planning Association, 1981).

9 For an example of a hurricane loss estimate, see Tampa Bay Regional Planning Council, *Tampa Bay Hurricane Loss and Contingency Planning Study* (St. Petersburg, FL: Tampa Bay Regional Planning Council, 1983). The council inventories residential, commercial, industrial, and institutional properties and develops five scenarios of loss from possible storms corresponding to the five Saffir-Simpson hurricane intensities. Using SLOSH (Sea, Lake, and Overland Surges from Hurricanes) model data produced by the National Hurricane Center, the council estimates the property damage from standing water, storm surge, wave action, and winds for each scenario. For examples of earthquake loss estimates, see National Research Council, *Estimating Losses from Future Earthquakes* (Washington, DC: National Academy Press, 1989). This publication, which has been issued by FEMA as an Earthquake Hazards Reduction Series publication, provides an in-depth review of earthquake loss estimation methodology.

10 For a positive assessment of the importance local governments accord to hazard priorities, see David R. Godschalk, David J. Brower, and Timothy Beatley, *Catastrophic Coastal Storms: Hazard Mitigation and Development Management* (Durham, NC: Duke University Press, 1989); for a negative assessment of the importance of hazard priorities on local government agendas, see Peter Rossi, James Wright, and Eleanor Weber-Burdin, *Natural Hazards and Public Choice: The State and Local Politics of Hazard Mitigation* (New York: Academic Press, 1982).

11 Behavioral surveys are reviewed by Earl J. Baker, "Public Attitudes toward Hazard Zone Controls," *Journal of the American Planning Association* 43 (1977): 401–8.

12 For an application of benefit-cost analysis, see R. J. Burby et al., *Cities under Water: A Comparative Evaluation of Ten Cities' Efforts to Manage Floodplain Land Use* (Boulder: Institute of Behavioral Science, University of Colorado, 1988).

13 See Peter J. May and Walter Williams, *Disaster Policy Implementation: Managing Programs under Shared Governance* (New York: Plenum Press, 1986).

14 See William Spangle and Associates, Inc., *Land Use Planning after Earthquakes* (Portola Valley, CA: William Spangle and Associates, Inc., 1980).

15 See P. J. Pizor, "Making TDR Work: A Study of Program Implementation," *Journal of the American Planning Association* 52, no. 2 (Spring 1986), 203–11. See also F. S. Bangs and C. Bagne, eds., *Transferable Development Rights* (Chicago: American Society of Planning Officials, 1975).

16 For impact fee approaches, see Thomas Snyder and Michael Stegman, *Paying for Growth* (Washington, DC: Urban Land Institute, 1987). See

also James Frank and Robert Rhodes, eds., *Development Exactions* (Chicago: Planners Press, 1987).

17 Reviews of several computer programs for decision support, simulation, and modeling are provided in S. A. Marston, ed., *Terminal Disasters: Computer Applications in Emergency Management* (Boulder: Institute of Behavioral Science, University of Colorado, 1986).

18 For a technical discussion of GIS, see P. A. Burrough, *Principles of Geographic Information Systems for Land Resources Assessment* (New York: Oxford University Press, 1986). See also Jeffrey Star and John Estes, *Geographic Information Systems: An Introduction* (Englewood Cliffs, NJ: Prentice Hall, 1990).

19 For a review of the increase in governmental liability suits based on losses from disasters, see Jon A. Kusler, "Liability as a Dilemma for Local Managers," *Public Administration Review* 45 (January 1985): 118–22.

7 Planning, training, and exercising

In cities and counties across the United States, a large-scale technological or natural disaster can occur at any time, leaving death and destruction in its wake. One need only remember September and October of 1989, when millions of people were directly affected by Hurricane Hugo on the East Coast and by the Loma Prieta earthquake in California. The majority of disasters are responded to by the local governments in the jurisdictions where they occur, because local elected officials have an inherent or a statutory responsibility to protect lives and property with coordinated response. The individual who fulfills this critical responsibility on behalf of local elected officials is the emergency manager.

Achieving the coordinated response of community emergency services is not easy. To mount an effective response to a disaster, the emergency manager must have leadership ability and managerial skills and must have, in addition, a thorough knowledge and understanding of emergency planning, training, and exercising—and the relationships among them.

The purpose of this chapter is to help the emergency manager use planning, training, and exercises to develop an effective response within the community. The chapter begins with a case study illustrating how planning, training, and exercising contributed to effective response in the medical evacuation in Pinellas County, Florida, in 1985—the largest medical evacuation in U.S. history. Next, the chapter discusses planning: current approaches to planning (including the integrated emergency management system—IEMS), the types of plans presently required, formats and levels of plans, and, most important, ways of organizing local government to conduct emergency planning. Since IEMS is now a widely used approach to planning, the discussion will address some of the potential difficulties its implementation may involve. This also relates to the next logical step—training the key decision-making personnel and responders in implementing the emergency plan—and that is discussed next. Finally, the chapter discusses the last key step in achieving effective response—the development of a program for conducting exercises to permit evaluation and improvement of the emergency plan.

The entire discussion applies to emergency managers in general, whatever the size and population of the jurisdiction. Although vulnerability and threats vary, every community needs to develop an emergency preparedness program that permits effective response. (A program to improve response with planning, training, and exercising is also applicable to building an effective capacity for recovery, which is often overlooked by the emergency manager.)

Case study: The largest medical evacuation in U.S. history

As a prelude, let's look in detail at a relatively recent disaster to see how the three elements of planning, training, and exercising can result in effective response when they are properly integrated into the emergency management program.

In late August 1985, the largest single-state peacetime evacuation in the history of the United States was undertaken in response to the threat of Hurricane Elena. As the hurricane approached the Florida Gulf Coast, local officials in nineteen coastal counties issued mandatory evacuation orders, and more than one million residents moved to safe areas.

Pinellas County was among those evacuated. A heavily populated coastal county, Pinellas was one of four large urban counties of the Tampa Bay Region that had been conducting comprehensive hurricane evacuation planning since early 1980. All four counties had conducted two large, full-scale regional hurricane exercises as part of the evacuation planning; the last exercise was completed fewer than thirty days before Hurricane Elena.

The damage statistics for Pinellas County alone indicate the immensity of the problem that county and municipal emergency management officials faced.

Deaths 4

Injured (hospitalized) 76

Injured (not hospitalized) 395

Evacuees 350,000+

Shelters opened 70

Persons sheltered 114,000

Dwelling units destroyed 256

Dwelling units damaged 7,707

Estimated damage $100 million

Even more remarkable is the fact that, in addition to evacuating over 350,000 threatened residents and sheltering 114,000 evacuees during a three-day period, Pinellas County undertook the largest medical evacuation in the history of the United States: 211 patients in three hospitals and 1,860 residents of nineteen nursing homes were moved to safe areas.

Pinellas County's effective response—which is discussed further below—was based on the attention that county emergency management officials had paid to planning, training, and exercising.

Planning

In late 1979, Pinellas County emergency management officials reviewed medical facility evacuation plans and found that for both the county as a whole and individual medical facilities, hurricane evacuation planning was almost non-existent; any plans that were in place were inadequate or impossible to implement. (For example, for licensing purposes a medical facility might have had to designate a shelter—but careful review revealed the shelter itself to be in an evacuation zone.)

The most serious problems were in nursing home evacuation planning, especially because, in a major hurricane, thirty-five nursing homes would be at risk from storm surge flooding. Emergency management officials felt that a concentrated, cooperative effort was necessary to improve the nursing home evacuation component of the county emergency plan. In addition, reviews of individual nursing home plans indicated a need for detailed guidelines to assist nursing home administrators, who have a statutory obligation to develop a preparedness plan.

To ensure that nursing home administrators were active and engaged participants in the planning process—and that any resulting plans not only met licensing requirements but were also realistic and capable of being implemented—a nursing home disaster committee was formed, consisting of representatives from emergency management, the local health department, and selected at-risk nursing homes. The emergency manager provided general direction to the committee and, through the committee, was able to work with all seventy-five nursing homes in the county. Thus, although the committee had no legal standing, it served a coordinating function.

As a starting point, the committee used a site-specific hazard vulnerability analysis that had been completed during the Tampa Bay comprehensive hurricane evacuation planning in 1980–81 (see Figure 7–1; the hazard vulnerability analysis is also discussed in detail in the section on plan development at the local level). The analysis was distributed to all nursing homes and incorporated into the county emergency plan. The committee also used a concept of operation that the emergency manager developed for the plan after the hazard analysis was completed: a general overview of how the evacuations would be undertaken. The committee then directed its efforts toward improving planning and plan implementation, focusing particularly on establishing a nursing home warning and communication system, reviewing transportation needs, and completing transfer agreements between evacuating and host facilities. Although the committee was concentrating on nursing home plans, its work provided the emergency manager with information that could then be incorporated into the county emergency plan, for example, the number of patients that could be transported by bus and the number that would require ambulances.

Warning and communication system   Because the nursing homes were not required to have radio communication, they were not a part of the county warning system. As a first step toward improving the situation, the emergency manager suggested the creation of a call-down system linking all nursing homes to the county warning point. (Under this system, the county warning point calls a designated "lead" nursing home, which in turn calls a designated number of other nursing homes. The branching process continues until all nursing homes have received the warning.) The committee coordinated the creation of the call-down system, which was incorporated into the individual nursing home plans and into the county emergency plan.

To further enhance communication capability, the emergency manager assigned a Radio Emergency Associated Citizens Team (REACT) group to work with evacuating and host nursing homes. (REACT is a volunteer communications group that operates AM and FM citizens band radio equipment.) The committee worked on coordination and oversight; many nursing homes joined REACT and purchased radios for daily and emergency use.

Figure 7–1   Portion of the site-specific hazard vulnerability analysis completed for nursing homes in the Tampa Bay region.

Name and address	Phone (813)	Elevation	Surge heights by hurricane category[a]				
			1	2	3	4	5
Tierra Pines Convalescent Center 7625 Ulmerton Rd. Largo, FL 34643	535-9833	19'				23.0	23.7
Village at Countryside 1410 4th St. N. Safety Harbor, FL 33572	726-1181	27'					
West Bay Nursing Center 400 State Rd., 584 West Oldsmar, FL 34677	855-4661	10'			11.5	16.4	15.0

[a]Height (in feet) above mean sea level (MSL) of the storm surge, by hurricane category, at that location.

Transportation needs   The committee's second major focus was transportation. A detailed plan was worked out and incorporated into the county emergency plan. The transportation plan specified numbers of patients to be moved, numbers and types of assigned transportation resources, host facility contacts, and location of host facilities (see Figure 7–2). Nursing homes were required to plan on their own for trucks to move supplies and mattresses.

In the course of planning for transportation, the emergency manager had to determine whether county resources—that is, buses—would be made available to help the nursing homes evacuate, even though nursing home licensing regulations required the homes to have their own transportation agreements (with private bus companies, car and truck rental companies, and so forth). In practice, regardless of any separate transportation agreements, medical facilities are usually assisted by government-provided transport during an evacuation. In view of that, it was felt that consideration should be given to establishing a policy of assisting nursing homes with transportation assets (buses and other vehicles) for evacuation. The emergency manager made this general policy decision after discussion with the nursing home disaster committee.

Transfer agreements   The third major focus for the committee was transfer (or mutual aid) agreements (see Figure 7–3). To ensure coordination among nursing homes, the committee provided mutual aid agreements to evacuating and host nursing homes, to be completed and included in each nursing home's disaster plan. These agreements outlined the understandings between facilities

Figure 7–2   Excerpt from Pinellas County *Hurricane Evacuation Implementation Guide* showing evacuating nursing homes in order of priority.

Order	Lvl. Evac.	Name Address Facility phone Disaster rep. & phone	Required number regular buses	Required number buses w/lift	Required number ambulances	Evaluate to (1 + 2) Address & phone Num. received by shelter facility Grid
1A	Level A	Maria Manor Nursing Home 10300 4th St. N. St. Petersburg 33702 576-1025	3L	2L	10	St. Paul's School 1900 12th St. N. St. Petersburg 823-6144
		Peg McDonald 576-1025				# Received: 268 Grid: 627B
		Grid: 459A Evac. Zone: 14 Elevation: 4'	Avg. census: 268 By bus: 248 By amb.: 20			
		Remarks: Multiple trips required				# Received: 0 Grid:
1B	Level A	830 North Shore Dr. St. Petersburg 33701 894-2102	1s	1L	3	First Congregational Church 240 4th St. N. St. Petersburg 898-6785
		Mr. Richard E. Tappan 894-2102				# Received: 35 Grid: 651
		Grid: 202A Evac. Zone: 17 Elevation: 4'	Avg. census: 41 By bus: 35 By amb.: 6			Leisure Manor - S30 336 4th Ave. N. St. Petersburg 896-4171
		Remarks: 2nd phone # 823-1646				# Received: 6 Grid: 651

with respect to transfer of patients and of medical information, transportation costs, and so on.

Guidelines During the committee's work, it became clear that guidelines for developing the nursing home plans would be helpful. The emergency manager requested such guidelines from the state of Florida Department of Health and Rehabilitative Services (HRS)—but the HRS had none. It responded by inviting the emergency manager to submit a proposed plan format. He did so, and his suggested format was subsequently approved by the HRS and distributed to all nursing homes in Florida.

In designing the format, the emergency manager was particularly concerned to ensure that homes that followed the format would develop individual plans closely resembling the county's emergency plan. The planning guide ultimately distributed by the HRS stressed the importance for nursing home administrators of coordinating with their county's plan.

Figure 7–3 Sample mutual aid agreement.

Mutual Aid Agreement

or

Statement of Understanding

Between

_____ **and** _____
(Name of facility)   (Name of support agency)

_____   _____
(Address)   (Address)

_____   _____
(Telephone)   (Telephone)

Purpose To provide the "Facility" with pre-arranged support of alternative emergency resources, as needed during actual disaster situations, to minimize suffering and loss of life, injury, or property damage, (i.e., emergency supplies, evacuation, patient transportation, housing, subsistence, etc.)

Mission The "Support Agency" agrees to furnish the "Facility" goods, services, or facilities during time of actual disaster as follows:
The "Facility" agrees to pay the "Support Agency" a normal and reasonable fee for all goods and services rendered.

Execution The "Support Agency" will make the terms and conditions of this statement of understanding known to those who might have to respond, possibly on a 24-hour basis, and make such telephone numbers available to the "Facility" so that the necessary goods and services are reasonably available at any time.

_____   _____
(Date)   For the support agency

                                   _____
                                   For the facility

Training

To ensure that those who would have to implement the countywide plan fully understood it, emergency management and health department representatives began conducting training for upper-level nursing home management—nursing home administrators and directors of nursing. The classes were held at a central location and focused on the overall county evacuation plan, including the portions that pertained to nursing homes. This training was followed by in-service training at individual nursing homes, where the emergency manager and the nursing home administrator made a joint presentation of the county plan as a whole, the nursing home portion of the county plan, and the individual nursing home plan.

In addition, nursing home staffs had the opportunity to become familiar with the transportation provided for in the county plan. As part of their training, staff at some nursing homes (observed by staff from other nursing homes) practiced loading and unloading buses, including those with wheelchair lifts. The practice gave them an idea of the time involved and allowed them to spot potential problems.

Exercising

Two full-scale regional hurricane exercises complemented the concentrated planning and training efforts. (In addition, the nursing home call-down warning system was activated and exercised at least quarterly.) Nursing homes were encouraged to play an active role in the exercises, participating in the decision-making, warning, transportation, and evacuation components. During both exercises, administrators and staff from all nursing homes were invited to observe at the evacuating and receiving facilities.

During the first exercise, held in May 1982, forty-six patients were moved from two nursing homes to host facilities by means of two regular and two wheelchair-lift school buses (school buses were the means of transportation specified in the county plan). In July 1985 a second exercise was held, with all nursing homes participating in the warning and decision-making portions of the exercise and four conducting voluntary evacuations. The county provided the evacuating facilities with seven school buses, including three with wheelchair lifts. One nursing home exercised the portion of its individual plan that called for rental trucks to be used to transport supplies and bedding.

The lessons learned from the exercises were incorporated into the county and individual nursing home plans.

Response

When Hurricane Elena struck, the planning, training, and exercising that had been undertaken in Pinellas County paid off. The nineteen nursing homes in the county were evacuated in an average time of just over six hours. The individual nursing home disaster plans were implemented by 698 nursing home employees and 140 volunteers. Any emergency manager who has been involved in the evacuation of even a single medical facility can understand what was accomplished during this operation. The nursing homes evacuated by plan, not by individual order. In other words, an individual nursing home did not have to wait for a call ordering it to evacuate. The county issued a "level-B evacuation order," and all nursing homes that the plan designated as required to evacuate under a level-B order began to take action. This greatly helped the emergency manager and the emergency operations center maintain operational control of, and support for, an evacuation of that magnitude.

As in any large-scale evacuation, there were unforeseen problems. For example, one nursing home had to evacuate into an American Red Cross public shelter because the planned sheltering facility was not prepared to accept all of the home's patients. Although such an arrangement had not been included in the county plan, it succeeded because the individual nursing-home plans required the staff to remain with and care for the patients—thus relieving the Red Cross workers of the responsibility to do so.

Plans and planning

To develop insight into emergency planning and its relationship to effective response, the emergency manager should first understand approaches to disaster planning. A review of the characteristics of the two principal approaches—military planning and the integrated emergency management system—will clarify the origins of some planning requirements and explain difficulties that may be encountered in planning at the local level. Other topics discussed in this section are federal and state requirements as to type of plan; plan formats; and levels of plans. Organizing local government to conduct emergency planning is discussed in the subsequent section.

Two approaches to disaster planning: The military and IEMS

As is discussed in Chapter 1, emergency management has been shaped by two principal policy streams: responses to natural disasters, and civil defense. Because the responsibility for protecting the population from attack has traditionally been assigned to agencies operating under the Department of Defense, the plans and planning guides used in emergency management, even today, are derived from those used in military planning. They are highly structured and similar in format and organization to military plans, although a recent trend—especially in Comprehensive Hurricane Evacuation Planning—is to develop plans more suited to the civilian government environment than to the military.

Trying to superimpose the military approach on a municipal or county government inevitably leads to problems because the military is oriented toward planning, whereas local government is not. The very organization of the military is designed to develop, support, and implement rigidly formatted plans: a portion of each staff section is assigned planning responsibilities, and all military planners are trained in the same planning processes and formats. In contrast, the only local government department whose exclusive task is to plan is the planning department—and general planners rarely receive training in emergency planning.

The second principal approach to emergency planning derives from the integrated emergency management system (IEMS), which FEMA is currently promulgating. In contrast to past emergency plans, which might have addressed a single hazard (a hurricane, a nuclear attack, an earthquake), IEMS supports the development of multihazard plans with functional annexes and, if necessary, hazard-specific appendixes. But this approach, too, has several disadvantages, foremost of which is the creation of voluminous documents that response agencies find cumbersome to use, and not only because of their size. To become acquainted with the response to a particular hazard, such as a hurricane, one must read the entire plan. This makes it difficult to acquaint local government officials with response plans for individual hazards, which is the usual method of briefing and preparation.

Keeping in mind some of the inherent problems created by both the military and the IEMS approach to planning, let's look in detail at requirements for types of plans, plan format, and levels of plans.

Federal and state requirements: Types of plans

This chapter cannot specify all federal and state planning requirements. Emergency managers must consult the FEMA civil preparedness guides (CPGs) and, to determine local requirements, their own state statutes and administrative rules. In doing so, emergency managers should be alert to the fact that the system of state and federal regulations contains contradictions, a number of which are highlighted in the following pages.

In general, FEMA recommends that each jurisdiction develop a comprehensive emergency operations plan (EOP) encompassing all hazards that pose a significant threat to the community—including nuclear attack. Current regulations call for a generic, or all-hazard, EOP in keeping with the IEMS concept.

For a state or local emergency management agency to be eligible for funds under FEMA's Emergency Management Assistance (EMA) program, one requirement is that its EOP conform to the regulations outlined in the appropriate CPGs. A state agency must have a FEMA-approved EOP, and a sub-agent (local jurisdiction) must have an EOP approved by the appropriate local chief executive and accepted by the governor or other authorized state official. In short, FEMA has tied EMA grants directly to plan development and approval. Unfortunately, this often results in plans that meet funding requirements rather than community needs.

The objectives of emergency management planning vary, depending on the CPG being used. According to CPG 1–5, *Objectives for Local Emergency Management* (July 1984), the objective of emergency planning is to develop and maintain a comprehensive EOP on the basis of a hazard analysis, existing resources, and current operational capabilities to deal effectively with any kind of emergency—whether natural, technological, or civil. However, according to CPG 1-8, *Guide for Development of State and Local Emergency Operations Plans* (October 1985), the objectives of emergency management planning at the state and local level are to

Foster a nationwide systematic approach to state and local planning for emergency management

Develop plans supporting a capability for prompt, coordinated response to large-scale disasters or threats simultaneously by all levels of government

Provide a basis for assured continuity of government (COG) at all levels for the duration of large-scale disaster situations and other major emergencies

Improve the operational utility of emergency plans

Promote uniformity in principles, policies, and concepts of operations and compatibility of organizations and systems to facilitate coordinated response

Reduce redundancy in plan documentation.

Differences between the objectives outlined in the two CPGs are apparent, and this might be confusing. Regardless, the IEMS approach entails the development of multihazard, functional plans that treat emergency management activities generically, without reference to a particular hazard. EOPs that address only a single hazard, such as hurricane, nuclear attack, or earthquake, will not be accepted for review by FEMA.

Generic planning may not meet the needs of every jurisdiction; in some cases, complete, hazard-specific plans may be more appropriate for the local level. This has proved to be the case, for example, in Comprehensive Hurricane Evacuation Planning, where one of the standard work products for communities involved in SLOSH (Sea, Lake, Overland Surges from Hurricanes) basins is a hurricane evacuation implementation guide. This guide contains all the information a jurisdiction needs to respond to a hurricane threat, including warning, decision making, and direction and control. Interestingly, hurricane evacuation implementation guides (discussed in more detail below) are usually prepared with federal funding in support of hurricane evacuation planning—but they are developed separately from the generic EOP plans. Although the guides have proven effective, jurisdictions encounter difficulties when they attempt to integrate an implementation guide into a generic local EOP.

Plan format

The format of a local plan is usually dictated by either FEMA or state guidelines. FEMA guidelines are discussed in detail below. Many states have established standardized formats for local plans to ensure compatibility with the state plan (and, although the required state format normally follows the FEMA guidelines, divergences do exist). Emergency managers should work closely with the state emergency management office to be sure that the local EOP adheres to established rules and procedures. Unless the state emergency management office permits some experimentation in the design of a local plan, flexibility is limited.

Complicating the situation for emergency managers is the inconsistency that plagues the planning process, from the level of departmental and support plans to the level of federal guidelines. Emergency managers must be prepared to deal with contradictions and sort out what is necessary for their jurisdictions to meet *both* funding requirements *and* community needs.

FEMA guidelines state that there is no standard format or organization for a local EOP. Nevertheless, CPG 1-8, *Guide for Development of State and Local Emergency Operations Plans* (October 1985), recommends that the EOP have the following three components: (1) the basic plan; (2) functional annexes in support of the basic plan; and (3) hazard-specific appendixes in support of each functional annex. Figures 7–4 and 7–5 outline the relationship of the three recommended components. According to CPG 1-8, the basic plan provides overall information, whereas the annexes cover specific responsibilities, actions, and procedures for functions such as law enforcement or public works. Appendixes to the functional annexes address unique characteristics of specific hazards.

CPG 1-8 also provides suggested formats for each of the three components. But, despite the guidelines' indication that there is no standard format, in practice the approval of the local EOP for purposes of obtaining EMA funding may depend on adoption of the suggested format.

Basic plan According to CPG 1-8, the basic plan should provide an overview of the jurisdiction's concept of emergency management, including authority and responsibility, and should contain the following nine elements:

1. Introduction
2. Purpose
3. Situation and assumptions
4. Concept of operations
5. Organization and assignment of responsibilities
6. Administration and logistics
7. Plan development and maintenance
8. Authorities and references
9. Definition of terms.

CPG 1-8A (*Guide for Review of State and Local Emergency Operations Plans*, September 1988) states that EOPs submitted under Comprehensive Cooperative Agreements (CCAs) between FEMA and the state must be consistent with the

Figure 7–4 Relationship of the components within an EOP.

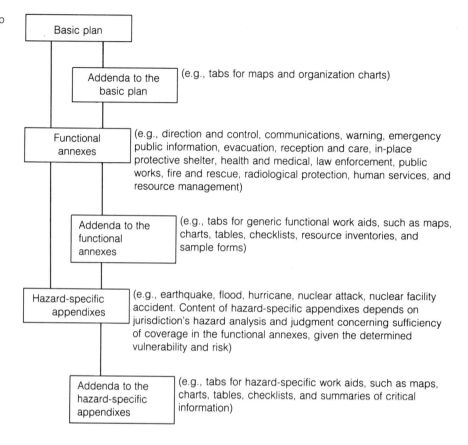

Figure 7–5 Using evacuation and direction and control as examples of functional annexes, this diagram of a portion of an EOP illustrates the relationship between the basic plan, the functional annexes, and the hazard-specific appendixes.

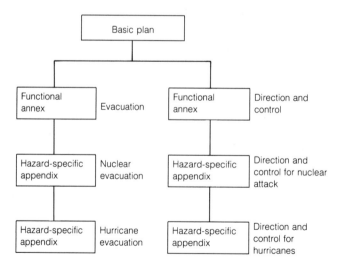

guidelines set forth in CPG 1-8 (CCAs are the means whereby the states apply for and receive assistance from FEMA). In addition, CPG 1-8A assigns to each state emergency management office the responsibility for reviewing the EOPs of all EMA participants. CPG 1-8A also provides the reviewer with a "cross-walk," or check sheet, that uses the exact format suggested in CPG 1-8. This crosswalk is the basis on which the state reviewer decides whether the local jurisdiction has met its planning requirements.

Annexes Annexes are the elements of the EOP that focus on operations. An annex is used to define a function—for example, warning—and to clarify who is responsible for carrying that function out. CPG 1–8 provides detailed guidance on the development of functional annexes. FEMA or state guidelines normally dictate the number of functional annexes and the areas they cover, but several informal guidelines can help the emergency manager develop the content of annexes:

The role of an annex is to clarify the basic plan where necessary. (This allows the basic plan to be shorter.)

The needs of the basic plan should govern the number and types of annexes.

Each annex should deal with one function of an operation.

Each annex should be prepared by the agency or office that has responsibility for the operational function it describes.

The annexes should not include matters covered by standard operating procedures.

As is the case with recommended formats for the basic plan, the federal guidelines relating to annexes contain inconsistencies (and there are generally state requirements to be dealt with, as well). For example, depending on the federal source consulted, "Firefighting," "Fire Service," and "Fire and Rescue" are all recommended titles for the same functional annex. In addition, depending on the CPG being used, the number of functional annexes ranges from thirteen to eighteen.

Typical titles for functional annexes are shown in the list that follows. The list is not inclusive, and the particular annexes required will depend on local requirements and needs.

Direction and Control

Communications

Warning

Emergency Public Information

Education and Training

Evacuation

Shelter (Reception and Care)

Medical Health

Law Enforcement

Public Works

Fire and Rescue

Transportation

Human Services (Welfare)

Reporting Procedures

Continuity of Government

Damage Assessment

Radiological Defense.

The format suggested in CPG 1-8 for annexes is parallel to the format recommended for the basic plan.

Appendixes   The purpose of dividing the EOP into a basic plan, annexes, and appendixes is to give the plan flexibility. However, a user attempting to gain general information about a specific hazard may find that a plan designed to meet FEMA's specifications is confusing rather than flexible. For example, in CPG 1-8, *Guide for Development of State and Local Emergency Operations Plans*, the hazard-specific Appendix E.1, "Evacuation in Response to Threat of Nuclear Attack," is part of the Evacuation annex. A user interested in *all* actions related to a specific hazard—such as nuclear attack—must consult every generic annex plus any appropriate hazard-specific appendixes to each annex. The sample plans in CPG 1-8 show hazard-specific appendixes related to nuclear attack under Direction and Control, Emergency Public Information, Evacuation, In-Place Protective Shelter, and Radiological Protection. A user who is relatively new to the field, unfamiliar with the plan, or in need of a rapid overview of responsibilities would find this arrangement of material cumbersome at best.

One way to increase the accessibility of the EOP is to create implementation guides, which might be used as appendixes giving full coverage to a particular threat. (Implementation guides are rather like the self-contained "situation plans" called for in FEMA's emergency planning course.) As noted earlier, hurricane evacuation implementation guides have been well received by the local governments that use them (see sidebar). Not only are such guides helpful for response, but they may also be better tools for training and exercising. Although the guides repeat information that appears elsewhere in the EOP, that may not be a serious concern, given that the plans for some communities are from six to twelve inches thick in any case.

Implementation guides in hurricane evacuation planning   Although implementation guides are not addressed in FEMA's emergency planning course or in the CPGs, they have been incorporated into hurricane evacuation planning since 1979, when the Jacksonville, Florida, District of the Corps of Engineers prepared the Lee County Flood Emergency Evacuation Plan. This plan, or implementation guide, addressed three critical elements of emergency response: warning, evacuation, and shelter. The Tampa Bay Region, Florida, Hurricane Evacuation Plan, completed in June 1981, expanded the implementation guide to seven chapters: Introduction, Hurricane Hazards and Vulnerability, Warning, Issuance of Evacuation Order (Legal Authority and Decision Making), Direction and Control, Evacuation (Evacuation of Elderly and Disabled, Traffic Control, Shelter, Transportation, and Critical Services), and Regional Coordination of Evacuation Activities.

The county guides used in the Tampa Bay region provide the detailed guidance necessary to prepare for and respond to a hurricane threat. They include all required evacuation orders, proclamations, resolutions, emergency broadcast messages, and ordinances. Pinellas County further expanded the approach in 1984 to include a draft recovery implementation guide, which includes all ordinances that may be required during the immediate emergency and short-range recovery periods. The topics covered include direction and control, search and rescue, debris clearance, security, medical care, restoration of services, emergency transportation, sheltering and mass feeding, intergovernmental resource distribution, damage assessment, and debris removal.

The guides do not use either the format or the style that is standard for emergency plans but are written in a format and style similar to those of the day-to-day administrative documents that normally flow through local government.

As the preceding discussion indicates, there are inherent problems in emergency planning guidance. Although conflicts between recommended state and federal guidelines are largely beyond the emergency manager's control, he or she can work with local government departments and local support agencies to ensure as much compatibility among plans as possible. One way to do this is to provide training and to encourage attendance at state- and FEMA-sponsored courses. As we have seen, the usefulness of such efforts was borne out in Pinellas County.

Levels of plans

There are four levels of plans, reflecting four levels of action and responsibility: state plans, regional plans, local plans, and departmental and support-agency plans.

Emergency managers should be aware that plans are often developed in what may appear to be a backward process: a plan is written at the local level, then integrated into a regional plan or made part of a hazard-specific annex to a state plan. This process, however, reflects the realities of implementation. The plan is designed by those who will implement it.

Although the bottom-up approach has advantages from the standpoint of implementation, it is sometimes more advantageous to develop an overall concept—for example, the state's response to earthquakes or hurricanes—and then to create compatible supporting plans written by lower levels of government. The disadvantage of this method is that it can give rise to turf battles between the various levels of government, harming the development of cohesive operations plans.

State plans   State emergency operations plans allow the states to exercise their authority and contribute their resources in such a way as to meet the federally established goal of mobilizing all levels of government in a unified emergency organization. Furthermore, the state plan is the principal document through which the state government communicates its commitment to emergency management to other levels of government, to disaster support agencies, and to the private sector. Finally, state plans, which are usually very general, provide an operational and policy framework for local planning and response.

As is discussed in the previous section, many states have required formats for both the state and local EOPs, and conflict can arise when the state requirements do not fall precisely within the FEMA guidelines.

Regional plans and studies   During the 1980s, as more coastal states received funding for Comprehensive Hurricane Evacuation Planning, plans were developed on a regional basis (especially in Florida). In most cases, studies to assist in plan development were undertaken by regional planning organizations such as planning councils. The disadvantage of this approach is that, in some areas, plans or implementation guides were written by general planners who had had little or no background in dealing with disasters. But the regional approach did have a significant advantage: the general planning background of the regional planners influenced the format of the implementation guides—which, as has been mentioned, do not use the standard EOP format and are therefore much more accessible to local government users.

Local plans   In the IEMS approach, a local EOP describes the jurisdiction's response to the threats identified in a hazard vulnerability analysis. For all four phases of comprehensive emergency management—preparedness, response, recovery, and mitigation—the local EOP provides organization, assigns responsibilities, outlines direction and control, and identifies resources that allow the jurisdiction to respond to disaster. Unlike the plans developed at the state level, local EOPs are true operations plans. In other words, they provide the specific guidance necessary for coordinated action, including direction and control and the assignment of emergency forces and resources.

Departmental and support-agency plans In many communities, the real failure in planning takes place at the level of departments and support agencies. A law enforcement annex may be written by a police officer or sheriff's representative, on the basis of responsibilities assigned in the plan. An annex on shelter may be written by a member of the local Red Cross chapter. One problem, when departments and support agencies write implementation plans for the jurisdiction's EOP, is that staff of the departments and agencies generally lack sufficient training or guidance for writing such plans. A second problem is that the formats used by support agencies differ from those used by the local government. Medical facilities that have planning requirements for licensing purposes have their own formats; the American Red Cross and Salvation Army have their own plan requirements, and also use different formats. As coordinator of the EOP, the emergency manager should ensure that departments and support agencies receive the guidance they need to make appropriate and useful contributions to the plan.

Plan development at the local level

The basis for a coordinated, effective response to a disaster is the jurisdiction's emergency plan. Although the process of developing a plan may be difficult, the process itself will be invaluable in the event of a disaster. Sharing knowledge and working together to develop the plan create a foundation that can be key to implementing the plan successfully.

Given the obstacles and the problems that can arise from conflicting planning guidance and relative lack of planning expertise in the local government environment, it is all the more important that the emergency manager understand the obstacles and approach plan development in a logical, coordinated way. The six sections that follow offer guidelines for ensuring an organized plan development process.

Understand the obstacles

Before beginning to plan, the emergency manager must take a realistic look at the local planning environment. The simple truth is that planning is not and will not be easy, and the emergency manager must be aware of the formidable obstacles before attempting to coordinate local government departments and local support agencies for planning.

There are three principal obstacles: (1) the lack of planning expertise within local governments and within the support agencies on which many emergency services depend, (2) the lack of formal training in planning among emergency managers themselves, and (3) the belief among emergency personnel that detailed planning is really unnecessary.

To whom can the emergency manager turn for assistance in updating or creating a plan? Ordinarily, the only trained planners in the local government are those in the planning department, but their background is most likely in general—rather than in emergency—planning. Staff in other local government departments are highly unlikely to have been trained in planning of any kind. Furthermore, the support agencies that usually participate in plan development have limited or no emergency planning experience. Thus, responsibility for planning falls primarily on the shoulders of the emergency manager, and the quality of the plan depends largely on his or her ability to organize a planning committee and coordinate its efforts.

But emergency managers themselves rarely have specific training in planning. In fact, only limited training is currently available. In the early 1980s, the Emergency Management Institute's professional development series began to include a one-week course in planning. Other plan-specific courses are also available at EMI. Given the importance of this aspect of their responsibilities, emergency managers should take advantage of the few courses available.[1]

The third obstacle to local planning is the belief held by many emergency personnel that the EOP should be simply two or three pages long—and that in the event of an actual disaster, the locality will "fly by the seat of its pants." Although, as a number of chapters in this book point out, there are dangers to an excessively detailed plan, too brief a plan is equally to be avoided. Disaster response operations require comprehensive plans.

Review and update the hazard vulnerability analysis

Many emergency managers underrate the importance of a hazard vulnerability analysis (HVA), which is an extremely important document in efforts to improve emergency planning. The effort expended to develop a detailed HVA will pay dividends at a later time—for example, support agencies can also use a detailed HVA as the basis for their plans. In particular, the emergency manager should avoid preparing an HVA that fulfills the FEMA requirements but provides little or no information for planning.

To create an HVA or update an existing one, the emergency manager should work with agencies that have the necessary expertise to gather technical data. For example, in the area of hazardous materials planning, the detailed information that organizations gather to fulfill SARA Title III requirements can yield valuable data for an HVA. In Pinellas County, the SLOSH analysis conducted as part of Comprehensive Hurricane Evacuation Planning provided material for the HVA.

After the HVA is reviewed and updated, the emergency manager must consider the EOP in relation to it: Does the EOP currently emphasize the high-probability threats? Does it use emergency personnel and resources appropriately? Such questions enable the emergency manager to decide what level of revision is necessary for the EOP. He or she can then begin to develop a planning committee.

Organize a planning committee

Although the emergency manager is responsible for overall plan development, he or she accomplishes this task with the assistance of the planning committee. The emergency manager is ordinarily responsible for the plan concept, including the assignment of agency responsibilities to support that concept. The final version of the basic plan is also the responsibility of the emergency manager. The annexes and appendixes, however, are developed by the planning committee, under the emergency manager's guidance. The major task facing the emergency manager is providing enough guidance to the planning committee to ensure that its contributions to the plan (the annexes and appendixes) will require minimum additional reworking before being incorporated into the plan.

In organizing a planning committee, an emergency manager has two principal options: to create a temporary, ad hoc committee, or to use the existing organizational structure, including those organizations (both inside and outside the local government) with disaster support responsibilities. The second approach is preferable. In this approach, each organization designates a permanent representative, who continues to serve his or her own organization but also functions as part of the planning committee.

Whether ad hoc or permanent, the planning committee should include representatives from all local government departments and agencies with emergency responsibilities, from disaster support agencies, and from the private sector (for example, power companies, private nursing homes, industry). Although the general planning department does not ordinarily have emergency responsibilities, it should have a representative on the committee because it has the capability to develop technical data for use in the planning process. (Most planning departments undertake population projections, maintain data on roads and transportation, and project future growth.)

A local planning committee under the general direction of the emergency manager might include representatives from local government departments such as public information, risk management, public works, purchasing, personnel, social services, planning, public health, parks and recreation, buildings, and general services. The committee might also include the medical examiner, the property appraiser, the sheriff, and a representative from the school board. Representatives of support agencies such as the Red Cross and Salvation Army would ordinarily be included, as well as staff from the local electric, gas, and telephone companies. Finally, local hospitals and nursing homes, the airport, and the National Guard might be represented.

Relatively early in the planning process, it may become apparent that the planning committee should be broken down into subcommittees or groups. For example, to ensure the full participation of a number of medical facilities, it may be desirable to organize a nursing home and hospital subcommittee.

A word of caution: the emergency manager should ensure that an organization's representative on the committee is the person who will actually be doing the work of planning. Although it may seem desirable to have the head of an entire agency participate on the committee, it is more important that the representative be someone with time to engage actively in planning.

If the planning committee learns about emergency management planning as a group, the documents it produces will be more likely to prove usable by the emergency manager. An innovative emergency manager will arrange for FEMA or state instructors to conduct an emergency planning course for his or her jurisdiction's planning committee only, thus significantly improving the jurisdiction's ability to plan.

Devise a schedule

To schedule the development of the plan, begin with the date for submission—which will depend on a combination of federal, state, and local requirements—and work backward. Figure 7–6 is an example of timing and sequence for development of a county plan.

Publish a planning directive

A planning directive, or guidance paper, is instrumental in a planning effort. The emergency manager uses the directive to ensure that all members of the planning committee are moving in the same direction at the same time. The directive should be signed by someone whose authority will ensure compliance by the participating agencies—for example, the mayor or the local government manager. At a minimum, the planning directive should address the following subjects, although the precise contents can be modified to reflect local needs:

Purpose
Authority

Objectives
Concept (of the plan)
Schedule for plan development
    1. Milestones
    2. Sequence
Organization for planning
Assignment of responsibilities for plan development
Development of annexes
    1. Format
    2. Content
Review and approval
Special instructions

Evaluate the draft plan

As the emergency manager consolidates the products submitted by the planning committee and incorporates them into the draft plan, he or she will be evaluating the overall breadth and depth of the EOP: is it complete enough, and does it include sufficient detail? Although plans vary from community to community, certain issues arise in virtually every disaster situation, and one indication of the completeness of a plan is whether it addresses these issues. As for determining

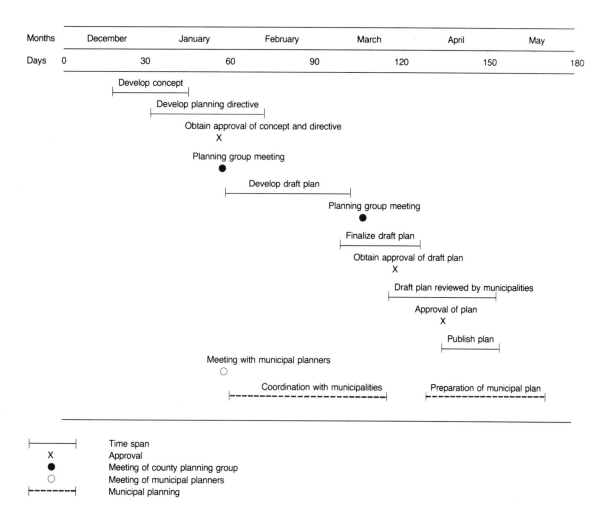

Figure 7–6   Sample schedule for development of a county emergency operations plan.

the appropriate level of detail, that is not easy to do. Many emergency managers find out the hard way—that is to say, after a disaster—what should have been in the plan. One thing to keep in mind, however, in evaluating the breadth and depth of the EOP is that the first reason for developing a plan is to improve response capability. The second reason is to meet funding requirements. Unfortunately, in many communities funding requirements take priority over response capability.

The eleven sections that follow consider issues that experience has shown to be important but that are nevertheless often overlooked in local emergency management plans. Only after ensuring that the plan fully addresses these issues should the emergency manager submit the final plan to elected officials for approval—the last step before the plan is distributed to all departments, agencies, and organizations with emergency management responsibilities or concerns.

Lines of authority and succession   The first thing the emergency manager needs to do is ensure that the appropriate legal framework is in place to allow decision making and action during disasters, particularly with respect to lines of authority and succession. For example, in Pinellas County, a quorum of the county commission is required to pass ordinances and issue orders and resolutions, but when Hurricane Elena threatened the county, the emergency manager was unable to gather a quorum of the county commission. Fortunately, several months earlier, an emergency ordinance had been passed specifying procedures for declaring an emergency and authorizing certain actions when a quorum of the county commission was unable to meet. As permitted by the ordinance, the actual order to evacuate several hundred thousand people was signed by an assistant county administrator. By clarifying lines of authority and making explicit provision for unusual situations, the ordinance made it possible for emergency actions to be undertaken with all due speed.

Exhibit 7-A is the text of the ordinance used in that situation. (All exhibits are at the end of this chapter.)

Ordinances   In addition to having specific ordinances on the books, it is also important to have fill-in-the-blank ordinances available for immediate approval by the governing body. As Hurricane Hugo approached, emergency managers in some coastal communities began searching for examples of resolutions declaring a state of local emergency. When such resolutions are ratified by the local governing body, they allow the local government to implement certain emergency actions. The time to prepare such resolutions, however, is not when a hurricane is approaching. Generic resolutions should be created ahead of time and included in the EOP. Should a disaster occur, the document is modified as necessary, and the governing body signs the resolution. Exhibit 7-B an example of a resolution declaring a state of emergency for a county.

Other ordinances that should be prepared ahead of time and included in the EOP are those establishing a curfew and controlling price gouging. Examples of such ordinances that can be modified to meet the needs of any community are given in Exhibits 7-C and 7-D. Finally, a generic evacuation order should be a standard part of every EOP. Exhibit 7-E is a sample evacuation order developed for a hurricane threat.

Broadcasting emergency information   With the necessary legal framework in place and ready-to-use ordinances available in the EOP, the emergency manager still must ensure that information about a disaster can reach the public. Today, more and more emergency managers are including emergency broadcast system (EBS) messages in the EOP. Because many communities have cable television companies, the local warning system should include the capability to override cable TV, either by video or by audio. A cable TV video override shows emergency information in full screen script or in a scroll across the bottom of the screen. In some communities, non-English warning messages may also be important.

Responses to citizens' questions It is also necessary to ensure that the EOP includes provision for an agency that can answer citizens' questions about the disaster. A citizens' information center or rumor control office is a necessity in all communities. If possible, it should be located in or adjacent to the emergency operations center to ensure a continuous flow of up-to-date information for callers. The information center can be staffed by volunteers. Consideration should also be given to including a device that allows citizens with hearing impairments to call in and receive information.

Evacuation of medical facilities Experience indicates that the best shelter for an evacuated medical facility is another medical facility. As a last resort, patients might be moved to another type of shelter, but such an approach led to problems in Hurricanes David, Elena, and Hugo. In light of those experiences, emergency managers should cooperate with local medical facilities to develop the approach that is best for the community. Including medical facility evacuation in the EOP gives the emergency manager significant flexibility in responding to any type of disaster affecting a hospital or nursing home. Figure 7–2, extracted from a local EOP, shows information on nursing homes. The critical information included in the plan is average patient census; buses required for transport by type (regular or with lift); names and telephone numbers of contacts; and the sheltering facility. Also important is the number of patients to be transported by bus and the number requiring ambulance transport. (Many emergency managers think that only ambulances can be used to evacuate a hospital or nursing home, but in fact a number of patients can usually be moved by bus.) Although Figure 7–2 is oriented toward hurricanes, the information it contains would help with initial response to any type of disaster.

Persons with special needs: Disabled and elderly residents A number of citizens in the community have special needs and require assistance during any evacuation. Some states now require local emergency management offices to maintain lists of persons requiring assistance, who voluntarily register their names. Whether required to do so or not, the emergency manager should devise a viable program to obtain and update registrations—and, even more important, to provide assistance when required. A comprehensive special needs program will integrate local social service organizations, home health agencies, and transportation agencies into a workable system to identify, locate, and, when necessary, assist residents who cannot evacuate on their own.

Information on how to register can be placed on TV or in newspapers or can be included with mailings such as utility bills. In larger jurisdictions, registration may be computerized; in smaller localities, it may be maintained on a card system. Figure 7–7 is an example of a registration form.

In the area of special needs, a registration program is only half the battle; the emergency manager must also ensure that the appropriate help is available when it is needed. For example, because the emergency management office itself often has limited transportation resources, the emergency manager must be sure to include in the plan the agencies or organizations that do have such resources.

Although a registration program for persons with special needs can be of enormous help in the event of a disaster, the emergency manager must be

Figure 7–7   Example of a registration form for evacuation of citizens with special needs.

Name: _____   Age: _____
          (Last)   (First)

Street no.: _____   Street name: _____   Apt./lot #: _____

Bldg.: _____   Floor: _____   City: _____   Zip: _____

Complex name: _____   Mobile home park (X): _____   Fire dist.: _____

Phone: _____   Deaf (X): _____   TDD (X): _____

Evacuation planning data

Evac. only for hurricanes (Y/N): _____   Evac zone #: _____   Zone color: _____   Level: _____

Evac. for any hazard (Y/N): _____   Grid: _____

Nature of disability: _____
(Be very specific)   _____

Is oxygen required? How many liters per minute (What's valve set on—1, 2, 3)? _____

Citizen's mobility (X):   Ambulatory _____   Wheelchair _____   Bedridden _____

Have wheelchair (Y/N)? _____   If bedridden, can be moved in wheelchair (Y/N)? _____

Type of transport and shelter are decided by above info. and personal visit

Type of transport (X):   Van/bus _____   Wheelchair _____   Ambulance _____

Evac. facility (X):   Shelter _____   Special care _____   Nursing home _____   Hospital _____

Number of people to accompany: _____   Pre-select shelter: _____

Family doctor: _____   Phone: _____

Emergency contact: _____   Phone: _____

Contact's relationship to citizen: _____

Notes: _____
                    (Special equipment, etc.)

Registration taken by: _____   Date: /   /

Personally visited by: _____   Date: /   /

Figure 7–8 Routing of last-minute transport requests for evacuation assistance.

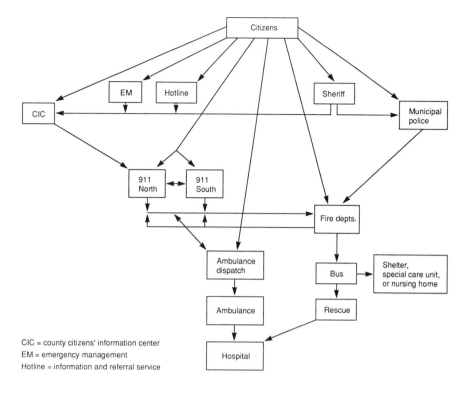

CIC = county citizens' information center
EM = emergency management
Hotline = information and referral service

aware that, historically, such programs identify but a small percentage of the residents actually requiring assistance. Many disabled persons prefer to keep their circumstances private and will seek assistance only when an emergency occurs. If the emergency manager has not prepared for this eventuality, the last-minute calls may overwhelm the communication system and prevent disabled residents from obtaining the assistance they require.

Figure 7–8 is an example of a system designed to take last-minute calls for assistance. Notice that if a citizen calls *any* response agency, including 911, the call will eventually be routed to an agency that controls or dispatches transportation assets. Because citizens tend to "shotgun" their calls (that is, call multiple agencies with the same request for assistance)—and possibly have three or four response agencies answering the same call—the calls must be controlled and coordinated to take maximum advantage of limited assets.

An emergency manager devising plans to assist residents with special needs should be aware of yet another issue—one that has, in part, been created by law and that affects most communities. Because of the Diagnosis Related Group (DRG) program, significant numbers of citizens with various illnesses are being released from hospitals much earlier than they would have been in the past and are living in the community; in many cases, they are being cared for by home health care agencies. The problem is that, in the event of a disaster, for sheltering purposes such persons may fall into a grey area. Those who require medical care cannot go to an American Red Cross shelter, yet those who have been recently released from a hospital cannot be readmitted. (The federal government will not reimburse a hospital if a patient is readmitted for the same problem within seven days of the most recent release).

The DRG program poses a tremendous challenge to the emergency manager. One possible solution is the establishment of "medical shelters" under the supervision of the local health department; there may be other solutions. The problem is nowhere near being resolved. The important thing is for the emergency manager to be aware that the problem exists and to set aside time during the planning process to explore its extent within the community.

Demographics may also have an effect on emergency response. In most communities, particularly in the Sun Belt, the average age of the population is steadily rising, and the emergency manager should examine the jurisdiction's demographics closely to determine the effect of elderly residents on emergency response. Two issues need to be considered: a long-term shelter operation is harder on elderly people than on others, and many elderly residents require transportation assistance.

If elderly residents go to a public shelter, they may place demands on the Red Cross that it is not normally prepared to meet. As an example, many older residents may require assistance in obtaining and taking medication. Furthermore, the overall condition of many elderly people has been found to deteriorate as the shelter duration is extended. Emergency managers should consider incorporating provisions into the EOP whereby the local Red Cross chapter would establish a health maintenance program to closely monitor elderly persons staying in shelter.

In communities with large numbers of elderly residents, the plan should include provision for buses to transport those who no longer drive. Buses can move along predetermined routes in the threatened area or can go to a designated pickup point. There are many alternatives, depending on the situation within the jurisdiction; the important point is not to overlook these individuals when developing the EOP.

Search and rescue   How often after a tornado or hurricane strikes is it reported that the local law enforcement agency rushed into the damaged area and lost the use of a number of vehicles because of damage or flat tires? To guard against such eventualities, the emergency manager should ensure that the EOP includes a structured approach to search and rescue (SAR). Teams should be organized and prepared to conduct SAR operations in heavily damaged areas. Comprehensive SAR plans should include air, boat, vehicle, and foot operations; the actual situation will dictate the precise approach. The important thing is to include in the EOP a framework for a structured response. In addition to volunteer groups, the following agencies and departments are normally included in SAR operations: public works, to clear debris to permit movement of fire/EMS and law enforcement vehicles; fire/EMS, to undertake rescue and medical treatment of the injured; law enforcement, to provide security and to oversee identification of bodies; and various support organizations, such as the National Guard and private contractors, to clear debris and assist as necessary.

Response versus recovery planning   Poor recovery planning is characteristic of emergency management programs throughout the country. Emergency managers tend to concentrate on response—but recovery operations actually require much more detailed planning. (This weakness in the planning effort affects not only the local level. An informal review of several state plans found only minimum reference to recovery operations.) Chapter 9, on the recovery process, contains a detailed discussion of the kinds of issues likely to arise during the recovery period and the ways in which the emergency manager can address them in the EOP.

Intergovernmental resource distribution   During the immediate recovery period, a community stricken by disaster will receive a huge influx of supplies and equipment from other parts of the country. The handling and distribution of these resources should be addressed in the EOP. The emergency manager may, for example, wish to designate recovery staging areas, recovery centers, and distribution points throughout the jurisdiction. The plan should also establish a system for requesting resources and directing their flow. Figure 7–9 is a sample distribution system for a county. This system addresses the request for, and distribution of, supplies down to local government and individuals.

The county preselects staging areas and the teams to operate them. A typical staging area team would initially be composed of representatives from public works, the Red Cross, the Salvation Army, the gas and electric companies, law enforcement, the National Guard, municipalities, and volunteer groups. To operate efficiently, the teams must be able to communicate—by radio, for example. Road signs prepared ahead of time can direct incoming vehicles to the appropriate staging areas. Recovery centers can be established by municipalities and, in unincorporated areas, by fire districts. Distribution points are sited in heavily damaged areas, where victims require supplies such as food, water, and clothing. These distribution points can be staffed by representatives of the local jurisdiction and of an appropriate agency, such as the Red Cross or Salvation Army.

Security Although very few communities think through security operations before a disaster occurs, a number of actions can be undertaken ahead of time and included in the plan. For example, signs can be made to designate security checkpoints and restricted areas (such signs might read "Checkpoint Ahead: I.D. Required" or "Restricted Area: Authorized Entry Only"). In addition, procedures can be developed specifying what forms of identification will be accepted at security checkpoints and how identification will be recorded. Procedures can also be developed for allowing individuals into heavily damaged areas; these procedures may include control sheets and tags for display. Figure 7–10 is a sample control sheet and tag. (Note that the tag is the same kind that most law enforcement agencies already use to tag evidence.)

The plan can also establish a system to ensure that judges are on hand to process persons apprehended during the immediate recovery period. Remember that, in large-scale evacuations, judges are among those evacuated—unless a system is established whereby they become part of overall disaster operations. Pinellas County has established a justice emergency operations center staffed by a judge, a state attorney, a public defender, a clerk of circuit court, and administrative staff. This team is prepared to issue emergency orders, conduct preliminary hearings, or process mass arrests.

Incident command An incident command system (ICS) is an on-scene emergency response system that fire service departments throughout the United

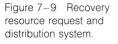

Figure 7–9 Recovery resource request and distribution system.

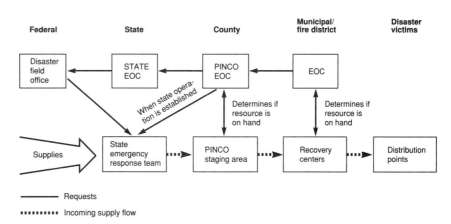

States are adopting. It provides for basic direction and control, including decision making and coordination among multiple responding agencies (for example, fire, emergency medical services, police, volunteer agencies).

The emergency manager who decides to adopt such a system must also decide how to integrate it into the EOP: does it go under Direction and Control, Evacuation, Shelter, or Fire, or under the heading of some other generic function? The problem is that incident command includes a little bit of everything—and is therefore difficult to "place" in the generic annexes recommended by current guidelines. One option is to treat the ICS as if it were a hazard-specific appendix, with the heading, for example, of "Response to Local Disasters: Incident Command System."

Training

Having a plan does not in itself enable a community to respond effectively to a disaster. Experience shows that if responders do not fully understand procedures or responsibilities, serious problems will arise during efforts to respond to an incident. To implement the EOP, therefore, emergency staff and disaster support agencies must also be trained in the plan's overall concept, their own responsibilities under it, and the procedures it sets forth. Training helps ensure that response agencies fully understand the plan. Failing to provide training is like giving a law enforcement officer a weapon without providing instruction on how to load, aim, and fire. The weapon becomes useless—and possibly dangerous. Similarly, a community with emergency plans that no one understands or knows how to implement is at an enormous disadvantage in the event of a disaster. This sections discusses the dimensions of a training program and support for training.

Dimensions of a training program

A training program should be three-dimensional: it should take advantage of programs and courses available through FEMA or the state, it should include

Figure 7–10 Sample control sheet and tags for use at security checkpoints.

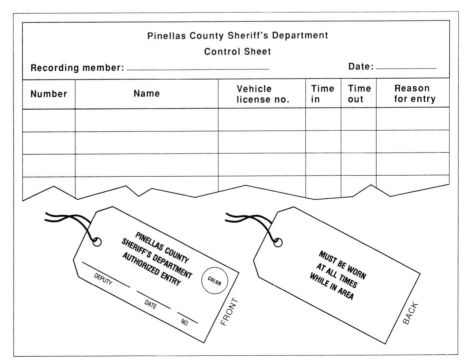

locally based training, and it should reach not only response agencies but the general population.

The drawback of FEMA and state training programs is that each jurisdiction is in competition with other municipalities, counties, and states across the nation to obtain funding to attend. (Even if a jurisdiction wants to fund attendance itself, the number of places available in each course is controlled by FEMA or the state.) The limited availability of FEMA and state training makes the second dimension—an internal training program—particularly important. Furthermore, whereas training conducted by FEMA or the state is fairly general (that is, it covers broad topics such as planning or exercising), the primary goal of an internal training program is to ensure that response agencies fully understand, and can act on, the roles assigned to them in the EOP. The third dimension of training is that designed for the community at large. For a response effort to be effective, citizens must know the proper responses to disasters and must also follow instructions. They need training in both areas.

Training provided by FEMA and the state   Both FEMA and the states publish schedules showing subjects, locations, and dates of training. As noted earlier, the emergency manager should give priority to attending the Emergency Management Institute's professional development series. The emergency manager should also take advantage of EMI training that is available for fire, police, hospital, and school personnel.

Going through a training program together encourages participants to view themselves as a team. The integrated emergency management course presented at the Emergency Management Institute and at field locations is an excellent example of the team approach to training. For this course, the jurisdiction's entire emergency operations center staff is isolated for training and a follow-up exercise.

As mentioned in the section above on the planning committee, the emergency manager should try to arrange for the planning committee to attend the EMI emergency planning course under similar conditions. Other groups that should be trained *as* groups are damage assessment teams, EOC staffs, and decision makers (elected and appointed officials).

Applications to attend EMI courses must be made through the state emergency management office.

Internal training   The emphasis of internal training should be on the concepts of operation and key components of the EOP that directly involve the group being trained, but an overview of the plan is also necessary to ensure that participants understand how they fit into the big picture. To ensure a full understanding of the EOP and the emergency management program, the best technique is for the emergency manager and the agency head to conduct training jointly. The emergency manager focuses on the overall program and the EOP, while the agency head focuses on the agency plan.

Internal training can be done on-site at local fire and police stations or at medical facilities. It should be offered to all local government departments with emergency management responsibilities, to Red Cross volunteers, to elected officials, and, if appropriate, to the military. The following agencies should be among those to receive presentations on the EOP: fire (all shifts), law enforcement (all shifts), the Red Cross, the school board, school bus drivers, school principals and assistant principals, hospital staffs, nursing home staffs, municipal and county departments, elected officials, ambulance operators, and the EOC staff.

Fire and police departments normally offer their own professional development courses. The emergency manager may be able to take advantage of these by offering emergency management training at the local fire and police academies. Although this training may be difficult to arrange (the courses are highly structured, with little time available for outside subjects), it will help improve fire fighters' and police officers' understanding of their roles in a coordinated response; it also gives the emergency manager an opportunity to make contact with individual police officers, fire fighters, and supervisors.

Another issue of importance besides who should be trained is how the training should be conducted. Technology has considerably broadened the range of available options. Communities throughout the country are likely to have access to closed circuit television, cable channels, and videotapes, all of which can be enlisted in the service of training. Contracts for local cable companies with permits for specific service areas may actually include a commitment to emergency preparedness.

Community education　When disaster strikes, citizens are expected to take certain actions or to follow the instructions of emergency management personnel. Preparing citizens for such an event must therefore be a part of the emergency management training program. The primary means of communicating with citizens are written materials (circulars, newspapers, handouts), television (talk shows, spot announcements, interviews, specials), radio (talk shows, interviews), cable television (government access, talk shows, training tapes), and individual presentations (to schools, clubs, community groups).

In particular, the government access channel on cable television can be enormously helpful to the emergency manager: FEMA programs, locally produced training programs, and any other material that would help educate the public can be shown repeatedly. (For example, a program on hurricanes might be run three times a day during June, July, and August.) The emergency management department can prepare tapes to familiarize citizens with various aspects of the EOP. In communities with large numbers of retirees who are home during the day, such programs are likely to reach a wide audience.

Training support

Any emergency management training program requires equipment. At the top of the list will be a 35-mm camera, a television camera, a 16-mm movie projector, a 35-mm slide projector, a VCR, and television monitors. (FEMA has both a publications catalog and a motion picture catalog.) Because of their cost, in most communities these items must be programmed over several years. Tapes and films will require additional expenditures. Only limited training support is available from higher levels of government, and what is available may not meet local needs or conditions. Thus, emergency managers should generally rely on training programs they have developed themselves (these may include slide or video presentations) and on support from within the jurisdiction.

Exercising

Disasters are ordinarily rare events, so the EOP is likely never to have been implemented. Exercising is therefore the primary way for the emergency manager to test and evaluate the components of the plan to determine whether they will work in an actual emergency.

There are four principal reasons to evaluate the EOP: (1) to detect deficiencies in the EOP (example: the warning annex does not include hospital notification); (2) to detect deficiencies in the overall emergency management system (example: agencies were not adequately trained in plan implementation); (3) to identify potential personnel and staff problems (example: shifts are not organized for optimum response); and (4) to detect problems with the functioning and operation of equipment. Constructive evaluation of the EOP—by means of exercises—is the basis of necessary plan revisions and, ultimately, of more effective response.

Progressive exercises

FEMA recognizes the value of exercising and suggests three types of exercises for incorporation into the emergency management program. These exercises are progressive; that is, they become more difficult as the response agencies' level of training and operational capability increase. CPG 1-3, *CCA General Program Guidelines* (June 2, 1987), outlines a tabletop exercise, a functional exercise, and a full-scale exercise. (Emergency managers need to be aware that FEMA updates CCA program requirements annually.) In addition, FEMA and individual states currently teach an excellent detailed course in exercise design that emergency managers should make every effort to attend.[2]

The tabletop exercise is a simple exercise requiring minimal preparation. It is an excellent vehicle for training officials and other key responders and decision makers in selected components of the EOP. Its purpose is to detect potential problems with coordination and to determine the appropriateness of assigned responsibilities. It also reveals potential problems in response procedures and can help determine requirements for further training.

To undertake the exercise, selected officials and key staff gather in an informal setting, such as a conference room, and are presented with a scenario and related problems devised by the emergency manager (for example, the scenario might involve a hazardous materials incident, and an attendant problem might be the evacuation of a mobile home park). This kind of setting is conducive to free discussion, and participants have the opportunity to practice solving relatively simple problems in a low-stress environment. To maintain informality, neither time schedules nor written messages are generally prepared in advance or in detail, unless absolutely necessary in the exercise.

Once emergency personnel have achieved a certain level of familiarity with the EOP—through tabletop exercises and other training efforts—they are ready for a functional exercise, which is much more complex than the tabletop exercise and may take up to three months to develop. This exercise is designed to test an individual function—such as direction and control—or multiple functions, such as decision making, warning, and direction and control. The functional exercise (which normally includes the use of written, telephone, or radio messages) can also be used to test and evaluate selected activities within a function, such as message flow and radio communications within the direction and control system. Another example would be the use of simulated advisories from the National Hurricane Center to exercise the decision-making process for a hurricane.

A functional exercise must include testing and exercising the direction, control, and warning functions coupled with a realistic activation of the EOC. Factors that build stress into the exercise include the type of activity being evaluated, time constraints, and the complexity of the problems requiring response actions or policy decisions.

FEMA requires that each jurisdiction accepting EMA funds conduct a functional exercise in each of three years during a four-year period. The exercise scenario (i.e., natural, technological, or civil) must be different each year.

The full-scale exercise is the highest level of exercise and the culmination of the exercise program. The full-scale exercise is designed to evaluate the operational capability of the emergency management system over a substantial period of time. It tests major components and subcomponents of the EOP through realistic scenarios that create a high-stress environment. FEMA requires each jurisdiction accepting EMA funds to complete one full-scale exercise every four years.

A full-scale exercise requires extensive preparation time—more than three months—because actions specified in the EOP must actually be undertaken: response agencies must be employed, resources moved, shelters opened, buses dispatched, and so on. EOCs are normally fully activated as part of a full-scale exercise.

Since the full-scale exercise is usually highly visible to both the press and the community, the emergency manager should provide timely public notification of the exercise and be prepared to address any concerns.

Medical facilities and the exercise program

Although the emergency manager should establish and maintain control of the local exercise program, he or she should be aware that local medical facilities are required to conduct disaster exercises to obtain licenses or accreditation. Both to control costs and to increase the overall effectiveness of the local emergency management exercise program, emergency managers should encourage local medical facilities to participate in the community exercises rather than conduct independent exercises.

The Joint Commission on Accreditation of Health Care Organizations requires hospitals to conduct two exercises annually, one of which must involve the arrival of patients at the hospital for emergency care as part of a mass casualty incident. To conduct such an exercise realistically, the hospital must contact local fire services, emergency medical services, and ambulance services. If hospitals conduct their own exercises independently of each other and of the local emergency management exercise program, local fire services, emergency medical services, or ambulance services may receive separate requests for support from more than one hospital. Such uncoordinated efforts significantly increase costs for the supporting response agency. (One local ambulance company saved a great deal of money when it stopped supporting sixteen different exercises that health-care facilities had scheduled independently and began supporting three exercises scheduled at jointly agreed-upon times.)

The emergency manager might:

Include hospital representatives when developing the exercise program

Design exercises that will generate enough patients to meet hospital accreditation requirements

Establish a team spirit among medical facility staffs and local response agencies by allowing medical staffs to observe or participate in field training (training conducted off-site)

Schedule hospital staff to observe triage, transport, and staging at the exercise site

At the very least, ensure that the emergency management department always plays a role in medical facility disaster drills, even if only in the area of communications.

One last concern about the participation of medical facilities in scheduled exercises: exercises are almost invariably scheduled during the day, but varying the time for disaster drills and exercises will pay dividends in an actual emergency. Thus, with the approval of participating medical facilities, the emergency manager should consider scheduling an exercise during other shifts—for example, after 5:00 in the evening and before 8:00 in the morning.

Organizing an exercise program

Emergency managers should consider going beyond the FEMA exercise requirements and conducting localized disaster exercises at least twice a year in different parts of the jurisdiction. This section discusses several aspects of organizing such a program.

Exercise committee   Establishing an exercise committee is an excellent way to organize a local exercise program. The committee has three purposes: (1) to develop a local exercise program that meets the requirements of all participating agencies; (2) to devise a schedule for the exercises; and (3) to determine general exercise scenarios and locations. The actual exercise can be developed either by the committee or by the agency charged with incident command or overall direction and control.

Depending on the situation in the community, the emergency manager may or may not be the committee chairperson (if, for example, the fire chief might be more acceptable to the other agencies represented on the committee, the emergency manager would simply be a committee member). In addition to the emergency manager, a community exercise committee might include representatives from the fire department, law enforcement (sheriff), the local hospital, emergency medical services, and ambulance services. This is only a basic roster and should be expanded according to the needs of the jurisdiction. Some communities, for example, include on their exercise committees representatives from the Red Cross, nursing homes, and even private industry.

Announced versus unannounced exercises   At some point in the development of the exercise program, someone will suggest conducting unannounced exercises. There are two problems with doing this: a high level of efficiency and training is required to do well on unannounced exercises; and it is difficult to conduct an unannounced exercise for organizations that are in a response mode on a daily basis because a real emergency may occur at the same time as the exercise, and keeping the responses separate may be difficult. In one community, local hospitals that had asked to participate in an unannounced exercise were told only that an exercise would be conducted at some time during a particular month. The actual exercise was conducted at 8:00 in the evening, with an on-duty shift that had never participated in even an announced exercise and that therefore did very poorly. After the critique, the hospitals chose not to participate in further unannounced exercises.

Although exercises of some components of the plan—such as EOC activation, alerting and call-back of personnel—can be conducted unannounced and are worthwhile, ongoing activities and routine emergencies make it difficult to test other components in an unannounced format. The decision whether to undertake an unannounced exercise should be given careful thought.

A document describing the exercise   The success of an exercise depends partly on whether the participants understand the exercise. The emergency manager can help ensure that understanding by providing participants with a document describing the goals, components, and conduct of the exercise. The outline that follows is an example that emergency managers can follow when organizing such a document. Of course, each emergency manager will modify the outline according to the jurisdiction's needs and the scale and type of exercise.

Introduction
Purpose of Exercise
Objectives of Exercise
Exercise Time Schedule
Exercise Organization
　1. List of Participants
　2. Controllers
　　a. Composition
　　b. Function
　　c. Responsibilities
　3. Observers

General Description of Scenario
Activities by Participants in Exercising Components of the EOP
  1. Warning and Alerting
  2. Decision Making
  3. Direction and Control
  4. Evacuation
      a. Shelter Activation
      b. Traffic Control
      c. Emergency Transportation
      d. Medical Facilities
      e. Special-Needs Population
List of Exercise Events
Preparation of Exercise Messages
Training
Special Instructions
Critique

Critique of the exercise Critiques of the exercise are prepared by the controllers—the individuals who are responsible for ensuring that the exercise is conducted according to plan and that the objectives are reached. (These critiques are consolidated into one by the agency sponsoring the exercise.) Controllers closely monitor the exercise, keeping notes that will be used afterward in the critique. Normally, each controller evaluates a separate component of the plan—the component in which he or she is especially knowledgeable—but in a small community, one controller may look at everything. Generally, except for the emergency manager, controllers are from outside the response agencies participating in the exercise (that is, they are from the state or another local jurisdiction). Figure 7–11 is a sample critique sheet that can be adapted for all jurisdictions.

Although FEMA's view is that the emergency manager should participate in the exercise rather than in the evaluation, several arguments can be made

Figure 7–11 Sample critique sheet for an exercise.

Name _____
Agency _____

Please check the evaluation you feel best indicates the quality of performance in the left column. Then provide a *reason* for that rating. (Note: Do not give as a reason for notification being poor was that it was late. Be specific. Why was it late? Give a *reason*.) In the right column, give your *recommendation* for improving performance in the future.

Evaluation	Reasons	Recommendation
Activity		
Very good _____ Good _____ Poor _____ Very poor _____		
Activity		
Very good _____ Good _____ Poor _____ Very poor _____		
Activity		

that the emergency manager is the best person to evaluate the EOP and the emergency management program. First, neither the plan nor the program should require the presence of the emergency manager for implementation; it is therefore sensible to conduct an exercise under conditions in which he or she is not a participant. Second, the emergency manager is the person most familiar with the plan and the program and should therefore have a major role in both designing and evaluating the exercise. Problems that might escape someone less familiar with the program will be picked up by the emergency manager. Despite FEMA's recommendation, therefore, emergency managers should consider not participating in every exercise.

An initial oral critique should be conducted immediately after the exercise, while everything is fresh in the participants' and controllers' minds. The discussion should be followed by a detailed written critique prepared by the emergency manager, who can then use it to make appropriate changes to the EOP. The written critique should be sufficiently detailed to cover the overall preparation and conduct of the exercise and, most important, the problems encountered and the solutions recommended.

Computer simulations There is a strong trend toward integrating computer technology into exercise programs. Emergency managers currently have access to a computer-generated exercise package distributed by FEMA through state offices of emergency management. The package includes generic exercise scenarios for events such as a tornado, an incident involving mass casualties, a nuclear accident, and a flood. The program is flexible enough to allow the emergency manager to determine the level of play and participation (for example, whether to exercise only the incident command system or to activate the EOC). Local data are then input to tailor the exercise to the community. Experience with the package to date indicates that it is an excellent tool for developing exercises.

Another way to use computers in conducting an exercise is to prepare exercise messages and store them in the computer database; they will be automatically input into the exercise scenario at specified intervals. The messages can be sent to either an on-site or an off-site printer, depending on the participants' location. This technique allows several EOCs to be exercised at the same time (for example, at a number of different municipalities within a county) and permits better overall control of the exercise. Emergency managers using this approach, however, are cautioned to have printed copies of messages on hand at each location for manual input in case of a malfunction.

Budgeting for exercises Almost any aspect of an emergency management program—including exercises, which require participation by departments other than the emergency management department—is vulnerable to changes in funding. Eventually, other local government departments that have been participating in exercises will begin to question the emergency manager about how this or that use of personnel or resources will be reimbursed. A limited budget can have a significant effect on the exercise program, particularly on full-scale exercises. As an example, a local government might not be able to activate its EOC for a full-scale exercise because the cost of turning on the internal phones for one day might be $500 (the cost incurred is for each phone for an entire month, even though only several hours are actually required for the exercise). Lack of funding can limit the use of buses, ambulances, and even emergency personnel.

Let's look at a typical exercise held in communities across the country and explore some means of reducing expenses. Figure 7–12 shows how an exercise involving mass casualties is usually conducted. To make the exercise as realistic as possible, volunteers are moulaged (given simulated injuries) and actually moved from the triage area to participating hospitals via ambulance or rescue vehicles. Depending on the size of the community, five to ten ambulances might be used to shuttle patients to participating medical facilities. But do the ambulance personnel need training in running ambulances back and forth between the hospitals and disaster sites? Not likely, because they run red lights and sirens daily as part of their routine duties. Hospitals, however, will specifically request that ambulances be used to make the exercise realistic for their staff. An excellent compromise is shown in Figure 7–13.

In this variation, patients are still used in the triage area and in the hospital emergency room, but ambulances do not move between the disaster site and the hospital. Victims are triaged and tagged at the disaster site. Normal radio communication is then made with the hospital concerning transport and the types of injuries. A victim is loaded onto an ambulance at the disaster site; the ambulance drives to a nearby drop-off area and unloads, then returns to the staging area for another patient. At the same time, separate radio communications are made to a patient holding-area on the hospital grounds. A victim who has previously been tagged with the same injuries is loaded into another ambulance and rides the short distance to the emergency room. That ambulance then returns to the patient holding-area and waits for the next patient.

This approach cuts costs not only by reducing the number of ambulance units involved but also by saving fuel (since long runs to the hospital are avoided) and by reducing liability (because the emergency vehicles are off the street while participating in the exercise).

The same technique can be modified to support hospital exercises involving mass casualties, which must be conducted to meet hospital requirements. A single ambulance moving patients from a holding area around the corner from the emergency room can provide the requisite realism to make the exercise a success. The field communications on patient transport can be established at any remote location—either inside a building, using a base station radio, or outside, using mobile communications. Again, exercise participants use one radio frequency to coordinate patient medical and transport information and another to manage the movement of patients from the patient holding-area outside the hospital. Such an exercise can be arranged relatively quickly, and costs are controlled by keeping support minimal. Yet this pared-down approach still makes it possible to exercise components of the EOP.

Recovery exercises

Exercising the complete plan includes conducting a recovery exercise. Recovery exercises can be designed to fit any of the required formats, from tabletop to full scale. A full-scale recovery exercise might include sending search and rescue teams into designated areas, establishing security for heavily damaged areas, establishing recovery staging areas, and airlifting paramedic teams into areas not

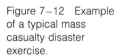

Figure 7–12   Example of a typical mass casualty disaster exercise.

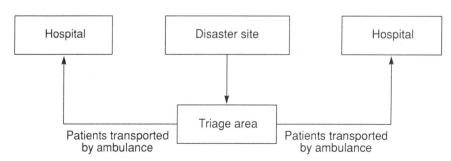

Figure 7–13 Example of a compromise mass casualty disaster exercise.

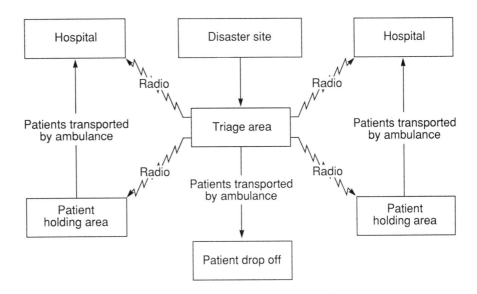

accessible by vehicle. Had such an exercise been conducted in Hurricane Hugo's strike area, severe problems after the hurricane might have been avoided.

Conclusion

The primary purpose of this chapter has been to illustrate the value of planning, training, and exercising in developing effective response. Developing effective response is not easy, and the emergency manager—who is responsible for ensuring the protection of all of our citizens when disaster strikes—must be given more assistance and training than is currently available. Fortunately, professionalism among emergency managers is on the rise, and change is gradually occurring in all aspects of emergency management. These and other developments must continue.

First, it must be recognized that the military system of planning is not appropriate to local government planning purposes. Indeed, as more planners without military experience have become involved in emergency planning, there has been a gradual move away from the military-style plan, particularly in the Comprehensive Hurricane Evacuation Planning conducted in the coastal areas of the United States. This may prove to be the future direction for planning in the local government environment. But even with the gradual move away from military planning models, local emergency managers still require guidance on standard formats. Such guidance facilitates training at all levels and should be implemented and endorsed by all agencies with disaster response responsibilities.

Second, the professionalism of the emergency manager must be upgraded through more stringent hiring standards and must be further enhanced through training. The basis of an effective comprehensive emergency management program is an emergency manager with a strong background in planning: the emergency manager must receive intensive training in developing emergency plans—a one-week course is not sufficient. One need only look at the degree requirements for general planners or at the extensive training provided military officers to see why emergency managers are pressing for further professionalization. The job requires it.

Third, once the emergency manager is trained, the entire planning committee should be trained, as well. Recognizing the value of this approach on the operational side, FEMA schedules local government operational staffs at the Emergency Management Institute for emergency training and exercising. This concept should also be applied to the planning committee if, in fact, planning capability is to be improved at the local level.

Fourth, the use of computer simulations to help train and exercise the emergency manager and emergency personnel at the local level must be expanded.

With these changes, citizens will be better protected against the ever-present threat of disaster.

1 Two recently developed degree programs will significantly increase emergency managers' planning expertise: the first is in Emergency Administration and Planning at the University of North Texas in Denton, Texas; the second is in Emergency Disaster Management at Thomas A. Edison State College in Trenton, New Jersey.

2 As the first step in progressive exercising (that is, before the tabletop exercise), the FEMA course in exercise design includes an orientation seminar to familiarize participants with plan, procedure, organization, and so forth. Similarly, orientation seminars can be given to elected officials and to EOC staff before they participate in a tabletop exercise.

Exhibit 7–A.

AN ORDINANCE DESIGNATING THE CHAIRMAN OF THE BOARD OF COUNTY COMMISSIONERS OR, IN HIS ABSENCE, THE VICE-CHAIRMAN OR ADMINISTRATOR, OR HIS DESIGNEE, IN THIS SUCCESSION, AS THE OFFICIAL WITH AUTHORITY TO DECLARE A STATE OF EMERGENCY IN THE EVENT OF A NATURAL OR MANMADE DISASTER OR THE IMMINENT THREAT THEREOF; AUTHORIZING SUCH OFFICIAL TO TAKE CERTAIN EMERGENCY MEASURES RELATING THERETO; PROVIDING FOR IMPOSITION OF A CURFEW; PROVIDING FOR REGULATION OF THE USE OF WATER; PROVIDING FOR PROHIBITION OF PRICE GOUGING; PROVIDING PENALTIES; PROVIDING FOR CONFLICT AND SEVERABILITY; PROVIDING AN EFFECTIVE DATE.

WHEREAS, because of the existing and continuing possibility of the occurrence of natural or manmade disasters or emergencies and destruction resulting therefrom, and in order to ensure readiness of Pinellas County to adequately deal with such disasters and generally provide for the protection of the public health, safety, and welfare and to preserve the lives and property of the people of Pinellas County, it is hereby determined to be in the best interest of Pinellas County that the following Ordinance be adopted.

NOW, THEREFORE, BE IT ORDAINED BY THE BOARD OF COUNTY COMMISSIONERS OF PINELLAS COUNTY, FLORIDA:

SECTION 1 It is the intent of the County to designate a County official to declare a Local State of Emergency in the event of a natural or manmade disaster or emergency, or the imminent threat thereof, and to authorize certain actions relating thereto when a quorum of the Board of County Commissioners is unable to meet.

SECTION 2 Pursuant to Chapter 252, Florida Statutes, which authorizes the waiver of procedures and formalities otherwise required of political subdivisions to take whatever prudent action is necessary to ensure the health, safety, and welfare of the community in the event of a state of emergency, when a quorum of the Board of County Commissioners is unable to meet, the Chairman of the Board of County Commissioners, or Vice-Chairman in his absence, or the County Administrator, or his designee, is empowered to declare a Local State of Emergency whenever he shall determine that a natural or manmade disaster or emergency has occurred or that the occurrence or threat of one is imminent and requires immediate and expeditious action.

SECTION 3 "Emergency" means any occurrence, or threat thereof, whether accidental, natural, or caused by man, in war or peace, which results or may result in substantial injury or harm to the population or substantial damage to or loss of property. (F.S. 252.34(2))

SECTION 4 A state of emergency shall be declared by Proclamation of the Chairman or the Vice-Chairman in his absence, or by the County Administrator, or his designee, in the absence of the Chairman or Vice-Chairman. The state of emergency shall continue until the Chairman or Vice-Chairman in his absence or County Administrator, or his designee, in the absence of the Chairman or Vice-Chairman, finds that the threat or danger no longer exists and/or until an emergency meeting of a quorum of the Board of County Commissioners can take place and terminate the state of emergency by proclamation.

SECTION 5 A proclamation declaring a state of emergency shall activate the disaster emergency plans applicable to Pinellas County and shall be the authority for use or distribution of any supplies, equipment, materials, or facilities assembled or arranged to be made available pursuant to such plans.

SECTION 6 Upon the declaration of a State of Emergency, pursuant to this Ordinance, Emergency Ordinances Nos. 85-16A, 85-16B, 85-16C, and 85-16D shall be effective during the period of such emergency to protect the health, safety, and welfare of the community.

The purpose of this Ordinance is to provide authority and enforcement power for whatever action is necessary, including the following:

A. Suspend or limit the sale, dispensing, or transportation of alcoholic beverages, firearms, explosives, and combustibles.
B. Establish curfews, including but not limited to the prohibition of or restrictions on pedestrian and vehicular movement, standing, and parking, except for the provision of designated essential services, such as fire, police, emergency medical services, and hospital services, including the transportation of patients, utility emergency repairs, and emergency calls by physicians.
C. Utilize all available resources of the County government as reasonably necessary to cope with the disaster emergency, including emergency expenditures not to exceed $50,000.
D. Declare certain areas off limits.
E. Make provisions for the availability and use of temporary emergency housing and the emergency warehousing of materials.
F. Establish emergency operating centers and shelters in addition to or in place of those provided for in the County's Emergency Plan.
G. Declare that during an emergency it shall be unlawful and an offense against Pinellas County for any person, firm, or corporation to use the fresh water supplied by the County or any City for any purpose other than cooking, drinking, or bathing.
H. Declare that during an emergency it shall be unlawful and an offense against Pinellas County for any person, firm, or corporation operating within the County to charge more than the normal average retail price for any merchandise, goods, or services sold during the emergency. The average retail price as used herein is

defined to be that price at which similar merchandise, goods, or services were being sold during the ninety (90) days immediately preceding the emergency or a mark-up which is not a larger percentage over wholesale cost than was being added to wholesale cost before the emergency.

I.   Confiscate merchandise, equipment, vehicles, or property needed to alleviate the emergency. Reimbursement shall be within sixty (60) days and at customary value charged for the items during ninety (90) days previous to the emergency.

J.   Allow the Chairman, Vice-Chairman, or, in their absence, the County Administrator, or his designee on behalf of the County, to call on the National Guard of the Army, Coast Guard, or other law enforcement divisions as necessary to assist in the mitigation of the emergency or to help maintain law and order, rescue, and traffic control.

SECTION 7   Nothing in this Ordinance shall be construed to limit the authority of the Board of County Commissioners to declare or terminate a State of Emergency and take any action authorized by law when sitting in regular or special session.

SECTION 8   Any person, firm, or corporation who refuses to comply with or violates any section of this Ordinance, or the emergency measures which may be made effective pursuant to this Ordinance, shall be punished according to law and, upon conviction for such offenses, shall be punished by a fine not to exceed Five Hundred Dollars ($500.00) or by imprisonment not to exceed sixty (60) days in the County jail, or both. Each day of continued noncompliance or violation shall constitute a separate offense. In addition to the foregoing, any licensee of Pinellas County found guilty of violating any provision of this Ordinance, or the emergency measures which may be made effective pursuant to this Ordinance, may have his license suspended or revoked by the Board of County Commissioners of Pinellas County.

Nothing herein contained shall prevent the County from taking such other lawful action in any court of competent jurisdiction as is necessary to prevent or remedy any refusal to comply with, or violation of, this Ordinance or the emergency measures which may be effective pursuant to this Ordinance. Such other lawful action shall include, but shall not be limited to, an equitable action for injunctive relief or any action at law for damages.

SECTION 9   In the event this Ordinance conflicts with any other Ordinance of Pinellas County or other applicable law, the more restrictive shall apply. If any phase or portion of this Ordinance is held invalid or unconstitutional by any court of competent jurisdiction, such portion shall be deemed a separate, distinct, and independent provision and such holding shall not affect the validity of the remaining portion.

SECTION 10   This Ordinance shall take effect upon acknowledgment from the Secretary of State that this Ordinance has been duly filed.

Source: Pinellas County, FL, *Hurricane Evacuation Implementation Guide.*

Exhibit 7–B.

WHEREAS, the National Hurricane Center recognizes the danger to coastal residents of Florida from Hurricane _____, by posting a Hurricane _____ from _____ to _____; and

WHEREAS, Pinellas County has high evacuation times in order to evacuate residents from the hazards of a hurricane; and

WHEREAS, the current forecast error of the National Hurricane Center does not allow for a confident prediction of the track of Hurricane _____ at that point in time coinciding with Pinellas County's high evacuation times; and

WHEREAS, Hurricane _____ has the potential for causing extensive damage to public utilities, public buildings, public communication systems, public streets and roads, public drainage systems, commercial and residential buildings and areas; and

WHEREAS, Chapter 252.38(6)(e), Florida Statutes, provides authority for a political subdivision such as Pinellas County to declare a State of Local Emergency and to waive the procedures and formalities otherwise required of political subdivisions by law pertaining to:

1. Performance of public work and taking whatever action is necessary to ensure the health, safety, and welfare of the community;
2. Entering into contracts;
3. Incurring obligations;
4. Employment of permanent and temporary workers;
5. Utilization of volunteer workers;
6. Rental of equipment;
7. Acquisition and distribution with or without compensation of supplies, materials, and facilities;
8. Appropriation and expenditure of public funds.

NOW THEREFORE IT IS RESOLVED by the Board of County Commissioners of Pinellas County, Florida, in _____ Session, this _____ day of _____ 19__ that Hurricane _____ poses a serious threat to the lives and property of residents of Pinellas County and that a State of Local Emergency shall be declared, effective immediately for all territory within the legal boundaries of Pinellas County, and that all unincorporated and incorporated areas shall be embraced by the provisions of this Resolution.

BE IT FURTHER RESOLVED that the Board of County Commissioners hereby exercises its authority and waives the procedures and formalities required by law of a political subdivision, as provided in Chapter 252.38(6)(e), Florida Statutes, and Section 2.04 (k), Pinellas County Charter.

Commissioner _____ offered the foregoing Resolution and moved its adoption, which was seconded by Commissioner _____, and upon roll call the vote was:
    Ayes _____
    Nays _____
    Absent and Not Voting _____

_____
    (Time)

Source: Pinellas County, FL, *Hurricane Evacuation Implementation Guide.*

Exhibit 7–C.

AN ORDINANCE RELATING TO PROVISIONS FOR A LOCAL EMERGENCY; PROVIDING THE PURPOSE AND INTENT OF THE ORDINANCE; PROVIDING FOR A CURFEW; PROVIDING PENALTIES; DEFINING THE TERRITORY EMBRACED; PROVIDING AN EFFECTIVE DATE.

WHEREAS, the Board of County Commissioners of Pinellas County, Florida, has declared a state of local emergency, pursuant to Section _____, Florida Statutes, and to County Ordinance No. _____.

WHEREAS, Chapter 252.38(6)(e), Florida Statutes, provides authority for a political subdivision such as Pinellas County to declare a state of local emergency and to waive the procedures and formalities otherwise required of political subdivisions by law pertaining to:

1. Performing public work and taking whatever action is necessary to ensure the health, safety, and welfare of the community;
2. Entering into contracts;
3. Incurring obligations;
4. Employment of permanent and temporary workers;
5. Utilization of volunteer workers;
6. Rental of equipment;
7. Acquisition and distribution with or without compensation of supplies, materials, and facilities;
8. Appropriation and expenditure of public funds.

NOW THEREFORE, BE IT ORDAINED by the Board of County Commissioners of Pinellas County, Florida:

SECTION 1. PURPOSE AND INTENT OF ORDINANCE   The Board of County Commissioners of Pinellas County, Florida, finds and declares that in order to protect and safeguard the safety, health, and welfare of the people of Pinellas County, the herein contained emergency regulations are necessary.

SECTION 2. CURFEW   Until rescinded by further County Ordinance, during this state of emergency there shall be a general curfew throughout Pinellas County between the hours of 7:00 P.M. and 7:00 A.M.; provided, however, that this shall not apply to regular members of the law enforcement bodies. Regular employees of local industries, while traveling to and from their jobs, are exempt, provided they have identification if stopped by any law enforcement personnel. Local industries are requested to do everything possible to provide identification to such of their employees as shall be traveling during the hours of the curfew.

SECTION 3. PENALTIES   Any person who knowingly violates any provision of this Ordinance shall, upon conviction, be punished according to law and shall be subject to a fine, not exceeding the sum of $500.00, or imprisonment in the County jail for a period of sixty (60) days, or both such fine and imprisonment. In addition to the penalties set forth above, Pinellas County or the Pinellas County Water System is authorized to shut off the water supply to such violators.

SECTION 4. TERRITORY EMBRACED   All territory within the legal boundaries of Pinellas County, Florida, including all unincorporated and incorporated areas, shall be embraced by the provisions of this Ordinance.

SECTION 5. EFFECTIVE DATE   This Ordinance shall take effect upon a declaration of local emergency as authorized by County Ordinance No. 85-16.

Source: Pinellas County, FL, *Hurricane Evacuation Implementation Guide.*

Exhibit 7-D.

AN ORDINANCE RELATING TO PROVISIONS FOR A LOCAL EMERGENCY; PROVIDING THE PURPOSE AND INTENT OF THE ORDINANCE; PROVIDING FOR THE PROHIBITION OF PRICE GOUGING AND OVERCHARGING FOR MERCHANDISE SOLD BY LICENSEES OF PINELLAS COUNTY, FLORIDA, AND PROVIDING FOR PENALTIES INCLUDING BUT NOT LIMITED TO SUSPENSION OR REVOCATION OF THE PINELLAS COUNTY OCCUPATION LICENSE; DEFINING THE TERRITORY EMBRACED; AND PROVIDING AN EFFECTIVE DATE.

WHEREAS, the Board of County Commissioners of Pinellas County, Florida, has declared a state of local emergency, pursuant to Section _____, Florida Statutes, and to County Ordinance No. _____.

WHEREAS, Chapter 252.38(6)(e), Florida Statutes, provides authority for a political subdivision such as Pinellas County to declare a state of local emergency and to waive the procedures and formalities otherwise required of political subdivisions by law pertaining to:

1. Performing public work and taking whatever action is necessary to ensure the health, safety, and welfare of the community;
2. Entering into contracts;
3. Incurring obligations;
4. Employment of permanent and temporary workers;
5. Utilization of volunteer workers;
6. Rental of equipment;
7. Acquisition and distribution with or without compensation of supplies, materials, and facilities;
8. Appropriation and expenditure of public funds;

NOW THEREFORE, BE IT ORDAINED by the Board of County Commissioners of Pinellas County, Florida:

SECTION 1. PURPOSE AND INTENT OF ORDINANCE The Board of County Commissioners of Pinellas County, Florida, finds and declares that in order to protect and safeguard the safety, health, and welfare of the people of Pinellas County, the herein contained emergency regulations are necessary.

SECTION 2. PROHIBITING PRICE GOUGING It is hereby ordained and declared to be unlawful for any licensee of Pinellas County to charge more than the normal average retail price for any merchandise sold during the state of local emergency. The average retail price as used herein is defined to be that price at which similar merchandise was being sold during the ninety (90) days immediately preceding the state of local emergency, or a mark-up that is not a larger percentage over wholesale cost than was being added to wholesale cost before the state of local emergency.

SECTION 3. PENALTIES Any person who knowingly violates any provision of this Ordinance shall, upon conviction, be punished according to law and shall be subject to a fine not exceeding the sum of $500.00, or imprisonment in the County jail for a period of sixty (60) days, or both such fine and imprisonment. In addition to the penalties set forth above, Pinellas County or the Pinellas County Water System is authorized to shut off the water supply to such violators.

SECTION 4. TERRITORY EMBRACED All territory within legal boundaries of Pinellas County, Florida, including all unincorporated and incorporated areas, shall be embraced by the provisions of this Ordinance.

SECTION 5. EFFECTIVE DATE This Ordinance shall take effect upon a declaration of local emergency as authorized by County Ordinance No. _____.

Source: Pinellas County, FL, *Hurricane Evacuation Implementation Guide.*

Exhibit 7–E.

EVACUATION ORDER
WHEREAS, a State of Local Emergency has been declared because of the serious threat to the lives and property of residents of Pinellas County from Hurricane _____.

Now, therefore, pursuant to Chapter 252.36 (5)(e) of the Florida Statutes and Governor's Executive Order 80-29, as the Chief elected official of Pinellas County I hereby order Evacuation Level ___, of the Pinellas County Hurricane Evacuation Plan, to be implemented in order to protect the citizens of Pinellas County from the effects of Hurricane _____.

All persons residing in Evacuation Zones _____ through _____ must evacuate their homes immediately and go over designated evacuation routes to safe areas or shelters.

This includes residents of all Evacuation Zones colored _____, _____, _____, _____, _____, in official Hurricane Evacuation Public Information tabloids or maps.

It is further ordered that all persons residing in mobile homes or travel trailers, in any part of Pinellas County, evacuate immediately.

Any person not abiding by this Order is guilty of a misdemeanor of the second degree and subject to penalties established under Chapter 252.50 of the Florida Statutes.

Done this _____ day of _____ _____, 19_____.

_____
Chairman, Pinellas County
Board of County Commissioners

Source: Pinellas County, FL, *Hurricane Evacuation Implementation Guide.*

Managing disaster response operations

Local governments must cope with two types of crises: emergencies such as house fires and automobile accidents that happen every day, and crises that are commonly called disasters. House fires, automobile accidents, and other crises like them are what might be called "routine emergencies": though painful, they are familiar events. They happen with some regularity and, in a general way, can be anticipated or expected. Although their consequences may be catastrophic for those directly involved, the impact of routine emergencies is rarely felt throughout a community. To deal with such crises, local governments have specific organizational arrangements. House fires are handled principally by fire services, automobile accidents by police departments. In contrast,

disasters may be defined as nonroutine events in which societies or their larger subsystems (e.g., regions or communities) are socially disrupted and physically harmed. The key defining characteristics of such events are (1) length of forewarning, (2) magnitude of impact, (3) scope of impact, and (4) duration of impact.[1]

Compared with routine emergencies, disasters are events that significantly interfere with the social life of a large part of the community. The ratio of damage to remaining local resources (the impact ratio) tends to be high and often requires that resources be marshalled from outside the community.

A disaster changes the very character of a community, affecting the conditions under which disaster operations are carried out. Russell Dynes, E. L. Quarantelli, and Gary Kreps have grouped the changes that affect disaster operations under six headings: uncertainty, urgency, emergency consensus, expansion of the citizenship role, deemphasis of contractual and impersonal relationships, and convergence.[2]

Uncertainty arises from the fact that the disaster agent is "new": it creates demands different from those created by routine emergencies. Generally two types of demands arise in disasters—agent generated and response generated—and none of them is routine (they may even be unique). Agent-generated demands derive from the particular disaster agent: for example, flooding may generate a need for sandbags to protect against high water. Response-generated demands derive from the execution of response operations: logistics may need to be devised for the provision of food, shelter, and clothing. In addition to being nonroutine, the demands created by disasters may lie outside the usual capacity of community organizations and require responses characterized by innovation and flexibility. The uncertainty that is connected with the new and possibly unique nature of the demands is made more intense by a sense of urgency in the face of extensive human suffering and property damage.

"Emergency consensus"—also a characteristic change arising in disaster situations—is spontaneous agreement among officials and responders about priorities. For example, victim care (such as rescue, medical attention, and shelter) usually assumes first priority. Expansion of the citizenship role is another change. Particularly in the short run, disasters are associated with high levels of community solidarity and desire to assist with response efforts. At the same time, contractual and impersonal relationships tend to be deemphasized: legal definitions of prop-

Figure 8-1 Mount Pleasant, South Carolina, after Hurricane Hugo (1989).

erty ownership tend to relax, for example, and people sense the need to improvise, innovate, and generally "do things differently." Finally, people converge on the impact area, some to check on or help family or friends, some to help the authorities, and some to satisfy their curiosity. Individuals, private organizations, and governmental organizations at all levels also send equipment, clothing, food, medicine, and sometimes work teams to disaster sites.

In addition to changing the way citizens behave, disasters change the way citizens view local officials and emergency managers. In normal times people expect custodial behavior of officials, but during disasters they demand action and leadership.[3]

This chapter examines management of the response phase of disaster (just before, during, and immediately after impact), with an emphasis throughout on the role played by planning. After a brief discussion of the general relationship between the emergency plan and response management, the chapter examines the key to disaster response—the emergency operations center (EOC). The topics discussed are the EOC's functions, location, and structure; the decision-making climate inside the EOC; special issues for EOCs; and disaster declarations.

One foundation of good decision making during the response phase is realistic expectations about the likely actions of victims and emergency responders. The behavioral responses of both those groups are discussed next.

The organization of six generic response functions is then considered. Generic functions are actions or activities that may be useful in various disaster events (activities such as emergency medical care, search and rescue, protection of property).

Finally, the chapter surveys the recent evolution of the role of emergency manager and highlights the qualities needed by an emergency manager.

Relationship between the emergency plan and response management

What is an emergency plan, and how is it related to the response phase of emergency management? If disaster response is defined as a series of decisions by emergency managers, planning can be viewed as the framework for decision making: it structures the options from which a decision maker can choose. In other words, a plan is composed of decisions made during "normal" times to help guide decisions during a disaster. And because disasters rarely occur repeatedly in the same community, much of the "real time" of being an emergency manager is spent *planning*.

The emergency plan is linked to the response phase in two important ways. First, during the planning process, the major agent-generated and response-generated demands are identified and strategies are developed for meeting them. The plan itself documents the strategies. Then, in the response phase, the strategies are evaluated and implemented. The second connection between planning and response management is exercises (drills). Such activities are usually mandated in the comprehensive emergency plan, but they should also be viewed as part of the emergency planning process. Some exercises test overall response capabilities, such as communication, and others test generic functions, such as evacuation or sheltering.

Organizational aspects of response

The functions of local emergency management units remain fairly constant, although the structures vary tremendously among municipalities. Dennis Wenger, E. L. Quarantelli, and Russell Dynes have identified eight types of local emergency management organizations, ranging from "real" organizations with a full-time staff and director to arrangements whereby a fire or police chief is

Figure 8–2   First responder and media representative at a hazardous materials incident.

designated the emergency management coordinator but serves without staff or with minimal staff.[4] Whatever the structure of the local emergency management unit, the key to disaster response is the emergency operations center (EOC). The EOC serves as the master coordination and control point for all counter-disaster efforts.

The EOC is a function, a place, and a structure. It also is characterized by a very distinctive climate—a climate that cannot help but affect decision making in the EOC. The emergency manager must consider, as well, several special issues relevant to the operation of the EOC. A final important organizational consideration during the response phase—a consideration that begins but does not end with the EOC—is disaster declarations.

The EOC as function, place, and structure

As a place, the EOC differs greatly from one municipality to another, but the functions are much less variable. Structurally and administratively, too, EOCs show only small variation.

Functions of the EOC   The EOC is responsible not only for assembling and directing local government response but also for communicating with all other levels of government, with the private sector, and with the public (both the public at large and the public at risk). E. L. Quarantelli has highlighted the six primary functions of the EOC: coordination, policymaking, operations management, information gathering and record keeping, public information, and hosting visitors.[5] Although all these functions are critical, coordination is often viewed as central.

Coordination focuses on response-generated demands. It requires assessing the threat and marshalling organizational resources for concerted action to counter the threat. Consequently, the EOC is responsible for ensuring that responder organizations are working together and understand one another's missions and responsibilities. This understanding develops during the planning process and is codified in the comprehensive emergency plan: the plan provides the framework for coordination, specifying task assignments, organizational responsibilities, chains of command, and resource provisions. Within this framework, the EOC commander deals with implementation issues and mobilization problems of the moment; but the foundation of coordination is established before the disaster event.

The second function of the EOC is to make the policy decisions that guide the overall community response to the disaster. These are broad decisions that affect the nature of the response, rather than specific operational deci-

Figure 8–3 Emergency Operations Center, Carroll County, Maryland.

sions. (The comprehensive emergency plan outlines the management strategy, or general approach, for particular disaster threats, ordinarily by specifying the generic functions that will be used in response to various disaster agents.) For example, EOC policy may specify that an evacuation is to be executed, whereas the particular routes of egress may be left to the discretion of the police department command post.

The third function of the EOC is operations management, which is the action undertaken to meet agent-generated demands. How will resources and personnel be deployed to counter dangers associated with the specific disaster agent? In a disaster, the constellation of agent-generated demands changes with time. Some threats can be effectively handled or countered and either disappear or substantially decline, lessening the need for personnel and resources. Meanwhile, new threats may require that additional resources and personnel be redeployed from initial assignments. The operations function requires continuous monitoring of the threat and review and reassignment of resources to ensure optimum communitywide response.

The fourth function of the EOC is gathering information. The local EOC must collect and disseminate a variety of disaster-relevant information, as well as store it for future use. This does not mean that the EOC should become a kind of library or that a massive information function is necessary. It simply means that some simplified form of record keeping should be devised and maintained during emergencies.

The information gathered by the EOC is of various types. Damage assessment is used to support other EOC functions. Information is also gathered on the execution of the disaster response itself, including the timing and effectiveness of management decisions. Such information is useful in after-action assessments to improve future management and in recovery funding requests. The EOC must also collect and distribute to responder organizations information about the nature of the threat and effectiveness of response. Finally, elected officials, other EOCs, and government agencies often request information from the EOC about communitywide response efforts.

Another function of the EOC is to disperse public information, both to the general public and to the public at risk. A third important audience is the mass media, which are an important channel of communication to both publics. Because serious operational problems can arise when inaccurate or inconsistent information is disseminated, the EOC should be the point of contact with all media. Responder organizations should not have independent contact with the media. Centralizing the public information function in the EOC and placing it under the supervision of the public information officer (PIO) ensures that a consistent message is disseminated and makes it easier for the media to obtain authoritative information in the first place. (Although the public information *function* should be considered a part of the EOC, the public information *office* need not be physically located within the EOC; demand for information is high in the aftermath of a disaster, and the presence of eager media representatives may be disruptive to the decision-making process in the EOC.)

In communicating with the population at risk, the PIO shares responsibility with the managers of various generic functions, such as warning, evacuation, and sheltering. At a minimum, an emergency management plan must include the capacity to disseminate information that allows citizens to determine whether or not they are at risk. This aspect of public information was not well handled, for example, during the reactor accident at Three Mile Island: many people defined themselves as in danger when, in terms of likely radioactive plume movement, they were probably not. From the standpoint of emergency operations, inaccurate perception of risk can create substantial difficulties. For instance, in the case of evacuations, if too many people define

Figure 8–4 Emergency Operations Center, Cumberland County, Pennsylvania. Controlling information flow is critical for a coordinated response.

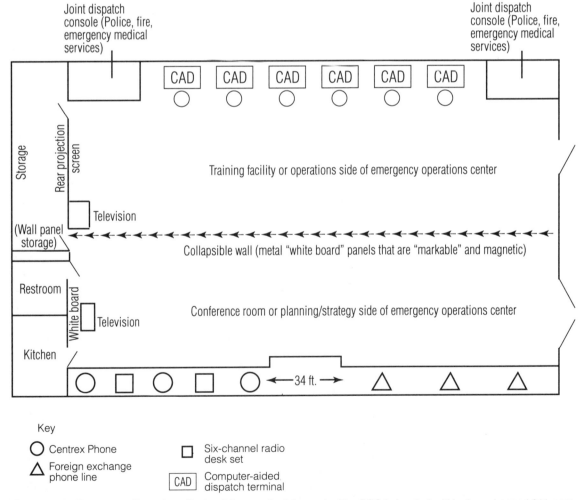

Key

○ Centrex Phone
△ Foreign exchange phone line
□ Six-channel radio desk set
CAD Computer-aided dispatch terminal

Figure 8–5   Emergency Operations Center, Minneapolis, Minnesota. The EOC is located within the enhanced-911 computer-aided dispatch center.

themselves as in danger, exit routes can get clogged and shelters overloaded. In contrast, if those at risk fail to recognize their condition, they may hesitate to comply with emergency measures. A well-conceived public information effort can greatly reduce the potential for such problems.

Finally, the EOC must be able to host visitors. EOC managers often do not anticipate that visitors (usually VIPs—for example, President Carter at Three Mile Island—and local or regional elected officials) will arrive on site. It is routine for the mayor and council members to appear. In large-scale disasters, particularly those with regional impact, the number of visitors increases. Because the operational structure of an EOC cannnot easily accommodate visitors who do not have a specific response function, staff should be available to escort visitors to the EOC, explain operations, and direct them to a space that permits them to observe—but not interfere with—operations.

There are a variety of ways in which an EOC might be organized to fulfill the six functions just delineated. One strategy, called FIRESCOPE (Firefighting Resources of Southern California Organized for Potential Emergencies), is a planning-based regional emergency response system that incorporates both the planning process and the functions of the EOC. The planning and resource evaluation part of FIRESCOPE, referred to as the Multiagency Coordination System (MAC), is operated by a multiagency coordination committee (composed of agency directors) and is divided into two functions: (1) a software-based system called the Fire Information Management System that stores data for fire management and (2) the Operations Coordination Center, which implements policy devised by MAC.

The EOC component of FIRESCOPE, called the Incident Command System (ICS), is an organizational structure composed of four sections: operations, planning, logistics, and finance. The ICS is activated at the time of a fire and executes the functions described for an EOC. Each of the four sections is broken down into units that correspond to the important generic functions of fire control and management. The ICS thereby provides a unified command structure and a defined set of interorganizational responsibilities for responder agencies. Although this system is designed to deal only with fires, it represents an effective general strategy for undertaking the EOC functions. The Incident Command System in particular is a type of structure that could be generalized to a variety of threat situations.[6]

The EOC as a place Physically, EOCs vary greatly, especially at the local level. At other levels of government (particularly states), the EOC has a permanent location as well as permanent equipment. Although such an arrangement may be an ideal to strive for, the limited funding available to local government makes it more likely that EOCs will be in temporary housing. The EOC might be in space that is captured and configured at the time of an emergency, though its contents should be planned in advance. However, the equipment needed to operate an EOC effectively—equipment such as telephone lines and other communications equipment—would limit the number of suitable spaces. Although all EOCs should contain certain equipment and supplies, lists of required resources are most important.[7]

It is not unusual, particularly when only one geographic segment of a community is affected, to find a field operations center located at or near the place of impact. When such centers are inappropriately called EOCs, confusion may result. In effect, they are branches of the main EOC, places where information is gathered for forwarding to the main EOC and where decisions made at the main EOC may be referred for implementation. Field operations centers can greatly enhance the effectiveness and timeliness of disaster response but should not be confused with the EOC itself.

In a large-scale disaster, it is also common for support organizations such as police, fire, and public works departments to operate command posts—their own operations centers. Sometimes these units are based in routine dispatch areas. The important point, however, is that these command posts, or functional centers, focus on the response operations of single organizations. The directives for response policy and operations come from the main EOC.

All command posts ordinarily have representatives at the main EOC. These representatives receive directives from the EOC director or controller and pass them on to their departmental command posts. The command posts receive the directives, call upon their own standard operating procedures or devise on-the-spot strategies, and then dispatch only their own personnel and resources. Thus, the main EOC commands the activity of all municipal departments—either directly or through the layers of operational or functional centers.

Representation, staffing, and command   In addition to police, fire, and public works, a number of other agencies and organizations generally have representatives at the EOC. For example, if emergency medical services are not part of a fire department, their representatives are present. Representatives of private utilities and the Red Cross or Salvation Army (as charged with sheltering and victim welfare) also routinely appear in an EOC. Depending on the nature of the disaster, there may be representatives of organizations such as the National Weather Service, FEMA, the U.S. Forest Service, or the U.S. Geological Survey. Staff from relevant county or state organizations, particularly emergency services departments, may be present. (A local EOC may be activated when a county or state EOC is not. But when the EOCs of larger government organizations are activated, it is appropriate for the local unit to have a representative at the county or state EOC.)

The EOC is staffed by officers with responsibilities for specific functions. Typically, every EOC has officers for communications and for public information. Many EOCs also have officers for damage assessment and for operations and resources planning. All these officers may have staff, housed sometimes in the EOC, more often off site, to assist them in their duties.

The actual management of an EOC during a disaster is handled by an EOC coordinator or director. The chief executive officer of the community—e.g., the mayor or the local government manager—often takes the leadership role in coping with the disaster (e.g., declaring a local emergency, ordering an evacuation) relying on the emergency manager and department heads for advice on decisions.

There are two common patterns for management of a local EOC during a disaster. In one pattern, the EOC coordinator is the emergency manager. This person consults with the EOC staff, recommends policy to the community leadership, clears policy with local officials (both elected and appointed), and implements the policy. In this pattern, the EOC coordinator works directly with local officials. In the alternative pattern, an emergency management committee is an advisory body separate from the EOC coordinator. The committee may include the directors of key departments—for example, fire, police, and public works—and representatives of the mayor. Disaster response policy may be either devised by the EOC coordinator and reviewed by the emergency management committee or devised by the EOC coordinator in consultation with the committee. In either case, all policy is cleared with elected officials through the advisory body and is then implemented by the EOC coordinator.

The second approach should not be mistaken for disaster management "by committee," which would generate numerous operational problems. The emergency management committee is simply a collection of technical experts (department heads) and political representatives who cooperate to develop an emergency response strategy for a particular event. In some types of

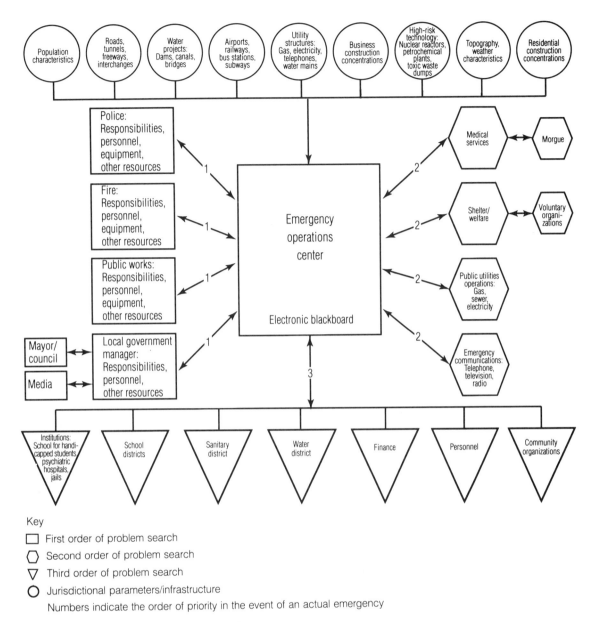

Key

☐ First order of problem search

◯ Second order of problem search

▽ Third order of problem search

○ Jurisdictional parameters/infrastructure

  Numbers indicate the order of priority in the event of an actual emergency

Figure 8-6 Emergency information system schema.

disasters—especially those involving unfamiliar agents and extended periods of impact, like the accident at the Three Mile Island nuclear plant—such advisory bodies can serve the vital function of explaining the changing nature of the threat to political decision makers, thereby freeing the EOC coordinator and the local chief executive to focus on operations management.

The decision-making climate of the EOC

As the master coordination and control point for all counter-disaster efforts, the EOC is a place of decision making. It is therefore important to examine the climate within the EOC—the social and psychological context within which decisions are made. It has been said that no kitchen generates the kind of heat found in the EOC; particularly for the inexperienced, the pressure is immense.

Psychological stresses placed on emergency responders will be examined in a later section; the focus here is on stresses affecting the decision-making climate within the EOC.

To appreciate the climate of an EOC, one needs to understand four characteristics of the environment: (1) pressure to take action, (2) limited and uncertain information, (3) shifting priorities, and (4) overlapping lines of authority and responsibility.[8]

Perhaps the most pervasive and formidable environmental characteristic is pressure. The air is thick with the pressure to take action—to prevent or alleviate human suffering and physical destruction. This pressure is intensified, first, by the presence of representatives of the mass media, who may themselves feel the need to help stop suffering; this often translates into close questioning and scrutiny of those in authority. The pressure is also intensified by the presence of political officials, who are observing, and may be involved in, policy decisions. These officials will be either directly or indirectly responsible to the citizenry (after the disaster), and they therefore closely follow the actions of the emergency manager. Finally, the pressure is intensified by shortage of time: during disaster events, decisions must sometimes be made quickly if they are to have any effect at all.

The decision climate of the EOC is also influenced by limited and uncertain information. During the response period, there is little time to gather information, and available information tends to be partial and imperfect. The EOC may be acquiring its information from only a single source until other sources become available. Even when an EOC has access to a number of sources, the information it receives may be conflicting.

A third aspect of the EOC environment is shifting priorities. The principal priorities of emergency management are to minimize loss of life, personal injury, and property damage. The actions that support these priorities, however, change during the course of the event, generally for one of three reasons. The agent-generated demands may change; for example, a levee may fail during a riverine flood, endangering a different part of town. The response-generated demands may change; for example, one shelter may fill with evacuees, requiring that a second shelter be designated. Information may change; for example, previously unavailable data may indicate unsuspected dangers.

Finally, the EOC climate is characterized by stress that arises from overlapping lines of authority and responsibility, especially in connection with field operations and their management. During disaster response, when numerous organizations and agencies work in concert, interorganizational relationships are often characterized by resource sharing, collaborative dependence, and an overlapping authority and responsibility—arrangements that often produce conflict and frustration. For example, when task responsibility is unclear, performance may be slow, leading to resource imbalances between responders when time pressures are great and response demands are high. These frustrations are routinely communicated to the EOC, where allocators themselves experience the frustration of insufficient or slow-moving resources.

In summary, decision making at the EOC is carried on in a high-pressure, emotionally charged atmosphere. Though much of the pressure is probably unavoidable, the level of stress must be managed if reasonable decisions are to be made. A variety of mechanisms can reduce the level of stress. The first is careful planning, which means that plans for generic functions and standard operating procedures will have been developed already and can be implemented during response. A damage assessment function, for example, can help fill the EOC's information needs. A generic evacuation plan can be implemented when agent-generated demands require it. Regular exercises are a second way to mitigate the high pressure of the EOC environment. During exercises, staff grow accustomed to cooperating and come to understand the functions of other responder organizations. Thus frustration is less likely to turn into conflict, and conflicts that do arise are easier to manage. Psychological stress in the EOC is examined in a later section.

Special issues for EOCs

Several special issues are important in the operation of an EOC: activation and deactivation of the EOC; internal management of the EOC; EOC operations; and communications issues (channel capacity, multiple channels, and planning for a viable communications system).

Ideally, activation and deactivation of the EOC is addressed by the emergency plan. Ordinarily, the EOC is activated in response to environmental conditions, although these conditions may be somewhat agent specific. For example, an EOC may remain inactive or only partially activated at the issuance of a "hurricane watch" but be fully activated by a "hurricane warning." Deactivation is also usually specified in terms of prevailing conditions. Whatever the particular conditions that determine the activation of the EOC, the emergency plan should specify the person (and alternates) charged with activation and deactivation. At the local level, EOCs are usually activated by staff of the emergency management department, by the emergency manager or his or her designate, or by directive of the chief executive officer or his or her designate.

A second issue sometimes not given sufficient attention is the internal management of the EOC. As described earlier, the staff of the EOC is concerned exclusively with management of the disaster response. Like any office, however, the EOC creates demands through its own operation. In some disasters, EOC staff must remain either at or near the EOC around the clock. They require food, rest, and sanitary facilities. Supplies and reference materials must be brought to the EOC. To meet these and other demands, the plan must provide for staff support for the EOC. Support need not be elaborate but should be sufficient to see to the needs of the principal EOC staff.

The third issue is EOC operations. Specifically, EOC commanders should consider using microcomputers, which have great potential for fulfilling a variety of EOC needs.[9] Plans and checklists can be stored on disks for rapid access by EOC commanders and staff. Microcomputers can also facilitate record keeping, one of the primary functions of the EOC. Simulation programs can strengthen evacuation planning and management. Hurricane tracking software and flash flood models can also be used in response management. As well as contributing to EOC operations, microcomputers can serve other phases of disaster management; strengthen interagency relationships; and improve data storage and retrieval, budgeting, policy formulation, and communication with dispersed organizations.

Three other issues involve communications: channel capacity, the importance of multiple channels, and planning for a viable communication system. Channel capacity is important because the increased information needs associated with disaster can strain existing communication channels. Emergency plans must anticipate both the technical communication needs and the expanded personnel needs that accompany disaster. For example, if public telephone lines are used during emergency operations, is the carrying capacity of the equipment adequate for such needs? In some fixed sites, such as hospitals, capacities are likely to be adequate for most needs, but when sites for shelters or other operations are chosen at the time of the disaster, communication capacity should enter into the decision. There is one adjustment for communication capacity that almost never succeeds: the public is often advised *not* to use telephones during emergencies. Research indicates that such advice is routinely ignored. Moreover, public use of telephones has a number of positive effects during disasters: phones are used to confirm warnings, relay warnings to others, and check on friends and relatives during evacuations. Rather than discourage phone use, it is far more effective to anticipate it and to make the necessary accommodations in planning for the response phase. For example, additional trunk lines might be installed to increase carrying capacity, or multiple information telephone numbers might be used to spread the demand for information across existing city offices.

The existence of multiple communication channels is also important. Although the reason for a communication disruption is often related to the nature of the disaster, almost any communication mode can experience interference. Tornadoes and hurricanes destroy above-ground telephone lines. Floods, too, threaten telephone service. Volcanic ash disrupts radio transmissions. Electrical storms can interfere with microcomputer transmissions. Electromagnetic pulse may be associated with war-related attacks. Because communication is vital to disaster operations, special attention should be given to ensuring that multiple channels exist for every important communication link.

Finally, communication is far too important to be allowed to evolve during the response phase itself. Establishing a viable communication system is a central part of the emergency planning process. The contacts between organizations that arise naturally in planning will begin to structure communications. The system itself is laid out in the written plan; further refinements are facilitated by drills and exercises of the plan.

Disaster declarations

To those directly affected, every disaster is catastrophic and merits a "declaration." There are, however, a variety of governmental disaster declarations that may be issued independently of one another. Sometimes mayors, county executives, or governors issue formal declarations that may or may not involve special emergency powers (for the issuing government) or open special assistance funds. But with respect to disaster response and recovery, an emergency manager's primary concern is with the declaration made by the president of the United States under the Federal Disaster Relief Act. A federal declaration may be for either a "major disaster" or an "emergency" situation, each of which carries its own level of federal support for the affected community. FEMA coordinates both the evaluation of requests for disaster declarations and the distribution of resources.

At the local level, the disaster declaration process begins with damage assessment. As damage assessment continues, data should be carefully assembled in the EOC. The EOC commander should make a preliminary assessment of disaster consequences and advise the mayor about the appropriateness of a request for a presidential declaration. Although the scope and magnitude of damages are important determinants of declarations, a crucial criterion is that damages must outstrip the resources of both the local and state governments before federal resources may be used.[10]

Because a request for a presidential declaration involves a number of steps, the damage assessment that the local emergency manager provides the mayor with must be accurate and timely. The damage assessment process must proceed long enough for an accurate picture of conditions to be assembled and for supporting data to be generated, though not so long that assistance arrives too late.

If the mayor does decide to ask for a presidential disaster declaration, a formal process ensues. In the first step, the mayor formally requests the governor to declare an emergency at the state level; the request is usually accompanied by supporting data from the damage assessment records. The governor may have a state agency check the damage estimates, but it is the governor alone who ultimately decides whether to declare the state-level emergency and whether,

Figure 8–7   Interstate 880, Oakland, California, after the 1989 Loma Prieta quake.

further, to request a presidential declaration. If the governor requests such a declaration, FEMA dispatches a damage assessment team to survey damages, state and local capabilities, and the assistance required. (If the governor does *not* feel a presidential declaration is merited, the state has an obligation to provide resources, but the process of seeking a federal declaration stops; a mayor may not approach the federal government directly for such a declaration.) The director of FEMA reviews the report of the assessment team and makes a recommendation to the president about a declaration. The president makes the final decision.

Depending upon the type of disaster declaration, various kinds of federal assistance may be made available to the local government.[11] Presidential declarations also make assistance available directly to victims and their families, including low-interest recovery loans, temporary housing, counseling, tax refunds, and food stamps. In addition to resources, a presidential disaster declaration can provide a psychological boost to victims, emergency responders, and local officials. It is important that local emergency managers monitor both private and federal assistance to victims, to ensure that victims are aware of the range of services and avail themselves of those they require.

Behavioral responses to disasters

The substantial body of social scientific research dealing with human responses to disaster can help emergency managers tailor response plans and decision strategies to the likely reactions.[12] Familiarity with common patterns of response to disaster by victims and emergency personnel can reduce response time and focus managerial attention on other agent- and response-generated demands.

Victims' responses

Both the public and emergency managers often assume that people respond to disasters in a disorganized and disoriented way. In the popular press and in "disaster movies," disasters are managed by a few brave and clear-thinking folks who set an example for the masses of passive or frightened victims. Indeed, short-term responses to disasters are often thought to fall into two categories: stunned inaction (reflecting shock or temporary mental paralysis) or undirected, disorganized activity (like panic flight).

Neither category accurately captures the reaction of most people to disaster. Most people do not go into shock; and panic flight is rare (and occurs only under particular conditions). Rather, people tend to act rationally, given the prevailing conditions as they understand them. Because myths about shock and panic remain strong, it is important to document what people *do not do* in disasters.

Shock reactions and mental health problems   What has come to be called the disaster syndrome is a form of shock associated with docility, disoriented thinking, and sometimes a general insensitivity to cues in the immediate environment. This type of shock, sometimes also called the survivor syndrome, has been documented in wartime for many years.

In domestic disasters, however, emergency managers need to remember four important lessons from research into the disaster syndrome. First, this reaction appears to arise most frequently in sudden-onset disasters when the agent is unfamiliar to the public and particularly when the disaster leaves much physical destruction or death in its wake. Second, the disaster syndrome is transient: it rarely occurs outside the immediate post-impact period and ordinarily persists for only a few hours. Third, even when conditions are right, the syndrome seems to affect only a minority of the disaster-stricken population. In one of the few methodologically sound studies of this phenomenon, Charles Fritz and Eli Marks found that only 14 percent of their random sample of victims showed signs of the syndrome.[13] Finally, this type of psychological reaction seems to respond well to crisis intervention techniques and to other types of short-term professional mental health care.

In fact, disasters generally do not seem to be associated with significant increases in mental health problems in the affected population. This does not mean that disasters produce no long-term psychological consequences or that the consequences mostly pass unnoticed. Disaster victims experience stress and anxiety that can manifest themselves in a variety of symptoms. Documented reactions include sleep disruptions, anxiety, nausea, vomiting, bed-wetting, and irritability. Some of these symptoms show up much later than the disaster syndrome, although they tend to be equally transient. On the whole, though, individuals seem able to handle these symptoms with minimum need for outside intervention. Most important, short-term reactions to stress do not seem to interfere significantly with the ability of disaster victims to act responsibly on their own or to follow instructions from emergency responders.

Panic flight   Undoubtedly the most stubborn myth about human behavior in disasters is that panic flight will disrupt emergency operations. E. L. Quarantelli defines panic as "an acute fear reaction marked by loss of self-control which is followed by nonsocial and nonrational flight behavior."[14] Although panic flight is a staple of disaster movies, it is comparatively rare as a response to real-life emergencies.

The myth of panic flight may owe its origin in part to "observer error"— misinterpretation of the behavior of disaster victims. It is not irrational to want to put distance between oneself and a fire, or to move quickly away from crumbling buildings after an earthquake. In these examples, individuals have chosen to cope with danger by distancing themselves from the apparent source, but an observer may not have understood the contingencies to which the victims were responding.

Not all examples of panic flight can be explained as observer error. Although rare, panic does occur under special circumstances. Quarantelli has found that flight seems to occur under two specific conditions, both of which are defined in terms of individual perceptions: panic flight is related to what people *believe* is true, not necessarily to what *is* true. The first condition is that the individual feels helpless or unable to control the danger by his or her own actions. In other words, the individual believes he or she cannot eliminate the danger by attacking or manipulating its source. The second condition is that the individual believes that, as time passes, he or she may become unable to escape from the threat. Escape seems possible at the moment, but escape routes seem to be closing off. Panic flight occurs only under these conditions.

Although panic flight is not entirely unheard of in natural disasters, it does not happen often. When it does, it seems to involve a relatively small proportion of the people exposed to the threat, and flight itself does not usually persist for long.

The topic of panic often comes up when emergency managers discuss public information or issuing warnings. Authorities sometimes let their fear of creating panic stop them from properly informing the public about environmental threats. Some officials who have withheld information have claimed that a public panic would have posed dangers equal to those created by the environmental threat itself. Quarantelli's work—among a host of studies—indicates that such claims are simply unjustified.

Since the special conditions that can give rise to panic are circumstances over which emergency managers have no control, public officials are always better advised to share as much information as possible with citizens. When officials share information, citizens are more likely to view them as having special access to data and thereby as being more reliable or credible.[15] Moreover, when citizens have the same information as authorities, they are more likely to view the threat in the same terms as the authorities and to take the recommended protective actions.

Emergency responders

Emergency responders have also been the subjects of disaster mythology. The most prevalent of these myths are associated with role abandonment and with psychological stress.

Role abandonment   Concern about role abandonment is long-standing; Samuel Prince's 1920 study of the Halifax, Nova Scotia, explosion refers to it.[16] Louis Killian tackled the issue directly in his 1952 study of group memberships in disasters.[17] Killian's argument was that people are immersed in a variety of social groups—families, friendship networks, work groups, and so on— and that when disaster strikes, uncertainty can give rise to cross pressures, forcing people to choose between their obligations to different groups. Killian's data indicated that when cross pressures do arise, people most often resolve them in favor of the family. The Holland flood study data from the early 1950s seemed to reinforce this conclusion: the husbands who were interviewed reported that they took care of wives and children before going to their jobs.[18] And in the early 1960s, Harry Moore's research on tornadoes and on Hurricane Carla found that disaster victims tended to render aid to family and friends first.[19]

Although these studies have often been cited as support for the contention that in a disaster, emergency workers would abandon their jobs to tend to other roles, two points alone bring into question this interpretation of the three studies. First, all three studies dealt with group membership, not role (job) performance. Second, the studies dealt with citizens who did not have clearly or officially assigned emergency roles: in each study, family and friendship roles were contrasted with job roles that had nothing to do with emergency response or management.

These two points suggest that the three studies do not create a basis for the assumption that emergency workers would abandon their roles in time of disaster. Indeed, the authors of these studies did not make such claims. Rather, the issue has been raised most recently by lawyers and members of pressure groups (usually involved in litigation) who were seeking to stop the commissioning or licensing of nuclear power plants.

Other disaster studies undertaken by social scientists do provide important information about role abandonment. One of the clearest conclusions to be drawn from the studies is that people do indeed show great concern for their families during disasters. It can also be noted that the literature is virtually without examples of trained, full-time emergency personnel abandoning their work roles. Finally, it is apparent that job commitment persists despite concern for families and the pull of cross pressures.

In the early 1960s, Charles Fritz interpreted the available data on role abandonment.[20] Acknowledging that all people would be loyal to family in times of disaster, he came to three conclusions. First, people who have no officially defined emergency roles and who have not themselves been victims will converge on the disaster scene and render aid. Second, people who have no official disaster roles and who have been victims themselves will render aid to their households first, then to other family members, and then to neighbors and friends. Finally, people with officially defined disaster roles will execute those roles, but will do so under psychological stress until they know their families are safe.

The third point requires some comment. Most emergency response personnel—fire fighters, police, sheriffs, emergency medical technicians, civil defense staff, and other full-time personnel—have had some formal training in their emergency jobs. Disaster personnel are aware that disasters will strike and that their work may require separation from family and friends. This knowledge encourages emergency workers to develop personal ways of ensuring the safety of their families in their absence, such as instructing family members on appropriate protective actions and arranging mutual help agreements with neighbors and friends. Some emergency response agencies (particularly police) have institutionalized such concerns, creating standard procedures for checking on workers' families and giving reports to employees who are on the job during emergencies.

By supplying the "safety accounting" that people need if they are to continue working, practices such as these make role abandonment less likely. Available data on role abandonment appear to support this line of reasoning. Russell Dynes and E. L. Quarantelli have reported, "In over 100 disasters and in the course of interviewing over 2,500 organizational officials, . . . role conflict was not a serious problem which creates a significant loss of manpower."[21]

Psychological stress   The research does, however, make plain that emergency personnel experience psychological stress, although the stress does not seem to prevent effective functioning. Despite a shortage of data, it is possible to speculate about why stress does not appear to prevent emergency personnel from performing their duties.

First, people who devote their careers to responding to disasters tend to suffer from delayed, or cumulative, stress and to develop individualized coping mechanisms; these mechanisms may become more effective or less over time, but they nonetheless enable emergency workers to continue to do their jobs. Some workers, however, may respond to cumulative stress by becoming unable to face the job and either dropping out of emergency work, getting fired, or going on disability.

One may also speculate that the level of stress associated with emergency work may depend on the worker's particular role. Employees who work in the field, for example, rendering direct aid to victims or dealing with agent-generated demands, may experience less negative stress than others. Field workers can physically move around—which, according to research, mitigates some of the symptoms of stress. They also have the psychological satisfaction of being able to take direct, personal action to aid disaster victims.

Emergency workers who are confined to EOCs, however, experience stress in a different context. First, the EOC staff has the disadvantage of not being able to move around much. Second, because the EOC is the hub of communications, EOC workers receive information about the full scope of the disaster and all the suffering, no matter where it occurs. In contrast, field workers often know only what they see before them. Still another problem for EOC workers is little or no direct contact with disaster victims. Although they may hear that they are "helping," EOC workers rarely get to look a victim in the face and feel personally responsible for the help that was given. These conditions suggest that, in the planning phase, emergency managers need to develop strategies for reducing stress in the EOC and that, in the response phase, such programs need to be implemented at once. The strategies might include rotating EOC with field assignments, enforcing shift assignments to ensure that EOC workers have reasonable opportunities to sleep, and instituting a regular "break" structure to reduce the cumulative pressure on EOC workers.

Although field workers may be at an advantage over EOC staff in several respects, significant sources of stress are also built into the field response environment. Field workers feel firsthand responsibility not only for successes but also for failures. Those who are exposed to death, body handling, and morgue

Figure 8–8   Members of the National Guard assist at the site of the 1989 Sioux City airplane crash.

work experience special stresses. Dealing with death (especially in cases of dismemberment) has serious psychological consequences. Yet these stresses tend less to become a problem in the operations phase than to cause a delayed stress reaction. Treatment programs for cumulative stress should clearly be part of the professional emergency management environment.

Generic functions

Generic functions are actions or activities that may be useful in various disaster events. Evacuation, for example, may be needed in floods, hurricanes, volcanic eruptions, nuclear power plant accidents, or hazardous materials incidents. Generic functions are developed and planned in the pre-impact phase, although some decisions will have to be adapted to situational demands. All details, organization charts, and standard operating procedures are prepared in advance; generic functions are exercised (or form the focus of drills) like other plan components. During the response phase, generic functions are activated according to the response needs for the specific disaster agent.

Several generic functions were discussed earlier, in connection with the EOC. This section examines the prime tasks associated with six generic functions—warning system, evacuation, sheltering, emergency medical care, search and rescue, and protection of property—and identifies issues that arise during the response phase.

Warning system

Some form of warning system is used in almost every type of disaster. The warning system itself is an important communication channel to the population at risk. The emergency plan should address several components of warning systems as generic functions. The first of these components involves environmental monitoring. Warning systems are usually activated in response to environmental changes that could endanger persons or property. Thus, the portion of the emergency plan dealing with warning as a generic function should specify the primary environmental monitoring systems as well as the agencies responsible for their operation. For example, a county flood district might be in charge of projecting river capacity, flow rates, and crest timing. Plans for monitoring, especially when agencies other than the local emergency management department are involved, should also be designed to ensure twenty-four-hour coverage of monitoring systems.

Notification, another important component of warning systems, means informing authorities when monitoring systems have detected a threat. The conditions that constitute a threat demanding official action are usually defined in advance; in the plan, they often appear both in the generic functions under warning and in the annexes dealing with specific threats. The definition of a threat is usually hazard specific. The plan should specify the individual (and alternates) who should be notified for further assessment of a threat after a monitoring official has determined that the level of threat requires response.

The third component of warning systems, threat assessment, requires that the threat be evaluated and intensively monitored. The plan should specify the procedure for notifying other potential responder organizations and public decision makers if the evaluations indicate increasing seriousness. Decisions to warn or evacuate populations need to be made by legally constituted authorities (at the local level that is usually the mayor, although arrangements may differ across jurisdictions). Emergency managers should be prepared to present such authorities with data describing the threat as well as with recommendations for protective actions. Once a decision to warn is made, the standard operating procedure for warnings would be implemented.

Evacuation

Evacuation is a frequently used generic function that constitutes a protective measure in itself.[22] The principle of evacuation is to move citizens from a place of relative danger to a place of relative safety, via a route that does not pose significant danger. A key concern in the decision to use evacuation is potential risk to evacuees. The destination as well as the route must be scrutinized and included in the risk assessment. The generic function plan should provide for the EOC commander to assess alternative protective measures (such as shelter in place) before advising that evacuation be initiated.

For the most part, the evacuation process is considered routine. Police or other law enforcement departments usually serve as lead organizations and the evacuation is carried out according to the standard operating procedures of the organization involved. The emergency plan, however, should address a number of issues in connection with the evacuation function.

Both the decision to evacuate and the warning message come under the purview of warning systems. The evacuation itself comes under the purview of the evacuation plan. The plan identifies the lead agency, designates the agencies that play supporting roles, and defines their responsibilities to the lead agency. In particular, the lead agency must carefully coordinate the timing and conduct of the evacuation with the organizations providing shelter and with those involved in barricading or marking routes of egress (usually public works). The plan also establishes procedures for choosing evacuation routes, for changing routes as the threat progresses, and for maintaining the flow of vehicles.

Generally, the evacuation plan addresses three types of movement. The first is the movement of residents who do not own or have access to private vehicles. Such residents require transportation, which in turn requires that emergency managers identify vehicles to be used and their locations. A protocol also needs to be developed—usually in connection with the warning function—to inform residents that transportation is available, where boarding stations are located, and what possessions may be transported. In particular, the logistics of moving household pets should be addressed.

The second and third types of movement addressed are the evacuation of residents with special requirements: handicapped residents and institutionalized populations. Handicapped residents may need specialized vehicles and sometimes specialized staff. Although many handicapped citizens—for example, those who are in wheelchairs—require minimal special treatment, evacuation planning should also specify procedures for people requiring considerable attention, such as those who are bedridden. The evacuation of institutions such as prisons, jails, hospitals, schools, and convalescence centers will, in most cases, be managed by the institutional staff, but the lead agency for evacuation must coordinate such efforts. Public schools require particular care. Because the evacuation of schoolchildren evokes strong family feelings, advance planning with both school authorities and parents is necessary. Such planning should review options for evacuations (will students be evacuated and then released to parents, or released and then evacuated with their parents?), likely modes of transportation, likely routes, and the location of appropriate shelter space.

Victim sheltering and welfare

Victim sheltering and welfare is a need that always arises after evacuations and must often be addressed even after small-scale disasters. Reference here is only to emergency or temporary sheltering: the provision of food, clothing, and sleeping and sanitary facilities for a period lasting from a few hours to a few days. Provisions for more-extended temporary or permanent housing of disaster victims appears under recovery in the emergency plan and is not normally addressed in the sections dealing with the response phase.

The generic function plan should designate a coordinator for shelter operations to work with groups that operate shelters (usually the Red Cross and Salvation Army, but sometimes many others, including the local government). The shelter operations coordinator should establish procedures for dealing with those in charge of three other generic functions: evacuation, emergency medical services, and search and rescue. The generic function plan should include a decision logic for determining how many shelters should be opened and where they should be located. Ordinarily this logic will draw its data from the damage assessment function.

A variety of routine issues arise in connection with victim sheltering and welfare; most of these are normally addressed in detail by the standard operating procedures of the shelter providers, particularly the Red Cross. The EOC commander should be consulted on a number of these decisions, however. A prime concern is the development of a system for recording who is in the shelter so that information can be provided to victims' relatives and friends and accurate counts for feeding and sleeping facilities can be made. Emergency managers also need to develop a decision guide to assess whether victims and evacuees are going to require clothing and sleeping facilities during their time at the shelter. The requirement for sleeping space complicates shelter logistics and sometimes limits the locations that can feasibly be designated shelter. When sheltering includes sleeping, shower and bathroom facilities must also be considered. Meals further increase the logistical complexity of sheltering. If meals are to be provided, shelter coordinators must consider how many; whether they will be hot, cold, or both; whether cooking can be done on site; how food will be transported; and where it can be stored. The presence of family pets in shelters can be problematic if their needs are not anticipated. Finally, sheltering plans must take account of children's needs, particularly if there is any chance that children may be separated from their parents for any significant time. Routine provisions for children should include entertainment, nursery facilities, and staff for reassurance. In most cases, the operational aspects of the shelters will be handled by agencies with vast experience; coordination through the EOC is an important planning milestone, however.

Emergency medical care and morgues

Emergency medical care and morgues are generic functions normally executed by specially trained staff operating specially equipped facilities. The generic function plan should specify the lead organization or person for emergency medical services (EMS). In some jurisdictions and during some types of emergencies, the local EMS system operates on its own, with a minimum of direction from and contact with an EOC. In large-scale disasters, however, contact with the EOC and the monitoring of the EMS function increase. The generic function plan may contain decision rules for field locations of emergency medical facilities and procedures for the transportation of victims and emergency responders who require care. At a minimum, the plan should include lists of hospitals and other medical facilities (and the nature of their equipment and staff) for use by the EOC staff.

In most jurisdictions, the establishment of morgues and the handling of the dead are regulated by law. Emergency plans normally specify decision rules for locating temporary morgues and for using permanent morgues, procedures for transporting the dead, and procedures for claiming bodies. Usually some procedure is mandated for maintaining in the EOC the records of both the identified and the unidentified dead.

Search and rescue

Unlike most other generic functions, search and rescue (SAR) often takes place in loosely structured situations under uncertain authority. The relative lack of structure makes it particularly important that the generic function plan identify a coordinator or lead organization and include a roster of organizations available for SAR work. Because volunteers (sometimes even victims) are routinely involved in rescue, some plans include a procedure for documenting their presence and incorporating them into established groups. The SAR coordinator should have direct access to all resource and equipment lists held in the EOC. Furthermore, procedures should be established to maintain communication between the SAR function and those responsible for sheltering and EMS.

Unplanned contact with the mass media during SAR operations is a serious operational problem. Such contacts can result in the inappropriate release of victims' names or photographs, harassment of victims or their families, and inappropriate release of information on the progress of disaster operations. To minimize such difficulties, explicit procedures should be developed for managing media relations. Strategies might include controlling access to operations areas, assigning a staff member or PIO to monitor and accompany media represent-atives, or briefing both SAR teams and reporters on the ethics of releasing information.

Finally, emergency managers should give some attention to the "urban heavy rescue" component of SAR. Heavy rescue refers to recovering victims from the wreckage or debris of urban buildings and is currently an important issue in earthquake preparedness planning. At a minimum, the SAR plan should contain a list of the available heavy rescue equipment, a logic for what kinds of buildings to excavate first in the event of multiple collapses, and a protocol for coordinating traditional, debris-removal rescue efforts with high-technology efforts to search for victims.

Security and protection of property

For the most part, security and protection of property, like evacuation, is con-sidered a routine generic function and is not given extensive attention in the plan. As with evacuation, the details of this function are in the standard operating procedures of the organizations delivering the service. Several decision-making issues do merit some attention, however. It is critically important that a lead agency be established and that clear lines of authority and coordination be delineated among all involved organizations. Security requires strong lines of interorganizational communication and a close connection between the security function and the EOC, damage assessment, and sheltering.

Securing the impact area is a priority throughout the emergency. This requires that three issues be addressed in the plan. First, rules must be established to determine which agency is in charge at the scene—usually the first responder. A procedure should also be devised for the first responder to use in relinquishing control of the scene to other agencies. Second, the plan should specify what access to the impact area will be permitted. Access control is exceptionally difficult to establish and maintain for any period of time. It commonly gives rise to public hostility and creates heavy demands on emergency responders. Thus, the decision to control access needs to be made carefully, usually on the basis of protecting citizens from dangers in the impact area. Access control should be accomplished by means of a pass system if at all possible and should be main-tained only as long as necessary. In general, access control operates best when the area to be controlled is small, contains relatively few people, and has only a few possible access routes. Pass systems functioned well for short periods in the small communities affected by the eruptions of Mt. St. Helens (most of these communities included fewer than one hundred households). Finally, when control over the impact area must be maintained for some time, some sort of patrol system or surveillance will be needed to protect property. Looting is much rarer than is generally believed, and minimal patrol forces are ordinarily all that is necessary to secure an area. It is important, however, that the public *feel* secure. When access to an impact area is limited, residents often express anxiety about property loss; the visible presence of uniformed patrols generally has a reassuring effect.

The changing role of emergency managers

This chapter has focused on the management of disaster response operations. Although a number of local government elected and appointed officials play important roles in disaster response, the central role is that of the emergency manager. As recently as the mid-1950s, emergency services in most U.S. jurisdictions were fragmented: the official or department responsible for planning or response depended on the kind of emergency involved—for example, hurricane, flood, volcanic eruption, train derailment. The public was vaguely familiar with the position of "civil defense director," filled by a largely invisible figure who was presumably attached to "defense authorities" and charged with "civil defense duties." Most people viewed police and fire fighters—those who handled everyday, personal emergencies—as the principal emergency services personnel.

But during the past thirty years, particularly in the United States, it has become increasingly clear that comprehensive emergency management cannot be handled by police and fire fighters as an adjunct to their normal duties (although they continue to have an important role in the emergency management system). For various reasons, including changing human settlement patterns and lack of enforceable zoning restrictions, natural disasters are affecting more people than ever before. In many cases, people themselves—not hazards—create the problems: more people than ever before are choosing to live in floodplains, on slopes subject to mudslides and landslides, in unreinforced dwellings near faults, too close to the spillways of dams, and in other places subject to the ravages of nature. It is also clear that risks from technological sources are increasing. This changing—and expanding—hazard environment has been in part responsible for the greater concern with emergency management at all levels of government. In the mid-1970s, an increasing number of jurisdictions began to develop full-time emergency management positions.

The establishment of the position, however, did not at first clearly establish the duties of the incumbent. Indeed, the job is evolving and will do so for some time. On the basis of the experience of the 1980s, it is possible to begin to specify desirable characteristics for emergency managers and to begin placing parameters on the job.

First, since disasters are affecting more people than ever before, emergency management is at the political forefront. Thus, an effective emergency manager must have some political acumen and must certainly understand the processes of government. With the politicization of the role of emergency manager, the invisibility of the position ended.

Second, in an environment in which more and different natural and technological hazards are affecting the public, the technical knowledge required of an emergency manager is becoming greater and more diverse. An emergency manager can no longer survive with a general understanding of civil defense and a little knowledge of a few natural hazards. Although the depth of technical information need not be great, an emergency manager must be familiar with the characteristics of a variety of hazards, be able to determine when expert help is needed, and know where to get that help.

As the needs for political acumen and increased technical knowledge imply, emergency managers must also cultivate communications skills and the ability to coordinate people and organizations. This chapter has made clear that disaster response is a many-faceted operation requiring a variety of people and organizations to act in concert. Comprehensive emergency management—mitigation, preparedness, response, and recovery—depends on the coordinating skills of emergency managers.

In summary, an emergency manager needs to possess political, technical, and administrative skills. In addition, success sometimes depends on the ability to share this expertise with the public, fellow emergency responders, and elected and appointed officials. Furthermore, the job is made particularly challenging by the fact that before a disaster, the public—and sometimes elected officials—believe that the emergency manager should be invisible; but after a disaster, the emergency manager is held strictly accountable.

1   Gary A. Kreps, "Future Directions in Disaster Research," *International Journal of Mass Emergencies and Disasters* 7 (November 1989): 215–43.

2   Russell R. Dynes, Enrico L. Quarantelli, and Gary A. Kreps, *A Perspective on Disaster Planning* (Newark, DE: Disaster Research Center, University of Delaware, 1972).

3   Robert Wolensky and Edward Miller, "The Everday versus the Disaster Role of Local Officials," *Urban Affairs Quarterly* 16 (June 1981): 483–504.

4   Dennis Wenger, Enrico L. Quarantelli, and Russell R. Dynes, *Disaster Analysis: Emergency Management Offices and Arrangements* (Newark, DE: Disaster Research Center, University of Delaware, 1987). In June 1979, the U.S. Conference of Mayors adopted a policy resolution urging that municipalities create permanent, stand-alone offices of emergency services.

5   Enrico L. Quarantelli, *Studies in Disaster Response and Planning* (Newark, DE: Disaster Research Center, University of Delaware, 1979).

6   The FEMA monograph series includes a detailed description of the FIRESCOPE system. FEMA, *The California FIRESCOPE Program* (Emmitsburg, MD: National Emergency Training Center, Emergency Management Institute, 1987).

7   An exhaustive discussion of EOC equipment is outside the scope of this chapter, but good basic lists may be found in a variety of reference books, including Roger Herman, *Disaster Planning for Local Government* (New York: Universe Books, 1982).

8   John A. Granito, *Improving Crisis Decision-Making* (Washington, DC: FEMA, 1989).

9   Drabek has described a variety of advantages associated with using microcomputers in emergency management. He has also reviewed the factors that impede and that encourage use of microcomputers. See Thomas E. Drabek, "Microcomputer Implementation Patterns among State and Local Emergency Management Agencies," in *Simulators V: Proceedings of the SCS Simulators Conference*, ed. A. B. Clymer and V. Amico (San Diego, CA: Simulations Councils, Inc., 1988).

10 A detailed examination of the processes used by the executive branch in evaluating requests for disaster declarations is included in National Gov-

ernors' Association, *Comprehensive Emergency Management: A Governor's Guide* (Washington, DC: Emergency Preparedness Project, National Governors' Association, 1979).

11 The U.S. Conference of Mayors has prepared a detailed listing of assistance available to local governments under various levels of disaster declarations. U.S. Conference of Mayors, *Emergency Management: A Mayor's Manual* (Washington, DC: Executive Director's Office, U.S. Conference of Mayors, 1980).

12 Thomas E. Drabek, *Human System Responses to Disaster: An Inventory of Sociological Findings* (New York: Springer-Verlag, 1986).

13 Charles Fritz and Eli Marks, "The NORC studies of Human Behavior in Disaster," *Journal of Social Issues* 10, no. 3 (1954): 26–41.

14 Enrico L. Quarantelli, "The Nature and Conditions of Panic," *American Journal of Sociology* 60 (November 1954): 267–75.

15 Ronald W. Perry and Michael K. Lindell, *Living with Mt. St. Helens: Human Adjustment to Volcano Hazards* (Pullman: Washington State University Press, 1989).

16 Samuel Prince, *Catastrophe and Social Change* (New York: Columbia University Press, 1920).

17 Louis Killian, "The Significance of Multiple Group Membership in Disaster," *American Journal of Sociology* 57 (January 1952): 309–14.

18 Instituut voor Sociaal Onderzoek Nederlandse Volk Amsterdam, *Studies in Holland Flood Disaster* (Washington, DC: National Academy of Sciences Press, 1955).

19 Harry E. Moore, Fred Bates, Marvin Layman, and Vernon Parenton, *Before the Wind: A Study of Response to Hurricane Carla* (Washington, DC: National Academy of Sciences–National Research Council, 1963).

20 Charles Fritz, "Disasters," in *Contemporary Social Problems*, ed. Robert Merton and Robert Nisbet (New York: Harcourt, Brace and World, 1961).

21 Russell R. Dynes and Enrico L. Quarantelli, "The Family and Community Context of Individual Reactions to Disaster," in *Emergency and Disaster Management*, ed. H. Parad, H. Resnik, and L. Parad (Bowie, MD: The Charles Press, 1976).

22 Ronald W. Perry, *Comprehensive Emergency Management: Evacuating Threatened Populations* (Greenwich, CT: JAI Press, 1985).

9 Recovery from disaster

Although most sizable communities in the United States conduct some emergency management planning, relatively few include the recovery period in the planning process. Why should local officials plan for recovery?

The aftermath of a disaster poses a monumental challenge to local public officials, who must be prepared to cope with demands encompassing every aspect of community life. Victims must be sheltered and cared for, essential services resumed, properties repaired and rebuilt. In short, recovery involves the restoration—and, in some cases, the improvement—of community life. In the aftermath of a disaster, the combination of disaster-related demands, governmental requirements, and public pressures challenges local officials to make decisions rapidly, often in great number and of great breadth—yet actions that are both quick *and* wise cannot be taken without adequate preparation.

Advance planning for recovery yields significant benefits in the event of a disaster. First, the recovery period is a valuable opportunity to influence the community's future development. If local officials do not take charge, they may find that property owners and business interests step into the breach. To avoid reconstruction projects that are unplanned or uncoordinated at the neighborhood or community level, local officials must be in a position to expedite the local public decision-making process—they must, in other words, have a recovery plan. Second, the recovery planning process virtually requires local officials to study the experience of other communities that have recovered from disaster. Local officials can learn, for example, how to prepare for issues likely to arise during recovery; how to deal effectively with other levels of government; and how to control demand for scarce or strained resources. Third, support for mitigation tends to be highest immediately after a disaster, and local officials must be prepared with specific plans and policies to take advantage of the opportunity for mitigation efforts. For instance, in a community subject to recurrent floods, flood control measures may include major structural projects and require a significant amount of capital. The plans for such major mitigation efforts should be drawn up well in advance of a flood (or other foreseeable disaster) so that they will be available in the immediate aftermath of the event.

This chapter presents a view of recovery drawn largely from research conducted in communities recovering from disasters. (Although in preparation and response there are differences between technological and natural disasters, the recovery process for both is essentially the same.) The chapter first presents a brief overview of recovery, including the timing and components of typical recovery functions. The next topic is research findings on the short- and long-range effects of disaster. Since recovery is a process that includes not only the physical restoration of the community but also the psychological healing of its residents, a section is included on the recovery needs of disaster victims and workers.

The central portion of the chapter presents a framework for an efficient, effective recovery. On the basis of research conducted in fourteen recovering communities, the framework outlines major components associated with successful recovery and suggests strategies for achieving such success.

Although local governments are the front lines of response in disaster, the federal government and the state government may provide financial and other assistance. The framework identifies good intergovernmental relations as central to the recovery process; building on this theme, the chapter considers in some detail the nature and implications of federal and state assistance. Assistance provided by the volunteer sector is also briefly discussed.

The chapter concludes with an examination of mitigation, one of the most important—and most neglected—aspects of recovery. As noted earlier, recovery presents an excellent opportunity to undertake mitigation efforts; in many cases, such efforts are also required by the federal and state governments providing assistance. Local government officials must be prepared to meet such requirements, and they must also be prepared for the obstacles that typically arise when mitigation efforts are undertaken.

Overview of the recovery process

Recovery is an ongoing process whose "beginning" and "end" are difficult to pin down; recovery may continue for many years or even decades after a disaster. Sometimes recovery is represented as bands of time in which response and

Figure 9–1 On the evening of May 31, 1985, forty-one tornadoes touched down in Pennsylvania. The photos show the community of Albion, one of the most severely damaged areas.

recovery are distinct, with long-term recovery "following" short-term recovery. In practice, however, there is no clear distinction between the response and recovery phases or between short- and long-term recovery. Rather than think in terms of short- or long-term recovery, it is more useful to focus on the functions typically required by the recovery process.

As the accompanying sidebar indicates, recovery encompasses all domains of community life. A community may have developed in the course of two centuries but may rebuild after a disaster in just a few years. Long-term recovery is characterized by repair or reconstruction of buildings and structures, the evaluation of building codes and land use regulations, and consideration and implementation of mitigation measures.[1] Also part of the recovery process are the planning and administrative activities necessary to identify and secure the requisite resources. Because all domains compete for a fixed number of dollars available for recovery, decisions (whether explicit or not) about allocations among domains significantly shape the strategy for recovery. For example, most communities give top priority to job-generating or economic-base recovery. Resort areas may therefore favor restoration of tourist hotels over residential rebuilding.

Although the precise pattern and timing of local recovery vary widely, depending on the type and magnitude of disaster and the resources and priorities of the affected jurisdictions, a number of functions—listed in Figure 9–2—are common to the recovery process. It is important to note that the functions and time frames shown in the figure are representative rather than definitive or prescriptive. For example, the duration of phases 1 and 2 may vary considerably; each may last many weeks or months, and full reconstruction and recovery may take years.

As the figure indicates, during the early stages of recovery many activities occur simultaneously. No one person or office is responsible for all tasks, and the activities listed will be uncoordinated and unrelated unless local officials take clear and appropriate action. The seven categories of functions shown in the figure are those that local officials are likely to be required to oversee, although other categories may surface in a particular community.

Community recovery Below is a brief listing of some recovery activities in each of the four main areas of community life.

Residential: The repair or reconstruction of houses, home furnishings, and vehicles; the temporary and permanent rehousing of displaced residents; the settling of insurance claims for damage to personal property.

Business: The repair or reconstruction of economically viable commercial, industrial, and retail establishments; the restoration of retail sales, business-related tax revenues, and employment to at least predisaster levels.

Public services and facilities: The resumption of water, sewer, electric, telephone, and other basic services; the restoration of public transportation, parks, and recreational areas; the repair or reconstruction of public schools, libraries, hospitals, clinics, police and fire stations, and other municipal buildings or structures; the continuation of progress on community projects that were planned or under construction before the disaster.

General population: The return of certain social indicators (such as birth, death, and crime rates; levels of alcoholism and child and spouse abuse; and levels of welfare payments) to predisaster levels; the implementation of programs to restore or improve the quality of life for local residents.

Categories of functions	Time (in weeks) after the disaster				Long-term reconstruction
	Phase 1		**Phase 2**		
	1	**2**	**3**	**4 ⟶ 12**	
Information gathering and assessment	Assess damage relative to prior plans; determine physical, social, economic, and environmental impact Determine level and type of disaster assistance needed and identify available resources Clarify objectives and policies with respect to obtaining assistance, and assign expediters		Continue assessing damage and identifying needs and sources of assistance		
Organizational arrangements	Create ad hoc recovery task force Deal with convergence of volunteers and with donated goods		Establish recovery coordinating organization: acquire or hire needed staff Develop local plan for recovery, and implement recovery component of state plans		
Resource mobilization	Expedite disaster relief Restore vital community services and facilities Obtain cooperation of local contractors		Clarify available resources Identify possible sources of outside aid and investment for repairs and rebuilding Coordinate local and outside resources		
Planning, administration, and budgeting	Review and revise existing plans Develop community plan for restoring affected structures, facilities, and systems Acquire vacant land Secure hazardous property and facilities		Develop a master plan for community development, taking account of local hazards and incorporating a recovery plan for damaged areas Refine the plan and obtain necessary approvals Obtain state and local appropriations to implement the plan		
Regulation and approval	Review, revise, and implement existing building codes, permit processes, land use controls Assess need for special ordinances (e.g., construction moratoriums) and permits		Obtain approval for special ordinances and for needed regulating and permitting programs Get appropriations for new programs		
Coordination and interorganizational relations	Coordinate activities of key community service agencies Establish interlocal, regional, state, and federal liaisons Create any new coordination mechanisms needed for intergovernmental and interorganizational relations Work with local and national church groups to gain assistance Form interfaith group to help with citizens' unmet needs		Apply for state and federal aid		
Monitoring and evaluation	Establish mechanisms for monitoring and feedback Widen contacts with local civic and nonprofit groups assisting citizens with housing and other needs		Determine data needs Incorporate results of planning studies into revised emergency preparedness plans Review all available sources of assistance Assess need for organizational change Establish and implement auditing system		

Figure 9–2 Steps for long-term disaster recovery. The duration of phases 1 and 2 may vary considerably, depending on the type and magnitude of the disaster and the capability and sophistication of the local and state governments affected. This time frame is offered as generally representative and not definitive.

In the aftermath of a disaster, a complex web of relationships forms among government officials at all levels. In addition, citizens, business people, and consultants—architects, engineers, and planners—may all be engaged in some aspects of recovery. Local officials should therefore anticipate a large number of participants in the recovery process; but the participants' interests and expertise may vary widely within a community and from one community to another. As a result, the recovery planning process and the organization of local recovery may take many forms. A local emergency manager would do well to prepare a list of recovery functions and tasks on the basis of types of potential disasters and the conditions and capabilities of the community. In preparing such a list, the emergency manager must remember to include additional functions that may arise in connection with requirements for state and federal assistance.

In summary, Figure 9–2 is designed to encourage broad thinking about the recovery process as a whole and about the multiple, simultaneous, ongoing activities in a recovering community. It is not an exhaustive checklist of actions to take.

Recovery research studies

Several groups of researchers have studied recovery from disasters over the long term. The earliest comparative work was that of J. Eugene Haas et al., *Reconstruction Following Disaster* (1977); it was followed by H. Paul Friesema et al., *Aftermath: Communities after Natural Disasters* (1979); and James D. Wright et al., *After the Clean-Up: Long-Range Effects of Natural Disasters* (1979).[2] In addition, a few researchers have documented the experiences of single communities. The role of local government in the long-term recovery process has not been given comprehensive analysis.

The book by Haas and his colleagues grew out of research on recovery from two 1972 disasters: the earthquake in Managua, Nicaragua, and the flood in Rapid City, South Dakota. In addition, Haas and his colleagues used secondary sources to analyze earthquake recovery in San Francisco (1906) and in Anchorage, Alaska (1964). Haas's group were among the first to describe the recovery process and to identify mitigation opportunities that arise during the recovery period: "Disaster recovery is ordered, knowable, and predictable. The central issues and decisions are value choices that give varying emphasis to the early return of normalcy, the reduction of future vulnerability or opportunities to improve efficiency, equity, and amenity."[3]

Friesema and his colleagues found that even major disasters had no long-term effects on a community. Wright's team reached similar conclusions. The findings of both groups of researchers were weakened, however, by the methodology used to "measure" recovery. Friesema's team relied on aggregate data gathered over the course of a decade in four communities. The data were gathered primarily from secondary sources, were confined primarily to economic effects, and were about ten years old and from a very small number of communities. Wright's study, too, used aggregate data, analyzing the effect of natural disasters by comparing 1960 and 1970 census data from communities that had—and had not—experienced natural disasters.

Indicators based on aggregate data can mask severe effects on individuals. In addition, some communities can externalize many of the consequences and costs of disaster; that is, they can use financial and other assistance from the state and federal government (as well as donations from business) to supplement their own limited ability to pay for the disaster-related losses.

More recent research using other methodologies, such as Robert C. Bolin's *Long-Term Family Recovery from Disaster* and Anthony M. Yezer and Claire B. Rubin's "The Local Economic Effects of Major Natural Disasters," does find long-term negative effects on families and communities.[4]

Figure 9–3   Downtown Santa Cruz, California, shortly after the 1989 Loma Prieta earthquake.

Figure 9–4   Most injuries, deaths, and destruction from earthquakes are caused by falling debris from unreinforced buildings.

Figure 9–5   Floodwaters created by Hurricane Elena destroyed this beach house.

Recovery for disaster victims and for emergency workers

The physical effects of disaster are fairly obvious: injury and death, ruined buildings, the suspension of normal life. Psychological effects are more difficult to detect and describe, particularly the long-term effects on victims. Few studies have measured the effects of disaster on individuals or families over many years. Far more is known about the short-term psychological effects of disaster. In the case of emergency workers, for example, research has shown that

disaster work can be an extremely gratifying occupation; saving lives and providing tangible goods to people in distress is obviously a highly important activity. But disaster work also presents significant emotional and physical challenges as well as risks to the worker. Exposure to distressing sights and sounds coupled with difficult working conditions may lead to physical illness or emotional problems. It can also lead to "burnout" with the worker unhappy and unable to perform successfully.
. . . But when workers are given appropriate support in a work situation designed to accomplish organizational goals while at the same time addressing human needs, they usually find their lives enriched by this work, and they are able to maintain a sensitive and caring attitude toward victims.[5]

The National Institute of Mental Health (NIMH) has supported research efforts to aid both disaster victims and emergency service workers. In presidentially declared disasters, states may request federal funds from NIMH to provide victims with special mental health services; in some recent disasters, emergency workers have also been included in the grant applications prepared by local mental health agencies. (NIMH assistance is one of the special forms of assistance triggered by a presidential declaration.)

Public concern about the needs of emergency workers is easy to understand. In the aftermath of a disaster, many emergency service providers work long hours under highly stressful conditions. Moreover, those whose family members have been killed or injured or whose property has been damaged are subject to the same stresses that victims are. As an NIMH study put it, emergency workers are the important people who "rescue the endangered, treat the wounded, and support the bereaved. But what do the caregivers themselves need: How can they best be supported in what is often gruesome, unexpected, and exhausting work?"[6]

Although the line between workers and victims may not always be clear-cut, the situations of emergency workers generally differ from those of victims in several ways. For example, emergency workers are protected by extensive training that helps them cope effectively. Since workers usually have not suffered personal loss, they do not have to undergo significant changes such as relocation. At the same time, workers may face difficult situations—such as recovering bodies—that victims may avoid. In addition, emergency responders make life and death decisions and feel responsible for the consequences of those decisions.

A psychologist with extensive disaster experience has identified three major types of stressors that affect emergency workers:

1. Event stressors. Three such stressors are personal loss or injury, traumatic stimuli, and mission failure or human error. Any one of these factors can increase a person's susceptibility to negative stress reactions.
2. Occupational stressors. These include heavy work loads; long hours; pressure to accomplish difficult tasks quickly; and periods of low activity and little pressure interspersed with sudden events that demand great concentration and physical exertion.
3. Organizational stressors. Rescue, relief, and security units usually give high priority to protecting their personnel and enabling them to accomplish tasks successfully. However, the intimate relationship between the worker and the organization—especially at a time of prolonged contact and heightened emotion—can render the organization a source of stress for the worker. During disasters, workers spend more time on the job and identify strongly with the goals of the organization. Organizational deficiencies—such as poor communication or administrative problems—affect the work in a more immediate and personal way than they might during routine times.[7]

In addition to these three factors, any postdisaster situation will involve special institutional and political conditions peculiar to the setting and the time.[8]

Christine Dunning notes that a review of the limited research on emergency workers subsequent to disaster participation suggests "that deployment does cause psychological, physical, and/or behavioral impairment, both temporary and, in a few cases, permanent."[9] While acknowledging the need for more research on the effects of disaster on emergency workers, Dunning observes that "the information available points to the urgent need for administrators to act to prepare for incidences of psychological injury among workers."[10]

A framework for local recovery

On the basis of fourteen case studies done in the early 1980s, Claire B. Rubin, Martin Saperstein, and Daniel Barbee developed a framework for thinking about the recovery process at the local level of government (Figure 9–6).[11] These researchers found that in communities where the speed and quality of recovery was greater, local officials had found ways to (1) ensure more productive intergovernmental relationships, (2) compete effectively for scarce resources, and (3) better manage community-level decision making during the postdisaster period. Of these three aspects of an effective recovery, effective intergovernmental relations was paramount. (Effective recovery, while not a measurable entity, was considered by the authors to be an efficient process that included attention

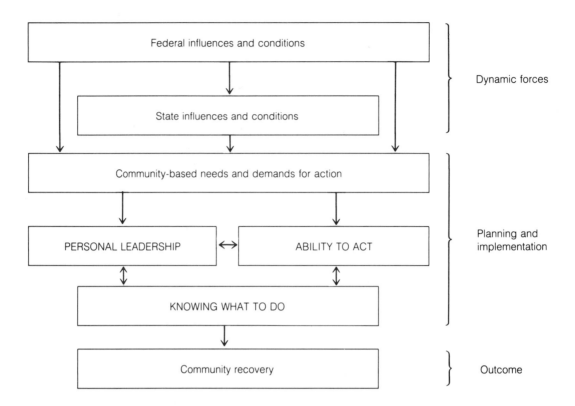

Figure 9–6   Framework for the recovery process.

to mitigation measures against a repeat of the hazard that had caused the previous disaster.)

Figure 9–6 shows the elements of recovery and the relationships among them. The three major elements—personal leadership, ability to act, and knowing what to do—are necessary to ensure an efficient community recovery and are the three elements over which local officials have the most control. Leadership, ability to act, and knowledge are possessed to some degree by every community, can be manipulated (e.g., increased, decreased, purchased, hired, learned), and interact with each other in predictable ways. Although no one of these elements is sufficient, leadership and the ability to act can together ensure an expeditious recovery. Disaster-specific knowledge can be acquired quickly once the two other elements are in place.

The remaining elements shown in Figure 9–6 represent the basic characteristics and conditions of the community before the disaster event. The entire framework may seem to indicate a one-way process, but the interactions are actually cyclical and interrelated. For example, under certain conditions—such as repeated experience with the same disaster agent—local officials may be able to influence some of the factors outside their normal zone of control. Experienced and aggressive local leaders have, in fact, affected federal, state, and private external agents. After extremely destructive events, such as Hurricane Camille (1969) and Hurricane Agnes (1972), federal laws, regulations, and policies were changed in response to complaints from local and state officials about federal disaster assistance programs in effect at the time.

Although major hurricanes, tornadoes, or other disaster agents often affect several counties or several states, patterns of response and recovery vary widely because of the variables that are mentioned above and shown in Figure 9–2. Furthermore, as cities that have had frequent experience with one hazard will testify (Corpus Christi, Texas, with hurricanes, or Ft. Wayne, Indiana, with

Key elements of the recovery process This list can be used not only as a checklist for developing a local recovery plan but also as a rating scheme for determining the relative strengths and weaknesses of municipalities within a county or within a group of neighboring counties.

Personal leadership

Local decision making
Priority of intergovernmental relations
Redevelopment of damaged areas
Long-range view of rebuilt community
Ability to marshal internal and external resources

Ability to act

Availability of state and federal resources
Reliance on local rather than external resources
Local administrative and technical capability
Horizontal and vertical intergovernmental relationships

Knowing what to do

Local knowledge of requirements for state and federal assistance
Identification of sources of assistance
Realistic, flexible, and current preparedness plans

riverine floods), each hazard occurrence has different characteristics, depending on conditions such as wind, time of day or night, or tides.

The sections that follow deal with each of the three major elements in turn, describing—on the basis of research—actions that can be taken to strengthen a community in that area.[12]

Personal leadership

Rubin, Saperstein, and Barbee found that personal leadership is manifested in five principal ways during the recovery period. The components of personal leadership should be developed before the disaster, although their presence (or absence) may become obvious only during the response or recovery period.

Local decision making As soon as possible after a disaster, local officials must decide what they want to do and who is to participate in the planning and implementation of the recovery. Research indicates that local public officials fare best when they are clear about how they want to recover, who they want to help plan and implement the recovery, and what mitigation measures they prefer to adopt.

Priority of intergovernmental relations Research indicates that local officials must understand the importance of the intergovernmental process, undertake action to ensure intergovernmental cooperation early in the postdisaster period, and see to it that cooperative efforts are implemented by both executive and administrative staff. In essence, both leadership and the ability to act are involved.

Redevelopment of damaged areas A broader perspective and a wider array of reconstruction options can result if heavily damaged areas are viewed as redevelopment sites. Local planners should consider a block or neighborhood planning approach rather than first allowing individual property owners to make solo decisions. In an area newly cleared of existing structures, there may be an opportunity to change land uses or to rebuild safer, higher-quality structures. Local decision makers should take a broad approach to planning, including investigating the special powers available to redevelopment authorities under state law. In some states, such as Colorado, the ability to gain access to land and change its uses and ownership have been expedited following a disaster. In other words, "taking powers" may be streamlined.

Long-range view of rebuilt community Researchers in communities that had experienced major disasters observed that when top elected or appointed local officials (or private-sector leaders willing to accept public office) showed foresight about the future of the community, their vision facilitated goal setting and making progress toward those goals. (It should be noted, however, that relatively few local leaders were able to combine such foresight with the ability to assess community values and desires and to provide effective leadership during the recovery period.)

Ability to marshal internal and external resources Strong, capable leadership increases the likelihood of obtaining the necessary resources to repair damage in the community. Researchers found that communities that had been well managed in normal times were more likely to rise to the special demands of disaster recovery. Skill and predisaster experience with public management as well as well-established predisaster interorganizational relationships were essential for accomplishing recovery. Consequently, communities that had

---

Battling disaster profiteering
Hurricane Hugo did much more than bludgeon South Carolina with ferocious winds—it spawned thousands of complaints of price gouging.

Left without electricity and scrambling to replenish water supplies and food, citizens were outraged by what they encountered after the Sept. 21 hurricane.

The earliest price gouging complaints involved items such as ice, food, gasoline and flashlight batteries.

Reports of five-pound bags of ice being sold for $10 and packages of two batteries priced from $4 to $6 were not rare occurrences. In addition, those looking to make a quick profit were charging $3 for a loaf of bread or a gallon of gasoline.

Vendors appeared in some of the worst-hit counties with electric generators loaded in the back of pickup trucks. The generators, in hot demand as people struggled to save food in their refrigerators and freezers, were selling for $700 to $1,000—nearly twice their normal price.

State and local officials did not wait long to respond to the price gouging. Within 48 hours after Hugo made its ungracious visit to Charleston, the City Council enacted an emergency ordinance barring price gouging.

Violators were subject to fines of up to $200 and jail terms of up to 35 days. Charleston Mayor Joe Riley spoke for many angry citizens when he said he would take personal pleasure in participating in the arrest of anyone attempting to take unfair advantage of citizens of the storm-ravaged city.

Responding to the emergency ordinances passed by Charleston and the surrounding counties, the local prosecutor established a price-gouging hotline for citizens. Within a week of Hugo, 52 people were charged with price gouging in the two-county area.

The emergency ordinances made it a misdemeanor to sell items for more than the price that existed immediately prior to Hugo. Local merchants, however, were allowed to recover any increased costs incurred in obtaining goods and merchandise. The emergency ordinances and the wide been muddling along before the disaster hit were very much at a disadvantage in coping with massive disaster-related demands for services, funds, and other resources.

Ability to act

The ability to act decisively and effectively during the recovery period depends on a number of factors, such as ease of access to state and federal resources and the condition of city-county-state relations. The sections that follow briefly discuss the four factors found by researchers to influence most significantly local officials' ability to act. In each case, the emphasis is on what local officials can *do* to position their communities for a speedy and well-planned recovery from disaster.

Availability of state and federal resources   In most cases of successful recovery, state and federal government plays an essential role in providing resources, which vary widely at the state level. In disasters of considerable magnitude, a relatively large number of counties or municipalities are often competing for the same state and federal dollars and for the attention of the same limited number of staff administering their disbursement. The ability to obtain the

---

publicity they brought slowed instances of price gouging.

South Carolina Gov. Carroll Campbell signed an executive order on price gouging four days after Hugo devastated more than half the counties in South Carolina. The order prohibited overcharging for food, fuel, shelter, items used for the protection of life or property, clothing and other essentials in any county subject to the state of emergency.

Shortly after Hugo, the Department of Consumer Affairs extended its normal hours of operation to 8 p.m. each evening and all day on Saturdays to handle the rising number of questions and complaints coming through a toll-free hotline. The crush of calls was so great that the telephone company said 70 percent of those calling were unable to get through.

In an effort to alert the public about the types of consumer abuses occurring in the state, thousands of fact sheets were distributed, along with model home repair contracts and lists of questions the public should ask before allowing anyone to work on their homes or property.

Efforts to distribute information on consumer fraud were hampered by the number of broadcast stations knocked off the air by Hugo. Many citizens, however, were warned not to do business with anyone until they asked to see a driver's license and wrote down the name, address and driver's license number. The department also recommended that citizens write down the license plate number of vehicles used by people making home repairs.

Shortly after, the department began receiving complaints about repair workers refusing to show identification. One elderly couple failed to ask for identification from an individual who promised to repair their roof if they paid him $500 in advance. Unfortunately, they never saw the contractor or their $500 again.

Source: Excerpted from Steven W. Hamm, "Battling Disaster Profiteering," *State Government News*, March 1990. © 1990 The Council of State Governments. Reprinted with permission from *State Government News*.

resources without serious delays therefore depends on the alacrity with which local officials bring their grantsmanship skills to bear. And it should also be noted that states themselves vary in their ability to obtain federal assistance and their willingness to quickly pass it on to county governments. (Counties are important because the presidential declaration names the counties included for federal assistance.)

Reliance on local rather than external resources   Although some dependence on external resources (financial as well as specialized personnel) is to be expected after a disaster, excessive dependence can cause loss of local control and can delay the recovery process. Small to medium-sized communities that have sustained a high ratio of damage to existing structures and systems are most likely to become dependent on state and federal resources. However, by effectively asserting local leadership and organizing its administrative capability, a small community can maximize control over its recovery and its future.

Local administrative and technical capability   Local administrative and technical mechanisms in place before the disaster usually contribute significantly to expeditious recovery. Administrative mechanisms that become important in the aftermath of a disaster are land use controls, building codes, inspection and enforcement procedures (for example, building permits), mutual aid pacts for public safety and public works activities, and contracting agreements (for example, for removal of debris). Technical mechanisms include maps and detailed assessments of known hazard areas or zones (for example, floodplains, seismic zones, and landslide areas).

A related need is for careful documentation of all disaster-related expenses—documentation such as disaster survey reports and records of repairs and of personnel time. A community that has a good record-keeping system in place will be better able to track disaster-related expenditures.

Horizontal and vertical intergovernmental relationships   Relationships across municipalities and among local, state, and federal officials are needed. Administrative staff should call emergency management issues and needs to the attention of local public leaders. Key personnel such as department heads and emergency managers should remind local chief executives or elected officials of the need for ongoing emergency management planning, exercises, and drills. Interagency and interorganizational relationships within a community are essential to effective recovery. Although a municipality and a county may both possess emergency management capability, they may not be able to effectively respond to and recover from a widespread disaster unless they have worked out plans to coordinate their efforts. Similarly, long-standing municipal-county rivalries or antagonisms will not go away when disaster strikes; they should be worked out under normal conditions.

Knowing what to do

For purposes of community recovery, local officials who know what to do are familiar with the requirements for obtaining assistance, have researched all possible sources of assistance, and have ensured that community preparedness plans can be implemented if disaster strikes.

Local knowledge of requirements for state and federal assistance   Local officials in communities subject to known hazards or at chronic risk should investigate *before* a disaster the procedures, requirements, and benefits of state and federal assistance programs. After a disaster, collecting the necessary information for completing a request for a presidential disaster declaration can be an onerous task. (FEMA provides a brochure on how to request a presidential declaration.) It is imperative that communities become familiar before a crisis occurs with the categories about which they will need information. Localities that have been hit by a disaster are often unfamiliar with the Small Business Administration's programs and FEMA assistance programs, particularly the Public Assistance Program, which requires local matching funds for the repair and restoration of public facilities.

Identification of sources of assistance Local officials must not only identify sources of assistance; they must also target their requests for assistance as specifically as possible. Communities fare best when officials know whom to

---

Nags Head, North Carolina, pre- and post-disaster plan The Hurricane and Storm Mitigation and Reconstruction Plan was adopted by the board of commissioners on October 10, 1988. Although the plan is tailored for coastal communities, many parts of it would apply to the preparation for or response to any natural disaster.

This plan is part of a program that is a unique blend of planning management tools, town ordinances and policies, interagency cooperative agreements, and specific police powers legislated to the mayor. The purpose of the program is three-fold: the town is preparing to take action for a major natural disaster; the town has adopted laws that will provide for an orderly rebuilding response in the event of a disaster; and the town has approved planning management tools that will reduce the numbers of people and value of property at risk after a storm.

The plan does the following:

Establishes various building moratoriums based on the severity of damage to ensure that damaged structures are not rebuilt and occupied prior to passing building code and safety inspections.

Establishes a Reconstruction Task Force of thirteen individuals who will advise the board of commissioners on a wide range of safety and reconstruction issues.

Establishes health and welfare requirements for issuing building permits to repair storm-damaged structures.

Establishes use standards and building setback requirements for ocean hazard areas to ensure that structures are placed a safe distance from the ocean.

Establishes requirements for the recombination of land under certain circumstances.

Establishes conditions for declaring hazardous and damaged structures and structures in public trust areas as public nuisances.

Establishes policies for the reconstruction of private and public roads.

Establishes a program for rapid acquisition of land for open space, parks, recreation areas, and historic or scenic areas.

Establishes a program where the town will use a facilitator-consultant to advise the town and its citizens about the types of emergency assistance and post-storm aid that are available and will assist with securing aid for programs that are most needed.

Establishes a Mutual Building Inspector Assistance Program where the town can borrow inspectors from other local governments to help ensure that buildings are safe to occupy and that damaged buildings are rebuilt in a safe manner.

Source: Excerpted from J. Webb Fuller, "Nags Head, North Carolina," *Public Management* 71, no. 12 (December 1989): 24.

ask, what to ask for, and under what authority state and federal agencies may assist. Officials in the communities that have been most successful in identifying and obtaining assistance relied on networks of professional contacts as well as personal contacts at previous places of employment.

Realistic, flexible, and current preparedness plans   Realistic preparedness plans are required for all phases of a disaster. (Again, FEMA provides informational materials that help with preparedness plans. The "Digest of Federal Programs," specifically for recovery, can be very useful. It's best to read these materials before a disaster rather than after.) Such plans must be broad and flexible; recent field work suggests that they be *current* as well, since many communities may have met the other criteria but, by not updating their plans, will have rendered them useless. For example, field investigation into the recovery experience in South Carolina after Hurricane Hugo (1989) revealed that some of the public shelters used were dangerous (too close to sea level) and that not enough alternative sites for citizen assistance centers had been identified. As a hurricane that caused serious damage one hundred miles inland, Hugo provided emergency preparedness personnel with many surprises.[13]

Federal and state assistance

Because communities that experience major disasters receive federal and state disaster assistance, recovery does not refer to basic community survival; no ghost towns have resulted from natural disasters in recent times. (In the Soviet Union, however, the nuclear disaster at Chernobyl caused that community to be evacuated and abandoned for the foreseeable future.) Some communities have decided to relocate (partially or entirely) because of fear of future disasters, but that has been a calculated decision rather than an involuntary occurrence.[14]

Since the early 1980s, the amount of federal and state assistance provided to local governments following disasters has increased, but the added assistance has been accompanied by more complex intergovernmental relations and the imposition of further requirements. When a disaster is damaging enough to warrant a presidential declaration, the resulting web of intergovernmental relationships can greatly complicate local freedom to make public policy choices, allocate resources, and implement programmatic decisions that will affect the future of the community.

As a case in point, consider the experiences of two major urban counties in California—Marin and Santa Cruz—that, in 1982, experienced floods and mudslides of sufficient magnitude to merit a presidential disaster declaration. Although eighteen counties in the San Francisco Bay area were deemed eligible for some form of federal disaster assistance, Marin and Santa Cruz were the focus of detailed case studies. Researchers investigating the recovery process in the two counties found that coordination among the various levels of government was one of the most significant factors in the two widely diverging patterns of response and recovery.

Events in the Bay area leading to the disaster began in early January 1982.[15] Moderate to heavy rainfall during a four-day period brought moisture to the upper levels of soil faster than percolation could occur. On steep, unstable slopes, the fluidity of the saturated soil and the great weight of the rainwater caused the soil to collapse. (Each acre of the wettest slopes received a rainfall mass of more than five million pounds.) Although extremely high water was reported in numerous local streams, flooding alone was not the worst problem. Most of the damage was caused by a combination of flooding and slope failure.

Many neighborhoods and communities were isolated when access roads were either washed out or covered by slides. Thousands of people were evacuated

Federal disaster aid in 1987 and 1988 In 1987 severe rains, snowstorms, floods, tornadoes, and seismic disturbances led the president to sign twenty-three disaster declarations that ultimately provided nearly $400 million in aid (excluding federal emergency aid and fire suppression assistance). The federal funds supplemented recovery efforts in fourteen states, three commonwealths, and two Pacific Ocean trust territories.

In 1988, the federal financial obligation was less than $32 million (excluding expenditures for forest fires, which are handled by the U.S. Department of Agriculture rather than by FEMA). Weather, fires, and other natural phenomena resulted in eleven presidentially declared disasters, the lowest number for any year during the decade. In the preceding five years, FEMA had responsibility for an average of twenty-seven presidentially declared disasters each year, with a total federal obligation of $766 million.

The chart below details the dates, recipients, and causes of 1988 presidentially declared disasters.

1988 PRESIDENTIALLY DECLARED DISASTERS
(excluding fires)

Date declared	Recipient of funds	Incident
January 8	Hawaii	Storms, mudslides, and flooding
January 16	Marshall Islands	Tropical storm Roy
January 20	Guam	Typhoon Roy
January 20	Northern Marianas	Typhoon Roy
February 5	California	Storms and flooding
March 11	Alaska	Fire
July 28	Iowa	Heavy rains and tornadoes
September 29	California	Wildfires
October 5	Texas	Hurricane Gilbert
November 23	Arkansas	Storms and tornadoes
December 2	North Carolina	Storms and tornadoes

Source: FEMA press releases no. 88–78 (December 31, 1988) and no. 87–102 (December 31, 1987).

from their homes. Phone service was disrupted throughout the area for days, and water systems were badly damaged in the city of Santa Cruz and in the Inverness area of Marin County.

Joint federal and state damage estimates indicated that 6,300 residences were damaged, including 231 that were destroyed. Dollar estimates of damage were $109 million to public facilities and $172.4 million to private property. There were thirty-three deaths, twenty-four of which were due to landslides and mudslides.

The accompanying sidebars detail researchers' findings in the aftermath of the disaster.

Federal aid to disaster-stricken communities

Federal disaster assistance is provided under the Disaster Relief Act of 1974, P.L. 93–288, as amended, which is implemented by FEMA following a presidential disaster declaration. A community is eligible for a presidential declaration if the impact of the disaster is beyond the "efforts and available resources of
(*continued on page 248*)

Case study: Recovery in Marin County, California   Project teams visited Marin County twice—shortly after the disastrous rains of early 1982 and again a little more than two years later. When the researchers first began investigating the recovery process in Marin County, they had difficulty singling out *local* public priorities from the array of issues and problems that arose in the aftermath of the disaster. This difficulty was compounded in cases in which a federal Interagency Hazard Mitigation Team (IHMT) had been appointed. (IHMT is used mainly for water-related disasters.) The IHMT introduced a new, strong federal presence and shortened the time frame for mitigation decisions. Within fifteen days of the disaster, the IHMT had already identified two sites—Corte Madera and Inverness—for priority attention. However, interviews with county officials indicated that the mitigation priorities identified by the IHMT were not necessarily those that local officials would have selected.

IHMT members and local officials also disagreed about how easily an identified problem could be solved. For example, a number of years before the rains of 1982 fell, a structural solution to the flooding problems in the Corte Madera flood zone had been undertaken with the support of the U.S. Army Corps of Engineers. However, local protests had halted the multimillion-dollar project when it was three-quarters completed. The corps estimated that the project in its uncompleted state was only one-third effective—and that if the project had been completed as designed, there would have been little or no damage downstream of San Anselmo.

Not surprisingly, the IHMT selected this unfinished flood control project as a priority mitigation effort for Marin County. Federal officials viewed the cost of completion—$600,000—as nominal, reasoning that it was less than the cost of two or three homes in this affluent county. County officials interviewed by the project team reasoned, however, that the county government had incurred only $60,000 in damage to public property during this very severe storm, so why should it invest ten times that amount to prevent future losses? In addition, citizens in several jurisdictions within the Corte Madera flood-control district objected to raising the funds. Since relatively few property owners had sustained major losses, why should a much larger number of residents pay the taxes required to raise $600,000 when they had not been (and were not likely to be) affected by flooding?

The involvement of ad hoc citizen or interest groups did not appear to be significant, although existing groups (such as taxpayer groups in the Corte Madera project area and environmental groups in the Inverness area) were active in championing the causes for which they had been created.

City-county relations   Although only one city administrator in Marin County was interviewed, city-county relations seem to have been good during and after the disaster. These good relations were an extension of the good relations that existed during normal times, when city and county officials had regular meetings, telephone contact, and communication.

In the first few days after the main flooding, each municipality used its equipment and personnel to take care of its own needs; then each shared what it could with other jurisdictions. During the recovery period, the county dealt with the state on behalf of the communities within its boundaries.

County-state relations   The county's perception of the state's role was generally positive. State activities in the affected localities ranged from the direct assistance of the National Guard to advocacy of local needs to federal officials. At the same time, the state aided the federal government by explaining, or seconding, federal insistence on mitigative steps by local governments. Because the state is the co-signer of the federal-state agreement required by a presidential disaster declaration, all local paperwork and requests must go through the state—a requirement that local officials sometimes considered onerous.

Shortly after the presidential declaration was issued, the state geologist made several suggestions for state legislation and actions:

Creating landslide-protection zones along the coast, in which particularly stringent building requirements would be put into effect and remedial measures taken for existing buildings

Undertaking a comprehensive, statewide "critical area and slope stability investigation" to pinpoint land prone to mudslides or landslides

Requiring that prospective home and apartment buyers receive mandatory notification of stability problems.

The geologist further commented that his department had "shelved a landslide hazard prevention legislative package because of the [state] administration's across-the-board fiscal retrenchment" the previous fall. The California Division of Mines and Geology was aware of many actions needed to reduce the landslide hazard. According to the IHMT's first progress report, however, that agency's ability to "encourage communities to adopt and implement land use regulations, construction standards and emergency plans in unstable slope areas" remained problematic.

Marin County depends heavily on income from property taxes and on state and federal transfers. In addition, the county has the unusual resource of the San Francisco Foundation, a private foundation with a special trust fund dedicated to the benefit of Marin County. After the disaster, the county and its cities received about $3.5 million from the foundation, which they primarily used as the local share of disaster assistance grants.

As a general-charter county, Marin County has the usual local authority and powers of counties in California.

Like all other jurisdictions in the state, it is subject to the limits of Proposition 13, under which a taxing measure must be placed on the ballot for voter consideration and must receive a two-thirds vote to be sustained. Needless to say, few tax-generating measures are passed. The research team therefore regarded it as unlikely that many flood control and other hazard mitigation measures requiring extraordinary revenues would be undertaken.

County-federal relations Although state officials were involved throughout, the focal point of interaction was the relationship between county and federal officials. County officials, particularly those engaged in preparing and reviewing the damage survey reports (DSRs), had numerous difficulties in dealing with FEMA staff or their designees. Since the county had about three hundred sites for which DSRs had to be prepared, there were many opportunities for disagreement. The conflicts stemmed from definitional questions over mudslides vs. landslides (landslides are not covered under the National Flood Insurance Program [NFIP]) and over what constitutes repair vs. permanent restoration. The county and federal officials also argued about the meaning of the law providing for public assistance and about engineering estimates.

The county officials were very dissatisfied with the process of preparing DSRs and with FEMA's disposition (or lack thereof) of the DSRs. The research team thought that at the heart of many of the disagreements over individual DSRs was the fact that the FEMA staffers simply wanted to restore the damaged areas, whereas the county (and local) officials wanted to improve them. For example, county officials wanted to shore up a section of a hillside that had experienced a slide that dumped debris on a roadway, whereas federal officials were willing to pay only for clearing the debris off the roadway.

(continued on next page)

(*continued from previous page*)

The restoration vs. betterment issue is one that arises frequently because FEMA is constrained in what it can pay out for public assistance under its enabling legislation, administrative regulations, and policy decisions. And in California the issue was exacerbated by the unusual nature and great number of landslides and mudslides and by the problematic issues of coverage under the NFIP.

Mitigation measures   Before the disaster of 1982, the county administration had taken several mitigative steps:

In 1973, the county adopted a general plan that placed a high value on environmental integrity, making it clear that development should not harm the environment. That plan contained an environmental hazards element that pertained to new development.

Special mapping was done for hazard-prone areas, such as Inverness.

As a participant in the National Flood Insurance Program, the county had revised (as of 1981) the flood hazard areas.

The county had undertaken some slope stability and hydrology studies.

Shortly after the disaster, county officials began to think about the needs of the Inverness area, which had sustained extensive damage. The county committed $90,000 to an engineering firm to study the area's needs and to make recommendations regarding reconstruction in Inverness. (It could not be determined whether the county initiated this effort on its own or whether it did so because it knew that IHMT had marked Inverness as a priority for attention.) The county planner expected that a special comprehensive plan would be needed for the Inverness community, which would probably require changes in land use regulations and building standards in the area. Examples of potential changes were the prohibiting of all new development in the upper reaches of the stream valley and the improving of the floodproofing of

existing buildings. The proposed changes were expected to generate considerable controversy in Inverness.

County and state representatives were part of the IHMT from the very beginning. The county planning director was the local representative on the team. As mentioned earlier, the two main sites for mitigation efforts identified by the IHMT were Corte Madera and Inverness. The former would require the completion of a structural solution—a flood-control system. The latter would entail mainly nonstructural measures (e.g., land use, building code changes) and perhaps some structural measures (e.g., pumps, dredging). Apparently FEMA held up the processing of claims and dollars for public assistance via the processing of payments for individual site DSRs until Marin County demonstrated it was making "good faith" efforts to achieve the two priority mitigation projects just mentioned.

Interviewers' perceptions   The burden of response and much of the recovery fell on the public works and planning departments because of the large amounts of mud that slid and the attendant land use issues.

The widespread and numerous mudslides raised a number of questions, including some about the types of landslides, mudslides, debris slides, etc., covered by the National Flood Insurance Program; the aggressive role of the federal members of the IHMT after a nonflood (i.e., mudslide or landslide) event; FEMA's insistence that the state's hazard initiation plan be an active one, taking into account the multihazard risk facing the affected areas; and the position of the Reagan administration regarding reductions in federal financial involvement in local recovery.

Marin County is an especially interesting example of a jurisdiction with notable public capacity and capability as well as a nationwide reputation for the affluence of its residents. Yet the conservative attitude of the local taxpayers about raising local taxes, together with the ceiling imposed by the state's Proposition 13, resulted in a questionable commitment to long-term mitigation measures on the part of the county and the cities within its boundaries. Similarly, limitations of both personnel and resources seem to have restricted the state's ability to mitigate the landslide hazard; witness the efforts of the California Division of Mines and Geology.

On the positive side, the harmonious and carefully cultivated city-county relations that existed before the disaster worked well in the stressful postdisaster period. Similarly, the county quickly involved itself in the mitigation planning activities of the federally initiated IHMT, which allowed it both to anticipate and to participate in choices and decisions being made for the county.

Update on Marin County Slightly more than two years after the presidentially declared disaster in California on January 7, 1982, the research team went back to Marin County to review the progress the county had made in achieving its recovery and mitigation goals. In its first site visit report, the team noted two priority sites for mitigation measures during recovery: the Corte Madera Creek project and Inverness. The IHMT, which provided a strong federal presence and involvement soon after the disaster, had significantly influenced the selection of those priority sites.

At the time of the second visit, relatively little progress had been made in connection with the Corte Madera Creek project, which required local political decisions and the conclusion of litigation, which was expected to take several years. Since the final decisions rested with the courts, the county could not directly affect the timing or outcome of the project.

In Inverness, notable progress had been made. Inverness is an unincorporated area of the county, where development is in three steep and rugged canyons. Shortly after the disaster declaration, the county hired an engineering firm to prepare designs for repairs to public structures and to recommend policies for new construction to mitigate future damage. The county accepted and acted on both of these products, although the county planner commented that improving the safety of existing structures was far more difficult and would take many years.

Finally, several communities in the county had decided to undertake and pay for flood mitigation efforts.

During its second visit, the research team observed a growing willingness to "pay for government" by a population that only a few years before had supported Proposition 13. Local progress toward recovery and mitigation goals in San Rafael, Santa Venetia, Novato, Petaluma, and also in Inverness suggested that the events of 1982 (and those of 1983, as well) had led local officials to find the funding for projects citizens wanted. In some of these areas, local tax increases had been necessary.

As noted earlier, the county administration had been highly competent in normal times. What was unusual was the amount of time and attention paid to regular, routine meetings on, and training in, emergency management. For more than a decade before the 1982 declaration, the county had held regular emergency drills even though no major disasters had occurred. The fact that the San Andreas fault goes through the county helps ensure the concern and attentiveness of county officials. The continual attention to emergency management and the regularly maintained coordination and training activities allowed the county to swing smoothly into action to handle an emergency.

Source: Adapted from Claire B. Rubin et al., *Community Recovery from a Major Natural Disaster* (Boulder: Program on Environment and Behavior, University of Colorado, monograph no. 41, 1985).

Case study: Recovery in Santa Cruz County, California   Officials in Santa Cruz County said the timing for the transition from response to recovery varied with the type of activity. The stream and high-water damage was repaired quickly, and within two weeks the public works department was planning recovery actions. In contrast, the road repair took a long time to complete, which meant that the beginning of the recovery period for that segment of reconstruction activities came later. In the early days after the disaster, virtually all county staffers assisted with operational jobs, regardless of their usual duties. For example, professional staff went to the severely stricken areas to help provide the manual labor needed to protect property and stem further destruction (e.g., to clear away mud and debris from buildings and roadways). After a few days of such tasks, several staffers switched to planning or analysis, which they thought would make a more meaningful contribution to understanding and coping with the disaster recovery and mitigation.

Identifying the county government's own priorities amid the array of recovery issues and problems was further complicated by the priority site selected by the Interagency Hazard Mitigation Team (IHMT). In Santa Cruz County, the IHMT report cited only one location, San Lorenzo Valley, although that is a large geographic area. County officials did not disagree with that site as a priority for attention, but they did think that some refinement and more specific target areas would be more appropriate to the county's agenda for mitigation.

City-county relations   Relations between city and county officials in Santa Cruz County were troubled. The research team did not delve very deeply into the emergency response phase, since most of the issues about recovery from, and mitigation of, the landslides and mudslides arose later. Nevertheless, from brief discussions of emergency preparedness and

response, it became clear that there had been problems. One was that the county had been reluctant to activate the emergency operations center (EOC) because the EOC was vulnerable to flooding, potentially endangering the safety of the emergency services personnel. A second problem was disagreement between city and county emergency personnel as to basic needs and priorities. Officials in some of the cities did not think the county had been responsive to their needs during the response period.

Ultimately, a grand jury investigation criticized the intergovernmental activities and relationships. (Some individuals characterized the investigation as "politically inspired." On the other hand, several persons commented that some county officials had overreacted to the report.) Although the research team did not know the details of the investigation, the formation of the grand jury and the controversy over its actions reflected troubled relations between city and county officials. It appeared that city and county officials had not met regularly before the disaster and that relations even under normal conditions had been strained. The stresses of disaster response and recovery had exacerbated existing difficulties.

County-state-federal relations   There was considerable wrangling over the damage survey reports (DSRs). Ultimately, disagreements over which projects were eligible and which federal assistance would be made available resulted in the scheduling of regular meetings—weekly for two months after the disaster, and then biweekly—with the congressional representative and top county, state, and federal officials in attendance. County officials who were interviewed attributed the necessity for such meetings to their special needs for relief and assistance and to the heavy demands they made on FEMA. Some local officials accused FEMA of not being familiar enough with the area, saying the agency should have relied more on local people—particularly with regard to selecting mitigation "opportunity" sites and feasible measures.

Mitigation measures The county-state-federal interchange about recommended hazard mitigation measures also caused a major stir. For reasons never explicitly identified, the county government did not name an individual to be its representative on the IHMT until late April, about fifteen weeks after the declaration was issued. This delay angered FEMA officials and raised questions about the county's commitment to hazard mitigation. As it turned out, county officials were in fact thinking about land use and other restrictions that would be necessary during the recovery period in the San Lorenzo Valley, although they were not doing so in the context of the team effort. The county representative assigned to the team in April was a member of the county planning department.

In the San Lorenzo Valley, a host of issues about land use controls, particularly in the Love Creek section of that valley, had been simmering. The IHMT report describes the terrain and hazard potential in San Lorenzo Valley as follows:

The San Lorenzo River Basin was the most heavily affected area in the declared counties. Almost every problem found in this disaster was evident in the San Lorenzo Valley. Landslide, mudslide and flooding caused loss of life and numerous injuries, loss of access and utilities, and damage and destruction of many buildings and facilities.

An estimated 14 people were killed by landslide and mudslide in the San Lorenzo Valley. Reliable information on damages in San Lorenzo Valley is not available because the information is on a countywide basis. However, of the over 400 families from San Lorenzo Valley who registered at the Disaster Assistance Center, 39 reported their homes were destroyed, 152 reported major damage, and 217 reported minor damage.

The Team is very concerned about the safety of developments in San Lorenzo Valley and concluded that the hazards, their severity and likelihood of occurrence must be determined before further development is allowed. Once the hazards are evaluated, new development and reconstruction should only be allowed if they can be reasonably safe from damage. Since most of the deaths in this disaster occurred in San Lorenzo Valley, the county should implement a warning and evacuation plan.

More specifically, the IHMT report listed the following work to be done: (1) identify significant hazards in San Lorenzo Valley; (2) evaluate the effects of these hazards; (3) review and evaluate applicable land use regulations, construction standards, and other existing hazard mitigation measures; (4) evaluate measures that could mitigate these effects; and (5) recommend appropriate mitigation measures.

As noted earlier, county officials did not dispute the selection of San Lorenzo Valley for mitigation attention, but they favored a narrower, site-specific focus. Furthermore, some county officials were highly concerned about the potential cost and, equally, about the political feasibility of achieving mitigation—especially in the developed portions of the valley.

Interviewers' perceptions In Santa Cruz County, the bulk of the response work—including removing debris, cleaning up mudslides, and cleaning creeks—fell to the public works department. That department, together with the planning department, also had the lead role in the recovery process. For reasons not fully known, the planning department appeared to have a secondary rather than primary role in recovery planning. The county representative to the IHMT was in the planning department.

Fundamental to the conflict over the IHMT's recommendations was the fact that the county's building codes and land use controls had not been adequate to protect life and property

(continued on next page)

(continued from previous page)
from the disaster. The changes needed were a major community issue, one that sparked controversy because of the varying philosophies of the key actors involved as well as varying ability and willingness to pay (directly and indirectly) for them. Whether or not the recovery outcome was influenced by the IHMT's efforts remains to be determined. The extent to which the team's recommendations were implemented may be a significant indicator of the future of recovery and mitigation in the county.

As mentioned earlier, the location of the emergency operations center (in the basement of the county administration building) made it susceptible to flooding, and therefore the decision to activate was delayed. As a result, during the early hours after the emergency, centralized, effective leadership at the county level was not as good as many city officials would have liked.

It did seem surprising that four months after the disaster, the county planning officials were not aware of federal Executive Order 11988 or its California counterpart: both the federal and state floodplain regulations require that every reconstruction project proposal include efforts to reduce the potential for future losses. Such requirements are the basis for the activities of the IHMTs. A related limitation, noted earlier, was the fact that the county did not name a representative to the IHMT until late April 1982.

Update on Santa Cruz County

During the spring of 1982, Santa Cruz County had many problems to deal with, ranging from inadequate emergency preparedness to the need for extensive changes in land use regulations in an area of delicate ecological balance. Population concentrations are unusual in Santa Cruz County, which includes almost 190,000 persons. About 50,000 persons live in the canyon areas; about half of those live in unincorporated areas. The ability to mitigate natural hazards is limited because so much of the land within the county forms canyons, the population is scattered rather than concentrated, and many persons live in areas without strong local government.

Aside from susceptibility to flooding (both coastal and inland), the county has three major earthquake faults within its boundaries. A number of the persons who live deep in the canyon areas are reclusive—they live without electricity and municipal water and sewer services and they want minimal contact with public officials. It is therefore difficult to identify all the people and structures at risk, let alone enlist their support for mitigation activities.

By the winter of 1983, when the research team was on site the second time, the county had taken several major actions to reduce its vulnerability to future flood and landslide hazards. The county had thoroughly revamped its emergency management operation (including substantially rewriting its operations manual and establishing a second emergency operations center); completed several of the land use control actions recommended by the IHMT; and generally accomplished many changes that would improve the county's preparedness for a future disaster.

When county officials were asked what they were doing differently after the 1982 disaster declaration, they listed the following: (1) changes in county regulations regarding location of new construction and critical facilities; (2) several programs for the public to ensure better personal preparedness; (3) condemnation of twenty-eight (intact) houses in the Love Creek area, most of which had since been moved or torn down; and (4) condemnation of two hundred structures in other parts of the county.

In addition to the major mitigative actions recommended by the IHMT, county officials in Santa Cruz undertook a variety of other measures to facilitate the county's recovery and improve its future preparedness. Many taxpayers had changed their attitude about government spending. After the 1982 and 1983 floods and related devastation in Santa Cruz, citizens were more willing to pay for flood, mudslide, and landslide prevention measures and better understood the need for certain land use regulations.

At the time of the team's second visit, county land use regulations required a geologic hazards analysis of development sites. County officials were to make field visits and personally review all sites of new construction. Four county employees performed these site inspections and also did erosion control work. It is not known whether these requirements and staffing arrangements were continued.

The county mounted a public information campaign to provide citizens with more information about hazards and preparedness. In the fall of 1983, the county mailed residents a tabloid with information on natural hazards. County officials also organized a series of community meetings at which county geologists spoke with citizens about the geologic hazards from which they were at risk. In addition, the county stepped up its erosion control work.

Other mitigative steps included setting up about one hundred private road-assessment districts as a new mechanism for coordinating private response; establishing a watershed review process for the Soquel Creek area; and improving a flood alert system.

County-state relations County officials acknowledged help from the state after both the 1982 and 1983 disaster declarations. Yet they viewed the state as a "mild" advocate of their needs and interests vis-à-vis the federal government and would have liked stronger support from the state. "The state should defend its children,"

explained one county official. In addition, local officials thought the state offered too few disaster recovery programs.

County-federal relations As noted earlier, initial county-federal relations were filled with tension and conflict. County officials acknowledged that they were very aggressive and argumentative regarding public assistance from FEMA. They defended their outspokenness, saying that for a relatively small county government the paperwork was extremely burdensome, the amount of federal aid and assistance was too little and hence "devastating" to a small community, and the administrative process for achieving and implementing the DSRs was "overwhelming." When the project team made its second visit, county officials were less agitated about the process, but they were still very vocal about the problems. Cash flow was a continuing concern for the county because of slow payments by the federal agencies.

The public works officials, on whom most DSR-related work fell, commented on the grey areas in the process. Some public assistance projects that the county put forward to FEMA for payment eligibility determination were answered with a "probably no," rather than with a "yes" or "no." When the possibility for project funding was thought to exist, county officials had pursued it. In Santa Cruz, county officials felt that they "had chased the carrot too far" on occasion. In addition, the public works department spent about $250,000 on engineering consultations that were necessary to supplement the existing staff to meet the workload. These expenditures of both time and money were the types of efforts that contributed to the feeling that the administrative burden was overwhelming. FEMA was viewed as not offering enough financial assistance to make recovery possible, yet as placing heavy demands on local officials after a disaster.

(continued on next page)

(continued from previous page)
Santa Cruz County public works officials advised others in their situation to document everything. They recommended recording project details from the engineering perspective (including photos) and documenting how time and money were spent. The details would help later with presentations and the inevitable appeals. They would also help if a subsequent disaster wiped out the earlier project for which a DSR had been prepared.

The officials also recommended being as specific as possible in requests to federal officials for equipment and expertise. It was also considered important to know how to ask for things—for example, if you are asking the state for help from the National Guard, you might be better off calling for a training exercise rather than for disaster response assistance.

Source: Adapted from Claire B. Rubin et al., *Community Recovery from a Major Natural Disaster* (Boulder: Program on Environment and Behavior, University of Colorado, monograph no. 41, 1985).

states, local governments, and private relief organizations in alleviating the damage, loss, hardships, or suffering." (Although most of the disasters that occur in the United States each year are not of sufficient magnitude to be eligible for a presidential declaration, communities can apply for assistance through a variety of other state and federal programs.)

Usually, FEMA monitors the development of disasters to determine if they warrant federal assistance. Before, during, and after a disaster the FEMA regional director (RD) is in close contact with federal agencies that have disaster assistance responsibilities as well as with the governor's office in the affected state and with the state emergency management agency. Before requesting a presidential declaration, state disaster officials, in coordination with other state and local officials and FEMA regional staff, survey the extent of public, private, and agricultural damage. If federal aid is needed, the appropriate state officials contact the RD for advice and assistance. The governor then makes the formal request for federal assistance to the president through the RD.

When the president declares a disaster or emergency, the governor, appropriate members of Congress, and federal agencies are notified immediately.[16] At that time, the FEMA director appoints a federal coordinating officer. As soon as possible thereafter, the political subdivisions eligible for federal assistance are designated, as is the kind of assistance to be made available. FEMA administers grants to the states from the president's Disaster Relief Fund and directly coordinates the disaster assistance functions of all federal agencies.

The sudden arrival of numerous federal and state agency representatives in a disaster-stricken community heralds a new phase of intergovernmental relationships. Because local officials deal with disasters infrequently, they are much less experienced than their state and federal counterparts. For a local official, a disaster may be a once-in-a-lifetime event; for a state official, it may be one of a dozen such events in a year; and for a federal official, it may be one of twenty presidentially declared disasters in a given year.

The presence of federal and state representatives adds complexity to the recovery process, as do burgeoning federal and state regulations. Recent federal policies and executive orders, for example, require the coordination of mitigation and recovery. Certain federal grant programs impose on state and local governments substantial financial and administrative responsibility for recovery, such as fixed shares of state and local matching funds. Taken together, intergovernmental relationships and federal and state mandates significantly shape the administrative, political, and economic context of recovery.

It is important to note that even after receiving a presidential declaration, a community may still have difficulty obtaining federal aid to assist with reconstruction. In recent years, block grant programs have left little discretionary federal funding available for long-range recovery.[17] There are numerous federal categorical grant programs, but each must be applied for individually. Although disaster-impacted communities get preferential treatment, each program has a fixed budget and budget cycle limitation.

State and local relations

As a partner in the federal-state agreement signed after a presidential disaster declaration, state government has a number of specified responsibilities, including oversight of local mitigation efforts. States also play an important role in the disbursement of federally provided Individual and Family Grants Assistance, Public Assistance, and other special programs and assistance triggered by a presidential declaration.

Each state's laws, executive orders, and regulations specify gubernatorial and other state powers regarding state financial and programmatic assistance to localities. The state is represented in a community by the governor's authorized representative, who works closely with the federal coordinating officer and others in the disaster field office that FEMA establishes soon after a disaster is declared.

Local-state relations vary widely. Researchers studying fourteen recovering communities found that the majority of local officials offered generally negative assessments of local-state relations—primarily because, in the view of the local officials, states were unable to provide needed technical assistance or significant financial assistance.[18] Furthermore, local dependence on federal programs to fund recovery led to more direct county-federal contacts. Although state officials are in the loop of intergovernmental relationships, the desire to bypass the state level intensified when local officials wanted quick decisions or ready cash from the federal government for major projects under the Public Assistance grant program. Under such circumstances, state government was often perceived not only as another layer of government to go through but also as one that did not yield substantial assistance. The negative view of state government was common and occurred even in cases in which outside researchers observed that the state had in fact provided significant effort and assistance. Local officials' perceptions may have been partly attributable to the fact that, in presidentially declared disasters, a state's role is dwarfed by that of the federal government.

In summary, local, state, and federal officials tend to have differing and sometimes incompatible perceptions of their roles in recovery, the priorities during recovery, the importance of postdisaster mitigation efforts, and the proper locus and form of recovery decision making.[19] The intergovernmental context provides both problems and opportunities for the exercise of local strategic choice during the recovery period. Case studies of communities stricken by disaster provide detailed illustrations of conflicting expectations and the complexity of the intergovernmental relations process.[20]

The Red Cross and other voluntary assistance

Thus far, the chapter has focused on local government services and assistance in the aftermath of a disaster. Also at work during response and recovery are many civic and religious organizations, as well as unaffiliated volunteers.

The most likely source of immediate assistance in caring for disaster victims is the Red Cross, but other private voluntary organizations, such as the Salvation Army and the Mennonite Disaster Service, also complement or supplement public-sector efforts. Such groups, along with individual volunteers, often work with victims on a one-to-one basis. Their assistance ranges from replacing clothing or household goods to providing personal counseling. Mennonite Disaster Service volunteers help low-income disaster victims clean and rebuild their homes.

Chartered by Congress in 1905, the Red Cross is responsible for helping meet the human needs created by a disaster. Furthermore, "that charter is not only a grant of power but an imposition of duties."[21] In other words, although the American Red Cross is a private organization, it is *required* to provide assistance after a disaster. Actually, the Red Cross is usually on-site well before the decision to issue or not issue a presidential declaration is made. Furthermore, the Red Cross will assist regardless of what that decision is.

After a presidentially declared disaster, the Red Cross is virtually an arm of the federal government: "The authority vested in the Red Cross makes unnecessary the issuance of special permission or license by state or local government

How to apply for financial aid from FEMA   Regardless of the type of disaster you may face as a leader of the community, your budget may not provide the funds necessary to maintain normal government functions during and after a disaster. The Federal Emergency Management Agency (FEMA) has several informative publications on this subject, but the time to wade through them is not in the hours or days following a disaster. This article provides a "cookbook" approach to obtaining Federal Aid through FEMA's Disaster Assistance Programs. Preparedness is the key to recovering from any disaster. Contact FEMA to receive publications and guidelines of the Community Disaster Loans under section 414 of the Disaster Relief Act of 1974, Public Law (PL) 93-288, 42 United States Code (USC) 5187. Read the guidelines carefully and review them occasionally so you will be prepared in your community's moments of crisis.

General information   The Associate Director of State and Local Programs and Support (SLPS) is responsible for making loans to local governments that have suffered a substantial loss of revenues as a result of a major disaster or emergency. Loans are based on an assessment of need and may not exceed 25 percent of the operating budget for the local government's fiscal year in which the disaster occurs.

Local governments are eligible for only one loan after a single event; however, the loan may be awarded in either the fiscal year in which the disaster occurred or in the following fiscal year. These funds are used to continue normal operation of the government or to assist in disaster-related needs, including state and local efforts to save lives and protect property, public health and safety or to avert or lessen the threat of a disaster.

Eligibility   As long as the local government can show that it has lost a significant portion of its revenue, including its tax base, and this loss will interrupt the day-to-day operation of the government, it may apply for a disaster assistance loan.

Any county, city, village, town, district, any Indian tribe or authorized tribal organization, or Alaska Native village or organization, and any rural community or unincorporated town or village or any other public entity may be eligible for federal assistance. The jurisdiction must be located within the area designated by the Associate Director, SLPS, as eligible for disaster assistance. Private, nonprofit, educational, utility, emergency, medical and custodial care institutions are not local governments and are not eligible for a Community Disaster Assistance Loan. The following are guidelines used to determine for the Red Cross to activate and carry out its relief program; nor can any state, territory, or local government deny the right of the Red Cross to render its services in accordance with the congressional mandate and its own policies and under its own administration."[22]

In addition to the congressional charter, the Red Cross has a statement of understanding with FEMA outlining its responsibilities in the event of any disaster in which FEMA is involved. For example, the Plan for Federal Response to a Catastrophic Earthquake enumerates special powers and responsibilities for the Red Cross in case of a catastrophe.

What is unique about the Red Cross from an organizational standpoint is that it rapidly implements a full-scale relief operation encompassing a broad range of functions and relying on both paid staff and volunteers brought in from near and far. During a disaster relief operation, the Red Cross provides mass care (shelter and food); direct financial and material assistance to families; emergency

---

loans to a local government:

1. Whether there are sufficient funds to meet the current fiscal year operating requirement.
2. Availability of cash or other liquid assets from the prior fiscal year.
3. Current financial condition considering projected expenditures for local governmental services and availability of other financial resources.
4. Ability to obtain financial assistance or needed revenue from state and other federal agencies for direct program expenditures.
5. The relationship of annual receipts to debt service.
6. Displacement of revenue-producing business due to property destruction.
7. Danger of municipal insolvency.

Application procedures The local government must submit several forms to FEMA to begin the loan process, including FEMA form 90-7, Community Disaster Loan Application, and FEMA form 90-5, Application for Loan Cancellation. These forms are available from FEMA, but in the event of a disaster all correspondence must go through the Governor's Authorized Representative and the FEMA Regional Office to the Associate Director, SLPS. At this level the FEMA regional director will review the application to verify that all documents are in order before

submitting them to the Associate Director, SLPS.

Loan application The local government must prepare and submit a Community Disaster Loan Application with accompanying justification of financial need based on the actual and projected expenses, as a result of the disaster, for the fiscal year in which the disaster occurred and the three succeeding fiscal years. Required forms include: a Summary of Revenue Loss and Unreimbursed Disaster Related Expenses, a Statement of the Applicant's Operating Results-Cash Position, a Debt History, Tax Assessment Data and Financial Projections. Also required are the local government's financial reports for the three fiscal years immediately prior to the disaster year.

While the steps are many, and the reading is much, these steps must be taken to adequately present the need for financial assistance. For further information, contact Office of Disaster Assistance Programs, FEMA, Room 714, 500 C St. SW, Washington, DC 20472, (202) 646-3683.

Source: From the April 15, 1990, "IEMS News," a FEMA-funded quarterly insert to the International Association of Fire Chiefs newsletter, *IAFC on Scene.*

Figure 9–7   Marilyn
Quayle helping to fill out
forms at a FEMA
assistance center.

health care; and assistance with rebuilding and repair of housing. In addition, the Red Cross undertakes a comprehensive damage assessment to determine the extent of the relief effort and its potential cost.[23]

Red Cross services are provided to victims of events ranging from a fire in a single-family home to a large-scale natural disaster. In this context, it is worth noting that the definition of *disaster* used by the Red Cross is much broader than that applied by FEMA. To the Red Cross, "the magnitude of a disaster may be such as to simultaneously affect tens of thousands of people in several states, or it may bring suffering and anguish to just a few persons in one apartment building or group of houses."[24]

Postdisaster mitigation

Mitigation has been defined as "deciding what to do where a risk to the health, safety, and welfare of society has been determined to exist; and implementing a risk reduction program."[25] Since most natural disasters result from known hazards, the disaster event, if not its date, can be anticipated and, to some extent, planned for. For instance, in a community where floods have been frequent, flood control measures may include major structural projects and may require a significant amount of capital. Structural flood protection measures, such as dams, dikes, or levees, ordinarily have a long lead time and require millions in state and federal funds. The plans for such major mitigation efforts should be drawn up well in advance of a flood (or other foreseeable) emergency so that they will be available during the immediate aftermath of a disaster. Mitigation measures are a desirable means of reducing the impact of future disasters; as noted earlier, they are also mandatory for some types of public assistance.

Mitigation requirements

States that have received a presidential disaster declaration are required to engage in hazard mitigation planning as set forth in Section 409 of P.L. 100–

707 (amending the Disaster Relief Act of 1974, P.L. 93–288). Section 409 (406 in the 1974 act) requires that the "state or local government shall agree that the natural hazards in the areas in which the proceeds of the grants or loans are to be used shall be evaluated and appropriate action shall be taken to mitigate such hazards, including safe land-use and construction practices." That requirement is the basis for multihazard analysis and mitigation efforts in the aftermath of a disaster. The governor's signature on the federal-state agreement that is a condition of a presidential disaster declaration commits the state and its localities to mitigation efforts. Both to receive assistance from FEMA and to be eligible for payments by the National Flood Insurance Program, local officials must, in turn, ensure that the community meets specified mitigation requirements.

In 1980, the federal government began using Interagency Hazard Mitigation Teams (IHMTs) to improve interagency cooperation in the postdisaster period

---

The disaster application center One of the most important objectives after a disaster is to inform individuals of the assistance available to them in the recovery process. Following a disaster declaration, FEMA may establish one or more disaster application centers (DACs) in the disaster area.

Centrally located, the DAC is a "one-stop" application center easily accessible to all persons affected by the disaster. Representatives of federal agencies, state and local governments, private relief agencies, and other organizations that can provide assistance or counseling are available to register and advise disaster victims. These centers are kept in operation as long as required by the situation. In addition, mobile teams may be sent to assist persons in areas without easy access to a DAC.

The DAC is open to the public no sooner than the fourth day after the president's declaration of disaster. This provides sufficient time for staff training, locating an appropriate site and equipment, public information on the application process and DAC location, and briefings to familiarize local officials with DAC operations and procedures.

There is no single best DAC configuration. The configuration is often modified to make it easier for individuals to get information and obtain the help available from the various agencies represented.

The size of the DAC and extent of agency participation depend on the extent of the disaster, the size of the affected community, the availability of facilities, and the capability of agencies to participate.

A DAC is commonly located in a gymnasium or large meeting hall. The optimum facility would have the following characteristics: a large main room; one or more smaller rooms for group presentations, staff lounge, and storage; adequate lighting for completion of forms; controlled access, preferably with one "entrance" and one "exit" door; arrangements to secure the DAC when it is closed; functioning rest rooms; and sufficient parking for staff and victims.

Local officials are responsible for providing the facility and basic furniture, such as folding tables and chairs. (Local disaster plans should include provision for providing DAC facilities.) FEMA and state DAC staff provide their own office supplies and signs. Local officials should also be prepared to provide crowd control, security, and janitorial services. Any office "amenities" that can be provided by local officials, such as access to a copy machine, are welcomed and can be helpful in assuring good service to citizens.

Most DAC managers and other FEMA DAC staff members are "reservists," which means that they work
(*continued on next page*)

and to monitor mitigation efforts during recovery. Currently, an IHMT is convened only after a water-related hazard results in a presidential declaration. The FEMA regional director appoints each team, which includes key federal agency representatives as well as representatives of state and local government. Some states, such as California, also have begun to use a team approach after disasters.

Although in theory the IHMT can be most effective in focusing early attention on mitigation needs, in practice the essential thing is what is actually done to implement the team's recommendations. On occasion, lack of follow-up by federal or state officials and lack of money in needed programs have made this process more a paper exercise than a real activity.

In addition to having to fulfill Section 409 requirements, state and local governments may have mitigation obligations under the National Flood Insurance Program, the Interagency Agreement for Post-Flood Disaster, the Executive

(*continued on page 256*)

(*continued from previous page*)

intermittently and may not have developed an administrative relationship with the regular FEMA staff. Often FEMA will dispatch a core DAC staff and will rely on borrowed state employees or local hires for additional staff. These additional employees are usually trained on site a day or so before the DAC opens. Training usually consists of a "crash course" on the basic application form and the various assistance programs. The DAC manager often works with a high degree of autonomy.

Local participation in the DAC is encouraged. Often there are questions about debris removal, restoration of utility service, zoning and other local matters. Some communities have developed their own programs to assist disaster victims, ranging from low-interest home repair loans to small business loans. These programs are often helpful to supplement or fill gaps in federal and state programs.

Individual assistance programs that may be available through agencies located at the DAC usually include:

Temporary housing for disaster victims whose homes are uninhabitable. Minimum essential repairs may be made to owner-occupied residences in lieu of other forms of temporary housing.

Disaster unemployment assistance and job placement assistance for those

unemployed as a result of the disaster.

Individual and family grants of up to $10,000 to meet disaster-related necessary expenses or serious needs when those affected are unable to meet such expenses or needs through other programs. (The amount may vary depending on federal regulations and individual state participation.)

Legal counseling.

Crisis counseling and referrals to appropriate mental health agencies.

Loans to individuals, businesses, and farmers for repair, rehabilitation, or replacement of damaged real and personal property and some production losses not fully covered by insurance.

Agricultural assistance, including technical assistance; payments covering a major portion of the cost to eligible farmers who perform emergency conservation actions on farmland damaged by the disaster; and provision of federally owned feed grain for livestock and herd preservation.

Veterans' assistance, such as death benefits, pensions, insurance settlements, and adjustments to home mortgages held by the Veterans Administration.

Tax relief, including state tax assistance and help from the Internal Revenue Service in claiming casualty losses resulting from the disaster.

Source: Gary Milliman, City Administrator, Fort Bragg, California.

Organizational sources of hazard and disaster information

Organization	Hazard expertise
American Institute of Architects Foundation 1735 New York Ave., N.W., Washington, DC 20006 202/785–2324	Mainly earthquakes and floods
American Planning Association 1313 East 60th St., Chicago, IL 60637 312/947–2082	Mainly earthquakes and floods
American Society of Civil Engineers 345 East 47th St., New York, NY 10017 212/705–7496	All hazards
American Red Cross National Office of Disaster Services 18th and E Sts., N.W., Washington, DC 202/857–3718	All hazards
Applied Technology Council 2471 East Bayshore Rd. (#517), Palo Alto, CA 94303 415/857–3718	Earthquakes
Bay Area Regional Earthquake Preparedness Project Metro Center 10 18th St., Oakland, CA 94607 415/642–6722	Earthquakes
Building Officials and Code Administrators 4051 West Flossmoor Rd., Country Club Hills, IL 60477 312/799–2300	All hazards
Building Seismic Safety Council 1015 15th St., N.W., Washington, DC 20005 202/347–5710	Earthquakes
California Seismic Safety Commission 1900 K St., Sacramento, CA 95814 916/322–4917	Earthquakes
Central United States Earthquake Consortium 2001 Industrial Park Drive Box 367, Marion, IL 62959 618/997–5659	Earthquakes
Clark University Center for Technology, Environment, and Development 950 Main St., Worcester, MA 01610 508/751–4622.	Technological
Disaster Research Center University of Delaware Dept. of Sociology, Newark, DE 19711 302/451–2581	All hazards
Earthquake Engineering Research Institute 2620 Telegraph Ave., Berkeley, CA 94704 415/848–0972	Earthquakes
Federal Emergency Management Agency 500 C St., S.W., Washington, DC 20472 202/646–2500 FEMA has ten regional offices (in Boston, New York, Philadelphia, Atlanta, Chicago, Kansas City, Denver, Dallas, San Francisco and Seattle).	All hazards

(*continued on next page*)

(continued from previous page)

National Information Service for Earthquake Engineering (NISEE) Earthquake Engineering Research Center 1301 South 46 St., Richmond, CA 94804−4698 415/231−9401	Earthquakes
National Science Foundation Division of Biological and Critical Systems 1800 G St., N.W., Washington, DC 20550 202/357−9545	Natural hazards
Natural Hazards Research and Applications Information Center University of Colorado IBS Building #6 Campus Box 482, Boulder, CO 80309 303/492−6818	Natural hazards
Natural Disaster Resource Referral Service P.O. Box 2208, Arlington, VA 22202 703/920−7176	Natural hazards
Oak Ridge National Laboratory Energy Division X-10 Hazard Management Group Bldg. 4500N, Rm. H24-6206, Oak Ridge, TN 37831 (615) 576-2716 Attn: John Sorensen	Technological/civil
Southern California Earthquake Preparedness Project 6850 Van Nuys Blvd., Van Nuys, CA 91405 213/787−5310	Earthquakes
Structural Engineers Association of California 217 2nd St., San Francisco, CA 94105 415/974−5147	All hazards
University of Pittsburgh Environmental Health and Safety Office B-80 Benedum Hall 3900 O'Harris St., Pittsburgh, PA 15261 412/624−9544	All hazards/civil
U.S. Geological Survey Office of Earthquakes, Volcanoes, and Engineering 905 National Center, Reston, VA 22092 703/648−4000	Geologic hazards
U.S. Dept of Commerce, National Oceanic and Atmospheric Administration (NOAA), National Weather Service Office, Silver Spring, MD 20910 301/427−8090	All weather hazards (storms, tornadoes, hail, thunderstorms)

Orders for Floodplain Management and Protection of Wetlands, and the National Earthquake Hazards Reduction Program. Furthermore, some states have their own mitigation requirements, as do some communities. For example, a California law requires all local governments to include a seismic safety element in their general plan.

Approaches to mitigation

In practical terms, mitigation measures fall into the categories of structural and nonstructural. Structural measures include dams, levees, dikes, and debris basins.

Nonstructural measures include the acquisition of high-risk properties, conversion of the land to green space or low-density uses, and the purchase of flood or earthquake insurance. The phases of disaster—response, recovery, mitigation, and preparedness—are not clear-cut, and there is no one "right time" to begin postdisaster mitigation efforts. Much depends on the type and magnitude of the disaster and on the capability and sophistication of the affected community.

There is no doubt that mitigation measures can save lives, protect property, and prevent suffering. If improved public safety is not enough of an incentive, emergency managers and other local officials should be prepared to point out that failure to take action to alleviate a known risk can create liability for the local government and its agents. Although it can often be demonstrated that the costs of mitigation are significantly smaller than the benefits it affords, the worth of mitigation goes beyond dollar savings alone. Social impact assessments to identify the broader societal value of mitigation are a promising area for future research.

Unfortunately, the greatest amount of attention to mitigation—as well as the largest amount of federal financial assistance—occurs only *after* a disaster has struck and a community has received a presidential declaration. Consequently, mitigation receives more attention in the postdisaster setting than it does before a disaster.

The important examples of predisaster mitigation are associated with earthquakes and hurricanes. For example, FEMA has assisted the Southern California Earthquake Preparedness Project and the Bay Area Earthquake Preparedness Project. Some counties in Florida, North Carolina, and South Carolina have received FEMA assistance to undertake in-depth hurricane vulnerability analyses and evacuation planning. FEMA also contributed to the development of a computer-based system called HURRIVAC, which was used in September 1989 to identify the low-lying areas likely to be affected by Hurricane Hugo, enabling the governor of South Carolina to order those areas evacuated.

Obstacles to mitigation

Hazard mitigation measures are essential to protect the public against a recurrence of the disaster that has just occurred. However, when executed effectively, hazard mitigation usually entails a complex, often not well understood set of activities. Because mitigation is hard to achieve, dealing with it realistically and practically is especially important. Some of the messy realities of implementing mitigation are listed below.

Complexity A good hazard mitigation program dealing with only a single hazard, such as riverine floods, may involve sophisticated long-range planning, a mix of structural and nonstructural measures, and extensive staging or scheduling. Multihazard analysis and multihazard mitigation planning are even more complex than single-hazard efforts. For these reasons, capable personnel with backgrounds in planning are essential to the recovery and mitigation effort.

Long lead time Local public leaders and managers should be aware that recovery may take many years. In addition, some structural mitigation measures, such as dams, dikes, and levees, may take many years or even decades to complete. Thus, effective mitigation after a disaster requires the foresight to envision how a community or a region will look several years ahead.

Resistance to mitigation Mitigation at the local level is complicated by the variety of motivating and inhibiting factors at work at any given time in a community, region, or state. Research reveals that even communities that have experienced frequent disasters do not necessarily give more attention to mitigation or implement such measures more expeditiously or effectively than communities with only rare disaster occurrences.[26] In the wake of a disaster, many competing forces influence the pattern and speed of recovery and reconstruction. Usually, citizens are impatient to rebuild their homes and businesses. Development and real estate interests are often the source of additional pressures to rebuild as quickly as possible, with little or no attention to mitigation. Public officials and civic leaders will have to be persistent in keeping key local actors aware of the need to mitigate against future disasters.

Local government capacity and will   Research by Claire B. Rubin and Daniel Barbee has identified several key variables affecting local strategic choices for recovery (including attention to mitigation). As discussed earlier, the key determinants are local leadership, ability to act, and knowing what to do. The interaction among these determinants has led to various recovery and mitigation outcomes.[27]

In a later report on their recovery research, Rubin, Saperstein, and Barbee describe the leadership, administrative capabilities, vision, and intergovernmental support required to achieve a successful recovery from disaster:

Guiding recovery on the basis of a future image of the community rather than simply of near-term expediency appears to produce better long-term results. That it also appears to be politically costly for local leaders suggests that local leaders need help in guiding community recovery and mitigation, and a careful examination of state and federal policies and programs is warranted in order to be sure they help, not hinder, effective local recovery.[28]

Mankato, Minnesota, is an example of a community that prepared to take action. After experiencing a 1965 Minnesota River flood that caused millions of dollars in property damage, the citizens of Mankato decided to take a new, activist approach to the city's problems. Although Mankato had experienced floods before, none had been as damaging as the 1965 flood. The citizens began to take a strong interest in the scope and capacity of their local government. They hired professional management, aggressively sought out resources, and rebuilt in an attractive and functional way—including taking steps to mitigate future flood hazards.[29]

Conclusion

This chapter has highlighted the importance of the recovery period and the need to anticipate the demands that recovery will probably create. The experiences of communities stricken by disaster provide a valuable, realistic view of the recovery period. Lessons learned by such communities can be of great use to those yet to undergo a major disaster. Although purely local circumstances influence the speed and effectiveness of recovery, a number of functions and issues are common to nearly all recovering communities.

Other levels of government as well as many voluntary organizations are prepared to provide financial and other assistance to localities affected by disaster. Local public managers must be familiar with their own resources and with other sources of assistance; they must know, as well, how to take effective advantage of outside resources.

Finally, public managers must be prepared to help the *people* of a community recover—victims and their families, emergency workers, and volunteers. Residents of a community stricken by disaster may experience extreme stress in the subsequent weeks and months. Local officials striving to restore utilities, repair roads, and plan for future development must not lose sight of the less visible damage wreaked by disaster.

1   Claire B. Rubin, "The Community Recovery Process in the United States after a Major Natural Disaster," *International Journal of Mass Emergencies and Disasters* 3, no. 2 (August 1985): 9–28.

2   J. Eugene Haas, Robert W. Kates, and Martyn J. Bowden, *Reconstruction following Disaster* (Cambridge: MIT Press, 1977); H. Paul Friesema et al., *Aftermath: Communities after Natural Disasters* (Beverly Hills, CA: Sage Publications, 1979); James D. Wright, Peter H. Rossi, Sonia Wright, and Eleanor Weber-Burdin, *After the Clean-up: Long-Range Effects of Natural Disasters* (Beverly Hills, CA: Sage Publications, 1979).

3   Haas et al., *Reconstruction*, xxvi.

4   Robert C. Bolin, *Long-Term Family Recovery from Disaster* (Boulder: Institute of Behavioral Science, University of Colorado, monograph no. 36, 1982); Anthony M. Yezer and Claire B. Rubin, "The Local Economic Effects of Natural Disasters" (Boulder: Natural Hazards Research Center, University of Colorado, working paper no. 61, 1988).

5   Jean Garrison, in the preface to *Disaster Work and Mental Health: Prevention and Control of Stress among Workers*, ed. Don M. Hartsough and Diane G. Myers (Rockville, MD: Center for Mental Health Studies of Emergencies, National Institute of Mental Health, 1985), iv.

6   Hartsough and Myers, eds., *Disaster Work and Mental Health*, iii.18.

7   Don M. Hartsough, "Stress and Mental Health Interventions in Three Major Disasters," in *Disaster Work and Mental Health*, 5, 13, and 20.

8   Discussion of institutional and political contexts of the stress experienced by emergency workers can be found in Thomas Drabek, "Institutional and Political Contexts," and William J. Staehle, "Discussion," both in NIMH/CMHSE, *Role Stressors and Supports for Emergency Workers*, proceedings from a 1984 workshop sponsored by NIMH and FEMA (Rockville, MD: Center for Mental Health Studies of Emergencies, National Institute of Mental Health, 1985).

9   Christine Dunning, "Intervention Strategies for Emergency Workers," in Mary Lystad, ed., *Mental Health Response to Mass Emergencies* (New York: Brunner/Mazel, 1988), 287.

10   Ibid., 304. For further information on the psychological aftermath of disasters, refer to the current publication list of the Natural Hazards Center at the University of Colorado. See also Lystad, ed., *Mental Health Response*; and Thomas E. Drabek, *Human System Responses to Disaster: An Inventory of Sociological Findings* (New York: Springer-Verlag, 1986).

11   Claire B. Rubin with Martin D. Saperstein and Daniel G. Barbee, *Community Recovery from a Major Natural Disaster* (Boulder: Program on Environment and Behavior, University of Colorado, monograph no. 41, 1985).

12   Rubin, "Community Recovery Process," 11–12.

13   Claire B. Rubin and Roy S. Popkin, forthcoming report.

14   Rubin, Saperstein, and Barbee, *Community Recovery*, 12.

15   The description that follows is based on case studies of Marin and Santa Cruz counties in Rubin, Saperstein, and Barbee, *Community Recovery*.

16   A declaration of "emergency" requires federal assistance to avert or lessen the danger of an impending catastrophe; a declaration of "disaster" requires federal assistance after the catastrophe has occurred.

17   For detailed information on available assistance, see FEMA, *A Guide to Federal Aid in Disasters*, DAP 19 (Washington, DC: FEMA, March 1987); and FEMA, *Digest of Federal Disaster Assistance Programs* (Washington, DC: FEMA, 1989).

18   Rubin, Saperstein, and Barbee, *Community Recovery*, 20.

19   Ibid., 18–20.

20   See Haas et al., *Reconstruction following Disaster*; and Rubin, Saperstein, and Barbee, *Community Recovery*.

21   American Red Cross, *Disaster Services Regulations and Procedures*, ARC 3001 (Washington, DC: American National Red Cross, January 1982).

22   Ibid.

23   American Red Cross, *Disaster Services Regulations and Procedures*, Disaster Operations Management, ARC 3015 (Washington, DC: American National Red Cross, November 1984).

24   American Red Cross, *Disaster Services Regulations* (1982).

25   William Petak, "Emergency Management: A Challenge for Public Administration," *Public Administration Review* 45 (January 1985), 3–6.

26   Rubin, Saperstein, and Barbee, *Community Recovery*, 22–23.

27   Claire B. Rubin and Daniel G. Barbee, "Disaster Recovery and Hazard Mitigation: Bridging the Intergovernmental Gap," *Public Administration Review* 45 (January 1985): 61.

28   Rubin, Saperstein, and Barbee, *Community Recovery*, 43.

29   The example of Mankato, Minnesota, is based on Nancy Girouard, "Creative Management in a Small City," *Public Management* (October 1978): 2–4; and on Claire B. Rubin's 1989 telephone interview of William Bassett, city manager of Mankato at the time Girouard's article was written.

Part three:
Daily operations
and
legal issues

10 Day-to-day management

The goal of emergency management is to coordinate a unified response to a crisis: to prevent or minimize threat when possible; to respond quickly and effectively when prevention is not possible; and to help restore normalcy as quickly as possible. The emergency manager need not be able to perform all the tasks required in a given situation, but he or she must be able to identify needs that may arise and ways of meeting them.

This chapter looks at emergency management from the perspective of the local emergency manager's day-to-day concerns. As other chapters have noted, emergency management agencies differ widely in size, structure, and placement within the local government. But all emergency management offices must undertake certain basic functions—and to do so, they must have certain systems in place. Some of these systems are for the kinds of internal managment required of *any* agency of local government; for example, all local government departments have planning and administrative functions. Other internal systems pertain specifically to emergency management: for example, emergency management agencies undertake exercises, maintain resource inventories, oversee operations for routine emergencies, and implement response to low-probability, high-risk hazards (such as 100-year floods). In this chapter, the term *microsystems* will be used to refer to all systems that facilitate the day-to-day internal management of emergency services.

Cooperative external relationships go hand-in-hand with good internal management to enable an emergency management program to operate effectively. For example, the emergency planning process must take account of the risk management policies of the local government. Similarly, it is through public policy that the local government expresses its commitment—including its financial commitment—to public safety. These are just two examples of systems outside the official bounds of the emergency management program that nevertheless have a significant influence on emergency operations. Although these *macrosystems*, as they will be referred to in this chapter, are outside the emergency manager's control, it is in his or her interest to establish cooperative and understanding relationships with them and to integrate their policies and needs into emergency planning efforts. Taken together, these macrosystems form the context within which the emergency management program must work.

The microsystems

One way of looking at the microsystems of an emergency management department is to ask what capabilities the department must have in order to function. First and foremost, an emergency management department needs what every other local government department needs: a mission, staff to implement the mission, and funds to support the mission. The second prerequisite for emergency management is *information*; reliable, accurate resource lists are fundamental to any emergency management program. Third, the emergency management department must be able to *retrieve and manipulate* information.

Daily operations, personnel, and budget

An emergency management department is defined by its mission. This section discusses how the mission translates into daily operations. In other words, what do emergency managers and their staffs *do*—particularly when they are not in the midst of a disaster?

Of the four phases of emergency management, the immediate response phase usually receives the most media attention and is therefore most familiar to the public. But those within the field know that mitigation, preparedness, and recovery make significant demands on an emergency manager's time and attention and are in no way less important than response. Moreover, every emergency manager has the routine responsibilities involved in running a local government department, such as handling personnel and budgeting. This section also examines personnel and budget considerations, with an emphasis on the special problems that can arise in staffing and funding emergency management programs.

Daily operations The accompanying sidebar lists an emergency manager's duties during nonemergency periods. Viewed from a broad perspective, the activities cover a range of needs in the areas of mitigation, preparedness, and recovery. To bring such daily operations into clearer focus, let's take as an example an emergency manager in a south central state subject to frequent tornadic storms.

For this manager, enforcing building codes and advocating the adoption of mobile home tie-down regulations are priorities in the area of mitigation. Preparedness activities include activating storm spotting, priming warning systems, and working closely with the local office of the National Weather Service to track storms and monitor their effects. Response activities include working with public safety staff to gather damage reports and providing the media, the public, and local officials with current and accurate information. In the recovery phase, the emergency manager works with support agencies to help individual citizens; with public works agencies to undertake debris removal, reconstruction, and damage assessment; and with elected officials to undertake further mitigation efforts.

Several of the nonemergency responsibilities outlined in the sidebar merit special mention. For example, developing a public education program may be an uphill battle during nonemergency periods, but such a program is essential to a viable emergency management program. Testing and exercising, two other principal duties enumerated in the sidebar, are the second- and third-best ways to determine the effectiveness of an emergency plan—the most effective being an actual disaster. Testing and exercising may be mandated by local ordinances or by state or federal regulation. State or federal regulation most often comes into play when a jurisdiction receives funding from other governmental sources, such as FEMA's Emergency Management Assistance program.

In addition to the tasks enumerated in the sidebar, two other responsibilities that lie outside the response phase require significant investments of time and energy on the part of the emergency manager and staff.

Although visibility may not be a federally prescribed duty, failure to achieve it can seriously undermine other well-intentioned efforts. Effectiveness and credibility are directly related to the level of participation and interest that emergency managers and their staff are *observed* demonstrating; in the event of a disaster, the manager who has attended meetings of department heads, made a point of communicating with staff throughout the local government, and kept in touch with the community will fare best.[1]

An emergency manager who wants to know the level of public safety awareness in the community or the resources that are available must go into the community.

Town meetings and professional conferences are opportunities to acquaint residents and colleagues with particular incidents and problems and to learn about problems, resources, and developments outside one's own office. Speaking to and visiting with volunteer and service groups gives emergency managers additional opportunities for public education and provides a chance to learn about residents' concerns.

Another important task of the emergency manager involves civil defense. Much of the literature on emergency management relates to the integrated emergency management system (IEMS), all-hazard planning, and general preparedness. Although the sidebar does not refer to preparedness for nuclear and conventional attack, any federal funding for local emergency management is contingent on the emergency manager's ability to demonstrate that civil defense enjoys high priority. National Security Decision Directive Number 259 states that the federal civil defense program will continue to support all-hazard integrated emergency management at state and local levels to the extent that this

---

Local emergency management duties during nonemergency periods

Identify and analyze the effects of hazards that threaten the jurisdiction

Work closely on a cooperative basis with local government departments and community organizations to develop emergency management plans and capabilities

Inventory personnel and material resources from governmental and private sector sources that would be available in an emergency

Assist in the establishment of mutual aid or cooperative assistance agreements to provide needed services, equipment, or other resources in the event of an emergency

Coordinate with industry to develop industrial emergency plans and capabilities in support of local government plans

Identify resource deficiencies and work with appropriate officials on measures to correct them

Work with local officials to develop a hazard mitigation program to eliminate or reduce potential hazards

Develop a public education program

Develop an emergency operations center (EOC) as a site from which key officials can direct operations during an emergency

Establish an emergency public information system

Develop and maintain emergency communications systems

Establish a system to alert key public officials and warn the public in the event of an emergency

Develop continuity of government procedures and systems

Establish and maintain a shelter and reception and care system

Develop a training program for emergency response personnel

Develop a program of tests and exercises

Keep the chief executive of the jurisdiction fully informed on emergency management activities

Prepare, submit, and justify the annual emergency management budget

Secure technical and financial assistance available through state and federal programs

Source: Adapted from Federal Emergency Management Agency, *Objectives for Local Emergency Management* (Washington, DC: U.S. Government Printing Office, July 1984), II–7.

is consistent with and contributes to preparedness of the nation in the event of an attack.[2]

Personnel   The personnel selected and trained to support the emergency manager range from full-time salaried staff (as in large urban areas) to part-time assignments for local government employees (which might be the case in mid-sized cities) to trained volunteers (as is true in many small communities). Table 10–1 shows the federally recommended staffing levels for jurisdictions of various sizes.[3] These staffing levels are guidelines—not mandates—and are subject to a host of considerations, not the least of which is budget. A jurisdiction with a population of 25,000–100,000 may not have the budgetary capacity to fund and support two to three staff persons. A jurisdiction that is not threatened by many hazards will not feel the public pressure for emergency preparedness that a jurisdiction in a high-risk area will feel. Moreover, an emergency manager who does not receive federal assistance may be less likely to invest personnel and resources in mitigation and preparedness than an emergency manager who must meet federal program requirements to receive funding.

FEMA also recommends that for jurisdictions greater than 25,000, the emergency manager be full-time. Criteria for the selection of the emergency manager include experience in administration, organization, planning, budgeting, and coordination; skills in dealing with people; and experience in emergency management activities.[4]

An issue in the selection of the emergency manager and staff is the fact that the emergency management department reflects its bureaucratic situation. In many areas, for example, emergency management is part of the local public safety department (police or fire) and is often headed by a uniformed public safety officer. This arrangement has a number of benefits: resources are more numerous and personnel more available for emergency purposes. In addition, emergency operations are based on routine public safety functions. Responses to incidents involving mass casualties, for example, are usually a primary responsibility of a fire department, which is where emergency medical services are also often housed.

However, being a member of a certain department can severely limit the emergency manager. In the wake of a disaster, a number of tasks must be accomplished that require time, coordination, and some degree of specialized knowledge. Unless the individual doing double duty as a public safety official and emergency manager has had the time and energy to acquire a general knowledge of emergency management in addition to the specific skills and training required within the department, the coordination function of emergency management is lost. As the accompanying sidebar shows, the fire chief/emergency management coordinator of Hutchins, Texas, was called on to serve in both roles simultaneously—and his was not an enviable position.

Many states, such as Texas, require their political subdivisions to participate in emergency programs.[5] Meeting the statutory requirement by assigning emergency management duties to a public safety employee may respond to the letter of the regulation but fails to respond to its spirit.

When resources permit, the emergency management function is independent or is an arm of the local governing body (for example, an extension of the mayor's office or a division of the city manager's office). Either arrangement solves some of the problems just described by providing the emergency manager with a broader scope of interests and activity. Attending meetings with planning and response experts outside one's own agency or department is crucial to the resource inventory, the emergency manager's most critical tool. Work with voluntary and social agencies gives the emergency manager a better grasp of the needs and strengths of the community. Ready access to

Table 10–1 Local
emergency program
management staffing.

Population	Workyears
Over 1,000,000	6–20
250,000 to 1,000,000	4–8
100,000 to 250,000	3–5
25,000 to 100,000	2–3
Under 25,000	½–2

Note: These workyear estimates must be augmented by
local assessment of the hazardous conditions of the
jurisdiction. The vulnerability of the population,
emergency management tasks necessary for full
preparedness, and other local conditions must guide
staffing decisions.

When the emergency manager wears two hats In September 1985, in the small city of Hutchins, Texas, a multiple-alarm fire occurred at a plant that manufactured kitchen countertops. Hutchins's fire chief also served as its emergency manager. *During* the incident, the fire chief (who was also the only paid fire fighter for the city) was responsible for:

Directing fire suppression activities of his arriving volunteer force

Overseeing protection of his fire fighters in light of the hazardous materials involved in the fire

Serving as liaison with the other fire departments responding under mutual aid agreements

Working with federal environmental officials to mitigate groundwater and soil contamination caused by runoff from fire suppression activities.

Concurrently, as the city's emergency management coordinator, the fire chief was also responsible for:

Working with police from a neighboring city and with the county sheriff's office to close roadway access to the area

Ordering and overseeing the evacuation and relocation of nearby elementary school students

Responding to media requests for access to the scene and information about activities

Keeping the city's leadership informed of the status of operations.

After the emergency phase, the fire chief would be:

Overseeing salvage and overhaul of the burned structure

Conducting the investigation to determine the cause of the fire and preparing his department's report for the facility's insurer

Remaining available to fight other fires, as necessary

Overseeing ongoing training of his volunteers in fire suppression, emergency medical care, and hazardous materials incident response

Responding to the elected leadership on questions of budget, policy, and fire service delivery, and to citizen questions and complaints.

As emergency management coordinator, the fire chief would also be responsible for:

Working with the city's schools and businesses on preparedness efforts and evacuation planning

Serving as the city's point of contact for weather emergency planning and response

Working with volunteer groups that provide disaster relief to citizens

Preparing assorted emergency plans as required by county, state, or local ordinance.

elected officials (who will ultimately be held responsible by the citizenry) provides for more open communication and greater understanding of the public's needs and perceptions.

But either arrangement also has disadvantages. If the emergency management office is an independent department, the emergency manager may focus on the administrative aspects of the job to the neglect of operational aspects. This will be a problem because, if an elected or appointed official is to explain to the public what actions are being taken at a disaster site and why, he or she must have an emergency manager who knows. Theories, statistics, probabilities, and plans will not have a fraction of the public impact of a ten-second television appearance. An emergency manager with little knowledge of response operations and limited public contact may find that he or she also has little credibility as a coordinator.

Perhaps the biggest problem for an independent emergency management office is budgetary vulnerability. When local officials look for ways to cut expenses, they look hardest at, and cut deepest into, what may be perceived by the public as nonessential services—which can be loosely defined here as services other than police, fire, and sanitation collection. Having a police officer or fire fighter assume emergency management functions (with no pay increase) seems to be a popular solution to the problem of a tight budget and may even be a workable one—until a situation like the one in Hutchins, Texas, occurs.

When emergency management is an arm of the local governing body, competition for funds may be less fierce, but the political battles will be more formidable.

Clearly, emergency management is not a responsibility easily assumed by one person or half a person, although in many small jurisdictions economics dictates that this be the case. When resources permit, emergency management offices should have enough staff so that emergency operations can be carried out without severely disrupting either ongoing management activities or the health of the emergency manager or staff. Once the emergency phase of a disaster has passed, other aspects of the emergency management program require ongoing attention and effort: communications, radiological protection, shelter planning, training, resource development, public information, and administration.

Budget Because emergency management offices are part of local government, the budget processes in emergency management are essentially the same as they are for the parent organization. In Dallas County, Texas, for example, the county emergency manager submits his or her own budget to the county's Court of Commissioners. In addition, each of the twenty-four cities within the county submits its own budget to its own city council. In Laurence County, Tennessee, the emergency management functions are housed in the emergency management department of the city of Laurenceburg, which informally provides emergency management services to the county. The city prepares a departmental budget and submits it to the mayor in competition with all other city departments. Although the emergency management department functions as a city and county organization, there is no formal reimbursement from the county. Instead, the county provides in-kind support, such as computer programming assistance. Although this informal system works in Laurence County, most joint operation programs have a formal agreement for reimbursement. In Atlanta, Georgia, the emergency management bureau is separate from both city and county. The bureau submits two budgets—one to the city (for 66 percent of its expenses) and one to Fulton County (for 33 percent of its expenses).

Justifying the need for and expenditure of public monies is no small task, and securing financial resources over and above those granted by local taxpayers is a formidable problem. When an office must justify requests to taxpayers (through their representatives), to the internal bureaucracy (competing departments), to the state (as regulators), and to the federal government (as grantors), it's a wonder that the emergency management program—mitigation, preparedness, response, and recovery—gets any attention at all. Even more daunting is the fact that the emergency management program must be maintained when disasters are *not* occurring if it is to be up and running when disasters *do* occur.

Marketing an emergency management program to elected officials and to the public is tough. Preparedness is widely endorsed in theory, but funding preparedness can be difficult when needs exceed dollars—which is a common condition in local government. Federal funding is one way to supplement the local funding available for emergency management programs, specifically through the Emergency Management Assistance (EMA) funding program. Whereas other federal programs make monies available to partially reimburse local governments for expenses incurred in declared disasters, EMA funds are available in the absence of a declared disaster or actual emergency. When local budgets are tight, obtaining EMA funds can help to "sell" emergency management by showing that funds for the emergency management program are available from outside the jurisdiction that oversees, and directly benefits from, the program.

EMA "provides matching funds for salaries, travel, and administrative expenses to conduct emergency planning and develop operational capabilities," usually up to 50 percent of eligible personnel and administrative costs.[6] Because this grant program is administered by the states, any jurisdiction seeking application guidance should contact its state emergency management office. EMA funds are limited, so there is no guarantee that a local government's first application will be approved. However, it is useful to continue to apply because recipient jurisdictions do drop out of the program.

Local budget processes need not be changed to qualify for EMA monies, as Dallas, Laurenceburg, and Atlanta illustrate. In Dallas, EMA funds are requested by and granted to the city of Dallas and Dallas County independently of each other. In Laurenceburg, EMA funds are requested by and granted to the city. And in Atlanta, the emergency management bureau requests and is granted EMA funds, with which it then reimburses the city and the county: 66 percent to the city of Atlanta and 33 percent to Fulton County. A jurisdiction applying for EMA funds should, however, develop a system to collect supporting data and report it in a format that is acceptable to the state and to FEMA. (State emergency management offices are empowered to help local jurisdictions set up such a system.)

Another approach to marketing an emergency management program and enhancing resource capabilities is to establish a cooperative agreement with the private sector. The city of Pampa, Texas, has entered into just such an agreement. School district, city, county, and state officials worked with representatives of the Hoescht-Celanese Chemical Company to make a joint effort to respond to both the letter and the spirit of SARA Title III. Because of this joint effort, both the chemical industry in Pampa and the government tried to ensure compliance with federal regulations; others in the chemical industry were induced to seek guidance in compliance efforts; and the city's fire department received industrial funding to enhance its capability to respond to chemical emergencies.[7]

Although most jurisdictions have emergency reserve funds to reimburse expenses incurred in disasters, each community establishes its own set of criteria for using these funds. Such funds are generally tightly regulated and are not available for day-to-day operations or even for small emergencies. When and if federal disaster declarations are received for damage to public property, the federal funds may be used to reimburse the emergency reserve fund.

Resource lists: Keeping the planning process current

Like daily operations, personnel, and budgeting, resource lists are one of the crucial "microsystems" on which the emergency management program depends. Determining what resources a community has—or does not have—with which to respond to a disaster is the most critical part of hazard analysis. As previous chapters have made clear, hazard analysis requires systematic identification of all potential natural and technological threats to which a community could be subject, and one of the principal end products of the analysis is a list of local and external resources and information about how to access them. For example, if the community has chainsaw crews, portable generators, or stockpiles of sand, an emergency manager needs to be able to reach the people who can authorize use of the personnel, equipment, or supplies to implement relief activities.

The resource list should have information on how to obtain emergency assistance on a twenty-four-hour basis: that means office phone numbers, home numbers, pager numbers, cellular phone numbers, and the identification numbers of persons who are accessible only by radio. An unpublished phone number

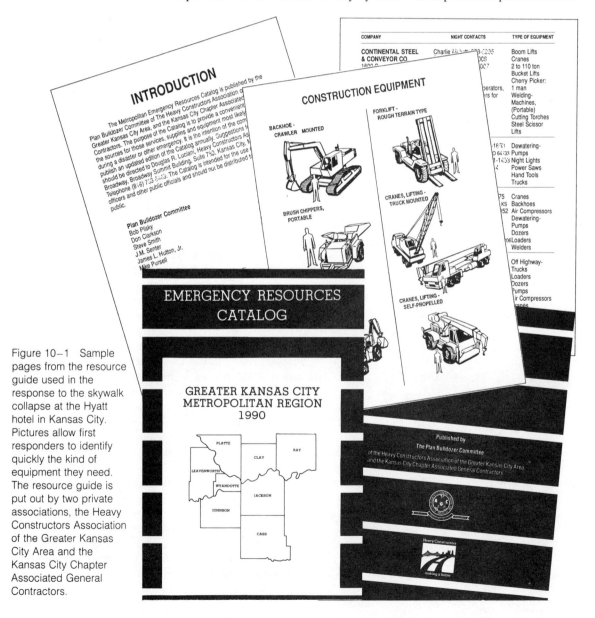

Figure 10–1 Sample pages from the resource guide used in the response to the skywalk collapse at the Hyatt hotel in Kansas City. Pictures allow first responders to identify quickly the kind of equipment they need. The resource guide is put out by two private associations, the Heavy Constructors Association of the Greater Kansas City Area and the Kansas City Chapter Associated General Contractors.

for police, fire, or weather information will enable an emergency manager to obtain—or give—critical information when normal communication channels are overloaded.

Building a list of available resources is quite a job, but it's a small one compared with the task of identifying and securing the resources that the local community does *not* have. To obtain services outside the local jurisdiction, the emergency manager or staff must identify providers, establish twenty-four-hour contacts, negotiate price agreements, and establish payment procedures. Redundancy must be built into external resource lists: a single provider may lack the capacity to provide the necessary volume of goods or services; may be unable to respond to more than one emergency at a time; or may not be in business when called upon.

Resource lists, whether software or manual, are far and away the most important and useful information systems that emergency managers have at their disposal. The lists themselves may be keyed to location, vulnerability (according to incident or population type), or provider capacity. Because levels of capacity rise and fall continually, resource lists are out-of-date virtually the moment they are printed. Businesses change staff, locations, and phone numbers, and services may be added or discontinued—but only rarely are such changes brought to the attention of the emergency manager. Noting changes as they are discovered is one way to keep lists current, but the information should be verified regularly,

Figure 10–2   Heavy equipment from the private sector being used in the aftermath of the Hyatt disaster.

frequently, and thoroughly. Although contacting every resource is time-consuming and may be costly, it's a vitally important activity that pays for itself when disaster strikes.

In addition to building redundancy into the lists and diligently verifying the currency of entries, another way of testing the reliability of resource lists is to hold frequent exercises and regularly critique response effectiveness in actual disasters. One of the best ways of monitoring changes in resource types and capacities is to conduct such critiques. Many jurisdictions routinely critique their own responses to major incidents, noting deficiencies and changes in resources, revising lists as necessary, and rewriting plans to reflect the changes.

Information and management systems

The information systems, management systems, and other software and manual programs that are discussed here are not in themselves "microsystems," but they *are* valuable tools for dealing with internal management needs. They are elements of emergency management that are incorporated into the office's standard operating procedures.

Information systems may be either software packages that are purchased or software or manual packages that are developed. Unlike management systems, information systems are designed to respond to the problems of a disaster in its acute stages, especially response and the early stages of recovery. Information systems provide emergency personnel with the best information available when a situation is, or threatens to become, critical. An example of an information system is an automatic sensor system that triggers pumping operations in actual or potential flooding situations. Sensor alarms alert personnel to the developing situation and tell them what problem is occurring, where, how serious it is or may become, what areas may need to be evacuated, and what routes would be open if the problem became acute.

A management system, in contrast, is most useful when situations are not critical. In the example of flooding given above, a management system would

---

Seismicity data and services The National Geophysical Data Center (NGDC) Earthquake Data Base holds information on more than 500,000 earthquakes, known or suspected explosions, coal bumps, rockbursts, quarry blasts, and other earth disturbances recorded worldwide for the period 2100 B.C. to 1987. It includes (where available) date and origin time of the event, location, depth, magnitude, maximum intensity, and related earthquake phenomena (including faulting, tsunamis, volcanism, and resulting casualties and property damage). *Summary of Earthquake Data Base*, a publication available free from NGDC, describes the data base in detail.

The Earthquake Data Base was formed from data furnished by the U.S.

Geological Survey (in earlier years by the U.S. Coast and Geodetic Survey and the National Oceanic and Atmospheric Administration), the California Institute of Technology (Pasadena), the University of California (Berkeley), the California Division of Mines and Geology (Sacramento), the Canadian Earth Physics Branch, the Institute of Physics of the Earth of the USSR, the Earthquake Research Institute of Japan, and about 20 other worldwide sources. NGDC and the World Data Center A for Solid Earth Geophysics provide a variety of data outputs from this extensive data base to the scientific and engineering communities.

Source: National Geophysical Data Center, NOAA, Boulder, CO.

be most useful in designing the responses that support personnel would under-take—responses such as activating the transportation resources that might be needed in an evacuation, notifying drivers, designating pick-up or staging areas to which vehicles would report, and identifying shelter facilities and capacities. Management systems are most often used in the preparation, mitigation, and late recovery phases of an emergency management program.

Information systems Prepared information systems can be extremely useful in organizing an emergency management program and are very popular. A primary reason for their popularity is that the emergency manager may not have enough time, resources, knowledge, or energy to scrutinize, weigh, and select the best alternative for action.

Computerized systems do, of course, also present problems. They require computer hardware. They also require that users know, or be free to learn, how to operate them. For a small jurisdiction, hardware and extra personnel or time may be difficult to obtain. In large jurisdictions, the problems do not usually involve hardware and personnel but arise simply from the magnitude of the task: obtaining, entering, and keeping current an enormous amount of data. In any case, information systems have to be tailored to fit the needs and capacities of each jurisdiction.

An example of an information system with direct benefits to the consumer as well as to the professional community for which it was designed is the enhanced 911 telephone system used in many parts of the country to summon emergency assistance. It displays on a computer screen the address and tele-phone number from which the call is being made. The product makes it possible for someone to request assistance without speaking, which is espe-cially important for the very young, the speech impaired, and the injured. By reducing confusion about the location of an incident, the system improves response capability. In addition, it provides access to sources of information other than the individual(s) or property immediately threatened, for example, when a request for assistance comes from a neighbor, passerby, or other uninvolved witness.

Other information systems that are useful and widely available address chemical emergencies. Some of these programs were created by public-sector agencies involved with the chemical industry, and others originated in the private sector. Volume II of the U.S. Coast Guard's *Chemical Hazard Response Information System (CHRIS)* manual provides material safety data sheets (MSDSs) on more than 2,000 substances for emergencies "that occur during the water transport of hazardous chemicals." *CHRIS* is available both in hard copy and on IBM-compatible software (see Figure 10–3).[8] The Association of American Railroads provides similar information (in hard copy and on software) on an estimated 3,900 substances regulated by the U.S. Department of Transportation and often carried by rail.[9]

In the private sector, the Chemical Manufacturers Association (CMA) maintains a variety of programs to help emergency responders not only iden-tify hazardous substances at the site of an incident but also contact the owners of spilled substances for off-site and on-site assistance. Off-site assistance may involve providing local health officials with information on potential envi-ronmental impact and on probable health effects. On-site assistance might mean company officials visiting the scene of an incident and advising emer-gency personnel about fire suppression tactics and protective measures.

Four of CMA's services merit special mention: CHEMTREC (Chemical Transportation Emergency Center), HIT (Hazard Information Transmission), the MSDS Library, and CRC (Chemical Referral Center). Through CHEM-TREC, twenty-four-hour assistance is available to emergency responders through an 800 telephone number.[10] Operators can access a computer data bank that

Hazardous materials information exchange (HMIX) The HMIX is a hazardous material information clearinghouse and exchange system designed to provide federal, state, local, and private-sector organizations with a means of sharing valuable and timely information about the prevention of, preparation for, and mitigation of hazardous materials emergencies. The HMIX serves as a central source of reliable information to prepare for potentially dangerous occurrences. It is not intended, however, to provide assistance during an actual emergency.

How the system works Information is available in two ways:

1. Through an electronic bulletin board. If you have a personal computer, a modem (300, 1200, or 2400 baud), and any communication software (set at no parity, 8 data bits and 1 stop), you can access the bulletin board by dialing commercial (708) 972-3275 or toll free 1-800-874-2884. This service is free; the caller pays only for long-distance phone charges. A user is allotted 60 minutes of access time per day, which can be used at one time or through a series of calls. The bulletin board is available twenty-four hours a day, seven days a week.
2. Through a toll-free telephone call. If you have no computer capability or need help using the electronic bulletin board, dial toll free 1-800-PLANFOR (752-6367). Illinois residents dial 1-800-367-9592. An information systems technician is available to provide assistance Monday through Friday, from 8:30 a.m. to 4:30 p.m. central time.

Bulletin board features The bulletin board is completely user friendly! That is, you always see a list of acceptable commands and a brief explanation of each. The bulletin board includes a "bulletin listing" that provides up-to-date items of immediate interest (e.g., current rulemaking action) and seven "information conferences" that contain information on the following topics:

1. Federal training courses
2. Public- and private-sector hazmat information
3. Calendar of conferences
4. Instructional material and literature listing
5. Toll-free (800) numbers and on-line data bases
6. Laws and regulations
7. Contacts
8. Agency-specific communication conferences: Department of Transportation and the Federal Emergency Management Agency.

Source: Federal Emergency Management Agency, Technological Hazards Division, and Department of Transportation, Research and Special Programs Administration.

holds information on more than six hundred thousand chemicals and chemical products. The HIT system—for responders whose emergency departments can afford mobile telephones, computer terminals, and printers in the field—transmits hard-copy data on substances directly to on-site personnel (see Figure 10–4).[11] The MSDS Library holds manufacturers' material safety data sheets and is accessible to emergency responders via facsimile equipment. CRC is a nonemergency service for the public; like CHEMTREC, it is accessed through an 800 telephone number.[12] It provides health and safety information about chemicals and chemical products by directing the caller to the spokesperson for the company that manufactures the substance in question or, if regulatory questions are involved, to the appropriate governmental agency.

Management systems A number of management software systems deal with the siting of local facilities that manufacture, store, or transport hazardous chemicals; the systems also provide plume modeling to identify populations potentially threatened by airborne toxics. From a managerial perspective, such programs are excellent tools for preparing for potential threats. From an operational perspective, however, the best source of information on which to rely when coordinating relief during an actual emergency is information from direct service providers—the first responders.

Software programs such as the Emergency Information System are useful during the planning process and during recovery. They teach the user what information to secure, how to organize it, and how to retrieve data. During the planning process, these programs can provide valuable guidelines for response capabilities and can suggest issues that officials may not have con-

Figure 10–3 Example of a material safety data sheet from the U.S. Coast Guard's *Chemical Hazard Response Information System.*

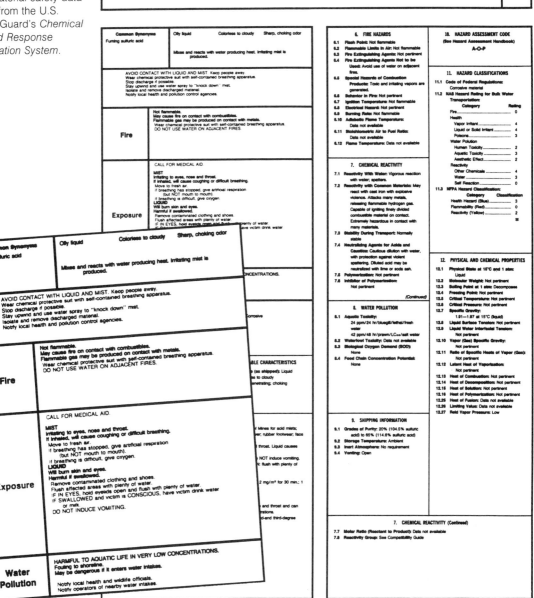

sidered exploring. During recovery, these systems are essential for tracking and sorting large numbers and many types of data and for organizing them into coherent reports.

One of the most widely used management systems, especially in fire service management, is the Incident Command System (ICS), which was developed after fires in southern California went out of control in 1970. ICS consists of procedures for controlling personnel, facilities, equipment, and communications.[13] A subsystem of the National Interagency Incident Management System (NIIMS), ICS was developed through a cooperative effort of agencies on the local, state, and federal levels. Whereas the purpose of the full NIIMS program is "to provide a common system that fire protection agencies can utilize at local, state, and federal levels," ICS was "designed to be used for all kinds of emergencies, and is applicable to both small day-to-day situations as well as very large and complex incidents."

The design requirements for ICS were to:

Provide for operations involving a single agency within a single jurisdiction; multiple agencies within a single jurisdiction; and multiple agencies from multiple jurisdictions

Provide an organizational structure that could be adapted to any emergency or incident to which fire protection agencies would respond

Be applicable and acceptable to users throughout the country

Be easily adaptable to any technology

Be easily expanded in a logical manner

Figure 10–4 Through the Hazard Information Transmission (HIT) system, a service of the Chemical Manufacturers Association, emergency departments that have mobile telephones, computer terminals, and printers in the field can receive direct transmissions of hard-copy data on chemical substances.

```
OLEUM

                              TODAY'S DATE   09/08/86

     INDEX   003330                   LAST UPDATE   08/13/86


     F&A      Colorless to dark brown, fuming oily liquid
     ODOR     Sharp, choking, penetrating
     DOT CL   CORM  Corrosive Material

     W-WATER  Reacts violently

                              F.P.      -            ID #   NA1831
          IMO #  8.0          V.D.   2.8-  .0        ID #   UN1831
          CAS   8014-95-7     B.P.   137- 288
          RTEC  WS5605000     F.L.%    .0-  .0
          RQ    RQ-1000       I.T.      -

     OBSERVATIONS
       Acute inhalation exposure will cause difficult breathing or choking
       and could lead to potentially fatal pulmonary edema.  Contact with
       liquid or fumes will result in severe, painful burns.  *****
       Dangerously reactive with a wide range of materials.

     NATURE OF PRODUCT
       Poisonous, corrosive liquid which may be fatal if inhaled. Violent
       reaction with water. Material reacts with water to form clouds of
       acid vapors. May ignite other combustible materials (wood, paper,
       oil, etc.). Container may rupture violently in heat of fire. Vapors
       extremely irritating and corrosive to skin, eyes and respiratory
       tract. Contact causes severe burns to skin and eyes. Contact of
       material or vapor with eyes may cause blindness. Runoff from fire
       control or dilution water may cause pollution. Reaction with
       combustible materials will cause the release of dense, white fumes.


     IN CASE OF ACCIDENT
       Keep unnecessary people away; isolate hazard area and deny entry.
       Stay upwind; keep out of low areas. Wear self-contained breathing
       apparatus (positive pressure) and chemical protective clothing
       (CPC)(acid suit).  CPC provides little or no thermal protection and
```

Have basic, common elements of organization, terminology, and procedures

Be effective, and be simple enough to ensure low operational maintenance costs.

ICS uses common terms; modular organization; integrated communications; a unified command structure; consolidated action plans; manageable span of control; predesignated incident facilities; and comprehensive resource management.

The value of ICS lies in its potential for broad practical application. Although originally developed for fire suppression, it is gradually being adopted by groups with other emergency responsibilities, and it promises to introduce a degree of certainty into conditions that, by definition, are uncertain. A caveat should be entered here: ICS approaches incident control from the task, tactical, and strategic perspectives of the fire service and appears to assume a large, well-organized, and probably urban fire department. The system may not be appropriate for local governments with small or mid-sized fire departments and may require considerable refitting for nonfire emergency activities. Regardless of the size of the community, the ICS application should be flexible enough to allow for local differences in organization, politics, and needs. ICS should therefore be reviewed for applicability before it is adopted.

The macrosystems

As has been mentioned, emergency management operations take place within a context over which the emergency manager has only limited influence. The four sections that follow highlight several particularly important aspects of that context and provide guidelines for emergency managers on how to work within them.

Risk management

Like emergency management, risk management recognizes that change is continuous and requires ongoing planning and management processes. Risk management is also similar to emergency management in seeking to mitigate the effects of, prepare for, respond to, and recover from disasters. Unlike emergency management, however, risk management is directed inward—toward preserving and protecting the assets and financial health of an institution. Whereas the emergency manager defines a worst-case scenario in terms of lives lost, injuries suffered, and private or business property damaged, a risk manager views a worst case in terms of the largest amount of public property loss. The important distinction to bear in mind is that risk management originated in the field of insurance and seeks to preserve and protect property; emergency management originated in the field of public safety and seeks to preserve and protect people. However, the emergency manager deals daily with the risk management aspect of the field in budget preparation, allocation of internal resources, and the mitigation or, if possible, avoidance of risk. Moreover, the emergency manager and the risk manager have a common interest in mitigating the effects of and facilitating recovery from a disaster.

After a disaster event, collection and documentation of all disaster-related costs is vital, and both the emergency manager and the risk manager are involved. In the event of a large-scale disaster, the emergency manager will be the person charged with obtaining from the private, business, and public sectors the damage information on which any federal disaster declaration will be based. After such a declaration is issued, private citizens and businesses will be able to receive assistance directly from the federal government through FEMA. Uninsured

Components of a damage risk forecasting system   The basic components of a system to model the effects of disaster situations consist of machine-readable data files, applications software (models), a processing system and operating software, and output devices (plotters and printers). Together, these components form the overall system structure. The relationships between them are depicted in Figure A and further briefly described.

Data files   Various kinds of data files can be used in the development of the system data base. The basic determination of data files is influenced by (1) the elements of information which are required for planning purposes, and (2) the availability of information already in machine-readable form (or readily transformable into a machine-readable state within cost and time constraints).

Five basic kinds of files are required for our example of earthquake damage/ risk analysis. It should be noted, however, that there are various ways of describing these kinds of files. In some cases, depending upon existing data file availability, a number of combinations and "cross-overs" could exist.

1. Geophysical files consist of mapped polygons (areas) of known geologic features and conditions. These files provide the basic information necessary to determine the extent and severity of ground motion. Separate files could contain data on groundwater depths, etc.
2. Topographic files generally portray the shape and elevation of the surface terrain. Such physical characteristics will show the location of mountains, valleys, rivers, and can include human-created features (e.g., landfills, reservoirs, land use patterns) which influence the topography.
3. Network files document major arterials, rail lines, and underground power, fuel, and water lines. Just about anything that consists of various links and nodes can be included within these kinds of data files. Grid reference or geolocator systems can also be included as network data.
4. Structural files can be of many varieties and are obtained or developed depending upon the planning need. Typically, these files include data on residential, commercial, and industrial buildings grouped by various occupancy classes; bridges, critical facilities, dams, power generating or storage facilities, sanitation plants, etc.
5. Demographic files describe the location and characteristics of the population at risk. These kinds of files are generally developed initially

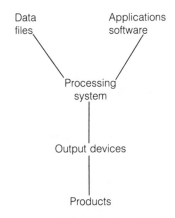

Figure A   System structure.

from census data and can be stored and aggregated in several ways. For earthquake hazard vulnerability modeling, it is convenient to use the census block as the basic demographic unit. To be useful in population damage and risk modeling, the data should be viewed over time as well as space. The night-to-day, home-to-work shift in population location in major urbanized areas can be significant, and modeling only the residential night-time population can produce unrealistic results for planning daytime or at-work scenarios. Data files are depicted in Figure B.

Models Models may be classified and described in several ways. For purposes of this description, "geophysical" and "socioeconomic" models of earthquake hazard vulnerability will be used.

Geophysical The most common geophysical models related to earthquakes are those which provide an estimate of earth shaking intensity and/or estimates of peak acceleration of the earth. These models compute shaking intensity or ground acceleration for a given point location, e.g., the centroid of a census block. They take into account fault location, location and length of rupture, level of energy release (magnitude), seismic wave attenuation through the earth, and effects of local ground conditions. The outputs of these models are generally numeric and can be related to a pre-established scale of observed or measured effects. The most commonly used scales for earth shaking intensity are the Modified Mercalli or the Rossi Forel Scale.

Another geophysical model important in damage vulnerability modeling is the liquefaction model. Developing a liquefaction model requires good information on subsurface geology, soil conditions, and groundwater depth as well as information on shaking intensity and duration. The combination of data within the model can produce results which will determine the potential for the earth to liquefy at any given location. The outputs of a liquefaction model can be descriptors such as "probable," "possible," or "negligible."

Socioeconomic Socioeconomic models attempt to determine the

(*continued on next page*)

Demographic
Structures
Networks
Topographic
Geophysical

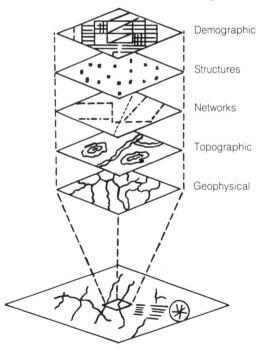

Figure B Basic file structure.

(continued from previous page)

probable effects of geophysical models to topography, structures, networks, and population. The models can be run separately or in combination so that the results of one will automatically become the input to another.

The results of these models can be reported in several ways. In general, information useful to planners could be produced as reports or maps showing number and/or percentage of structures/networks damaged; estimates of actual, or percentage of, dollar value lost; homeless households (shown as temporary or permanent); treatable injured (measured from all causes); and deaths. Depending upon the model used, such data can be aggregated at several levels: census block, census tract, or block groups. Currently there are a number of socioeconomic modeling projects underway, but as yet no acceptable standard has been developed.

The Applied Technology Council under a FEMA contract has recently developed Damage Probability Matrices (DPMs) for a wide variety of

structural classifications. These DPMs could form a standard baseline for use in damage vulnerability modeling. The development of models which will show injuries and deaths from structural and nonstructural causes is progressing slowly, and more research should be done in this area.

The relationship of data files and models is shown in Figure C.

Processing system   The processing system which integrates data file content with model applications software must be capable of handling large volumes of data. The system to be used should have room for both data file expansion and additional models.

Source: Excerpted from Terence Haney, "Application of Computer Technology for Damage/Risk Projections," in Sallie A. Marston, ed., *Terminal Disasters: Computer Applications in Emergency Management* (Boulder: Institute of Behavioral Sciences, University of Colorado), 97–101.

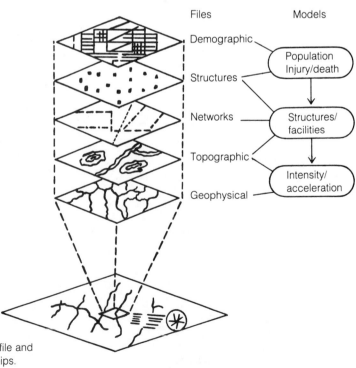

Figure C   Data file and model relationships.

public-sector losses are also eligible for partial federal reimbursement. Risk managers become active in disaster recovery in documenting for the federal government how a jurisdiction's insurance policy did and did not apply to various losses. Some communities use the risk management office to coordinate cost collection for damages.

Public policy

Managing an emergency management program is, in many respects, like managing other services. Like other managers, the emergency manager often serves as a bridge between direct service providers and policymakers, and as such has the opportunity to affect policy. Because the emergency manager does not have direct authority in the policy arena, his or her effectiveness is heavily contingent on context, and liaison activities are extremely important. When things are not going wrong on a grand scale, it may be difficult to catch the attention of the public and the governing body, let alone hold it long enough to affect policy— but more than one elected or appointed official has lost his or her position because of insufficient attention to preparedness activities or an inability to manage in an emergency. A large part of daily operations should therefore be devoted to risk assessment (a standard staff activity is monitoring an incident that has the potential for escalation) and to advocacy (or marketing) of the program.

The city of Pampa, Texas, provides a fine example of establishing and maintaining liaisons, in this case with the private sector. The Chemical Manufacturers Association had initiated the CAER (Community Awareness and Emergency Response) program as a means of meeting requirements under SARA Title III. In 1985, Pampa recognized that the core of the CAER program matched the needs and goals of its own emergency management program (which were to ensure protection of the community from industrial accidents and to maintain a positive working relationship between industry and community representatives—conditions essential for the city, as a participant in the local emergency planning committee, to meet the goals of SARA Title III). Taking advantage of the momentum generated by the CAER program in the private sector, Pampa expanded the municipal emergency management program using CAER's functional guidelines: "(1) Inform local residents about industry operations; (2) Integrate plant emergency response plans with local coordinated emergency response plans; and (3) Test and modify coordinated plans through regularly scheduled field exercises."[14] Implementation of the CAER guidelines broadened the community's involvement in emergency management and merged the planning efforts of the public and private sectors.[15] Moreover, this proactive cooperation between industry and local government became the foundation of the city's economic development efforts.

Considering that a significant percentage of new jobs are created when businesses expand at their existing locations, it makes sense to have a forum for positive public-private communication. In Pampa, opportunities for public-private cooperation that have arisen since the city's adoption of the CAER functional guidelines have had several positive results both for industry and for the city. The chemical industry has found municipal guidance more forthcoming and more relevant to the industry's licensing efforts; municipal assistance has also been valuable in enabling the industry to meet SARA Title III requirements and in extending the availability of state and federal emergency management training programs to private-sector contingency planners. In addition, the city helped one local plant to develop an expansion project and another to broaden and diversify its product line.

The city has benefited as well, through (for example) the receipt of private-sector funding for emergency response equipment, training for public employees, and access to training facilities.

Adoption of the CAER guidelines brought the public and private sectors together in efforts to mitigate, prepare for, respond to, and recover from disaster. Emergency management in Pampa has been plucked from obscurity and made visible to the entire community it was designed to serve. This is one example of how the role of the emergency manager is changing. It is not enough to write a plan, sound the sirens, and circle the wagons. The manager of today, engaging in liaison activities, is a teacher, an advocate, an advisor, and a facilitator, as emergency manager Steve Vaughn was in attempting to match the needs and resources of the city of Pampa with the needs and resources of the chemical industry.

Mastering Title III paperwork

Processing Title III information   Here are some tips for handling and processing Title III and other types of hazmat information:

1. Decide what it is you want to accomplish with the information.
2. Appoint an individual(s) to be in charge of processing and handling the information. All department personnel should know the identity and the location of this individual. Your intent may be that all chemical facilities mail information to the department's hazmat coordinator, but this does not always happen. Frequently, facilities send information to the local fire station, the fire chief, the fire marshal, or the fire inspector. Unless all members of your department are aware who has been assigned to handle it, Title III information is likely to be lost or misfiled.
3. Date all incoming materials. This provides a record as to when chemical facilities complied with reporting requirements. The local emergency planning committee or a facility's insurance company may request the date of compliance. Some insurance companies require, as a condition of insurance, that facilities they insure comply with reporting requirements.
4. Start a separate file for each reporting facility. Since Material Safety Data Sheets and Tier I and II reporting forms look alike, it is important to keep facility files separate. Setting up a file on each facility helps reduce the chance of losing or misfiling information.
5. Provide your department's inspectors and station officers with information on proper reporting procedures and special information requests. Fire inspectors are often asked questions about compliance requirements for Title III. A flyer explaining compliance details can be prepared for department personnel to hand out. It also can be made available to the local emergency planning committee for distribution when requested.
6. Develop form letters for requesting clarification or additional information from facilities. This reduces the number of letters you need to write. Develop a form letter with a checklist of often-requested items, so that you need only check the appropriate box and address the letter. . . .

Tips for developing useful preplans   Develop a cover page for each facility. The cover page should provide an overview of the facility and the major hazards and precautions to be observed during emergency operations. The information on the cover page might include:

1. Name and address of the facility
2. Emergency contact numbers for facility representatives
3. Types of operations conducted at

As teachers, emergency managers and staff members speak to school groups, industry groups, and service clubs, communicating information about different risks the community faces and encouraging participation in mitigation activities. Emergency managers and staff should use these speaking opportunities to educate citizens about what occurs during disasters, types of damage to expect, precautions to take, ways the local government can be expected to respond, and the sort of assistance it can provide to individuals. In this endeavor, schools, employers, and public service organizations all have contributions to make, as do the National Weather Service and the local media.

In school districts throughout the Southwest, for example, the onset of the spring tornado season often prompts large-scale tornado drills. National Weather Service field offices, the media, local emergency officials, and school adminis-

---

the facility, such as manufacturing chemicals, storage and distribution
4. The size, quantity and types of container for stored chemicals that are of concern to the fire department
5. Any special precautions to be observed.

Next, develop a map showing the location of chemicals stored within the complex. This need not be highly detailed. The intent is to show personnel the location of chemicals of special concern within the complex. This information is critical in order to implement proper strategy and tactics during an incident.

The following items can be included on the map:

1. Specific location of chemicals within the facility
2. Location of sewer system openings
3. Street intersections
4. Utility cutoffs and other special building systems
5. Other specific hazards which can be indicated easily on a map.

The last page of the occupancy guide sheet can provide additional information that can influence emergency operations.

This might include:

1. Size of building
2. Building suppression systems

3. Hydrant and water supply information
4. Sewer system and drainage information to use in determining where the chemical runoff will go
5. Emergency telephone numbers of facility personnel
6. Evacuation information for the immediate area, including the number of residents and special-risk facilities such as nursing homes and schools
7. Hours of operation for the facility and the number of employees on-site
8. Any information that might be of special concern during initial operations.

When you develop this information, keep it simple and easy to use. Maps and diagrams with highly detailed symbols and reference charts will be difficult to use. If you provide too much information or information which is too detailed, it will not be used. If you provide too little information, personnel may not have the basic information they need to manage the incident effectively. The secret is to find the middle ground that will accomplish the job.

Source: Excerpted from William H. Stringfield, "Mastering Title III Paperwork," *Fire Command* (January 1989): 24–26. Reprinted with permission from *Fire Command*® (Vol. 56, No. 1), copyright© 1989, National Fire Protection Association, Quincy, MA 02269.

trators cooperate to undertake activities that remind children and their parents to be prepared for tornadic or severe thunderstorm activity.

Many employers take advantage of the season to bring in speakers on the nature and effects of tornadoes; and public service organizations (Lions and Rotary clubs, for example) focus on storm awareness and preparedness.

The National Weather Service "spotter" training is intensive during this season. The service conducts classes for amateur radio operators, who will work with local officials to provide field reports of rainfall amounts and hail activity, early notification of potential trouble spots, and confirmation of funnel or tornado sightings.[16]

Because local media have the ability to reach and teach so many people, it's critical that emergency managers and public safety officials work with, not around, the media at all times. To protect the emergency manager's credibility with citizens, it's also important that officials provide the media with information that is as full and as accurate as possible.

Topical issues—technological and natural disasters outside the jurisdiction—can provide focal points for public education efforts. Local residents often learn about such emergencies when the emergencies draw the attention of the broadcast media. Being available for public forums and local talk shows dealing with incidents that have occurred elsewhere is an effective way to reach a large audience, but it requires that the emergency manager and staff make special efforts as a part of daily operations.

First, they must keep abreast of the changes in local policy and procedures. An emergency manager who doesn't know local policies risks making promises that cannot be kept or statements that cannot be supported. For example, an emergency manager might offer public facilities as storm shelters although a city council was considering closing those facilities because of budget shortfalls; or might advise citizens how to dispose of household hazardous waste although the jurisdiction has not yet developed a policy for handling hazardous waste.

Second, the department must have the resources to educate staff quickly and extensively on matters that may not be part of the local risk experience and must then activate the resources to respond. Earthquakes, for example, are not part of the risk experience of Dallas, Texas, but because of the substantial Hispanic population in Dallas, the Mexico City earthquakes of 1985 demanded a response on the part of Dallas officials (see sidebar).

Liaison activities also arise from daily events that give emergency managers opportunities to work with groups that lie outside both the public and the business sectors but that effectively provide relief assistance. The American Red Cross, the Salvation Army, Meals-on-Wheels, and Visiting Nurses associations are examples of such groups. Not so well known, perhaps, are hobbyists' clubs. Four-wheel-drive vehicle clubs, all-terrain vehicle clubs, and amateur radio operator clubs are often called on to help deliver emergency supplies when roads are impassable, to search for lost persons in underdeveloped areas, and to provide emergency communications when normal channels break down. The services of these groups are needed, are effective, and reduce the role the public sector has to fill. Thus it will be well worth the effort for the emergency manager to work with these groups as their advocate and student. The emergency manager should advocate official recognition of their contributions. In addition, by taking the time to visit with group members and attend or address group meetings, the emergency manager can have a better idea of what each group can and cannot do.

As emergency planning is increasingly incorporated into professional organizations, emergency managers have greater opportunities to act as advocates of preparedness, mitigation, and relief activities. The American Public Works Association, for example, has recently established an emergency management division that expands the focus of its member organizations to include the community impact of construction or of structure failure, prestaging equipment, staffing and supplies in preparation for incidents (such as hurricanes), coordination with local officials to enhance delivery of relief services, and training in self-protection for employees of the member organizations, not only in relation to job safety but also in areas of personal safety.

In the areas of code development and enforcement, the emergency manager can affect public policy by assisting in an advisory capacity those whose work in mitigation may be more narrowly focused. Floodplain designation and management, fire code enforcement, hazardous materials transportation routing restrictions, and building code enforcement are all areas that lie outside the traditional role of the emergency manager but that are at the core of his or her daily efforts at mitigation and preparation. Although emergency managers may not be directly involved in preparation of building or fire safety codes (dual-role

---

Dallas responds to the Mexico City earthquakes By Friday morning, it was clear that we would have to organize. Calls from concerned family members and friends were coming in to the American Red Cross and Dallas Emergency Preparedness offices, the Dallas Concilio (a planning and coordinating agency for Hispanic service organizations), and ham radio operators throughout the Dallas area. A coalition of these four groups was forged to provide the bilingual communications skills, the administrative expertise and support, and the technical expertise that were needed to respond to the requests for information on earthquake victims in Mexico.

Saturday at 9 A.M. the hotline number provided by Southwestern Bell went into operation, whereupon a "kidnapping" occurred—the Dallas public affairs director saved us in the early hours by pressing into service bilingual residents attending a meeting on the sixth floor of City Hall. These volunteers came to the EOC and staffed the phones until the Dallas Concilio members arrived, were briefed, and took their places. The "angels" from the sixth floor continued to drop in and out of the hotline operation to relieve Concilio volunteers of phone duty.

Initially, calls were coming in at the rate of 200 per hour. It was surprising to learn, during those early hours—and even as late as Monday morning—that we were taking calls from people who,

for more than forty-eight hours, had been unsuccessful in getting through to *any* authority to report a missing friend or family member.

According to Southwestern Bell, we received more than 1,290 inquiries during the nine hours of operation on Saturday. Volunteers responded to 800 additional inquiries on Sunday and to another 135 by noon on Monday. Although callers were told that no word should be expected from Mexican ham radio operators before forty-eight hours, within thirty-six hours ham radio operators handling hotline calls managed to locate more than 20 percent of the friends and family whom callers were trying to reach.

On Sunday, the Cable News Network carried a nationwide story on the Dallas "earthquake hotline," and Dallas volunteers found themselves taking inquiries from elsewhere in Texas, from New York City, Oklahoma City, Connecticut—and from Mexico.

On Monday, as the pace of incoming calls slowed, volunteers began calling search initiators for more complete information when it was needed. The inquiries continued to go out as long as the questions came in.

Source: Adapted from briefing notes of John H. Pickett, coordinator of the Office of Emergency Preparedness for the City of Dallas, Mexico City Earthquakes, September 19, 1985.

emergency managers excepted), they are directly concerned with the effects of floods, fires, chemical accidents, and building collapses. FEMA, for example, has many publications about wind damage to structures and actions that may be taken to mitigate such damage; so does the National Oceanic and Atmospheric Administration (NOAA). By sharing the information to which they have access, emergency managers help make planning officials more aware of considerations other than those pertaining to engineering and regulations.

Emergency managers could and should solicit printed materials on fire safety and flood prevention and insurance to distribute to groups and individuals with whom they deal. In addition, they should encourage other public officials to use and distribute literature and training materials on disaster preparedness, relief organizations, and community resources.

Working with local utilities to protect power and water resources in support of emergency operations is an easy, and often overlooked, way to enlarge the effectiveness of emergency operations. Some emergency operations centers include permanent work stations for representatives of local utilities, and it is not uncommon for utility representatives to monitor the development of a situation, interact with both the public and utility personnel to ensure that power is available to support response operations, and keep the local government apprised of a utility failure so that the government can initiate compensatory activity.

Finally, diplomatic skills should have high priority for emergency managers. Emergency managers are coordinators—not commanders—and should strive to learn the skills that are needed to deal empathetically with the community, to facilitate mitigation and preparedness, to coordinate a response that is effective, and to oversee a recovery that works. Disasters do not respond to the efforts of single individuals, and the emergency manager must work to identify, assemble, and coordinate the resources that will serve the community best.

Cost recovery system

Basic to the establishment and implementation of any cost recovery system is an understanding of what is expected of local government under federal and state disaster assistance programs. Setting up a cost recovery system that will be activated in the event of a disaster is wise, for there is little time to research cost recovery options once a disaster has occurred. Maintaining receipts and records during an actual disaster operation will prove difficult enough.

The mission of a cost recovery system is "to provide a timely, accurate, quantitative cost collection system to document [costs] for management purposes [and] disaster assistance claims and assist in the subsequent recovery plan."[17] As mentioned earlier, a jurisdiction's risk manager can be of invaluable assistance in both setting up and carrying out this process.

It is recommended that a "trigger" be established to initiate the posting of disaster-related expenses to an incident-specific cost collection system. At the American Red Cross, for example, when an event is of such magnitude that response and recovery costs are expected to exceed $2,500, a disaster relief (DR) number is assigned, and all further references to that incident are made in terms of that DR.[18] Because initial damage assessments are completed within twenty-four hours of the event, related expenses are identified very early.

In the public sector, disaster-related costs range from the dollar value of damage to buildings, vehicles, and equipment, to labor costs for incident-related activities, to the cost of using materials and equipment. The information must be gathered on a "per unit" basis: per hour (for labor and equipment use), per square foot or cubic yard (for materials), per square mile or acre foot (for area covered), or according to the number of items, weight, or mileage.

Unfortunately, capturing disaster-related costs from administrative records does not necessarily mean that the monies spent will be recovered. Establishing a disaster contingency fund is therefore recommended, as insurance policies may contain exclusions and deductible amounts that can substantially affect a local budget. If damage is sufficiently severe, a federal disaster declaration may be requested, which, if approved, could reimburse up to 75 percent of a local government's disaster-related expenses.

It should be noted that full cost recovery of disaster-related expenses is no more probable than full cost recovery of routine emergency services. That every dollar spent by a jurisdiction in a disaster will be reimbursed is no more likely than that every patient transported to the hospital by a publicly operated emergency medical system will be able to pay for that ambulance service. However, a good percentage of disaster-related costs may be recovered if insurance has been purchased and if efforts are made to research and apply for available relief funds.

Special populations

The emergency management community is fortunate in that, for some years now, social service and public safety agencies have been identifying the needs of special populations. Although the willingness or capacity to respond to those needs varies widely among jurisdictions, it is incumbent on the emergency manager to consider special populations whenever disaster threatens or strikes.

Representatives of special populations should automatically be included in the resources inventory discussed in an earlier section. Translators, regional hospital councils, chambers of commerce, religious support groups, and a local council of churches may all be helpful in assisting certain segments of a population in response and recovery. The Dallas Concilio, for example—a planning and coordinating agency for Hispanic service organizations—was unfamiliar to many in the Dallas community before the Mexico City earthquakes of 1985; this group is now considered to be a critical resource. Councils of churches throughout the nation have been enormously effective in helping victims and their families deal with the trauma that so often follows aircraft accidents, building collapses, or other mass casualty incidents. Support groups that have arisen in response to the influx of Asians and Central Americans often assist public-sector officials in their work with disaster victims of various cultural groups.

As important as identifying resources is identifying critical facilities. These may include sites, structures, and institutions that, if affected by an emergency, may enlarge the scope of impact by exacerbating the problem (a fire at a hazardous waste treatment center might release a toxic cloud); reducing a department's ability to respond (as when emergency response routes are blocked by traffic jams near sports arenas); or presenting a secondary problem greater than the primary one (as when a small fire results in a major power outage at a hospital complex).

Institutions that exist in most jurisdictions and pose special problems to emergency responders include nursing homes, in which patients' limited mobility requires special evacuation procedures; hospitals, where life-sustaining equipment may preclude patient evacuation; or schools and jails, where provision must be made for transporting, relocating, and fully accounting for each member of the evacuated group. Most incarceration facilities are administered by county, state, or federal officials on a twenty-four-hour basis, and their evacuation is usually handled by nonmunicipal personnel. However, the same degree of custodial attention is not maintained in local school districts, so the evacuation of schools and child-care centers presents special problems that the local emergency manager should be prepared to address.

In some cities, building managers of high-rise structures and general managers of hotels and motels have evacuation exchange plans, wherein occupants are routinely transported to another, safe building when a particular structure is threatened.

Proaction and advocacy

Active and visible participation in community affairs, cooperation and communication with public- and private-sector counterparts, the maintenance of an up-to-date resource list, and the application of software systems and hard-copy databases are just some aspects of day-to-day operations in today's emergency management department. However disparate the activities, they share a common purpose, which is to maintain a local program capable of mitigating, preparing for, responding to, and recovering from disaster.

The management *of* crisis is always preferable to management *by* crisis. This is particularly the case in emergency management, where the emphasis is not on reacting to disaster but on proaction to lessen the impact when disasters do occur. A proactive approach to public safety requires persistent and well-reasoned advocacy. Preparing a community to deal with a crisis that has not occurred is difficult—obtaining financing and cooperation from the beleaguered representatives of a ravaged jurisdiction may be easier than making a scheduled budget request—but the potential savings in lives and property justify the effort.

1   Although the overall focus of this discussion is *nonemergency* duties, visibility *during* an emergency is equally important. The emergency manager, of course, cannot leave the EOC, but the presence of emergency management staff at field command posts can have a number of positive effects: staff at a command post are in a good position to identify the need for resources and take steps to obtain them; staff can relay valuable information to the EOC; first responders will note the staff's willingness to assist; and staff presence at a command post reinforces the post's role as an integral part of the coordinated response effort. Of course, such positive results have a prerequisite: sufficient visibility during nonemergency times to establish an atmosphere of trust and cooperation.

2   National Security Decision Directive Number 259, February 4, 1987.

3   See FEMA, *Objectives for Local Emergency Management* (Washington, DC: U.S. Government Printing Office, July 1984), II-8.

4   Ibid., II-9.

5   *Texas Disaster Act of 1975*, Vernon's Texas Codes Annotated, Government Code Chapter 418, "Emergency Management," 70th [Texas] Legislature, 1987. See also Executive Order of the Governor, WPC-87-6a.

6   FEMA, *Objectives*, II-5.

7   Steve Vaughn, "Emergency Management Program, City of Pampa, Texas," September 1988, photocopy.

8   U.S. Department of Transportation, U.S. Coast Guard, *Chemical Hazard Response Information System* (CHRIS), Commandant Instruction M1645.12A (Washington, DC: U.S. Government Printing Office, November 14, 1984), 1-1.

9   Association of American Railroads, *Emergency Handling of Hazardous Materials in Surface Transportation* (Washington, DC: Association of American Railroads, February 1987).

10 Chemical Manufacturers Association, *National Chemical Response and Information Center* (Washington, DC: Chemical Manufacturers Association, n.d.).

11 Chemical Manufacturers Association, *Hazard Information Transmission Program* (Washington, DC: Chemical Manufacturers Association, n.d.).

12 Chemical Manufacturers Association, *National Chemical Response and Information Center.*

13 All information on the Incident Command System is from *Incident Command System*, Fire Protection Publications (Stillwater: Oklahoma State University, 1983).

14 Chemical Manufacturers Association, *Community Awareness and Emergency Response* (Washington, DC: Chemical Manufacturers Association, n.d.).

15 Steve Vaughn, Emergency and Environmental Management Director, Pampa, TX, September 1988, private communication.

16 Trained by the National Weather Service and operating under the authority of local officials, storm spotters are cadres of amateur radio operators who volunteer their time and equipment during severe weather activity. They travel with moving storms to report existing and developing weather conditions as well as incidents of street flooding, vehicular accidents, traffic signal malfunctions, or any other type of information that a local government would need to have.

    Under the auspices of the Federal Communications Commission, these volunteers are able to dedicate a radio frequency that is normally reserved for amateur operation to the exclusive work of assisting civil officials during emergencies. Because they operate on short wave and use their own equipment, they are usually able to avoid the problems of lost communication capabilities that often occur in emergencies.

    See National Weather Service, *Amateur Radio and the National Weather Service* (Fort Worth, TX: June 1977).

17 Dallas, TX, *Master Emergency Operations Plan*, Annex E, Appendix 3 (Dallas, TX: December 1986).

18 American Red Cross, *Disaster Services Regulations and Procedures*, no. 3003, section E, subsection 3, para. e, "Financial Funding, Authorities, and Procedures" (Washington, DC: American Red Cross, January 1987).

11 Liability issues

Decisions made and actions taken in emergency management activities can result in liability suits and judgments. Local officials involved in emergency management must therefore understand the legal implications of their actions. The legal issues associated with emergency management are shaped by both state and federal law, so local officials must be familiar with applicable state as well as federal law.

Under state law, the legal issues involve negligence and state statutory requirements. Under federal law, the legal issues involve federal constitutional claims and federal statutory issues.

Negligence occurs when the careless action or inaction of employees or volunteers causes injuries or property damage. Claims of negligence are issues of state law and are brought in state court. Federal constitutional rights are involved in claims resulting from land use regulation, emergency powers of law enforcement officers, limitations placed on citizens during a disaster, or business inspections. Claims based on federal statutes could be for employment discrimination or environmental contamination. Claims of constitutional or federal statutory violations are brought in federal court.

Liability under state law

During the past thirty years, major changes have occurred at the state level in the immunity of governmental jurisdictions from tort liability, or suits involving claims of negligence filed by citizens, businesses, or interest groups. A tort is an act that harms a person or property. A tort occurs when a person acts or fails to act in conflict with the rights of others and thereby harms another directly or indirectly. A tort claim is a civil action for personal injuries or property damage resulting from negligent conduct, rather than a criminal suit that involves intentional misconduct.[1] In the field of emergency management, for example, a tort could involve a failure to warn citizens of a known hazardous materials release or a failure to provide adequate time for an evacuation order in a natural disaster.[2] Individuals have filed tort actions against public agencies for failing to respond to their emergency needs, and businesses have filed suits claiming that the response was mismanaged and caused a business interruption.[3]

Before 1960, few states allowed civil suits against public organizations. The state (including local government units) was protected by sovereign immunity, statutory immunity, or immunity based on case law. Today the situation is very different: in many states, individual citizens and private businesses may file civil suits against public organizations for injunctive relief (court orders) and money damages payable from the public treasury.

The English common law principle of sovereign immunity was the basis of the immunity from civil suit of most states and their political subdivisions. Simply stated, sovereign immunity meant that the king could do no wrong; the sovereign and his representatives were immune from civil claims. When this doctrine was incorporated into U.S. law, it bestowed immunity on the federal government, the states, and the states' political subdivisions.[4]

In 1960 only five states and the District of Columbia allowed suits against a state or its political subdivisions, but during the next ten years tort law changed in fifteen states, and during the 1970s it changed in twenty-seven more. The remaining three states addressed the issue of immunity in the 1980s.[5] By 1987 every state had acted either to abolish, retain, or alter the protection provided by the principle of sovereign immunity. Today, all states limit tort claims against governmental units; but they use different means of doing so. In some states, constitutional provisions prohibit suits. In others, statutes address aspects of liability claims. In thirty-one states, comprehensive tort liability statutes have been adopted that delineate the scope of liability; areas of immunity; procedural requirements for making claims against governmental units, officials, employees, agents, and volunteers; damage limitations; indemnification provisions; and means

Figure 11-1   Tort liability in emergency planning: Summary of state law.

State	Sovereign immunity	Governmental/ proprietary immunity	Definition of disaster includes technological emergencies	Statutory immunity for emergency activities	Includes broad definition of emergency management*	Requires a local plan	Other
			Elements of state emergency management acts				
Alabama	PW/1 (State R)			31-9-16	x	x	4
Alaska	A/2		x	26.20.140	x	x	
Arizona	A/2		x	26-314	x		
Arkansas	R		x	12-75-128	x	x	4
California	PW/2		x	8657	x	x	
Colorado	PW/2	x	x	24-33.5-903	x	x	5
Connecticut	PW/1	x	x	Sect. 28-13	x		4
Delaware	PW/2		x	Sect. 3116	x		3
Florida	PW/2		x	(Broad immunity recognized in case law)	x		3
Georgia	PW/1	x	x	38-3-35	x	x	4
Hawaii	PW		x	128-18	x		4
Idaho	PW/2		x	46-1017	Limited	x	
Illinois	PW/2		x	1117	x	x	3,4
Indiana	PW/2		x	10-4-1-8	x	x	
Iowa	PW/2		x			x	3,4
Kansas	PW/2		x	48-915	x	x	
Kentucky	PW/1	x	x	39.433	x	x	4
Louisiana	A		x	29.613	x	x	
Maine	PW/2		x	37-B 822	x	x	3
Maryland	PW/1	x	x	12-105			
Massachusetts	PW/2		x	31 Sect. 12A	Limited		
Michigan	PW/2	x	x	30.411	x		
Minnesota	PW/2		x	466.07 (local) 3.736 (state)			3
Mississippi	PW/2		x	33-15-21	x		3
Missouri	PW/1	x	x				3
Montana	PW/2		x	10-3-111	x	x	3
Nebraska	PW/2		x	81-829.55	x	x	3,4
Nevada	A/2		x	414.110	x		3
New Hampshire	PW/1		x	107:12	x		3
New Jersey	PW/2			55:13A-6 Hazardous materials response			3

of providing insurance.[6] Finally, case law also determines the nature of claims against governmental units.

Negligence and immunity from liability

Each state in its laws, regulations, and court decisions recognizes individual and business rights. Tort law protects these rights by providing those who have been harmed by a public employee or agent with a means of seeking compensation for the loss. Clearly, public officials and government units are not always liable for injuries and property damage resulting from disasters and response efforts: the key is to clarify when legal accountability exists and when immunity exists. Through a process that protects both the interests of the person injured and

Figure 11-1—Continued

State	Sovereign immunity	Governmental/ proprietary immunity	Elements of state emergency management acts				
			Definition of disaster includes technological emergencies	Statutory immunity for emergency activities	Includes broad definition of emergency management*	Requires a local plan	Other
New Mexico	PW/2		x	41-4-4			
New York	PW/2		x	9193	x		
North Carolina	PW/1	x (local only)	x	166 A-14	x	x	3,4
North Dakota	PW/1		x	37-17.1-16	x	x	3
Ohio	PW/1	x	x	5915.10	x		4
Oklahoma	PW/2		x	63 S. 683.14	x		
Oregon	PW/2		x	401.170	x		
Pennsylvania	PW/2		x	7303(c)	x	x	
Rhode Island	A/2	x	x	30-15-15	x		
South Carolina	PW/2		x	15-78-60 (19)	x		
South Dakota	PW/1	x	x	33-15-38	x	x	3
Tennessee	PW/2		x	58-2-129	x		
Texas	PW/2	x	x	418.022	x	x	
Utah	PW/2	x	x	63-30-16	x		
Vermont	PW/1	x		20 Sect. 7	x		3
Virginia	PW/1	x	.x	44-146.23	x	x	
Washington	A/2		x	38.52.180	x	x	5
West Virginia	A/2		x	15-5-11(a)	x		4
Wisconsin	A/1 (local)			166.08(e)			
	R (state)		x	895.48(e)		x	
Wyoming	A/2			19-5-113	x	x	3

Key

A	Abolished sovereign immunity
PW	Partially waived sovereign immunity
R	Retained sovereign immunity
1	State statutes permit suits in specific areas.
2	Adopted a comprehensive tort liability statute, which defines the scope of the liability of public agencies; establishes what forms of immunity exist; discusses procedures for bringing suit; and sets limits for damages, if any.
3	Purchase of insurance constitutes waiver of immunity.
4	Liability claims are reviewed by a state claims board, commission, or appeals court rather than by a state court.
5	State assumes financial liability for claims arising out of emergency situations.
*	Broad definition of emergency management: any emergency management activity, including planning, organizing, administering, responding, and cleaning up. A blank in this column means that the statute does not mention immunity.

those of the governmental jurisdiction, state tort law is used to systematically analyze and resolve liability claims.[7]

In each state the law defines the scope of governmental liability for acts of negligence and specifies whether immunity is recognized in special circumstances. Immunity may derive from constitutional provisions, case law, or statutory provisions. The extent to which governmental jursidictions and their employees may be liable is shaped by the principles of negligence, discretionary immunity, the governmental/proprietary function test, the private liability test, and statutory immunity.

Negligence is either a failure to do what the reasonable and prudent person would have done under the circumstances or an action that unintentionally harms another. It occurs when a person owes a duty to another but fails to exercise due skill, diligence, or care, with the result that the other person is injured. The elements of negligence include:

The existence of a duty, recognized by law, for a person (the governmental agency, employee, or agent) to conform to a defined standard of care (or conduct). This standard of care may evolve from common law (previous practice or judicial decision) or from a statute

A failure to carry out the standard of care or prescribed duty

A connection between the action of the governmental agency, employee, or agent and the resulting injury to a third party such that the law recognizes the action as the legal cause of the harm

Actual loss or damage to the interests of the injured party.[8]

All suits involving negligence have all these elements in common; a failure to satisfy any one of these elements defeats a claim of liability. A determination of negligence depends upon the facts and circumstances in the case, the conduct of the alleged wrongdoer, and whether the actions of the wrongdoer did in fact cause the injury or harm. Even slight differences in facts among liability cases may lead to alternative conclusions.

The starting point for a finding of negligence is the existence of a duty— imposed by common law or by statute—that establishes a standard of conduct. Common law generally imposes a duty of care on any persons (citizens, businesses, and government officials or employees) to recognize when their conduct creates a risk of harm to others and to use reasonable attention, perception, memory, knowledge, intelligence, and judgment in their actions.[9] For example, a school has a common law duty to repair or place off limits unsafe playground equipment. If an unsafe condition on school property exposes children to obvious hazards, the school is under an obligation to repair it or provide warning. Another example: managers of emergency shelters have a common law duty to recognize obvious hazards and either repair them or provide a warning. A third example: state courts have held that public works departments have a duty to repair known road hazards in a reasonable time and to place unsafe recreational areas off limits.[10] Giving notice that a specific danger exists and that the danger creates a significant threat is a critical component of the duty to repair a hazard or protect the public safety. In emergency situations, warnings should be given of specific dangers such as hazards in the roadway. Duty of care for the welfare of others is thus based on (1) a significant threat to the welfare of others, (2) a known hazard or danger, and (3) the public agency's control of the property in question. Unless a specific danger to an individual is present, public jurisdictions are generally not held liable for a failure to provide police protection or to protect the public safety.

In addition to the general common law duty of care, many states impose specific statutory duties on public organizations, such as the duty to inspect day-

Duty to control employee's behavior   In a case involving the federal government under federal law—a case brought against the Bethesda Naval Hospital under the Federal Tort Claims Act (FTCA)—the U.S. Supreme Court held that federal government employees were negligent in allowing a fellow serviceman to leave the facility in an intoxicated condition. Although the Court held that the government was not responsible for the injuries caused by an intoxicated employee, it determined that the government *was* liable for injuries caused by employees who observed and who allowed the intoxicated employee to leave with a loaded rifle. By adopting rules that prohibit the possession of firearms in the work area and by requiring all personnel to report the presence of any firearm, the government had assumed a responsibility to act in a careful manner.

The government was not held responsible for the injuries caused by the intoxicated employee because he was not on duty and was thus acting outside the scope of his job. He was acting on his own and not as a representative of the government as his employer. In addition, the employee's act of firing the rifle was considered by the Court to be an intentional and willful action, and the FTCA prohibits claims against the government for employee conduct that is intentional and willful.

Although the case involves the federal government under federal law, state and local officials should ensure that all emergency management personnel understand organizational and statutory duties, and carefully comply. In a similar claim, state courts would consider whether statutory duties could form the basis of organizational liability even though an immunity provision might exist in the emergency management statute.

Source: *Sheridan* v. *United States*, 56 LW 4761, United States Supreme Court, 1988.

---

care centers, repair traffic controls, enforce workplace safety requirements, or inspect public buildings. The statutes may simply establish a duty or standard of care, with or without specific mention of civil penalties for failure to comply. When a statute provides for civil actions, penalites, or damages, the court will adopt the statute's standard of care and penalties. Under these circumstances, liability may simply be imposed by a demonstration that the statute was violated.

For example, a state statute may require state and local agencies to prepare and keep current an emergency preparedness plan for natural, technological, or civil disasters. If a local government failed to prepare a plan and a disaster occurred, a citizen could file suit claiming that the governmental unit had failed to carry out a statutory duty and was therefore liable for losses.

Discretionary immunity   Tort law is intended to address the claims of individuals harmed by the actions of public officials and employees, but not to address them to such an extent that well-qualified persons would be discouraged from serving in public positions.[11] Public officials therefore enjoy immunity for discretionary judgments and decisions made within the scope of their positions. State legislatures adopted discretionary immunity to free the public official from fear of tort liability if a decision were to result in harm to another. Discretionary immunity further evolved from a concern on the part of the courts and legislatures not to interfere with the executive decision-making process, which would violate the principle of separation of governmental powers.

Discretionary actions are policy decisions that chart the direction and extent of policies, programs, and activities. They are distinguished from activities that implement policies, such as operational or ministerial actions. Questions that clarify whether a decision is a discretionary action include the following:

Does the decision involve a basic governmental policy or program?

Does the decision chart the course or direction of a program, activity, policy, or objective (as opposed to a decision that is required to implement the policy)?

Does the decision require the exercise of basic policy judgment or expertise on the part of the governmental actor?

Does the governmental agency have the proper authority to make the decision?[12]

If the decision of the governmental agency or official involves these elements, the decision is discretionary and protected by immunity. If one or more of the questions are answered in the negative, further inquiry is necessary, and liability may result. Examples of discretionary actions would include allocating funding for programs and activities; developing criteria for evaluating emergency management programs and activities; establishing programs and activities—including their goals and strategies; and making decisions about evacuations and sheltering.

Discretionary immunity is intended not to exempt public officials from liability but, rather, to insulate them while they exercise their judgment. Discretionary immunity exists only when an official acts with proper authority; thus, it is critical that emergency managers understand the scope of their duties and the limitations of their authority. When local emergency managers or officials make decisions based on broad responsibilities and authority, they may be taking discretionary actions and thus be immune from civil suit in state court.

Governmental/proprietary test In fifteen states, another source of immunity from tort liability derives from the distinction between governmental activities traditionally performed by public agencies and governmental activities that are proprietary (or businesslike) ventures.[13] Traditional activities receive immunity, even though the employee or agent may be negligent and cause harm to another. Proprietary activities do not receive immunity.

Traditional activities are essential services traditionally performed for the public good, and they include, among others, issuing licenses and permits,

---

Duty based on common law As a landowner, a governmental unit has the same duty to maintain property that a private individual has. The duty requires that the public entity exercise reasonable care under the circumstances and maintain property in a safe condition. Signs in a state recreational area stated that no swimming was permitted in the park, but local kids hung a rope from a tree and used it as a swing to jump into the water. Although authorities knew about the rope, knew that the area had been used for some time as a swimming hole, and knew that a number of young people had been injured, no action was taken to remove the rope and stop the swimming. When a visitor was injured, the court held that the recreational agency had known kids were using the unsafe area and had failed to stop them. The sign prohibiting swimming did not change the government's duty to act and correct a known danger. A governmental unit has an obligation to act when a known danger exists on public property. If the danger cannot be corrected, people should be prohibited from entering the area.

Source: *Mesick* v. *State*, 504 N.Y.S. 279, N.Y. Sup. Ct., App. Div., 1986.

conducting inspections, and protecting public safety.[14] Proprietary functions are those that are similar to private-sector business ventures. These activities include services such as public transit, parking garages, municipal hospitals, recreation programs, and garbage collection. Because the activities are similar to private ventures, immunity is not granted, and if an injury results from the negligence of a public agent providing these services, the courts hold the public sector to the same standard of care required of a private business.[15]

The law in each of the fifteen states defines what activities are governmental functions and thus what activities will have immunity. States that recognize the governmental/proprietary function test usually consider public safety, law enforcement, and fire fighting to be governmental functions and allow these agencies to operate with immunity. Similarly, emergency management departments are generally designated public safety operations performing a traditional governmental function and therefore immune from suit.[16] However, because the activities designated governmental functions do vary from state to state, emergency management officials in states that recognize this form of immunity should be sure they know precisely which activities qualify as governmental functions.

Florida's private liability test   The Florida Supreme Court altered the governmental/proprietary function test to create a new form of immunity for the public sector. The court noted that under the Florida Comprehensive Tort Liability Statute, public agencies are liable "to the same extent as a private person under like circumstances."[17] The statute thus recognizes existing duties as defined for individuals and businesses, and provides a means to compensate persons harmed by a violation of these duties. If under the same circumstances, there is no private duty of care, then there is no public duty. If a duty does not exist for a private person under the same circumstances, then there is no duty or liability for the public actor.

To clarify liability, the court established four types of activities:

1. Legislative, permitting, licensing, and executive officer activities
2. Enforcement of the laws and the protection of the public safety
3. Capital improvements and property control operations
4. The providing of professional, educational, and general services for the health and welfare of citizens.

The Florida Supreme Court held that there would be no tort liability for the action or inaction of governmental officials or employees in carrying out the "discretionary functions" of categories 1 and 2. There could be liability for activities within categories 3 and 4.[18]

Under Florida law, actions of the legislature, city council, commissions, and executive officers belong to category 1 and are not subject to tort liability. Similarly, governmental action to enforce compliance with the laws or to protect public safety does not carry with it a private common law duty of care, and there is therefore no public duty.

In the provision of professional, educational, medical, and general services as well as capital improvements, the private sector recognizes a standard of care. Because a common law duty of care exists in the private sector, a public agency could be held to the same standard.[19]

Activities undertaken by state and local emergency management units generally fall within the functional framework of public safety. The planning and policy recommendations of local emergency officials and staff could fall within the scope of category 1 functions and be immune from suit. The administration and response duties of emergency management personnel could be included in category 2 and thus could be protected activities.

At the present time, only Florida courts have adopted this "private liability test." Other state comprehensive tort liability statutes do, however, have provisions stating that public entities are liable to the same extent as private entities under the same circumstances.[20] And other state courts interpret the provisions as the Florida courts have.

Statutory immunity　Some state laws specifically provide immunity for public employees and volunteers from tort liability in suits involving public safety functions and emergency management activities.[21] The scope of immunity provided by such laws, however, varies in a number of ways.

The most encompassing state laws grant broad immunity for *any* emergency management activity and any public employees or agents engaged in such activities (for example, planning, conducting drills, carrying out recovery efforts). These states provide statutory immunity for *any* emergency management activity regardless of whether there is a declared disaster or emergency.

Laws in other states grant statutory immunity in specific circumstances, such as in a type of emergency management activity (for example, the response phase) or in a type of emergency situation (for example, a natural disaster). Immunity provisions thus could provide protection for responders only for some activities—those named in the emergency management statute—or for actions relating to the type of emergencies addressed in a state emergency management statute.[22] Some state statutes apply only to natural or civil disasters and do not mention technological emergencies.

Vicarious liability and indemnification　Many managers, employees, and volunteers are concerned about their individual liability in emergency management activities. Individual liability as compared to the liability of the governmental jurisdiction is shaped by the principles of vicarious liability and indemnification. If officials and employees do not have immunity from civil claims arising from performance of their official duties, vicarious liability and indemnification provide a means of insulating them.

In some states, indemnification of employees, officials, and agents is required by statute: in the case of a suit, the employing governmental jurisdiction must provide legal counsel and pay damages.[23] In addition, many states hold the employees harmless; the governmental unit does not seek restitution from the employee, although the unit is not prohibited from taking disciplinary action against an employee whose actions justify punishment.

If state law does not require an employer to provide counsel and pay a judgment, the employer may nevertheless be liable under the principle of vicarious liability. According to this principle, an employer is responsible for the actions of its employees or agents and is therefore vicariously liable (through the employee or agent) for wrongful actions. The law usually requires that the official be acting within his or her authorized role and excludes actions that are intended to harm others (intentional torts).

Emergency managers, staff, and volunteers must understand that just as there are limits to immunity, there are limits to the protection provided by indemnification and vicarious liability. Statutes granting indemnification extend qualified protection for ordinary negligent acts; they do not protect employees from personal liability for gross negligence, willful misconduct, or actions outside the scope of their jobs.[24]

The Supreme Court of Wyoming in *Danculovich* v. *Brown* defined willful or wanton misconduct as highly unreasonable behavior—behavior that is an extreme departure from ordinary care in a situation in which danger is apparent. Wanton or willful misconduct involves an intent to cause injury and is more than a mere mistake resulting from inexperience, confusion, thoughtlessness, or inattention.[25]

State action　Some state liability statutes entirely prohibit civil suits against officials, employees, and agents and require that claims be made only against the agency or jurisdiction, with the jurisdiction held responsible for actions of their officials, employees, and agents.[26] Official actions performed within the scope of a person's duties and responsibilities are thus "state action": action on behalf of the state. A suit filed against an emergency management employee or volunteer for actions undertaken while serving a public entity is a claim against the employee or volunteer in his or her official capacity as a representative of the governmental unit. But if the alleged violation involves actions outside the individual's duties, the courts may consider the claim to be against the employee or agent in his or her individual capacity.[27] Because the employee was not acting in his or her official capacity, the employer may not be responsible. The employee may be held individually liable.

The term *employee* may be defined as an officer, official, employee, or agent of a governmental entity, including elected or appointed officials and persons acting on behalf of any governmental entity in any official capacity in the service of the governmental entity.[28] An employee may be compensated or not and full- or part-time. The definition of employee does not usually include independent contractors, although exceptions may be made by statute to allow for the immunity of paid contractors who assist in an emergency or disaster.[29]

A complication may arise when local government employees and officials serve in a dual capacity as employees of the political subdivision (fire service, police department, or emergency management department) and as members of a state-created local emergency planning committee (LEPC). As long as state law defines *employee* to include members of commissions, boards, or committees, the members' actions would be those of official agents of the state.

Questions of liability, however, may be more complex. The court could determine, on the basis of the circumstances or facts, that the actions of an LEPC member were outside his or her role and authority as an LEPC member but within his or her capacity as a local governmental employee. Local governmental employees who are also LEPC members should understand their authorized role and its limits. The courts could view actions outside the "state" LEPC role as actions of a local governmental employee—for which the local governmental *employer* could be held liable.

Whether a volunteer represents a private business or nonprofit corporation, is self-employed, or is a private citizen who is not employed, as long as the governmental unit has the authority to appoint the volunteer—and does so— the volunteer's actions are official actions on behalf of the governmental unit. Thus, if a suit is brought against a volunteer emergency management worker, he or she is an official agent of the governmental unit. The state court thus considers such a suit either as against the volunteer in his or her "official capacity" or as against the appointing governmental unit, rather than against the agent in his or her individual capacity.[30]

Liability under federal law

As noted in the introduction to the chapter, claims that involve constitutional rights or federal statutory violations are brought in federal court. For employees or agents of emergency management departments, such claims could involve civil rights violations.

Civil rights violations

In 1871 the U.S. Congress passed civil rights legislation (42 U.S.C. section 1983) to protect civil rights from abuse by governmental officials. Section 1983 is intended to provide a remedy when state law is inadequate or when a state remedy, though adequate in theory, is not available in practice. Claims for unintentional or negligent actions involving rights that are protected by state law may not be brought in federal court under section 1983. (The Supreme Court has repeatedly stated that claims involving negligence should be made at the state level.)

Section 1983 of the federal code renders public officials at the state and local levels personally liable for actions that deprive individual citizens or businesses of any rights, privileges, or immunities secured by the U.S. Constitution and federal laws. Elected officials, employees, agents, or contractors of the state or its political subdivisions, as well as public authorities of varied purposes, may be held liable under section 1983.[31] Under section 1983, city and county jurisdictions, too, may be sued for constitutional deprivations when the jurisdiction officially implements a policy statement, ordinance, regulation, or decision.[32] Although state emergency management statutes may include immunity provisions for negligent actions, the immunity does not extend to suits involving federal constitutional or statutory violations.

The states themselves, however, are immune from suit in federal court under section 1983. State assets are unreachable in federal court because the Eleventh Amendment bars the federal judiciary from imposing, in a private citizen's suit, any money judgment that must be satisfied from state funds. But federal courts can issue an injunction to deal with objectionable state conduct and may require the state to pay the claimant's attorneys' fees.[33]

Definitions

Due process and probable cause

Due process is required under the Fourteenth Amendment, which provides that no state shall deprive any person of life, liberty, or property without due process of law. The amendment requires public entities to follow procedures that give both adequate *notice* of any action that will result in a deprivation of life, liberty, or property and an *opportunity to be heard* before the deprivation.

Procedural due process refers to the steps a public agency must take to ensure that a decision is fair. For example, public employers are required to notify an employee of a pending disciplinary action or adverse action. The employer should give the employee an opportunity to explain why the disciplinary action should not be taken. For job terminations, the employer must provide a hearing for the employee before an impartial body. The employee may be represented and given an opportunity to cross-examine witnesses.

Substantive due process refers to the substance of a decision rather than the process used in reaching it. Substantive due process involves the rationality or justification of the government's decision. If the court believes that the decision is arbitrary, with no rational basis, the decision will be considered a violation of the Fourteenth Amendment.

Probable cause refers to the Fourth Amendment's requirement that before an arrest may be carried out, there must be reasonable grounds for the action. Thus, before making an arrest, a police officer must pursue reasonable avenues of investigation, especially when it is unclear whether a crime has taken place. In the context of emergency management, the courts recently held that law enforcement officials during an emergency had reasonable grounds for arresting a citizen when he traveled through a roadblock in attempting to return to his home. (*Miller* v. *Campbell County, WY*, 722 F.Supp. 687 [D.WY, 1989]).

Before the U.S. Supreme Court's decision in *Monroe v. Pape* in 1961, section 1983 had been narrowly construed.[34] Its use was restricted by early decisions that had confined application of the statute to violations of federally protected rights by state laws or by acts of state officials authorized by state law. If an official acted beyond the scope of his authority, the act was held not to be state action; in other words, it was not "under color of law" and was therefore beyond the enforcement power of section 1983.[35]

The *Monroe* decision changed this limited view of section 1983. *Monroe* involved a suit for damages against the city of Chicago and thirteen police officers as individuals. The suit alleged that city police unlawfully and violently invaded and searched the plaintiff's home, then arrested and detained him illegally. The Supreme Court stated that a suit could be brought against the policemen even though their actions were unauthorized by state law or local ordinance and that their acts were violations of the plaintiff's constitutional rights.

Rights protected under section 1983 As noted earlier, section 1983 protects rights guaranteed under federal statutes and the U.S. Constitution.

What sorts of actions provoke claims of violation of federal statutes? One category of action that can lead to liability is the failure to administer federal programs in the manner required by the relevant statute. For example, damages have been assessed against state officials for failing to process hospital

---

Remedies

Remedies means actions sought by an injured party; they may include money damages, a declaratory judgment, an injunction, or some combination.

Money damages means financial compensation awarded to a party to help offset direct losses. *Punitive damages* may be awarded to punish a wrongdoer and to deter future wrongful conduct. *Nominal damages* are money awarded to a party that won but was not due compensation. The party may have brought the lawsuit to determine its rights.

Declaratory judgment is a court order stating that the party was right and was improperly treated.

Injunction is a court order that deters parties from taking an action or requires parties to perform an action.

Courts

Precedence refers to the establishment by a court of standards or rules of law that must be followed by certain other

courts. Decisions of the U.S. Supreme Court must be followed by all courts in the United States. Decisions of a U.S. circuit court of appeals must be followed by all federal courts within that circuit. A state supreme court decision must be followed by all state courts within the state.

Trial court is the level where the facts of the case are heard. At the trial level, the judge—at times with the assistance of a jury—hears evidence, determines the facts, applies relevant law to those facts, and makes a decision.

Appellate level is the level where trial court decisions are appealed on grounds of law. An appellate court does not challenge the facts of the case except in extraordinary circumstances. Rather, it checks to see whether the law was applied properly in the situation. If the law was not applied properly, the case may be returned (or remanded) to a lower court for a new trial or for further consideration, depending on the instructions of the appellate court. Federal and state court systems have their own appellate courts.

certificates of need, which is required under federal social security laws, and for failing to prepare individual treatment plans for foster care children, as required under Title IV-A of the Families with Dependent Children program.

In addition to the potential for statutory violations, emergency management activities can affect citizens' constitutional rights. The U.S. Supreme Court has held that damages may be awarded when public officials violate the *settled* constitutional rights of citizens, recipients of benefits, or businesses. Three principal categories of constitutional rights are most likely to provoke claims against public officials in the course of their efforts to protect the lives and property of citizens in an emergency: rights protected by the First Amendment, by the Eighth Amendment, and by the Fourteenth Amendment.

First Amendment rights protected by section 1983 include freedom of speech and freedom of association. It is a violation of such rights, for example, for public officials to discharge employees for supporting an unsuccessful candidate for local office, speaking out on public issues, or joining an employees' association.[36] In disasters, local officials sometimes limit freedom of association, the use of public communication channels, or entry into evacuated areas, all of which pose the potential for violation of First Amendment rights. Before restricting the rights of citizens affected by a disaster, an emergency manager or other public official must be confident that he or she has good reason for doing so. Government may inhibit the speech, assembly, and association of citizens when there is a clear and present danger to property, the restrictions are imposed to protect the general welfare, or individual actions interfere with the activities of the government. The First Amendment protections apply to state and local governments through the Fourteenth Amendment. Local officials should recognize that their actions in responding to a disaster could conflict with citizens' rights. Before implementing emergency management decisions, officials should consult legal staff to minimize the adverse effects of their actions.

Local law enforcement officials are commonly subject to Eighth Amendment claims by arrestees, who contend that excessive force was used. Use of force by a law enforcement official should be both reasonable and justified by the situation. On the one hand, law enforcement officials should not hesitate to use force when the situation requires it. On the other hand, the force should be reasonable. In the case of *O'Neal* v. *DeKalb County*, the use of gunfire to disarm an armed hospital patient was not deemed excessive in light of the obvious danger the patient posed to other patients and staff.[37] Emergency workers must understand what level of force may be permitted

Liability of government contractors and private citizens Government contractors and private citizens who act as agents of state or local jurisdictions may be held liable for violations of individual constitutional rights. The U.S. Supreme Court held that contracting out services does not relieve the government, the contractor, or an agent of the obligation to respect a citizen's constitutional rights. Under the Eighth Amendment, a public entity is obligated to provide adequate medical treatment to those in its custody. This is true even though the medical service is provided by a private physician under a contract. Thus, individuals who manage or supervise shelters during an emergency may have an obligation to provide medical services to citizens in their care. State immunity provisions would not protect a public agency, workers, or volunteers who violate the constitutional rights of citizens.

Source: *West* v. *Atkins*, 56 L.W. 4664, 1988.

in the course of their duties. Such questions can become crucial in the case of emergency management activities such as evacuations, where it is not uncommon for emergency workers to encounter resistance from evacuees.

The Eighth Amendment also requires public officials to act. Deliberately ignoring the medical needs of a prisoner, arrestee, or inmate who can seek no other means of medical care has been considered by the federal courts to be cruel and unusual punishment and a violation of the Eighth Amendment. In addition, law enforcement officers have a duty to intercede on behalf of a citizen whose constitutional rights are being violated by other public safety officials.[38]

The due process provision of the Fourteenth Amendment (see "Definitions") is involved if state emergency management statutes allow emergency management officials to seize property for use in disaster response and relief efforts. The due process provision requires that officials have reasonable grounds for taking a person's property and that they provide some compensation for the seized property.

Relief   A citizen filing a successful suit under section 1983 may be awarded monetary damages and attorneys' fees. In addition, the plaintiff may request injunctive relief, or a court order prohibiting the governmental actor from carrying out a public policy or conducting a program in a specific manner. Finally, the court may issue a declaratory order making a statute, ordinance, regulation, policy, or procedure unconstitutional.

Defenses   Official or *unqualified immunity* from section 1983 suits has been granted to state legislators, judges, and prosecutors.[39] The purpose of this form of immunity is to foster the effective functioning of government by freeing public officials from the threat of personal liability in the performance of their duties.

This absolute immunity, however, is not available to officials in the executive branch or to local governments. State and local officials, employees, and their agents (but not local governments) have only *qualified immunity*. An official acting within the scope of his or her authority is immune from liability if he or she acted reasonably and is not depriving a person of *settled, protected rights*. The Supreme Court has stated that a violation of an individual's rights by a public official, employee, or agent can no more be justified by ignorance or disregard of settled, indisputable law than by actual malice.[40]

A supervisor cannot be held personally liable for the acts of subordinates unless the supervisor personally participates in the tort to some degree. The supervisor may be liable only if he or she directed, participated in, approved of, was present at, or had knowledge of a subordinate's misconduct, or if the supervisor's inaction caused or contributed to the misconduct.[41]

Although local governments are considered persons under section 1983, they do not enjoy even qualified immunity for their official actions. Municipalities are strictly liable for acts that implement an official policy of the governmental unit and that violate statutory or constitutional rights.[42] Local government organizations may be held liable even though the law was not settled at the time of the harm.

Employment discrimination

Title VII of the Civil Rights Act of 1964 (amended by the Equal Employment Act of 1972) prohibits discrimination on the basis of race, color, sex, religion, or national origin in all practices, conditions, and privileges of employment.[43] Other statutes prohibit discrimination on the basis of handicap, age, or military service. Discrimination occurs when decisions relating to a job are influenced

Emergency powers: Destruction of private property   Under 42 U.S.C. section 1983, landowners filed suit against state and local officials in federal court for destroying the value of their property on Sinaloa Lake. Plaintiffs claimed that the public officials' decision to breach the Sinaloa Lake dam was without notice and was not based on reasonable grounds or a legitimate governmental purpose. Government officials have broad discretion to use police powers in emergency or crisis situations, but there are limits to these powers. When the use of governmental powers is excessive, without justification, or for malicious reasons, there is a violation of substantive due process rights protected by the Fourteenth Amendment to the Constitution.

On March 2, 1983, heavy rains and dangerously high water levels in Sinaloa Lake led officials of Simi Valley to evacuate residents living below the dam. State officials from the California Division of Safety of Dams (DSOD) took steps to lower the level of the water behind the dam. The Army Corps of Engineers inspected the dam and concluded that it was stable.

On March 4, without advising residents, state DSOD officials decided to breach the dam to drain the lake, but the decision was not implemented immediately. By March 5 the water level of the lake had fallen to between ten and twelve feet below the high water mark. City officials determined that the emergency was over and advised residents that it was safe to return to their homes below the dam.

By March 8, DSOD officials had decided not to breach the dam and promised residents that the water level of the lake would be maintained at 22 feet below the high water mark to enable property owners to use the lake for recreation. On March 10, senior officials of DSOD again decided to breach the dam. Homeowners were advised of the decision the next day— only a few hours before the dam was to be breached.

The homeowners claimed that the actions of the state officials in breaching the dam and destroying the lake amounted to a taking of their property without due process.

The U.S. Court of Appeals for the Ninth Circuit agreed with the homeowners and held the state officials liable. The court stressed that although government officials have broad discretion to act during emergencies, the discretion does not apply when the officials know no emergency exists or when they act with reckless disregard of the actual circumstances. The court concluded from the facts of the case that there was no justification for DSOD's failure to give the homeowners an opportunity for a hearing, however abbreviated.

The court noted that a government entity's police and emergency powers go far beyond crisis management and that the city has the power to protect its citizens by breaching a dam it considers potentially—though perhaps not imminently—dangerous. In this situation, however, government officials seemed determined to destroy the dam for no legitimate reason and to conceal that decision until the last possible moment to prevent the homeowners from taking advantage of available legal processes.

The exercise of emergency powers is particularly subject to abuse. Emergency decision making is, by its nature, abbreviated and normally does not admit of consultation with those who may be affected. Judicial review, as this case illustrates, is often greatly curtailed or nonexistent. Exigent circumstances often prompt actions that severely undermine the rights of citizens—actions that might have been eschewed if there had been time for more careful reflection or if the safeguards that normally constrain government action had been operative.

Source: *Sinaloa Lake Owners Ass'n.* v. *City of Simi Valley*, 864 F.2d 1475, United States Court of Appeals, Ninth Circuit, 1989.

by any of these factors. Federal law requires both public and private employers to manage personnel and administer programs and activities in an environment free from discrimination.

Many states have enacted similar statutes applicable to both public and private employers. In addition, state emergency management statutes may require state and local governmental bodies and other organizations and personnel who carry out emergency management functions to do so equitably and impartially.[44]

Discrimination charges   Under many federal employment discrimination laws, either an individual or a group of employees may file suit. An individual employee who claims discrimination files a charge of *adverse treatment* with the Equal Employment Opportunity Commission (EEOC). The employee demonstates that he or she is protected by one of the statutes and has been discriminated against by the state or local employer. The EEOC reviews the claim and determines the validity of the charge. The claim may lead to a suit filed in federal district court against the employer by the EEOC. If the EEOC believes the charges are unjustified, the individual may file suit. The public entity then has an opportunity to justify its actions. If the court finds that the employer's justification is reasonable, the employee still has an opportunity to demonstrate during the trial that the justification was a pretext for discrimination.

When a group of employees files charges with the EEOC, it would claim that the employer's personnel practices or policies have an *adverse impact* on

---

Federal antidiscrimination statutes   The federal statutes listed below, in addition to Title VII of the Civil Rights Act of 1964, require state and local emergency management officials to develop personnel practices and procedures that are free from prohibited discrimination. Practices to which the statutes apply include recruitment, interviewing, selection, promotion, training, discipline, and performance evaluation; the statutes may also affect work assignments.

The Pregnancy Disability Act of 1978 forbids discrimination on the basis of pregnancy, childbirth, or related medical conditions. The act requires employers to treat pregnancy and related conditions like any other short-term disability (42 U.S.C.A. section 2000e).

The Equal Pay Act of 1963 (amended in 1974 to include public employers) prohibits wage and salary differentials on the basis of sex for substantially equal or similar work. The federal Equal Employment Opportunity Commission has enforcement authority (P.L. 88–38).

The Age Discrimination in Employment Act of 1967 (amended in 1974, 1978, and 1987) prohibits discrimination against persons over the age of forty in all aspects of employment (P.L. 94–135 as amended by 95–478).

The Vocational Rehabilitation Act of 1973 prohibits discrimination on the basis of handicap in any program or activity receiving federal financial assistance or in any agency holding a contract with the federal government for goods or services of more than $2,500. The law requires employers to make reasonable accommodations to employ handicapped individuals (P.L. 93–112 and 95–602).

Government agencies that receive federal funding are prohibited from discriminating against Vietnam-era veterans and must develop affirmative action plans to eliminate past, present, or future discrimination (42 U.S.C.A. section 2011–2014).

them. The claim could involve race, color, sex, religion, or national origin. In an adverse impact claim, the employees do not have to demonstrate discriminatory intent but must simply show by statistics that employment practice had an adverse impact on their protected group. The employer may be able to defend against this type of claim by demonstrating that the employment practice was a business necessity or that the requirement was a bona fide occupational qualification.

Relief If a federal court determines that discrimination has occurred, it may issue a court order requiring the employer to reinstate the plaintiff, appoint the plaintiff to a position, institute quotas, establish an affirmative action plan, or award retroactive seniority or back pay. In addition, the court may award attorneys' fees to the prevailing party.

Prevention of discrimination claims Good management is the key to preventing complaints of discrimination. Emergency managers should consider the following steps:

Take uniform action with respect to assignment of work, promotion, training opportunities, discipline, and discharge. Employees who file discrimination claims believe they are being treated differently from others. Follow agency policies in a uniform manner and be prepared to justify exceptions.

Explain your actions. Many discrimination charges result when employment or work-related decisions are not explained to those who are affected by them.

Base decisions on job-related factors. Employees expect decisions to be made on a rational basis. Job-related decision criteria provide an excellent basis for making and *justifying* decisions. Such criteria ensure that decisions have an objective basis and protect against claims of subjective preference.

Deal with complaints and disagreements quickly and clearly. Avoiding an employee who is displeased by an employment action may lead to further confusion and charges of discrimination. Listen to the employee's side before explaining the basis of the decision. Good communication can prevent later confrontation and claims.

Hazardous materials requirements

The threat posed by hazardous materials has become increasingly visible since the late 1970s. Hazardous materials incidents can be deadly or cause extensive injury and property damage and can occur in our own backyards. Planning and coordination can minimize potential losses from such disasters, and emergency workers play a key role in such planning and coordination.[45]

Federal Superfund legislation adopted in 1980 provided for the cleanup of toxic waste sites and hazardous chemicals spills on the ground, but the 1984 disaster in Bhopal, India, made it apparent that the release of a highly toxic substance into the air posed special problems for emergency response.[46] By the time emergency personnel reach the scene, an airborne substance has already begun to affect public health and the environment.

To encourage and support state and local emergency planning efforts and to provide local governments and residents with information about potential chemical hazards, Congress included emergency planning requirements and community right-to-know provisions in Title III of the Superfund Amendments and Reauthorization Act (SARA) of 1986. SARA Title III is now the primary vehicle for facilitating emergency planning, preventing accidents, and preparing facilities and the surrounding community to respond to a release of hazardous material on the ground *or* in the air.

Title III of SARA requires the governor of each state to appoint a state emergency response commission. The state commissions designate local emergency planning districts and committees to be in charge of developing an emergency response plan for their communities. The state commissions supervise the activities of the local committees and review the plans they develop.

As part of the planning process, local districts and committees identify available resources that can be called on to respond to a hazardous materials emergency. Local committees also devise means to maintain information on hazardous materials transported through, stored in, or produced in the community. Local planning committees are required to review the plan annually (more frequently as circumstances merit); conduct exercises of the plan; and make recommendations to the state commission, local governmental units, and hazardous materials facilities with respect to resources that may be required to implement the plan effectively. Fixed facilities that transport, store, or produce hazardous materials must cooperate in the planning and information gathering process.[47]

The community right-to-know provisions of SARA Title III require the local committee to make specified information available to the general public during normal working hours. The information includes the local emergency response plan, documents indicating what hazardous materials exist in the community, and forms describing the nature of toxic chemical releases.

Civil penalties exist for any person or business other than a governmental entity who violates the reporting requirements of SARA Title III.[48] A fine of up to $25,000 may be assessed by a federal district court for a failure to report toxic and hazardous chemicals. An additional fine of up to $10,000 may be assessed against any person other than a governmental entity who fails to submit material safety data sheets or provide information to health professionals.[49]

A citizen may file in federal district court a civil action under Title III against the administrator of the U.S. Environmental Protection Agency, a state governor, or the state emergency response commission for failure to respond to a request for information within 120 days after the date of receipt of the request.[50] A citizen may also file a claim in federal district court against a state emergency response commission for failure to fulfill its obligations under Title III. Title III, however, authorizes only injunctive relief against a state commission; it does not authorize money damages or penalties. The court may thus issue an injunction, or court order, requiring the commission to comply with Title III.[51]

Title III does not create a federal "cause of action," or legal basis for a suit, for citizens who wish money damages from the state commission, individual members of commissions or committees, or the governor. Unless there is a cause of action or statutory basis for a suit, the claim against the commission or local government would be dismissed.[52] Title III therefore does not impose liability on local governmental units or officials for a failure to plan effectively for hazardous materials emergencies.

Although federal law imposes emergency-planning and record-keeping requirements on state and local government officials, the basis of liability remains an issue of state law. Liability under Title III of state commissions, local committees, and their individual members is limited by provisions of the act; however, Title III does not restrict the right of persons to seek enforcement of their rights or relief under any other federal or state statute.[53] Citizens who feel they have been harmed by a state commission, a local committee, or individual members of these bodies may file an action with a state court or a state commission or board that reviews claims; thus, liability depends on the law of the state.

Conclusion

Government officials and employees, representatives of business, and individual citizens who participate in emergency management programs and activities serve in an environment in which the threat of liability suits in state and federal courts is ever-present.

Although the threat of personal and organizational liability exists, state law provides qualified immunity to protect the interests of state and local government units. The immunity, whether discretionary, governmental/proprietary, private liability, or statutory, provides extensive protection for official agents of state and local government units who perform their duties within the prescribed limits of their roles and responsibilities. Because the immunity is qualified, however, it can be lost if the member's actions are willful or wanton. Threats of suits and the potential loss of personal resources are protected against by statutory indemnification provisions, which encourage public servants, paid and nonpaid, to carry out their official obligations knowing that their governmental employer will provide counsel and pay judgments in the event of a suit.

Liability under federal law entails duties, obligations, and liabilities separate from those under state law. The immunity provided under state law does not preempt duties imposed by federal law, such as obligations to avoid employment discrimination. To prevent suits, emergency managers and staff must be familiar with federal statutory requirements and constitutional rights.

Knowing when to raise questions with legal counsel and ask for clarification of the law is a management responsibility. Emergency management officials, employees, and volunteers should consult legal counsel to discuss their duties, authority, status as agents of state and local government units, immunities, and indemnification. Legal counsel can clarify the scope of individual and organizational liability so that all individuals who serve during emergencies can focus their attention on preserving the peace, saving property from loss, and protecting citizens.

1 Howard L. Oleck, *Tort Law Practice Manual* (Englewood Cliffs, NJ: Prentice-Hall, 1982), 19.
2 *Brown* v. *MacPherson, Inc.* 545 P.2d. 13 (WA, 1975).
3 *Tavarez* v. *O'Malley*, 826 F.2d. 670, United States Court of Appeals, Seventh Circuit, 1987.
4 Osborne M. Reynolds, *Handbook on Local Government Law* (St. Paul, MN: West Publishing Co., 1982), section 192.
5 John C. Pine, "Changes in the Tort Liability of Governments under State Law," *Governmental Risk Management Manual*, supplement no. 62 (Tucson, AZ: Risk Management Publishing, 1986).
6 John C. Pine, *Tort Liability Today: 1986 Update* (Washington, DC: Public Risk Insurance Management Association and the National League of Cities, 1987).
7 *Restatement of the Law*, Torts 2d (St. Paul, MN: American Law Institute Publishers, 1965), section 281.
8 See *Restatement of the Law*, section 281.
9 John C. Pine and Robert Bickel, *Tort Liability Today: A Guide For State and Local Governments* (Washington, DC: Public Risk Management Association and National League of Cities, 1986), 5.
10 *Fox* v. *City of Columbia*, 196 S.E.2d 105 (SC, 1973); *Strohofer* v. *City of Cincinnati*, 451 N.E.2d 787 (OH, 1983); *Larson* v. *Township of New Haven*, 165 N.W.2d 543 (MN, 1969).
11 See Pine and Bickel, *Tort Liability Today*, 2.
12 *Evangelical United Brethren Church* v. *State*, 407 P.2d 440, 445 (WA, 1965).
13 Reynolds, *Local Government Law*, section 193.
14 *Ross* v. *Consumers Power*, 363 N.W.2d 641 (MI, 1984); *Zovala* v. *Zinser*, 333 N.W.2d 278 (MI App., 1983).
15 *Crenen* v. *Nox*, 611 S.W.2d 651 (TX App., 1980).
16 John C. Pine, *Tort Liability of Governmental Units in Emergency Actions and Activities* (Washington, DC: Federal Emergency Management Agency, 1988), 4.
17 *Trianon Park Condominium Assn.* v. *City of Hialeah*, 468 So.2d 912 (FL, 1985).
18 See *Trianon*, 915.
19 See *Trianon*, 917.
20 See Pine, *Tort Liability of Governmental Units*. Kansas, Nebraska, Nevada, Oklahoma, Rhode Island, Texas, Virgina, and Washington are the states that have such a provision in their comprehensive tort liability statute.
21 See Pine, *Tort Liability of Governmental Units*, 13. The states with such laws are Alaska, Kansas, South Carolina, and Utah.
22 See Pine, *Tort Liability of Governmental Units*, 14. States that limit immunity to actions related to hazards specifically named in the emergency management statute are Hawaii, Idaho, Kansas, Massachusetts, Montana, Oregon, Pennsylvania, and Tennessee.

23 Ill. Stat. Ann. 127.1302; La. Rev. Stat. Ann. 13:5108.2; Utah Code Ann. section 63–30–2.

24 *Archie* v. *City of Racine*, 826 F.2d 480, United States Court of Appeals, Seventh Circuit, 1987.

25 *Danculovich* v. *Brown*, 593 P.2d 187 (WY, 1979).

26 Col. Rev. Stat. section 24–33.5–902; Wis. Stat. Ann. section 893.82(3).

27 *Daniels* v. *Conn*, 382 So.2d 945 (LA, 1980).

28 Ala. Code section 11–93–1(2) 1975.

29 Ariz. Rev. Stat. Ann. section 12.820 1094.

30 For members of either a state emergency response commission (SERC) or an LEPC who serve in a dual capacity (in a volunteer capacity as a member of the SERC and as an employee of a chemical company), the courts could under some circumstances determine that the member's actions were representing not the state but the chemical company. If a member knew of the use or existence of a chemical but did not reveal the information to the LEPC, the court could conclude that the actions were on behalf of the company rather than the LEPC. The court will look at the facts of the situation to determine whom the member represents. Under some circumstances, the court could conclude that the LEPC member's actions were not on behalf or for the good of the state but on his or her own behalf or for his or her company. As long as the member is participating with the LEPC in good faith, for the public good rather than for private gain, in the public service, then the court would probably determine that the member's actions are as a representative of the SERC, the LEPC, or the state.

31 State officials range from the governor in *Scheuer* v. *Rhodes*, 416 U.S. 232 (1974), to prison officials in *Procunier* v. *Navarette*, 434 U.S. 555 (1978). For private organizations that perform public functions, see *Wright* v. *Arkansas Activities Association*, 504 F.2d 25, United States Court of Appeals, Fifth Circuit, 1987.

32 *Monell* v. *Department of Social Services of the City of New York*, 436 U.S. 658, United States Supreme Court, 1978.

33 *Quern* v. *Jordan*, 440 U.S. 332, United States Supreme Court, 1979.

34 365 U.S. 167, United States Supreme Court, 1961.

35 Ibid.

36 See, e.g., *Taylor* v. *Cochran*, 830 F.2d 900, United States Court of Appeals, Eighth Circuit, 1987.

37 *O'Neal* v. *DeKalb Co.*, 850 F.2d 653, United States Court of Appeals, Eleventh Circuit, 1987.

38 *O'Neal* v. *Krzeninski*, 839 F.2d 9, United States Court of Appeals, Second Circuit, 1988.

39 For decisions concerning state legislators, see *Tenny* v. *Brandlove*, 341 U.S. 367, United States Supreme Court, 1951. For decisions concerning judges, see *Pierson* v. *Ray*, 386 U.S. 547, United States Supreme Court, 1967.

40 *Wood* v. *Strickland*, 420 U.S. 308, United States Supreme Court, 1975. *Harlow* v. *Fitzgerald*, 457 U.S. 799, United States Supreme Court, 1984.

41 See *Reimer* v. *Short*, 578 F.2d 621, United States Court of Appeals, Fifth Circuit, 1978; *Ford* v. *Byrd*, 544 F.2d 194, United States Court of Appeals, Fifth Circuit, 1976; and *Harris* v. *Chanclor*, 537 F.2d 203, United States Court of Appeals, Fifth Circuit, 1976.

42 *Owen* v. *City of Independence*, 445 U.S. 622, United States Supreme Court, 1980.

43 42 U.S.C.A. section 2000e et. seq.

44 E.g., N.C. Stat. Ann. 166A–12.

45 Environmental Protection Agency Rules. *Federal Register* 51:211 (November 17, 1988), 41570.

46 "Title III: Emergency Planning and Community Right to Know," *EPA Journal* 13, no. 1 (January–February 1987).

47 42 U.S.C. Ann. section 1103.

48 42 U.S.C. Ann. section 11022 and 11023.

49 42 U.S.C. Ann. section 11021 and 11–43(b).

50 42 U.S.C. Ann. section 11046.

51 42 U.S.C. Ann. section 11046(g).

52 42 U.S.C. Ann. section 11046(f).

53 42 U.S.C. Ann. section 11046(g).

Part four:
The future of
emergency
management

12 Future directions

This chapter anticipates the future of emergency management by discussing relevant demographic trends; reviewing a number of emerging issues; and examining relations between academic researchers in emergency management and practitioners. The chapter concludes by briefly discussing the movement toward formalizing the profession and by surveying the basic challenges the profession must meet and the satisfactions it can offer.

Demographic change and future risk

Recent major disasters such as Hurricane Hugo, the Loma Prieta earthquake, and the Huntsville, Alabama, tornado are grim reminders of our nation's vulnerability to disaster. Most communities in the United States, large or small, are at risk from some type of natural hazard; many are exposed to multiple risks. While television viewers nationwide were watching scenes of the damage suffered by the Charleston, South Carolina, area during Hurricane Hugo, few were aware that the same area had been rocked by a major earthquake in 1886 and is still considered vulnerable to earthquakes. Even communities not visibly at risk from natural hazards are subject to technological hazards.[1] Moreover, the risk from natural and technological hazards is compounded by demographic trends that increase vulnerability: increasing population density; increasing migration to hazard-prone areas; and the growth of those segments of the population that are especially vulnerable to losses from disaster.

As the population continues to concentrate in urban areas, more and more people are exposed to the risks that those areas face. For example, some of the most violent earthquakes ever recorded in the United States were those centered on New Madrid, Missouri, in 1811 and 1812. At the time, the area was sparsely populated; if earthquakes of a similar magnitude were to occur today—and that region is still at risk—a major disaster would result. Conversely, the Loma Prieta earthquake, M 7.1 on the Richter scale, was a relatively moderate event—but because it occurred in the densely populated San Francisco Bay area, it caused billions of dollars' worth of damage.[2]

The second significant demographic trend is the movement of population and capital into hazard-prone areas of the country. For example, the rate of population growth along the Pacific, Atlantic, and Gulf coasts is high compared with that in most of the rest of the United States.[3] Partly because of this movement into high-risk areas, the annual per capita loss from natural hazards is expected to double during the 1970–2000 period, with the greatest losses resulting from such hazards as tornadoes, hurricanes, landslides, and earthquakes.[4] Referring to the hurricane hazard, one observer defined the problem as "continuing urban growth in high-risk coastal areas without a corresponding growth in our ability to protect developed property or to evacuate expanded populations in threatened areas."[5] The deaths and the billions of dollars in property damage caused by Hurricane Hugo are reminders of the risks people accept in choosing to live and work in attractive—but potentially deadly—environments.

The third factor contributing to increased risk is rapid growth among some

Figure 12–1 Disabled citizen at risk.

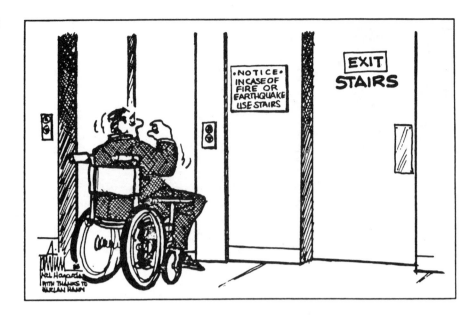

of the most vulnerable groups in society—elderly people, disabled people, minorities, and poor people. Physical, social, and cultural barriers put members of these groups at greater risk from hazards. Elderly and physically disabled people, for example, generally have more difficulty evacuating threatened areas; non-English-speaking minority groups may have problems taking proper protective actions because of language difficulties or a distrust of the authorities; and poor people often live in the most vulnerable structures. One of the primary tasks of emergency managers and policymakers is to devise effective strategies to help reduce the risk of particularly vulnerable segments of the population.

Because all three of the trends just described can be expected to continue, a comprehensive emergency management program should include close monitoring of changes in population density and composition as well as changes in settlement and transportation patterns. Such information will be crucial to shaping emergency plans in the years ahead. A comprehensive emergency management program should also reflect an awareness of a broad range of emerging issues.

Emerging issues

Chapter 1 listed a number of "emerging issues" that Thomas Drabek identified in a 1983 address to the Senior Executive Policy Center. This section provides a second look at several of those issues and discusses others as well. The issues discussed here involve the substance of emergency management in the 1990s and beyond, and they concern virtually every jurisdiction. The next nine subsections discuss mitigation; predisaster planning for recovery; natural disaster predictions; the psychological effects of disaster; the public perception of risk, and public policy; legal concerns; values and professional responsibilities; the role of the private sector; and federal, state, and local relations. In large part, it is by emergency managers' efforts in these areas that their success will be judged.

Mitigation

The view that the emergency manager's realm is limited to planning for and responding to disaster is losing currency. The emergency manager, to remain effective, must participate in governmental efforts to mitigate natural and technological hazards. As Beverly A. Cigler has observed,

the fatalistic assumption that natural disasters will happen and all we can do is cope is slowly being altered, leading to increased reliance on governmental action. . . . Citizens perceive that effective public management can decrease risks from such threats as the transportation of hazardous substances and explosions at fixed sites.[6]

The public perception that government should protect citizens from disasters or from the potential effects of disasters, or at least should make citizens whole following any disaster, expands the emergency manager's job.

Because mitigation relies on long-term, sometimes expensive measures to reduce vulnerability, "marketing" mitigation to a community can be extremely difficult. One reason for the difficulty is that the payback on mitigation investments may not be evident until the 100-year flood or the earthquake (whose recurrence period is unknown) occurs. In addition, the forces opposing mitigation are generally better organized and financed than those favoring such measures. The two sides in the conflict are likely to be developers and property owners, on the one hand, and a shifting alliance (depending on the particular issue) of public officials, such as building safety and zoning officials, on the other hand. Furthermore, as William Spangle and Associates, Inc., has noted, the diffusion of responsibility for key actions among various agencies is a common obstacle to implementation of seismic safety policies:

Seismic safety policies are usually the creations of the planning staff and planning commission, but responsibility for key actions often rests with others. For example, the building department enforces building codes; the public works department carries out the strengthening of public facilities; the fire department conducts safety inspections of commercial and industrial buildings; and the emergency services department assesses risks and prepares to respond. Each city and county has its own organization and names for the departments, but all these functions are rarely combined. Thus, putting together a successful program to implement seismic safety policy always requires cooperation among departments.[7]

Yet another obstacle to mitigation is attitudes about personal property and government regulation.[8] Without a strong constituency to support mitigation, elected officials may find it politically risky to take a stand in favor of programs that may abridge what some people hold to be their rights.

Although resistance to mitigation can be difficult to overcome, emergency managers are ideally situated to do so: of all those in the community, they have the greatest understanding of the potential hazards and are in the best position to develop a sound rationale for the adoption of mitigation measures. In addition, emergency managers can call upon their contacts and colleagues in other sectors of the community—for example, academicians, representatives of business and nonprofit organizations, and representatives of school- and community-based groups—to contribute their expertise, time, or influence to the campaign. Precisely because the opposition can be formidable, it is up to the emergency manager to play a leadership role in advocating mitigation.

Predisaster planning for recovery

A second major issue facing the contemporary emergency manager is the increasing importance assigned to pre-event planning for post-event recovery (PEPPER). Typically, decisions about recovery and reconstruction have been made after a disaster has struck, at a time when the community's systems, resources, and psychological resilience are already fully taxed. Effective planning for recovery ensures that policymakers have the tools they need to cope with the chaotic postdisaster environment. Plans and policies to guide decision making and facilitate the recovery process must be in place before the event. In developing the recovery plan, the emergency manager must be sure to work with eventual users. As is the case with any other element of the plan, the emergency manager's role is not to write the plan, but to make the recovery planning process happen.

Natural disaster predictions

Our increased ability to predict the occurrence of many kinds of natural disasters provides valuable lead time, enabling emergency managers to implement such emergency operations as public warnings and evacuations. Over the years, this increased predictive ability has been due to advances in science (such as greater knowledge about weather phenomena) and in technology (such as the advent of sophisticated computer programs that allow for the analysis of complex variables and for the development of innovative modeling techniques).

One area where some progress has been made—although much more remains to be done—is in the forecasting of coastal storms. The National Weather Service is at the center of an operational coastal storm prediction system that has become more mature through the years. This system was credited with helping to reduce the loss of life along the Atlantic Coast following Hurricane Hugo in 1989.[9] Systems for predicting such disaster agents as tsunamis and floods are also in operation.

Our scientific knowledge of earthquakes, however, has not advanced enough to permit accurate short-term prediction of these phenomena. Such a prediction would specify the time, location, and magnitude of an earthquake. Although much research in the United States and elsewhere has focused on this problem and some progress has been made, we are still a long way from having an operational earthquake prediction system in place. Yet earth scientists remain confident that someday reliable earthquake predictions will become a reality and will be as useful to emergency managers as hurricane forecasts are today.[10]

When it is possible to predict a natural disaster, emergency managers are key to the outcome. It is clear, for example, that to produce the desired public responses to impending threats, city and county emergency managers must be integrated into natural disaster prediction systems. Emergency managers should attempt to acquire some general understanding of the technological features of prediction systems as well as a clear notion of the role they themselves will play in those systems relative to other groups and organizations, including those at the state and federal levels. The people involved in the technological aspects of disaster prediction are important, but so are emergency managers, who determine and implement local policies and plans regarding such vital emergency actions as preparedness, warning, and evacuation. A cooperative effort is needed to realize the opportunities offered by natural disaster prediction for reducing the toll of a disaster.

Psychological effects of disaster

Social science research, described in more detail in a later section of this chapter, is contributing to growing understanding of the often profound and lasting psychological effects of disasters on victims and responders alike. Anyone who has been through a disaster may experience psychological aftereffects. Psychologists have found that postdisaster stress may be slow to manifest itself and that it is experienced by a significant proportion of victims and emergency workers. They do not agree, however, on what influences the development and course of the symptoms or on how widespread the effects are.[11]

The emergency manager must expect and plan for psychological effects on both victims and responders. Post-traumatic stress disorder is a medically recognized impairment for which treatment and prevention programs have been developed, but rapid and effective assessment and intervention are necessary to

Assisting victims Before, during, and after a search and rescue (SAR), keep the family members and close friends of the lost person apprised of the steps which are being taken to find, care for, transport, protect and otherwise assist the victim. Anxious people are starving for information. Regular, accurate, verifiable information is extremely important. If you don't provide official information, family members and friends will grab onto any rumor or distorted piece of information that happens to appear.

Appoint one SAR official to perform the task of family liaison. Too many officials in contact with the family members produces confusion and feelings of insecurity in the victims or family members and leaves SAR personnel open to stating contradictory information.

Acknowledge the fears, anger and anxieties of the victim's family and friends. Early acknowledgment and acceptance of even uncomfortable feelings can do much to prevent the potential for . . . family interference in the latter stages of an SAR.

Keep the media away from the family members to avoid intensifying their stress.

Provide safe, quiet, private places where families can gather.

Take care of the basic needs of family members such as warmth, shelter, and food.

Group the family members together. In situations where the family is large and where family members are disruptive, advise the family that you will share all information with one member who can then act as a family spokesman/liaison.

Once you have located the victim(s), assist them in orienting themselves

to place and time. Tell them approximately where you are, how long they have been missing, the current date and the time. People lost in wilderness areas are at times quite out of touch with time.

Talk to the victims. They need lots of reassurance and guidance. This is particularly important if they have been injured.

When appropriate, a gentle touch of the person's hand or shoulder may be extremely helpful.

Tell victims what you plan to do *before* you do it. Surprises are not a good idea for a traumatized person who is very anxious.

Discuss strategies and techniques with the victim when appropriate. Relaying a summary of the plan before it is initiated can do much to encourage cooperation from the victim.

Little kindnesses such as retrieving and protecting the victim's equipment are very much appreciated.

Encourage victims to express themselves and to talk to you whenever they wish.

Be honest. Any falsehood may complicate the situation later. You don't have to provide victims with every minute detail, but be honest in whatever you do say to them. If you don't know something for sure, tell victims that and try to assure them that you will get that information for them as soon as possible.

Source: Jeffrey T. Mitchell, "Critical Incident Stress Management," *Response!* (September/October 1986): 24–25. Reprinted with permission of RESPONSE!, copyright 1986: Jems Publishing Co., Inc.

The critical incident stress debriefing

A critical incident stress is any event which overwhelms the capacities of a person to psychologically cope with the incident. It may be a large-scale catastrophe like the Mexico City earthquake, but it is more likely a smaller, less dramatic event such as a missing child who turns up murdered in a wooded area. The type of event is not as important as the impact the event has on the people exposed to it. When the impact is negative and powerful, search and rescue people may benefit from a critical incident stress debriefing (CISD).

A CISD is a psychological and educational group process designed specifically for emergency workers with two purposes in mind. First, the CISD is designed to mitigate the impact of a critical incident on the personnel. Second, the CISD is designed to accelerate normal recovery in normal people who are experiencing the normal signs, symptoms, and reactions to totally abnormal events.

The CISD is led by a trained mental health professional or a specially trained CISD team and usually takes three hours to complete. People from a given SAR gather together to discuss their reactions to a bad event. Debriefings are usually only done after powerful events—not after routine situations.

The ideal time is 24 to 72 hours after an incident, although some are done earlier and others much later.

Workers are encouraged to discuss their own feelings and reactions. The event is talked about, but not for critiquing purposes. Instead, people express themselves and their reactions to their work in the field.

The CISD is structured in the following way:

An *introduction*, in which the ground rules, such as confidentiality, are set down.

The *fact phase*, in which the situation and the aspects of the situation which made it difficult to experience are briefly reviewed, with an emphasis on how those facts produced emotions.

The *thought phase*, in which the participants are able to state their first thoughts upon exposure to the worst part of the incident.

The *reaction phase*, in which participants can state their overall feeling or emotional reaction to the situation.

The *symptom phase*, in which the group can discuss the cognitive, physical, emotional and behavioral symptoms which occurred at the scene, within a few days or weeks after the incident.

The *teaching phase*, in which the group leader provides reassurance that what the members of the group are experiencing is a set of normal reactions to a bad incident and that they are not going crazy.

The *re-entry phase* is the concluding phase, in which people get a chance to ask questions and clarify what has occurred. Referrals for additional help and helpful summary statements can then be made by the leader and CISD team members.

Source: Adapted from Jeffrey T. Mitchell, "Critical Incident Stress Management," *Response!* (September/ October 1986): 24–25. Reprinted with permission of RESPONSE!, copyright 1986: Jems Publishing Co., Inc.

prevent long-term aftereffects and to accelerate the healing process. The emergency manager should establish ongoing programs for emergency response personnel to help them learn to recognize and deal with the stresses arising from emergency work. Such programs might include training peer counselors to assist co-workers. In addition, emergency managers should ensure that response personnel participate in critical-incident stress debriefing programs with mental health professionals in the immediate aftermath (within the first week) of a disaster or traumatic incident. These debriefing sessions are designed to deal with the psychological and emotional reactions to the experience and, optimally, can bring together personnel from various organizations (such as law enforcement, fire, and emergency medical personnel and public works and utility workers—who are likely to be among the immediate responders to a disaster). As two mental health practitioners have written, "Prevention and recovery from

---

Suggested readings on disasters and mental health Following are a few publications dealing with critical incident debriefing published by the National Institute of Mental Health. Requests for one complimentary copy of any of the publications listed below should be addressed to: Office of Scientific Information, Public Inquiries, National Institute of Mental Health, Room 15C-05, 5600 Fishers Lane, Rockville, MD 20857.

Disaster Work and Mental Health: Prevention and Control of Stress Among Workers, by Don M. Hartsough and Diane G. Myers, DHHS Pub. No. (ADM) 85-1422. This publication focuses attention on the need to increase understanding of the health and mental health effects of disaster work and provides a model training package for teaching emergency organizations and their workers how to prevent, ameliorate, and treat mental health problems arising out of emergency work.

Prevention and Control of Stress Among Workers: A Pamphlet for Team Managers, DHHS Pub. No. (ADM) 87-1496. This pamphlet contains information for managers to help them assist disaster workers in avoiding unnecessary stress on the job. It suggests interventions before, during, and after a disaster.

Prevention and Control of Stress Among Workers: A Pamphlet for

Workers, DHHS Pub. No. (ADM) 87-1497. This pamphlet provides information on common sources of stress among disaster workers and methods of ameliorating mental health problems resulting from such stress. It suggests interventions to workers that may be helpful before, during, and after a disaster.

Training Manual for Human Service Workers in Major Disasters, by Norman L. Faberow, DHHS Pub. No. (ADM) 86-538. This publication is designed for use in developing an effective response to emotional problems that may occur when a major disaster disrupts the functioning of individuals, families, communities, and regions.

Field Manual for Human Service Workers in Major Disasters, DHHS Pub. No. (ADM) 87-537. This manual has been designed to accompany the emergency worker into the field. Its aim is to provide the worker with essential information necessary to understand both human response to disaster and ways of addressing such responses.

Source: "Rescue for the Rescue Workers," Jim Rose, Pat Rheaume, and Tim Hunter, *Public Risk* (March/April 1990): 12. Reprinted with permission from *Public Risk* magazine, published by the Public Risk Management Association.

exposure to these traumatic situations is the responsibility of emergency organizations in collaboration with mental health professionals."[12]

Public perception of risk and public policy

The public perception of risk strongly affects the emergency manager's work. An informed public can be a major ally: awareness can lead to action, including pressure on legislators and other policymakers. For instance, increasing public concern about the release of hazardous materials used in industry led to hazardous materials right-to-know legislation in the 1980s. Public outcry following transportation accidents such as the 1989 *Exxon Valdez* oil spill in Alaska and the 1990 *American Trader* spill off the coast of southern California generated protective legislation and renewed interest in alternative means of transportation. Furthermore, the public perception of risks associated with nuclear power plants has significantly affected the siting, construction, and operation of nuclear facilities across the United States. In short, an informed and concerned public wields a significant amount of power, and a wise emergency manager will ensure that the public *stays* informed so that public power—and public policy—contribute to the strength of the emergency management program.

Perception of risk and communication   The emergency manager's first task is to understand the nature of the risks to which the community is subject and to learn to use the terminology associated with those risks. (An emergency manager who doesn't know the difference between a watch and a warning won't be of much use when a tornado threatens.) Next, the emergency manager must develop an ability to express technical information in terms that citizens and public officials can easily understand; for example, how does a tsunami "work"? What is the magnitude of difference between an earthquake that measures 5.0 on the Richter scale and one that measures 7.0? Communicating the nature and magnitude of risk—in terms that the public can understand—is essential to garnering support for every phase of the emergency management program. It is particularly important for mitigation because a public that is not aware of its vulnerability is not likely to take steps to lessen it. And when disaster is imminent, public safety may depend on the quick, accurate, and forceful communication of risk.

The emergency manager should also work with public officials and the media to ensure that *their* communications will be useful to the community. Officials may need assistance in understanding and articulating information about hazards. By working closely with the media, the emergency manager can see to it that information released to the public is both accurate and helpful. A good relationship with local media has an added benefit: it may allow the emergency manager access to the vast technical resources possessed by the major media, which can be extremely helpful during a disaster. For instance, helicopters normally used by news services for monitoring and reporting on local traffic conditions can be used for aerial damage assessment or rescue work; news teams' microwave video vans, or "minicams," can transmit vital information from key disaster sites to assist emergency responders; movie crews' mobile lights and generators can be used at collapsed buildings or other rescue sites. Furthermore, the media can be engaged to help change some of the attitudes and behavior that put people at risk. As has been pointed out, "better linkages between the public media and the community of hazard-mitigation researchers and practitioners—whether the linkages are scientific, technological or service-oriented—can make anti-hazard efforts more effective and, more important, can accelerate the shift in both the public's and the expert groups' thinking toward effective pre-disaster initiatives."[13]

Public policy options Emergency managers have widely varying effects on policy. One state-level emergency manager is currently well-known in Congress and throughout the United States, whereas others are obscure even within their own organizations. How can emergency managers affect policy? They must empower themselves. There is no single formula for success, but there are multiple strategies that emergency managers need to perfect (see sidebar).

Emergency managers interested in affecting public policy are faced with three major options: (1) adopt nothing new but continue to carry out existing policies; (2) adopt no new policies but improve the implementation of existing policies and programs; or (3) initiate proposals for major changes in existing policies.[14] In determining which option to pursue, the emergency manager must carefully evaluate his or her position in the public policy arena and the available tools and approaches.

The first challenge is simply to get *on* the public policy agenda; the second challenge is to stay there. Emergency managers must make their concerns part of the way a municipality, a state, the federal government, and private businesses do business. They must be alert to events or trends that could create an opening for change. Change can come quickly if the timing is right, and the time is most often right in the immediate aftermath of a disaster.

To increase their effect on policy, emergency managers can build a coalition of groups in support of emergency management issues. Fire officials, building officials, the local engineers' association, and university faculty members can unite with the emergency manager to present much more persuasive arguments for mitigation, for example, than any of them could alone. In addition, emergency managers cannot possibly hope to have any effect on land use practices unless they know and work with planners and planning and zoning boards.

Ultimately, the effect of emergency management thinking on public policy depends on leadership. In the 1990s, emergency management professionals at every level of government—and the public and corporate leaders whom they

---

Strategies for having a greater impact on public policy

1. Use "windows of opportunity" (e.g., heightened levels of awareness and interest in the aftermath of a disaster) to create change.

2. Identify and cultivate a wide range of potential allies, both inside and outside the organization.

3. Get yourself on the agenda of individual lawmakers; provide them with programs they can champion. Help them to be heroes.

4. Be a source of accurate, easily understood, and timely information.

5. Be sensitive to the various needs of the diverse constituencies that make up your community.

6. Emphasize teambuilding among agencies, and identify and work toward common goals.

7. Help bridge the gap between specialists' and politicians' views of reality by effectively communicating the risk of disaster.

8. Remove financial disincentives for emergency management programs by devising nontraditional funding mechanisms, such as incentives, public-private joint ventures, and federal (or state) and local joint programs in which federal (or state) funding is matched at the local level by in-kind contributions.

advise—are likely to face increased public scrutiny of how they do their jobs before, during, and after disasters, and a perceived lack of leadership is likely to be the most damaging indictment.

In summary, affecting public policy is difficult and not apt to become easier. The following points, made in 1982, are equally valid in the 1990s:

Public policy agendas at all levels are crowded with other issues, [and] the economizing pressures which have been exerted at all levels and jurisdictions of government have lowered staffing levels within existing operating agencies and made it difficult to keep up with routine work, much less to meet new challenges. Public understanding of natural hazards risks and public support for measures to cope with those risks are at comparatively low levels in contrast to other issues.[15]

Legal issues

Like other officials, emergency managers face legal issues in the course of their work. Legal issues can be complex, but legal advice is generally available through the employing jurisdiction. Emergency managers should be wary, however, of allowing such advice to substitute for a clear personal understanding of the legal implications of their actions.

Liability is the principal legal issue that arises from the administration of an emergency management program. Although some states provide protection from liability, such protection may not cover every emergency management action, and it is essential that emergency managers familiarize themselves with the precise protection afforded them under state law. It is also essential that emergency managers be aware of the principal areas of potential conflict between emergency management actions and statutory or constitutional rights. Consider the aftermath of the Loma Prieta earthquake: owners and residents of damaged buildings sought access to buildings that were in danger of total collapse, while the building and fire safety officials who were responsible for public protection sought to restrict access to the buildings. On the one hand, the action taken to reduce hazards may be viewed by the courts as infringing on private property rights. On the other hand, failure to take protective action in response to a known hazard can render public officials liable for damage to persons or property.

The best protection against infringement of rights is to ensure that

Regulatory measures are implemented and enforced fairly and systematically

The decision-making process is open, reasonable, and defensible

The exercise of police power is necessary for public protection and is not arbitrary, unreasonable, or discriminatory

When privately owned property is employed for public purposes, due process is followed.

The complexity of legal issues may seem daunting, but the emergency manager has at least the guideposts provided by statutory and constitutional law and legal precedent.

Values and professional responsibilities

As emergency managers play an ever-wider role in the public policy arena, it becomes increasingly important that they work from a solid base of professional skills and values and have a clear perception of their professional responsibilities. At the same time that academics and professional organizations are debating professional standards for emergency managers' education, training, and experience, practitioners active in the field are defining their values and professional responsibilities. Like any new profession, emergency management must be guided, in defining its values and responsibilities, by an openness to change, independent thinking, and tolerance for differing opinions.

Values Years of experience dealing with emergency managers have shown that despite their diverse backgrounds, emergency managers have relative singleness of purpose. The emergency management profession places highest value on the following:

Protection of life and property Emergency managers' basic mission is to enhance citizens' safety and security in the face of a wide range of threats.

Improvement of the quality of life By enhancing the preparedness of individuals and families as well as of business and government, emergency managers can greatly minimize the effects of disaster and facilitate recovery.

Protection of the environment Emergency managers are focusing more and more on protecting both people and an increasingly fragile environment from the harm caused by toxic materials and technological hazards.

Responsiveness to disaster victims, and responders' inner as well as physical needs Emergency managers are advocating intervention and prevention programs to help disaster victims and responders cope with the psychological aftereffects of the trauma.

Responsiveness to the special needs of society's diverse populations Emergency managers are tailoring programs to meet the needs of populations that are particularly vulnerable to disaster, such as people with disabilities, and to take into account the varying cultural and linguistic requirements of the community's members.

Promotion of justice and equity Emergency managers promote equal access to services and communitywide outreach.

Provision of mutual assistance and support Emergency managers value cooperation with co-workers and the sharing of ideas, plans, and programs to make their colleagues' jobs easier.

Proactiveness in approaching problem solving Emergency managers value a proactive, forward-thinking attitude to anticipate both the barriers they may encounter and the new tools they may be able to harness to simplify their jobs and improve their effectiveness.

Professional responsibilities What are emergency managers' professional responsibilities? The primary ones are to know the community they serve; to follow sound management principles in carrying on their work; and to set a good example to others.

Knowing the community Planning for disasters cannot occur in a vacuum; plans and programs reflect the values, views, and convictions of the emergency manager and other public officials and the plurality of interest within the community. Emergency managers must reach beyond the boundaries of their own convictions and views and embrace the diversity and pluralism of the organizations and institutions in their environment.

In particular, the emergency manager's job carries with it the responsibility of contributing to the creation and implementation of sound public policy in the context of his or her particular environment. For instance, in earthquake-prone areas, a program to strengthen structures likely to collapse in an earthquake may permanently or temporarily displace low-income renters. Thus, the rehabilitation program will eventually increase the life safety of the building's occupants, which is a valued outcome, but the short-term effect of evicting tenants from what may be the only housing they can afford is unacceptable. In such a case, emergency managers' professional responsibility would lead them to work as hard to ensure that tenants are protected as they would to urge adoption of the seismic strengthening program.

Knowing the community also means being able to foresee and plan for the potential social and economic effects of disasters. Experience has shown that when disaster strikes, many of society's problems are exacerbated: marginal business enterprises fail; displaced families join the chronically homeless in needing shelter and assistance; and relief agencies may be overwhelmed. The scramble for relief funding may cause funds to be diverted from other domestic programs, leaving those other needs unmet. The essence of emergency management is being prepared to deal with the unexpected. The more emergency managers anticipate the effects of disaster in their own community, the more effective the community's response and recovery will be.

Following sound management principles   Confronting complex problems and competing demands from constituencies requires emergency managers to develop skills in identifying, analyzing, and selecting alternatives. Their jobs also require them to participate in setting goals and objectives and measuring progress, effectiveness, and operational efficiency. In addition, they must ensure the continuing professional development of themselves, their staff, and their organizations. Doing all of that properly requires following sound management principles.

In particular, emergency managers must be prepared to participate in making difficult choices that weigh individual freedom against community good. For instance, should people be allowed to rebuild, time after time, in the same susceptible site, such as a barrier island, which is likely to be inundated by storm surge or ravaged by hurricane time after time? If they are afforded such freedom and consequently suffer repeated losses, should they receive public assistance to recover from their losses? What is the extent of government's obligation to protect people and property from potential natural disasters? In working with other public officials to address these types of issues, emergency managers must bring sound management principles to bear while also being sensitive to community values and attitudes toward the role of government.

Setting a good example   Emergency managers must set the example. This means they should adhere to high standards of professionalism and should demonstrate commitment, effective leadership, and a strong sense of teamwork. It also means they have a special responsibility to their employers and communities to maintain a high degree of personal readiness to meet the effects of disaster. They must constantly promote and take preparedness and mitigation actions within their own homes, families, and organizations. Family members and staff need constant retraining, drills, and exercises so that appropriate response actions occur naturally when an emergency occurs. Emergency managers must be sure that they and those closest to them avoid neglecting the very principles of sound emergency preparedness they preach to the community at large.

The role of the private sector

The role of the private sector in emergency management is growing. Examples of disaster mitigation investments and emergency preparedness actions on the part of major employers abound, particularly in geographic areas where the risk of disaster is well documented. In California, for example, the earthquake threat has persuaded corporate and business leaders to engage actively in planning, preparedness, and mitigation actions, to such an extent that some of the measures taken by businesses exceed the efforts and investments of local governmental agencies.

In the major population centers in California, it is not unusual for corporations to be involved in hazard mitigation, emergency planning, employee training and exercising, stocking of emergency supplies, and provision for back-up power, data processing, and other critical services. In addition, corporations that have taken the lead—in particular, several banks and financial institutions—have generously shared their expertise and assisted others. Brokers of corporate emergency planning guidelines include the Golden Gate (San Francisco) Chapter of the American Red Cross and California's two regional earthquake preparedness projects, the Bay Area Regional Earthquake Preparedness Project (BAREPP) and the Southern California Earthquake Preparedness Project (SCEPP).

Similar dedication of company time and resources is harder to achieve, of course, in smaller firms with access to fewer resources and in geographic areas where evidence of vulnerability to disaster is less convincing. Moreover, even in larger firms in times of economic downturn, programs with longer-term payoffs are generally viewed as more expendable than programs with direct contributions to short-term profits: the corporate emergency planner may be among the first to be laid off. Because preparedness programs at small firms may be non-existent—and those at large firms may be vulnerable—cooperation between the public and private sector in identifying risk, mitigating vulnerability, and preparing for disaster is particularly important.

Emergency preparedness has become a major concern at several of southern California's theme parks, especially Disneyland and MCA/Universal City Studios. Disneyland maintains supplies of food and water sufficient to feed ten thousand people for five days. The park also keeps rescue equipment, medical supplies, and emergency communications equipment on hand for use in evacuations and rescues, and it provides home and work-site preparedness training to employees. The MCA/Universal City Studios site has back-up power generators and enough food, water, and medical supplies to support visitors for between three and seven days. Staff are drilled regularly and have been trained in first aid, cardiopulmonary resuscitation, and evacuation procedures. Universal Studios also supports earthquake awareness efforts through its earthquake attraction on the studio tour. To maximize the educational value of the attraction, the studio worked closely with local public safety officials and educators in creating it.

Partnerships among business, government, and nongovernmental organizations have emerged nationwide, and their growing strength, impact, and numbers point the way to increased regional cooperative efforts, both formal and informal. For instance, in the Kanawha Valley of West Virginia, a 100-member group of representatives from business, industry, government, hospitals, the media, and volunteer emergency response and support organizations has formed the Kanawha Valley Emergency Preparedness Council (KVEPC). A private, non-profit organization, KVEPC has developed coordinated emergency plan elements for industry and government, provides emergency preparedness educational activities, and plays a major role in developing early warning systems and emergency communications for the valley's residents. And a pioneering business-government-volunteer organization in Los Angeles initiated by the mayor and several corporate leaders in 1983 (see sidebar) has already been duplicated in another region of California and has attracted attention across the United States and in several other countries.

Government–private-sector cooperative efforts are also emerging in response

BICEPP: A business and industry initiative   When Los Angeles Mayor Tom Bradley invited eighty corporate executives to a meeting in 1983, few had included emergency management in their corporate structures, and even fewer had created positions for emergency management coordinators. The mayor and other city officials made it clear to the executives that they needed to be prepared to be "on their own" for about seventy-two hours in the aftermath of a major earthquake because government personnel and resources would be fully committed to emergency response during that period. The mayor called on the executives to make a personal commitment to their companies and employees to prepare for disaster response and recovery, and the business leaders took the mayor's request to heart.

With city support, a core group of representatives of several major Los Angeles businesses formed a voluntary organization they named BICEPP, the Business and Industry Council for Emergency Planning and Preparedness. Based on the concept of business helping business to plan for survival, BICEPP's mission is to encourage emergency preparedness throughout the business sector and assist in the development and preparation of emergency response and recovery plans.

Initially, only a handful of corporations participated in the organization, sharing ideas and working to encourage emergency preparedness throughout the Los Angeles area business community. But from its modest beginnings, BICEPP has grown to be a healthy nonprofit corporation boasting an annual paid sponsorship of more than eighty southern California companies. As the organization has matured, its operations have become more complex, requiring the services of a policy advisory board, elected officers, an executive committee, and part-time paid staff. In keeping with its objectives of disseminating information and promoting and facilitating emergency management, BICEPP sponsors meetings, workshops, and seminars on topics of interest to the membership and produces the quarterly *BICEPP News*, which consists primarily of articles written by BICEPP's business members and state and local leaders. BICEPP also maintains a resource library in space provided by the Los Angeles chapter of the American Red Cross. The library includes examples of individual corporate emergency plans, materials developed for various BICEPP training activities, and other documents, slides, and videotapes useful in promoting emergency preparedness and organizing for response and recovery.

Seminars and workshops are BICEPP's primary means of encouraging interaction and mutual support among persons responsible for emergency preparedness in their companies. Topics are developed by subcommittees of BICEPP members and reflect current interests of the membership. BICEPP seminars distinguish themselves from others available in southern California because of their private-sector orientation. For instance, BICEPP's seminar on the Loma Prieta earthquake focused specifically on lessons learned by the San Francisco Bay area business community. Other BICEPP seminars have covered such topics as "Hazardous Materials: What Business and Industry Need to Know," "Recovery Planning, Business Survival," and "Earthquake Planning for Your Data Processing Center."

Although BICEPP is committed to continuing to focus on the Los Angeles area, it is responsive to requests for information and assistance from other areas. With BICEPP assistance, a sister organization has emerged in neighboring San Bernardino and Riverside counties: IBCEP, the Inland Business Council for Emergency Preparedness. And a New Zealand company has become a corporate BICEPP sponsor.

For more information, write to BICEPP, P.O. Box 57905, Los Angeles, CA 90057.

to increasing concern about the fact that 50 percent of the nation's missile and space business and about 75 percent of the microchip industry are located in California and are vulnerable to earthquakes. Defense contractors are currently working with the American Defense Preparedness Association, the Business and Industry Council for Emergency Planning and Preparedness (BICEPP), local government, and the Department of Defense, and all are supporting a Defense Industry Decade for Natural Disaster Reduction in the 1990s.

Along with increasing its involvement in mitigation and preparedness, the private sector has also increased its participation in response and recovery. Businesses' increasing contributions in these areas were clear in the two largest disasters in the United States in 1989: Hurricane Hugo and the Loma Prieta earthquake. Charitable aid from private firms around the world converged on those two sites, including everything from cash to generators, flashlights, cellular phones, drinking water, and boxcars full of plywood, to service such as free storage at storage facilities.

The charitable donations from major businesses that poured into the Bay area after the Loma Prieta earthquake included $1.4 million from major league baseball and $1 million from Anheuser-Busch. Other corporate givers included Chevron, Shell Oil, Pacific Gas and Electric, and Levi Strauss. International firms active in Bay area markets made contributions of as much as $1 million each, including Hanson Industries of Great Britain and Sony, Toyota, and Nissan of Japan. The California State Department of Transportation received two twenty-two-ton hydraulic excavators valued at $180,000 each from Komatsu. Corporate involvement can be expected to play a significant role in relief from future disasters.

Businesses, of course, are victims as well as heroes in disasters. Even small-scale disasters can put smaller firms out of business by destroying stock and wrecking storefronts and offices. Businesses that operate with small profit margins rarely have much money to invest in insurance, mitigation, or preparedness. Larger firms that suffer damage are often better able to cope with the effects.

Public-sector emergency managers should assist small local businesses by helping them to understand and prepare for the risks they face. Local business groups such as chambers of commerce can provide a means of educating small businesses about preparedness. The emergency manager can make planning guidance (such as checklists and information about basic steps to protect employees) available to the business community. FEMA has developed guidance for business and industry in its *Disaster Planning Guide for Business and Industry* and *Disaster Mitigation Guide for Business and Industry*. To meet the needs of small businesses in earthquake country, emergency managers can disseminate such tools as the *Guidelines for Local Small Businesses in Meeting the Earthquake Threat*, developed by SCEPP.[16]

To maintain the economic viability of any region in the aftermath of disaster, a healthy private sector is as necessary as a healthy public sector. A community's recovery from disaster depends on both.

Federal, state, and local relations

Enabling legislation in the 1950s distributed responsibility for civil defense, flood insurance, and disaster relief among federal, state, and local governments, but this shared responsibility has often been marked by conflict over priorities and funds.[17] The federal government, for its part, can exert various forms of influence—including financial influence—on state and local emergency management programs. At the state and local levels, the desire is to continue to receive federal funding while remaining as independent as possible of federal constraints.[18]

Federally administered dollars are critical to a wide range of state and local emergency management programs, and as states and local jurisdictions face limitations on their ability to raise revenues, their reliance on federal money increases. Federal funds, however, are distributed according to federal priorities (and may be accompanied by requirements and regulations that conflict with state and local needs). For example, in 1977 Congress enacted the Earthquake Hazards Reduction Act and appropriated $53 million to implement the act; but ten years later, when the state and local levels needed more funding for earthquake hazards reduction, total federal funding under the act was $66 million, the equivalent of a one-third *decrease* in purchasing power. And only about $1.3 million—or 2 percent—of that amount supported state and local hazard reduction projects. (For fiscal year 1990, however, Congress appropriated an additional $20 million for earthquake hazard reduction programs, a level of spending expected to be maintained for FY 1991.)

Another area of potential conflict between the federal and other levels of government is the relative priority assigned to preparedness for nuclear attack. Although some state and local emergency management agencies support attack preparedness as a first priority, others believe that limited resources would be better spent on preparedness for technological and natural hazards. FEMA's continuing commitment to attack preparedness may create difficulties for state and local agencies concerned about other hazards. Although very different selection criteria may apply to nuclear attack shelters and shelters that would be appropriate for other hazards, such as flooding, FEMA's administrative priorities in preparing its 1990 budget were that

FEMA will continue to identify shelters, building on the present shelter data base, that may be needed in the event of a nuclear attack. Although emphasizing protection against attack hazards, many shelters identified within the State can provide some protection against other hazards as well.[19]

Federal, state, and local emergency management agencies tend to come together in two situations: first, in the event of disaster, and second, in the pursuit, dispersal, and regulation of federal moneys; and neither situation is particularly conducive to the development of close working relationships. To obtain the greatest benefit from their work together, emergency managers throughout federal, state, and local systems must strive to understand the differences between their perspectives and to overcome the barriers to cooperation that such differences can create.

Disaster research and emergency management

A symbiotic relationship exists between the field of disaster research and the emergency management profession; as producers of knowledge, disaster researchers often must turn to emergency managers for information vital to the studies they undertake. And emergency managers become users of the knowledge produced by disaster researchers, relying upon it to inform their decision making.

Because emergency managers can learn valuable lessons from studies of hazards and disasters, it is important that emergency managers and professionals in related fields know something about the field of disaster research. This section of the chapter offers a brief glimpse into that field and some suggestions about how emergency managers can tap the growing body of knowledge it provides. (Although this discussion focuses on social science disaster research, emergency managers should also acquaint themselves with applicable research in the physical sciences, such as seismology and meteorology.)

The origins of the field of disaster research in North America can be traced to Samuel Prince's study of the 1917 Halifax, Nova Scotia, disaster. Since Prince's study, the field has evolved into a small but well-established area of research conducted largely by university-based researchers. They represent a range of social science disciplines—including anthropology, political science, psychology, and public administration—but this breadth is a relatively recent development.

Through much of its history, disaster research was dominated by geographers and sociologists, who tended to work and communicate primarily with others in their own disciplines. Their training, moreover, led them to emphasize certain topics and approaches and neglect others. Geographers, for example, focused largely on predisaster issues such as mitigation and the perception of hazards. Sociologists focused primarily on group and organizational responses to disasters.

Trends in disaster research

One trend in disaster research today is an increase in interdisciplinary work and in the involvement of researchers from a wide mix of social science disciplines. In addition, sociologists are now investigating subjects that once caught the attention only of geographers, and vice versa. As a result, the field of disaster research is being enriched by the growing diversity of topics studied and by the emergence of researchers who are calling attention to previously neglected areas of research.[20] To mention only a few such instances, legal researchers are studying the legal aspects of mitigation and preparedness, political scientists the formu-

---

Some key areas of research

Mitigation   Federal, state, and local floodplain management

The impact on mitigation of the perception of hazards

The role of financial institutions in earthquake hazard mitigation

State and local government adoption of mitigation measures

Factors that help shape the effectiveness of various mitigation measures

The use of research results in mitigation and preparedness programs.

Preparedness   The effectiveness of warning and evacuation planning

The role of hazard information dissemination programs in preparedness

Socioeconomic implications of earthquake prediction

Preparedness planning for predicted hazard events

Problems associated with preparedness planning at the local, state, and federal levels.

Response   Community response to disaster warning

The role of the mass media during the response period

Differences in the impact of disaster on various population groups

The nature of search and rescue operations

The effectiveness of disaster assistance from government and voluntary organizations.

Recovery   The long-term effects of disaster

The nature of family recovery from disaster

The problems of community recovery from disaster

Opportunities for postdisaster hazard mitigation.

Source: William A. Anderson et al., "Emergency Management Practice and Research in the United States," *Proceedings of the Coordination Council for North American Affairs– American Institute in Taiwan Joint Seminar on Research for Multiple Hazards Mitigation* (Tainan, Taiwan: National Cheng-Kung University, 1984): 591–93.

lation and adoption of disaster policy, and land use planning researchers means of incorporating hazard reduction measures into the disaster recovery process. Furthermore, interdisciplinary teams are shedding light on such previously neglected topics as the experiences of physically disabled persons in hazardous situations and the consequences of earthquake prediction.

A second significant trend in disaster research is the growing internationalization of the field.[21] One of the principal manifestations of this is the growing worldwide contact among researchers, and U.S. researchers are at the center of this development. Through publications, conferences, workshops, and individual meetings, U.S. researchers are exchanging research results with colleagues in Canada and Europe as well as in such faraway locales as Australia, Japan, Taiwan, and the People's Republic of China. Institutions such as the Disaster Research Center at the University of Delaware host visiting scholars and have trained numerous foreign researchers. Furthermore, U.S. researchers play leading roles in such organizations as the International Sociological Association's Research Committee on Disasters, which facilitates the cross-cultural exchange of ideas through international conferences and through the *International Journal of Mass Emergencies and Disasters.*

One potential stimulus for new ideas in emergency management is the International Decade for Natural Disaster Reduction designated in December 1987 by the United Nations General Assembly. The concept was initially promoted by Frank Press, president of the U.S. National Academy of Sciences. The U.N. has urged all countries to pursue their own research and hazard reduction programs and to cooperate with other nations to reduce the threat of natural disasters in the 1990s. Some Decade activities have already been initiated in the United States: through funding by federal agencies, a U.S. National Decade Committee was formed at the National Academy of Sciences, and several conferences have been held in the United States under the Decade theme.

A third major trend in disaster research is the increasing expectation that researchers communicate their findings to emergency management practitioners and not only to academic colleagues. The next subsection of this chapter explores techniques that policymakers and emergency managers can use to build links to the disaster research community in order to make use of the knowledge it produces.

How researchers can increase the use of their research results

1. Become active in associations and organizations to which both knowledge producers and knowledge users belong.

2. When designing a research project, keep in mind the specific groups that may use the results.

3. During the course of the project, be sensitive to ways in which the research might be modified to meet emerging user needs or changed definitions of the problem.

4. Plan to produce at least one product that is aimed at a potential user group.

Source: Adapted from Joanne M. Nigg, "Frameworks for Understanding Knowledge Dissemination and Utilization: Applications for the National Earthquake Hazards Reduction Program," in *A Review of Earthquake Research Applications in the National Earthquake Hazards Reduction Program: 1977–1987*, ed. Walter W. Hays (Reston, VA: U.S. Geological Survey, 1988), 23.

Links between the two communities

Because the field of disaster research has its own culture—its own set of norms and values, its own special language—even the highly motivated emergency manager needs time and effort to obtain, understand, and make use of the findings of disaster research, which are sometimes hidden in obscure documents that might seem incomprehensible at first glance. Despite the difficulties involved, emergency managers must learn how to overcome the cultural barriers that separate them from disaster researchers and must establish continuing ties with them.

As noted earlier, most disaster researchers—whatever their field—are employed by universities, which means that they are affected in some way by the desire to gain tenure and promotion and receive the recognition of their peers. The usual path to professional recognition is to conduct research that can be shown to follow the rules of scientific inquiry and contribute to the knowledge base in a particular discipline. To those outside the field, much disaster research may seem to have been selected with little regard for its potential practical application but because it will appeal to university colleagues. Nevertheless, the gap between the disaster research community and the emergency management community can be—and often is—bridged. Disaster researchers have many reasons to work in the field apart from the rewards granted by the university community, including a genuine interest in reaching out to practitioners and ensuring that research findings are disseminated in a form that practitioners can use.

The culture of disaster research can be thought of as a continuum: at one end are researchers actively committed to reaching out to practitioners; at the other end are their more passive colleagues (passive, that is, in terms of seeking contact with practitioners). The "active" disaster researcher develops and maintains ties to the emergency management community and aggressively pursues innovative approaches to information dissemination, rather than relying on the usual journal article to do the job. Humanitarian concerns often motivate such researchers, but other factors that encourage activism include the expectations of research funding agencies, the increasing professionalism of emergency managers, and the existence of formal opportunities for interaction between researchers and emergency managers, such as the Annual Natural Hazards Workshop held at the University of Colorado by the Natural Hazards Research and Applications Information Center.

Figure 12–2 The "gap" between researchers and practitioners.

Emergency managers   Disaster researchers

Furthermore, responsibility for widening the use of research findings cannot be laid at the feet of researchers alone. Practitioners have a corresponding responsibility to interact with researchers to make their needs and interests known. Meetings such as the previously mentioned Natural Hazards Workshop provide the perfect setting for such contacts.

Another way to encourage practitioner-oriented research is for practitioners to participate in observation visits to disaster sites. For instance, qualified emergency management personnel can apply to participate in the Earthquake Engineering Research Institute's (EERI) Learning from Earthquakes program, which sponsors post-earthquake investigations by multidisciplinary teams. EERI also sponsors seminars, and publishes reports to disseminate the teams' findings. The reports are available to all interested parties.

A further option is to create local practitioner-researcher teams to conduct on-site investigations of specific issues of concern to the team. An experiment with this approach joined a Natural Hazards Research and Applications Information Center researcher with a multidepartmental team of emergency management practitioners from the city of Los Angeles to investigate the Loma Prieta earthquake. Indications are that joint researcher-practitioner teams can provide special advantages: for example, strengthening links between governmental jurisdictions and nearby research and educational institutions and improving understanding of each others' needs and capabilities. Participation in such a team might lead researchers to take a special interest in the concerns of their own communities, and participating emergency managers might acquire a better understanding of proven field investigation techniques.

Dissemination and application of research results

Despite the difficulties involved, there is evidence that some of the information being produced by disaster researchers is reaching and being applied by emergency managers.[22] Disaster research findings are informing the decision making of organizations throughout the country and are reflected in the plans, procedures, and training efforts of entities at all levels of government as well as the private sector. For example, research results on disaster warning and education have found their way into organizations such as the U.S. Geological Survey and the National Weather Service. Among other things, these organizations have incorporated into their procedures disaster research findings on risk perception, public response to warning signals, and the special needs of different population groups confronting disaster. Similarly, a national broadcasting organization relied on disaster research results to develop guidelines for broadcasting disaster information. Also at the national level, organizations like FEMA and the American Red Cross have been major consumers of disaster research information. FEMA has relied upon the body of knowledge on emergency preparedness to develop instructional material and training courses for emergency managers, and the Red Cross has used similar information for training purposes and for its shelter program.

Disaster research is also being applied at the state and local levels. State and local emergency management officials have reported using Thomas Drabek's work on search and rescue and on the emergency management profession in courses for emergency managers and policymakers.[23] Local emergency managers in various parts of the country have incorporated findings by Ronald Perry and other scholars on emergency evacuation into the planning process for hurricanes, floods, and tsunamis.[24] Preparedness organizations such as SCEPP and BAREPP have relied heavily on disaster research in developing their preparedness and training materials. One BAREPP official said that such information proved its worth during the response to the 1989 Loma Prieta earthquake.[25]

As these few examples indicate, the gap between the disaster research and emergency management communities can be closed, allowing valuable information to be applied to emergency management problems. Such outcomes are often due at least in part to emergency managers' deliberate efforts to obtain information produced by disaster researchers.

Information dissemination system

In the United States, information on hazards and disasters is disseminated through a loosely knit information system. (Although this "system" is fragmented, there are enough connections between the groups that disseminate information to warrant thinking of them as part of a system.)

What are the components of this system? First, of course, are the researchers who provide the information that is to be disseminated. Among the users in this system are the policymakers and emergency managers who require information to carry out their responsibilities. Another part of the system is governmental and quasi-governmental bodies such as FEMA, the National Science Foundation, the U.S. Geological Survey, the National Weather Service, and the National Academy of Sciences, which fund or conduct their own research, fund dissemination, or carry out their own dissemination programs. Professional organizations such as the Association of Flood Plain Managers, the National Coordinating Council on Emergency Management, and ICMA are another important component of the system. Because of the credibility these professional organizations have in the eyes of their constituents, they often play a particularly important role in calling attention to and interpreting new information.

The picture would not be complete without mention of clearinghouses and libraries. The best of them, such as the Natural Hazards Research and Applications Information Center (NHRAIC) at the University of Colorado, offer information in the variety of formats that is often required to facilitate the use of research findings. The NHRAIC provides information on hazards through

---

Key factors in the application of research

The policies of funding agencies have a major impact on the dissemination and application of findings. Agencies that fund disaster research, such as the National Science Foundation (NSF) and the Federal Emergency Management Agency (FEMA), encourage researchers to interact with the emergency management community and to devise strategies to disseminate their research results to practitioners. Funding agencies have sponsored research projects and conferences to help researchers better understand how to help practitioners use their research results.

Communication between researchers and practitioners facilitates the application of results. Communication can break down barriers to mutual understanding.

Involving potential users in research planning increases the chances for the application of research results.

Dissemination through different formats and channels may be required before users can apply a new body of knowledge. In such instances, redundancy should be encouraged.

Source: Robert K. Yin and Gwendolyn B. Moore, *The Utilization of Research: Lessons from the Natural Hazards Field* (Washington, DC: Cosmos Corporation, 1985), 69–81; and Working Group on Earthquake Hazards Reduction, *Earthquake Hazards Reduction: Issues for an Implementation Plan* (Washington, DC: Office of Science and Technology Policy, 1978), 62–63.

its library and publications program and views its primary role as linking researchers and practitioners. Its Annual Natural Hazards Workshop is one of the major ways it does this.

The Disaster Research Center (DRC) library has one of the world's premier collections of documents relevant to emergency management. Its archives contain both published and unpublished reports on natural and technological disasters, as well as an extensive collection of disaster plans from jurisdictions around the country. Although the major mission of the DRC is to conduct research, its library is a vital resource used by scholars and practitioners alike.

Whereas the NHRAIC and the DRC are examples of organizations in the information dissemination system that provide information on a broad range of hazards and disasters, SCEPP and its sister organization BAREPP focus more, as their names imply, on earthquakes. SCEPP and BAREPP constitute a joint southern and northern California preparedness effort. SCEPP, whose offices are in Los Angeles and San Diego, was created in 1980; BAREPP, located in Oakland, was formed a few years later. Both programs are supported by FEMA and the state of California. As part of their efforts to encourage earthquake preparedness in the two regions of California they represent, both programs attempt to serve as links between researchers and practitioners by maintaining information resource centers and interpreting and packaging information for users.[26]

Ties exist between many of the groups that constitute the disaster information dissemination system in the United States, although not all groups are directly linked to one another. The four organizations briefly discussed above, however, do have rather definite connections. For example, they are aware of one another's activities, and many of the professionals in the four organizations share information and ideas at workshops and conferences. Nevertheless, information dissemination in the disaster field is still quite fragmented, often resulting in gaps in the system, duplication of effort, and a user community that is often confused as to where to turn for vital information.

The role of changing information technology

One of the promises of computer information technology is that it may help reduce some of the fragmentation of the information dissemination system. Some of the key hazard information organizations are already providing computer access to their databases. For example, the National Center for Earthquake Engineering Research at the State University of New York at Buffalo has a computerized database of hazard and disaster literature that is accessible to local and national users. Although creating and maintaining such databases is currently time-consuming and expensive, in the future computer-linked databases may significantly facilitate the dissemination of hazard information.

Some researchers and practitioners in the field have called for the creation of a truly national center for the dissemination of disaster information. One vision is that such a center would be staffed by research utilization specialists sensitive to user needs and would link users to existing sources of information rather than create duplicate archives.[27] Perhaps such a center would be the logical place to maintain the integrated disaster-loss database called for by some in the field. In the meantime, emergency information dissemination efforts, such as the network initiated in 1987 by the United Nations Disaster Relief Organization (UNDRO), suggest intriguing future possibilities (see sidebar).

The profession of emergency management

Although no hard and fast rules currently dictate who may claim the title of emergency manager, the decade of the 1980s saw a surge in interest among both academics and practitioners in formalizing emergency management as a profession. Emergency management is evolving as a discipline primarily within the field of public administration, although it also considerably overlaps crisis management within the field of business administration. Following a 1983 FEMA initiative, efforts to bring emergency management into the mainstream of public administration education were undertaken jointly by FEMA, ICMA, and the National Association of Schools of Public Affairs and Administration (NASPAA). The results of these efforts included an emergency management workshop for public administration faculty at FEMA's Emergency Management Institute and the 1985 publication of a special issue of *Public Administration Review*, the journal of the American Society for Public Administration.

FEMA is also funding a grant project being carried out by the National Coordinating Council on Emergency Management (NCCEM), a national nonprofit professional organization established in 1952, to define and develop professional standards. NCCEM's Advisory Council on Professional Standards is exploring issues of certification and requirements, including training, education, and experience, which will affect the future of the profession by ensuring that basic standards are met or that those who enter the profession have basic skills.

Emergency managers should support efforts to define and formalize emergency management education and the emergency management profession. Such efforts can only strengthen the education and training available to practitioners. Emergency managers should also participate as trainers and students in available courses—and lobby for more. If emergency managers are to be agents of change, they require continuing education to stay abreast of the advances in technology, science, and management that can affect emergency management plans and policies.

This and previous chapters have included considerable discussion of the development of emergency management, the information and skills that emergency managers need to have at their disposal, the issues and challenges they will

UNIENET To make its disaster-related information accessible to the emergency management community throughout the world, UNDRO initiated a computerized information network in mid-1987, called UNIENET (United Nations International Emergency Network). This system links microcomputers around the world with the UNIENET central computer via telephone lines, enabling any computer on the network to communicate with any other. While the network is managed by UNDRO, it is a cooperative effort involving several organizations concerned with emergency management. UNIENET features an electronic mail system and several bulletin boards and databases. The electronic mail permits information to be sent from one terminal to another, while the bulletin boards contain bibliographic information, relatively short reports on current disaster situations, and other information provided both by UNDRO and by the other organizations cooperating in this effort. Several available databases provide users with more detailed information, which may be searched for specific information of interest, for example, the UNDRO disaster situation reports. As the system is developed further, it is expected that more databases will be added, as well as bulletin boards provided by other organizations concerned with emergency disaster management.

Source: Adapted from Charles Kerpelman, "International Disaster Management Information Network," *UNDRO NEWS* (January/February 1988): 9–11 (updated October 1990).

confront, and ongoing efforts to professionalize the field. It should be apparent that emergency management is first and foremost management: directing the use of resources to solve problems. Emergency managers face diverse players and priorities in a complex environment filled with obstacles to accomplishment and achievement. By observing and exercising sound management and organizational principles and practices, borrowed from the fields of public administration and business management, they will be able to effect positive change in the way government and business go about their business in their communities.

Emergency managers must also be willing to do a hard job and to make a commitment to the future of the community that employs them. For as public servants they get the really tough problems, the ones with multiple constituencies and limited funding.

Furthermore, emergency managers can make a difference in people's lives—an exciting but daunting prospect. So emergency managers can't do their jobs half-heartedly because, when disaster arrives, not only will the ineffective emergency manager be exposed but the community will suffer needlessly. Emergency managers must therefore not only be committed to, but must also live up to, the responsibility placed on them.[28] For them, as for anyone in the public trust, the real proof ultimately is in the *doing*. Good intentions are not enough.[29]

1 E. L. Quarantelli, *Sociobehavioral Responses to Chemical Hazards: Preparations for and Responses to Acute Chemical Emergencies at the Local Community Level* (Columbus: Disaster Research Center, Ohio State University), 3.

2 Some observers have suggested that burgeoning Third World cities are even more at risk from natural hazards than urban areas in the United States. Construction in Third World cities, for example, is often less disaster-resistant than construction in cities in more industrialized nations. See Spenser W. Havlick, "Building for Calamity," *Environment* (November 1986): 6–45.

3 David R. Godschalk, David J. Brower, and Timothy Beatley, *Catastrophic Coastal Storms* (Durham, NC: Duke University Press, 1989), 2.

4 William J. Petak and Arthur A. Atkisson, *Natural Hazard Risk Assessment and Public Policy: Anticipating the Unexpected* (New York: Springer-Verlag, 1982), 199.

5 Godschalk, et al., *Catastrophic Coastal Storms*, 4.

6 Beverly A. Cigler, "Current Policy Issues in Mitigation," in *Managing Disaster: Strategies and Policy Perspectives*, ed. Louise K. Comfort (Durham and London: Duke University Press, 1988), 40–41.

7 William Spangle and Associates, Inc., Martha Blair-Tyler, and Penelope A. Gregory, *Putting Seismic Safety Policies to Work* (developed for Bay Area Earthquake Preparedness Project, October 1988), 3.

8 Cigler, "Current Policy Issues in Mitigation," 47.

9 Roy Popkin, "Hurricane Hugo Was a Disaster . . . and a Victory," *Hazard Monthly* (November 1989), 7.

10 Dennis S. Mileti, Janice R. Hutton, and John H. Sorensen, *Earthquake Prediction Response and Options for Public Policy* (Boulder: Institute of Behavioral Science, University of Colorado, 1981).

11 *The National Earthquake Hazards Reduction Program: Commentary and Recommendations of the Expert Review Committee 1987* (Washington, DC: FEMA, 1987), 31.

12 Norma S. Gordon and Carl A. Maida, "Emer-gency Service Workers: Coping with the Stress of Caring," *BICEPP News* (Spring 1989): 14.

13 Stephen Rattien, "The Role of the Media in Hazard Mitigation and Disaster Management," in *Communication When It's Needed Most: How New Technology Could Help in Sudden Disasters*, report of the International Disaster Communications Project (The Annenberg Washington Program, Communications Policy Studies, Northwestern University, 1989), 52.

14 Petak and Atkisson, *Natural Hazard Risk Assessment*.

15 Petak and Atkisson, *Natural Hazard Risk Assessment*, 434–35.

16 FEMA, *Disaster Planning Guide for Business and Industry*, FEMA 141 (Washington, DC: FEMA, 1987); FEMA, *Disaster Mitigation Guide for Business and Industry*, FEMA 190 (Washington, DC: FEMA, 1990); and Southern California Earthquake Preparedness Project, *Guidelines for Local Small Businesses in Meeting the Earthquake Threat* (Los Angeles: SCEPP, 1982).

17 Peter J. May, "FEMA's Role in Emergency Management: Examining Recent Experience," *Public Administration Review* 45 (January 1985): 40, 41.

18 Ibid., 41.

19 "Testimony of the Honorable Julius W. Becton, Jr., Director, FEMA, Before the Subcommittee on Military Installations and Facilities, Armed Services Committee, House of Representatives, March 15, 1989," *FY 1990 Congressional Civil Defense Testimony*, FEMA-179 (Washington, DC: Office of Civil Defense, FEMA, June 1989), 12.

20 See, for example, Thomas E. Drabek, *Human System Responses to Disaster: An Inventory of Sociological Findings* (New York: Springer-Verlag, 1986).

21 Russell R. Dynes, "Cross-Cultural and International Research: Sociology of Disaster," *International Journal of Mass Emergencies and Disasters* 6 (August 1988): 101–29.

22 Robert K. Yin and Gwendolyn B. Moore, *The Utilization of Research: Lessons from the Natural Hazards Field* (Washington, DC: Cosmos Corporation, 1985).

23 See, for example, Thomas E. Drabek, Harriet L. Tamminga, Thomas S. Kilijanek, and Christopher A. Adams, *Managing Multiorganizational Emergency Responses: Emergency Search and Rescue Networks in Natural Disasters and Remote Area Settings* (Boulder: Institute of Behavioral Science, University of Colorado, 1981); and Thomas E. Drabek, *Emergency Management: Strategies for Maintaining Organizational Integrity* (New York: Springer-Verlag, 1990).

24 See, for example, Ronald W. Perry, Michael Lindell, and Marjorie Greene, *Evacuation Planning in Emergency Management* (Lexington, MA: D.C. Heath, Lexington Books, 1981); and Ronald W. Perry and Alvin Mushkatel, *Disaster Management* (Westport, CT: Greenwood Press, 1984).

25 Personal communication to William A. Anderson.

26 James D. Goltz and Paul J. Flores, "Innovative Planning and Knowledge Transfer: The History of the Southern California Earthquake Preparedness Project (SCEPP)," in *A Review of Earthquake Research Applications in the National Earthquake Hazards Reduction Program: 1977–1987*, ed. Walter W. Hays (Reston, VA: U.S. Geological Survey, 1988), 34–58; and Richard K. Eisner, "Advocacy of Earthquake Preparedness: The Bay Area Regional Earthquake Preparedness Project (BAREPP)," in Ibid., 59–64.

27 Working Group on Earthquake Hazards Reduction, *Earthquake Hazards Reduction: Issues for an Implementation Plan* (Washington, DC: Office of Science and Technology Policy, 1978), 66.

28 Adapted from a class lecture by Professor Marc J. Roberts at the John F. Kennedy School of Government, Harvard University, June 1989.

29 Paraphrase of a statement by Daniel J. O'Donaghue, president, O'Donaghue Associates, at a City of Los Angeles Recovery and Reconstruction Workshop, Lake Arrowhead, CA, September 24, 1989.

Bibliography

This bibliography is highly selective and represents informed judgments about materials of interest to local officials. It is intended to supplement the endnotes to individual chapters. The bibliography is arranged by chapter for the convenience of the reader, although some items cover a number of the topics explored in the text. Such references will, therefore, be shown in each applicable chapter.

1 The evolution of emergency management

Barton, Allen H. *Communities in Disaster: A Sociological Analysis of Collective Stress Situations*. Garden City, NY: Doubleday, 1969.

Blanchard, B. Wayne. *American Civil Defense 1945–1984: The Evolution of Programs and Policies*. Emmitsburg, MD: FEMA, 1984.

Burby, Raymond J., Steven P. French, Beverly A. Cigler, Edward J. Kaiser, David J. Moreau, and Bruce Stiftel. *Flood Plain Land-Use Management: A National Assessment*. Boulder, CO: Praeger, 1985.

Clary, Bruce B. "The Evolution and Structure of Natural Hazard Policies." *Public Administration Review* 45 (January 1985): 20–28.

Cuny, Frederick C. *Disasters and Development*. New York: Oxford University Press, 1983.

Drabek, Thomas E. *Emergency Management: Strategies for Maintaining Organizational Integrity*. New York: Springer-Verlag, 1990.

_____. *Human System Responses to Disaster: An Inventory of Sociological Findings*. New York: Springer-Verlag, 1986.

_____. *The Professional Emergency Manager: Structures and Strategies for Success*. Boulder: Institute of Behavioral Science, University of Colorado, 1987.

_____. *Some Emerging Issues in Emergency Management*. Emmitsburg, MD: National Emergency Training Center, FEMA, 1984.

Dynes, Russell R. *Organized Behavior in Disaster*. Lexington, MA: Lexington Books, 1970.

Foster, Harold D. *Disaster Planning: The Preservation of Life and Property*. New York: Springer-Verlag, 1980.

Hoetmer, Gerard J. "Emergency Management." *Baseline Data Report 15*, no. 8. Washington, DC: ICMA, August 1983.

May, Peter J., and Walter Williams. *Disaster Policy Implementation: Managing Programs under Shared Governance*. New York: Plenum Press, 1986.

National Governors' Association. *1978 Emergency Preparedness Project: Final Report*. Washington, DC: NGA, 1978.

Perry, Ronald W. *Comprehensive Emergency Management: Evacuating Threatened Populations*. Greenwich, CT: JAI Press, 1985.

_____. *The Social Psychology of Civil Defense*. Lexington, MA: Heath, 1982.

Petak, William J., and Arthur A. Atkisson. *Natural Hazard Risk Assessment and Public Policy: Anticipating the Unexpected*. New York: Springer-Verlag, 1982.

Vale, Lawrence J. *The Limits of Civil Defense in the USA, Switzerland, Britain and the Soviet Union: The Evolution of Policies since 1945*. New York: St. Martin's Press, 1987.

2 Organizing for emergency management

Bosworth, Susan Lovegren, and Gary A. Kreps. "Structure as Process: Organization and Role." *American Sociological Review* 51 (October 1986): 699–716.

Drabek, Thomas E. *Human System Responses to Disaster: An Inventory of Sociological Findings*. New York: Springer-Verlag, 1986.

_____. *The Professional Emergency Manager: Structures and Strategies for Success*. Boulder: Institute of Behavioral Science, University of Colorado, 1987.

Dynes, Russell R. *Organized Behavior in Disaster*. Lexington, MA: Lexington Books, 1970.

Dynes, Russell R., E. L. Quarantelli, and Gary A. Kreps. *A Perspective on Disaster Planning*. Disaster Research Center Report Series no. 11. Newark: University of Delaware, 1972.

Hoetmer, Gerard J. "Emergency Management." *Baseline Data Report* 15, no. 4. Washington, DC: ICMA, April 1983.

_____. "Emergency Management." *Baseline Data Report* 15, no. 8. Washington, DC: ICMA, August 1983.

_____. "How Prepared Is Your Community for Its Next Disaster?" *Emergency Management Review* 1 (Winter 1984): 6–9.

Kreps, Gary A. "Sociological Inquiry and Disaster Research." *Annual Review of Sociology* 10 (1984): 309–30.

_____, ed. *Social Structure and Disaster*. Newark: University of Delaware Press, 1989.

May, Peter J., and Walter Williams. *Disaster Policy Implementation: Managing Programs under Shared Governance*. New York: Plenum Press, 1986.

Perry, Ronald W. *Comprehensive Emergency Management: Evacuating Threatened Populations*. Greenwich, CT: JAI Press, 1985.

_____. "Evaluating Emergency Response Plans." *Emergency Management Review* 1 (Winter 1984): 20–24.

Quarantelli, E. L. *Criteria Which Could Be Used in Assessing Disaster Preparedness Planning and Management*. Newark: Disaster Research Center, University of Delaware, 1987.

Quarantelli, E. L., and Russell R. Dynes. "Response to Social Crisis and Disaster." *Annual Review of Sociology* 3 (1977): 23–49.

Rossi, Peter H., James D. Wright, and Eleanor Weber-Burdin. *Natural Hazards and Public Choice: The State and Local Politics of Hazard Mitigation*. New York: Academic Press, 1982.

Saunders, Sarah L., and Gary A. Kreps. "The Life History of Emergent Organization in Disaster." *Journal of Applied Behavioral Science* 23, no. 4 (1987): 443–62.

Wenger, Dennis E., E. L. Quarantelli, and Russell R. Dynes. *Disaster Analysis: Emergency Management Offices and Arrangements*. Newark: Disaster Research Center, University of Delaware, 1987.

Wright, James D., Peter H. Rossi, Sonia R. Wright, and Eleanor Weber-Burdin. *After the Clean-Up: Long-Range Effects of Natural Disasters*. Beverly Hills, CA: Sage Publications, 1979.

3 Coordinating community resources

Bolin, Robert C. "Response of the Elderly to Disaster: An Age-Stratified Analysis." *International Journal of Aging and Human Development* 16 (1983): 283–96.

Brouillette, John R. *The Department of Public Works: A Community Emergency Organization*. Disaster Research Center Report Series no. 3. Newark: University of Delaware, 1968.

Drabek, Thomas E., Harriet L. Tamminga, Thomas S. Kilijanek, and Christopher Adams. *Managing Multiorganizational Emergency Responses: Emergent Search and Rescue Networks in Natural Disasters and Remote Area Settings*. Boulder: Institute of Behavioral Science, University of Colorado, 1981.

Dynes, Russell R. *Organized Behavior in Disaster*. Lexington, MA: Lexington Books, 1970.

Fox, Gerald G. "Disaster Planning: Tale of Two Cities." *Public Management* 63 (January/February 1981): 7–11.

Kueneman, Rodney M., and Joseph E. Wright. "New Policies of Broadcast Stations for Civil Disturbances and Disasters." *Journalism Quarterly* 52, no. 4 (1975): 670–77.

Mulford, Charles L. *Interorganizational Relations: Implications for Community Development*. New York: Human Sciences Press, 1984.

Quarantelli, E. L. *Delivery of Emergency Medical Services in Disasters: Assumptions and Realities*. New York: Irvington, 1983.

Rogers, David L., and David A. Whetten. *Interorganizational Coordination: Theory, Research, and Implementation*. Ames: Iowa State University Press, 1982.

Wolensky, Robert P. "Toward a Broader Conceptualization of Volunteerism in Disaster." *Journal of Voluntary Action Research* 8, nos. 3–4 (1979): 33–42.

4 Reaching out: Getting the community involved in preparedness

Drabek, Thomas E. *Human System Responses to Disaster: An Inventory of Sociological Findings*. New York: Springer-Verlag, 1986.

Dynes, Russell R. *Organized Behavior in Disaster*. Lexington, MA: Lexington Books, 1970.

Dynes, Russell, and E. L. Quarantelli. "What Looting in Civil Disturbances Really Means." *Trans-action* (May 1968): 9–14.

Hewitt, Kenneth, and Ian Burton. *The Hazardousness of a Place*. Toronto: University of Toronto Press, 1971.

Jones, Charles O. *An Introduction to the Study of Public Policy*. Monterey, CA: Brooks/Cole, 1984.

Kartez, Jack D., William J. Kelley, and Michael K. Lindell. *Adaptive Planning for Community Emergency Management: A Management Brief*. Pullman: Washington State University, 1987.

Loewy, Kathleen K., and David Sink. "Political Realities of Local Emergency Managers." Paper presented at a conference of the American Society for Public Administration, April 1986.

Quarantelli, E. L. "The Controversy on the Mental Health Consequences of Disasters." In Robert J. Ursano, ed., *Groups and Organizations in War, Disaster, and Trauma*. Bethesda, MD: Uniformed Services University of the Health Sciences, 1987.

———. "Disaster Education: Its Substantive Content and the Target Audiences." Paper presented at conference, Emergency '88, London, November 29, 1988.

———. "The Nature and Conditions of Panic." *The American Journal of Sociology* (November 1954): 267–75.

———. *Organizational Behavior in Disasters and Implications for Disaster Planning*. Emmitsburg, MD: National Emergency Training Center, FEMA, 1984.

Sandman, Peter M. "Explaining Risk to Non-Experts." Paper presented at conference, Global Disasters and International Information Flow, Washington, DC, October 8–10, 1986.

Scanlon, Joseph. "Planning for Peace and War Emergencies—Learning from 70 Years of Disaster Research." *Disaster Management* 1, no. 2 (1988): 3–8.

———. "Political Leadership and Canadian Emergency Planning: The Role of the Mayor." In Richard T. Sylves and William L. Waugh, Jr., eds., *Cities and Disaster: North American Studies in Emergency Management*. Springfield, IL: Charles C Thomas, 1989.

Scanlon, Joseph, Suzanne Alldred, Al Farrell, and Angela Prawzick. "Coping with the Media in Disasters: Some Predictable Prob-

lems." *Public Administration Review* 45 (January 1985): 123–33.

Scanlon, Joseph, with Natalie Brisebois and Denise Lachance. *The Woodstock Tornado: An Unplanned Event*. Ottawa: Emergency Communications Research Unit, 1980.

Scanlon, Joseph, Jim Jefferson, and Debbie Sproat. *The Port Alice Slide*. Ottawa: Emergency Planning Canada, 1976.

Scanlon, Joseph, with Gillian Osborne. *The Response to the Medicine Hat Train Derailment and Collision of 1984: The City Tests Its Peacetime Emergency Disaster Plan*. Ottawa: Emergency Preparedness Canada, 1988.

Scanlon, Joseph, with Massey Padgham. *The Peel Regional Police Force and the Mississauga Evacuation: How a Major Police Force Handled a Chemical Emergency*. Ottawa: Canadian Police College, 1979.

Scanlon, T. Joseph, and Suzanne Alldred. "Media Coverage of Disaster: The Same Old Story." In Barclay G. Jones and Miha Tomazevic, eds., *Social and Economic Aspects of Earthquakes*. Ithaca: Cornell University Press, 1982.

Singer, Benjamin, and Lyndsay Green. *The Social Functions of Radio during a Community Emergency*. Toronto: Copp Clark, 1972.

United Nations Environment Program, Industry and Environment Office. *APELL Awareness and Preparedness for Emergencies at Local Level*. Paris: UNEP, 1988.

Wenger, Dennis E., Thomas F. James, and Charles E. Faupel. *Disaster Beliefs and Emergency Planning*. New York: Irvington, 1985.

5 Perspectives and roles of the state and federal governments

Auf der Heide, Erik. *Disaster Response: Principles of Preparation and Coordination*. St. Louis: Mosby, 1989.

Chartrand, Robert Lee, and K. C. Chartrand, eds. *Strategies and Systems for Disaster Survival: The Symposium on Information Technology and Emergency Management*. Rockville, MD: Research Alternatives, 1989.

Comfort, Louise K., ed. *Managing Disaster: Strategies and Policy Perspectives*. Durham and London: Duke University Press, 1988.

Drabek, Thomas E. *Human System Responses to Disaster: An Inventory of Sociological Findings*. New York: Springer-Verlag, 1986.

_____. *Some Emerging Issues in Emergency Management*. Emmitsburg, MD: National Emergency Training Center, FEMA, 1984.

May, Peter J., and Walter Williams. *Disaster Policy Implementation: Managing Programs under Shared Governance*. New York: Plenum Press, 1986.

Mitler, Elliot. *Natural Hazard Policy Setting: The Role of Political Influentials*. Boulder: Institute of Behavioral Science, University of Colorado, 1988.

Petak, William J., and Arthur A. Atkisson. *Natural Hazard Risk Assessment and Public Policy: Anticipating the Unexpected*. New York: Springer-Verlag, 1982.

Rossi, Peter H., James D. Wright, Eleanor Weber-Burdin, and Joseph Pereira. *Victims of the Environment: Loss from Natural Hazards in the United States, 1970–1980*. New York: Plenum Press, 1983.

U.S. General Accounting Office. *Disaster Assistance, Timeliness and Other Issues Involving the Major Disaster Declaration Process*. Report no. GAO/RCED-89-138. Washington, DC: GAO, 1989.

Wenger, Dennis, and E. L. Quarantelli. *Local Mass Media Operations, Problems, and Products in Disaster*. Disaster Research Center Report Series no. 19. Newark: University of Delaware, 1989.

Wenger, Dennis E., E. L. Quarantelli, and Russell R. Dynes. *Disaster Analysis: Emergency Management Offices and Arrangements*. Newark: Disaster Research Center, University of Delaware, 1987.

6 Disaster mitigation and hazard management

Advisory Committee on the International Decade for Natural Hazard Reduction. *Confronting Natural Disasters: An International Decade for Natural Hazard Reduction*. Washington, DC: National Academy Press, 1987.

Alesch, Daniel J., and William J. Petak. *The Politics and Economics of Earthquake Hazard Mitigation: Unreinforced Masonry Buildings in Southern California*. Boulder: Institute of Behavioral Science, University of Colorado, 1986.

Baker, Earl J. "Public Attitudes toward Hazard Zone Controls." *Journal of the American Planning Association* 43 (1977): 401–8.

Bangs, F. S., and C. Bagne, eds. *Transferable Development Rights*. Chicago: American Society of Planning Officials, 1975.

Blair, M. L., et al. *When the Ground Fails: Planning and Engineering Response to Debris Flows*. Boulder: Institute of Behavioral Science, University of Colorado, 1985.

Burby, Raymond J., et al. *Cities under Water: A Comparative Evaluation of Ten Cities' Efforts to Manage Floodplain Land Use*. Boulder: Institute of Behavioral Science, University of Colorado, 1988.

Burrough, P. A. *Principles of Geographic Information Systems for Land Resources Assessment*. New York: Oxford University Press, 1986.

Coleman, Ronny J., and John A. Granito, eds. *Managing Fire Services*. Washington, DC: ICMA, 1988.

Dames and Moore. *The October 17, 1989 Loma Prieta Earthquake*. Los Angeles: Dames and Moore, 1989.

Drabek, Thomas E., Alvin H. Mushkatel, and Thomas S. Kilijanek. *Earthquake Mitigation Policy: The Experience of Two States*. Boulder: Institute of Behavioral Science, University of Colorado, 1983.

Earthquake Engineering Research Institute. *Reducing Earthquake Hazards*. El Cerrito, CA: EERI, 1986.

Erley, D., and W. J. Kockelman. *Reducing Landslide Hazards: A Guide for Planners*. Chicago: American Planning Association, 1981.

FEMA. *Integrated Emergency Management System Mitigation Program Development Guidance*. FEMA 122. Washington, DC: FEMA, 1987.

_____. *Landslide Loss Reduction: A Guide for State and Local Government Planning*. Washington, DC: FEMA, 1989.

_____. *Making Mitigation Work: A Handbook for State Officials*. DAP 12. Washington, DC: FEMA, June 1986.

_____. *National Earthquake Hazards Reduction Program: Fiscal Year 1987 Activities*. Report to Congress. Washington, DC: U.S. Government Printing Office, 1988.

Frank, J., and R. M. Rhodes, eds. *Development Exactions*. Chicago: Planners Press, 1987.

French, S., and M. Isaacson. "Applying Earthquake Risk Analysis Techniques to Land Use Planning." *Journal of the American Planning Association* 50, no. 4 (Autumn 1984): 509–22.

Godschalk, David R., and David J. Brower. "Mitigation Strategies and Integrated Emergency Management." *Public Administration Review* 45 (January 1985): 64–71.

Godschalk, David R., David J. Brower, and Timothy Beatley. *Catastrophic Coastal Storms: Hazard Mitigation and Development Management*. Durham, NC: Duke University Press, 1989.

Interagency Hazard Mitigation Team Report. *Hurricane Hugo*. Washington, DC: FEMA, 1989.

Jaffe, M., J. A. Butler, and C. Thurow. *Reducing Earthquake Risks: A Planner's Guide*. Chicago: American Planning Association, 1981.

Kasperson, Roger E., and K. David Pijawka. "Societal Response to Hazards and Major Hazard Events: Comparing Natural and Technological Hazards." *Public Administration Review* 45 (January 1985): 7–18.

Kusler, Jon A. "Liability as a Dilemma for Local Managers." *Public Administration Review* 45 (January 1985): 118–22.

Lee Plan. Fort Myers, FL: Lee County Planning Division, 1989.

Marston, Sallie A., ed. *Terminal Disasters: Computer Applications in Emergency Management*. Boulder: Institute of Behavioral Science, University of Colorado, 1986.

May, Peter J., and Walter Williams. *Disaster Policy Implementation: Managing Programs under Shared Governance*. New York: Plenum Press, 1986.

McPhee, John. "The Control of Nature: Los Angeles against the Mountains." *The New Yorker*, September 26 and October 3, 1988.

Mileti, Dennis S. *Natural Hazard Warning Systems in the United States: A Research Assessment*. Boulder: Institute of Behavioral Science, University of Colorado, 1975.

National Research Council. Advisory Board on the Built Environment. *Multiple Hazard Mitigation: Report of a Workshop on Mitigation Strategies for Communities Prone to Multiple Natural Hazards*. Washington, DC: National Academy Press, 1983.

National Research Council. Commission on Engineering and Technical Systems. *Reducing Losses from Landsliding in the United States*. Washington, DC: National Academy Press, 1985.

———. *Estimating Losses from Future Earthquakes*. Panel Report. Washington, DC: National Academy Press, 1989.

National Response Team. *Hazardous National Emergency Planning Guide*. Washington, DC: U.S. Environmental Protection Agency, 1987.

Petak, William J., and Arthur A. Atkisson. *Natural Hazard Risk Assessment and Public Policy: Anticipating the Unexpected*. New York: Springer-Verlag, 1982.

Pizor, P. J. "Making TDR Work: A Study of Program Implementation." *Journal of the American Planning Association* 52, no. 2 (Spring 1986): 203–11.

Platt, Rutherford H. *Regional Management of Metropolitan Floodplains: Experiences in the United States and Abroad*. Boulder: University of Colorado, 1987.

Rogers, George O., and Jiri Nehnevajsa. *Behavior and Attitudes under Crisis Conditions: Selected Issues and Findings*. Pittsburgh: Center for Social and Urban Research, University of Pittsburgh, 1984.

Rossi, Peter H., James D. Wright, and Eleanor Weber-Burdin. *Natural Hazards and Public Choice: The State and Local Politics of Hazard Mitigation*. New York: Academic Press, 1982.

Smith, T. P. *A Planner's Guide to Low-Level Radioactive Waste Disposal*. Chicago: American Planning Association, 1982.

Snyder, Thomas, and Michael Stegman. *Paying for Growth*. Washington, DC: Urban Land Institute, 1978.

Southwest Florida Regional Planning Council. *Hurricane Evacuation Study Update: 1987*. Fort Myers, FL: SWFRPC, 1987.

Spangle, William, and Associates, Inc. *Land Use Planning after Earthquakes*. Portola Valley, CA: Spangle, 1980.

Star, Jeffrey, and John Estes. *Geographic Information Systems: An Introduction*. Englewood Cliffs, NJ: Prentice-Hall, 1990.

Zimmerman, Rae. "Public Acceptability of Alternative Waste Management Services." In Dennis Peck, ed., *Psychosocial Effects of Hazardous Toxic Waste Disposal on Communities*. Springfield, IL: Charles C Thomas, 1989.

7 Planning, training, and exercising

Anderson, William A. "Tsunami Warning in Crescent City, California, and Hilo, Hawaii." In *The Great Alaska Earthquake of 1964: Human Ecology*. Committee on the Alaska Earthquake of the National Research Council. Washington, DC: National Academy of Sciences, 1970.

Baker, Earl J. "Hurricane Elena: Preparedness and Response in Florida." *Florida Policy Review* (Winter 1986): 17–23.

———. "Predicting Response to Hurricane Warnings: A Reanalysis of Data from Four Studies." *Mass Emergencies* 4 (1979): 9–24.

Cross, John A. "Longitudinal Changes in Hurricane Hazard Perception." *International Journal of Mass Emergencies and Disasters* 8 (March 1990): 31–47.

FEMA. *CCA General Program Guidelines.* CPG 1–3. Washington, DC: FEMA, June 1987 (revised May 1988, September 1988, September 1989, December 1989).

_____. *Guide for Development of State and Local Emergency Operations Plans.* CPG 1–8. Washington, DC: FEMA, October 1985 (revised September 1988).

_____. *Guide for Review of State and Local Emergency Operations Plans.* CPG 1–8A. Washington, DC: FEMA, October 1985.

_____. *Objectives for Local Emergency Management.* CPG 1–5. Washington, DC: FEMA, July 1984.

Lindell, Michael K., and Ronald W. Perry. "Warning Mechanisms in Emergency Response Systems." *International Journal of Mass Emergencies and Disasters* 5 (August 1987).

Mileti, Dennis S. *Natural Hazard Warning Systems in the United States: A Research Assessment.* Boulder: Institute of Behavioral Science, University of Colorado, 1975.

Perry, Ronald W. *Comprehensive Emergency Management: Evacuating Threatened Populations.* Greenwich, CT: JAI Press, 1985.

Perry, Ronald W., and Alvin H. Mushkatel. *Minority Citizens in Disasters.* Athens: University of Georgia Press, 1986.

Post, Buckley, Suhuh and Jernigan, Inc. *Hurricane Hugo Assessment: Review of Hurricane Evacuation Studies Utilization and Information Dissemination.* Washington, DC: U.S. Army Corps of Engineers and FEMA, 1990.

Quarantelli, E. L. *Evacuation Behavior and Problems: Findings and Implications from the Research Literature.* Newark: Disaster Research Center, University of Delaware, 1980.

Rogers, G. O., A. P. Watson, J. H. Sorensen, R. D. Sharp, and S. A. Carnes. *Evaluating Protective Actions for Chemical Agent Emergencies.* Oak Ridge, TN: Oak Ridge National Laboratory, 1990.

Sorensen, John H., Barbara M. Vogt, and Dennis S. Mileti. *Evacuation: An Assessment of Planning and Research.* Oak Ridge, TN: Oak Ridge National Laboratory, 1987.

Weston, Roy F., Inc. *Identification and Analysis of Factors Affecting Emergency Evacuations.* Washington, DC: Nuclear Management and Resources Council, 1989.

8   Managing disaster response operations

Drabek, Thomas E. *Emergency Management: The Human Factor.* Emmitsburg, MD: National Emergency Training Center, FEMA, 1985.

_____. *Human System Responses to Disaster: An Inventory of Sociological Findings.* New York: Springer-Verlag, 1986.

Foster, Harold D. *Disaster Planning: The Preservation of Life and Property.* New York: Springer-Verlag, 1980.

Herman, Roger. *Disaster Planning for Local Government.* New York: Universe Books, 1982.

Lindell, Michael, and Ronald W. Perry. *Behavioral Foundations of Emergency Response Planning.* New York: Hemisphere, forthcoming.

Perry, Ronald W. *Comprehensive Emergency Management: Evacuating Threatened Populations.* Greenwich, CT: JAI Press, 1985.

Quarantelli, E. L. *Evacuation Behavior and Problems: Findings and Implications from the Research Literature.* Newark: Disaster Research Center, University of Delaware, 1980.

Quarantelli, E. L., and Russell R. Dynes. "Response to Social Crisis and Disaster." *Annual Review of Sociology* 3 (1977): 23–49.

Wenger, Dennis E., E. L. Quarantelli, and Russell R. Dynes. *Disaster Analysis: Emergency Management Offices and Arrangements.* Newark: Disaster Research Center, University of Delaware, 1987.

9   Recovery from disaster

Bolin, Robert C. *Long-Term Family Recovery from Disaster.* Monograph no. 36. Boulder: Institute of Behavioral Science, University of Colorado, 1982.

Burby, Raymond, et al. "Coping with Natural Hazard Damages to Public Facilities." Chapel Hill: Center for Urban and Regional Studies, University of North Carolina, 1990.

Drabek, Thomas E. *Human System Responses to Disaster: An Inventory of Sociological Findings.* New York: Springer-Verlag, 1986.

Farberow, Norman L., and Norma S. Gordon. *Manual for Child Health Workers in Major Disasters.* Rockville, MD: Center for

Mental Health Studies of Emergencies, National Institute of Mental Health, 1981.

FEMA. *Digest of Federal Disaster Assistance Programs*. Washington, DC: FEMA, 1985 and additions.

———. *Making Mitigation Work: A Handbook for State Officials*. DAP 12. Washington, DC: FEMA, June 1986.

Friesema, H. Paul, et al. *Aftermath: Communities after Natural Disasters*. Beverly Hills, CA: Sage Publications, 1979.

Haas, J. Eugene, et al. *Reconstruction following Disaster*. Cambridge: MIT Press, 1977.

Hartsough, Don M., and Diane G. Myers. *Disaster Work and Mental Health: Prevention and Control of Stress among Workers*. Rockville, MD: Center for Mental Health Studies of Emergencies, National Institute of Mental Health, 1985.

Lystad, Mary, ed. *Innovations in Mental Health Services to Disaster Victims*. Rockville, MD: Center for Mental Health Studies of Emergencies, National Institute of Mental Health, 1985.

———, ed. *Mental Health Response to Mass Emergencies*. New York: Brunner/Mazel, 1988.

NIMH/CMHSE. *Role Stressors and Support for Emergency Workers*. Proceedings of a 1984 workshop sponsored by NIMH and FEMA. Rockville, MD: Center for Mental Health Studies of Emergencies, National Institute of Mental Health, 1985.

Petak, William J., ed. Special issue on emergency management. *Public Administration Review* 45 (January 1985).

Rubin, Claire B. "The Community Recovery Process in the United States after a Major Natural Disaster." *International Journal of Mass Emergencies and Disasters* 3, no. 2 (August 1985): 9–28.

Rubin, Claire B., and Daniel G. Barbee. "Disaster Recovery and Hazard Mitigation: Bridging the Intergovernmental Gap." *Public Administration Review* 45 (January 1985): 57–63.

Rubin, Claire B., with Martin Saperstein and Daniel G. Barbee. *Community Recovery from a Major Natural Disaster*. Program on Environment and Behavior Monograph no. 41. 1985. Boulder: University of Colorado, 1985.

Wright, James D., Peter H. Rossi, Sonia R. Wright, and Eleanor Weber-Burdin. *After the Clean-Up: Long-Range Effects of Natural Disasters*. Beverly Hills, CA: Sage Publications, 1979.

Yezer, Anthony M., and Claire B. Rubin. "The Local Economic Effects of Natural Disasters." Natural Hazards Research Center Working Paper no. 61. Boulder: University of Colorado, 1988.

10 Day-to-day management

Drabek, Thomas E. *Emergency Management: Strategies for Maintaining Organizational Integrity*. New York: Springer-Verlag, 1990.

———. *The Professional Emergency Manager: Structures and Strategies for Success*. Boulder: Institute of Behavioral Science, University of Colorado, 1987.

Emergency Preparedness News. Published biweekly by Business Publishers, Inc., 951 Pershing Dr., Silver Spring, MD 20910.

FEMA. *Digest of Federal Disaster Assistance Programs*. DR&R-21. Washington, DC: FEMA, 1989.

———. *Hazard Identification, Capability Assessment, and Multi-Year Development Plan*. CPG 1–34. Washington, DC: FEMA, January 1987.

"44 CFR Part 206: Robert T. Stafford Disaster Relief and Emergency Assistance Act; Implementation, etc.; Final Rules." *Federal Register*, January 12, 1990, pp. 2284–2318.

Hazard Monthly. Published monthly by Research Alternatives, Inc., 966 Hungerford Drive, Rockville, MD 20850.

Public Management 71, no. 12 (December 1989). Six feature articles relating to emergency management.

Quarantelli, E. L. *Emergent Citizen Groups in Disaster Preparedness and Recovery Activities*. Newark: Disaster Research Center, University of Delaware, 1985.

———. *The Functioning of the Local Emergency Services Offices in Disasters*. Newark: Disaster Research Center, University of Delaware, 1985.

U.S. Congress. "Robert T. Stafford Disaster Relief and Emergency Assistance Act of 1988" (P.L. 100–707). Washington, DC: Government Printing Office, November 23, 1988.

11 Liability issues

Community Right-to-Know Deskbook. Washington, DC: Environmental Law Institute, 1988.

Davis, Kenneth Culp. *Administrative Law Text*. St. Paul, MN: West, 1972.

Fordham, Jefferson B. *Local Government Law*. Mineola, NY: Foundation Press, 1986.

Franklin, Marc A., and Robert L. Rabin. *Tort Law and Alternatives*. Mineola, NY: Foundation Press, 1987.

Freilich, Robert H., and Richard G. Carlisle. *Section 1983 Sword and Shield: Civil Rights Violations and the Liability of Urban, State and Local Government*. Washington, DC: American Bar Association, 1983.

Frug, Gerald E. *Local Government Law*. St. Paul, MN: West, 1988.

Gellhorn, Walter, Clark Byse, and Peter L. Strauss. *Administrative Law*. Mineola, NY: Foundation Press, 1979.

Gunther, Gerald. *Constitutional Law*. Mineola, NY: Foundation Press, 1985.

Huffman, James. *Government Liability and Disaster Mitigation*. Lanham, MD: University Press of America, 1986.

Keeton, W. Page, Dan Dobbs, Robert Keeton, and David Owen. *The Law of Torts*. St. Paul, MN: West, 1984.

Mancini, Marguerite R. *Emergency Care and the Law*. Rockville, MD: Aspen Systems, 1981.

Pine, John C. *Emergency Management Liability*. Washington, DC: FEMA, 1988.

_____. *Liability in Emergency Planning*. Washington, DC: U.S. Environmental Protection Agency, 1988.

_____. *Tort Liability of Governmental Units in Emergency Actions and Activities*. Washington, DC: FEMA, 1988.

Pine, John C., and Robert Bickel. *Tort Liability Today: A Guide for State and Local Governments*. Washington, DC: Public Risk Insurance Management Association and the National League of Cities, 1986.

Pine, John C., and Patricia Hollander. *Public Administrator and the Courts*. Asheville, NC: Research Publications, 1986.

Reynolds, Osborne M. *Reynolds' Handbook on Local Government Law*. St. Paul, MN: West, 1982.

Smith, Russell A., Harry T. Edwards, and R. Theodore Clark, Jr. *Labor Relations Law in the Public Sector*. New York: Bobbs-Merrill, 1974.

Tribe, Laurence H. *American Constitutional Law*. Mineola, NY: Foundation Press, 1978.

12   Future directions

Advisory Committee on the International Decade for Natural Hazard Reduction. *Reducing Disasters' Toll: The United States Decade for Natural Disaster Reduction*. Washington, DC: National Academy Press, 1989.

Alesch, Daniel J., and William J. Petak. *The Politics and Economics of Earthquake Hazard Mitigation*. Boulder: Institute of Behavioral Science, University of Colorado, 1986.

American Red Cross. *San Francisco Corporate Disaster Planning Guide*. 2d ed. San Francisco: Red Cross Disaster Resource Center, Golden Gate Chapter, American Red Cross, 1986.

Auf der Heide, Erik. *Disaster Response: Principles of Preparation and Coordination*. St. Louis: Mosby, 1989.

Barton, Allen H. *Communities in Disaster: A Sociological Analysis of Collective Stress Situations*. Garden City, NY: Doubleday, 1969.

Bay Area Regional Earthquake Preparedness Project. "Taking Care of Business." *Networks Earthquake Preparedness News* 4, no. 2 (Summer 1989).

Comfort, Louise K., ed. *Managing Disaster: Strategies and Policy Perspectives*. Durham and London: Duke University Press, 1988.

Drabek, Thomas E. *Human System Responses to Disaster: An Inventory of Sociological Findings*. New York: Springer-Verlag, 1986.

_____. *The Professional Emergency Manager: Structures and Strategies for Success*. Boulder: Institute of Behavioral Science, University of Colorado, 1987.

Dynes, Russell R. *Organized Behavior in Disaster*. Lexington, MA: Lexington Books, 1970.

FEMA. *Disaster Mitigation Guide for Business and Industry*. FEMA 190. Washington, DC: FEMA, 1990.

_____. *Exemplary Practices in Emergency Management: Business and Industry Council for Emergency Planning and Preparedness*. Monograph Series no. 4. Emmitsburg, MD: National Emergency Training Center, FEMA, 1986.

_____. *The National Earthquake Hazards Reduction Program: Commentary and Recommendations of the Expert Review Committee 1987*. Washington, DC: FEMA, 1987.

Godschalk, David R., David J. Brower, and Timothy Beatley. *Catastrophic Coastal Storms: Hazard Mitigation and Development Management*. Durham, NC: Duke University Press, 1989.

Hill, Lawrence J. *Studies of Postdisaster Economic Recovery: Analysis, Synthesis, and Assessment.* Washington, DC: FEMA, 1987.

May, Peter J., and Walter Williams. *Disaster Policy Implementation: Managing Programs under Shared Governance.* New York: Plenum Press, 1986.

Mitchell, Jeffrey T. "Assessing and Managing the Psychological Impact of Terrorism, Civil Disorder, Disasters, and Mass Casualties." *Emergency Care Quarterly* 2, no. 1 (May 1986): 51–58.

National Research Council. *Confronting Natural Disaster: An International Decade for Natural Disaster Reduction.* Washington, DC: National Academy Press, 1987.

Perry, Ronald W., and Alvin H. Mushkatel. *Disaster Management: Warning Response and Community Relocation.* Westport, CT: Greenwood Press, 1984.

———. *Minority Citizens in Disasters.* Athens: University of Georgia Press, 1986.

Petak, William J., and Arthur A. Atkisson. *Natural Hazard Risk Assessment and Public Policy: Anticipating the Unexpected.* New York: Springer-Verlag, 1982.

Rattien, Stephen. "The Role of the Media in Hazard Mitigation and Disaster Management." In *Communication When It's Needed Most: How New Technology Could Help in Sudden Disasters*, report of the International Disaster Communications Project. Washington, DC: Annenberg Washington Program, Communications Policy Studies, Northwestern University, 1989.

Southern California Earthquake Preparedness Project. *Guidelines for Local Small Businesses in Meeting the Earthquake Threat.* Los Angeles: SCEPP, 1982.

Spangle, William, and Associates, Inc., Martha Blair-Tyler, and Penelope A. Gregory. *Putting Seismic Safety Policies to Work.* Developed for Bay Area Earthquake Preparedness Project, October 1988.

Tierney, Kathleen, William J. Petak, and Harlan Hahn. *Disabled Persons and Earthquake Hazards.* Boulder: Institute of Behavioral Science, University of Colorado, 1988.

Working Group on Earthquake Hazards Reduction. *Earthquake Hazards Reduction: Issues for an Implementation Plan.* Washington, DC: U.S. Office of Science and Technology Policy, 1978.

Yin, Robert K., and Gregory D. Andranovich. *Getting Research Used in the Natural Hazards Field: The Role of Professional Associations.* Washington, DC: Cosmos Corp., 1987.

Yin, Robert K., and Gwendolyn B. Moore. *The Utilization of Research: Lessons from the Natural Hazards Field.* Washington, DC: Cosmos Corp., 1985.

List of contributors

Thomas E. Drabek (Editor, and Chapter 1) is professor of sociology at the University of Denver, where he was department chair during 1974–1979 and 1985–1987. He has written numerous books and articles on group and organizational responses to large-scale disasters. From 1986 to 1991 he was co-editor of the *International Journal of Mass Emergencies and Disasters*. He currently serves as president of the Research Committee on Disasters of the International Sociological Association. He holds a bachelor's degree from the University of Denver and a master's degree and doctorate from Ohio State University.

Gerard J. Hoetmer (Editor, and Introduction) is assistant executive director for program development, public policy, and consortia for ICMA. In addition, he manages ICMA's public safety program, overseeing grants and contracts from the National Institute of Justice, FEMA, other federal agencies, and private foundations. During the 1980s, under a cooperative agreement with FEMA, he designed and conducted a training course attended by nearly two thousand local chief executive officers and emergency management personnel. He represents ICMA on many committees and task forces and has written and lectured widely on local government emergency management and other public safety issues. Before joining ICMA, Mr. Hoetmer was assistant to the fire chief and aide to the city manager in Aurora, Colorado. He holds a master's degree in public administration from the University of Colorado.

William A. Anderson (Chapter 12) is head of the Hazard Mitigation Section at the National Science Foundation. Previously he was professor of sociology at Arizona State University. He has also taught at Kent State University and Ohio State University, and served as field director at the Disaster Research Center. He has served on panels and committees at the National Academy of Sciences, the Council on Environmental Quality, and the Office of Science and Technology Policy. His degrees are in sociology and include a bachelor's degree from the

University of Akron, a master's degree from Kent State University, and a doctorate from Ohio State University.

Barbara A. Block (Chapter 10) is an emergency preparedness specialist with the city of Dallas, Texas. She works primarily in the areas of public assistance grants in federally declared disasters, severe weather preparation and response, radiation detection/monitoring instruction, and hazardous materials regulation, serving as liaison to the Dallas County Local Emergency Planning Committee's Subcommittee on Transportation. She previously served as assistant director of disaster services for the Dallas County chapter of the American Red Cross, and holds a bachelor's degree in anthropology (urban emphasis) from the University of Texas at Dallas.

Guy E. Daines (Chapter 7) is the director of civil emergency services for Pinellas County, Florida. He previously served as director of emergency management for Pinellas County. He holds a bachelor's degree from Eastern Kentucky University and a master's degree from Webster College. Mr. Daines also served in the U.S. Army in various planning and training assignments and is a graduate of the U.S. Army Command and General Staff College at Fort Leavenworth, Kansas. He has worked as a consultant to both public and private agencies and is a past president of the Florida Emergency Preparedness Association.

Tom Durham (Chapter 5) is chief of the Natural Hazards Branch of the Tennessee Emergency Management Agency (TEMA). During his tenure with the agency, he has worked closely with the leadership of the National Emergency Management Association, the National Coordinating Council for Emergency Management, and other national organizations interested in strong local emergency management programs. His experience overseas includes hazard management projects in Brazil, Venezuela, Nicaragua, and Bolivia, undertaken through the auspices of the U.S. Agency for International Development and Partners of the

Americas. Mr. Durham has a master's degree in urban and regional planning. Before joining TEMA, he worked in The Gambia, West Africa, as a community development specialist.

David F. Gillespie (Chapter 3) is professor of social work at Washington University in St. Louis. Previously he served as director of the doctoral program in social work at Washington University, assistant professor at Michigan State University, and research assistant professor in the Center for Social Welfare Research at the University of Washington in Seattle. He holds bachelor's and master's degrees in sociology from California State University at Los Angeles, and a doctorate in sociology from the University of Washington. He has undertaken studies for a number of nonprofit and private organizations, including the National Science Foundation, the Department of Health and Human Services, the American Red Cross, and Union Electric Company.

David R. Godschalk (Chapter 6) is professor of city and regional planning at the University of North Carolina at Chapel Hill. His professional experience includes serving as a city planning director in Gainesville, Florida; as vice-president of a planning consulting firm in Tampa; and as a planning faculty member at Florida State University. He has been editor of the *Journal of the American Institute of Planners* and a member of the governing boards of the American Planning Association and the American Society of Planning Officials. In the field of hazard mitigation he has done a national study supported by the National Science Foundation and worked with local governments in preparing coastal hazard management plans. In 1989 he completed a four-year term on the Chapel Hill town council. He holds a bachelor of arts degree from Dartmouth, a bachelor of architecture degree from the University of Florida, and a master's degree and doctorate in planning from the University of North Carolina.

Gary A. Kreps (Chapter 2) is professor and chair of the Department of Sociology at the College of William and Mary. He completed his doctoral studies in sociology at Ohio State University. In addition to his academic work, he has served as staff officer, consultant, or member of four National Academy of Sciences–National Research Council committees on emergency and hazards management, and as a member of the National Academy of Public Administration panel on Three Mile Island. For the past several years, with support from the National Science Foundation he has been engaged

in archival research on the roles of improvisation and preparedness during the emergency period of natural disasters.

Shirley Mattingly (Chapter 12) is director of emergency management for the City of Los Angeles. She serves as chair or vice-chair of several local and regional panels, including her county's emergency preparedness commission and the policy board for the Southern California Earthquake Preparedness Project. In addition, she has served on the U.S. National Committee for the Decade for Natural Disaster Reduction and the Expert Review Committee for the National Earthquake Hazards Reduction Program. She holds a bachelor's degree from Occidental College and a master's degree from the University of California at Los Angeles. She was a Fulbright scholar at Quito, Ecuador, and completed the Senior Executive Program for State and Local Government at the Kennedy School of Government at Harvard University.

Ronald W. Perry (Chapter 8) is professor of public affairs and director of the doctoral program in public administration at Arizona State University. Dr. Perry has conducted research on disaster preparedness and response for more than twenty years. He has served on National Academy of Sciences–National Research Council committees on emergency management and is currently co-editor of the *International Journal of Mass Emergencies and Disasters*.

John H. Pickett (Chapter 10) retired in 1990 as emergency manager of Dallas, Texas, a post he had held since 1978. Mr. Pickett is a past president of the National Coordinating Council on Emergency Management and serves on the National Urban Search and Rescue Task Force Advisory Committee, the advisory committee for the 1991 Emergency Management Exposition in Las Vegas, and the Professional Standards for Emergency Managers Project Executive Committee. He holds a bachelor's degree from the University of Texas and a master of liberal arts degree from Southern Methodist University.

John C. Pine (Chapter 11) is associate professor in the Industrial and Agricultural Technology Program in the Department of Agricultural Engineering at Louisiana State University and A&M College. He is also adjunct professor at LSU's College of Business Administration. From 1980 to 1988, he was a management development associate with LSU's Public Administration Institute, where he directed management seminars and institutes for state and local officials.

Professor Pine, whose areas of research include administrative law, liability, federal and constitutional law, risk management, and occupational safety and health, is currently conducting projects supported by the U.S. Environmental Protection Agency, FEMA, and the Public Risk Management Association's Center for Public Risk Management. The author of several publications on legal issues in public administration, he is a liberal arts graduate of Southwestern at Memphis and holds a master's degree and doctorate from the University of Georgia.

Claire B. Rubin (Chapter 9) is a research scientist at the George Washington University Center for International Science and Technology Policy. She is also a consultant in public and emergency management. As a social scientist who specializes in public management aspects of natural hazards and disasters, she has initiated and managed numerous natural disaster research projects; created and conducted training programs; and designed and operated information dissemination and utilization systems. Ms. Rubin holds a bachelor's degree from Simmons College and a master's degree in political science from Boston University. She has published many articles, handbooks, and other documents on hazards and disasters. Before joining the staff at George Washington University, she was a fellow in public management at the Academy for State and Local Government, where she was director of the Natural Disaster Research Center. Previously she was director of contract research at ICMA.

T. Joseph Scanlon (Chapter 4) is professor of journalism and director of the Emergency Communications Research Unit at Carleton University in Ottawa. Since 1970 he has studied more than seventy emergency incidents, and his findings have appeared in reports, articles, and a dozen books. He lectures regularly at the Canadian Emergency Preparedness College and the Canadian Police College and heads a consulting firm, Scanlon Associates, Inc. Professor Scanlon holds a bachelor's degree in journalism and a diploma in public administration from Carleton University, and a master's degree in politics from Queen's University.

Lacy E. Suiter (Chapter 5) has been director of the Tennessee Emergency Management Agency since 1983. He serves on the Board of Visitors of the Emergency Management Institute at Emmitsburg, Maryland, and on the Board of Trustees of the National Association for Search and Rescue. He also represents state emergency management directors on the IEMS National Advisory Committee, and was appointed by the National Academy of Sciences to the U.S. National Committee for the Decade for Natural Disaster Reduction. In 1985 Mr. Suiter was president of the National Emergency Management Association, and in 1984–85 and 1988–89 he chaired the Central United States Earthquake Consortium. A lifelong resident of Nashville, Tennessee, he holds a bachelor's degree in general business from Middle Tennessee State University.

Illustration and table credits

Introduction   Figure 1: Emergency Preparedness Program, Pan American Health Organization. Figure 2: Robert E. Litan, "Earthquake! Planning and Paying for the 'Big One,'" *The Brookings Review* 8, no. 4 (Fall 1990): 43; map by Robert Wiser. Figure 3: Courtesy U.S. Geological Survey, National Earthquake Information Center. Figure 4: Courtesy U.S. DOT/RSPA; data gathered from DOT Form 5800.1. Tables 1 and 2: Robert E. Litan, "Earthquake! Planning and Paying for the 'Big One,'" *The Brookings Review* 8, no. 4 (Fall 1990): 44.

Chapter 1   Figure 1–1: Reproduced by permission of The Granger Collection, 1841 Broadway, New York, NY 10023. Figure 1–2: Photo from collections of the U.S. Army Corps of Engineers. Figures 1–3 through 1–5: Courtesy of American Red Cross. Figure 1–6: David McLoughlin, "A Framework for Integrated Emergency Management," *Public Administration Review* 45 (January 1985): 167, reprinted with permission from *Public Administration Review* © 1985 by the American Society for Public Administration (ASPA), 1120 G Street, N.W., Suite 500, Washington, DC 20005; all rights reserved. Figure 1–7: Courtesy of the National Oceanic and Atmospheric Administration.

Chapter 2   Figure 2–1: Adapted from IEMS National Advisory Committee, *The CEO's Disaster Survival Kit* (Washington, DC: U.S. Fire Administration, FEMA, 1988), app. C.

Chapter 3   Figure 3–1: Photo by Jo. L. Keener, copyright © 1989—IFPA Houston. Figure 3–2: Courtesy of American Red Cross. Figure 3–3: Adapted from John C. Bush, *Disaster Response: A Handbook for Church Action* (Scottdale, PA: Herald Press, 1979), 154–55.

Chapter 4   Figure 4–1: Message of Mayor Norm Tremblay to the Citizens and Businesses in the City of Live Oak, in *Citizen's Emergency Action Guide* (Live Oak, TX, 1988), i. Figure 4–2: Reprinted by permission of First Interstate Bank of California, Los Angeles, CA. Figure 4–3: Reprinted from "Get Ready for Hurricanes." © 1987 Children's Television Workshop. Big Bird © 1987 Jim Henson Productions, Inc. All rights reserved.

Chapter 5   Figure 5–1: Reproduced by permission of the Pennsylvania Emergency Management Agency. Figure 5–3: FEMA, *National Earthquake Hazards Reduction Program: Five Year plan for 1989–1993* (Washington, DC: FEMA, 1989), 6. Figure 5–4: U.S. Food and Drug Administration, "Preparedness and Response in Radiation Accidents," FDA-83-8211 (Rockville, MD: FDA, August 1983), 37. Figure 5–5: Frederick C. Cuny, *Disasters and Development* (New York: Oxford University Press, 1983), 109.

Chapter 6   Figure 6–1: Adapted from D. R. Godschalk, D. J. Brower, and T. Beatley, *Catastrophic Coastal Storms: Hazard Mitigation and Development Management* (Durham, NC: Duke University Press, 1989), 19. Figure 6–2: Southwest Florida Regional Planning Council, *Hurricane Evacuation Study Update: 1987* (Fort Myers, FL: SWFRPC, 1987), II-B-3. Figure 6–3: D. R. Godschalk and D. J. Brower, "Mitigation Strategies and Integrated Emergency Management," *Public Administration Review* 45 (January 1985): 68, reprinted with permission from *Public Administration Review* © 1985 by the American Society for Public Administration (ASPA), 1120 G Street, N.W., Suite 500, Washington, DC 20005; all rights reserved. Table 6–1: Adapted from Godschalk et al., *Catastrophic Coastal Storms*, p. 6 [compiled from W. J. Petak and A. A. Atkisson, *Natural Hazard Risk Assessment and Public Policy* (New York: Springer-Verlag, 1982), tables 5.3, 5.8, 5.9, and 5.10].

Chapter 8   Figure 8–1: Photo reproduced by permission of the Charleston (SC) *News and Courier*. Figure 8–2: Courtesy of FEMA. Figure 8–3: Photo courtesy of Carroll County (MD) Emergency Operations Center. Figure 8–4: Photo courtesy of the Office of Emergency Preparedness, Cumberland County, PA. Figure 8–5: Courtesy of Minneapolis Emergency Communications. Figure 8–6: Adapted from Louise K. Comfort, "Improving Organizational Decision-Making Capacity in Emergency Management: A Design for an Interactive Emergency Management System," in Sallie A. Marston, ed., *Terminal Disasters: Computer Applications in Emergency Management* (Boulder: Institute of Behavioral Science, University of Colorado, 1986), 186. Figure 8–7: Photo by Lt. Tom Carr, Collapse Rescue Team, Montgomery County (MD) Department of Fire and Rescue Services. Figure 8–8: Photo by T/SGT Pat Kenaley, 185 TFG, Iowa Air National Guard.

Chapter 9   Figure 9–1: Photos courtesy of Pennsylvania Emergency Management Agency. Figure 9–2: Adapted from Claire B. Rubin, "Natural Disaster Recovery for Local Public Officials" (Washington, DC: Academy for Contemporary Problems, 1979), 8. Figure 9–3: Photo by Bill Lovejoy/*Santa Cruz Sentinel*. Figure 9–4: San Francisco Fire Department photo; thanks also go to IAFC. Figure 9–5: Photo by Michael Ewen/*Tallahassee Democrat*. Figure 9–6: Adapted from Claire B. Rubin et al., *Community Recovery from a Major Natural Disaster*, Program on Environment and Behavior Mon-

ograph no. 41 (Boulder: University of Colorado, 1985), 18. Figure 9–7: Photo reproduced by permission of the Charleston (SC) *News and Courier*.

Chapter 10   Figure 10–1: Plan Bulldozer Committee, *Emergency Resources Catalog* (Kansas City, MO: Heavy Constructors Association of the Greater Kansas City Area and the Kansas City Chapter Associated General Contractors, 1990), 7, 14. Figure 10–2: © *Kansas City Star*, Kansas City, MO. Figure 10–4: Excerpted from Chemical Manufacturers Association, *Hazard Information Transmission* (Washington, DC: CMA, n.d.). Table 10–1: FEMA, *Objectives for Local Emergency Management* (Washington, DC: U.S. Government Printing Office, July 1984), II-9.

Chapter 11   Figure 11–1: Adapted from John C. Pine, *Tort Liability of Governmental Units in Emergency Actions and Activities* (Washington, DC: FEMA, July 1988), apps. A and B.

Chapter 12   Figure 12–1: Reproduced with permission from *Natural Hazards Observer* 13 (October 1988): 1. Figure 12–2: Adapted from *Natural Hazards Observer* 6 (July 1988): 4; reproduced with permission.

Index

Page numbers in italics refer to illustrations

Legal issues, 102, 154–156, 178, *194–196,*
    227, 285, 320
    see also Liability
LEPC, *see* Local emergency planning com-
    mittee (LEPC)
Liability, 24–25, 157, 257, 320
    defenses, 301
    government contractors, *300*
    private citizens, *300*
    reduction strategies, *158*
    under federal law, 297–305
    under state law, 289–297, 297–298, 305
Liberal, Kansas, drought, ca. 1930, *8*
Lifeline systems, 142
Lindell, Michael, 87
Lines of authority, 102–104, 178, 210
Liquefaction model, *279*
Live Oak, Texas, and emergency guide, *85*
"The Local Economic Effects of Major Natu-
    ral Disasters," 228
Local emergency planning committee
    (LEPC), 103, 297
Local Exchange, *76*
Loewy, Kathleen, 97
Loma Prieta earthquake, 1989, xxiii, *75, 76,*
    121, 161, *229,* 311, 320, 325, 330
London, England, fire, 1666, 6
Long Beach, Mississippi, *9*
Long-Term Family Recovery from Disaster,
    228
Looting, 23, *35*
LORCS, *see* League of Red Cross and Red
    Crescent Societies (LORCS)
Love Canal, New York, xxx, 18, 140, 141

MAC, *see* Multiagency Coordination System
    (MAC)
Macrosystems, 277–287
Macy, John, 19
MAD, *see* Mutually assured destruction
    (MAD)
Management issues, *24*
Management systems, 272–273, 274–277
Managua, Nicaragua, earthquake, 1972,
    228
Mandated coordination, 58
Mankato, Minnesota, flood, 258
Marin County, California, flood, 1982, 238,
    239
Marks, Eli, 20
Material safety data sheets (MSDSs), 26,
    273–274, *275,* 305
Maximum envelope of water (MEOW), *149*
May, Peter, 19
MCA/Universal City Studios, and emergency
    preparedness, 323
McKinley, William, 11
McNamara, Robert, 15, 16
Meals-on-Wheels, 284
Media relations, *24,* 74, 284
    and disaster myths, 89
    exercise coverage, 98
    Gander air crash, *96,* 97

honesty issues, 96
national media, 95
postdisaster period, 94–97
and risk communication, 318
and search and rescue, 221
and warning systems, 92–93
see also Communication; Information
Medical care, *see* Emergency medical care
Medical facilities
    evacuation of, 179
    exercises with, 188
Mennonite Disaster Service, 249
Mental health, 83, 214
Mental health services, 67, 70, 230, *317*
MEOW, *see* Maximum envelope of water
    (MEOW)
Mexico City, earthquake, 1985, xxii, 74, 88,
    284, *285,* 287, *316*
Miami, Florida, civil unrest, xxxii
Miamisburg, Ohio, train derailment, 1986,
    63, *64–65*
Microsystems, 263–277
Military assistance, *69,* 70
Military planning, 193
    approaches to, 167
Minneapolis, Minnesota, Emergency Opera-
    tions Center, *206*
Minnesota River, flood, 1965, 258
Mississauga derailment, 1978, 81, *82,* 92,
    99
Mississippi River, flood, 1912, *7*
Mitchell, Jeffrey T., *315, 316*
Mitigation, 23, 90–91, 97, 103, 134–135,
    136, 138, 242, 245, 246–247, 312–313
    approaches to, 256–257
    chemical disasters, 140
    and communication of risk, 318
    comprehensive plan for, *152*
    definition, 131, 252
    earthquakes, xxii
    elements of, 131–132
    federal policy evolution, 132–134
    flood hazards, 121
    goals of, 157
    hazard information systems, 156–157
    hurricanes, *237*
    insurance, 156
    marketing of, 313
    obstacles to, 257–258
    plans, 153–154
    process of, 133–138
    public costs of, 156
    and public policy, 157–159
    regulations, 154–156
    requirements of, 252–254, 256
    research, *327*
    strategies preparation, 151–153
    uses of, 134
    see also Postdisaster mitigation
Mobilization of personnel, 51
Mobilization of resources, 32, 42, 43, 51, 60,
    106, 109–111, 182–183, *227,* 234
    identification of, 305
    resource lists, 270–272

Municipal Management Series

Emergency Management:
Principles and Practice for Local Government

Text type
Times Roman, Helvetica

Composition
EPS Group Inc.
Baltimore, Maryland

Printing and binding
Arcata Graphics/Kingsport
Kingsport, Tennessee

Design
Herbert Slobin